T0142887

IFIP Advances in Information and Communication Technology

598

Editor-in-Chief

Kai Rannenberg, Goethe University Frankfurt, Germany

IFIP – The International Federation for Information Processing

IFIP was founded in 1960 under the auspices of UNESCO, following the first World Computer Congress held in Paris the previous year. A federation for societies working in information processing, IFIP's aim is two-fold: to support information processing in the countries of its members and to encourage technology transfer to developing nations. As its mission statement clearly states:

> IFIP is the global non-profit federation of societies of ICT professionals that aims at achieving a worldwide professional and socially responsible development and application of information and communication technologies.

IFIP is a non-profit-making organization, run almost solely by 2500 volunteers. It operates through a number of technical committees and working groups, which organize events and publications. IFIP's events range from large international open conferences to working conferences and local seminars.

The flagship event is the IFIP World Computer Congress, at which both invited and contributed papers are presented. Contributed papers are rigorously refereed and the rejection rate is high.

As with the Congress, participation in the open conferences is open to all and papers may be invited or submitted. Again, submitted papers are stringently refereed.

The working conferences are structured differently. They are usually run by a working group and attendance is generally smaller and occasionally by invitation only. Their purpose is to create an atmosphere conducive to innovation and development. Refereeing is also rigorous and papers are subjected to extensive group discussion.

Publications arising from IFIP events vary. The papers presented at the IFIP World Computer Congress and at open conferences are published as conference proceedings, while the results of the working conferences are often published as collections of selected and edited papers.

IFIP distinguishes three types of institutional membership: Country Representative Members, Members at Large, and Associate Members. The type of organization that can apply for membership is a wide variety and includes national or international societies of individual computer scientists/ICT professionals, associations or federations of such societies, government institutions/government related organizations, national or international research institutes or consortia, universities, academies of sciences, companies, national or international associations or federations of companies.

More information about this series at http://www.springer.com/series/6102

Luis M. Camarinha-Matos · Hamideh Afsarmanesh ·
Angel Ortiz (Eds.)

Boosting Collaborative Networks 4.0

21st IFIP WG 5.5 Working Conference
on Virtual Enterprises, PRO-VE 2020
Valencia, Spain, November 23–25, 2020
Proceedings

 Springer

Editors
Luis M. Camarinha-Matos ⓘ
NOVA University of Lisbon
Monte Caparica, Portugal

Hamideh Afsarmanesh ⓘ
University of Amsterdam
Amsterdam, The Netherlands

Angel Ortiz ⓘ
Polytechnic University of Valencia
Valencia, Spain

ISSN 1868-4238   ISSN 1868-422X (electronic)
IFIP Advances in Information and Communication Technology
ISBN 978-3-030-62414-9   ISBN 978-3-030-62412-5 (eBook)
https://doi.org/10.1007/978-3-030-62412-5

This Springer imprint is published by the registered company Springer Nature Switzerland AG
The registered company address is: Gewerbestrasse 11, 6330 Cham, Switzerland

Preface

Collaborative Networks (CNs) play a key role in the ongoing process of digital transformation in industry and services. Although the CN area is relatively young, its history is longer than two decades, as is also reflected in the series of PRO-VE conferences. A number of major milestones can be identified through these decades in the CN's "revolution." The theme of the conference this year recognizes this fact and focuses on launching new ideas for its latest milestone.

As we look back in time, the first generation of the CN area was developed around the concept of extended enterprises and virtual enterprises. The focus of this first generation was to achieve the right design for these kinds of networks, to identify its constitutive elements, and to promote organized collaboration. The second generation of the CN area focused on better application of the ICT concepts and technologies to complement developments of its first generation. Furthermore, the idea of the breeding environment rose as the natural key concept to support different life cycle stages of the collaborative networks. The third generation of the CN area focused on supporting the inter- and trans-CN collaboration and networks co-creation. We can summarize these earlier milestones of the CN area as follows:

- Collaborative Networks 1.0 – primarily addressing the operation and management of goal-oriented networks, including the supply chains, extended enterprises, virtual enterprises, and virtual organizations.
- Collaborative Networks 2.0 – primarily addressing and supporting the complete life cycle of CN breeding environments, including the business and social ecosystems, industry clusters, industrial districts, and professional virtual communities.
- Collaborative Networks 3.0 – primarily addressing the interplay among multiple CNs, including those of the inter- and trans-value system networks, and co-creation networks.

However, the dynamic world of collaborative networks continue to evolve and need to be formalized in order to face new emerging aspects, e.g., to properly deal with the exponential increase in availability of both data and intelligence, the continuous increase in digitalization, and the better positioning of the role of humans in highly collaborative, dynamic, and resilient networks, among others. Research and development on CN is now beginning to address its fourth milestone, namely the Collaborative Networks 4.0, for which some of its main distinctive features include addressing: hybridization in CN structure, where network entities constitute organizations, people, intelligent systems, and machines; formation of distributed cognitive systems; collaborative decision making among humans and intelligent autonomous systems; managing big data; mass collaboration; and collaborative creativity. These raise a large number of new challenges for the CN area, specifically related to the rights and liabilities, monetization, accountability, ethics, trust, coping with risks and disruptions, as well as the need for the creation of new collaboration culture and business models for collaborative value creation. These topics, among others, are challenges being tackled by the fourth generation of the CN area and constitute the contents of this proceedings book.

We would also like to further note, that this year, the PRO-VE conference took place under extraordinary circumstances. Although the conference was planned and organized to be held in its regular format, as in all previous editions, in Valencia, Spain, during September 2020, the world's dynamics changed from the beginning of the year, and the uncertainty increased dramatically throughout the year, due to the COVID-19 pandemic. Therefore, the conference could only be held in virtual format, while this proceedings book was prepared with the same quality requirements as in previous years.

In fact, the situation created by this pandemic further reveals the timeliness of the conference motto, reaching its full sense worldwide. Today more than ever, everyone realizes the need to network and boost collaboration between varied partners, including governments, non-profit organizations, enterprises, professionals, and public citizens, across many sectors such as health, logistics, manufacturing, food, agriculture, and news media, while facilitating their work under tight restrictions and characteristics, such as speed, resilience, flexibility, quality, reliability, and trustworthiness.

Most approaches that have been applied so far, as well as the solutions which are adopted to mitigate the impact of the COVID-19 pandemic around the world, have already been addressed in the past PRO-VE conference series. Considering this crisis, we conclude that the performed research and developed applications in the CN area have been fundamental for facing these complicated times. Nevertheless, we also realize that there are many new challenges emerging and in need of innovative contributions.

PRO-VE 2020 addresses diverse viewpoints on timely CN 4.0 challenges. The conference provides a forum for sharing experiences, discussing trends, and identifying opportunities, thus introducing innovative solutions for the new generation of collaborative networks in the era of digital transformation. Understanding, modeling, and proposing solution approaches to these challenges require contributions from multiple and diverse areas and disciplines, including: computer science, manufacturing, industrial, electrical and computing engineering, social sciences, organization science, and technologies, among others, which are well tuned to both the interdisciplinary nature of the research and development on CN 4.0, as well as the spirit of the PRO-VE working conferences.

PRO-VE 2020 was the 21st event in this series of successful conferences, including: PRO-VE 1999 (Porto, Portugal), PRO-VE 2000 (Florianopolis, Brazil), PRO-VE 2002 (Sesimbra, Portugal), PRO-VE 2003 (Lugano, Switzerland), PRO-VE 2004 (Toulouse, France), PRO-VE 2005 (Valencia, Spain), PRO-VE 2006 (Helsinki, Finland), PROVE 2007 (Guimarães, Portugal), PRO-VE 2008 (Poznan, Poland), PRO-VE 2009 (Thessaloniki, Greece), PRO-VE 2010 (St. Etienne, France), PRO-VE 2011 (São Paulo, Brazil), PRO-VE 2012 (Bournemouth, UK), PRO-VE 2013 (Dresden, Germany), PROVE 2014 (Amsterdam, The Netherlands), PRO-VE 2015 (Albi, France), PRO-VE 2016 (Porto, Portugal), PRO-VE 2017 (Vicenza, Italy), PRO-VE 2018 (Cardiff, UK), and PRO-VE 2019 (Torino, Italy).

This proceedings book includes selected papers from the PRO-VE 2020 conference. It provides a comprehensive overview of major challenges that are being currently addressed, and specifically recent advances in various domains related to the collaborative networks and their applications. There is therefore a strong focus on the following areas related to the selected main theme for the 2020 conference:

- Collaborative models, platforms, and systems for digital transformation
- Business ecosystems and collaboration in Industry 4.0
- Hybridization of collaboration – organizations, people, machines, and systems
- Big data analytics and intelligence
- Collaborative cyber-physical systems
- Distributed cognitive systems
- Risk, performance, and disruptions in collaborative networked systems
- Semantic data/service discovery, retrieval, and composition, in a collaborative networked world
- Ethics, trust, culture of collaboration, and sustainability in CNs
- Value creation, collaboration monetization, and social impact of collaborative networks
- Intelligent platforms supporting collaborative systems
- Collective intelligence and collaboration in advanced/emerging applications
- Collaborative manufacturing and factories of the future, e-health and care, food and agribusiness, and crisis/disaster management

We are thankful to all the authors from academia, research, and industry, for their contributions. We hope this collection of papers represents a valuable tool for those interested in research advances and emerging applications in collaborative networks, and in identifying future open challenges for research and development in this area. We very much appreciate the dedication, and the time and effort spent by the members of the PRO-VE International Program Committee who supported us with the selection of articles for this conference and provided valuable and constructive comments to help authors with improving the quality of their papers.

November 2020

Luis M. Camarinha-Matos
Hamideh Afsarmanesh
Angel Ortiz

Organization

PRO-VE 2020 – 21st IFIP Working Conference on VIRTUAL ENTERPRISES

Valencia, Spain, November 23–25, 2020

Conference Chair

Angel Ortiz   Polytechnic University of Valencia, Spain

Program Committee Chair

Luis M. Camarinha-Matos   NOVA University of Lisbon, Portugal

Program Committee Co-chair

Hamideh Afsarmanesh   University of Amsterdam, The Netherlands

Program Committee

Antonio Abreu, Portugal
Hamideh Afsarmanesh, The Netherlands
Cesar Analide, Portugal
Dario Antonelli, Italy
Américo Azevedo, Portugal
Thomas Beach, UK
Frédérick Bénaben, France
Peter Bernus, Australia
Xavier Boucher, France
Jeremy Bryans, UK
Luis M. Camarinha-Matos, Portugal
Wojciech Cellary, Poland
Rob Dekkers, UK
Filipa Ferrada, Portugal
Adriano Fiorese, Brazil
Adrian Florea, Romania
Rosanna Fornasiero, Italy
Gary Fragidis, Greece

Cesar Garita, Costa Rica
Ted Goranson, USA
Juanqiong Gou, China
Paul Grefen, The Netherlands
Dmitri Ivanov, Germany
Tomasz Janowski, Poland
Javad Jassbi, Portugal
Eleni Kaldoudi, Greece
Dimitris Karagiannis, Austria
Adamantios Koumpis, Germany
Matthieu Lauras, France
Leandro Loss, Brazil
António Lucas Soares, Portugal
Laura Macchion, Italy
Patricia Macedo, Portugal
Kyrill Meyer, Germany
Istvan Mezgar, Hungary
Paulo Miyagi, Brazil

Arturo Molina, Mexico
Ovidiu Noran, Australia
Paulo Novais, Portugal
Adegboyega Ojo, Ireland
Ana Inês Oliveira, Portugal
Martin Ollus, Finland
Angel Ortiz, Spain
A. Luis Osório, Portugal
Hervé Panetto, France
Iraklis Paraskakis, Greece
Adam Pawlak, Poland
Jorge Pinho Sousa, Portugal
Raul Poler, Spain
Ricardo Rabelo, Brazil
João Rosas, Portugal

Hans Schaffers, The Netherlands
Jens Schütze, Germany
Volker Stich, Germany
Chrysostomos Stylios, Greece
Klaus-Dieter Thoben, Germany
Lorna Uden, UK
Paula Urze, Portugal
Katri Valkokari, Finland
Rolando Vallejos, Brazil
Agostino Villa, Italy
Antonio Volpentesta, Italy
Lai Xu, UK
Christian Zinke, Germany
Peter Weiß, Germany

Special Session Organizers

Special Session on Boosting Sustainability through Collaboration in Agri-Food 4.0

Mareva Alemany, Spain
Jorge Hernandez, UK
Hervé Panetto, France

Special Session on Digital Innovation Hubs for Digitalising European Industry

Francisco Blanes, Spain
José Ferreira, Portugal

Special Session on Collaborative Networks for Health and Wellness Data Management

Elena Pessot, Italy
Marco Sacco, Italy
Daniele Spoladore, Italy
Andrea Zangiacomi, Italy

Special Session on Skills for Organizations of the Future

Adrian Florea, Romania
Luis M. Camarinha-Matos, Portugal

Technical Sponsors

**IFIP WG 5.5 COVE
Co-Operation infrastructure for Virtual
Enterprises and electronic business**

Society of Collaborative Networks

Project

Organizational Co-sponsors

Nova University of Lisbon

Contents

Data and Knowledge Services

Blockchain and Knowledge Graphs

Maintenance, Compliance and Liability

Digital Transformation

Skills for Organizations of the Future

Collaboration in Open Innovation

Collaboration in Supply Chain

Simulation and Analysis in Collaborative Systems

Product and Service Systems

Collaborative Business Ecosystems

Evaluating and Influencing the Performance of a Collaborative Business Ecosystem – A Simulation Study

Paula Graça[1,2(✉)] and Luís M. Camarinha-Matos[1(✉)]

[1] Faculty of Sciences and Technology and Uninova CTS, NOVA University of Lisbon, Campus de Caparica, 2829-516 Caparica, Portugal
cam@uninova.pt
[2] Instituto Superior de Engenharia de Lisboa, Instituto Politécnico de Lisboa, Rua Conselheiro Emídio Navarro 1, 1959-007 Lisbon, Portugal
paula.graca@isel.pt

Abstract. In a Collaborative Business Ecosystem, organisations collaborate to acquire and accomplish more innovative and challenging market opportunities. But the sustainability of collaboration requires continuous performance improvement. To this end, well-defined performance indicators can be used to both assess the collaboration level and act as an influence mechanism to induce an improvement in the collaborative behaviour of the participating organisations. By varying the importance (weight) of the adopted set of indicators, it is possible to study the variations in behaviour towards improvement, not only at organisations' level but also at the level of the ecosystem as a whole. In order to assess this hypothesis, this paper contains a case study based on simulation and agent-based modelling whose behaviour is shaped according to actual data on collaboration collected from three companies in the area of the IT industry. Various scenarios are simulated and described.

Keywords: Collaborative networks · Business ecosystem · Performance indicators · Simulation · Agent-Based modelling

1 Introduction

The challenges of dealing with market turbulence, disruptive events, and the increasingly competitive levels induced by globalisation motivate companies to engage in collaborative processes as a way to acquire agility and resilience [1]. This trend is followed by increasing digitalization and supporting technology, providing environments conducive to business collaboration. Moore [2], inspired by natural ecosystems, first introduced the term Business Ecosystem. On the other hand, Camarinha-Matos and Afsarmanesh [3], consider a business ecosystem as a form of a Collaborative Network (CN). As such and aiming to emphasise the collaboration aspect, we have adopted the term Collaborative Business Ecosystem (CBE) [4].

In this context, it is crucial to be able to evaluate the performance of the CBE and the potential gains that organisations can achieve. For the management of individual companies, there are well-defined performance assessment methods and indicators.

L. M. Camarinha-Matos et al. (Eds.): PRO-VE 2020, IFIP AICT 598, pp. 3–18, 2020.
https://doi.org/10.1007/978-3-030-62412-5_1

As an example, Kaplan and Norton [5] introduced the balanced scorecard (BSC). This method encompasses key performance indicators aligned with the vision and strategy of companies. Although there is extensive literature research that mentions the benefits of collaboration, only limited contributions to performance assessment in CNs can be found. Some authors have suggested using BSCs in CNs [6, 7], and some approaches have been applied to supply chains (SCs) [8–10]. However, and although they are important contributions, they do not constitute a common line of reasoning to adopt as a strategy for the design of performance indicators for CBEs [3]. Other areas of research identify value creation in collaboration and provide relevant contributions to this topic. As an example, in [11], the authors propose a method to evaluate the alignment of the value systems (VS) of the members of a CN [12]. Other examples propose a variety of methods and metrics to assess the performance of supply chain collaboration (SCC) [13–16]. Finally, the area of social network analysis (SNA), draws insights from the patterns of relationships linking social actors [17], from which metrics tailored to CBEs can be inspired. As another important contribution, we can mention [18, 19], where the authors also inspired by SNA, propose performance indicators for CNs, based on collaboration benefits and to measure social capital.

The purpose of this paper is to present a simulation study to evaluate a CBE through the performance indicators previously proposed [20]. We further aim to be able to change CBE's behaviour through an influence mechanism, varying the weight of the adopted indicators. The study uses the Performance Assessment and Adjustment Model (PAAM) proposed in [21] and tunes it with actual data from three companies in the area of the IT industry. These companies operate in the same ecosystem, two of them being ranked in the FT 1000 – Europe's Fastest Growing Companies 2020 [22]. Organisations in the ecosystem are differentiated into classes of responsiveness that correspond to different profiles. Such classes constrain the evolution of members' behaviour when assessed and influenced by the proposed mechanism. Some readjustment is expected from organisations to improve their behaviour and that of the whole ecosystem. There is a natural tendency (in the same way as individuals) to evolve in the sense that they are evaluated.

The remaining sections are organised as follows: section two presents the simulation model of the CBE, briefly describing the performance assessment and proposing an influence mechanism anchored in theories of inter-organisational networks; section three contains the experimental evaluation, presenting simulation scenarios using actual data from the three organisations considered, as well as a discussion of outcomes; the last section summarises the results, describes ongoing research and identifies future work.

2   A Simulation Model of a CBE

For this simulation study, we adopt the Performance Assessment and Adjustment Model (PAAM) [21] illustrated in Fig. 1. A CBE is characterized by an environment populated by organisations that interact collaborating to accomplish market opportunities. The interactions referred to here as collaboration opportunities (*CoOps*) are

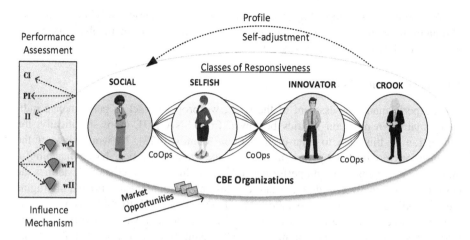

Fig. 1. PAAM (Performance Assessment and Adjustment Model) for a CBE.

represented by "links" between the organisations (the "nodes"), weighted by the number of *CoOps* (*#CoOps*) exchanged over a period of time.

The organisations in the CBE have different profiles, revealing different collaborative behaviours according to the classes of responsiveness considered in Table 1. Each class (i.e. Social, Selfish, Innovator, and Crook) is characterized by three factors (parameterizable decimal values between from 0 and 1), namely contact rate, accept rate, and new products rate, which model the organisation in terms of its propensity to invite other members of the CBE to collaborate, accept invites or tend to accept opportunities involving innovation.

Table 1. Example of parameterization (decimal values between 0 and 1) to characterize the organisations' classes of responsiveness in the PAAM model.

Profiles of Organizations					
Classes of Responsiveness [0..1]		**Social**	**Selfish**	**Innovator**	**Crook**
Contact rate	Willingness to invite others to collaborate	0,7	0,1	0,7	0,3
Accept rate	Readiness to accept invitations	0,6	0,2	0,8	0,3
New products rate	Tendency to accept opportunities related to innovation	0,2	0,2	0,6	0,3

A "Performance Assessment" system composed of a set of performance indicators (CI – Contribution Indicator, PI – Prestige Indicator and II – Innovation Indicator) proposed in [20, 21], can evaluate the CBE, and also act as a factor of influence by varying the importance (weight) of the adopted indicators by the CBE. This "Influence Mechanism" is likely to induce a readjustment of organizations, thereby improving their profile and that of the CBE.

We use the PAAM model to set different simulation scenarios, varying the number of organisations of each class of responsiveness and, for each of them, also varying the rate of each factor that characterizes it.

2.1 Performance Assessment

For the performance assessment of the CBE, we propose a set of performance indicators mainly inspired on metrics borrowed from SNA [17], more specifically, the application of this area to inter-organisational contexts [23]. Network view of the organisations connected by ties, as well as the strength of ties, has a meaningful influence on its behaviour and performance [23]. In this line, Coleman [24] defines the closure of social networks (direct or indirect links between all the actors) and highlights their importance as a form of social capital. On the other hand, Burt [25] considers the density of a network as a form of closure, since contacts in a dense network (meaning more links) are in close communication. Moreover, Burt [25] also identifies social capital but in terms of brokerage structural holes (weak ties between groups), allowing a competitive advantage for those whose relations cross the holes. Freeman, in [26, 27], also mentioned in Burt [28], proposes the betweenness centrality as a method to assesses the brokerage of these structural holes in the network.

According to predominant research where SNA is applied to inter-organisational contexts, Zaheer et al. [23] identify findings in a three-layer analysis: i) *"dyadic"* (nature of ties) – strong ties among organisations increase trust between them, lowering transaction costs and increasing benefits; ii) *"ego"* (organisations) – high degree centrality is favourably related to their performance, as well as structural holes and closure generate social capital; iii) "the *whole network*" – research focuses on measures such as centrality, density, cliques [29], and small-worlds [30], the findings of which are too extensive to be discussed here, even though there is very little work on business networks [29].

The performance indicators used in this simulation study, briefly described in Table 2, follow the lines of research mentioned above. Based mainly on metrics of density and weighted centrality in SNA [26, 27, 31, 32], are designed to assess individual organisations and the CBE as a whole.

The purpose of this paper is not to discuss the performance indicators which were proposed in earlier works, but rather to apply them to evaluate collaboration in the CBE, and check how they can influence the organisations to improve their behaviour, also resulting in ecosystem improvement.

2.2 Influence Mechanism

The behaviour of a CBE evolves according to some factors that influence the establishment of relationships between the organisations. The inter-organisational relations influence organisational learning and innovation, including organisational change, by promoting or constraining their access to information, physical, financial, and social resources [33]. Ahuja et al. [34] introduced the concept of *"micro-foundations"* as the fundamental drivers of networks at every level of analysis, i.e. the basic factors driving the formation, persistence, dissolution and content of ties in the network. The same

Table 2. Performance Indicators to assess the collaboration of organisations and CBE as a whole.

Performance Indicators	
Contribution Indicator of an Organisation (CI$_i$) and the CBE (CI$_{CBE}$)	
$CI_i in/out = \dfrac{C_D(O_i) in/out}{C_D(O^*) in/out} = \dfrac{\sum_j O_{ij} \#CoOp_{ij} in/out}{\max \sum_j O_{ij} \#CoOp_{ij} in/out}$	Assesses the contribution of organisation O$_i$ in terms of the number of accepted/created (in/out) collaboration opportunities (#CoOp).
$CI_{CBE} in/out = \dfrac{\sum_i [C_D(O^*) in/out - C_D(O_i) in/out]}{C_D(O^*) in/out * (\#O - 1)}$	Assesses the degree to which the most popular/active organisation [max degree centrality C$_D$(O*) in/out] exceeds the contribution of the others.
$CI_{CBE} t = \dfrac{\sum_i \#CoOp_i}{\#O}$	Ratio of the total number of collaboration opportunities (#CoOp) created/accepted in the CBE by the total number of organisations (#O).
Prestige Indicator of an Organisation (PI$_i$) and the CBE (PI$_{CBE}$)	
$PI_i = \dfrac{C_B(O_i)}{C_B(O^*)} = \dfrac{\sum_k \sum_j O_{kj}(O_i)}{\max \sum_k \sum_j O_{kj}(O_i)}$	Assesses the prominence/influence of organisation O$_i$ in terms of the number of collaboration opportunities (#CoOp).
$PI_{CBE} = \dfrac{C_B(CBE)}{\max C_B(CBE)} = \dfrac{\sum_i [C_B(O^*) - C_B(O_i)]}{C_B(O^*) * (\#O - 1)}$	Assesses the degree to which the most prominent/influent organisation [max betweenness centrality C$_D$(O*)] exceeds the contribution of the others.
Innovation Indicator of an Organisation (II$_i$) and the CBE (II$_{CBE}$)	
$II_i = \dfrac{\#NewPd_i}{\#PortPd_i}$	Measures the ratio of the number of new products/services/patentes (NewPd$_i$) of the organisation O$_i$ by the total portfolio (PortPd$_i$) created.
$II_{CBE} = \dfrac{\sum \#NewPd_i}{\sum \#PortPd_i} * r(\#VO, \#NewPd)$	Calculates the ratio of innovation of the organisations in the CBE, weighted by the correlation between the collaboration (participation in Vos) and new products/services/patents [r(#VO, #NewPd)].

Note: The values of the indicators are normalised between [0..1].

authors [34] identify four primary micro-foundations to explain the genesis and evolution of networks, namely Agency, Opportunity, Inertia, and random and exogenous factors. Moreover, they argue that these micro-foundations operate through "*micro-dynamics*" to form, dissolve or maintain ties, resulting in the accumulation of changes that affect the structure of the network and are consequently reflected in changes in its "*Structural dimensions*".

Table 3 summarizes the framework of network dynamics of Ahuja et al. [34], describing the four micro-foundations, their microdynamics at the level of node assortativity and tie pattern, and their structural dimensions concerning the ego-network and the whole-network. The authors state that in order to explore the idea of the dynamics of the network, its architecture can be conceived in terms of the nodes that compose it, the ties that connect the nodes, and the patterns that result from those connections. The proposed PAAM model of a CBE is consistent with this view, as it is represented by a network of nodes (the organisations) whose collaboration creates ties (opportunities that they send and receive), forming patterns of connections according to their profile. As such, the micro-foundations of Ahuja et al. are suitable for mapping the different profiles of organizations in the CBE, allowing the design of the proposed influence mechanism, considering, as the authors argue [34], that they determine the evolutionary path of networks at all levels of analysis.

Table 3. A framework of networks dynamics (Source: Ahuja et al. [34]).

Networks Dynamics				
Micro-foundations	Agency	Opportunity	Inertia	Random/ Exogenous
Description	Refers to the focal actor's motivation and ability to shape relationships and create a beneficial connection or dissolve a non-profit relationship, or to shape an advantageous structure	Firms form alliances with firms they have prior alliances with or with the partners of their partners. Both of these emerge from the logic of trust and convenience	Refers to the durability of social structures as well as the social processes through which the actions of the focal actor are influenced, directed and conditioned by institutional norms and pressures	Considers that the emergence of network structures may result from exogenous factors from outside the network or from simple random processes, whether generated inside or outside the network
Microdynamics Nodal assortativity driven	Homophily, heterophily, prominence attraction	Proximity, common goals, common identity	Habits, networking propensity, collaborative expertise	
Tie pattern driven	Brokerage, closure	Transitivity, repetition, referral	Dense clusters with few bridging ties, low connectivity	
Structural dim. Ego-network	Centrality, structural holes, closure			
Whole-network	Degree distribution, connectivity, clustering, density, degree			

Using the framework of Ahuja et al. [34] and based on the network-change behaviour according to the identified micro-foundations and respective microdynamics, we propose an influence mechanism in which the significance (weight) assigned by the CBE Manager to each performance indicator, is expected to influence the behaviour of the organisations. The assumption is that in the same as with individuals, organisations tend to perform according to the way they are evaluated.

As such, we can map the organisations' profiles considered in the simulation model in Fig. 1, into the micro-foundations identified in Ahuja et al. [34] to help to understand changes in their behaviour according to their microdynamics, when influenced by the adopted performance indicators. We can consider the Agency and Opportunity micro-foundations as having a Social profile since both have a propensity to collaborate, nevertheless, Agency is more likely to collaborate with a diversity of organisations (homophily and heterophily) expanding new ties, and those from Opportunity type tend to collaborate with partners they already know and trust (transitivity, repetition, and referral). Moreover, the Agency also has more entrepreneurial behaviour, spanning structural holes (brokerage) to gain benefits from this social capital. From the above, we mapped the Agency with our Innovative profile and the Opportunity with our Social profile. The Selfish profile that can be identified with the Inertia micro-foundation comprises organisations with more conservative behaviour and a low rate of collaboration (low connectivity), due to the propensity to keep the same partners. Finally, the Crook profile can be associated with a collaboration rate due to exogenous and random factors, although these types of factors are also associated with all micro-foundations on a smaller scale [34]. Table 4 describes a possible parameterization of organisations' profile, expressed in terms of their classes of responsiveness.

Table 4. Possible parametrization (decimal values between 0 and 1) of the organisations' classes of responsiveness according to the microdynamics of the mapped micro-foundations.

Profiles of Organisations					
Profiles		Social	Selfish	Innovator	Crook
Micro-foundations		Opportunity	Inertia	Agency	Exogenous/ Random
Contact rate	Willingness to invite others to collaborate	0,7	0,1	0,7	n/a
Accept rate	Readiness to accept invitations	0.6	0,1	0,8	n/a
New products rate	Tendency to accept opportunities related to innovation	0,2	0,2	0,6	n/a

(left side row label: Classes of Responsiveness)

Considering the characterization of the organisations' classes of responsiveness in Table 4, and a weight defined by the CBE manager to each performance indicator (*wCI, wPI, wII*) as exemplified in Table 5, the influence mechanism can be set.

Table 5. Example of weights (values between 0 and 5) assigned to performance indicators.

Weights of P. Indicators		
wCI	wPI	wII
4	2	1

Table 6 summarizes the proposed influence mechanism. A given factor of influence (FI%) acts differently in the behaviour of the organisations according to their classes of responsiveness. The weight of each indicator is associated with the attribute of the class of responsiveness for which it has the most significant influence, i.e. the Contact rate is related to the CI, the Accept rate to the PI and the New products rate to the II. As such, the influence on an organisation (O_i) is calculated by increasing its class of responsiveness by a percentage calculated by the factors FI_{wCI}, FI_{wPI}, and FI_{wII}, represented by formulas (1), (2) and (3). A factor ($\pm F_e$) is also considered in the formulas to add an exogenous/random positive or negative influence.

$$contact_{rate}(O_i) + = contact_{rate}(O_i) * wCI * \frac{FI}{wCI+wPI+wII} + F_e \qquad (1)$$

$$accept_{rate}(O_i) + = accept_{rate}(O_i) * wPI * \frac{FI}{wCI+wPI+wII} + F_e \qquad (2)$$

$$newProduct_{rate}(O_i) + = newProduct_{rate}(O_i) * wII * \frac{FI}{wCI+wPI+wII} + F_e \qquad (3)$$

Table 6. Influence mechanism of a Collaborative Business Ecosystem.

Influence Mechanism				
Classes of Responsiveness	Perf. Indicator	Related to	Weight	Factor of Influence (FI %)
Contact rate	CI	It is related to activity	wCI	$FI_{wCI} = wCI * \dfrac{FI}{wCI + wPI + wII}$
Accept rate	PI	It is related to prominence/influence	wPI	$FI_{wPI} = wPI * \dfrac{FI}{wCI + wPI + wII}$
New products rate	II	It is related to innovation	wII	$FI_{wII} = wII * \dfrac{FI}{wCI + wPI + wII}$

2.3 Behaviour of the Agents

The simulation model (PAAM) was designed using AnyLogic tools [35]. Accordingly, the CBE is an environment (the business ecosystem) populated by agents (the organisations). The profile of organisations is modelled by probability distributions [35] to simulate their behaviour according to the defined classes of responsiveness. Figure 2 shows a simplified model of a social organisation using agent-based modelling (ABM), statecharts, and system dynamic (SD). The resources of the organisations are maintained in stocks divided into three main groups: *Research&Development*, *Consulting,* and *Inner tasks.* When an organisation receives a new market opportunity (*newMarketOp* composed of a task and number of required resources), it uses a Bernoulli distribution parametrized by the *contactRate* (4) to invite others to collaborate. The recipient organisation uses a Bernoulli distribution parametrized by the *acceptRate* (5) or the *newProductsRate* (6) if the opportunity involves innovation. The higher the parameters, the more likely it is to create collaboration opportunities (*CoOps*), if there are available resources. A triangular distribution is used to generate the number (between a min and max) of business units to distribute to the partners (7).

$$invite_{toCollaborate} = bernoulli(contactRate) \tag{4}$$

$$accept_{collaboration} = bernoulli(acceptRate) \tag{5}$$

$$accept_{collaboration} = bernoulli(newProductsRate) \tag{6}$$

$$businessUnits_{toDistribute} = triangular(minUnits, maxUnits) \tag{7}$$

3 Experimental Results of the Simulation Model

For the experimental evaluation, we parameterized the PAAM simulation model using actual data accrued in 2019 from three companies operating in the same business ecosystem in the area of the IT industry. The data collected includes the resources (number of persons) allocated by function (research and development, consulting and

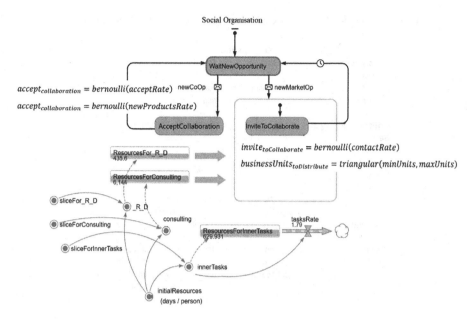

Fig. 2. Simplified model representing the behaviour of a social organisation in the CBE.

inner tasks), number of market opportunities received and accepted (characterised by a minimum, maximum and typical duration in days/person), the partners to whom invitations to collaborate were sent or from whom invitations were received, and the number of products/services created (total, innovative and in collaboration). The data also allowed to estimate the organisations' classes of responsiveness (contact rate, accept rate and new products rate) to configure the behaviour of the agents of different profiles.

Organisation1 is expert in delivering responsive web applications and high fidelity mobile apps, using agile platforms in complex environments and large infrastructures, where they excel in architecture and systems integration. Table 7 shows a sample of data collected from Organisation1 in the year 2019. Organisation2 operates as a consultant and integrator with solutions focused on cybersecurity and networks, providing highly specialized services to government and business markets. Table 8 shows a sample of data collected from Organisation2 in the year 2019. Organisation3 is a system integrator with solutions focused on information management, using the best of breed technologies that best apply to the requirements and objectives of solutions to various market sectors. It also has partnerships with Universities for R&D processes. Table 9 shows a sample of data collected from Organisation3 in the year 2019.

The data of the three organisations are consolidated in Table 10 to parameterize the PAAM model. Here, the attributes of the classes of responsiveness are the average between the minimum and maximum values, where applicable.

Table 7. Sample of data collected in the year 2019 from the Organisation1.

Organisation1					
Resources (persons)	R&D 1		Consulting 46		Inner tasks 15
Market Opportunities	Received 178	Accepted 136	Duration (days/person) min mode max		
Collaboration Ops. Sent	Invites sent min max		Contact rate min max		Business units min max
Partner1	22				7,2%
Partner2	23		0,56		6,8%
Partner3	19				6,4%
Partner4	12				4,0%
Total	76				
Received	Invites received min max		Accept rate min		max
Total	0	0			
Products/ Services	Total portfolio 136		Innovative		New products rate
	In collaboration 2		min 5	max 9	min 0,04 max 0,07

Table 8. Sample of data collected in the year 2019 from the Organisation2.

Organisation2					
Resources (persons)	R&D 0		Consulting 14		Inner tasks 2
Market Opportunities	Received 98	Accepted 88	Duration (days/person) min 0 mode 10 max 30		
Collaboration Ops. Sent	Invites sent min max		Contact rate min max		Business units min max
Partner5	1	1			5,5% 5,5%
Partner6	1	3	0,03	0,08	5,5% 16,7%
Partner7	1	2			1,7% 3,4%
Partner8	0	1			0,0% 4,7%
Total	3	7			
Received	Invites received min max		Accept rate min		max
Partner9	1	2	100%		
Partner10	1	1	100%		
Partner11	1	1	100%		
Total	3	4	1,00		
Products/ Services	Total portfolio 80		Innovative		New products rate
	In collaboration 3		min 10	max	min 0,13 max

Table 9. Sample of data collected in the year 2019 from the Organisation3.

Organisation3					
Resources	R&D		Consulting		Inner tasks
(persons)	2		28		3
Market Opportunities	Received	Accepted	Duration (days/person)		
			min	mode	max
	27	15	30	60	100
Collaboration Ops.	Invites sent		Contact rate		Business units
Sent	min	max	min	max	min max
Partner12	1	2			0,8% 1,7%
Partner10	2	3	0,47	0,73	3,0% 4,5%
Partner13	1	2			0,4% 0,8%
Partner8	3	4			1,2% 1,7%
Total	7	11			
	Invites received		Accept rate		
Received	min	max	min	max	
Partner12	3	4	70%	80%	
Partner10	2	3	50%	60%	
Partner13	3	4	80%	90%	
Partner8	6	7	90%	100%	
Partner14	8	10	30%	50%	
Partner15	2	3	50%	70%	
Partner16	1	2	100%	100%	
Partner17	2	3	50%	50%	
Partner18	1	2	70%	100%	
Partner19	4	5	30%	50%	
Partner20	1	2	100%	100%	
Total	33	45	0,30	1,00	
Products/	Total portfolio		Innovative		New products rate
Services	16				
	In collaboration		min	max	min max
	6		10		0,63

Table 10. Consolidated samples of data from the Organisation1, Organisation2 and Organisation3.

	Organization1	Organization2	Organization3
Resources	value	value	value
Total (persons)	62	16	33
Total (days/person)	13640	3520	7260
R&D	2%	0%	6%
Consulting	74%	87%	85%
Inner Tasks	24%	13%	9%
Market Opportunities	min	mode	max
Duration (days/person)	0	20	100
Classes of Responsiveness	value	value	value
Contact rate	0,56	0,06	0,60
Accept rate	0,00	1,00	0,65
New products rate	0,06	0,13	0,63
Units to Distribute	min max	min max	min max
	4,0% 7,2%	0% 16,7%	0,4% 4,5%

The PAAM model in Fig. 3, shows a simulation scenario populated by 20 organisations to totalise a similar number of organisations considered in the data samples: 10 organisations with the Organisation1's profile (Social), 4 with the Organisation2's profile (Selfish) and 6 with the Organisation3's profile (Innovator). The model was executed for one year in a simulated environment [35], using the Poisson's distribution [35] to create 2000 market opportunities, plus 20% of opportunities with innovation. The model supports any combination of each profile and any distribution of market opportunities to be possible to create and analyse several simulation scenarios.

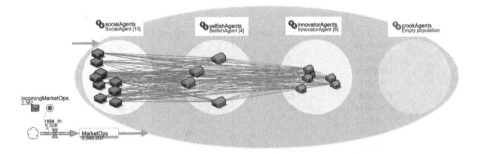

Fig. 3. PAAM set with a simulation scenario using 10 social agents, 4 selfish and 6 innovators.

Table 11. Performance indicators CI and PI (normalized) for organisations and the CBE as a whole, before and after applying the influence mechanism.

Performance Assessment before Influence					Performance Assessment after Influence				
Profile	O_i	CI_i in	CI_i out	PI_i	Profile	O_i	CI_i in	CI_i out	PI_i
Organisation1 (Social)	0	0,03	0,52	0,00	Organisation1 (Social)	0	0,00	0,67	0,00
	1	0,00	0,60	0,00		1	0,00	0,88	0,00
	2	0,03	0,56	0,00		2	0,00	0,88	0,00
	3	0,00	0,48	0,00		3	0,00	0,75	0,00
	4	0,00	0,44	0,00		4	0,00	0,71	0,00
	5	0,00	0,60	0,00		5	0,02	0,38	0,00
	6	0,00	0,96	0,00		6	0,00	0,54	0,00
	7	0,00	0,76	0,00		7	0,00	0,71	0,00
	8	0,00	0,68	0,00		8	0,00	0,92	0,00
	9	0,00	0,80	0,00		9	0,00	0,54	0,00
Organisation2 (Selfish)	10	0,78	0,12	0,00	Organisation2 (Selfish)	10	1,00	0,08	0,08
	11	0,86	0,04	0,00		11	0,67	0,08	0,00
	12	0,95	0,00	0,00		12	0,72	0,08	0,00
	13	1,00	0,08	0,10		13	0,67	0,04	0,00
Organisation3 (Innovator)	14	0,76	1,00	1,00	Organisation3 (Innovator)	14	0,50	0,92	0,89
	15	0,62	0,52	0,06		15	0,72	0,79	1,00
	16	0,51	0,92	0,66		16	0,54	0,67	0,47
	17	0,49	0,52	0,02		17	0,54	0,83	0,58
	18	0,51	0,36	0,02		18	0,57	0,88	0,78
	19	0,54	0,52	0,11		19	0,48	1,00	0,50
CI_{CBE} t = 13,1					CI_{CBE} t = 14,8				
CI_{CBE} in = 0,68			PI_{CBE} = 0,90		CI_{CBE} in = 0,71			PI_{CBE} = 0,79	
CI_{CBE} out = 0,50					CI_{CBE} out = 0,40				

We can now assess the CBE using the performance indicators, before and after applying the influence mechanism, assuming the weights of the performance indicators defined in the example in Table 5 (*wCI = 2, wPI = 4, wII = 1*) and a factor of influence FI = 15%. Table 11 displays the results achieved in this CBE before and after being influenced. This assessment does not include performance indicator II, as not enough actual data has been collected in the scope of this paper, to allow its calculation.

Analysing the results in Table 11, we can see that due to the profile of organisations considered as Social, have an Accept rate = 0, the indicators more related to prominence and influence (CI_{in} and PI) are almost all equal to zero. Even after de influence mechanism with a weight *wPI = 4*, the PI indicator remains almost unchanged, which means that an exogenous positive (*+Fe*) factor may have to be applied to reverse this trend. However, using the graphical representation (Ghephy tool [36]) of the network formed by the CBE (Fig. 4), we can perceive the influence of the mechanism, as more organisations gained prestige by acquiring a higher PI. As a result, the PI_{CBE} has improved (lower value) showing a more uniform collaboration in the CBE.

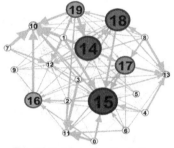

(A) PI ranking before the influence.   (B) PI ranking after the influence.

Fig. 4. Shows the PI ranking before (A) and after (B) the CBE was influenced: the nodes' size is related to the PI. i.e., the larger the node, the higher the value of the indicator; the links' strength is weighted by the number of collaboration opportunities exchanged by the organisations.

Regarding the results related to the CI indicator in Table 11, graphically represented in Fig. 5 and Fig. 6, no significant changes can be observed in the contributions of the organisations (CI_{in} and CI_{out}). It is an expected result since the influence mechanism used a low weight *wCI = 2*. However, the $CI_{CBE}t$ has improved, which means more collaboration opportunities created in the CBE. The $CI_{CBE}in$ has increased, signifying more bias in accepted collaboration opportunities, but a levelling out of the created collaboration opportunities in the CBE.

In conclusion, the simulation scenarios presented show that the collaborative behaviour of the organisations in a CBE can be measured by the adequate performance indicators and can be influenced. This approach allows the CBE Manager to orchestrate the network, by varying the weights of the indicators, thus promoting its performance and sustainability. Organisations, in turn, can gain more knowledge and business by engaging in more collaboration opportunities by becoming more influential (scenario of Fig. 4), popular (scenario of Fig. 5), active (scenario of Fig. 6), or innovative.

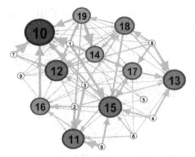

(A) CI$_{in}$ ranking before the influence.   (B) CI$_{in}$ ranking after the influence.

Fig. 5. Shows the CI$_{in}$ ranking before (A) and after (B) the CBE was influenced: the nodes' size is related to the CI$_{in}$. i.e., the larger the node, the higher the value of the indicator; the links' strength is weighted by the number of collaboration opportunities received by the organisations.

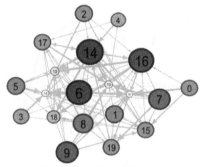

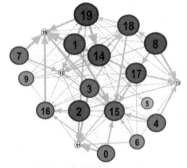

(A) CI$_{out}$ ranking before the influence.   (B) CI$_{out}$ ranking after the influence.

Fig. 6. Shows the CI$_{out}$ ranking before (A) and after (B) the CBE was influenced: the nodes' size is related to the CI$_{out}$. i.e., the larger the node, the higher the value of the indicator; the links' strength is weighted by the number of collaboration opportunities sent by the organisations.

4   Conclusions and Further Work

The experimental results using the PAAM model showed that it is possible to simulate a CBE populated by organisations, represented by agents, whose behaviour evolves according to different profiles, represented by classes of responsiveness. A performance assessment composed of a set of proposed indicators can evaluate the CBE, and act as an influence mechanism according to the weight of each of the adopted indicators. Several scenarios can be set using any combination of organisations of different profiles. The considered profiles are parametrised and tuned using actual data from organisations in the area of the IT industry to create more realistic scenarios.

The ongoing work is related to the improvement of the simulation model and influence mechanism, introducing exogenous and random factors that can influence positively and negatively the collaboration behaviour of the organisations in the CBE.

Future work includes the inclusion of the Innovation Indicator (II) calculation in the PAAM model and fine-tuning more complete simulation scenarios, to better understand the dynamics of a CBE to induce a better self-adjustment towards an improvement of the organisations and the CBE as a whole.

Acknowledgements. This work benefited from the ongoing research within the CoDIS (Collaborative Networks and Distributed Industrial Systems Group) which is part of both the Nova University of Lisbon (UNL) - Faculty of Sciences and Technology and the UNINOVA - CTS (Center of Technology and Systems). Partial support also comes from Fundação para a Ciência e Tecnologia through the program UIDB/00066/2020, and European Commission through the project DiGiFoF (Nr. 601089-EPP-1-2018-1-RO-EPPKA2-KA).

References

1. Ramezani, J., Camarinha-Matos, L.M.: Approaches for resilience and antifragility in collaborative business ecosystems. Technol. Forecast. Soc. Chang. **151**, 119846 (2020)
2. Moore, J.F.: Predators and prey: a new ecology of competition. Harvard Bus. Rev. **71**(3), 75–86 (1993)
3. Camarinha-Matos, L.M., Afsarmanesh, H.: Collaborative networks: a new scientific discipline. J. Intell. Manuf. **16**(45), 439–452 (2005)
4. Graça, P., Camarinha-Matos, L.M.: The need of performance indicators for collaborative business ecosystems. In: Camarinha-Matos, L.M., Baldissera, Thais A., Di Orio, G., Marques, F. (eds.) DoCEIS 2015. IAICT, vol. 450, pp. 22–30. Springer, Cham (2015). https://doi.org/10.1007/978-3-319-16766-4_3
5. Kaplan, R.S., Norton, D.P.: The Balanced Scorecard: Translating Strategy into Action. Harvard Business Press, Boston (1996)
6. Duan, L.N., Park, K.H.: Applying the balanced scorecard to collaborative networks. In: 2010 6th International Conference on Advanced Information Management and Service (IMS), pp. 131–134. IEEE (2010)
7. Schmitt, J., Trang, T.N., Kolbe, M.: Steering information technology in collaborative networks. In: First International Conference on Resource Efficiency in Interorganizational Networks-ResEff 2013, pp. 180 (2013)
8. Bhagwat, R., Sharma, M.K.: Performance measurement of supply chain management: a balanced scorecard approach. Comput. Ind. Eng. **53**(1), 43–62 (2007)
9. Motadel, M.R., Amiran, H., Etemad, S.H.: Presenting a mathematical model for evaluation of the (effectiveness of) supply chain management through balanced scorecard approach (a case study of isaco corporation). In: Not (2012)
10. Chang, H.H., Hung, C.-J., Wong, K.H., Lee, C.-H.: Using the balanced scorecard on supply chain integration performance - a case study of service businesses. Serv. Bus. **7**(4), 539–561 (2013)
11. Camarinha-Matos, L.M., Macedo, P.: A conceptual model of value systems in collaborative networks. J. Intell. Manuf. **21**(3), 287–299 (2010)
12. Macedo, P., Camarinha-Matos, L.M.: A qualitative approach to assess the alignment of value systems in collaborative enterprises networks. Comput. Ind. Eng. **64**(1), 412–424 (2013)
13. Ramanathan, U.: Performance of supply chain collaboration - a simulation study. Expert Syst. Appl. **41**(1), 210–220 (2014). 21st Century Logistics and Supply Chain Management
14. Vereecke, A., Muylle, S.: Performance improvement through supply chain collaboration in Europe. Int J. Oper. Prod. Manag. **26**(11), 1176–1198 (2006)

15. Ramanathan, U., Gunasekaran, A., Subramanian, N.: Supply chain collaboration performance metrics: a conceptual framework. Benchmarking Int. J. **18**(6), 856–872 (2011)
16. Ramanathan, U., Gunasekaran, A.: Supply chain collaboration: Impact of success in long-term partnerships. Int. J. Prod. Econ. **147**, 252–259 (2014)
17. M. O Jackson. *Social and economic networks*, volume 3. Princeton university press Princeton, 2008
18. Camarinha-Matos, L.M., Abreu, A.: Performance indicators for collaborative networks based on collaboration benefits. Prod. Plan. Control **18**(7), 592–609 (2007)
19. Abreu, A., Camarinha-Matos, L.M.: An approach to measure social capital in collaborative networks. In: Camarinha-Matos, L.M., Pereira-Klen, A., Afsarmanesh, H. (eds.) PRO-VE 2011. IAICT, vol. 362, pp. 29–40. Springer, Heidelberg (2011). https://doi.org/10.1007/978-3-642-23330-2_4
20. Graça, P., Camarinha-Matos, L.M.: A proposal of performance indicators for collaborative business ecosystems. In: Afsarmanesh, H., Camarinha-Matos, L.M., Lucas Soares, A. (eds.) PRO-VE 2016. IAICT, vol. 480, pp. 253–264. Springer, Cham (2016). https://doi.org/10.1007/978-3-319-45390-3_22
21. Graça, P., Camarinha-Matos, L.M.: Evolution of a collaborative business ecosystem in response to performance indicators. In: Camarinha-Matos, L.M., Afsarmanesh, H., Fornasiero, R. (eds.) PRO-VE 2017. IAICT, vol. 506, pp. 629–640. Springer, Cham (2017). https://doi.org/10.1007/978-3-319-65151-4_55
22. Kelly, M.: FT 1000: the fourth annual list of Europe's fastest-growing companies (2020)
23. Zaheer, A., Gözübüyük, R., Milanov, H.: It's the connections: the network perspective in interorganizational research. Acad. Manag. Perspect. **24**(1), 62–77 (2010)
24. Coleman, J.S.: Social capital in the creation of human capital. Am. J. Sociol. **94**, S95–S120 (1988)
25. Burt, R.S.: The network structure of social capital. Res. Organ. Behav. **22**, 345–423 (2000)
26. Freeman, L.C.: Centrality in social networks conceptual clarification. Soc. Netw. **1**(3), 215–239 (1978)
27. Freeman, L.C.: A set of measures of centrality based on betweenness. Sociometry **40**(1), 35–41 (1977)
28. Burt, R.S.: Reinforced structural holes. Soc. Netw. **43**, 149–161 (2015)
29. Provan, K.G., Fish, A., Sydow, J.: Interorganizational networks at the network level: a review of the empirical literature on whole networks. J. Manag. **33**(3), 479–516 (2007)
30. Barabási, A.-L.: Linked: the new science of networks. Am. J. Phys. **71**(4), 409–410 (2003)
31. Opsahl, T., Agneessens, F., Skvoretz, J.: Node centrality in weighted networks: generalizing degree and shortest paths. Soc. Netw. **32**(3), 245–251 (2010)
32. Brandes, U.: A faster algorithm for betweenness centrality. J. Math. Sociol. **25**(2), 163–177 (2001)
33. Ferreira, M.P., Armagan, S.: Using social networks theory as a complementary perspective to the study of organizational change. BAR Braz. Adm. Rev. **8**, 168–184 (2011)
34. Ahuja, G., Soda, G., Zaheer, A.: The genesis and dynamics of organizational networks. Organ. Sci. **23**(2), 434–448 (2012)
35. Borshchev, A.: The Big Book of Simulation Modeling: multimethod Modeling with AnyLogic 6. AnyLogic North America (2013)
36. Bastian, M., Heymann, S., Jacomy, M.: Gephi: An open source software for exploring and manipulating networks (2009)

Exploring the Barriers and Mitigation Strategies in Digital Business Ecosystem Development: A Case Study from Engineering Material Supply Service Provider

Qingyu Liang[✉], Juanqiong Gou, Wenqiang Li, and Long Huang

School of Economic and Management, Beijing Jiaotong University,
Beijing, China
{qingyu.liang, jqgou, 20201206, 19125658}@bjtu.edu.cn

Abstract. At present, more and more companies are aware of and have the incentive to promote the construction and development of collaborative platforms, to improve collaboration to cope with many uncertainties such as market turmoil and increased competition. At the same time, with the emergence of emerging digital technologies, the concept of a digital business ecosystem is becoming more and more prominent. DBE development is a long-term evolutionary process, and there are many barriers in the practice. The current research on DBE is mainly conceptual and theoretical, and the barriers in the development process of DBE in the practice are still lack of exploration. Therefore, the purpose of this study is to summarize and analyze the key barriers in the practice of the enterprise through empirical investigation. According to the case companies' mitigation measures and related literature research, we proposed some relevant suggestions and research ideas to solve the barriers.

Keywords: Digital business ecosystem development · Collaborative platforms · Mitigation strategies · Case study

1 Introduction

The market turbulence and increased competition brought about by globalization have encouraged companies to engage in collaboration to gain flexibility and elasticity. With the advent of new organizations, platform structures, and enabling technologies, this trend provides an advantageous environment for business collaboration. A growing number of enterprises are aware of this trend and motivated to push forward the construction and development of collaborative platforms, and the concept of the digital business system is created gradually [1]. DBE can be understood as a social and technological environment composed of collaborative and competitive individuals, organizations, and digital technologies that jointly create value through Shared digital platforms [2]. The main characteristics of DBEs are platform, symbiosis, co-evolution, and self-organization [3]. The core of DBE is the platform. DBE transcends the boundary of traditional industries by virtue of digital collaborative platforms and promotes more open collaboration and competition.

L. M. Camarinha-Matos et al. (Eds.): PRO-VE 2020, IFIP AICT 598, pp. 19–30, 2020.
https://doi.org/10.1007/978-3-030-62412-5_2

At present, the number of enterprises begins to pay attention to DBE development and actively build it of their own. The systematic architectural design is viewed as the means to improve their quality of service. Enterprises energetically promote the construction and development of collaborative platforms to build their own DBE. Commonly, the DBE platform is based on the transformation and upgrade of the traditional supply chain [4]. The traditional supply chain core enterprises gradually build the DBE through the development and operation collaboration platform, promoting collaboration among participants. In the existing researches of DBE, most scholars carry out relevant researches in the idealized state that the DBE has been constructed completely. In the literature on DBE development, [5] proposed a framework, at the theoretical level, for the formation and management of a DBE through a three-stage approach: creation, monitoring, and evaluation. [6] introduced the challenges of top-down and bottom-up DBE development through the comparison of DBE development cases between China and Germany. In practice, the development process of DBE is a complex system engineering, which has many barriers. Currently, the development process of DBE has not been discussed or paid enough attention in the literature.

Authors consider that it is vital to study the barriers in the development of DBE. Firstly, it is the basis of subsequent theoretical and conceptual studies. Besides, real enterprise case studies are more valuable and relevant to the practice of enterprises in the same field. Therefore, the purpose of this study is to analyze the development process of DBE in case enterprises through empirical research, focusing on the key barriers and mitigation strategies in the development process of DBE.

The following tow research questions will be the core of the paper:

A: What are the key barriers for enterprises in DBE development?
B: What are the measures taken by the case enterprise to mitigate barriers during the DBE development?

We used the empirical method, through the collection and analysis of the interview data and text data of the relevant personnel of the case enterprise. We reviewed the process of DBE development of the case enterprise, and to summarize and analyze the key barriers in the process. We summarized and analyzed the barrier mitigation strategies of enterprises in the process of DBE development, and provides theoretical support for the corresponding strategies based on the relevant literature research.

The significance of this paper lies in: in practice, it can provide a reference for enterprises in the same field or other industries in DBE development, at the same time, in the academic field, it complements the relevant content of key barriers in DBE development, and provides a new practical perspective for the follow-up DBE related research.

The rest of the paper is organized as follows: the second section outlines the research methods of this paper, the third section summarizes and analyzes the key barriers and mitigation measures in the DBE development process, and the last section summarizes the full text and provides some future research.

2   Methods

2.1   Data Collection

Our research data are from China Railway Material Trade CO., Ltd. (hereinafter referred to as "MTC"), which was established in December 2010 and is a wholly-owned subsidiary of China Railway Group Limited and one of the world's top 500 enterprises. MTC is mainly responsible for the centralized procurement and supply management of materials for large engineering projects directly managed by the China railway. As a supply chain service provider, MTC has been taking "supply guarantee, quality guarantee, cost reduction" as the service target, serving the whole supply chain network.

In the early stage of its establishment, MTC mainly provided services for China railway's material supply chain, and gradually established second-level subsidiaries, including e-commerce companies and rail logistics companies, to continuously improve its professional services. With the suppliers and logistics providers participating in the service of engineering projects, MTC gradually attaches importance to its own supply chain upgrading and optimization. In 2015, MTC paid attention to the application of digital technology, built a business collaboration platform (BCP), made all offline businesses online, implemented the company's system and business management methods through the platform, and realized the internal control of MTC itself. In 2018, MTC valued the management of the entire supply chain and realized the management of the entire supply chain through the implementation of technologies such as data sharing and system interoperability. Starting from 2019, MTC builds its own supply chain intelligent collaborative service platform, hoping to become a demonstration enterprise of supply chain ecological services in China.

China Railway Group Limited is one of the world's top 100 enterprises and a leading enterprise in China's railway construction. It has more than 40 secondary subsidiaries and more than 150 tertiary subsidiaries. The whole China Railway Co., Ltd. has a huge ecological environment. This paper mainly introduces the DBE development process of China Railway products trade service provider-MTC. MTC has 10 subsidiaries and 3 branches. The ecology of China Railway Co., Ltd. is shown in Fig. 1.

To explore the key barriers in the development of DBE, it is necessary to understand the strategic planning of MTC from the perspective of the industry background, and further understand the barriers and solutions at various stages of its development. Since long-term tracking and multiple interviews are helpful to obtain relevant information, this paper takes deep rebound as the most important way to obtain data. in the current research on DBE, there is relatively little literatures on empirical research methods, which also encourage the use of empirical research methods to carry out DBE research [2], which proves the rationality of the selected method.

In view of the research problem, we conducted 6 semi-structured interviews on MTC including the technical developers of the commodity trade enterprises' BCP platform, the CEO of the commodity trade company, the business personnel of the two subsidiaries, and the relevant personnel of the commodity trade service bureau. Different managers, technicians, and business personnel from different departments were

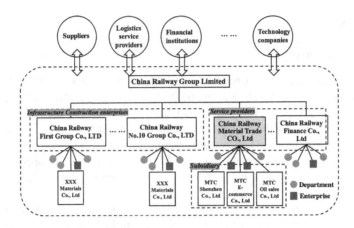

Fig. 1. China railway group limited ecological map

selected to systematically understand the BCP platform from various perspectives. The accumulation of years of practical experience helped them form their own unique understanding. They are all involved in the development, construction, and use of the platform within DBE, and have a relatively accurate grasp of some of the barriers. At the same time, we also collected a large number of text materials within MTC, and participated in two reports of MTC, so as to better understand the initial vision of the enterprise and the relevant strategic planning of the enterprise.

We maintain the flexibility of the conversation throughout the interview so that the interviewees can freely explain their experiences. We also take special care to ensure that there is no leading conversation [7]. The interview followed the semi-standard protocol [8], and questioning interviewees were based on interview design outline. At the same time, according to the respondent's answers and ideas, they were asked follow-up questions to obtain detailed information as far as possible and to avoid the bias of the evidence brought by the interviewees' mistakes or negligence (Table 1).

Table 1. Types of data collected and descriptions

Type of data	Description
Onsite semi-structured interviews	17 h of audio interview recordings with participants from different levels including the managing director, technology officer
Organizational documentation	(1) Approximately 450 pages of digital collaborative platform design report, feasibility report, planning, etc. (2) Approximately 1300 pages of internal meeting summary, Risk Management Regulations, Business Management Approach, etc. (3) There are five ppt documents (120 pages) about logistics collaboration center design report, platform design report, which mainly include the functions, technologies and business strategies, etc.

2.2 Data Analysis

We conduct data analysis from the perspective of interpretation, following the principle of interpretative research [9]. We followed the selective coding technique to code the number of interviews obtained. Data analysis and data collection is a continuous iterative process. When the data can be interpreted by literature, we will merge it into the theme model. When a new theme appears, but there is not enough literature data support, we will conduct follow-up interviews. Finally, the coded theme model was submitted to a group of scholars and enterprises for review, whose responsibility was to challenge the potential logic and data accuracy. Until the group agreed that the topic model was logical and accurate [9], we stopped coding.

To answer our first research question: what are the major barriers for enterprises in DBE development? we sorted out the answer records of different interviewees and identify some key factors.

The DBE development process of MTC can be divided into three stages. In the first stage, MTC focus on collaborative platform construction within the organization to achieve information sharing within the entire organization. In the second stage, MTC pays attention to collaboration platform construction among organizations in the supply chain environment to realize business collaboration among different organizations. In the third stage, MTC is building an ecological intelligent collaborative service platform, focusing on serving the whole ecology and realizes the value co-creation among organizations with the identity of the core enterprise. Therefore, this paper will mainly explore the main barriers in the process of DBE development from the following three stages.

Stage1:Business collaboration platform construction within the organization
Stage2:Business collaboration platform construction among the organizations
Stage3:Intelligent collaborative service platform construction in the ecosystem

According to the existing literature analysis, the barriers analyzed in this article are truly the challenges in front of the current research of DBE [2]. This article also sorts out some barriers that have not been mentioned in the literature and further research the questions based on the interview records.

The second research question studies the strategies to overcome the barriers of DBE development. Firstly, starting from the innovative measures taken by the research objects MTC of this paper, we summarized the strategies taken by MTC to overcome the barriers in different DBE development stages. Then we identified the relevant literature to provide theoretical support for the corresponding strategies. Comparing the case study results with the literature, we proposed the mitigation strategies that organizations can adopt to alleviate the dilemma in DBE development.

3 Barriers and Mitigation Strategies in DBE Development

This section presents the findings of our qualitative research on the barriers and mitigation measures in DBE development. We discuss the barriers that MTC faces according to the different development stages. After identifying each barrier, we discuss the mitigation strategies implemented by MTC and suggest possible propositions based on relevant literature.

3.1 Stage 1: Business Collaboration Platform Construction Within the Organization

According to the analysis of the interview data, we find that there are two key barriers in the first stage of the DBE development of MTC. On the one hand, MTC has a large number of independent systems, such as risk management system, e-commerce system, bidding system and so on. Due to the lack of data sharing, data re-entry and data accuracy lead to the complexity of the business and a lot of uncertainty. How to realize the system integration and data sharing in MTC organization becomes the key barrier in the first stage. On the other hand, one of the most important characteristics of construction industries is the existence of a large number of temporary project sites. [10] mentioned there is a time and space gap between the job site and the office that causes duplication of data and information, lack of data and information, and associated confusion. So, MTC is facing another key barrier is the management of the project sites.

The incompatibility of platform and system, and the different standards of data and information presentation, storage, exchange, processing, and communication have been the main obstacles in the process of enterprise collaboration [6]. Data standardization and system interoperability have always been key issues in the area of DBE [11]. According to the analysis of the interview data, MTC keeps trying to remove barriers in data sharing and process integration. MTC began to construct a business collaboration platform within the enterprise to solve the problem of data sharing by sharing a set of platform, and has achieved some progress.

The project site of the construction industry can be understood as an opportunity-driven temporary organization, which is difficult to be fixed and in a dynamic process. Because it is difficult to be controlled by the platform system, some scholars describe it as shadow system or illegal system [12]. The Shadow System that exists outside the current legal system (BCP) can be understood as the network formed by people spontaneously. It is another network established by people outside the legal system (BCP) through informal channels. In practice, it can be understood that people or group are resistant to use the new platform and still deal with transactions according to the old habits, or the new platform has no practical help or pays no attention to their existence for people or group, and they still rely on traditional Excel or Database to deal with transactions or according to their own experience to deal with some things that the BCP will not record. For example, Different individuals and groups in construction make different messy evaluations of interacting events, which leads to them taking different actions [13]. This will lead to a lot of uncertainty outside the BCP control.

In the case of MTC, the Shadow System is mainly reflected in the construction site. There are still a lot of behaviors that are not recorded in BCP system. It is a key barrier for the development of the DBE platform that the existence of the Shadow Network supports or opposes the legal system, which needs to be paid attention to. At present, many researches have focused on the use of RFID and other technologies to achieve the implementation of data collection in the project site [10]. Through the investigation and research of a large number of the BCP users, MTC has begun to attach importance to the explicit of the shadow system, MTC are still mining more Shadow System forms in the organization and constantly made the Shadow Network explicit by using emerging technology, such as IoT, Blockchain and so on.

P1: Pay attention to the data sharing and system integration, and constantly mining Shadow System and make it explicit

3.2   Stage2: Interconnection Among Organizations in Ecosystem

In the process of building a collaborative platform within the organization, many businesses handled by BCP platform involve multiple participants in the supply chain. However, as the construction of BCP mainly serves the internal of the organization, MTC cannot provide services for external participants. As a result, MTC began to build a business collaboration platform among organizations, and the second phase of DBE development began.

Through the analysis of the interview data, we find that there are two main obstacles to MTC in the second stage of the development of disadvantaged commercial enterprises. On the one hand, with the increase of business participants, the business complexity behind system integration and data sharing is becoming increasingly prominent. On the other hand, the traditional collaborative process between organizations is connected by business processes. With the increase of business complexity, the collaborative process between organizations becomes a complex scenario, needs attention.

As mentioned above, heterogeneity has always been the focus of attention in the collaborative process. In the second stage of DBE development, MTC is also trying to use various technologies to realize the system connection among organizations in the whole ecological network. With the increase of DBE participants in the business, including various organizations, personnel, processes, emerging technologies and other multi-party interaction and collaboration, the complexity of the business continues to increase, and the business gradually becomes a "black box". Traditional DBE platform developers have been looking at the complexity of business from a technical perspective, trying to solve business problems with emerging digital technologies, but the barriers have not been well solved. For example, MTC only has one material demand list, but it will be supplied by different suppliers, and multiple supply lists will be generated. Although all the lists can be recorded by the platform, the naming methods and data representation of goods by different enterprises will cause MTC to need a lot of manual understanding and refilling.

Therefore, in the process of collaborative, a lot of uncertainty and complexity come from collaborative business will be generated. With the rapid growth of collaboration business quantity, many problems cannot be solved only by data sharing. In a word, it is business barriers behind many technical problems. We need critical attention to the business-related issue since technology integration is not the biggest problem [11].

For the problem of data interoperability in collaborative networks, scholars have begun to pay attention to it. [14] proposed a systematic methodology and a set of mechanisms for the federation of four typical types of knowledge sources shared within

CNs, to realize federation of varied knowledge sources in administrative CNs. Authors consider enterprises need to pay attention to the business complexity behind technology heterogeneity. Only by analyzing the complexity of the business, can we take appropriate technology to solve the corresponding barriers.

Digitally enable networks and ecosystem fuel complexity by fostering hyper-connection and mutual dependencies among human actors, technical artifacts, processes, organizations, and institutions [15]. Authors consider the collaboration of different organizations will bring a lot of uncertainty and complexity by means of a digital collaborative platform. It would be certain and manageable if the connection or collaboration is standard and controllable. In the integration process, the problem of the border crossing will be involved [16]. In the process of organization collaboration, there are many boundary conflicts. Including different organizational culture, information level does not match, data standards are not unified, and so on. Authors consider that the boundary is the carrier of complexity and uncertainty, so the boundary is not just a line, but a complex scenario that deserves attention.

Based on interviews with MTC personnel, MTC had sorted out several business scenarios including material demand, material procurement, material distribution, material handover and receipt, and reconciliation and settlement. Through scenario analysis, MTC focuses on a specific business and boundary conflicts involving multiple parties, and mitigate them.

P2: Pay attention to the business complexity behind the technology heterogeneity, and focus on the complexity and uncertainty in the organizational boundary during the business interaction between organizations.

3.3 Stage 3:Intelligent Collaborative Service Platform Construction-Driven by Collaborative Scenario

Aiming to solve the two barriers (Stage 2) mentioned above, MTC began to promote the construction of intelligent collaborative service platforms driven by collaborative scenarios. The platform divides the key links in the business process into different collaborative scenarios for analysis and begins to pay attention to the business complexity and uncertainty in the collaborative scenarios analysis.

As mentioned above, as business complexity and uncertainty increase, business gradually becomes a black box. How to deconstruct the black box has become a major barrier in the construction of DBE development platform in Stage 3. According to the interview, MTC began to pay attention to business scenarios and proposed an intelligent collaborative service platform driven by collaborative scenarios in traditional business processes. The business process is divided into specific business scenarios, mainly from uncertainty and complexity to try to deconstruct the business "black box".

The business process is redefined as the concept of "Scene chain" when MTC studies business activities with scenario methods, so it is also necessary to pay attention to the transmission and cascade effect in the scene chain. [17] proposed a risk identification approach in collaborative networks, paying attention to the cascade effect of risk. [13] focus on knowledge transfer and information exchange in different construction projects. Each scenario involves flows that produce a response and generate a succession of multi-directional flows until a particular function is satisfied and specific issues are resolved. Cascading effect is an inevitable and sometimes unforeseen chain of events due to an act affecting a system [18]. In the process of focusing on scenarios, MTC needs to pay attention to the cascading effect in the whole ecosystem, which may include data ecological governance, knowledge interoperability, risk cascade, etc.

As described in the case introduction section above, MTC has 10 subsidiary companies and 3 branch companies. The establishment of early subsidiaries was mainly divided around different types and regions, such as steel, oil, etc. The business form of each subsidiary is relatively fixed. With the transformation and development of Luban e-commerce company, it began to be responsible for the overall bidding and procurement of various materials. With the establishment of Luban e-commerce digital platform, material bidding and procurement are standardized and unified. How to find their own positioning, how to carry out collaborative development between each other, and how to seek value co-creation have become important challenges in the future.

MTC has begun to pay attention to the whole ecological collaboration problem under its own complex organizational structure. It is trying to build an intelligent collaborative service platform driven by collaborative scenarios. Starting from the business scenario of multi-party collaboration, MTC starts to provide intelligent services and further excavates the value co-creation possibilities among participating subsidiaries.

According to the interview, the development of DBE of MTC is in the third stage, and the intelligent collaborative service platform driven by collaborative scenarios is

Table 2. Barriers and measures in DBE development

DBE development stage	Barriers	Measures to overcome barriers	Corresponding proposition
Business collaboration platform construction within the organization	1. Data sharing and system interoperability 2. Shadow systems	1. Integration platform within the organization (BCP) 2.shadow system explicit	P1
Business collaborative platform construction among organizations	1. Business complexity behind technology heterogeneity 2. Boundary conflict of organizations collaboration	1. Focus on business (Business scenario) 2. Insights into organizational boundary scenario	P2
Intelligent collaborative service platform construction in ecosystem	1. Cascading effect 2. Collaborative value co-creation	1. Focus on cascading effect in the whole ecosystem 2. Intelligent collaborative service platform	P3

under development, and the specific obstacle solving measures have not been fully applied. Table 2 summarizes the main discussion in the third section.

P3: Pay attention to the uncertainty and complexity in the collaborative scenarios, and the cascading effect in the scenarios chain

4 Conclusion

This research analyzes the barriers and mitigation strategies faced by DBE development. The conclusions are mainly the following three aspects.

First, this paper summarizes the key barriers in the three stages of the DBE development process through empirical research methods, and traces the source of the specific barriers and analyzes them in detail. through the analysis of the barriers, the research of related literature, and the related measures taken by the enterprises, the possible mitigation strategies for each type of barrier are proposed and presented in the form of propositions.

Secondly, in the field of practice, the development of DBE is a complex system project and a continuous long-term evolution process. The case company MTC is currently progressing to the third stage. Many companies may still stay in the first or second stage, or even a different evolution path. We only aim at case companies and provide references for the development of DBE in the field of construction engineering.

Thirdly, the existing DBE research is mainly at the theoretical level, so it calls for more empirical articles [2]. Empirical articles will bring more new research problems in the academic field. This article mainly discusses the key barriers and mitigation measures companies face in the process of DBE development, supplements the literature in the field of DBE development, and puts forward new thinking and research questions on the related research of DBE in the form of propositions.

5 Future Research

The popularization and development of IoT technology provide new method for the solution of the shadow system. At present, in the construction industry, the solution to the problem of the shadow system is to collect behavior data with the help of some technologies, such as RFID [10]. The main solution is to use the digital method to show it on the platform. The project site is only a kind of shadow system which is concrete and obvious. There are many other shadow systems in the ecosystem. In the future, how to intelligently mine the shadow system and how to intelligently explicit the shadow system will become the key direction of collaborative platform optimization in the future.

As emphasized in the introduction of this paper, the development of DBE is a complex and systematic project, which is a long-term construction and operation process. DBE emphasizes the importance of digital technology, but according to MTC case study, some barriers cannot be solved by digital technology alone. It is necessary to return to the original business system and analyze the complexity and uncertainty of the business itself. Therefore, the future needs to carry out more empirical studies and accord real cases to explore more complex and uncertain situations in the construction industry business ecosystem.

The management method of complexity and uncertainty of the construction industry has always been the focus of scholars. [19] proposed a three-phase framework for the identification and categorization of uncertainty. And some scholars focus on lean management [20] or Soft Systems Methodology [13] to resolve the complexity of the construction industry. Taking the case of MTC as an example, the development of uncertainty and complexity analysis and manage methods has become the direction of future research.

Acknowledgments. Funding for this research was provided by the National Natural Science Foundation of China (61972029) and the project of Science and Technology Research and development Project of China State Railway Group Co., Ltd. "Research on key Technologies of Railway Data Service Architecture and Ownership Relationship" (K2019S011).

References

1. Graça, P., Camarinha-Matos, L.M.: Performance indicators for collaborative business ecosystems – literature review and trends. Technol. Forecast. Soc. Change **116**, 237–255 (2017)
2. Senyo, P.K., Liu, K., Effah, J.: Digital business ecosystem: Literature review and a framework for future research. Int. J. Inf. Manage. **47**, 52–64 (2019)
3. Senyo, P.K., Liu, K., Effah, J.: A framework for assessing the social impact of interdependencies in digital business ecosystems. In: Liu, K., Nakata, K., Li, W., Baranauskas, C. (eds.) ICISO 2018. IAICT, vol. 527, pp. 125–135. Springer, Cham (2018). https://doi.org/10.1007/978-3-319-94541-5_13
4. Attour, A., Peruta, M.D.: Architectural knowledge: Key flows and processes in designing an inter-organisational technological platform. Knowl. Manag. Res. Pract. **14**(1), 27–34 (2014)
5. D'Andrea, A., Ferri, F., Grifoni, P., Guzzo, T.: Digital ecosystem: The next generation of business services. In: Proceedings of the 5th International Conference on Management of Emergent Digital EcoSystems (MEDES 13), pp. 40–44. Association for Computing Machinery, Neumünster Abbey (2013)
6. Lenkenhoff, K., Wilkens, U Zheng, M., Süße, T., Kuhlenkötter, B., Ming, X.: Key challenges of digital business ecosystem development and how to cope with them. Procedia CIRP **73**, 167–172 (2018)
7. Myers, M.D., Newman, M.: The qualitative interview in is research: examining the craft. Inf. Organ. **17**(1), 2–26 (2007)
8. Kvale, S.: InterViews: An Introduction to Qualitative Research Interviewing. Sage, Thousand Oaks (1996)
9. Klein, H.K., Myers, M.D.: A set of principles for conducting and evaluating interpretive field studies in information systems. MIS Q. **23**(1), 67–94 (1999)
10. Wang, L., Lin, Y., Lin, P.: Dynamic mobile RFID-based supply chain control and management system in construction. Adv. Eng. Inf. **21**, 377–390 (2007)
11. Korpela, K., Hallikas, J., Dahlberg, T.: Digital supply Chain transformation toward blockchain integration. In: Proceedings of the 50th Hawaii International Conference on System Sciences, Waikoloa Village, HI, USA, pp. 4182–4191 (2017)

12. Stacey, R.: Complexity and Creativity in Organizations. Berrettkoehler, San Francisco (1996)
13. Behera, P., Mohanty, R.P., Prakash, A.: Understanding construction supply chain management. Prod. Plan. Control. **26**(16), 1332–1350 (2015)
14. Pang, B., Afsarmanesh, H., Gou, J., Mu, W.: Supporting transparent information/knowledge federation in collaborative administrative environments. In: Camarinha-Matos, L.M., Afsarmanesh, H., Antonelli, D. (eds.) PRO-VE 2019. IAICT, vol. 568, pp. 205–219. Springer, Cham (2019). https://doi.org/10.1007/978-3-030-28464-0_19
15. Benbya, H., Nan, N., Tanriverdi, H., Yoo, Y.: Complexity and information systems research in the emerging digital world. MIS Q. **44**(1), 1–17 (2020)
16. Tan, F., Pan, S., Liu, J.: Towards a self-organizing digital business ecosystem: examining IT-enabled boundary spanning practice of China's LeEco. In: International Conference on Information Systems, Dublin, Ireland, pp. 1–12 (2016)
17. Li, J., Bénaben, F., Gou, J., Mu, W.: A proposal for risk identification approach in collaborative networks considering susceptibility to danger. In: Camarinha-Matos, L.M., Afsarmanesh, H., Rezgui, Y. (eds.) PRO-VE 2018. IAICT, vol. 534, pp. 74–84. Springer, Cham (2018). https://doi.org/10.1007/978-3-319-99127-6_7
18. Cascade Effect: A Dictionary of Ecology. Encyclopedia.com
19. Gosling, J., Naim, M., Towill, D.: Identifying and categorizing the sources of uncertainty in construction supply chains. J. Constr. Eng. Manag. **139**, 102–110 (2013)
20. Meng, X.: Lean management in the context of construction supply chains. Int. J. Prod. Res. **57**, 3784–3798 (2019)

Developing Digital Business Ecosystems to Create Collaborative Value in Supply-Chain Finance

Xufan Zhao, Juanqiong Gou, and Wenchi Ying[✉]

School of Economic and Management, Beijing Jiaotong University,
Beijing, China
{19120631, jqgou, wcying}@bjtu.edu.cn

Abstract. Although many enterprises have been launching the supply-chain finance (SCF) to help firms solve financing problems and increase collaborative performance, the formation process remains limited. The "digital business ecosystem (DBE)" is a sound guiding theory that we adopt to study the process of SCF networks formation, while SCF offers a suitable phenomenon to research how to integrate the business ecosystems and digital platforms to shape DBE and its logic of value. Guided by this lens, we conduct an in-depth case study of a super-large infrastructure enterprise in China. This study reveals a process model which consists of focal IT/IS enablers, dominant types of ecosystems, and forms of ecosystems. Our findings contribute to existing body of literature, in the field of SCF and DBEs. Core firms of ecosystems can use the model to design and develop DBEs to co-create value in SCF with rational deliberation and planning.

Keywords: Collaborative networks 4.0 · Value creation · Digital business ecosystems · Supply-chain finance · Process model · Case study

1 Introduction

The existing research on collaborative networks (CN) is clarified into three stages that are defined as CN 1.0, 2.0 and 3.0. Specifically, CN 1.0 focus on goal-oriented networks such as virtual enterprises [1] and virtual organizations [2]. CN 2.0 focus on CN breeding environments [3] and CN 3.0 mainly discussed the interplay among multiple CNs (e.g., value system networks [4]). Research and development are now beginning to address the issues of CN 4.0, one of which is the formation of new business ecosystems focusing on collaborative value creation in the era of digital transformation.

Supply chain is a typical form of CN. With the growth of supply chains, a shortage of working capital faced by small and medium-sized enterprises (SMEs) always exists. Because of information asymmetry or financial risks (e.g., fake account receivable vouchers), SMEs' good business performance does not always result in loans from financial institutions. To address this issue, SCF was created as a type of financial products/services that consists of a set of collaborative organizations that are interdependent to co-create and extend supply-chain value through the exchange of services

© IFIP International Federation for Information Processing 2020
Published by Springer Nature Switzerland AG 2020
L. M. Camarinha-Matos et al. (Eds.): PRO-VE 2020, IFIP AICT 598, pp. 31–43, 2020.
https://doi.org/10.1007/978-3-030-62412-5_3

[5]. Simultaneously, SCF must be supported by Fintech that can combine digital technologies with financial business structures and process [6]. Thus, SCF is a suitable phenomenon for CN 4.0 research in the academia. However, research on the formation process of SCF networks remains limited.

Given that value co-creation and participant co-evolution are significant features of business ecosystems and Fintech enables SCF networks, DBE [7] is a suitable theoretical lens that we adopt to study the formation process of SCF networks and to address the research gap of CN4.0. DBE is defined as a self-organizing environment relies largely on synergy between different business entities through its platforms based on digital technologies during value co-creation [7]. Although the "what" question has been investigated in many studies, the "how" question (i.e. *"How is DBE shaped through the combination of the business ecosystems and digital platforms?"*) has yet to be explored, which lead to that logic of value co-creation in CN 4.0 or DBE is still in the black box. Thus, this study aims to uncover the formation process of SCF networks which contribute to collaborative value co-creation in CN 4.0. Guided by DBE theory, we conducted in-depth case analysis of China Communications Construction Co., LTD. (CCCC) and derive our research question: *how to develop a digital business ecosystem (DBE) to create collaborative value in supply-chain finance (SCF)?*

Process theory focuses on a series of activities to explain how specific outcomes evolve over time of the studied case [8]. Process models can make it easier for scholars and practitioners to understand the underlying mechanisms involved [9]. This study proposes a three-phase process model on DBE formation in the field of SCF. In each phase, the model reveals a kind of focal IT/IS enablers that triggers a value co-creating mechanism and further shapes corresponding dominant types of ecosystems. Thus, the process model reveals a complete process of formation of DBE and makes both important theoretical and practical contributions. First, by examining the value co-creation process of DBE for SCF and uncovering the key factor of DBE – focal IT/IS enablers, this study contributes not only to the SCF and CN 4.0 literature but also to DBE literature. Second, the core firms may use the findings to implement integration of digital fintech platforms and business ecosystems, and by doing so, increase the success rate of the adoption of SCF to co-create collaborative value.

2   Literature Review

2.1   Supply-Chain Finance (SCF) as a Typical Phenomenon of CN 4.0

Supply chain, a stable long-term goal-driven network composed of raw material suppliers, manufacturers, distributors, retailers and final consumers, is obviously one typical form of CN [10]. SCF is a value extension of the traditional supply chain by improving the management of the transaction, physical, and information flow at an inter-organizational level [11]. The supply chain collaboration dimensions has received significant attention in the research on SCF [12], which state that SCF is a collaborative entity primarily encompassing three participants: borrowers, banks and LSPs [13] as well as the integration of financing processes with customers, suppliers, and financial service providers [11].

Meanwhile, the development of e-commerce not only forces the improvement of supply chain sustainability, but also moves it into the digitalization era [14], digitization is increasingly emphasized in SCF [6]. Especially, Fintech, the acronym for financial technology, supports and enables many aspects of SCF, resulting in new business models, applications, processes or products [15]. Fintech describes the connection of the typical business activities in financial services and the existing internet-related technologies(e.g., cloud computing, mobile internet) or emerging information technologies(e.g., blockchain, AI) [16]. As we know, the new business ecosystems focusing on value co-creation in era of digital transformation is a hot topic of CN 4.0. Therefore, as a fintech-enabled business model which focus the supply chain value extension, SCF is clearly a typical practice phenomenon for CN 4.0 research. However, research on the formation process of SCF networks remains limited. Thus, DBE, the digital concept with the value co-creation and co-evolution as the important characteristics, is a suitable theoretical lens we can adopt to study this phenomenon and address the gap of CN4.0 in the academia.

2.2 Digital Business Ecosystem (DBE) Perspective Towards SCF

DBE comprises two main tiers: digital (ecosystem) and business (ecosystem) [17]. Digital ecosystem refers to a virtual environment consist of digital entities (e.g., software applications, hardware and processes) [18]. The concept of business ecosystem was introduced by Moore in the 1990s as an economic community supported by loosely-coupled interacting individuals and organizations who produce valuable goods and services [19]. Digital business ecosystem (DBE) derives from the natural evolution of business ecosystem for which strongly emphasis on the centrality of digital technology. DBE is defined as a socio-technical environment made up of different entities with collaborative and competitive relationships, including individuals, organizations and digital technologies, to achieve value co-creation through shared digital platforms [7]. The main characteristics of DBEs are platform, symbiosis, co-evolution and self-organization [20].

Given that DBEs has to integrate new technologies and to leverage digital platforms [7], it is important to understand how to strategically control platforms to benefit participants of business ecosystems [21]. Hence developing the DBE involves not only traditional business ecosystems but also digital technology platforms [22, 23], the combination of the two may contribute to new value co-creation in ecosystems of digital era (CN 4.0). However, research focused on the process of how DBE is shaped through the combination receives little attention. SCF, as the typical concept of DBEs which integrate digital technologies and financial business, offers us an opportunity to study the logic of value co-creation in DBE and also CN4.0 with a thorough discussion of collaborative networks and related ecosystems. From there, we derive our research questions: *how to develop a digital business ecosystem (DBE) to create collaborative value in supply-chain finance (SCF)?*

3 Research Methodology

The case research methodology is particularly appropriate for this study for three reasons. First, the research aims to answer the "how" question and is thus better addressed through inductive methods [24, 25]. Second, the case study is more effective to build a new theoretical model with its strength in exploring new conceptual arguments [26]. Third, the case study method is suitable for a process-based analysis concerning the "how" question [27].

Given the research question, three criteria were identified. First, the sample organization should be reasonably large, and have sufficiently complex supply chain relationships so that their types of ecosystems and value co-creation processes can be identified; Second, the company should establish its own supply chain finance systems, so that the theoretical insertion in this aspect has practical significance. Third, the sample companies were willing to provide enough detailed information to support the research, especially senior management.

CCCC is particularly suitable for our research purposes, as it is the second largest infrastructure enterprise in Asia, with a large and complex industrial chain network of design, construction and equipment manufacturing enterprises at its core. CCCC has successfully built a supply chain financial service platform covering all its equipment manufacturing enterprises. In addition, the company has given us sufficient authority and detailed information for promotion research.

3.1 Data Collection

Data was collected in two steps. Research access was first negotiated and approved in April 2019. Before onsite data collection, we systematically collected secondary data from various sources, including newspapers, magazines, books and the Internet, in order to accurately determine the appropriate direction and facilitate on-site interviews. Meanwhile, we selected and confirmed the theoretical lens [24] that we would employ in the study, and read both the classic and current literature. Based on the collection of secondary data, the adoption of SCF concepts and digital business ecosystem perspective, a preliminary theoretical model guides us for subsequent on-site data collection and analysis.

On-site data collection was then conducted at CCCC's headquarters and its subsidiaries, through meetings and telephone interviews, and from October 2019 to January 2020. We applied the top-down interview method [24], interviewing a total of 26 informants (see Table 1), including the director, CIO, project manager, product manager, among others. Each interview lasted approximately 30–120 min, and the questions were customized to the informants. Each digitally recorded interview was transcribed after and then formed a document total of more than 210 pages. The transcripts with the secondary data allowed for triangulation, which enabled greater substantiation of the constructs and hypotheses [28].

Table 1. List of interview.

Position/departments	The number of interviewees	Duration of the interview (per person)
Director of Xingyu Data	1	120 min
CIO of Xingyu Data	1	120 min
Senior managers in the procurement, strategy and IT of CCCC	3	120 min
Project manager of Fuhe bridge project in CCCC	2	90 min
Domain experts in SCF	2	90 min
Project manager of SCF project in CCCC	2	40 min
Mid-level managers in product, development, technology and market of Xingyu Data	15	30–40 min

3.2 Data Analysis

To organize the large volume of data, we focused on two themes: the history of SCF construction of CCCC and the IT/IS enablers for ecosystems evolution. The exhibition of the history could facilitate the development of people's familiarity with the strategies and activities for SCF formation, thus allowing them to identify the focal IT/IS enablers and different forms of ecosystems more easily, which is important to the understanding of DBE practices and theories. Focusing on the two sets of constructs-the focal IT/IS enablers and dominant types of ecosystems, we identified CCCC's three important phases for DBE development in SCF: developing an originally digital application of SCF, building a Fintech platform for potentially diverse applications of SCF and enriching digital business ecosystems of SCF through complementing diverse applications. Correspondingly, we conceptualized three structures of business ecosystems by identify its three main characteristics, and thereby outlined three ecosystems forms established by CCCC: a value-added business ecosystem, a financial technology (Fintech) ecosystem, and digital business ecosystems for SCF (See Table 2).

Data analysis was performed concurrently with data collection to take advantage of the flexibility afforded by the case study research methodology [28]. Based on the emerging data, to facilitate the examination of the value co-creation process of DBEs for SCF, we divided events and activities into three distinct phases: original applications of "Accounts Receivable Financing Vouchers" based on digital credit, unified Fintech platform for potentially applications based on core functionalities, and complementing diverse applications for CCCC manufacturing enterprises based on Fintech platform. The theoretical model was then verified and modified accordingly. To achieve theoretical saturation, the data analysis constantly iterative among the empirical data, the relevant literature, and the emerging model [24].

Table 2. A process model of DBEs development for SCF.

Phases	Developing an original digital application of SCF (e.g., Vendors' AR Financing)	Building a Fintech platform for potentially diverse applications of SCF	Enriching digital business ecosystems of SCF through complementing diverse applications
Focal IT/IS enablers for Ecosystems	*Digital assets and digital credit:* Vouchers with economic value can be digitalized as data assets which embody the credit endorsed by the core firms. Digitalization enables credit to be divided and then transferred to all the nodes of supply chain.	*Core functionalities of Fintech platform:* Because of the logic that digital credit is supported by data assets, three cascading core functionalities, e.g., asset digitization, information traceability and credit transferability, can be abstracted from then original applications.	*The Fintech Platform and applications:* Complementary applications are enriched according to concrete business needs and models (e.g., receivables financing, receive storage financing and financial leasing).
Dominant types of ecosystems	*A value-added business ecosystem:* The AR financing, as an original SCF application, is a kind of value-added service designed based on the supply-chain networks. The application centers on the core firms and connects upstream multi-tier suppliers and financial institutions around the core firm.	*A financial technology (Fintech) ecosystem:* The Fintech platform is constructed on the basis of core functionalities and then offer application developers with technical environment (e.g., interfaces) is provided to develop potentially diverse SCF applications.	*Digital business ecosystems for SCF:* Diverse SCF applications can be customized for different stakeholders, which enrich the DBEs. The core firm can coordinate multi-role actors to create collaborative value around the complementary SCF applications.
Forms of ecosystems			

4 Case Description

China Communications Construction Co., LTD. (CCCC) is the world's leading provider of super-large infrastructure integrated services. In 2017, a subsidiary of CCCC was established-Xingyu Data, dedicated to promoting the industrialization of cutting-edge technologies such as CCCC's supply chain finance. With Xingyu Data as the operating subject, CCCC has spent more than three years actively exploring the SCF practice for large infrastructure enterprises, and finally built an extensible and scenario-based supply chain finance service platform. Through credit digitization of core enterprises, this platform can effectively empower upstream and downstream enterprises in the supply chain to reduce management and operation costs, and help SMEs to solve the problems of financing. At present, with the bridge of digital credit-enabled fintech platform built by CCCC, digital business ecosystems (DBEs) in supply chain finance (SCF) has been established and full covered in CCCC equipment manufacturing enterprises. So, how did CCCC do it?

4.1 Original Applications of "Accounts Receivable Financing Vouchers" Based on Digital Credit

Relying on the business characteristics of long industrial chain and long construction period, CCCC has the problems of high asset-liability ratio and long cash flow cycle, which lead to rising prices for raw materials from upmarket suppliers. Against the background of fierce competition and rapid technological iteration, CCCC, as one of the leading infrastructure construction companies in Asia, is facing difficult challenges, as explained by Xingyu Data's director Wang:

> *For us, the company's procurement and management costs remain high. For the upper middle and small suppliers, it is difficult to obtain financing due to their insufficient credit. The information asymmetry between the credit parties is the root of these problems. We know very well that we were at a turning point in financial technology reform, and SCF offered an answer.*

At the beginning of 2016, SCF construction project of CCCC was officially launched. For Xingyu Data, as the actual implementation subject, the primary task is the concept design of future core products. "Account Receivable (AR) Financing Vouchers" was born in this context, which has the characteristics of quick disassembly, transferability and realizability. The vouchers record the trade data of core enterprises and suppliers based on the real business scenario.

AR Financing Vouchers can be used as regular payment means. Meanwhile, it is the credit symbol of the core firms involved, using the vouchers as the carrier to lend the credit endorsed by core firms to multi-tier suppliers, thereby the flow of data realizes the transfer of credit, "Digital Credit" from "Trade Data", and also "Commercial Credit" from "Financial Credit". It is the technology that empowers the credit of participants to be fully demonstrated, thereby facilitating the convenient and low-cost circulation in the supply chain and accelerating the bank's financing response.

The concept of the AR Financing Vouchers received more and more support, and verified in practical applications. The bid for the Fuhe Bridge project, undertaken by a subsidiary of CCCC, was opened in October 2017, with a total steel volume of 40,000 tons. During the checkout phase of the Fuhe Bridge project, CCCC used the vouchers as the payment means, the suppliers can sign them and use them to apply for account receivable financing. After the financing, the supplier re-quoted the purchase price according to the actual cost it beards. Then the procurement cost of the core enterprise was reduced by 48 yuan/ton, moreover, it only needed online operation for no more than 10 min, which greatly improved the efficiency and promoted the cooperation enthusiasm of the suppliers. As mentioned by Li, a project manager in charge of CCCC's SCF projects:

> From the perspective of actual benefits, the applications of the digital credit-enabled AR financing vouchers in the supply chain is indeed a win-win! For us, suppliers will no longer urge us as before, so cash flows are precipitated. And it also promotes the speed of the supplier's fund recovery.

4.2 Unified Fintech Platform for Potentially Applications Based on Core Functionalities

Value can only be realized if it is landed as soon as possible. The innovative concept of digital credit was recognized as the core to build a supply chain financial service platform, and CCCC's member enterprises requested the implementation as soon as possible. CIO Qi recalled:

> The organizational structure of CCCC is huge and complicated. Where should the platform start? In view of the uneven informatization degree of member companies, finally the overall idea of the platform building was "unify first, then customize!"

Then, building a unified SCF service platform became the primary goal of technology implementation. The unified platform collects business data by docking with business systems such as office, approval, and payment of the enterprise, and then grafts it to the bank, electronically reconstructs the industrial chain financial scene, which realizes the digitization of the entire industrial chain assets. Taking the SCF service platform as a bridge, the digital credit transmission channel among core enterprises, suppliers and financing institutions is opened up. Data of business flow, capital flow, logistics and information flow are transported from the enterprise side to the financing institutions side in the form of various electronic invoices, vouchers and receipts, realizing the "Four flows in one" and "Everything is credit".

The guarantee of data authenticity and reliability is permeated in the process of unified platform design and deployment. One is the agreement text standard is consistent. The platform agreement is based entirely on the traditional bank loan standard text, realizing the online 100% reproduction of the traditional offline financing and factoring text format, and the final electronic confirmation is performed by CS electronic signature. Another one is the true and reliable data source. The unified platform is grafted on the internal ERP systems, OA approval office systems and audit systems of the enterprises, so the platform's trade data is directly captured from the aforementioned systems.

The platform can connect with all financial institutions, realizing diverse supply chain financial applications, such as accounts payable reverse factoring, accounts receivable factoring, ABS, ABN, etc. After that, applications can be customized designed to meet various requirements of specific scenarios. The three characteristics of the unified platform provide the basis for its scalability. As product manager Jack explained:

> *Asset digitization, credit transferability, information traceability, are the three characteristics of our unified platform. Based on this, the platform realizes the unified docking of capital channels, conducts overall management of different types of financing service applications, and finally, through the construction of scenes, can customizes the design of financing service.*

4.3   Complementing Diverse Applications for CCCC Manufacturing Enterprises Based on Fintech Platform

Relying on stable supplier relationship and smooth existing information systems, equipment manufacturing sector became the first pilot unit to implement the customized SCF service platform. However, it was not easy to go from a unified platform to customization, as mentioned by project manager Li:

> *As a leading enterprise in the heavy equipment manufacturing industry in China, this sector has built mature OA systems, material ERP systems, Inspur systems and supplier portals. We must think about how the platform to integrate with the existing organizational structure, basic data, and authority system.*

In the second half of 2017, Xingyu Data successfully built a SCF service platform covering CCCC's equipment manufacturing enterprises. Based on the connection with existing mature systems, the platform realizes the online operation of the whole process of single business document provision, agreement signing and approval. On January 19, 2018, an upstream supplier of an CCCC equipment manufacturing enterprise successfully applied financing of 15.85 million yuan through its customized SCF service platform, which is the first online SCF business of Industrial and Commercial Bank of China to connect with a third-party platform.

As the payment means, electronic vouchers are transferred on the customized SCF service platform, the financial behavior is embedded into every node involved in the business process for convenient operation and seamless connection. With digital credit as the core and unified fintech platform as the driver, the original data comes from the business and serves the payment stage in the way of credit, so as to accelerate the flow of capital chain and finally return to the practical business. Intelligent contracts as legal protection, digital fintech (e.g., blockchain) enables trust assurance, integrate into a stable governance mechanism for participants. As director Wang illustrated:

> *Digital credit enables business demand, and fintech boosts platform functions. By virtue of CCCC's equipment manufacturing enterprises customized SCF service platform, the multi-participants are mutually beneficial and symbiotic.*

5 Case Analysis

5.1 Formation Process of DBEs Towards SCF

This study proposes a three-phase process model on DBE formation in the field of SCF. In each phase, the model reveals a kind of focal IT/IS enablers that triggers a value co-creating mechanism and further shapes corresponding dominant types of ecosystems. Thus, the process model reveals a complete process of formation of DBEs (See Table 2).

Specifically, the concepts of digital assets and digital credit enable an account receivable (AR) financing application and are the foundation of a value-added business ecosystem as well as the basis of core fintech functionalities in the second phase. Then, the three major functions, including credit transferability, information traceability and asset digitization, are abstracted from the AR financing application and used to construct the underlying architecture of Fintech platform, so that potentially diverse SCF applications and a corresponding Fintech ecosystem will be available. Finally, with the growth of number and diversity of SCF applications, the Fintech platform and complementary applications enable a prosperous and robust DBE for SCF with prosperous.

5.2 Developing an Original Digital Application of SCF

With the support of financial institutions, core enterprises revitalize idle credit lines and convert electronic vouchers. Given the vouchers can be used for payment, it has the characteristics of a currency-like and realizes the digitization of assets. In terms of the transferability of the vouchers, the business credit endorsed by the core enterprise is split and transmitted to the far end of the supply chain, realizing the digitization of credit. In this phase, digital assets and digital credit, as the focal enablers, realize the application of SCF based on the supply-chain networks. In this case, the core enterprise of Fuhe Bridge project applied AR financing vouchers as the payment means. It was obviously a win-win option to help suppliers solve the financing problems and simultaneously reduce their own procurement and capital costs. Thus, core enterprise serves as the center to promote the collaborative benefits, connecting upstream N-tier suppliers and financial institutions. Transferability of digital credit realizes the transmission of value, and achieves the tripartite value co-creation and co-evolution of participants, which form a value-added business ecosystem.

5.3 Building a Fintech Platform for Potentially Diverse Applications of SCF

The three core functionalities abstracted from the aforementioned original digital applications are identified as the focal enablers of the second phase. First, assets digitization, as the payment means, the detachable vouchers realize the circulation of data assets, thereby creating superimposed value; Second, credit transferability, breaking through the isolation of credit, the credit endorsed by core enterprises penetrates all levels of the supply chain; Third, information traceability, guaranteeing the data source be true and reliable, and the data transmission process cannot be tampered with. Credit transferability uniforms allocation of credit resources, asset digitization helps achieve credit appreciation, and information traceability ensures the safety and reliability. Therefore, these three are the basis of Fintech platform and provide the technical environment (e.g., interfaces) to develop potentially diverse SCF applications. In this phase, with the platform as the coordination locus, the applications innovation and potential externalities (e.g., inventory financing, strategic relationship financing and so on) provide flexibility, as the main sources of value creation. Participants achieve value co-creation by using technologies, services and applications of the platform. Finally, extracting digital-credit-enabled core functionalities into a digital platform to develop a financial technology (Fintech) ecosystem, which contribute to complementary applications for SCF in next phase.

5.4   Enriching Digital Business Ecosystems of SCF Through Complementing Diverse Applications

The business scenarios of the infrastructure industry are numerous, thus according to concrete business needs and models, diversified specific applications are developed, and become the focal IT/IS enablers in the third phase. Meanwhile, multiple scenarios lead to complex application stakeholders, forming business alliances/networks, which enrich DBEs for SCF. The core enterprises empowered by the Fintech platform serve as the new coordinated locus and diversified applications based on digital credit develop as a new source of value. The collaborative and cumulative interaction between different roles and their core capabilities of participants promote value co-creation and realize the symbiosis. Taking the case as an illustration, a customized SCF service platform for CCCC equipment manufacturing enterprises has realized complementing diverse applications (e.g., receivables financing, receive storage financing and financial leasing), which connect multiple types of participants, including multi-tier suppliers, multi-tier distributors, subsidiaries and financial institutions, together they build digital business ecosystems for SCF.

6   Conclusion

Because an increasing number of enterprises are launching supply chain finance while only a few know its process of formation, SCF construction by one Chinese super-large infrastructure enterprise was investigated in the present study, which suitable to adopt the DBE as the theoretical lens to improve both the research and practice in this field. Meanwhile, as a typical DBE, SCF, integrates business activities and digital fintech, offering a great opportunity to research on the process of how business ecosystems and digital ecosystems are combined to co-crate value in CN4.0. Thus, employing SCF and DBE as the theory basis, this paper provides a process model to help explain how to develop digital business ecosystems to create collaborative value for the successful adoption of supply chain finance by infrastructure enterprises. Specifically, the process model demonstrates that in each phase for DBE formation in SCF-developing an originally digital application of SCF, building a Fintech platform for potentially diverse applications of SCF and enriching digital business ecosystems of SCF through complementing diverse applications-requires particular focal IT/IS enablers: digital assets and digital credit, core functionalities of Fintech platform and the Fintech platform and applications. Moreover, the focal IT/IS enablers can trigger a value co-creating mechanism and further shapes corresponding dominant types of ecosystems, which serve as the source for focal enablers identification in the next phase. This research generates empirical insights into supply chain finance formation and has important implication for theoretical study on value co-creation of DBE. With respect to future research, there is a need to further develop both research and practice in the field of SCF by infrastructure enterprises by examining the specific effects of focal IT/IS enablers on formation of different types of ecosystems.

Acknowledgments. Funding for this research was provided by the National Natural Science Foundation of China (61972029), the Fundamental Research Funds for the Central Universities (2019RCW011) and the project of Science and Technology Research and development plan of China National Railway Group Co., LTD. "Research on key Technologies of Railway Data Service Architecture and Ownership Relationship" (K2019S011).

References

1. Camarinha-Matos, L.M., Afsarmanesh, H.: Virtual enterprise modeling and support infrastructures: applying multi-agent system approaches. In: Luck, M., Mařík, V., Štěpánková, O., Trappl, R. (eds.) ACAI 2001. LNCS (LNAI), vol. 2086, pp. 335–364. Springer, Heidelberg (2001). https://doi.org/10.1007/3-540-47745-4_16
2. Camarinha-Matos, L.M., Afsarmanesh, H., Ollus, M.: Virtual Organizations: Systems and Practices. Springer, Boston (2005). https://doi.org/10.1007/b102339
3. Camarinha-Matos, Luis M., Afsarmanesh, H., Ortiz, A. (eds.): PRO-VE 2005. ITIFIP, vol. 186. Springer, Boston, MA (2005). https://doi.org/10.1007/0-387-29360-4
4. Camarinha-Matos, L.M., Macedo, P.: A conceptual model of value systems in collaborative networks. J. Intell. Manuf. **21**(3), 287–299 (2010). https://doi.org/10.1007/s10845-008-0180-7
5. Ketchen, D.J., Crook, T.R., Craighead, C.W.: From supply chains to supply ecosystems: implications for strategic sourcing research and practice. J. Bus. Logist. **35**(3), 165–171 (2014)
6. Milian, E.Z., Spinola, M.D.M., de Carvalho, M.M.: Fintechs: A literature review and research agenda. Electron. Commer. Res. Appl. 34, 100833 (2019)
7. Senyo, P.K., Liu, K., Effah, J.: Digital business ecosystem: literature review and a framework for future research. Int. J. Inf. Manag. **47**(AUG), 52–64 (2019)
8. Shaw, T., Jarvenpaa, S.: Process models in information systems. In: Lee, A.S., Liebenau, J., DeGross, J.I. (eds.) Information Systems and Qualitative Research. Chapman & Hall, London (1997)
9. Gupta, S., Cadeaux, J., Dubelaar, C.: Uncovering multiple champion roles in implementing new-technology ventures. J. Bus. Res. **59**(5), 549–563 (2006)
10. Camarinha-Matos, L.M., Afsarmanesh, H.: Collaborative networks. In: Wang, K., Kovacs, G.L., Wozny, M., Fang, M. (eds.) PROLAMAT 2006. IIFIP, vol. 207, pp. 26–40. Springer, Boston, MA (2006). https://doi.org/10.1007/0-387-34403-9_4

11. Wuttke, D.A., Blome, C., Henke, M.: Focusing the financial flow of supply chains an empirical investigation of financial supply chain management. Int. J. Prod. Econ. **145**, 773–789 (2013)

12. Bals, C.: Toward a supply chain finance (scf) ecosystem – proposing a framework and agenda for future research. J. Purchasing Supply Manag. **25**(2), 105–117 (2019)

13. Liu, X., Zhou, L., Wu, Y.: Supply chain finance in China: business innovation and theory development. Sustainability **7**, 14689–14709 (2015)

14. Macchion, L., Moretto, A.M., Caniato, F., Caridi, M., Danese, P., Vinelli, A.: International e-commerce for fashion products: what is the relationship with performance? Int. J. Retail Distrib. Manag. (2017)

15. FSB: Financial stability implications from fintech, vol. 33 (2017)

16. Gomber, P., Koch, J.-A., Siering, M.: Digital finance and FinTech: current research and future research directions. J. Bus. Econ. **87**, 537–580 (2017). https://doi.org/10.1007/s11573-017-0852-x

17. Stanley, J., Briscoe, G.: The ABC of digital business ecosystems. Commun. Law J. Comput. Media Telecommun. Law **15**(1), 1–24 (2010)

18. Nachira, F., Dini, P., Nicolai, A.: A network of digital business ecosystems for Europe: Roots, processes and perspectives. Digital business ecosystem. European Commission Information Society and Media ((2007))

19. Moore, J.F.: Predators and prey: a new ecology of competition. Havard Bus. Rev. **71**(3), 75–83 (1993)

20. Folguera, A., et al.: Neogene growth of the patagonian andes. In: Folguera, A., et al. (eds.) The Evolution of the Chilean-Argentinean Andes. SESS, pp. 475–501. Springer, Cham (2018). https://doi.org/10.1007/978-3-319-67774-3_19

21. Koch, T., Windsperger, J.: Seeing through the network: competitive advantage in the digital economy. J. Organ. Des. **6**(1), 1–30 (2017). https://doi.org/10.1186/s41469-017-0016-z

22. Korpela, K., Mikkonen, K., Hallikas, J., Pynnonen, M.: Digital business ecosystem transformation - towards cloud integration. In: Hawaii International Conference on System Sciences, pp. 3959–3968 (2016). https://doi.org/10.1109/HICSS.2016.491

23. Korpela, K., Hallikas, J., Dahlberg, T.: Digital supply Chain transformation toward blockchain integration. In: Hawaii International Conference on System Sciences, pp. 4182–4191 (2017). http://hdl.handle.net/10125/41666

24. Pan, S.L., Tan, B.: Demystifying case research: a structured–pragmatic–situational (SPS) approach to conducting case studies. Information and Organization **21**(3), 161176 (2011)

25. Walsham, G.: Interpretive case studies in IS research: nature and method. Eur. J. Inf. Syst. **4**(2), 74 (1995)

26. Siggelkow, N.: Persuasion with case studies. Acad. Manag. J. **50**(1), 20–24 (2007)

27. Gummesson, E.: Qualitative Methods in Management Research. Sage, Thousand Oaks (2000)

28. Eisenhardt, K.M.: Building theories from case study research. Acad. Manag. Rev. **14**(4), 532–550 (1989)

Collaborative Business Models

Deriving Collaborative Business Model Design Requirements from a Digital Platform Business Strategy

Frank Berkers[1,2(✉)], Oktay Turetken[2], Baris Ozkan[2], Anna Wilbik[3],
Onat Ege Adali[2], Rick Gilsing[2], and Paul Grefen[2]

[1] Netherlands Organisation for Applied Scientific Research (TNO),
PO Box 96800, 2509 JE The Hague, The Netherlands
frank.berkers@tno.nl
[2] School of Industrial Engineering, Eindhoven University of Technology,
PO Box 513, 5600 MB Eindhoven, The Netherlands
[3] DKE, University of Maastricht, Maastricht, The Netherlands
a.wilbik@maastrichtuniversity.nl

Abstract. The widespread deployment of digital technologies has resulted in a hyperconnected context for business organizations. Currently many ventures, both start-ups and incumbents, consider engaging in a Digital Platform Business Strategy to create and capture value in collaborative ecosystems. This type of strategy strongly differs from a conventional Business Strategy in speed, scale, scope and interaction with the ecosystem. Business Models are used to realize a strategy, but little guidance and support exists for the specification of business models realizing a Digital Business Platform Business Strategy. This affects an organization's responsiveness to digital opportunities. To address this gap, this paper proposes a novel method to support the derivation of Business Model Design Requirements from a Digital Platform Business Strategic Objective. The method uses a Catalogue of Strategy Elements as a starting point to generate Subobjectives and Business Model Design Requirement Specification Cards as a structuring tool to facilitate the transformation of these Subobjectives into Business Model Design Requirements. The method is demonstrated using a historical platform case study. We show that our approach generates Business Model Design Requirements in a structured way and in line with Business Strategy. As a positive by-product the method creates options for business model evolution.

Keywords: Digital business strategy · Strategic objectives · Business model · Digital platform · Collaborative network

1 Introduction

Services in the current digital era and Digital Business Models typically depend on online connectivity between organizations and consequently on collaborative business networks [1]. Hyperconnectivity has dramatically expanded the potential applicability of value propositions, as digital technologies can serve for larger masses and different applications with increased speeds "at zero marginal cost". Increased scale, speed,

L. M. Camarinha-Matos et al. (Eds.): PRO-VE 2020, IFIP AICT 598, pp. 47–60, 2020.
https://doi.org/10.1007/978-3-030-62412-5_4

scope of business and multiple sources of value creation and capture are the key themes for a Digital Business Strategy [2]. Renowned Digital Platforms, like Amazon, Uber, AirBnB and many others have shown strong growth and gained much attention. Based on their yearly survey, McKinsey concludes that the best economic performers have taken advantage of Digital Platforms [3]. Their growth is attributed to their capability to establish network effects between supply and demand sides interacting on the platform [4]. In this development, many ventures, both digital natives, start-ups and incumbents, consider engaging in a Digital Business Strategy based on a Digital Platform. Digital Platform Business, however, involves a major strategic reorientation: from linear production to an ecosystem, leveraging network effects and transforming to digital business operations and customer centric products and processes. Because a Digital Platform facilitates transactions between multiple user sides, it can be considered to support a collaborative network.

Business Models are often positioned as realizations of strategy [5], whereas the strategy can be expressed as a set of statements that define what is critical or important to achieve to reach the long-term organizational goals [6]. The study by Cortimiglia et al. [7] based on a survey of 138 firms, is one of the very few studies we found studying how firms reconfigure their Business Models during the Strategy Making Process in practice. However, this study and other literature on strategy and business models do not provide a clear explanation or guidance about how Business Model Design takes place in context of the Strategy Making Process. Consequently, our research question of 'How a Digital Platform Business Strategic Objective can be translated into a set of Business Model Design Requirements in a structured way?' remains as of yet largely unanswered.

This paper proposes and demonstrates a method to guide the derivation of Business Model Design Requirements from a Digital Platform Business Strategic Objective. Acccordingly, we investigate the problem and we have developed the initial version of our method based on the literature. We performed a sequence of iterative focus group sessions with a team of researchers in the field. Using a real-life historical business case in the aviation industry, we applied the method to demonstrate its working and evaluate its validity. Our approach contributes to research by establishing a conceptual link from strategic objectives to business models. Furthermore, our approach contributes to practice by providing a method that specifies a set of requirements for business models that are in line with strategy.

In the next section, we introduce the theoretical background on the topics of Business Strategy, Digital Business Strategy and Platform Strategy. We discuss the link between Strategy and Business Models and introduce the definitions for our research. In Sect. 3, we describe the method that we propose. In Sect. 4, we demonstrate the working of the method in the context of the SABRE case and discuss the method, its limitations and future research directions. Finally, we conclude this paper in Sect. 5.

2   Theoretical Background

2.1   Digital Business Strategy

Varadarajan and Clark [8] state *'Business Strategy is generally explained in terms of the achievement and maintenance of competitive advantage in specific product-market domains.'*. Key strategic issues identified at the business unit level focus on maintaining and achieving competitive advantage and the integration & coordination of 'Arena, Advantage, Access and Activities'. One of the most commonly accepted Business Strategy tools is the Balanced Scorecard (BSC) [6]. The BSC is a framework that is used to set, link and monitor Strategic Objectives, generally defined as statements that define what is critical or important to achieve to reach the long-term organizational goals and that help to convert a mission statement into more specific plans and projects. In the BSC they are organized in four so-called Strategy Perspectives, being Growth & Learning, Internal Processes, Customer and Financial. Kaplan & Norton state that *'a business strategy can be viewed as a set of hypotheses about cause-and-effect relationships.'*. Quezada et al. [9] provide a method for identifying Strategic Objectives. It starts from vision and mission, identification of strategic themes and general Strategic Objectives. Then, based on external/internal (SWOT) analysis, specific objects are specified and aligned with the previous steps. From this a Strategy Map is generated and performance indicators are derived.

Digitalization and the internet do not only affect the business propositions, they also affect the rate of renewal of propositions by incorporation of new technologies. This continuously generates new opportunities and threats in an organization's context. Consequently, this requires organizations to update their strategies and this poses requirements on an organization's dynamic capabilities and its Strategic Decision Making Process [10]. Bharadway et al. [2] define Digital Business Strategy as *'an organizational strategy formulated and executed by leveraging digital resources to create differential value'*. They identify four Digital Business Strategy themes: Scope, Scale, Speed and Sources of Value Creation and Capture. Scope refers to the reach of the IT strategy in the Business Strategy, and it is based on the observation that IT systems can integrate internal processes as well as serve many different customer segments and use resources of ecosystem partners. Scale refers to the capability of scaling up or down the deployment of digital technologies, the use of data, within its own boundaries as well as that of partners. Speed refers to the extent in which an organization can, using digital technologies, learn and improve decision making, accelerate new product launches and dynamically orchestrate its supply chain. Sources of Value Creation and Capture refers to an organization's capability to create and capture value from information, its ecosystem and collaborative network partners, including Platform Business Models.

2.2   Business Models and Platform Business Models

Although the Business Model concept has become highly popular, it has also been subject to discussion and debate. In order to provide clarity on the concept, several authors have made substantial attempts to review the definition and use of the Business

Model [11, 12]. Business Models are considered to provide realizations of strategy [5, 11], yet based on the research by Cortimiglia et al. [7], we see that Business Model Design can be driven from observing opportunities in the market as well as more 'top-down' from the Strategy Making Process. Casadesus-Masanell and Ricart [5] indicate that a single strategy can be abstracted into many different Business Models.

Hagiu and Wright [13] define a platform as '*an organization that creates value primarily by enabling direct interactions between two (or more) distinct types of affiliated customers*'. Also in other definitions, the support of interactions, often commercial transactions, is central [13]. This interaction between two interdependent parties makes this business model differ to a large extent from more conventional models in which transformation of inputs into outputs is central. In a platform business model, the transactions are based on production of goods and services by multiple other parties. The platform supports these transactions. One of the key characteristics of a platform business model is the possibility to obtain and leverage network effects. Network effects occur if the presence of a certain type or number of customers attracts new customers. Eisenmann et al. [4] distinguish same-side and cross-side effects. In-depth case studies on AirBnB, Etsy and Uber reveal the, often overlooked yet crucial, effort that the platform organization has to put in, in order to achieve acceptance and critical mass for establishing network effects [14]. There are also several synonyms in use, e.g. two- or multi-sided business model or marketplace. Eisenmann et al. [4] distinguish the following four key elements of a Platform Business Model: Supply Side Users (1), ensuring supply of goods or services and Demand Side Users (2), in demand for the supplied goods and services. The Platform Provider (3) is the point of contact for the transaction and provides components (hardware, software, and service modules in an architecture) in most user transactions, rules (including standards, protocols, policies and contracts) to coordinate participants. The last element distinguished, Platform Sponsor (4), designs the components and rules, and determines who may participate in the network as platform providers and users. Oftentimes, this role coincides with the Platform Provider. A key strategic consideration is the extent to which these four elements are open to participation by other parties. A well-known example is the control that Apple store applies to the offered apps, versus the relative lack of control in the Android store. Platform Business Models are often based on digital technologies, although not often explicitly mentioned so.

3   A Method for Deriving Business Model Design Requirements from a Digital Platform Business Strategic Objective

Below, in Sect. 3.1 our research methodology is briefly described, which we link to definitions in 3.2. In Sect. 3.3 we present an overview of the method. In Sect. 3.4, we present a card and in Sect. 3.5 we introduce the process that guides the derivation Business Model Design Requirements. Section 3.6 introduces the Catalogue of Strategy Elements that help to derive Subobjectives from a Strategy Objective.

3.1   Research Approach

For the development of our method, as presented in this section, we have followed the step-wise Design Science Research approach as proposed in [15]. We briefly detail the distinct steps. The practical problem refers to the increased consideration by organizations to pursue a Digital Platform Business Strategy. The corresponding scientific gap targeted is the lack of guidance in the transformation of a Strategic Objective into Business Model Design Requirements ('problem & solution objectives' step in the DSR approach). The method we developed specifies five steps to take from a given Digital Platform Business Strategic Objective, to deriving Subobjectives, to translating and analyzing a set of forthcoming Business Model Requirements. The process is supported by a set of cards that facilitates the process. The specification of Subobjectives is facilitated by a Catalogue of Digital Platform Business Strategy Elements (see 3.6). We performed a sequence of iterative focus group sessions with a team of researchers in the field of Digital Strategy and Business Models ('development & design' step in the DSR approach). Using a historical case in the aviation industry (see 4.1), we demonstrate the working of the method and evaluate its validity ('demonstration & evaluation' step in the DSR approach) (explained in Sect. 4).

3.2   Definitions

We consider a Digital Platform Business Strategy as a specialization of the concept of digital business strategy. It is defined as a Business Strategy in which a Platform Business Model, enabled by digital technology, is central. A Digital Platform Business Model is then defined as a specification of the logic of value creation and value capture utilizing a Digital Platform. Similarly, we define a *Digital Platform Strategic Objective* as a Strategic Objective that targets at achieving or maintaining competitive advantage by means of a Digital Platform Business Model. Such Business Model will have to consider, among other aspects, the specific characteristics of Platforms and Digital Strategy, as well as fit within Business Strategy. A *Strategic Subobjective* (SSO) can be defined as a partial Strategic Objective that specifies for a given Strategy Element what should be achieved. A *Strategy Element* can be defined as a commonly recognized dimension or aspect of a (Digital Platform) Business Strategy. An overview is presented in Sect. 3.6. We refer to the ex-ante inputs for both designing and evaluating a Business Model as *Business Model Design Requirements*.

3.3   Method Overview

The process, depicted in Fig. 1, starts from a given Digital Platform Business Strategic Objective. Such SO may result from for example following a SWOT analysis in context of a Strategic Decision-Making Process. In order to be actionable as a set of design requirements, that SO needs to be specified further and transformed into statements that have meaning in the design of Business Models.

Next, 19 Business Model Design Requirement Specification Cards are provided. Each card represents one Strategy Element. On each card, the following three steps are supported. (1) Detailing of the SO into Strategic Subobjectives, (2) Next, for each SSO,

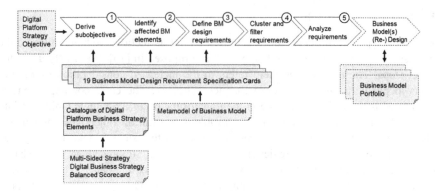

Fig. 1. Method to derive business model requirements

elements of a Business Model that would be affected by the SSO are identified (e.g., customer, activity). (3) These elements are then described in the form of a business model requirement. After the processing of all cards, the requirements are collected and filtered to avoid duplications and redundancy. As a last step the requirements are analyzed and prepared for further processing in the (re-)design of one or more Business Models in the Business Model Portfolio of the business organization.

The 19 Strategy Elements are captured in the Catalogue of Digital Platform Business Strategy Elements, as described in Sect. 3.6. The transformation of SSO to Business Model Requirements is based on the metamodel of the Business Model that is used by the business organization (see 3.4).

3.4   Business Model Design Requirements Specification Card

A specification card (SC) consists of three blocks: Strategic Subobjectives, Business Model Elements, and Business Model Design Requirements). These correspond with the first three steps of the requirements specification process depicted in Fig. 1. We discuss the three blocks (Fig. 2).

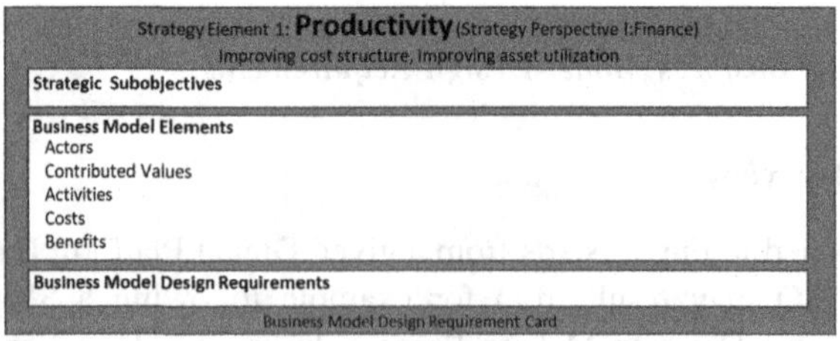

Fig. 2. A business model requirement specification card for the strategic element 1.

Strategic Subobjectives: The top line captures the number and name of the Strategy Element is the name of the Strategic Perspective. The second line describes a set of associated concepts (See Sect. 3.6). The empty space after the term Strategic

Subobjective is the room to describe the SSO as the desired future state of the business of the organization in context of the strategic objective and related to the Strategy Element in free format. In the case of the SC illustrated above: *"What does the digital platform business strategy imply for a revenue growth strategy?"* One can describe none, one or multiple SSOs.

Business Model Elements: In the left column of the middle part five elements of a Business Model metamodel are depicted. For this card, we deployed the metamodel of the Service-Dominant Business Model Radar (SDBM/R) [16], as we intend to provide requirements for a portfolio of Business Models specified and managed in that format. The SDBM/R is built on Service-Dominant logic [17], of which underlying principles correspond closely to typical digital services supported by Digital Platforms. In the five empty spaces, answers to the following questions can be briefly described: *What does the specified strategic subobjective imply for actors, as contributed value for an actor, as activity for an actor, as benefit for an actor, as cost for an actor?*

Because in the top section there can be multiple Strategic Subobjectives, it is also possible to provide multiple sets of answers.

Business Model Design Requirements: A Business Model Design Requirement specifies the conditions that one or more Business Models in the Business Model Portfolio should meet in order to achieve the formulated Strategic Objective. The identified elements of the middle section and the SSOs specified in the top section are used to formulate a requirement with the following structure to *'Actor provides contributed value (to user) by performing activity to get benefit at the expense of cost'*. The number of resulting requirements per Specification Card is not limited and need not be 1:1 corresponding to the number of described SSOs.

3.5   Method Application Process

The process consists of five steps. In the first three steps, Derive Subobjectives (1), Identify affected Business Model elements (2), Define Business Model Design Requirements (3), the 19 SCs as described above, are used one by one. Step 4 and 5 process the cards.

Cluster and Filter Requirements (4): As each card may capture multiple SSOs and multiple Business Model Requirements, the total resulting set of requirements may overlap. Consequently, all business model requirements are collected, clustered and filtered. Since the requirements have a set structure, the clustering can, e.g., be sorted in a database on the elements actor and activity. This may reveal similar or overlapping activities and value contributions. Then these can be inspected and harmonized. This may result in combining and rephrasing Business Model Design Requirements.

Analyze Requirements (5): The purpose of this final step is to understand the coherence of the set of Business Model Requirements on an aggregate level. What does the Strategic Objective imply for the organization in the collaborating network? What activities does the focal organization have to employ? Two ways of analyzing are proposed: i) build a Value Network [18] and ii) cluster activities for the focal organization. A Value Network can be built by mapping all identified Actors as nodes and the Value Contributions as directed arcs. Value Network Analysis allows to inspect how value is created and it also reveals how the Strategic Objective may affect value contributions beyond the focal organization. The clustering of activities of the focal organization can be done on the following categories:

- initial and preparatory activities, required to prepare for the operation of the business model;
- key operational activities, required to run the Business Model; and
- additional, enhancing activities, that are not necessarily part of the Business Model, but may improve the user experience or target additional segments.

This analysis thus helps to understand what the key activities are and how the business model can potentially be enhanced.

The final set of Business Model Design Requirements is, together with the Strategic Objective, then available to the organization to update the Business Model Portfolio by designing new Business Models and redesign or out phase others to realize the Strategic Objective.

3.6 A Catalogue of Digital Platform Business Strategy Elements

A Platform Business Strategy and a Digital Business Strategy are related but distinct. In order to be able to devise a complete Business Strategy, we integrate these theories, consisting of different elements, into a Catalogue of Strategy Elements (a commonly recognized dimension or aspect of a (Digital Platform) Business Strategy). The Catalogue is composed by confronting and clustering the Business Strategy Perspectives and the underlying elements of the BSC [6], with key dimensions from Digital Business Strategy [2], and key concepts in Platform Business Strategy theory, e.g. [4]. This has led to an update of the original four perspectives of the BSC. Firstly, the Customer Perspective is replaced by a Value Proposition Perspective, as in digital business -and specifically in platform business strategies-, organizations must deal with multiple interdependent segments of supply and demand. Secondly, the Internal Processes Perspective has been renamed as simply the Processes Perspective, since digital business processes typically cross boundaries of organizations. Lastly, an Ecosystem Perspective has been added as a separate perspective, since in digital business, and specifically in Platform Business Strategies, Sources of Value Creation and Capture typically require collaboration in the ecosystem. The Finance Perspective remained unaltered. The Learning & Growth Perspective has kept the same name, although new, digital, elements have been added. Each of five perspectives contains two or more elements, leading to 19 elements in total (Table 1).

In the method we have developed the Strategy Elements of this catalogue are used to specify one or more Strategic Objectives. For brevity, the full list of underlying source elements and the clustering are omitted.

Table 1. Five strategy perspectives and nineteen strategy elements for digital platform business strategy expanded from the balanced scorecard

Finance: Productivity strategy; Revenue growth strategy
Value Proposition: Supply-side and demand-side customers; Experience; Product/service attributes; Reusability; Intangible values
Ecosystem: Parties and relations; Network effects and critical mass; Governance and competition
Processes: Operations management; Customer management; Innovation; Decision making
(Digital) Learning & Growth: Human Capital; Organization Capital; Digital architecture; Platform evolution; IT infrastructure

4 Demonstration Using the SABRE Business Case

In this section, we demonstrate the method by illustrating the transformation of a single Strategic Objective to SSOs, and eventually to Business Model Requirements in the scope of the SABRE business case.

4.1 Introduction to SABRE

SABRE is an acronym for Semi Automated Business Research Environment. The project started as a joint initiative between American Airlines (AA) and IBM to create the world's first computerized airline reservation system in 1960. In 2000 SABRE was spun off AA and according to Reuters in 2014 it was the largest global distribution systems (GDS) provider for air bookings in North America. A GDS is a computer system supporting transactions between travel industry service providers and travel agencies. Currently, SABRE advertises itself as a travel technology company.

In 1953 the process of airline seat reservation was manual and error-prone, resulting in a mismatch between underutilized aircrafts. In 1964 a computerized system was launched. In 1976 130 travel agent offices used terminals to make passenger reservations directly in the system. This number grew to 130,000 in 1989. Also, in 1976, other airlines were admitted to the system, increasing the value for travel agents as well as other airlines. In the eighties, SABRE added functionalities for finding cheapest prices and allow consumers to access airline, hotel and car rental information and make their own reservations using personal computers. In the end of the eighties SABRE started commercially providing the software solutions to other airlines. In 2000 SABRE became an independent company. Currently SABRE provides several tools on an open online platform, integrating mobile services, pricing tools, reporting tools and booking systems. Overseeing these developments, we see the evolution of an information system, initially as a company internal system, to a system used with specific travel agents, to a platform serving multiple airlines and other travel services, serving both travel agents and customers directly. Based on these developments, we can condense this business case as follows:

- American Airlines spins off the SABRE brand and its system, at that point used by only American Airlines and American Airline affiliated travel agents.
- The SABRE company considers the opportunity to open this system for use by other airlines and other travel agents.
- The Strategic Objective we work with in this example is *"to establish profits with the SABRE platform"*.

4.2   Subobjectives and Business Model Requirements

In this section we present two of the five Strategic Perspectives with examples of the derived Strategic Subobjectives and the forthcoming Business Model Design Requirements.

Value Proposition :The subobjective resulting from the combination of the strategic objective and the Strategy Element (4) 'The experience and customer journey, including transactions; Relationship-Service/Partnership; Customer (demand and supply side) processes; interfaces and interactions' is:

> *"Overcome travel agents' loss of possibility to apply arbitration between airlines' offerings."*.

The forthcoming Business Model Design Requirement is:

> *"7. SABRE provides an alternative to arbitrage to travel agents by [activity] to get fees at the expense of operational costs."*.

Learning & Growth: The subobjectives resulting from the combination of the strategic objective and the Strategy Element (17) 'Digital architecture, and specifically Platform envelopment' are:

> *"Create a new proposition for both airlines (supply) and agents (demand) based on an existing booking platform and existing relations of one airline and travel agents. Use the new position to learn from demand and supply data for airlines.*
>
> *Leverage American Airlines' booking system. Build standardized interfaces. The booking system must be made open for use by third parties."*.

The forthcoming Business Model Design Requirement is:

> *"25. SABRE provides [contributed value] (to [user]) by acquiring and opening the booking platform, activating/transferring existing relations, setting up procedures to learn from data and creating standards to get start, increased adoption at the expense of investment."*.

4.3   Results of 'Analyze Requirements (5)'

The following table illustrates how a subset of the forthcoming Business Model Design Requirements, using their set structure can be organized in a database.

Value Network: Based on this information we can build a Value Network [18]. In the following Fig. 3, the different actors and the value contributions are depicted.

Major actors are depicted in full ellipses. Any (potential) revenue streams (e.g., fees) that were identified in the requirements are not depicted, since neither the form

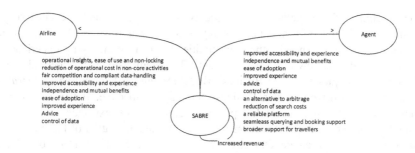

Fig. 3. Value network representation of resulting business model requirements (excerpt).

Table 2. Database structure for collecting requirements

From	Value contribution	To	Activity	Benefit/Cost
Agent	Insight and booking	Traveler	Querying and booking	Fees and operational costs
Airline	Airline services	Traveler	Servicing airlines	
American Airlines	Booking system (license, rights, code)	SABRE	Hand-over	Outsource opportunity
SABRE	Critical supply and demand	(initial) Airline; (initial) Travel Agent	Acquiring initial airlines and agents (on top of AA)	Income and position

nor quantity are determined. The core of the Business Model is the interaction between the travel agents and the airlines, facilitated by SABRE. To this end, SABRE has a value proposition to both sides of the platform. Other identified actors have been omitted in this view.

Activities: The activities can be taken directly from the database depicted in Table 2. An example of an 'initial phase' activity is: 'Opening the booking platform, creating interfaces'. An example of an 'operational phase' activity: 'Integrate interfaces and cross-organizational processes'. An example of an 'enhancing' activity is: 'Attract car rental offers of car rental providers by integrating and exposing offers'.

4.4 Discussion

Based on one Strategic Objective and 19 Strategy Elements and corresponding Business Model Design Requirement Specification Cards, 29 Business Model Design Requirements were derived. These requirements were expressed in the targeted business model structure and consequently presented as a database, as a Value Network and as categories of activities for the focal company. Below, we discuss the method and its outputs.

The outputs of the method, the Value Network (Fig. 3) and the clustering of activities provide not only a rather concrete outline of a Business Model, but also potential evolutions, defined by the opportunities to enhance the users' experience on both sides or address new customer segments. This demonstrates the method's capability to specify requirements for Business Model Designs that are *in line with strategy,* as this process is driven from a Business Strategy perspective. If the process were driven from a customer or market perspective, it can be expected that different, potentially conflicting, requirements result. Also, in the application of the method, we dealt with a single Strategic Objective. In practice the Strategic Decision Making Process yields multiple concurrent Strategic Objectives. The researchers believe that it would be possible to run the process in parallel for multiple Strategic objectives, until step (4) 'Cluster and filter requirements. Such approach would probably also increase the probability of encountering conflicting requirements. This could be remedied by either choosing a dominant requirement, or by taking multiple sets, as scenarios, forward in the Business Model Design phase.

By using the Catalogue of Strategic Elements in deriving the requirements, the method demonstrates that a complete set of strategic considerations *and the corresponding context information* can be taken aboard the specification of requirements. We believe this may avoid design-evaluation iterations.

The presented approach can be characterized as elaborate as the 19 different Specification Cards require substantial processing. However, as the scope of each of the cards is limited to the Strategic Element, the Strategic Objective and the context knowledge of the team, the task per card can be completed quickly.

As a design artefact, the method should be evaluated for its validity, utility and/or efficacy to make sure that it produces valid outcomes, it is considered useful by its intended audience, and it performs effectively and efficiently as intended. This demonstration of the method cannot show that the resulting Business Model Design Requirements, or the forthcoming designs, would be more complete, more effective or efficient than in a conventional situation. As future research, we are planning a set of evaluation activities for this purpose.

5 Conclusion

Digital technologies and hyperconnectivity have paved the way for new services and the pursuit of entirely new Business Strategies. A type of Business Strategy that has gained strong attention recently is the Platform Business Strategy. Such a strategy strongly differs from a conventional Business strategy in speed, scale, scope and interaction with the ecosystem. Although Business Models are often said to realize a strategy, little guidance and support exists for the specification of Business Models realizing a Digital Business Platform Business Strategy. This affects an organization's responsiveness to digital opportunities.

In this paper, we propose a novel method that we have developed to support the specification of Business Model Design Requirements of an organization given its Digital Platform Business Strategy. The method is demonstrated using the SABRE platform business case.

The application of the method demonstrates that following its steps, using the Specification Cards and the underlying Strategic Elements, produces a usable set of Business Model Design Requirements, as well as a resulting Value Network and clustering of activities. This provides the basis for a Business Model design, as well as possible evolutions to enhance the value proposition. Such basis could not by conventional methods, such as BSC, as these do not provide a transformation to the targeted business model structure. The outcome of the method is in line with the strategy and complete with respect to the Strategic Elements defined in the Catalogue. The latter element allows to take aboard specific and relevant context information into the specification of the business model requirements. This likely avoids design-redesign iterations.

Based on the demonstration and discussion of the method in context of a historical case, we can conclude that the method is usable to derive a set of Business Model Design Requirements in a structured way, given a Digital Platform Business Strategic Objective. A next step indicated by the DSR approach, is to formally evaluate the presented method in a real-life business application.

References

1. Camarinha-Matos, L.M., Afsarmanesh, H.: Collaborative Networked Organizations: A Research Agenda for Emerging Business Models. Springer, Heidelberg (2004). https://doi.org/10.1007/b116613
2. Bharadway, A., El Sawy, O.A., Pavlou, P.A.: Digital business strategy: toward a next generation of insights. MIS Q. **37**(2), 471–482 (2013)
3. Catlin, T.: The right digital-platform strategy (2019)
4. Eisenmann, T.R., Parker, G., Van Alstyne, M.W.: Opening platforms: how, when and why? SSRN Electron. J. (2008)
5. Casadesus-Masanell, R., Ricart, J.E.: From strategy to business models and onto tactics. Long Range Plann. **43**(2–3), 195–215 (2010)
6. Kaplan, R.S., Norton, D.P.: Linking the balanced scorecard to strategy. Calif. Manag. Rev. **39**(1), 53–79 (1996)
7. Cortimiglia, M.N., Ghezzi, A., Frank, A.G.: Business model innovation and strategy making nexus: evidence from a cross-industry mixed-methods study. R&D Manag. **46**(3), 414–432 (2016)
8. Varadarajan, P.R., Clark, T.: Delineating the scope of corporate, busines and marketing strategy. J. Bus. Res. **31**, 93–105 (1994)
9. Quezada, L.E., Cordova, F.M., Palominos, P., Godoy, K., Ross, J.: Method for identifying strategic objectives in strategy maps. Int. J. Prod. Econ. **122**(1), 492–500 (2009)
10. Eisenhardt, K.M., Zbaracki, M.J.: Strategic decision making. Management **13**(3), 17–37 (1992)
11. Al-Debei, M.M., Avison, D.: Developing a unified framework of the business model concept. Eur. J. Inf. Syst. **19**(3), 359–376 (2010)
12. Massa, L., Tucci, C.L., Afuah, A.: A critical assessment of business model research. Acad. Manag. Ann. **11**(1), 73–104 (2017)
13. Hagiu, A., Wright, J.: Multi-Sided Platforms **1** (2011)
14. Teixeira, T.S.: Airbnb, Etsy, Uber: Expanding from One to Many Millions of Customers (2019)

15. Peffers, K., Tuunanen, T., Rothenberger, M.A., Chatterjee, S.: A design science research methodology for information systems research. J. Manag. Inf. Syst. **24**(3), 45–77 (2007)
16. Turetken, O., Grefen, P., Gilsing, R., Adali, O.E.: Service-dominant business model design for digital innovation in smart mobility. Bus. Inf. Syst. Eng. **61**(1), 9–29 (2019)
17. Lusch, R.F., Vargo, S.L.: The service-dominant mindset 1 goods to service. In: Service Science, Management and Engineering, pp. 89–96 (2008)
18. Allee, V.: Value network analysis and value conversion of tangible and intangible assets. J. Intellect. Cap. **9**(1), 5–24 (2008)

A Method to Guide the Concretization of Costs and Benefits in Service-Dominant Business Models

Rick Gilsing[2(✉)], Oktay Turetken[2], Baris Ozkan[2], Frans Slaats[2],
Onat Ege Adali[2], Anna Wilbik[3], Frank Berkers[1], and Paul Grefen[1]

[1] Netherlands Organisation for Applied Scientific Research (TNO),
PO Box 96800, 2509 JE The Hague, The Netherlands
frank.berkers@tno.nl, p.w.p.j.grefen@tue.nl
[2] School of Industrial Engineering, Eindhoven University of Technology,
PO Box 513, 5600 MB Eindhoven, The Netherlands
{r.a.m.gilsing,o.turetken,b.ozkan,o.e.adali}@tue.nl,
f.h.slaats@student.tue.nl
[3] Department of Data Science & Knowledge Engineering, Maastricht
University, PO Box 616, 6200 MD Maastricht, The Netherlands
a.wilbik@maastrichtuniversity.nl

Abstract. Contemporary organizations increasingly transition to a service-orientation to better cater to the needs of customers. To offer the resulting complex service solutions, organizations collaborate in business networks to exchange services, which are typically conceptualized by means of service-dominant business models. As business models influence organizational performance, novel service-dominant business models should be evaluated with respect to how value in terms of costs and benefits is captured per actor. However, limited support is present in literature to guide the concretization of costs and benefits in networked, service-dominant settings to assess the viability of the model. In response, we propose a method to guide the concretization of costs and benefits in service-dominant business models. Building upon existing work in terms of networked value capture, we introduce design parameters to concretize costs and benefits and consequently guide the concretization of these parameters by means of a structured process.

Keywords: Service-dominant business model · Information governance · Business model viability · Business model evaluation

1 Introduction

Stimulated by factors such as globalization, rapid technological change and digitization, we see that many organizations transition to a service-orientation of business to offer novel value to customers or to better cater to customer needs. For instance, in the manufacturing domain, organizations such as Kone or IBM increasingly focus on servitization to extend current product offerings in order to create novel value or to enhance existing value propositions [1]. Similarly, driven by advances in IT, we

© IFIP International Federation for Information Processing 2020
Published by Springer Nature Switzerland AG 2020
L. M. Camarinha-Matos et al. (Eds.): PRO-VE 2020, IFIP AICT 598, pp. 61–70, 2020.
https://doi.org/10.1007/978-3-030-62412-5_5

observe that digital companies such as Netflix and Spotify move away from a sole focus on key product offerings (e.g. movie DVDs or music) and aim to provide digitally-enabled, integrated service solutions to better cater to the needs of customers [2].

To reduce the complexity that underlies these service-based solutions and to foster business agility with respect to offering services, many organizations engage in collaborative business networks, in which organizations exchange services and integrate resources to co-create value [3, 4]. The configuration of these networks in terms of actors in the network, resources deployed and services exchanged consequently defines how value is co-created.

Typically, the business model concept is used to conceptualize these service-driven collaborative networks, describing the logic of how value is created and captured by the network and what resources are leveraged or exchanged to support the business model [5]. Accordingly, these *service-dominant* business models can be used to explore how new service-driven business collaborations should be configured or structured, and how the resulting business model is positioned vis-à-vis strategy and operational processes. Business models are argued to influence organizational performance [6], which calls for the viable design of novel business models in terms of the balance of costs and benefits captured through participation [7].

In contrast to traditional business models, which typically reason from the perspective of a single focal organization, each actor in the business network of service-dominant business models is essential towards the co-creation of value. Accordingly, novel service-dominant business model designs should yield or establish a viable or acceptable scenario (in terms of costs and benefits) for *all* actors in the network. However, service exchange between actors towards the co-creation of value logically results in reciprocal costs and benefits [3], which in turn may result in opposite or conflicting desires, requiring negotiation in order to adequately concretize these costs and benefits. Moreover, especially in competitive settings, actors may not be inclined to share sensitive knowledge or make explicit strategic motives towards their concretization. As a result, this complicates the design and concretization of service-dominant business models, which consequently may threaten the performance of novel, collaborative service-driven initiatives.

Although tools and techniques have been proposed for the *design and representation* of service-dominant business models [8, 9], whereas some research has focused on the *evaluation* of network-oriented business models [10, 11], limited support is present in literature with respect to guiding the concretization of costs and benefits that are the result from participation in service-dominant business models, taking into account the need for governance in terms of how information is shared between actors in the business network and in what context (e.g. publicly shared or restricted to a set of actors). Such support in turn would help users or decision makers to evaluate novel service-dominant business models, exploring under what settings the business model is viable. In response, we pose the following research question to address this gap:

"How can the concretization of costs and benefits that result from the participation in service-dominant business models be supported to support its subsequent analysis?"

In this paper, we propose a method for guiding and analyzing the costs and benefits of service-dominant business models. The method entails a process description that is built upon three layers of knowledge to govern how information is shared in the network to concretize costs and benefits. On the basis of these layers, we introduce design parameters for the concretization of costs and benefits, for which the process description offers guidance on the steps taken to concretize these design parameters.

The remainder of this paper is structured as follows. Section 2 describes the background to our research and details how value is captured in service-dominant business models. In Sect. 3, we introduce the method and elaborate on the steps taken. Section 4 illustrates the working of the method. We conclude and summarise this paper in Sect. 5, making explicit how we aim to further improve the method.

2   Research Background

This section discusses the research background for this research. Specifically, we elaborate on the *design* of *service-dominant business models* and how *value is captured* within these business models.

Design of Service-Dominant Business Models – A business model describes the logic of how value is created and captured and how this is supported through its organizational and architectural infrastructure [5]. In contrast to traditional business models, which take the perspective of a single organization and focus on the novel recombination of internal and external resources and capabilities to propose value, service-dominant business models are explicitly *networked* in nature and focus on how value is co-created through service exchange between actors in the network [2].

Several tools have been proposed for the design and representation of service-dominant business models. For instance, Zolnowski et al. [9] propose the SDBMC, which is based on the Business Model Canvas [7] and takes the concepts of SDL at its basis, and accommodates users to represent the business network as 'stacked' BMCs. Contrastingly, Turetken et al. [8] propose the SDBM/R, which consists of a circular template taking the co-created value at its core, and enables users to map how actors in the business network contribute and capture value through participation. Given its descriptive power in terms of the business network, we use the SDBM/R for representing service-dominant business models for the remainder of this paper.

Value Capture in Service-Dominant Business Models – Value co-creation in service-dominant business models is based on service exchange, which results in reciprocal costs and benefits for the actors involved for the exchange [3]. The concretization of these costs and benefits depends on the perception and preferences of both actors involved for the exchange, and typically result in conflicting or opposite motives and desires. Accordingly, this requires negotiation to support the concretization of these costs and benefits. Next to this, costs and benefits may moreover be irrespective of exchange, and be the result of the performance of the entire network or business model (such as the corporate image generated through business model participation), or may solely relate to a single actor (such as operational costs). Note here that costs and benefits can be financial, but also non-financial in nature [2]. The balance of the total set of costs and benefits captured per actor consequently determines whether for the respective actor the business model design is viable or acceptable, which also depends on the strategic goals of the respective actor. For service-dominant business models to be viable, this property should hold for *all* actors in the business network.

Reypens et al. [12] propose a conceptual process for value capture in networked collaborations. Their work identifies two layers of concern, namely the *network* layer and the *stakeholder* layer, between which information is shared to support value capture. Value is co-created on the network level (for which all actors in the business model are involved) which results in actor specific costs and benefits that concern the stakeholder layer. However, using solely these two layers does not accommodate communication and information exchanges between *subsets* of *actors* that participate in a business model, such as the case for service exchange. The method we propose in the present study supports all three layers by its design.

3   Method Description

The proposed method entails a structured process description that guides actors for a service-dominant business model to concretize their respective costs and benefits, explicating how information is shared across the network. The balance of costs and benefits consequently obtained makes explicit how well each actor in the business network performs, allowing actors to judge whether this is viable or acceptable [7]. Although costs and benefits may be financial and non-financial in nature, the intangible and subjective nature of non-financial costs and benefits makes it difficult to quantify these in a structured way. Therefore, we support the concretization of the financial costs and benefits and contrast the resulting balance per actor to any non-financial benefits or costs that are also captured by this respective actor. Each actor should then judge whether the total balance of costs and benefits (e.g., both financial and non-financial) is acceptable.

As the backbone to our method, we first introduce the structure needed to support the concretization of costs and benefits obtained from participation in the service-dominant business model, addressing the need for increased governance on how information is shared and used. On the basis of this structure, we derive design parameters for the concretization of financial costs and benefits and describe via a step-wise process how these design parameters are concretized in a structured way.

3.1   Information Sharing Structure and Associated Design Parameters

Concretizing costs and benefits per actor resulting from a service-dominant business model design depends on the information that is needed to concretize or quantify these costs and benefits and where this information exists, which should be shared such that each actor can understand the balance of costs and benefits they accrue from participation. Taking into account that not all actors are willing to share sensitive information across the entire network [13], this demands a structure that supports the governance and sharing of information in service-dominant business models, which serves as the backbone for our concretization process.

Next to the *network* level and *actor* level (which we denote as *public level* and *private level* for the remainder) views identified for conceptualizing value capture in networked settings [12], we introduce a third level, the *restricted level*, which accounts for information that needs to be shared to support the concretization of costs and benefits as a result of service exchange between two or more actors. Accordingly, information for the concretization of costs and benefits can exist on the *public level* (visible to all actors in the business network), *private level* (visible to only a single actor) and on the *restricted level* (only visible to those actors that are involved for a particular service exchange). As such, in case sensitive information is shared for concretizing costs and benefits as a result of service exchange, this information can be shared on the *restricted level*, such that it is not visible to other actors in the business network.

Based on these levels of concerns, we derive three design parameters that are used to concretize and quantify the financial costs and benefits of the value model under-lying the service-dominant business model: *public parameters*, *restricted parameters* and *private parameters*. *The public parameters* are concretized by all actors in the network, and are used for public costs and benefits or provide the context for the concretization for restricted or private costs and benefits. For instance, a public parameter may refer to the number of expected customers of a service (if decided upon collaboratively), which in turn may affect how costs and benefits as a result of service exchange (restricted level) are quantified.

The *restricted parameters* are used to costs and benefits as a result of service exchange and are concretized by multiple-actors, those that are involved for the respective service exchange. As an actor may partake in multiple service exchanges in a service-dominant business models, the costs and benefits for these exchanges are to be concretized using different restricted parameters for each of these.

The *private parameters* are used to concretize private (actor specific) costs and benefits. Logically, only the actor that concerns these costs and benefits is able to concretize the associated private parameters.

3.2   Process to Guide the Concretization of Costs and Benefits

Through the highlighted structure, sharing of information is governed by means of the design parameters, which in turn serve as the building blocks for the concretization of the costs and benefits captured from participation in a service-dominant business models. To guide the concretization of these design parameters and consequently the costs and benefits captured, we follow the process description illustrated in Fig. 1. In the following subsections, we will elaborate on each step.

1. Determine information required to concretize costs and benefits

As a first step, each actor should determine what information is needed to con-cretize their respective costs and benefits and how this information is obtained, such that the costs and benefits can be translated into *public, restricted* and *private* parameters. For instance, the concretization of costs a result of service exchange may depend on information that is present at the other actor partaking in service exchange, such as the price this respective actor desires to set for offering the service or the

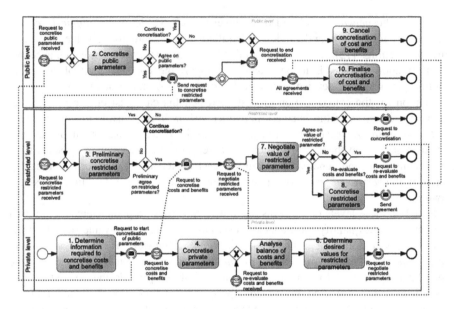

Fig. 1. Step-wise process for concretizing costs and benefits in service-dominant business models

frequency by which the service is paid for. Such information accordingly should be represented by *restricted parameters* to facilitate concretization of the costs and benefits per actor. Similarly, as costs and benefits may depend on the number of expected customers to the service offered for the business model, which may be collaborative discussed on the *public level*, *public parameters* are required to effectively capture this information. Therefore, the goal of this step is to understand how the costs and benefits can be concretized through the set of design parameters. As this step may concern *private parameters* as well, it is positioned on the *private level* of concern.

2. Concretize the public parameters

Next, actors collaboratively discuss and concretize the set of public parameters. As the public parameters concern all actors in the business network, it is positioned on the *public level*. Accordingly, actors share information publicly and collaboratively decide on what values are set for these parameters. As illustrated, this is an iterative step that may feature several rounds before the business networks agrees on the value set for the public parameters. In case no agreement is found on public parameters, the concretization process is terminated, requiring the business model design to be reconsidered.

3. Preliminary concretize the restricted parameters

The third step entails the preliminary concretization of restricted parameters and is positioned on the *restricted level*. As such, it only concerns those actors that are involved for a specific service exchange. Note that an actor in a service-dominant business model may partake in many service exchanges (and therefore require multiple restricted parameters to concretize the associated costs and benefits). The concretization is preliminary as actors should first analyze the total balance of costs and benefits to truly understand what settings of restricted parameters are desired. Nevertheless, as described for the process, the preliminary concretization of the restricted parameters may require several iterations to be concretized and may even make apparent that no viable or acceptable scenario can be found (as for instance the strategic preferences in terms of parameter settings for both actors involved are too distant).

4. Concretize private parameters

The fourth step entails the concretization of private parameters. As these parameters are only visible to and decided upon by a single actor, this step is positioned on the *private level*. Based on information that is available in-house, each actor determines what value should be set for these parameters, taking into account any information derived from the *public* and *restricted parameters*.

5. Analyze balance of costs and benefits

Once the values for the *public, restricted* and *private parameters* have been concretized, the resulting value of the costs and benefits should become apparent, which allows each actor to analyze the balance of the costs and benefits captured under the current settings. This should make explicit whether a viable or acceptable scenario is established for a respective actor, or whether settings (particularly for the restricted parameters) should be changed. As this analysis only concerns a single actor, it is positioned on the *private level*.

6. Determine desired values for restricted parameters

The next step involves what-if analysis with respect to the values set for the restricted parameters, to explore the balance of costs and benefits under different values for the restricted parameters. This is especially relevant in cases for which the initial values set (as explained for step 5) did not result in a viable scenario. Through what-if analysis, each actor can determine under what settings of the restricted parameters (which are subject to negotiation) a viable business scenario can be obtained. As this step is positioned on the private level, this exploration is not visible to other actors, such that actors do not necessarily have to share strategic motives or preferences.

7. Negotiate value of restricted parameters

Taking into account the knowledge obtained through step 6, the respective actors partaking in service exchange negotiate on what *final* values should be set for the restricted parameters. As illustrated by the process, this represents an iterative task with different outputs. In case both actors are able to agree on the value of restricted parameters, the process progresses to the next step. However, in case no agreement can be found, actors may be required to re-evaluate their balance of costs and benefits and to consider either different values for the respective restricted parameter or even different restricted parameters (involving different actors). In case negotiations break down, this may even result in termination of the concretization process, requiring the business model design to be altered.

8. Concretize restricted parameters

If both actors for a specific service exchange agree to a certain value for the restricted parameter, the restricted parameter accordingly can be concretized. Consequently, this agreement (without disclosing the value set) is forwarded to the public level.

9. Cancel concretization of costs and benefits

As explained, if concretization or negotiation on parameter settings break down, the costs and benefits accordingly cannot be concretized, which implies that the business model design should be reconsidered or altered (as either no agreement can be formed or no viable scenario can be obtained for all actors in the business network).

10. Finalize concretization of costs and benefits

Once an agreement has been received for all *restricted parameters*, which implies that under the current settings of the parameters each actor obtains a viable business scenario, the concretization process can be finalized. The final settings of the parameters consequently can be taken as a basis to further operationalize or implement the business model design. Logically, once the business model design becomes increasingly concrete, data availability increases, which facilitates parameters to be more accurately predicted or forecasted, potentially requiring the process to be revisited.

4   Illustrative Application of Method

To illustrate the working of the method, we apply the method to a practical case study. The case study focuses on providing a bike-sharing solution in large cities in Europe, which typically requires the integration and exchange of services between actors such as the *bike sharing service provider (BSSP)*, *municipality* and *bike maintenance provider (BMP)*. This collaboration can be represented through a service-dominant business model as illustrated in Fig. 2 (modelled using the SDBM/R [8]). As illustrated by the model, each actor captures value in terms of costs and benefits from participation, which should be concretized to assess the viability or performance of the business model design, for which we apply the proposed method. For this example, we focus specifically on the perspective of the BMP and the maintenance service it offers to the BSSP to ensure that bikes continuously can be used, and how this can be concretized using the method. A more detailed, quantified walkthrough of this concretization can be found in http://tiny.cc/PRO-VE.

The BMP determines that, to concretize its listed costs and benefits, it needs information on the bike usages per month (to concretize operational costs) and requires negotiation with the BSSP to set the maintenance fee (which depends on both parties) (Step1). For Step 2, the business network first collaboratively determines the expected number of bike usages (as a public parameter), whereas consequently the BMP negotiates a preliminary value for the *maintenance fee* with the BSSP (expressed through a restricted parameter) (Step 3). Next, the BMP concretizes the operational costs per Step 4 (using a private parameter related to the operational costs per customer

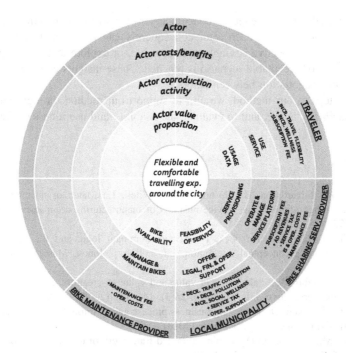

Fig. 2. Service-dominant business model design for bike sharing

and the public parameter related to the expected number of customers) current balance of costs and benefits. On the basis of the resulting profit balance (Step 5), both the BMP and BSSP seek after settings for the restricted parameter that result in an acceptable scenario for themselves (Step 6). This what-if analysis is private and not visible to others in the network. Based on the set of acceptable settings, the BMP and BSSP come together and negotiate on the final value of the restricted parameter (Step 7). If agreement is reached, the cost/benefit item *maintenance fee* accordingly can be concretized using the agreed upon parameter setting (Step 8). If both parties fail to reach an agreement, the network should come together and consider how the business model design should be altered (Step 9). Once all restricted parameters are concretized and agreed upon, the concretization process can be finalized (Step 10).

5   Conclusion and Future Work

In this paper, we have proposed a method to guide the concretization of costs and benefits for service-dominant business models, taking into account the need for increased information governance with regards to how information is shared in business networks, which is especially relevant for competitive business settings. Through the illustrated process, actors in service-dominant business networks can concretize in a structured way the costs and benefits they obtain through participation in the business model in isolated, partially-shared and shared contexts. We identify three design parameters based on knowledge or concern layers to aid this concretization. On the basis of this concretization, each actor consequently can judge whether the business model from their perspective is viable or acceptable, or explore under what parameter settings a viable or acceptable scenario is reached. These insights consequently can be used to support negotiation between actors.

As next steps to our method, we aim to support our method through (automated) tooling to facilitate its use, and to evaluate the usability and usefulness of the method.

References

1. Gebauer, H., Edvardsson, B., Gustafsson, A., Witell, L.: Match or mismatch: strategy-structure configurations in the service business of manufacturing companies. J. Serv. Res. **13**(2), 198–215 (2010)
2. Clauß, T., Laudien, S., Daxböck, B.: Service-dominant logic and the business model concept: toward a conceptual integration. Int. J. Entrep. Innov. Manag. **18**(4), 266–288 (2014)
3. Vargo, S., Maglio, P., Akaka, M.: On value and value co-creation: a service systems and service logic perspective. Eur. Manag. J. **26**(3), 145–152 (2008)
4. Grefen, P., Turetken, O.: Achieving business process agility through service engineering in extended business networks. BPTrends (2018)
5. Al-Debei, M., Avison, D.: Developing a unified framework of the business model concept. Eur. J. Inf. Syst. **19**(3), 359–376 (2010)
6. Casadesus-Masanell, R., Zhu, F.: Business model innovation and competitive imitation: the case of sponsor-based business models. Strateg. Manag. J. **34**(4), 464–482 (2013)
7. Osterwalder, A., Pigneur, Y.: Business Model Generation: A Handbook for Visionaries, Game Changers, and Challengers. John Wiley & Sons, New Jersey (2010)
8. Turetken, O., Grefen, P., Gilsing, R., Adali, O.: Service-dominant business model design for digital innovation in smart mobility. Bus. Inf. Syst. Eng. **61**(1), 9–29 (2019)
9. Zolnowski, A., Weiß, C., Böhmann, T.: Representing service business models with the service business model canvas - the case of a mobile payment service in the retail industry. In: 47th Hawaii International Conference on System Science (2014)
10. Gordijn, J., Akkermans, H.: Designing and evaluating E-business models. IEEE Intell. Syst. Appl. **16**(4), 11–17 (2001)
11. Gilsing, R., Turetken, O., Ozkan, B., Adali, O., Grefen, P.: A method for qualitative evaluation of service-dominant business models. In: European Conference on Information Systems (ECIS) 2020
12. Reypens, C., Lievens, A., Blazevic, V.: Leveraging value in multi-stakeholder innovation networks: a process framework for value co-creation and capture. Ind. Mark. Manag. **56**, 40–50 (2016)
13. Flint, D., Mentzer, J.: Striving for integrated value chain management given a service-dominant logic for marketing. In: The Service Dominant Logic of Marketing: Dialog, Debate and Directions, pp. 139–149 (2006)

Green Virtual Enterprise Breeding Environment: A Proposal of Web Platform Model for a Circular Economy

Fernando Zatt Schardosin[1]([envelope]), Carlos R. De Rolt[1],
Amanda M. L. Batista[1], Clerilei A. Bier[1], and Amanda A. Lentez[2]

[1] ESAG, Santa Catarina State University, Madre Benvenutta, 2037,
Florianópolis, SC 88035-001, Brazil
ferzatt@gmail.com
[2] CEART, Santa Catarina State University, Madre Benvenutta, 2037,
Florianópolis, SC 88035-001, Brazil

Abstract. This paper aims to present a proposal for a Green Virtual Breeding Environment (GVBE) grounded in Circular Economy to create Green Virtual Enterprises (GVE) for the deployment of green solutions for products and services. Through the life cycle of the products, in which, a product, for one organization is discarded and for another, input for new products. New solutions will be developed jointly by the GVBE component actors. Entitled as Reciclica GVBE it contributes to the management of residues focused on sustainability in an economically viable way. It will also contribute, with the population, organizations, and researchers to have a clearer view of the processes that involve waste management, which will allow for better citizen participation, greater responsibility on the part of companies, and new research on the subject.

Keywords: Green Virtual Breeding Environment · Green Virtual Enterprise · Circular economy · Industrial ecology · Collaborative network

1 Introduction

Over the last few decades, the concept of development has involved a large number and variety of conceptions and values, with new references for individual and collective rights, to balance the relations between humans and nature, however it still exists major debates on the nature of sustainable development, the necessary changes, the tools, actors and the benefits of the proposed changes. It is possible to affirm that there is a relative global consensus that the desired sustainable development must harmonize the mutual influences, between nature and society, and guide actions to promote harmony between human beings, humanity, and nature and overcoming challenges.

From the premise that development cannot exist if natural resources deteriorate, nor can nature be protected if economic growth does not consider impacts on environmental destruction. We can disagree of the need for capital reproduction about the tendency of the scarcity of natural resources, and perhaps start looking for an alternative development model that integrates social and economic interests, beyond the

L. M. Camarinha-Matos et al. (Eds.): PRO-VE 2020, IFIP AICT 598, pp. 71–80, 2020.
https://doi.org/10.1007/978-3-030-62412-5_6

limits of nature, and which necessarily demand a transformation of society and human relations with the environment to avoid a growing crisis, and even a possible collapse in the future [1–5]. In this sense and based on two main pillars: the use of resources and the awareness of their limits, the Brundtland Report [6] solidifies an approach that assumes that natural resources are not inexhaustible and that it is not possible to continue with economic growth without considering the variables environment and society, defending the preservation of environmental and cultural resources for future generations, respecting diversity and promoting the reduction of social inequalities.

There is a relative global consensus on environmental limitations and the urgent need for changes in the society thinking, for a desired sustainable development, with a focus on aspects and phenomena with a global scope, leading to the intensification of studies on environmental issues, as well as the regulation of industrial activity and its effects, and the establishment of relevant milestones and their results on sustainability, especially within the scope of the United Nations (UN), with the elaboration of objective and practical measures for the implementation of sustainable development to materialize and systematize conduct that will be followed by society. In this sense, the construction of the 2030 agenda for Sustainable Development, considering extreme poverty as the greatest global challenge and as an indispensable requirement for the effective achievement of sustainable development [7].

UN component countries have promulgated the 2030 agenda, in which they present 17 objectives for the sustainable development of the planet, among which: 8. Promote sustained, inclusive and sustainable economic growth, full and productive employment, and decent work for all; 9. Build resilient infrastructure, promote inclusive and sustainable industrialization, and foster innovation; 11. Sustainable cities and communities; 12. Ensure sustainable production and consumption patterns and 17. Develop partnerships and means of implementation [8]. To achieve these goals, actions will be needed that will disrupt how activities are being carried out and provide a new look at the world, including economic activities to promote sustainable development.

The Johannesburg Declaration [8] establishes that sustainable development is based on three pillars: economic development, social development, and environmental protection, thus reflecting the true scope of the theme, the definition is the result of the recognition that social and economic relations Economic conditions are so complex that sustainable development must be studied with a multidisciplinary focus, comprising economic, cultural, social structure and resource use aspects, among others.

Thus, the circular economy as a theory and resulting practices can present solutions to problems in this theme [9, 10], allied to the Green Virtual Enterprise Breeding Environment (GVBE) [10–14], whose concepts will be appropriately addressed in the course of this work. After all, GVBE and its Green Virtual Companies (GVE) represent promising aspects to address the sustainable challenges of production, logistics, and consumption towards the circular economy [14]. Therefore, this article proposes a GVBE based on the Circular Economy to create GVE for the development of green solutions for products or services. In an innovative perspective of developing technological tools, with alignment, not only for solving green problems but also for economic and social development [15].

Therefore, the research questions that guide this work are: 1. Development of new technologies in products and services by GVEs, through recycling or reuse of discarded materials; 2. Exchanges of materials between organizations that joined in GVBE; 3. Employment and income generation. This work is structured in addition to this introduction, follows with theoretical reviews about GVBE and Circular Economy, then presents the results with the presentation of Reciclica GVBE to finalize with a conclusion and suggestion for future work.

2   Green Virtual Breeding Environment (GVBE)

Collaborative networks consist of a variety of entities, such as organizations, people, govern, autonomous, geographically distributed and heterogeneous in terms of environment, culture, social capital, and objectives, but which collaborate to achieve common or compatible objectives [16]. Collaborative networks have different configurations, topologies, types, sizes, activities developed, and characteristics of the actors that compose them. They can be based on contracts, supply chains, or less formal or more dynamic forms of collaboration, such as virtual enterprise [17]. There are many different forms of such associations, including, strategic alliances, partner networks, industrial clusters, collaborations in research and development, collaborative manufacturing, complex co-production arrangements [18].

The collaboration process needs to mature over time and involves sharing information, resources, and responsibilities, risks, resources, results and rewards between partners, to plan, implement and jointly evaluate a program of activities for a common goal, either to solve a problem or to present an image of joint identity [20].

A collaborative network model is the Virtual Breeding Environment (VBE), which is characterized as a long-term strategic alliance between organizations, which provides an adequate environment for the rapid formation of goal-oriented networks, such as virtual companies, aiming at specific business opportunities [16]. VBEs are also known as a source or support networks, designed to offer the necessary conditions (for example, people, financier, social, infrastructure and organizational) to support the fast and fluid configuration of virtual companies [22]. Also known as a platform, it is a stationary group of organizational entities, although not static, that has developed a preparation to help in the case of a specific task or customer demand [21].

Green Virtual Business Creation Environments (GVBEs), can be understood as long-term strategic alliances of green companies and support institutions, designed to offer the conditions to support the fast configuration of Green Virtual Enterprises (GVE). The GVBEs, grounded in traditional bases of set up a suitable environment for the establishment of collaboration agreements, mutual operating principles, interoperable infrastructures, ontologies, and common trust, among others, to prepare its members to take part in potential GVEs, that will be settled when a business opportunity appears or it is identified by a member of the GVBE who acts as a broker [11]. GVBEs aim to offer the necessary conditions (people, financier, social, infrastructure, and organizational) to promote and efficiently establish work and sharing common principles to create sustainable value in a shared and collaborative way [14].

The difference between VBEs and GVBEs is that in these, the collaboration aims to create economies of scale in a recycling strategy and shared sustainable engineering efficiency. As a result, GVBEs seek to offer their members, the market and society a model of sustainable industrial development, characterized by economic growth combined with a low environmental impact compared to other traditional models of industrial development [11].

The Green Virtual Enterprise (GVE) emerges from the GVBE, which is characterized as a business model of tenable manufacturing and logistics network focused on offering, delivering, and retrieving green products, under a life cycle thinking, supported by its source network [12]. In this sense, the GVBE is in line with the principles defended by the circular economy, besides, it enables an environment favorable to innovation, exchanges, industry, and trade in developed products and services, bringing together the various actors that are related to this environment. In Sect. 3, the circular economy can be better understood.

3   Circular Economy

The circular economy (CE) involves a wide field of knowledge and performance, a review presented 114 definitions for the term and based on the concepts studied, the following understanding was formulated, the circular economy is an economic system that replaces the notion of "end of life" for reducing, reusing alternative goods and services, recycling and recovering materials in production, distribution and consumption processes. It operates at the micro (products, companies, consumers), meso (ecosystems) and macro (city, region, nation) levels, to achieve sustainable development while creating environmental quality, prosperity and social equity, for the benefit of current and future generations, being supported by new business models and responsible consumers [9].

The perspective of the life cycle of materials or products is thinking from the production to disposal and involves: a) prevention with the generation of waste by reducing consumption and new business models and value generation; b) the minimal use of materials and, preferably, materials of easy reincorporation in the production processes and fast and safe absorption by natural ecosystems (as is the case with biodegradable materials) and c) the end of life stage with adequate management of the materials in the post-consumption by directing them to a processing and reincorporation network in some production process or as an input for the generation of energy. To act with this perspective, the CE is based on the performance economy [23], Biomimetics [24], Cradle to Cradle design [25], and Industrial Ecology [26].

The performance economy has as pillars the extension of the product life cycle through more durable products and waste prevention, it also addresses the importance of selling services and not products to produce wealth and economy with less physical resources through value-added business as its core value [23]. Biomimetics has nature as a model, measure, and mentor, understanding that the more human processes are like natural cycles, the greater the chances of being effective [24].

The Cradle to Cradle design has as its central idea that resources are managed in a circular logic of creation and reuse, each cycle passage becomes a new 'cradle' for a given material creating a flow of "technical metabolism" of materials industrial [25]. Finally, Industrial Ecology is an interdisciplinary field of science that proposes a radical overhaul of the business model and intersectoral collaboration [26], with a view to sustainable economic development. It involves the exchange of resources between companies in a mutually beneficial way, closing their production cycles through the reuse or entry of the residues of one in the production process of the other, generating a "symbiosis".

The application of CE in waste management in a life cycle perspective depends on the interaction of local public authorities, final consumers, and the private sector [27], especially the industry that absorbs materials again in its processes, closing the cycle in an approach Industrial Ecology [28]. This requires communication and technology tools capable of fostering and making feasible [29], which is the purpose of the platform presented here, which is under development and whose pilot project will be applied in the city of Florianópolis, Santa Catarina.

The principles of CE are appropriate in the proposal presented in Sect. 4 of this paper, which contributes to the more sustainable management of waste in Brazil. Through GVBE companies can connect to develop new product and service technologies, considering the performance savings, Cradle to Cradle design, and biomimetics to obtain increasingly durable products, avoiding waste, facilitating the reuse, and biodegradation when the disposal is unavoidable. In turn, concerning existing waste, Industrial Ecology takes the collaborative network character of the proposal forward, enabling symbiosis between the organizations that joined in GVBE, in which the disposal of a material may be the raw material for the production process of another organization.

4   Reciclica GVBE

Considering the principles of Circular Economy presented in Sect. 3, Reciclica GVBE will be aimed at facilitating the reuse or reuse of discarded materials, using the end-of-life manufacturing approach to recover goods, parts, subassemblies or scrap, and shared resources for your direct use (reuse), repair, renovation, remanufacture, recycle or safe disposal [13], whereby one can make more efficient use of complementary skills or essential competencies of people and organizations, who will be called actors. The name Reciclica comes from the Portuguese words "reciclar" and "ciclo", the first meaning recycle, about the formation of new products from discarded materials, while the second meaning cycle, about the cyclical characteristic from of the circular economy. The name also contains the acronym CE (rECiclica) of circular economy and in Portuguese, it is pronounced in feminine, in honor of women and nature (also pronounced in the feminine in Portuguese), since both have vital cycles.

As shown in Fig. 1A, the GVBE was planned considering its useful life from its creation, which involves policy procedures, standards, vision, mission and values, criteria for selecting organizations and people that meet the readiness and preparation requirements [30] to compose this environment for emerging virtual companies. The operation stage involves governance of the GVBE, as well as conflict resolution, coordination of activities, infrastructure, and technology. The evolution phase is the growing stage of the GVBE with the formation of an increasing number of GVE, consolidating the model, finally, the dissolution stage is the phase in which the GVBE fulfilled its objectives or was transformed and does not support the maintenance of this model as expected.

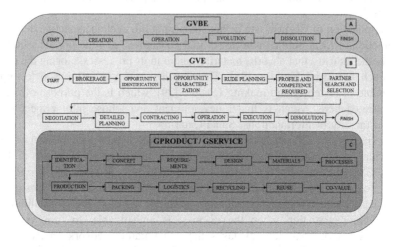

Fig. 1. Recíclica GVBE concept structure life cycle.

According to Fig. 1B, the GVEs that arise from their creation environment bring together actors who share the same objective, the broker of a GVE can be represented by the GVBE administrator or by any actor who has identified the opportunity, to characterized and elaborated preliminary planning, in which it will be foreseen from the objectives of the GVE until the products or services that will be made, going through the search and selection of partners [19] among the members of the GVBE, so that together they can prepare plans more detailed, remaining to operate at GVE until its dissolution, the results of which will be partly distributed among the participants and partly returned to GVBE [31], for platform maintenance and growth.

The green product or service developed by GVE (Fig. 1C) will consider the policies, rules, and regulations that govern all platform participants, to improve production processes that lead to minimizing impacts on the environment, in the meantime, new products or services are developed to meet the needs of consumers, in this sense, the waste resulting from the productive processes of any one of the GVBE actors may serve as input to the productive processes of another, as well as an opportunity for the formation of GVE to jointly develop new products based on new uses of waste in a continuous process of innovation, therefore, both producers and consumers may be present at GVBE, whose production process will be based on recycling, reuse, and co-value.

Therefore, the GVBE administrator or any actor, exercising the broker role, may see a problem or an opportunity that will require collective action, both in the external environment and in the GVBE, such as reusing packaging, recycling metals, plastic, glass, product design for use or new use after the end of its useful life. Considering the problem or opportunity and from the GVBE the actors will be gathered in GVEs from the registered profile, considering their skills and abilities, from an analysis of complementarity made by the manager or the broker, together they will develop the best solutions in Economics Circular. Besides, it will also be possible to share logistics and services, carry out trade, donate materials, loans, and use other resources among the platform's participants.

For a better understanding of the specificities of Reciclica GVBE, we briefly contextualize the normative scenario of Brazil, the country where the platform is under development. In this country there is a low propensity for the formation of collaborative networks, data show that less than 8% of innovations in the industry were promoted in cooperation between the years 2006 and 2017, showing limits to the joint performance of the actors, such as the lack of an environment that favors collaboration.

In 2010, the National Solid Waste Policy (PNRS) was instituted, which favors materials management focused on sustainability and the Circular Economy. According to scientific works that demonstrate the role of the State in promoting collaborative networks between organizations [32]. Through this legislation, the principle of shared responsibility among manufacturers, traders, consumers, and public agents for the life cycle of products was established to "minimize the volume of solid waste and waste generated, as well as to reduce the impacts caused to human health and environmental quality". The PNRS has a decentralizing character and it is up to the municipalities to implement a selective collection system, to elaborate a diagnosis of the situation of solid waste generated in their territory, as well as mechanisms for the creation of business, employment and income sources, through the valuation of materials through reuse or recycling, the reality of which shows many cities allocating urban waste to open-air dumps, and recyclable material collectors seeking to obtain some income from this waste.

Therefore, it is necessary to seek for alternative means to promote a more ecological environment, through the development of new technologies in products and services, through recycling or reuse of discarded materials, facilitating the exchange of materials between organizations and generating jobs and income.

The GVBE Reciclical was planned with the support of the World Wide Web, through an electronic website, whose modules enable: a) registration of actors; b) sharing products and services in a structured manner as well as selecting and finding products and services; c) conversation module; d) contractual instruments; e) means of financial transactions; and f) logistics [33]. Reference value information for the material, geographical distance between the participants, the ranking of materials most available by geographic areas, as well as other information will be included.

As a reference for the values of the materials, which are waste for some organizations and raw material for others, the tabulation of the Business Commitment for Recycling (CEMPRE), one of the main non-profit associations dedicated to the promotion of recycling in Brazil, will be used. The geographic distance information will be obtained by the geolocation feature. As transactions occur through the GVBE, a ranking of materials will be obtained, which can guide the creation of new businesses aimed at prolonging or closing production cycles.

Finally, other information will be presented, such as suitable disposal points and forms of disposal obtained from information from the entity responsible for collection. In the case of special wastes (electronics, batteries, tires, among others) that manufacturers must reverse logistics according to PNRS, the proposal is that the platform can promote intelligent methods of return and reuse of these materials assisting in compliance with legislation.

Other accessories services presented on the platform will be examples of initiatives focused on sustainability, CE and Industrial Ecology (IE) principles and good practices, public and private funding notices for projects aimed at sustainable development, legislation, carbon footprint calculator (for companies and people) and information about the responsible team. Such information will have educational content and will be transmitted interactively, with the help of videos and texts, using a simplified and creative language.

5   Conclusions and Further Research

The purpose of this article was to present a GVBE proposal grounded in the Circular Economy to create Green Virtual Enterprises (GVE) for the development of green solutions for products and services called Reciclica. The purpose of the platform is to contribute to waste management geared towards sustainability in an economically viable way, what, in the current model, is an expense for public agencies, in GVBE is a business opportunity.

Besides, Recíclica GVBE will help the population, organizations, and researchers to have a clearer view of the processes that involve waste management, which would allow for better citizen participation, greater responsibility on the part of companies, and new research on the subject.

Brazil is one of the most unequal countries in the world, in addition to preserving such exuberant and fundamental biomes, the use, and recovery of waste can represent a source of dignity, income, inclusion and, consequently, development. Sustainable development, especially in the case of emerging economies, must commit to improving the quality of life of people through productive inclusion, in this sense, even networks that have a global reach that develop in a virtual environment should preferably be able to contribute to improving the local context in which they are established.

The Recíclica GVBE, although intended for a global and scalable network, also promotes waste management geared towards sustainability at the local level, with information on conscious consumption and adequate waste disposal by the population. It also seeks to support an intersectoral collaboration system in the city, an action that collaborates with the surroundings but also facilitates transactions all over the world in the format of the CE and through the IE. Since CE is an area of interdisciplinary knowledge that proposes a radical reformulation of consumption habits and the business model with a focus on networking, it often needs encouragement to establish itself effectively. Therefore, the importance of the Reciclical GVBE platform to adopt a local-global approach, in harmony with SDGs 11 and 17 simultaneously.

Further research is needed to develop protocols for assessing the readiness of organizations to join the GVBE and preparedness for the formation of GVEs, as well as improving the governance of Reciclica GVBE.

Acknowledgments. The Recíclica GVBE is part of the Participact - Sustainable Technologies for Urban Waste Management project that receives funding and scholarship from Fapesc -

Fundação de Amparo à Pesquisa e Inovação de Santa Catarina and is developed within the Santa Catarina State University in Florianópolis.

References

1. Cabral, E.R., Santos, A.L.L.D., Gomes, S.C.: Social and environmental responsibility and local sustainable development: the case of the environmental education project and asset - PEAP. GEAS **4**, 91–107 (2015)
2. Camargo, A.L.B.: Desenvolvimento sustentável: dimensões e desafios. Papirus, Campinas (2010)
3. Guimarães, R.P.: Desenvolvimento sustentável: da retórica à formulação de políticas públicas. A geo. pol. do desenv. sust., 13–44 (1997)
4. Hopwood, B., Mellor, M., O'brien, G.: Sustainable development. Sust. Develop. **13**, 38–52 (2005)
5. Silva, C.L.D.: Desenvolvimento sustentável: um conceito multidisciplinar. In: Silva, C.L.D., Mendes, J.T.G. (eds.) Reflexões sobre o desenvolvimento sustentável: Agentes e interações sob a ótica multidisciplinar, pp. 11–40. Vozes, Petrópolis (2005)
6. Sustainable Development. https://sustainabledevelopment.un.org
7. Department of Economic and Social Affairs Un. https://sdgs.un.org/
8. United Nations. https://www.un.org/
9. Kirchherr, J., Reike, D., Hekkert, M.P.: Conceptualizing the circular economy: an analysis of 114 definitions. SSRN Electron. J. **127**, 221–232 (2017)
10. Romero, D., Molina, A.: Green virtual enterprise breeding environments: a sustainable industrial development model for a circular economy. In: Camarinha-Matos, L.M., Xu, L., Afsarmanesh, H. (eds.) PRO-VE 2012. IAICT, vol. 380, pp. 427–436. Springer, Heidelberg (2012). https://doi.org/10.1007/978-3-642-32775-9_43
11. Romero, D., Molina, A.: Green virtual enterprises and their breeding environments. In: Camarinha-Matos, L.M., Boucher, X., Afsarmanesh, H. (eds.) PRO-VE 2010. IAICT, vol. 336, pp. 25–35. Springer, Heidelberg (2010). https://doi.org/10.1007/978-3-642-15961-9_3
12. Romero, D., Molina, A.: Green virtual enterprise breeding environment reference framework. In: Camarinha-Matos, L.M., Pereira-Klen, A., Afsarmanesh, H. (eds.) PRO-VE 2011. IAICT, vol. 362, pp. 545–555. Springer, Heidelberg (2011). https://doi.org/10.1007/978-3-642-23330-2_59
13. Romero, D., Molina, A.: Forward - green virtual enterprises and their breeding environments: sustainable manufacturing, logistics and consumption. In: Camarinha-Matos, L.M., Afsarmanesh, H. (eds.) PRO-VE 2014. IAICT, vol. 434, pp. 336–346. Springer, Heidelberg (2014). https://doi.org/10.1007/978-3-662-44745-1_33
14. Romero, D., Noran, O., Afsarmanesh, H.: Green virtual enterprise breeding environments bag of assets management: a contribution to the sharing economy. In: Camarinha-Matos, L. M., Bénaben, F., Picard, W. (eds.) PRO-VE 2015. IAICT, vol. 463, pp. 439–447. Springer, Cham (2015). https://doi.org/10.1007/978-3-319-24141-8_40
15. Batista, A.M.L., Schardosin, F.Z., Bier, C.A., Rolt, C.R.D., Lautert, H.F., Darold, D.L.: A technological alternative for solid waste utilization with a emphasis on closed production cycles in circular economy. In: IEEE International Conference on Technology and Entrepreneurship, San Jose, CA, pp. 1–6 (2020)
16. Graça, P., Camarinha-Matos, L.M.: Performance indicators for collaborative business ecosystems — literature review and trends. Tech. Forec. Soc. Ch. **116**, 237–255 (2017)

17. Loss, L., Pereira-Klen, A.A., Rabelo, R.J.: Value creation elements in learning collaborative networked organizations. In: Camarinha-Matos, L.M., Picard, W. (eds.) PRO-VE 2008. ITIFIP, vol. 283, pp. 75–84. Springer, Boston (2008). https://doi.org/10.1007/978-0-387-84837-2_8

18. Polyantchikov, I., Shevtshenko, E.: Partner selection criteria for virtual organization forming. In: 9th International Conference of DAAAM Baltic: Industrial Engineering, Tallinn, Estonia, pp. 163–168 (2014)

19. Shamsuzzoha, A., Toscano, C., Carneiro, L.M., Kumar, V., Helo, P.: ICT-based solution approach for collaborative delivery of customised products. Prod. Plan. Control **27**, 280–298 (2016)

20. Camarinha-Matos, L.M., Afsarmanesh, H.: Collaborative networks. In: Wang, K., Kovacs, G.L., Wozny, M., Fang, M. (eds.) PROLAMAT 2006. IIFIP, vol. 207, pp. 26–40. Springer, Boston, MA (2006). https://doi.org/10.1007/0-387-34403-9_4

21. Duin, H., Thoben, K.D.: Enhancing the preparedness of SMEs for e-business opportunities by collaborative networks. In: Cruz-Cunha, M.M., Varajão, J. (eds.) E-Business Issues, Challenges and Opportunities for SMEs: Driving Competitiveness, pp. 30–45. IGI Global, Hershey (2010)

22. Romero, D., Molina, A.: Virtual organisation breeding environments toolkit: reference model, management framework and instantiation methodology. Prod. Plan. Control **21**, 181–217 (2010)

23. Stahel, W.R.: The Performance Economy. Palgrave-Macmillan, London (2010)

24. Benyus, J.M.: Biomimicry: Innovation Inspired by Nature. William Morrow & Company, New York (2002)

25. McDonough, W., Braungart, M.: Cradle to Cradle: Remaking the Way We Make Things. North Point Press, New York (2002)

26. Frosch, R.A., Gallopoulos, N.E.: Strategies for manufacturing. Sci. Am. **189**, 144–152 (1989)

27. Iacovidou, E., et al.: Metrics for optimising the multi-dimensional value of resources recovered from waste in a circular economy: a critical review. Clean. Prod. **166**, 910–938 (2017)

28. Sterr, T., Ott, T.: The industrial region as a promising unit for eco-industrial development - reflections, practical experience and establishment of innovative instruments to support industrial ecology. Clean. Prod. **12**, 947–965 (2004)

29. Costa, I., Massard, G., Agarwal, A.J.: Waste management policies for industrial symbiosis development: case studies in European countries. Clean. Prod. **18**, 815–822 (2010)

30. Romero, D., Galeano, N., Molina, A.: Mechanisms for assessing and enhancing organisations' readiness for collaboration in collaborative networks. Prod. Res. **47**, 4691–4710 (2009)

31. Karvonen, I., Salkari, I., Ollus, M.: Increasing collaboration preparedness and performance through VO inheritance. Serv. Oper. Manag. **6**, 293–312 (2010)

32. Schardosin, F.Z., Rolt, C.R.D., Batista, A.M.L., Penz, D., Amorin, B., Bier, C.A.: Inter-organizational collaborative networks: a systematic review. In: IEEE International Conference on Technology and Entrepreneurship, San Jose, CA, pp. 1–6 (2020)

33. Gillett, E., Brown, E.G., Staten, J., Lee, C.: Future View: The New Tech Ecosystems of Cloud, Cloud Services, and Cloud Computing, Forrester, for Vendor Strategy Professionals. Forrester Research (2008)

Collaboration Platforms

For a Dynamic Web Services Discovery Model for Open Ecosystems of Software Providers

Ricardo J. Rabelo[1(✉)], Hernesto A. Ruiz[1], and Maiara H. Cancian[2]

[1] UFSC - Federal University of Santa Catarina, Florianopolis, SC, Brazil
ricardo.rabelo@ufsc.br, hernesto4706@gmail.com
[2] Estácio University Florianopolis, Rodovia SC401 km 01, Florianopolis, SC, Brazil
maiara.cancian@estacio.br

Abstract. With the increasing adoption of business models relaying on Cloud Computing, digital platforms and servitization, IT providers have been transforming their solutions into services-based, having as a goal facilitating their binding to clients' applications. In this formed wide and open service-oriented environment, classical static services binding approaches are limited to support the business dynamics of Virtual Organizations (VO). As services would assure VO members' systems operation, a bad services selection may hazard that. We argue, though, that services selection criteria, largely based on QoS and costs, are not enough to provide higher confidence to VO members when selecting services from such open ecosystem of service providers. In this line, this paper proposes a more comprehensive and multi-criteria decision-making model for dynamic services discovery. A prototype has been implemented and results are discussed.

Keywords: Service Oriented Architecture · Dynamic services discovery · Web services · Ecosystem · Industry 4.0 · Collaborative networks · Virtual organization

1 Introduction

Collaborative Networks (CN) play a key role in Industry 4.0 realization. It provides theoretical foundations for some of its key issues, as networking, vertical and horizontal integration, sharing, co-engineering and interconnectivity, immersed in business models grounded on the Internet of Things, Services and People [1].

This has been imposing a much higher flexibility from companies' systems architectures. Firstly, in their classical transaction-based systems, usually designed in a quite fixed, pre-defined and hierarchical/vertical way based on the five-layer ISA-95 model[1]. Secondly, in their CN supporting systems, designed to execute *ad-hoc*, non-hierarchical/horizontal, interlayered and inter-company business processes (BP) [2, 3].

Computing reality has changed significantly in the last two decades. Cloud computing, service orientation and digital platforms, besides newer business models built

---

[1] https://www.isa.org/isa95/.

© IFIP International Federation for Information Processing 2020
Published by Springer Nature Switzerland AG 2020
L. M. Camarinha-Matos et al. (Eds.): PRO-VE 2020, IFIP AICT 598, pp. 83–97, 2020.
https://doi.org/10.1007/978-3-030-62412-5_7

up on top of this, have made disparate IT providers from digital ecosystems to start offering computing infrastructures and applications *as-a-service*, and that can be accessed remotely and on-demand [2, 4]. Following this trend, many industries and SMEs have changed their IT strategy. From the *acquisition* of large, off-the-shelf, on-premises and sometimes very expensive software packages and lock-in licenses, they have been gradually shifting to *servitization*, accessing only specific and much smaller software's functionalities when needed and paid-per-use [5]. These functionalities are called and modeled as *services* and generally called as *web services*.

This shift also happens because: i) companies have realized that some of the required functionalities for their BPs/systems are not feasible or interesting to be developed and/or maintained by their own as they may be already available in the market/ecosystem; ii) companies' business models, their products, management methods, etc., are more often changing, meaning some unpredictability in their near future software needs; and iii) only large IT providers (as *Google*, *Amazon*, etc.) are actually able to develop and maintain some complex software as IT and technology rapidly evolve, offering them as-a-service via their APIs [6, 7].

Within this context and regarding the usual SME limitations at several levels, this paper exploits the vision where companies adopt that service-oriented and sharing strategy when they form a Virtual Organization (VO) [1, 2], and that a services-based architecture/system would be dynamically created to support the execution of the involved (intra- and inter-organizational) VO's BPs [2].

In this vision, all such IT services providers would belong to diverse digital ecosystems, similarly to a wider VBE[2]. They would publish and make their IT assets available (their software services and, indirectly, their required computing infrastructure) in a logical entity called as *services federation* [2, 4, 8]. Providers keep their autonomy and legal independence, owning and providing software services' implementations and descriptions as well as the respective technical and business support. Companies can have access to them *as-a-service* [4, 8].

In this scenario, companies could then have access to a "infinite cloud" of services (the federation). Assuming there would potentially (and naturally) exist several software services functionally equivalent one to another, and that an inadequate selection may hazard the VO success and efficiency, this paper addresses the problem of how to select the most suitable services for the very current VO's BP needs.

This problem is known as *dynamic services discovery* [9]. In general, the approaches for services selection are essentially based on evaluating some services' quality of service (QoS) attributes [9]. We argue that the mentioned ecosystem and VO scenarios require additional aspects to consider so that companies can be more confident when selecting services for their daily operations. Yet, that companies could have the possibility to weight such aspects considering their current priorities and IT policies.

In this direction, this paper proposes a more comprehensive set of decision criteria for multi-criteria services selection, which works within a wider discovery model.

---

[2] VBE - Virtual organization Breeding Environment [1].

This is an ongoing proof-of-concept work being developed under the *design science research* (DSR) methodology, looking at a SME cluster of 34 Industry-4.0 IT software providers placed in the South of Brazil[3] as an initial basis for the criteria elicitation.

2 Basic Concepts and Summary of Literature Review

2.1 Dynamic Services Discovery

The selection of a software by companies normally takes a long time, is manually done, and use to consider aspects as price, supported functionalities, documentation, technical assistance, used technology, lock-in risks, providers branding, historical partnerships, impact on legacy systems and integration costs, among others [6, 10]. Many of these aspects are somehow embraced by the 31 *characteristics* of ISO/IEC 25010 standard[4] for systems and software quality evaluation. Yet, once the selection is settled, contracts usually last at least a month for SaaS mode, and much longer for on-premise software.

Regarding the beforehand mentioned vision and the intrinsic dynamics of VOs, such long selection process and the static/fixed binding of software services to BPs prevents VO formation and evolution from both being more agile and benefit from the huge variety of services nowadays ecosystems can offer [2, 9].

Service discovery refers to locating web services, evaluating their suitability considering functional and non-functional requirements, and to finally selecting one. It is considered as dynamic discovery when it is performed at run time [9, 11].

Searching for the suitable web services out of all the available ones in large-scale distributed federation-like entities can be very computationally complex [12]. Besides the selection criteria to be defined, it should also try to: i) respect the individual requirements and technology restrictions of every single BP's activity against the ones supported by every single candidate service; and ii) respect the end-to-end QoS of the entire BP all those activities are related to [13].

2.2 Literature Review

The envisaged discovery model involves several issues, for which many works in the literature have proposed different approaches. Given space restrictions, this section presents just a highlight of some of them.

Much research has been done about dynamic services discovery over the last fifteen years. Obidallah *et al.* (2016) [14] present a large overview of the different approaches for services discovery. In terms of selection criteria, QoS-based are by far the most adopted ones. However, no mentions were made to more appropriate criteria for discovery in large scale services repositories from disparate ecosystems of IT providers.

Camarinha-Matos *et al.* (2011) [15] created a matching-maker environment in a cloud where different partners of CN can offer their (non-software) services respecting

---

[3] https://manufatura.acate.com.br/.

[4] https://iso25000.com/index.php/en/iso-25000-standards/iso-25010, former ISO/IEC 9126.

the technical demands from a given manufacturer. Osorio *et al.* (2011) [16] and their subsequent works have presented an evolving services-based platform to support payment actions by users of tolling systems involving ecosystems of disparate providers. Thanks to open reference specifications, they can plug and play their solutions in the platform. However, these two works do not support dynamic discovery.

Correa *et al.* (2014) [17] devised a AHP-based multicriteria framework to select the best logistic service providers for given businesses out of a logistic providers cluster based on their historical performance regarding QoS indicators. Bezerra *et al.* (2018) [12] developed a system to dynamically discover web services from a services federation when faults are detected in SOA compositions. Perin *et al.* [9] implemented a web services dynamic discovery model integrated to the BPM level in way that SOA compositions can be created and dynamically evolve as businesses change. Bandara *et al.* (2015) [18] implemented a prototype where users can balance criteria regarding current processes' needs. These four works are just examples to show that QoS-based criteria are the most adopted approach in services discovery, sometimes combined with multi-criteria methods. Cancian *et al.* (2015) [19] conceived a model with 22 processes that should be supported to manage the federation/ecosystem of SaaS providers.

Despite the importance of the many contributions of current works, none works have proposed more comprehensive selection criteria better suited for dynamic services discovery in open and evolving IT SaaS/services providers ecosystems.

3 Services Selection Criteria

3.1 Elicited Criteria

Following the DSR methodology, an initial set of selection criteria for services discovery was created after a generalization and terminology harmonization based on a literature review. It was further submitted and discussed in a meeting with the mentioned IT cluster. Given that this research proposal can be considered as a state-of-the-art scenario, the discussions were open and tried to reason about near equivalent scenarios based on trends and on companies' experience and their empirical evidences.

Six dimensions of analysis have come up after that, which included the relevance of considering multi-criteria decision-making. They are described below.

3.1.1 Quality of Services (QoS)
QoS is a non-functional dimension defined as the ability to provide different priority to applications, users, data flows, or to guarantee a certain level of general quality. QoS is the largest used technical dimension to select software services and cloud providers, being also considered as a reference for setting up SLA (*Service Level Agreement*). There is a direct relation between SLA fulfillment and provider's reputation [10].

The list of QoS attributes varies a lot in the literature. The *Service Measurement Index* (SMI) initiative has elicited the 33 most relevant QoS attributes for SaaS/services- and cloud-based scenarios [20] (Fig. 1), extending a bit and adapting the attributes defined in ISO/IEC 25010.

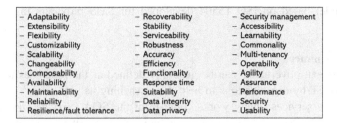

– Adaptability	– Recoverability	– Security management
– Extensibility	– Stability	– Accessibility
– Flexibility	– Serviceability	– Learnability
– Customizability	– Robustness	– Commonality
– Scalability	– Accuracy	– Multi-tenancy
– Changeability	– Efficiency	– Operability
– Composability	Functionality	– Agility
– Availability	– Response time	– Assurance
– Maintainability	– Suitability	– Performance
– Reliability	– Data integrity	– Security
– Resilience/fault tolerance	– Data privacy	– Usability

Fig. 1. SMI QoS attributes

3.1.2 Reputation

Reputation can be considered as a collective measure of trustworthiness calculated based on the referrals or ratings from members of a community. It can be measured in different ways considering different aspects, usually fed by personal experiences from users [21]. In business, it is basically interpreted as the higher the company's or the service's reputation the higher is its trustworthiness.

3.1.3 Trust

Trust represents the confidence level about an entity, which can be measured as a numerical value and transformed into indicators for decision-making. In business, it is basically interpreted as the trustier a company the less risky it is. Reputation systems are typically used to manage and to establish trust [22].

In the context of networked companies, Msanjilla *et al.* (2007) [23] has created a comprehensive framework to calculate trust by computing five dimensions: financial, organizational, social, technological and behavioral. They also pointed out that trust can be established between the trustor and the trustee, but it can also involve a third part and/or a regulatory institution, as a recognized intermediate entity to certify trust.

3.1.4 Development Quality

This criterion refers to the need of assuring that the potential evocable services are reliable as well as trustworthy and capable to attend the SLA requirements of different software compositions from their many client systems in different tenants [24].

The quality of a software is directly related to the quality of the development process [24]. Sun *et al.* (2012) [25] has highlighted the usual lack of information about the quality of the offered services, creating obstacles for their larger use by customers.

In order to provide higher levels of services quality, SaaS/services providers need to constantly improve their maturity [26]. Organizational maturity is the extent to which it explicitly and consistently deploys processes that are documented, managed, measured, controlled, and continually improved, indicating the organizational path of process improvement [26]. IBM, for example, has developed a services maturity model (called *OSIM*[5]) to assess services and SOA adoption, and to create blueprints to increase business and IT flexibility. Cancian *et al.* (2020) [19] have developed a 5-layer

---

[5] https://www.ibm.com/developerworks/library/ws-OSIMM/.

maturity model based on ISO 15504 developed for SaaS providers in collaborative networks.

3.1.5   Governance

In the IT context, governance can be generally defined as the processes to assure the proper use of IT by organizations to help them reaching its objectives[6].

In software services, many works come from the SOA (*Service Oriented Architecture*) area [27]. In essence, the more solid and comprehensive governance processes are implemented in an organization the more trustworthy the general quality of its services tends to be. IBM, for example, defines in its SOA governance model[7] 10 aspects to be governed throughout 26 processes, grouped into 4 categories. Another important work is the *SOA Governance Reference Model (SGRM)*[8], a generic process model used as a baseline to tailor SOA governance models for given organizations.

3.1.6   Collaboration

Collaboration in business can be defined as a working practice by which organizations work on a common purpose to achieve planned benefits [1]. In the context of CN, Correa *et al.* (2014) [17] have devised a model that calculates how risky a given partner is to be added to a given VO based on, among other elements, its successful experience in past VOs as well as when working together with some given partners.

In the context of SOA, this refers to how complex the integration of two heterogeneous services can be (as they should e.g. communicate and exchange documents), or how easier this can be given that some IT providers may have proper APIs to interoperate with each other thanks to existing business partnerships [2].

3.2   Multi-criteria Methods

Decision-making problems generally imply the selection of the best compromise solution. Besides the values calculated using diverse criteria, the final decision also depends on the decision maker's preferences and underlying policies not always formally calculated or capable to be explicitly expressed as decision criteria [28].

The literature presents several multi-criteria methods, being the *Analytic Hierarchy Process (AHP)* one of the most used ones. AHP allows the combination of quantitative and qualitative data, requiring a judgement about the relative importance (in terms of weights) between one criterion to another [29].

In services discovery, this means calculating a given value via weighting the criteria dimensions to further rank the most suitable services [18].

---

[6] *COBIT* and *ITIL* are two of very recognized IT governance models for general software and infrastructures.

[7] https://www.ibm.com/developerworks/library/ar-servgov/index.html.

[8] https://www.opengroup.org/soa/source-book/gov/p4.htm.

4 The Proposed Services Dynamic Discovery Model

This section presents the proposed model and multi-criteria algorithm for services dynamic discovery. Figure 2 illustrates the general view of the model.

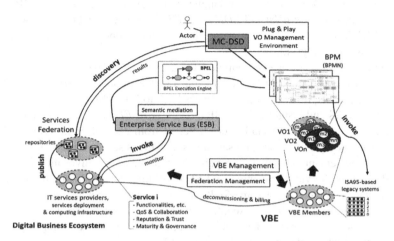

Fig. 2. Basic view of the dynamic discovery model

In general terms, the *Multi Criteria Dynamic Service Discovery* (MC-DSD) acts as a broker, doing a kind of e-procurement, bridging web services sellers and buyers within a digital marketplace. It corresponds to an improvement of a static service discovery module developed in a previous work [30], whose focus was on supporting a seamless ESB-based plug and play integration and semantics interoperation of VOs throughout their life cycle, adopting BP reference models. The whole model also joins the contributions developed for dealing with the VBE/VO management and governance [1, 31], federation management [5, 32], BPM-SOA integration [2, 9], and resilience/fault-tolerance support in the formed services composition when a VO is created [12].

The model works under the *publish-discovery-invoke* SOA reference architecture [10]. In the left side of the figure, the interested software services providers, as members of open and disparate IT ecosystems, prepare their IT assets in way they can be properly published using specific ITs in specific services repositories. Different deployment architectures can be applied for that. A set of metadata has to be added upon each published service, being some data given by the respective provider (e.g. services' functionalities), and some other data maintained and provided by the own Federation (e.g. services' reputation). The federation manages the performance of every provider and single service, updating the respective meta-data accordingly. The federation has a sort of processes used to manage itself and its members [5, 32].

The right side shows the VBE and its members (enterprises, industries, etc.), each one having its legacy systems, usually organized according to the ISA-95 layered model. One of the main goals of a VBE is to breed and launch VOs. VOs are mostly created as a response to business demands, and they have a life cycle [1]. The profile of the VO members m and the required BP depend on the unique business demands' characteristics. From the dynamic services discovery point of view, the goal is to find the very right services for the diverse BPs. BPM (*Business Process Management*) is a modern approach to help linking business modeling and IT systems [2, 9]. *BPMN* has become a standard *de facto* modeling language and different standards for BP models may be adopted, as *RosettaNet* and *EDIFACT*. *UBL*[9] has been used in this work [2, 30].

The MC-DSD allows different actors to tune the supported selection criteria to guide the discovery algorithm.

An internal engine takes every single BPs' activity and triggers a discovery action against the services federation, trying to find out the published services that fit the chosen requirements, bringing their references back to MC-DSD. It, in turn, selects the most suitable ones and instantiates the BP models. A *BPEL* file is generated as a result. Regarding that services are usually very different from each other in terms of implementation technologies, formats and semantics, this file is sent to a message bus, which is an ESB with semantics mediation capabilities that makes the invocation itself to the selected services. Services execution and SLA fulfillment are monitored so that they can be replaced in the case of some fault. All this is very explained in [2, 12, 30].

As VO members finish the execution of their BPs and hence the usage of the involved services, services are decommissioned, and the respective billing is generated regarding the SaaS mode and signed contract [12].

4.1   Discovery Model Rationale

A set of design principles has been adopted in the devise model:

---

i. System engineering: the model encompasses different systems from different organizations, each one having their business strategies, IT approaches, life cycles, governance models, and functional and legal responsibilities. This also means that both providers and consumers (i.e. the VO members' systems) can have very different levels of SOA/IT maturity and governance;

ii. Software engineering: providers should consider their services as loosely coupled, interoperable, and non-intrusive entities that, when orchestrated to support the VO operation, will form an integrated business service;

iii. Providers' services represent just one part of the required functionalities of the VOs' BPs. The other part is done by the own VO members' internal systems. VO members can also offer their shareable services via the Federation;

iv. Hybrid integration strategy: *Top-down* - providers can adopt different BP reference models to drive their services' functionalities design and granularity definitions. *Bottom up* - providers can use different implementation tenants and implementation technologies, exposing services via wrappers. A service-bus approach (via an ESB) is used to mediate interoperability. It can be created per

---

[9] https://www.oasis-open.org/committees/tc_home.php?wg_abbrev=ubl.

VBE, per VO or per Federation, and be deployed in their local servers or in a cloud. Each provider can offer its services under variable business models, versioning and services' lifecycle management, deployment topologies, redundancy policies, and security schemas;

v. Once a service is chosen by MC-DSD, it gets responsible for the entire operation related to the BP's activity it was bound to. The service can do all the needed operations on its own or, complementarily, invoke other providers' services;

vi. The way the VBE and the Federation/Ecosystem handle their members' and services' general performance is up to each one, regarding their bylaws and governance models. For instance, whilst the VBE should define its models (performance, trust, etc.) and manage, supervise, and keep up-to-date the related data upon its members as VOs are executed, the Federation should do the same as for their services and respective providers. Providers should publish their services' metadata and usage costs following the federation's information model. All these data are the ones used by MC-DSD for discovery;

vii. There is a meta (implicit or explicit) governance model, which harmonizes the different working principles of each model's entity to guarantee the whole model operation.

4.2   The MC-DSD Algorithm

The multi-criteria algorithm considers services' costs and the six dimensions described in Sect. 3: services' QoS and collaboration; providers and services' reputation; providers and services' trustworthiness; services' quality of software and providers' processes maturity; and providers' governance. It is assumed that the classical selection criteria (Sect. 2.1) and the providers' and services' collaboration levels are covered by those dimensions.

The model is generic. Besides the services' functionalities and their interfaces' information, the values and underlying information model each of those dimensions are expressed by the VBE, Federation and providers depend on each model "instantiation" case. Proper IT and tools should be used to model and implement all that[10]. Regarding this proof-of-concept work, it has been instantiated in the implemented prototype (see Sect. 5) as follows, also considering the targeted IT cluster's opinions:

---

[10] *OASIS, Mozilla* and *W3C* are examples of organizations that have been defining standards and providing some open source supporting tools.

- *QoS*: the 33 aspects proposed in [10, 20] were used, being expressed as numbers, considering their intrinsic scale. QoS is the basis for the dynamic SLA establishment [12] and also considers services performance ('collaboration') in past VOs;
- *Trust* and *Reputation*: the 5 dimensions proposed in [23] were used, measuring providers' trustworthiness as well as providers' and services' reputation. They are expressed in a scale varying from 0 (very low) to 10 (very high);
- *Cost*: it directly indicates the maximum acceptable cost to access/use the service, being expressed as a numerical value. It can also indicate a minimum cost, if it was the case;
- *Quality* and *Maturity*: the 5 levels proposed in [19] (and based on CMMI and ISO 15504) were used to express services' quality (in terms of capability) and provider's maturity (collaborative- and SaaS-based processes);
- *Governance*: the 7 levels proposed in [22] were used. In this case, the values are binary, indicating if the company supports it (1) or not (0).
- *Services functionalities*: they are expressed using the UBL BP reference model (as in [2]).

The algorithm is executed in seven steps. It is very similar to the ones applied in several related works, although varying in terms of selection criteria and the ecosystem environment it should work in:

For each VO, for each global BP, for each (sub)BP, for each activity, do:
Specify and configure selection criteria
Search for services in the Federation that fit the selection criteria
Apply a multi-criteria method
Rank the found services and select the best one
Bind the selected service to the respective BP's activity
Repeat until all activities have a bound service

In order to easy the algorithm configuration, user interfaces can hide some details, aggregate dimensions and/or group those values into high-level categories. For instance, instead of indicating numerical values for every single different 33 QoS aspects, (trained) users can just choose for *low, medium, high*, or even indicate that the given aspect is *irrelevant* to be considered in the search. The supporting system(s) should then make a link between such words/specification with the real numbers stored in the related information systems. For example, assuming a scale from 80% to 99.99% of *service availability*, the internal convention can stablish that it is *low* if the value is between 80% and 90%, *medium* if 90.1% and 95%, and *high* if higher than 95%.

The discovery algorithm will then look for services whose availability fits the given range. In the hypothetical governance model, it would be considered that services whose mean *availability* in normal conditions is lower than 80% are not allowed to be published and hence offered by the Federation.

Regarding the large numbers of items to be configured in a search for every single BP's activity of the global VO's BP, companies (each VO member) can have pre-configurations set up as by default (in general, per type of business, etc.) so that the discovery can run completely automatically as VOs get into execution; or users can only modify some items for very particular services' needs. Preliminary rougher searches may be done to better tune the chosen criteria and their parameters.

In the case no services are found out as the result, the search configuration should be redefined (via relaxing some aspects) and executed again. In the very worst case, when no services are found out after many attempts, the missing service(s) should be developed (by some VO member or by some ecosystem's provider), or the VO should find another way (i.e. another BP design) to accomplish the respective business.

Once having at least one service found out for the involved BP's activities, the next main step refers to weighting the degrees of importance between the chosen criteria.

In a large ecosystem composed of potentially hundreds of services providers, it is expected that several services can fit the search criteria for each BP's activity. The problem is then to select which service will be elected as the most suitable one. The essence of multi-criteria methods is helping in this, also based on the premise that it is basically impossible to find a given service that is the best in all the chosen criteria. Therefore, once many services are returned, it is necessary to compare them with each other, which is done via indicating priorities among the chosen selection criteria.

This is done at two levels: intra-criterion and inter-criteria. The first one is basically used for QoS, where the user should specify his preferences. For example, he could indicate that *availability*, *performance*, and *efficiency* should have higher priority than *security* and *assurance*. In the same way, in the inter-criteria level, he could indicate that *provider's governance* should have less priority than *service's costs*. Here again some pre-configurations can be set up as by default.

The AHP multi-criteria method [29] has been used. All those criteria should be compared against to each other to identify which criteria have higher priorities. A matrix is formed with the chosen criteria, and the found services are evaluated based on the defined priority. A subset of the best ranked services is kept. The best one is directly bound the BP's activity, and the remaining ones are kept for future usage.

5   Prototype and Results

Although the resulted outcome and focus of this research is represented by a qualitative model, a prototype has been implemented to generally evaluate its feasibility. This section summarizes that.

As already mentioned, the devised MC-DSD method is an improvement of the service discovery module developed in a previous and complex integration work [30], which only considered some QoS attributes and that were treated as having the same priority in the final services selection. New dimensions of analyses have been added (as described in Sect. 3.1) and a multi-criteria method (Sect. 3.2) has been used to define the different degrees of importance these dimensions have one to another.

The previous prototype [30] were partially reused and adapted to the devised model. Hundreds of services were generated and published adopting the UBL business process reference model as a basis, simulating that all ecosystem's software service providers and VO members would have prepared (tenant wrapping) their services following its specification (in terms of functional requirements, arguments, and data/document types), although with different granularity and implementing technologies. This and other adopted assumptions were explained in Sect. 4.1.

A hypothetical VO was created to produce a given product and the related tasks were distributed among the chosen partners. According to the UBL model, diverse BPs would be involved in this transaction, including the *'Ordering Process'* (one of the 68 UBL's BPs). Due to space restrictions, Fig. 3b only shows one part of it (modeled in BPMN), covering the acceptance and rejection of the business request. Many BPs will be normally involved in a VO regarding its full life cycle and the BP's needs of the customer order in place. From the execution point of view, the way the model treats one VO and one UBL BP is exactly the same than as for many VOs and multiple BPs.

VBE's partners information (see Sect. 4.1) have been previously stored in its database (implemented using the *SQL Express* tool). Services repositories were implemented using the *UDDI*, from W3C, using *JUDDI* tool. Services' information is registered in the *tModel* UDDI's structure in *XML*, being partially fed by the respective provider and partially fed by the Federation or VBE. Figure 3a presents an excerpt of the *tModel* of a given service, showing the service's reference (for its future invocation) and the meta data and respective values e.g. for its *reputation* and *trust*.

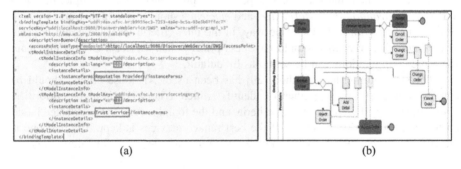

(a)   (b)

Fig. 3. (a) Example *tModel*. (b) UBL *Ordering Process* BP

For each BP's activity a configuration for services discovery is done (Fig. 4a). In this implementation, the user does that via scales instead of via absolute numbers. Before or after that the user sets up the degree of importance among the chosen criteria. The discovery itself is then performed and the AHP method is applied upon them regarding those criteria and indicated weights. A ranking is created once services are retrieved (Fig. 4b). The first ranked service is considered as the most suitable one for the *place order* activity and it is automatically bound to it.

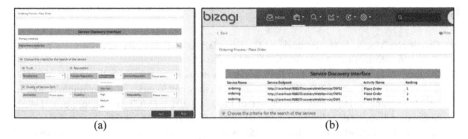

Fig. 4. (a) Discovery configuration. (b) Services ranking

6 Final Considerations

This paper has presented results of an ongoing research that aimed at devising a more comprehensive set of selection criteria for dynamic (web) services discovery that better fits a scenario of open ecosystems of software providers, including collaborative and virtual organizations.

The model is flexible in a way that more criteria can be added as new scenarios arise up. It was built as a proof-of-concept considering a local cluster of IT-based SMEs. The multi-criteria approach allows companies tuning the service discovery algorithm according to their current business needs, governance principles, and preferences.

A system prototype was implemented using open source tools and IT standards, in a controlled environment. It can be said that the federation concept and related digital platform represent an approach towards Collaboration 4.0.

According to the IT cluster, and despite the several adopted assumptions, results showed that the model is promising and seems to be comprehensive enough for dealing with evolving open ecosystems of SaaS-based providers. Foreseen obstacles identified by the cluster for the model adoption include: it can take a long time given the many issues to handle; demands some trust building; and it requires investments on governance, IT and human resources. It also calls for a new mindset and much higher complexity on how building and integrating disparate computing systems.

Next main steps of this research include: the consideration of the IT cluster's services to test the discovery model in a near-real business environment; and to define better strategies to decrease the searching algorithm's computing complexity.

Acknowledgements. This work has been partially supported by CAPES - The Brazilian Agency for Higher Education, project PrInt CAPES-UFSC "Automation 4.0".

References

1. Camarinha-Matos, L.M., Fornasiero, R., Ferrada, F.: Collaborative networks - a pillar of digital transformation. Appl. Sci. **9**(24), 5431 (2019)
2. Bezerra, R.O., Cancian, M.H., Rabelo, R.J.: Enhancing network collaboration in SOA services composition via standard business processes catalogues. In: Camarinha-Matos, L. M., Afsarmanesh, H., Fornasiero, R. (eds.) PRO-VE 2017. IAICT, vol. 506, pp. 421–431. Springer, Cham (2017). https://doi.org/10.1007/978-3-319-65151-4_38
3. Romero, D., Vernadat, F.: Enterprise information systems state of the art: past, present and future trends. Comput. Ind. **79**, 3–13 (2016)
4. Rabelo, R.J., Gusmeroli, S.: The ECOLEAD collaborative business infrastructure for networked organizations. In: Camarinha-Matos, L.M., Picard, W. (eds.) PRO-VE 2008. ITIFIP, vol. 283, pp. 451–462. Springer, Boston, MA (2008). https://doi.org/10.1007/978-0-387-84837-2_47
5. Cancian, M.H., Rabelo, R.J., Wangenheim, C.G.V.: Collaborative business processes for enhancing partnerships among software services providers. Enterp. Inf. Syst. **9**, 1–26 (2015)
6. Chou, T.: The End of Software: Finding Security, Flexibility, and Profit in the on Demand Future. SAMS Publishing, Indianapolis (2004)
7. Gansky, L.: The Mesh – Why the Future of Business is Sharing. Penguin Books, London (2010)
8. Sitek, P., Gusmeroli, S., Conte, M., Jansson, K., Karvonen, I.: The COIN Book - Enterprise Collaboration and Interoperability. COIN IP EU Project (2010)
9. Souza, A.P., Rabelo, R.J.: A dynamic services discovery model for better leveraging BPM and SOA integration. Int. J. Inf. Syst. Serv. Sector **7**(1), 1–21 (2015)
10. Khanjani, A., Nurhayati, W., Rahman, W.: Saas quality of service attributes. J. Appl. Sci. **14** (24), 3613–3619 (2014)
11. Ardagna, D., Baresi, L., Comai, S., Comuzzi, M.: A service-based framework for flexible business processes. IEEE Softw. **28**(2), 61–67 (2011)
12. Bezerra, R.O., Rabelo, R.J., Cancian, M.H.: Supporting SOA resilience in virtual enterprises. In: Camarinha-Matos, L.M., Afsarmanesh, H., Rezgui, Y. (eds.) PRO-VE 2018. IAICT, vol. 534, pp. 111–123. Springer, Cham (2018). https://doi.org/10.1007/978-3-319-99127-6_10
13. Moghaddam, M.: Simultaneous service selection for multiple composite service requests: a combinatorial auction approach. Decis. Support Syst. **120**, 81–94 (2019)
14. Obidallah, W.J., Raahemi, B.: A survey on web service discovery approaches. In: Proceedings of the 2nd International Conference on Internet of Things, Data and Cloud Computing, pp. 1–8 (2017)
15. Camarinha-Matos, L.M., Afsarmanesh, H., Koelmel, B.: Collaborative networks in support of service-enhanced products. In: Camarinha-Matos, L.M., Pereira-Klen, A., Afsarmanesh, H. (eds.) PRO-VE 2011. IAICT, vol. 362, pp. 95–104. Springer, Heidelberg (2011). https://doi.org/10.1007/978-3-642-23330-2_11
16. Osorio, L., Afsarmanesh, H., Camarinha-Matos, L.: A service integration platform for collaborative networks. Stud. Inform. Control **20**(1), 19–30 (2011)
17. Vieira, R.G., Alves-Junior, O.C., Rabelo, R.J., Fiorese, A.: A risk analysis method to support virtual organization partners' selection. In: Camarinha-Matos, L.M., Afsarmanesh, H. (eds.) PRO-VE 2014. IAICT, vol. 434, pp. 597–609. Springer, Heidelberg (2014). https://doi.org/10.1007/978-3-662-44745-1_59
18. Bandara, K.Y., Wang, M., Pahl, C.: An extended ontology-based context model and manipulation calculus for dynamic Web service processes. SOCA **9**(2), 87–106 (2013). https://doi.org/10.1007/s11761-013-0145-3

19. Cancian, M.H., Rabelo, R.J., Hauck, J.C.R.: Towards a capability and maturity model for collaborative Software-as-a-Service. Innovations Syst. Softw. Eng. **16**, 245–261 (2020). https://doi.org/10.1007/s11334-020-00360-9
20. Ferretti, S., Ghini, V., Panzieri, F., Pellegrini, M.: QoS-aware clouds. In: Proceedings IEEE 3rd International Conference on Cloud Computing, pp. 321–328 (2010)
21. Resnick, P., Kuwabara, K., Zeckhauser, R., Friedman, E.: Reputation systems. ACM Commun. **43**, 45–48 (2000)
22. Sabater, J., Sierra, C.: Review on computational trust and reputation models. Artif. Intell. Rev. **24**, 33–60 (2005). https://doi.org/10.1007/s10462-004-0041-5
23. Msanjila, S.S., Afsarmanesh, H.: Modeling trust relationships in collaborative networked organizations. Int. J. Technol. Transf. Commer. Indersci. **6**(1), 40–55 (2007)
24. Beecham, S., Hall, T., Britton, C.: Using an expert panel to validate requirements process improvement model. J. Syst. Softw. **76**(3), 251–275 (2005)
25. Sun, L., Singh, J., Hussain, O.K.: Service level agreement (SLA) assurance for cloud services: a survey from a transactional risk perspective. In: Proceedings 10th ACM International Conference on Advances in Mobile Computing Multimedia, pp. 263–266 (2012)
26. Knoke, B.: Innovation capability maturity within collaborations. In: Proceedings 25th International Conference on Advanced Information Systems Engineering, pp. 7–11 (2013)
27. Hojaji, F., Shirazi, M.A.: A comprehensive SOA governance framework based on COBIT. In: Proceedings 6th World Congress on Services, pp. 407–414 (2010)
28. Daghouri, A., Mansouri, K.: Multi criteria decision making methods for information system selection - a comparative study. In: Proceedings International Conference on Electronics, Control, Optimization and Computer Science, pp. 1–5 (2018)
29. Saaty, R.W.: The analytic hierarchy process - what it is and how it is used. Math. Model. **9**(3–5), 161–176 (1987)
30. Méndez, J.D., Rabelo, R.J., Baldo, F., Cancian, M.H.: A plug and play integration model for virtual enterprises. In: Camarinha-Matos, L.M., Afsarmanesh, H., Rezgui, Y. (eds.) PRO-VE 2018. IAICT, vol. 534, pp. 312–324. Springer, Cham (2018). https://doi.org/10.1007/978-3-319-99127-6_27
31. Rabelo, R.J., Costa, S.N., Romero, D.: A governance reference model for virtual enterprises. In: Camarinha-Matos, L.M., Afsarmanesh, H. (eds.) PRO-VE 2014. IAICT, vol. 434, pp. 60–70. Springer, Heidelberg (2014). https://doi.org/10.1007/978-3-662-44745-1_6
32. Cancian, M.H., Teixeira, C.P., Rabelo, R.J.: Supporting business processes for collaborative alliances of software service providers. In: Camarinha-Matos, L.M., Bénaben, F., Picard, W. (eds.) PRO-VE 2015. IAICT, vol. 463, pp. 467–478. Springer, Cham (2015). https://doi.org/10.1007/978-3-319-24141-8_43

Adoption of Digital Collaborative Networking Platforms in Companies: A Study of Twitter Usage in Finland

Heli Hallikainen[1(✉)] and Lili Aunimo[2]

[1] Business School, University of Eastern Finland, Joensuu, Finland
`heli.hallikainen@uef.fi`
[2] Haaga-Helia University of Applied Sciences, Helsinki, Finland
`lili.aunimo@haaga-helia.fi`

Abstract. Digital collaborative networking platforms have become increasingly important for companies. They are widely used for communication and co-creation with customers, suppliers and other actors in companies' value chains. This study takes one social media platform, Twitter, as an example of a digital collaboration platform and analyses patterns of Twitter usage among Finnish companies. The empirical part of the study is based on survey data (n = 554 companies) and Twitter usage data of 107 of the same companies. The research data is analyzed to explore the extent to which companies have adopted Twitter and for what purposes it is being used. The results of the study show that surprisingly few companies have a Twitter account and most commonly companies use Twitter to communicate about news and events to the large public. Hence, plenty of opportunities remain for taking social media platforms more efficiently in use for collaborative networking and co-creation.

Keywords: Digital collaborative networks · Social media adoption · Technology adoption · Company segmentation · Content analysis · Twitter

1 Introduction

For companies, digital collaborative networking platforms offer novel and efficient ways of communicating and interacting with customers, suppliers and other actors with regard customer service, product development, marketing and recruiting, among others. Collaborative networks consist of autonomous and heterogeneous entities that collaborate to achieve common or compatible goals through interaction that is made possible through computer networks [1]. Through collaborative networks, companies and their stakeholders may engage in co-creation activities that produce new value to all participants of the network. Many alternative digital platforms are available for such collaboration. Some of the platforms are used more for networking (e.g. Twitter, Facebook, LinkedIn) whereas other platforms are used more for co-creation (e.g. GitHub, Wikipedia and other open source and open media content communities). In addition to public collaborative networking platforms, companies also use various types of internal collaborative networking platforms [2]. Internal platforms are typically available only to named actors within the network. They have been found useful e.g. in

© IFIP International Federation for Information Processing 2020
Published by Springer Nature Switzerland AG 2020
L. M. Camarinha-Matos et al. (Eds.): PRO-VE 2020, IFIP AICT 598, pp. 98–110, 2020.
https://doi.org/10.1007/978-3-030-62412-5_8

the B2M (Business to Manufacturing) setting in the context of mass customization [3]. In this study, we focus on one publicly available social media platform, Twitter, and study patterns of its use among Finnish companies. Even though Twitter may be used as a platform for collaborative networking, it may as well also be used for several other purposes.

The Internet and online based social media platforms have changed customer and company behavior by providing new ways of searching, assessing, choosing and buying [4]. For companies, social media platforms enable new possibilities for interaction and collaboration with their network, including customers, suppliers and other actors within their value chains. Customer-generated and company-generated posts in social media represent one aspect of social media content, and overall, social media platforms provide a collaboration channel for companies. Indeed, social media platforms, including Twitter, enable the creation of virtual customer environments where online communities are formed around specific companies, brands and products [5]. Therefore, companies are increasingly placing their marketing efforts in such platforms and according to Barnes et al. [6] Twitter has proven to be a platform in which companies should focus their social media efforts.

Companies can use Twitter for various purposes and there hardly exists a "one-way-fits-all" approach in this respect. Some companies may utilize Twitter to disseminate corporate announcements [7], other companies utilize social media for employer branding [8], while some companies consider social media beneficial for employee recruitment [9]. Culnan, McHugh and Zubillaga [5] list that social media platforms may be fruitful for companies in terms of branding, e.g. in driving traffic, viral marketing, and customer loyalty and retention. Additionally, social media platforms can provide an additional channel for customer service and support and can help to gain insights in terms of company's product development [5, 10]. These are just some examples of the numerous ways in which companies can utilize and benefit of social media data, which surely has its own challenges and pitfalls in terms of validity and representativeness [e.g. 11, 12] yet such data may provide interesting insights for practitioners and academics, alike.

In this vein, the present study attempts to understand both the extent to which Twitter is being used by companies and for what purposes it is being used. Additionally, this study examines patterns of social media use within companies, and attempts to discover collaborative networks related patterns and sheds light on differences between companies operating in different businesses and in different industries. Specifically, the study first performs a company segmentation based on survey responses and thereafter, the study takes a detailed look on company characteristics that are associated with the identified segments. These results are then complemented by performing a content analysis on the Twitter posts generated by the companies that participated in the survey.

With this approach, the study contributes to the literature on technology adoption within companies, and particularly on corporate social media use as a platform for collaborative networking. The chosen approach can help other companies in positioning themselves in what comes to utilization of social media as a collaborative networking platform. Knowing where a company stands in relation to other companies may serve as a benchmarking tool and can provide valuable information when making strategic decisions on where to invest. As a majority of the existing research on information systems adoption relies on conventional research methods such as qualitative interviews and quantitative surveys, the present study also contributes to the academic literature by describing and applying a methodological approach that combines survey data with the objective metrics obtained from Twitter and the actual tweets issued by the companies. The latter type of data reflects a company's true activity in social media platforms.

2   Background of the Study

Theoretical background of this study is grounded on the literature on information technology and information systems adoption within companies [e.g. 13–16] as social media use represents adoption of a novel collaboration technology. Information technologies are universally regarded essential in enhancing the competitiveness and productivity of companies [15], yet there may exist several potential paths in realizing value from such technologies. Overall, social media platforms provide an important communication channel for companies [17, 18]. In addition to providing a communication and networking channel, social media platforms enable collaborative networks by offering a platform for direct interaction between different stakeholders, including customers, service providers and other actors in the value chain as well as current and potential employees.

Twitter is a social media platform with a growing number of users [19] and with an increasing emphasis in professional communications [6]. However, Twitter communication sets its own challenges on topic discovery, as tweets are short and limited to 280 characters. The global number of daily active Twitter users was 154 million users as of the fourth quarter of year 2019 [19], and this large mass of data generated by Twitter users has been considered a fruitful data source by several previous studies [20–22]. Grover et al. [21] sum up some of the advantages of this research approach as follows: Twitter data is freely available through the Twitter API, tweets can be analyzed objectively and the use of content analytics methods enables to classify tweets around themes and topics [21].

Freely available Twitter data may be collected for research purposes in several ways. Some researchers use the Twitter REST API in collecting tweets posted by selected Twitter accounts [20, 21, 23]. A limitation of this approach is that it only retrieves 3200 most recent tweets, thus creating a database with varying time periods depending on the activeness of the selected accounts. Other researchers have used the Twitter stream API to collect tweets from a certain time period [24, 25]. With this approach, the dataset is narrowed down by specific query words. Some researchers use the Twitter advanced search to manually complement the dataset [20].

Some studies classify tweets into predetermined topic categories [26, 27] while other studies focus on topic discovery [28]. Classification methods based on supervised machine learning have also been widely used [29, 30]. Tweet classification is widely used when topic classes are well-known and clear-cut. Topic discovery from Twitter data, on the other hand, is used when no previous knowledge exists of the topic classes or when those classes may change over time [30]. Topic discovery methods may be categorized as distance-based and probabilistic methods [31]. Probabilistic models typically consider a tweet as a mixture of topics. Latent Dirichlet Allocation (LDA) [32] is a well-known example of such a probabilistic model. It is a method that is commonly used to model the topics within a collection of natural language documents.

3   Methodology

3.1   Data Collection and Sample

The study uses a combination of survey data (n = 554) and Twitter data generated by the companies that participated in the survey. Survey data was collected using an online questionnaire sent out to companies operating in Finland, and data collection resulted in 554 valid responses. In the questionnaire, respondents were asked to indicate the extent to which their company utilized the so-called big data in their business on a Likert scale ranging from 1 = little or no use to 5 = heavy use. Additionally, the respondents were asked some background questions about the characteristics of the companies they represent. Majority of the respondents represented small (n = 378) and medium-sized (n = 133) companies, and 417 operated in B2B markets, in comparison to B2C markets (n = 137).

Additionally, a large database of approximately 15 million tweets was constructed using the Stream API provided by Twitter and by collecting all tweets between December 2018 and May 2019 where the language of the Twitter account was set to Finnish. This data was used to extract the tweets posted by those 554 companies that participated in the survey. This analysis revealed that only 107 of the participating companies had an active Twitter account, and hence the Twitter dataset used in this study consists of 16,801 tweets posted by 107 companies during a six-month period between December 2018 and May 2019. The information on the status (number of tweets posted from the account since its creation), followers, friends and favorites were retrieved using the Twitter API.

3.2   K Means Cluster Analysis

Data analysis was performed in several steps. First, using k means cluster analysis, the data was grouped into segments based on the survey responses on how companies reported to use big data in their business. K means cluster analysis does not permit a mathematical demonstration of an optimal solution for the number of clusters, and therefore we started the data analysis by comparing some alternative cluster solutions. A comparison of three-, four-, five- and six-cluster solutions shows that a five-cluster solution appears the most optimal, because a solution with six clusters produced two very similar middle segments. Three- and four-cluster solutions, on the other hand, identified the utmost segments but did not show that much variation between the middle segments. Hence, the study considered a five-cluster solution the most optimal and subsequent analyses examine patterns of Twitter use among the identified five segments with 205, 71, 96, 55 and 127 responses for segments 1-5, respectively.

3.3   Twitter Content Analysis

Based on the collected Twitter data, two types of data analysis were performed: 1) an overall analysis of the Twitter activity and 2) an analysis on the content of the tweets posted by the companies. Twitter activity was measured using the following indicators: statuses (number of tweets posted so far), followers (number of followers), friends (number of Twitter accounts followed by the company) and favorites (number of likes the company has created for the tweets of other Twitter users). Specifically, tweets were modelled and analyzed using Latent Dirichlet Allocation (LDA), which is "a generative probabilistic model for collections of discrete data, such as text corpora" [32, p. 993]. In this study LDA is applied on Twitter tweets, and each tweet is considered a mixture of a small number of topics and that each word's presence is attributable to one of the tweet's topics [31].

The LDA method was chosen because topic contents were not known beforehand and because LDA is commonly used to model topics in similar cases [31]. In this study, the researchers experimented with different numbers of topic categories and found out that tweets were most naturally divided into five different topic categories. Data analysis was performed using KNIME [33], with Newman et al.'s [34] and Yao, Mimno and McCallum's [35] implementations of the core algorithms. The implementation uses the "MALLET: A Machine Learning for Language Toolkit" topic modeling library [36].

4   Results

4.1   Segmentation Results

Using ANOVA in SPSS 25, we first looked at the characteristics of the identified segments in order to understand underlying factors that might shed light on some of the key differences between the segments derived using survey data and k means cluster analysis. Additionally, we looked at the Twitter activity of the identified segments to understand patterns of Twitter behavior by the companies. Surprisingly, only 107 companies had an active Twitter account, and we extracted the Tweets posted by these companies during a six-months' period ranging from December 2018 to May 2019. Results of this comparison shows that the difference in Twitter activity is not statistically significant, however, segment 3 is the most active user of Twitter in terms of status posts, followed by segments 2, 4, 1 and 5, respectively (Table 1).

Segment 1 consists of mainly smaller companies, the average number of employees being 50 and the smallest among the identified segments. Companies of this segment operate mainly in manufacturing and construction sectors. Companies in this segment are relatively passive in using Twitter and hence do not seem to be at the frontline in adopting information technologies.

Segment 2 is the second smallest in term of the number of employees, with the average number of employees being 90. Construction companies and companies providing professional, scientific, and technical services are the two largest industry sectors. Based on Twitter metrics, this segment has more Twitter status updates, followers, friends and favorites, compared to other segments.

Segment 3 represents larger companies with an average of 214 employees, the largest industry sector being manufacturing companies, followed by wholesale and retail trade. Regarding the use of Twitter, companies in segment 3 rank as the most active in posting tweets themselves but have a relatively low number of followers and friends in Twitter.

Segment 4 is mainly representative of manufacturing companies, followed by construction companies and companies providing real estate services. The average of company size is the largest, with the average of 405 employees. Based on Twitter metrics, companies in segment 4 are quite passive in using Twitter and have less followers and friends, compared to the other segments.

Segment 5 represents medium-sized companies, the average of company size being 194 employees. The largest representative industries in segment 5 are manufacturing companies, wholesale and retail trade, and construction companies. Overall, companies in this segment are not very active users of Twitter.

Table 1. The Twitter activity of the companies per segment. Values represent mean numbers of statuses, followers, friends and favorites by the companies belonging to a specific segment.

	Segment 1 N=25	Segment 2 N=23	Segment 3 N=24	Segment 4 N=14	Segment 5 N=21	F (p)
Statuses	1230	3284	3781	1402	1134	0.855 (0.494)
Followers	1189	3089	1706	739	1795	0.848 (0.498)
Friends	562	2056	429	129	269	1.066 (0.377)
Favorites	914	1237	667	288	611	0.944 (0.442)

4.2 Twitter Content Analysis

Next, we analyzed the Twitter activity of the companies based on the tweet dataset consisting of tweets from December 2018 to May 2019. Table 2 shows first the total number of tweets per segment, followed by the difference from the expected number of tweets in parenthesis. The expected number of tweets is calculated by multiplying the total number of tweets by the proportion of companies belonging to the segment. The difference is calculated as the frequency – expected. A negative value signifies that the companies in a specific segment tweet less than expected and a positive value means that there are more tweets than expected. Table 2 shows that companies belonging to segments 2 and 3 are unexpectedly active in posting tweets. To compare, companies in segments 1, 4 and 5 are unexpectedly inactive in posting tweets.

Table 2. The total number of tweets posted by the segment. Difference from the expected value is reported inside parenthesis.

	Segment 1 (n=25)	Segment 2 (n=23)	Segment 3 (n=24)	Segment 4 (n=14)	Segment 5 (n=21)
Total no of tweets 12/2018-05/2019	2836 (-1089)	4226 (615)	5666 (1896)	1296 (-902)	2777 (-520)

We took an effort to understand the purposes for which the identified segments mainly created content in Twitter. Using data obtained from Twitter and LDA method, five topic categories were identified from the Twitter data (n = 16,801). Specifically, five distinct topic categories were identified based on terms occurring in the tweets (Table 3).

Table 3. Topic categories identified using LDA. The terms have been translated from the Finnish language.

Topic	Main terms occurring in tweets	N (%)
National communications, general societal issues concerning the entire country	Equality, sustainable development, accessibility, elections	3069 (18%)
Local news related communications	Location names, vehicle, security, news, driver	4167 (25%)
Marketing, events such as sports events	League, welcome, company names and places	3393 (20%)
Local events related communications, especially local events and facts	Cities, health services, customer, services	3030 (18%)
Recruitment of personnel	Recruitment, position, application, task, company, service, euro	3142 (19%)

Chi-square test shows that the differences between segments and topics of the tweets is statistically significant (df = 16, sum of squared errors = 2054,399 and the p-value < 0,001). Using cross-tabulation, we took a deeper look at the activity of the companies belonging to identified segments in posting different types of content in Twitter (Table 4). Table 4 shows the absolute numbers of tweets per topic produced by companies in each segment. The figures in parenthesis show the deviation from the expected number of tweets. The expected frequencies of tweets are calculated as the probability of the topic in the tweet dataset multiplied by the number of tweets in the segment. The deviation is calculated simply as the frequency – expected. A negative value signifies that the companies belonging to the segment tweet about a particular topic category less than expected and a positive value means that there are more tweets about a topic category than expected.

Table 4. Cross tabulation of identified segments and main topic categories (Note: White cells indicate a deviation smaller than 100, light grey cells a deviation between 100–300 and dark grey cells indicate a deviation greater than 300.)

	Segment 1 (n=25)	Segment 2 (n=23)	Segment 3 (n=24)	Segment 4 (n=14)	Segment 5 (n=21)
National communications (n=3069)	1015 (497)	802 (30)	664 (-371)	161 (-76)	427 (-80)
Local news (n=4167)	429 (-274)	848 (-200)	2221 (816)	133 (-188)	536 (-153)
Marketing (n=3393)	461 (-112)	943 (90)	1255 (111)	157 (-105)	577 (16)
Local events (n=3030)	423 (-88)	820 (58)	759 (-263)	485 (251)	543 (42)
Recruitment (n=3142)	508 (-22)	813 (23)	767 (-293)	360 (118)	694 (175)

Based on the results (Table 4), companies in segment 1 are the most active in tweeting about topics that relate to national communications, and less active in tweeting about other identified topic categories. Segment 2 posts less about local news, but more than expected about national communications, marketing, local events and recruitment related topics. Segment 3 is the most active in tweets that relate to local news and marketing topics, while segment 4 shows activity particularly in posting about local events and recruitment related topics. Alike segment 4, segment 5 similarly posts more tweets than expected about local events and recruitment related topics, but also about marketing related topics.

5   Discussion

The study contributes to the literature on technology adoption within companies, and particularly on corporate social media adoption literature by examining the extent to which companies use Twitter, and for which purposes it is being used. Specifically, the study identified segments based on how companies reported to use data in their business, after which the study examined how the identified segments differed in terms of company's background characteristics and patterns of utilizing Twitter. Results of the study show that identified segments differ in their background characteristics and patterns of utilizing Twitter. As such, this study provides empirical results for practitioners and academics alike, and results of this study can serve as a benchmarking tool in helping companies to position themselves what comes to utilization of social media as a platform for collaboration in their networks.

The topic discovery performed on the tweets show that out of the six dimensions of collaboration characterizing collaborative networks and industry 4.0, [37], the dimension 2: Horizontal integration through global value chain networks is the most dominant among the companies of the study. This dimension involves networking along the entire value chain, including customers, suppliers, and business partners. The topics discovered are strongly related to communications, information sharing aiming at collaboration and marketing that is aimed at customers, consumers in particular. There is plenty of unused potential for collaborative networking with other stakeholders of the value chain. The results of the content analysis on companies' tweets show surprisingly few tweets that illustrate the dimension 6: New business models and customer access [37] of collaborative networks and industry 4.0. This dimension includes tweets between the company and empowered customers, and they are related to co-design, co-creation, and customer experience, among others.

Interestingly, results of this study show that the representative sample, i.e. medium and large-sized companies operating in Finland, are less active in utilizing Twitter compared to what was expected based on some recent reports and studies [6]. In the present study, approximately 20% of the companies were active in utilizing Twitter while e.g. Barnes, Mazzola and Killeen [6] reported that 96% of Fortune500 companies were present in Twitter. The difference may relate to the fact that in the present study, majority of the companies operated in B2B markets, in comparison to B2C markets, and companies in B2C sector typically acknowledge benefits of new technologies faster, compared to B2B sector [38]. On the other hand, it is likely that Fortune500 companies, in general, have more visibility in social media platforms, compared to small- and medium-sized companies, of which many are less well-known. Results of this study are in line with a recent study conducted in Finland [13] which reported that among Finnish companies, 53% had adopted at least one of the following social media platforms: Facebook, Instagram, LinkedIn, Pinterest, Periscope, Twitter, or Vimeo. More specifically, Koski et al. [13] reported that 20% of Finnish companies were involved in Twitter, but Twitter was only the fourth social media platform in popularity after Facebook, Youtube and Instagram. Hence, Twitter might not be the number one social media platform from the viewpoint of Finnish companies, while prior research indeed reports that Twitter use has several benefits, including building of company image and brand, co-innovation with customers, and potential in recruiting employees [13].

With regard the identified Twitter topic categories, the categories discovered by the LDA method are somewhat different from those expected. A tweet category that seems to be missing is "customer care" types of tweets which are typical in Twitter for companies such as airlines and other consumer service providers. This finding may relate to the fact that majority of the companies in the present study were primarily business-to-business companies. Also, tweets concerning corporate finance, and corporate policies regarding topics such as sustainability, did not form a separate group in the study. This may relate to a low number of publicly listed companies in the dataset as well as to the fact that publicly listed companies are often multinational, and hence, their tweets are typically posted from the parent organization's Twitter account and possibly in other language than Finnish. It is also noteworthy that such tweets are commonly posted through the company CEO's Twitter account [21], which this study did not control for.

6   Limitation and Future Research

This study is bound by limitations that provide suggestions for future research. We consider the combined use of survey data and Twitter metrics a strength of this study, however, it is noteworthy that data for the study was collected among Finnish companies, and hence, future studies are encouraged to use a similar research approach to extend these findings to other countries and organizational cultures. We believe that these results may be generalizable to other developed and digitally advanced countries as Finland ranks first among the 29 European Union countries in the Digital Economy and Society Index [39]. On the other hand, it is noteworthy that the Finnish population and Finnish companies, in general, are not as active in using Twitter compared to some other countries [13].

Also, the chosen research methods require some consideration. The use of Twitter data is also bound by some limitations, which are noted e.g. by Hino and Fahey [23]. The tweet database was constructed using the Stream API provided by Twitter, which has been shown to provide a biased sample [40]. However, as long as the number of retrieved tweets does not exceed 1% of the total volume of Twitter traffic, Twitter documentation suggests that all tweets are retrieved [40]. A relatively large volume of tweets was retrieved for the study, and the search query was set to retrieve posts that were issued by a Twitter account that had Finnish set as language. Some Twitter accounts may have an erroneous language code and tweets posted from such accounts were not included in the present dataset.

It is noteworthy that in the collected dataset, a relatively large number of tweets were issued by a few operators such as newspapers, event organizers and public organizations. This means that many of the tweets included posts about contemporary topics and news events, or announcements of forthcoming events, including e.g. music concerts and sports events. On the other hand, other types of operators, such as B2B companies, typically issue a much smaller number of tweets. Future research should evaluate whether having a more balanced tweet dataset would enable the LDA algorithm to identify more fine-grained social media platform usage patterns – shortness is one of the key characteristics of tweets, and in general, topic detection among tweets can be challenging [31]. Thus, techniques such as metadata enrichment, network structure of actors and enriching the tweets with term expansion techniques [41] should be experimented within future work on tweet topic discovery of company tweets.

Future research on collaborative networks in Twitter should better consider the network structure of Twitter data. The present study analyzed the Tweets of companies that had participated in the survey from the point of view of collaborative networking and its various dimensions. Future research should also analyze the retweets, replies and links between tweets issued by other actors in the network. The networking behavior of all actors of each company's value chain should be studied based on Twitter data. This would shed more light on which of the dimensions of collaborative networks or industrie 4.0 are present – and to what extant - in the Twitter behavior of companies.

7 Conclusions

This study sheds light on how widely Twitter is used by Finnish companies, Twitter representing an example of a collaborative networking platform for companies. To form a deeper understanding on how companies utilize Twitter for different purposes, the study used a combination of survey data (n = 554) and Twitter data generated by the companies that participated in the survey. In this study, Twitter user data and the tweets generated by the companies were examined. The content analysis is done with the LDA algorithm and it is based on Twitter data collected between December 2018 and May 2019.

Surprisingly, it turned out that only 107 of the 554 companies had an active Twitter account, and hence, companies in this study were less active in Twitter than expected. Interestingly, the identified segments differed in the extent to which they share content and follow others in Twitter. Specifically, segments 2 and 3, i.e. the relatively small companies from e.g. construction, manufacturing and retail sectors, were the most active in utilizing Twitter in content sharing and networking. The LDA-based content analysis reveals that most commonly companies use Twitter to communicate about news and events to the large public, followed by marketing and recruiting related content. Overall, the companies in Finland use social media less than expected and those that use it, prefer to use it for very traditional purposes, such as communications to the wide public. Hence, the present study shows that plenty of opportunities remain for taking social media platforms, such as Twitter, more efficiently into use for collaborative networking and co-creation.

Acknowledgements. This work was partly supported by the BIG-research program, funded by Business Finland (Finnish Funding Agency for Innovation) no 2710/31/2016. The authors also thank Senior Lecturer Harto Holmström at Haaga-Helia University of Applied Sciences who assisted in collecting the Twitter data.

References

1. Camarinha-Matos, L.M., Afsarmanesh, H.: Collaborative networks: a new scientific discipline. J. Intell. Manuf. **16**(4–5), 439–452 (2005). https://doi.org/10.1007/s10845-005-1656-3
2. Ferron, M., Massa, P., Odella, P.: Analyzing collaborative networks emerging in Enterprise 2.0: the Taolin Platform. Procedia Soc. Behav. Sci. **10**, 68–78 (2011)
3. Mourtzis, D.: Internet based collaboration in the manufacturing supply chain. CIRP J. Manufact. Sci. Technol. **4**(3), 296–304 (2016)
4. Alves, H., Fernandes, C., Raposo, M.: Social media marketing: a literature review and implications. Psychol. Mark. **33**(12), 1029–1038 (2016)
5. Culnan, M.J., McHugh, P.J., Zubillaga, J.I.: How large US companies can use Twitter and other social media to gain business value. MIS Q. Executive **9**(4), 243–259 (2010)
6. Barnes, N.G., Mazzola, A., Killeen, M.: Oversaturation & Disengagement: The 2019 Fortune 500 Social Media Dance. Center for Marketing Research of the University of Massachusetts Dartmouth, 9 January 2020. https://www.umassd.edu/cmr/research/social-media-research/2019-fortune-500.html. Accessed 7 Feb 2020

7. Prokofieva, M.: Twitter-based dissemination of corporate disclosure and the intervening effects of firms' visibility: evidence from australian-listed companies. J. Inf. Syst. **29**(2), 107–136 (2015)
8. Roper, S., de Carvalho, L.V., Guzman, F., Sivertzen, A.M., Nilsen, E.R., Olafsen, A.H.: Employer branding: employer attractiveness and the use of social media. J. Prod. Brand Manag. **22**(7), 473–483 (2013)
9. El Ouirdi, M., El Ouirdi, A., Segers, J., Pais, I.: Technology adoption in employee recruitment: the case of social media in Central and Eastern Europe. Comput. Hum. Behav. **57**, 240–249 (2016)
10. Martin-Domingo, L., Martín, J.C., Mandsberg, G.: Social media as a resource for sentiment analysis of airport service quality (ASQ). J. Air Transp. Manag. **78**, 106–115 (2019)
11. Stieglitz, S., Mirbabaie, M., Ross, B., Neuberger, C.: Social media analytics – challenges in topic discovery, data collection, and data preparation. Int. J. Inf. Manage. **39**, 156–168 (2018)
12. Tufekci, Z.: Big questions for social media big data: representativeness, validity and other methodological pitfalls. In: Eighth International AAAI Conference on Weblogs and Social Media (2014)
13. Koski, H., Pajarinen, M., Rouvinen, P.: What company characteristics are associated with the adoption of social media? Ind. Innov. **26**(8), 880–897 (2019)
14. Melville, N., Kraemer, K., Gurbaxani, V.: Information technology and organizational performance: an integrative model of IT business value. MIS Q. **28**(2), 283–322 (2004)
15. Oliveira, T., Martins, M.F.: Literature review of information technology adoption models at firm level. Electron. J. Inf. Syst. Eval. **14**(1), 110–121 (2011)
16. Siamagka, N.T., Christodoulides, G., Michaelidou, N., Valvi, A.: Determinants of social media adoption by B2B organizations. Ind. Mark. Manage. **51**, 89–99 (2015)
17. Cheng, X., Fu, S., de Vreede, G.J.: Understanding trust influencing factors in social media communication: a qualitative study. Int. J. Inf. Manage. **37**(2), 25–35 (2017)
18. Floreddu, P.B., Cabiddu, F.: Social media communication strategies. J. Serv. Mark. **30**(5), 490–503 (2016)
19. Statista: Leading countries based on number of Twitter users as of January 2020(2019). https://www.statista.com/statistics/242606/number-ofactive-twitter-users-in-selected-countries/. Accessed 7 Feb 2020
20. Albarrak, M.S., Elnahass, M., Papagiannidis, S., Salama, A.: The effect of Twitter dissemination on cost of equity: a big data approach. Int. J. Inf. Manage. **50**, 1–16 (2020)
21. Grover, P., Kar, A.K., Ilavarasan, P.V.: Impact of corporate social responsibility on reputation – insights from tweets on sustainable development goals by CEOs. Int. J. Inf. Manage. **48**, 39–52 (2019)
22. Ren, Y., Wang, R., Ji, D.: A topic-enhanced word embedding for Twitter sentiment classification. Inf. Sci. **369**, 188–198 (2016)
23. Hino, A., Fahey, R.A.: Representing the Twittersphere: archiving a representative sample of Twitter data under resource constraints. Int. J. Inf. Manage. **48**, 175–184 (2016)
24. Milajevs, D.: Retrieval of visually shared news. In: Ustalov, D., Filchenkov, A., Pivovarova, L. (eds.) AINL 2019. CCIS, vol. 1119, pp. 59–73. Springer, Cham (2019). https://doi.org/10.1007/978-3-030-34518-1_5
25. Xu, W.W., Chiu, I.-H., Chen, Y., Mukherjee, T.: Twitter hashtags for health: applying network and content analyses to understand the health knowledge sharing in a Twitter-based community of practice. Qual. Quant. **49**(4), 1361–1380 (2014). https://doi.org/10.1007/s11135-014-0051-6
26. Lin, J.S., Peña, J.: Are you following me? A content analysis of TV networks' brand communication on Twitter. J. Interact. Advert. **12**(1), 17–29 (2011)

27. Parganas, P., Anagnostopoulos, C., Chadwick, S.: 'You'll never tweet alone': managing sports brands through social media. J. Brand Manag. **22**(7), 551–568 (2015). https://doi.org/10.1057/bm.2015.32

28. Vicient, C., Moreno, A.: Unsupervised topic discovery in micro-blogging networks. Expert Syst. Appl. **42**(17–18), 6472–6485 (2015)

29. Ghiassi, M., Lee, S.: A domain transferable lexicon set for Twitter sentiment analysis using a supervised machine learning approach. Expert Syst. Appl. **106**, 197–216 (2018)

30. Missier, P., et al.: Tracking dengue epidemics using Twitter content classification and topic modelling. In: Casteleyn, S., Dolog, P., Pautasso, C. (eds.) ICWE 2016. LNCS, vol. 9881, pp. 80–92. Springer, Cham (2016). https://doi.org/10.1007/978-3-319-46963-8_7

31. Chinnov, A., Kerschke, P., Meske, C., Stieglitz, S., Trautmann, H.: An overview of topic discovery in Twitter communication through social media analytics. In: Twenty-First Americas Conference on Information Systems (2015)

32. Blei, D.M., Ng, A.Y., Jordan, M.I.: Latent Dirichlet allocation. J. Mach. Learn. Res. **3**, 993–1022 (2003)

33. Berthold, M.R., et al.: KNIME – the Konstanz information miner: version 2.0 and beyond. ACM SIGKDD Explor. Newsl. **11**(1), 26–31 (2009)

34. Newman, D., Asuncion, A., Smyth, P., Welling, M.: Distributed algorithms for topic models. J. Mach. Learn. Res. **10**, 1801–1828 (2009)

35. Yao, L., Mimno, D., McCallum, A.: Efficient methods for topic model inference on streaming document collections. In: Proceedings of the 15th ACM SIGKDD International Conference on Knowledge Discovery and Data Mining, pp. 937–946 (2009)

36. McCallum, A.K.: MALLET: Machine Learning for Language Toolkit (2002). http://mallet.cs.umass.edu. Accessed 18 June 2019

37. Camarinha-Matos, L.M., Fornasiero, R., Afsarmanesh, H.: Collaborative networks as a core enabler of Industry 4.0. In: Camarinha-Matos, L.M., Afsarmanesh, H., Fornasiero, R. (eds.) PRO-VE 2017. IAICT, vol. 506, pp. 3–17. Springer, Cham (2017). https://doi.org/10.1007/978-3-319-65151-4_1

38. Lacka, E., Chong, A.: Usability perspective on social media sites' adoption in the B2B context. Ind. Mark. Manag. **54**, 80–91 (2016)

39. European Commission: The Digital Economy and Society Index (2016). https://ec.europa.eu/digital-single-market/en/digital-economy-and-society-index-desi. Accessed 31 Jan 2020

40. Tromble, R., Storz, A., Stockmann, D.: We Don't Know What We Don't Know: When and How the Use of Twitter's Public APIs Biases Scientific Inference. SSRN Scholarly Paper No. ID 3079927. Social Science Research Network, Rochester, NY (2017)

41. Perez-Tellez, F., Pinto, D., Cardiff, J., Rosso, P.: On the difficulty of clustering company tweets. In: Proceedings of the 2nd International Workshop on Search and Mining User-Generated Contents, pp. 95–102 (2010)

From Digital Platforms to Ecosystems: A Review of Horizon 2020 Platform Projects

Henrique Diogo Silva[1,2(✉)] and António Lucas Soares[1,2]

[1] INESC TEC, Porto, Portugal
{henrique.d.silva,asoares}@inesctec.pt
[2] University of Porto, Porto, Portugal

Abstract. Digital platforms have, in the past decades, undergone a revolution, evolving from its technical roots so much that nowadays value is mostly generated, not by the technologies that power platforms, but by the ecosystem of applications, developers and users it is able to generate and support. In this paper, we seek to understand the importance industrial platform owners place on the community building and platform growth components of the platform development process by reviewing 50 Horizon 2020 financed projects that stand on the development of platforms. This evidence is leveraged for the case of a validation strategy definition for a platform ecosystem aiming at sharing production capacity. Key findings point to platform developing practices focused on the development of technical components to the detriment of the ecosystem generation element. We also shed light on how different business models and funding schemes impacted the steering of these platforms.

Keywords: Digital platforms · Digital ecosystems · Digital communities · Horizon 2020

1 Introduction

The concept of multi-sided markets that gathers consumers and producers together in the same environment has been around for a long time, coexisting in many industries with traditional product and service offerings [7, 8]. At its core, these analog platforms provide the infrastructure and base rules for the facilitation of interactions between different groups of users. These can vary from newspapers that join readers with advertisers, to record labels that link bands with listeners. Through the digitization of this paradigm, and with this infrastructure becoming software, the platform business model was rapidly propelled forward over traditional industries [14]. Digital platforms (DPs) became to allow for scalability and flexibility that would be very difficult to accomplish through traditional, even if already established, networks. Early examples of DPs thrived on this connecting of buyers and sellers, advertisers and consumers. In the last decade, however, platform owners have devoted more and more resources not just in the growing of user communities, but also in stimulating outside firms to create complementary innovations, in the form of their own products and services that make the core platform increasingly valuable [6]. Different authors see this phenomenon from different perspectives. [6] sees this as a push from what the authors call innovation

L. M. Camarinha-Matos et al. (Eds.): PRO-VE 2020, IFIP AICT 598, pp. 111–120, 2020.
https://doi.org/10.1007/978-3-030-62412-5_9

platforms and transaction platforms to blend and acquire characteristics from each other: innovation platforms (such as Apple's App Store) seek to not lose control over the distribution component of the business, by integrating typical transaction platform's characteristics; and transaction platform owners recognize that not all innovation comes from within and open its platform and user database to application developers. [19], drawing on the work of [9], go further by placing these complementary products and services as integral components of a platform's ecosystem and value chain. The authors point to how the platform itself is just a component of a larger bundle of systems and that the fate and survival of a platform hinges on the vibrancy of its downstream ecosystem. By opening its borders and taking software-based platforms as the infrastructure that powers an ecosystem of other products and/or services, platforms allow end-users to customize the platform to specific needs by bundling different sets of functionalities [1]. In sum: ecosystems, not platforms, attract and sustain users over long periods.

As part of its Digital Single Market package, the European Commission launched its first industry-related initiatives under the Horizon 2020 programme (H2020) with the combined EUR 50 billion mobilized from public and private investment for the digitisation of the European industrial sector. DPs take a central role in a variety of different calls that touch different sectors of the market. H2020 projects themselves pose an interesting research testbed for multiple reasons: (1) for many of the funding schemes, research, and technology organizations (RTOs) and industry are combined in the same working group; (2) strike a balance between pushing the boundaries of technological developments while delivering on market-ready products and/or services; and (3) bridge technology innovations with innovations on the business front. Leveraging these factors, this paper presents a review of how H2020 funded projects have adopted the platform paradigm for the industrial sector. More specifically, we set out to understand how these projects go beyond the technical understanding of platform and develop the user and application of ecosystems that complement the platform. In summary, the research question becomes: Have H2020 funded projects that stand on the development of DPs been able to generate and sustain user ecosystems?

2   Digital Platforms Towards Digital Ecosystems

As with many complex sociotechnical systems, conceptualizations of DPs vary according to the context that surrounds them. [15, 17] and [5] are some examples of Management and Information Systems researchers that have in the past decade compiled and categorized lists of some of these definitions. The most denoted separation is seen in the view of platforms from a technical point of view or from a more sociotechnical perspective. This first perspective sees DPs as extensible codebases to which complementary third-party modules can be added through the use of different interfaces, while this second perspective adopts a view that combines the technical (software and hardware) with the associated organizational processes and standards. Examples of conceptualizations that fall unto these two perspectives are: (1) "An IT-platform is defined as comprised of a technological base on which complementary add-ons can inter-operate, following standards and allowing for transactions among stakeholders, within the platform-centric ecosystem" [17]; (2) "Multisided platform (...) exists wherever a company brings together two or more distinct groups of customers (sides) that need each other in some way, and where the company builds an infrastructure (platform) that creates value by reducing distribution, transaction, and search costs incurred when these groups interact with one another" [13].

The concept of ecosystem suffers from some of the same conceptual ambiguity as DPs. While the term is often found close to DPs, the division between a technical perspective and a sociotechnical perspective is also prevalent. Having the metaphor originally been introduced to the IS field by [12], to describe the idea of a changing competitive environment, this division has more recently emerged on two fronts: an organizational perspective, exemplified by how [10] uses the concept of ecosystem to describe the way companies leverage platforms to become keystone actors in a specific sector of the market; and a technical view that points to ecosystem as a collection of the platform plus "apps" that interoperate with it and are more often than not supplied by third parties. Authors such as [9], and [19] place this vision of ecosystem at the core of the platform value chain. Ultimately, we can trace back some of the basic ideas of DP-based ecosystems in the collaborative networks community where competency management, value systems, system of metrics, and trust management are among the main elements for its success [2].

3 Methodology

The primary source of data utilized in this research was the main "Cordis - EU research projects under Horizon 2020" dataset, published by the EU Publications Office and retrieved on September 2019. We complemented the dataset by (1) collecting public project deliverables from each respective web page (when available); and by (2) querying standard scientific publications databases using each project's unique grant number.

An initial broad selection of projects was selected based on a range of terms, namely: "digital platform"; "multi-sided market"; "marketplace"; and "online platform". This phase resulted in seventy-four selected projects. During the second stage, we analyzed the short descriptions, topics and objectives of each project, excluding duplicates and non-related projects, reducing the number of projects to fifty-two. A third phase consisted of a careful assessment of extended descriptions and some of the initial (more mission descriptive) deliverables. During this phase, projects were selected based on a specific set of criteria. The selected projects all have to involve, in some capacity: (1) The creation of digital platforms for the industry in a business-to-business perspective; (2) the creation of digital platforms for the support of supply chains; and (3) the creation of digital platforms that support an ecosystem of users; We did not consider projects that concerned: (1) the development of non-digital platforms; (2) the development of single-sided platforms; (3) the development of digital platforms where the industry is not the primary target userbase; and (4) the development of new tools or mechanisms for already existing platforms. For the projects selected in this third phase, we took three main components into account: (1) the metadata of each project; (2) the available public deliverables that depict the work involved for the development of the platform in question; and (3) scientific publications published within the scope of the project.

It is also important to note that of the fifty considered projects, only fifteen have ended. The analysis process previously described considered this fact, and it reflects, where relevant, the caused shortcomings. We took as few assumptions as possible regarding future directions of these projects by basing our review on the direction set by each consortium (reflected in the more technical and business-driven deliverables).

4 Results and Discussion

Distribution of Projects Across Years. Since the beginning of the Horizon 2020 framework program in 2015, the number of projects that stand on the development of DPs for the industrial contexts has stayed relatively stable at around 9 per year, with a slight increase in 2018 to 14. This represents 0,21% of the entirety of the funded projects under the program in the considered time frame. These results are congruent with the time frame in which DPs started to become more and more prevalent in other sectors of the market. These numbers also seem to be in line with the review of research that focused on platforms across IS and Management journals conducted by [3]. Starting in 2009–2011 the authors point to the field growing, in terms of the number of publications, going from 1 in 2009 to 13 in 2015 and 22 in 2017.

Distribution of Funding Scheme Across Years. Figure 1 shows the breakdown of funding schemes over the years. Here we can note the increase in research interest around this topic, with the majority of projects being funded under the innovation action (IA) and research innovation action (RIA) scheme. By 2017, however, this trend starts to reverse and we begin to see a growing prevalence of the SME instrument that focuses on the feasibility and economic viability of innovations and works much closer to the market-ready solutions. This switch sees the funding redirected from projects that have a heavy research component, to projects that, although not devoid of research interest, are led by industry organizations themselves. Projects funded under the coordination & support action (CSA) scheme on the other hand are distributed through 2015, 2017, and 2019. This scheme is primarily related to projects that involve standardization, dissemination, policy dialogues and awareness-raising, and many of the platforms that emanate from these projects fall under these two last topics, as the WATERINNEU project that aimed at the creation of a *"marketplace to enhance the exploitation of EU funded ICT models, tools, protocols and policy briefs related to water"* is an example.

Distribution of Categories Across Years. The classification of DPs is another topic that is still not consensual between authors. Different authors have classified platforms according to model of governance or even ownership structure. Due to the nature of this review, we opted to categorize platforms according to its business model. This categorization divides platforms into three models: the (1) integrator platform, where the platform acts as a middle-man and intermediator between two entities (crowd-funding platforms such as Patreon are an example of this model) [4]; (2) in product

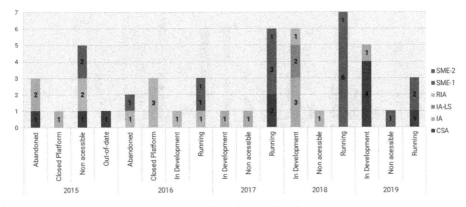

Fig. 1. Platform status by funding scheme across years

platforms, where the platform acts as the technological infrastructure where external contributors build on top of (Shopify is a clear example of this model) [4]; and (3) multisided platform model, where external users can freely interact with end-users without the direct interaction of the platform owner (eBay is an example of this model) [4].

Figure 2 presents the distribution of platforms, by its classification, across years. Here we can note a clear preference for integrator type platforms in the first year of the H2020 programme, that shifted towards the multisided business model in the later years. Given the tight time constraints this nature of funding implies, these results are in line with the business development complexity of each of the categories of platform. Integrator type platforms require a high level of synergy between the different components of the platform and a level of ecosystem development and bootstrapping that is difficult to achieve in the early years of platform development. Most integrator type platforms evolve from one of the other types (mainly multisided platforms). Apple's App Store success has much to do with the pervasiveness of the iPhone platform, and the Amazon Kindle platform to the success of Amazon as an (e)book seller. In the case of product platforms, these are mostly abstracted to the end-users, which adds a step of complexity in the ecosystem building process. This does not only mean that the platform owner has less control over the interactions of end-users with the platform, but also that the growth of the platform is very much tied with the engagement of a specific type of users. In the case of Shopify, these are other organizations or users that intent to sell some product or service, in the case of Squarespace these are users that need a website. Multisided platforms rely heavily on the platform owner's capacity to kickstart the ecosystem and get the platform to a level where platform externalities become a factor. These typologies of platform also lend themselves to dissemination through online and offline channels, which are most common in the projects of this nature.

Distribution of Platform Status Across Years. Figures 1 and 2 also show a breakdown of the current status of the DPs in relation to its business model category and funding scheme. The status of each platform was determined from the point-of-view of an external user and six status were considered: (1) *Running*, where platform use is

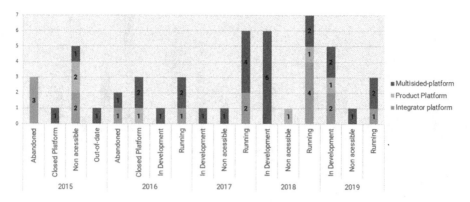

Fig. 2. Platform status by category across years

evident, and an alive ecosystem exists; (2) *Out-of-date*, where the platform shows sign of having been used in the past, but not in the last 6 months; (3) *Abandoned*, where no sign of platform use is present in the past year; (4) *Closed*, when the platform is not accessible to external users; (5) *Non Accessible*, in the cases where the platform is not reachable or not running anymore; and (6) *In Development* when the project is still ongoing, and no platform is available yet.

Overall we cannot consider these results as positive. For projects that started before 2018 only 33% (9 platforms) are running, with a large number of them being abandoned or closed. Of these 9 that are up and running, we can also say that they fall mostly under the multisided business model category (22%), and are funded under direct SME (Phase 1 & 2) instruments (22%).

It's also to note the high number of non accessible platforms for this time period. Platforms such as *Knowliah Community* place a high barrier to entry in the ecosystem by requiring that users use means outside of the platform itself to apply for membership, while *Amable*, requires potential users to go through an application type process to access the offered services. Although hurdles to entrance in an ecosystem can be useful as means of shaping the community of the platform, for platforms early in their lifecycle these can severely limit the capacity to bootstrap the ecosystem and get the network externalities that keep the platform viable in the long term. These need, then, to be paired with strong community engagement and dissemination activities, in order to get the intended user groups over these initial hurdles and into the platform's community. For the last 2 years, a large part of platforms are still in the initial development phase (13 platforms), and 10 can already be considered as running. In this group we still find the same prevalence of SME direct funding (for all but one project), and for the multisided business model (4), although 2018 saw the start of four platforms that fall into the integrator platform model.

Publications and Deliverables. When we look at the total scientific output of each of these projects the results follow what is expected given the different types of funding. RIA projects total a number of 135 publications on scientific journals and conferences, followed by IAs with 44 publications and 12 for CSA. Both the SME instruments combined, for the five years, a total of 5 publications. From this group of 196 publications, only a subset of 26 are directly related to the technical development, deployment, and management of DPs for the manufacturing sector, while the remaining focus on other components of the projects. These numbers point to a prevalence of DPs as the technological infrastructure that is leveraged for the development of new and innovative products and services, but at the same time to the lack of focus that many of these projects put on the development of the platform concept for the manufacturing sector.

A similar situation can be seen in the deliverables specific to each project. In these we found that most of these projects begin with sets of deliverables that center the technical and business development of the platform in its sector of the market through standard tools. Stakeholder analysis, competitor capabilities analysis, and business model development through standard tools were transversal through most of the projects. For some of the projects, such as *EuTravel* these processes are not limited to the start of the project, but an ongoing effort that is evident through several deliverables. When it comes to community engagement and ecosystem development, deliverables show that much of the effort is devoted to conventional dissemination strategies: conference and workshop participation, webinar presentations, and social media presence. Although this strategy allows for the reaching of a wider audience, it is often not focused on the intended target userbase of each project's DP. For most of the considered projects, this results from a lack of separation from what is the dissemination of the project itself, the platform and its ecosystem. This results in platforms with landing pages that describe reference architectures but fail to convey the competitive advantage in its adoption, platforms that become one-sided catalogs of suppliers, communities that fail to gain enough traction to be sustainable without the backing of H2020 funding.

5 Creating and Shaping Communities for DP Enabled Ecosystems: The MANU-SQUARE Case

Building on the manufacturing as a service concept, the H2020 MANU-SQUARE project [11, 16] aims at establishing a European ecosystem of organizations and other relevant stakeholders that, in a marketplace environment, can act as both supplier and client. The platform moves available capacity closer to production demand, further disrupting the traditional linear value network, allowing for the rapid and efficient creation of local value networks for innovative providers of products and services and the optimization and reintroduction in the loop of unused capacity that would otherwise be lost.

In order to develop an ecosystem that is able to outlast the H2020 funding stage, and based on the finding presented in the previous sections, the MANU-SQUARE project has focused its later stages (mid-2019 through mid-2021), in implementing a strategy for the growth of its ecosystem. This strategy leverages [18] high-level metrics to design validation strategies that focus not only on the technological constructs but also on the involvement of end-users and external developers in the platform development process and spans the three stages of the platform lifecycle: short, medium and long-term.

The short-term is the most inward step of platform development where platform owners establish the userbase, core components, and key functionalities provided. Despite its inward nature, dissemination and user engagement activities should start early on the platform building process. According to its target userbase platform owners can opt for online or offline strategies that leverage the press, social media, or already existing communities. To support these activities, on the technical and business side, platform owners have to focus on the scalability and composability of its main services. The focus on scalability will ensure that the platform functional and financial performance under different (higher or lower) levels of adoption while composability ensures the flexibility of the platform's components to be altered without affecting other components of the ecosystem. The interplay between these two characteristics allows for a flexible early platform that can be shaped by the use that end-user and developers give it (Fig. 3).

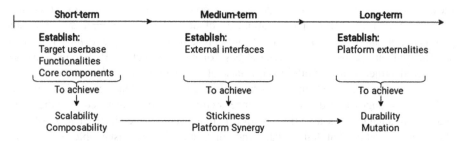

Fig. 3. MANU-SQUARE ecosystem development process

In the medium-term, and with key functionalities in place, the main focus can change to prioritize the implementation of robust and standard technical interfaces for third-party services (crucial for industries where other software tools have become standard and many times hard to replace). This switch implies that the main target of dissemination and engagement actions are now developers and owners of other digital products/services. Overall stickiness and platform synergy are to be considered crucial at this stage. These characteristics ensure that the platform keeps incentivizing persistent usage over time while keeping up the integration with third-party platforms.

Over the long-term, to leverage the externalities that the standing community generates more and more prevalence should be put into the durability and mutation. While durability ensures the capacity of the platform to be competitive in the market, mutation provides the community growth component by keeping alight the capacity of platform owners to pivot and generate new services based on the original platform or even to overtake the services of other platforms and absorb an existing community. These characteristics are to serve as guidelines for the shaping of the lifecycle of the MANU-SQUARE platform. By allying these with (1) the development of robust and standard technical interfaces and (2) the continuous engaging, online, and offline, of end-users we expect to invert the trend of H2020 funded platforms that fail to generate and sustain thriving communities.

6 Conclusion

This study shows that despite the prevalence of DPs as infrastructure in H2020 funded projects for the industry, there is still a lack of understanding of platforms as sociotechnical ecosystems that thrive on both developer and user engagement. Communication and dissemination activities often focus their efforts in the dissemination of the project itself, to the detriment of the growth of the platform ecosystem. We highlight how, under the H2020 umbrella, funding towards platform development has shifted to the direct funding of SMEs and how these funding schemes have resulted in platforms that remain active in the short term.

Horizon 2020 projects adhere to strict guidelines from the first proposal to the last formal review. Although this structure provides projects with clear goals and roadmaps, it can also narrow its growth potential. Although DPs are an integral component of today's market, how they can be deliberately designed and deployed is still a matter of debate. For many of what are currently considered the most successful and thriving platforms of different sectors, business models have changed drastically, core functionalities were added and removed, visions and missions were redirected. It is then crucial to, when designing and reviewing projects that focus on the building of DPs in its sociotechnical conceptualization, to factor in the room for the branching out of functionalities and goals that were not initially foreseen. DPs provide researchers and companies with unparalleled flexibility in the infrastructure and communities they are able to generate, the processes that lead the building of DPs need to also afford this same flexibility on the short, medium and long time-frames.

This research presents, however, several limitations. These include the difficulty in assessing the reliability of the data source used, the large number of projects that are still ongoing, with platforms in the development phase, and the lack of direct contact with both many of the considered platforms and the researchers and organizations involved in these projects. The process we introduce in Sect. 5 also lacks the required validation, as it still is an ongoing effort.

Acknowledgments. The work presented here was part of the project "MANU-SQUARE – MANUfacturing ecoSystem of QUAlified Resources Exchange" and received funding from the European Union's Horizon 2020 research and innovation programme under grant agreements No 761145.

References

1. Adner, R., Kapoor, R.: Value creation in innovation ecosystems: how the structure of technological interdependence affects firm performance in new technology generations. Strateg. Manag. J. **31**(3), 306–333 (2010)

2. Afsarmanesh, H., Camarinha-Matos, L.M.: A framework for management of virtual organization breeding environments. In: Camarinha-Matos, L.M., Afsarmanesh, H., Ortiz, A. (eds.) PRO-VE 2005. ITIFIP, vol. 186, pp. 35–48. Springer, Boston, MA (2005). https://doi.org/10.1007/0-387-29360-4_4

3. Asadullah, A., Faik, I., Kankanhalli, A.: Digital platforms: a review and future directions. In: PACIS, pp. 248 (2018). https://aisel.aisnet.org/pacis2018/248

4. Boudreau, K., Lakhani, K.: How to manage outside innovation. MIT Sloan Manag. Rev. **50** (4), 69 (2009)

5. Costa, E., et al.: On the use of digital platforms to support SME internationalization in the context of industrial business associations. In: Jamil, G.L. (ed.) Handbook of Research on Expanding Business Opportunities with Information Systems and Analytics, pp. 66–94. IGI Global, Hershey (2019)

6. Cusumano, M.A., et al.: The Business of Platforms: Strategy in the Age of Digital Competition, Innovation, and Power. HarperCollins, New York (2019)

7. Eisenmann, T.R., et al.: Strategies for two sided markets. Harvard Bus. Rev. **84**(10), 92 (2006)

8. Fichman, R.G.: Going beyond the dominant paradigm for information technology innovation research: emerging concepts and methods. J. Assoc. Inf. Syst. **5**(8), 11 (2004)

9. Gawer, A., Cusumano, M.A.: Platform Leadership: How Intel, Microsoft, and Cisco Drive Industry Innovation. Harvard Business School Press, Boston (2002)

10. Iansiti, M., Levien, R.: The Keystone Advantage: What the New Dynamics of Business Ecosystems Mean for Strategy, Innovation, and Sustainability. Harvard Business School Press, Boston (2004)

11. Landolfi, G., et al.: An ontology based semantic data model supporting a MaaS digital platform. In: 9th international Conference on Intelligent Systems 2018 (2018)

12. Moore, J.C., et al.: Information acquisition policies for resource allocation among multiple agents. Inf. Syst. Res. **8**(2), 151–170 (1997). https://doi.org/10.1287/isre.8.2.151

13. Pagani, M.: Digital business strategy and value creation: framing the dynamic cycle of control points. MIS Q. **37**(2), 617–632 (2013)

14. Parker, G., et al.: Platform Revolution. W. W. Norton & Company, Inc., New York (2016)

15. de Reuver, M., et al.: The digital platform: a research agenda. J. Inf. Technol., 1–12 (2017). https://doi.org/10.1057/s41265-016-0033-3

16. Silva, H.D., Soares, A.L., Bettoni, A., Francesco, A.B., Albertario, S.: A digital platform architecture to support multi-dimensional surplus capacity sharing. In: Camarinha-Matos, L. M., Afsarmanesh, H., Antonelli, D. (eds.) PRO-VE 2019. IAICT, vol. 568, pp. 323–334. Springer, Cham (2019). https://doi.org/10.1007/978-3-030-28464-0_28

17. Sun, R., et al.: Information technology platforms: conceptualisation and a review of emerging research in IS research. In: Australasian Conference on Information Systems, pp. 1–17 (2015)

18. Tiwana, A.: Platform Ecosystems: Aligning Architecture, Governance, and Strategy. Newnes, London (2013)

19. Tiwana, A., et al.: Research Commentary: Platform Evolution: Coevolution of Platform Architecture, Governance, and Environmental Dynamics (2010). https://doi.org/10.2307/23015636

Data and Knowledge Services

Towards a Reference Model for Knowledge Driven Data Provision Processes

Wei Min Wang[1]([✉]), Maurice Preidel[1], Bernd Fachbach[2], and Rainer Stark[1]

[1] Chair of Industrial Information Technology, Technical University of Berlin, Pascalstr. 8-9, 10587 Berlin, Germany
{w.wang, m.preidel, r.stark}@tu-berlin.de
[2] Virtual Vehicle Research GmbH, Inffeldgasse 21a, 8010 Graz, Austria
Bernd.Fachbach@v2c2.at

Abstract. Value creation in most business areas takes place in networks that involve a wide range of stakeholders from various disciplines within and beyond company borders. Collaboration in such networks require the exchange of knowledge that is manifested in digital artefacts and consequently in data. As the utilization of that "hidden" knowledge has become increasingly important, the provision of relevant data in sufficient quality has also become crucial. This article proposes a reference model for knowledge driven data provision processes that is developed within a research project at the Virtual Vehicle Research GmbH for a future networked engineering environment. It describes a systematic process to drive operationalization of data provision from knowledge requirements to identify, extract and provide raw data until the application of such data sets. Still, the model in its current state is only applicable by descriptive means and needs further development and validation in practical use cases.

Keywords: Data provision · Reference model · Knowledge discovery · Networked engineering

1 Introduction

Engineering is increasingly driven by data of various types and categories, especially in industry sectors with highly complex products such as the automotive and the railroad sector. Market demand and legal requirement are transformed into technical requirements. Product architectures are described in models and the maturity of the complex products is managed by KPIs. Numerical simulations that enable a deep insight in the behavior of a product long time before the first part is physically build requires various input data and produces a huge amount of result data. Moreover, an increasing number of development partners are involved, which have to be tracked adequately [1]. Above all Digital Twins of the product require an extensive dossier of numerous data and information about a specific real vehicle along the complete lifecycle [2, 3].

Communication and cross-disciplinary collaboration are crucial aspects of current vehicle development – either inside a company as well cross-enterprise. Looking at the

© IFIP International Federation for Information Processing 2020
Published by Springer Nature Switzerland AG 2020
L. M. Camarinha-Matos et al. (Eds.): PRO-VE 2020, IFIP AICT 598, pp. 123–132, 2020.
https://doi.org/10.1007/978-3-030-62412-5_10

same base of relevant and consistent data from different perspectives is relevant for high effectivity and quality [4]. Generic data provision services, context enrichment, and continuous aggregation are key aspects for future effective development and lifecycle integration [5]. A high quality of consistent data is the necessary base for agile engineering methodology, for networking collaboration as well as for wide-spread implementation of supporting data analytics and artificial intelligence (AI)-based methods for knowledge discovery (KD) [2]. Cross disciplinary development teams have to have efficient access to related data, to analogies from other development activities, to knowledge by analyzing available information [6] and to effect models from specific topics, domains and disciplines.

Hence, the extraction and utilization of potential knowledge from such large data sets has become even more important to industrial practitioners as they expect considerable potentials to optimize current processes and to enable novel business models [7]. In order to extract potential knowledge from large data sets, these have to be evaluated, e.g. by statistical analysis during data mining (DM) endeavors [6]. Therefore, data have to be identified, prepared and delivered. However, most existing reference models for Knowledge Discovery and Data Mining (KDDM) do not include detailed descriptions of such a data provision process per se, but rather point out single aspects (e.g. data prospecting [8]) or summarize it in few steps (e.g. data understanding and data preparation [9]). Additionally, existing KDDM reference model mainly focus on single projects. Hence, they lack the ability to support the establishment of novel data-driven product concepts such as product-service systems (PSS) [10] or smart products [11], which require a constant supply of operational data to enable customer specific service adaptions.

The efficient application of KDDM in engineering is also a subject to the K2 research project V-Lab – Future Engineering Lab at the Virtual Vehicle Research GmbH (V2C2). Collaboratively with industrial companies from the automotive and the railroad sector, innovative processes and tools for networked engineering in future are investigated. A key aspect of data provision of this research is to integrate KDDM activities as continuous activities within the organizational processes to enable streamlined and automated (or respectively AI-aided) knowledge exchanges. Therefore, the authors developed a generic reference model for data provision processes that considers the data provision as a part of the process organization. It refers to elements of current frameworks for KDDM and data provision (see Sect. 2) and suggests detailed process steps to for a systematic data provision process that drive operationalization of data provision from knowledge requirements to identify, extract and provide raw data until the application of such data sets (see Sect. 3.2). Moreover, technical and organizational prerequisites for the proposed model are pointed out (see Sect. 3.1).

2 State of the Art

In context of KDDM in product development, the role of data provision processes is to identify, collect and prepare relevant and reusable data in order to support knowledge (re)use in PDP [12]. For KDDM in industrial practice, the CRISP-DM (Cross Industry

Standard Process for Data Mining) reference model has been found to be the most widely used model compared to other models such as SEMMA (Sample, Explore, Modify, Model, and Assess) or KDD (Knowledge Discovery in Databases) [13, 14]. Therefore, the proposed reference model will only refer to CRISP-DM.

Within CRISP-DM, six phases are described: 1) Business Understanding, 2) Data Understanding, 3) Data Preparation, 4) Modelling, 5) Evaluation and 6) Deployment [9]. For the reference model, the phases 1–3 are most relevant, because those phases define the data need for the data mining project. The phases 4–6 are also considered, but as they highly focus on an actual data-mining model, there is a greater difference to the purpose of the reference model (data provision vs. data mining). Nevertheless, the phases 1–3 present a good overall framework as a starting point for creating a reference model for data provision. A clear understanding of the business objectives (phase 1) helps to focus on the right data in order to have a reasonable return on invest for real world applications. Data understanding (phase 2) is crucial for every data provision and data mining project: The available data must be understood from a domain knowledge perspective and needs to be linked to the identified business case from phase 1. Data preparation (phase 3) is all about making the data applicable for the business case. This is achieved by aggregating, cleaning and transforming the relevant data into a data structure, which is usable for subsequent phases. While CRISP-DM is a great starting point for the reference model for data provision processes, it also has notable limitations [15, 16]: Firstly, CRISP-DM is a framework for individual projects, whereas the reference model for data provision aims for continuous provision of relevant data in sufficient quality within business processes [6]. Secondly, CRISP-DM is a general framework suitable for many industries and use cases with a high abstraction level [17]. In contrast, the proposed reference model focuses on specific phases for data provision and the context of product development.

To evaluate further existing reference models for data provision processes, a literature review was conducted on Scopus (https://www.scopus.com) based on the keyword matrix presented in Table 1. The initial query results were reduced according to the limiting topic keywords (see Table 1) and to the period from 2009 to 2019.

Table 1. Keyword matrix applied for literature review

Search keywords (OR)	Limiting topic keywords (OR)
Data provision	Engineering
Data supply	Product development
Data retrieval	Data science
Data procurement	Data analytics
Data preprocessing	Produktentwicklung (German)
Information retrieval	Konstruktion (German)
Datenbereitstellung (German)	
Datenversorgung (German)	

The abstracts of the 57 remaining matches were then evaluated for direct (explicit mentions in abstract) or indirect (e.g. as paraphrase) references to the topic of data provision. After this step, 18 candidates remained of which 15 were available online.

As already noted in KDDM reference models, the evaluation of these sources also revealed that the data provision process per se is rarely considered specifically, but rather briefly mentioned as a component of application cases (e.g. data stream mining) or data management concepts [18–22]. Some authors use application cases to describe the potential benefits of analyzing data and its properties [23–25], but stay quite unspecific about how data is actually provided. Only one article by Thoben and Lewandowski provides a generic data provision framework for the utilization of operating data for product development [12]. Based on a closed-loop PLM approach [26], they describe four major requirements for a data provision process as well as a three-pillar concept comprising "Technical prerequisites", "Methodological concepts" and "Procedural implications" [12].

3   Reference Model for Data Provision Processes

As mentioned above, the proposed reference model draws on existing frameworks and integrates elements of those with typical stages of a generic data provision process. In contrast to CRISP-DM, the proposed model particularly addresses the data provision process and the causal relationships therein. Hence, it focuses is on the chronological and logical order of process steps as well as necessary input and output artefacts.

The proposed model is intended to support the establishment of a continuous data provision process within organizational process structures. To describe the elements of the reference model, the detailed steps are described in context of a hypothetical use case from the research project at V2C2. In that case, the simulation of a high-speed test (HST) has to be carried out during an engineering process in the automotive sector. In practice, HSTs are carried out to estimate the maximum speed of a vehicle. They can either be numerical simulations, physical simulations (road testing), or even a hybrid approach by combining numerical and physical simulation. The adequate method approach is selected according to the phase of development process and the availability of data or real parts. However, within the hypothetical scenario is assumed that there is a working simulation model for HSTs and that all relevant models, formulas and data are available. The implications for the proposed reference model for data provision process are described in the following section.

3.1   Technological and Organizational Prerequisites

To enable a streamlined and (partially) automated end-to-end data provision process, some essential technological and organizational requirements have to be met. For the reference model, the authors especially consider four clusters of prerequisites, which are described below. However, is has to be mentioned, that some of them are not realized yet or show a future scenario. In the context of the model development it is assumed that these prerequisites are already fulfilled.

Seamless Integration of the Processes: In order to enable an efficient and end-to-end data provision process, all organizational processes have to be modelled at a sufficient level of detail and implemented in operative business. Only then is it possible to create sufficient transparency regarding the need for knowledge, information and data [12]. Such a process modeling can be realized with an activity-based approach [27]. In this approach, all activities in the business context are regarded as a sequence of atomic activities (smallest, non-divisible activity), which are carried out by specific actors in order to achieve a specific goal in the process. These activities are described in the context of the environment in which they are embedded, namely the organization and its specific processes, the tools and IT systems used, and the physical and virtual artefacts used as input or produced as output. The activity-based approach enables a holistic description of the value-creating processes in the company and the identification of their reciprocity and dependencies [27].

Consistency of Data and Models: In order for data to be identified and extracted, the data itself or the artifacts in which they are manifested have to be available in the respective value network. This requires both vertical (e.g. across company departments) and horizontal (e.g. over the product lifecycle) consistency and traceability of the data. According to the Model-based Systems Engineering (MBSE) approach, digital models can be used to link development data from different disciplines and development phases. The consistent deployment of digital models in all organizational processes and their company-specific orchestration can reduce the complexity of distributed development tasks and ensure the traceability of information and data [28].

Integration of IT Systems and Their Respective Data Sources: In order to realize a comprehensive data supply process, it is also necessary to integrate the IT systems used to manage the meta and user data [12]. Following the Product Lifecycle Management (PLM) approach, a PLM backbone can be used for that purpose, e.g. by means of a PDM/PLM system. This system would play the role of a central data management instance for all engineering processes and integrate other IT systems (e.g. ERP, PPS), tools (e.g. CAx) and specialized data warehouses from other business units (e.g. sales) via defined interfaces. For this purpose, it must also be ensured that the organizational processes are sufficiently digitalized and that data arising from any organizational activities are entered into the corresponding system [12, 28].

Company-Specific Knowledge Model: The knowledge of a company constitutes the basic semantic framework on which all data provision and data application processes are based. This knowledge base must include knowledge about the company's own products, processes and tools as well as about the collaboration partners in the value creation network [12]. From a strategic point of view, it represents the background architecture of a company's value creation activities and therefore should

1. be reflected in the processes, models and tools
2. be implemented in the IT infrastructure (e.g. PLM backbone) and
3. be accessible to all internal company IT systems - and to some degree also to external collaboration partners (e.g. via standardized interfaces).

The implementation of such a knowledge base for linking different knowledge areas can be achieved, among other things, by means of semantic technologies (e.g. ontologies) [29–31]. Also, methods and tools from research areas such as Business Intelligence can provide suitable guidance to develop a basic semantic framework of company data (e.g. the Kimball bus matrix [32]).

3.2   Model Description

The proposed reference model for data provision processes can be divided into three generic phases: *Clarify need*, *Data acquisition* and *Data application* (Fig. 1).

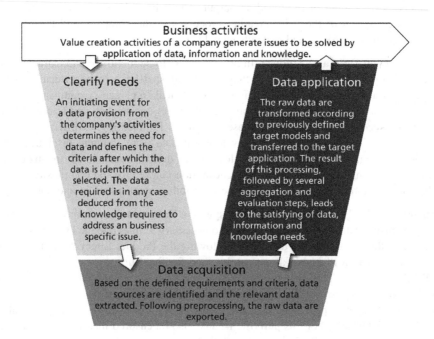

Fig. 1. Generic phases of the proposed reference model for data provision processes

Each of these phases comprises specific stages as well as artifacts that serve as input or result as output. The detailed stages of the model are illustrated in Fig. 2 and described in this section. In the phase of *Clarify needs*, the objectives for the data provision process are defined. As for any engineering activities, the initiator of a data provision process is always an issue that arises from a value creation activity of the respective organization [33]. By operationalizing this issue, the respective knowledge need can be identified (cf. business understanding in CRISP-DM [9]). In the present use case, the theoretical maximum speed of a vehicle at time X should be determined by a simulated HST in order to provide initial data for the variant definition of the engine and the transmission control. The knowledge need of a person who is hypothetically assigned with that task (e.g. a simulation engineer), can be described as: "What is the maximum speed that the vehicle can achieve at the given point in time X, according to the valid status of the relevant development data and simulation models, when linear acceleration is applied?" With the help of the company-specific knowledge base, this person can derive the relevant information from this question, e.g. which components and models need to be regarded for such a simulation. After identifying the relevant information carriers (e.g. documents or CAD models), relevant attributes (e.g. max. torque) and quality criteria (e.g. completeness, correctness) have to be determined. Based on this defined data need, the *Data acquisition* activities can be initiated. In the first step, the corresponding data (e.g. valid CAD models in the PDM system) have to be identified and localized. The type of source system (e.g. company-owned vs. external) also specifies the data provenance, which has a great influence on the quality of the data (e.g. reliability, correctness). The properties of the source systems further determine the effort to utilize the data. The source data model as well as the source data formats and types determine how attributes are encoded in the source system and how they can be extracted or transformed (cf. data understanding in CRISP-DM [9]). The identified data has to be extracted from the source systems then and stored temporarily for data pre-processing. During preprocessing, transformations take place with the aim of preparing the extracted data specifically for later use, for example, by deleting invalid data sets or scaling data with different dimensions. The pre-processed collection of raw data can then be loaded to dedicated storage locations (e.g. a data warehouse) (cf. data preparation in CRISP-DM [9]).

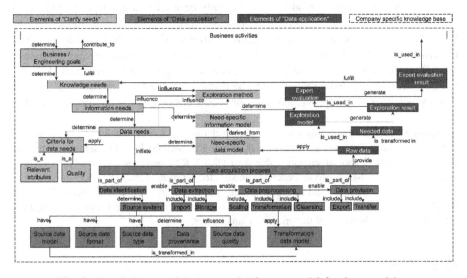

Fig. 2. Detailed steps of the proposed reference model for data provision

This raw data can then be further processed in *Data application*, depending on the requirements of the exploration method. This results in data that meet the defined data requirements and can be fed into an exploration model. This can be either an already existing analysis model (i.e. already trained and in use) or a new model that is to be which experts can assess whether the business issues have been adequately answered and thus the knowledge need have been satisfied.

4 Conclusion and Outlook

The proposed reference model for data provision processes suggests detailed generic stages to support and facilitate the operative implementation of such processes. Based on the HST example, the model elements were described and explained. In contrast to classical KDDM reference models such as CRISP-DM that are limited to support the implementation of individual DM projects, the detailed stages of the proposed model (see Fig. 2) allow companies to understand how they can integrate the data provision process as a continuous process in their business organization. Especially, in the light of novel data-driven product concepts and business models as well as the growing importance of digital twins, it is necessary to understand data provision not only as isolated activities within DM projects, but also as a continuous element of value creation activities. By establishing routines for knowledge-driven data provision processes, companies can exploit the potentials of advanced analytics as well as AI-capabilities to improve their engineering processes (e.g. shorten development time) as well as their products and services (e.g. by continuous adaption to customer requirements) [34].

However, the reference model so far can only be used as a descriptive model or a canvas to plan or analyze data provision processes. The stages within the model need to be further complemented with technological solutions and methodological approaches. In particular, the transformations from knowledge needs to information and data needs as well as vice versa pose great challenges and will require further research [12, 34]. Furthermore, the reference model has to be further validated on practical use cases to identify potentials for improvement both on a conceptual and methodological level.

Acknowledgements. The publication was written during the research within K2 research project V-Lab – Future Engineering Lab (Virtual Vehicle Research GmbH). The authors would like to acknowledge the financial support within the COMET K2 Competence Centers for Excellent Technologies from the Austrian Federal Ministry for Climate Action (BMK), the Austrian Federal Ministry for Digital and Economic Affairs (BMDW), the Province of Styria (Dept. 12) and the Styrian Business Promotion Agency (SFG). The Austrian Research Promotion Agency (FFG) has been authorized for the program management.

References

1. Vajna, S. (ed.): Integrated Design Engineering. Springer, Heidelberg (2014). https://doi.org/10.1007/978-3-642-41104-5
2. Barricelli, B.R., Casiraghi, E., Fogli, D.: A survey on digital twin: definitions, characteristics, applications, and design implications. IEEE Access **7**, 167653–167671 (2019). https://doi.org/10.1109/ACCESS.2019.2953499

3. Stark, R., Damerau, T.: Digital twin. In: The International Academy for Production Engineering, Chatti S., Tolio T. (eds.) CIRP Encyclopedia of Production Engineering, pp. 1–8. Springer, Heidelberg (2019). https://doi.org/10.1007/978-3-642-35950-7_16870-1
4. Neumann, F. (ed.): Analyzing and Modeling Interdisciplinary Product Development. Springer Fachmedien Wiesbaden, Wiesbaden (2015). https://doi.org/10.1007/978-3-658-11092-5
5. Voet, H., Altenhof, M., Ellerich, M., Schmitt, R.H., Linke, B.: A framework for the capture and analysis of product usage data for continuous product improvement. J. Manuf. Sci. Eng. **141** (2019)
6. Kurgan, L.A., Musilek, P.: A survey of knowledge discovery and data mining process models. Knowl. Eng. Rev. **21**, 1–24 (2006). https://doi.org/10.1017/S0269888906000737
7. Markus, M.L.: Toward a theory of knowledge reuse. Types of knowledge reuse situations and factors in reuse success. J. Manag. Inf. Syst. **18**, 57–93 (2015). https://doi.org/10.1080/07421222.2001.11045671
8. Anand, S.S., Büchner, A.G.: Decision Support Using Data Mining. Financial Times Management, London (etc.) (1998)
9. IBM: IBM SPSS Modeler Crisp-DM Guide (2016)
10. Exner, K., Stark, R., Kim, J.Y.: Data-driven business model a methodology to develop smart services. In: Proceeding of the 2017 International Conference on Engineering, Technology and Innovation (ICE/ITMC), pp. 146–154 (2017)
11. Porter, M.E., Heppelmann, J.E.: How smart, connected products are transforming companies. Harvard Bus. Rev. **93**, 96–114 (2015)
12. Thoben, K.-D., Lewandowski, M.: Information and data provision of operational data for the improvement of product development. In: Bouras, A., Eynard, B., Foufou, S., Thoben, K.-D. (eds.) PLM 2015. IAICT, vol. 467, pp. 3–12. Springer, Cham (2016). https://doi.org/10.1007/978-3-319-33111-9_1
13. Azevedo, A., dos Santos, M.F.: KDD, SEMMA and CRISP-DM: a parallel overview (2008)
14. Piatetsky, G.: CRISP-DM, still the top methodology for analytics, data mining, or data science projects - kdnuggets (2014). https://www.kdnuggets.com/2014/10/crisp-dm-top-methodology-analytics-data-mining-data-science-projects.html. Accessed 17 Apr 2020
15. Four problems in using CRISP-DM and how to fix them - kdnuggets (2020). https://www.kdnuggets.com/2017/01/four-problems-crisp-dm-fix.html. Accessed 17 Apr 2020
16. Wiemer, H., Drowatzky, L., Ihlenfeldt, S.: Data mining methodology for engineering applications (DMME)—a holistic extension to the CRISP-DM model. Appl. Sci. **9**, 2407 (2019). https://doi.org/10.3390/app9122407
17. Huber, S., Wiemer, H., Schneider, D., Ihlenfeldt, S.: DMME: data mining methodology for engineering applications – a holistic extension to the CRISP-DM model. Procedia CIRP **79**, 403–408 (2019)
18. Shentu, J., Zheng, M.: Mechanism design of data management system for nuclear power. Ann. Nucl. Energy **129**, 21–29 (2019)
19. Tan, J.S.K., Ang, A.K., Lu, L., Gan, S.W.Q., Corral, M.G.: Quality analytics in a big data supply chain: commodity data analytics for quality engineering. In: Proceeding of the TENCON 2016 – 2016 IEEE Region 10 Conference, Singapore, pp. 3455–3463 (2016)
20. Ramírez-Gallego, S., Krawczyk, B., García, S., Woźniak, M., Herrera, F.: A survey on data preprocessing for data stream mining: current status and future directions. Neurocomputing **239**, 39–57 (2017)
21. Madenas, N., Tiwari, A., Turner, C.J., Peachey, S., Broome, S.: Improving root cause analysis through the integration of PLM systems with cross supply chain maintenance data. Int. J. Adv. Manuf. Technol. **84**, 1679–1695 (2015). https://doi.org/10.1007/s00170-015-7747-1

22. Lin, H.-T., Chi, N.-W., Hsieh, S.-H.: A concept-based information retrieval approach for engineering domain-specific technical documents. Adv. Eng. Inform. **26**(2), 349–360 (2012)
23. Al-Utaibi, K.A., El-Alfy, E.-S.M.: Intrusion detection taxonomy and data preprocessing mechanisms. J. Intell. Fuzzy Syst. **34**, 1369–1383 (2018). https://doi.org/10.3233/JIFS-169432
24. Alkhalil, A., Ramadan, R.A.: IoT data provenance implementation challenges. Procedia Comput. Sci. **109**, 1134–1139 (2017)
25. Hassler, A.P., Menasalvas, E., García-García, F.J., Rodríguez-Mañas, L., Holzinger, A.: Importance of medical data preprocessing in predictive modeling and risk factor discovery for the frailty syndrome. BMC Med. Inform. Decis. Mak. **19**, 33 (2019). https://doi.org/10.1186/s12911-019-0747-6
26. Jun, H.-B., Kiritsis, D., Xirouchakis, P.: Closed-loop PLM. In: Taisch, M., Thoben, K.-D., Montorio, M. (eds.) Advanced Manufacturing. An ICT and Systems Perspective, pp. 79–87. CRC Press, Boca Raton (2007)
27. Lünnemann, P., Stark, R., Wang, W.M., Manteca, P.I.: Engineering activities — considering value creation from a holistic perspective. In: 2017 International Conference on Engineering (ICE/ITMC), pp. 315–323 (2017)
28. Eigner, M., Gilz, T., Zafirov, R.: Interdisziplinäre produktentwicklung - modellbasiertes systems engineering. PLMportal, München (2012)
29. Akmal, S., Shih, L.-H., Batres, R.: Ontology-based similarity for product information retrieval. Comput. Ind. **65**, 91–107 (2014)
30. Borsato, M.: Bridging the gap between product lifecycle management and sustainability in manufacturing through ontology building. Comput. Ind. **65**, 258–269 (2014). https://doi.org/10.1016/j.compind.2013.11.003
31. Stark, R., Wang, W.M., Pförtner, A., Hayka, H.: Einsatz von ontologien zur vernetzung von wissensdomänen in der nachhaltigen produktentstehung am beispiel des sonderforschungsbereiches 1026 – sustainable manufacturing (2014)
32. Kimball, R., Ross, M.: The Data Warehouse Toolkit. The Definitive Guide to Dimensional Modeling. Wiley, Indianapolis (2013)
33. Wang, W.M., Lünnemann, P., Preidel, M., Stark, R.: Wissen in Produktentwicklungsprozessen – Ein Aktivitäten-basierter Analyseansatz. In: Brökel, K., Grote, K.-H., Stelzer, R., Rieg, F., Feldhusen, J., Müller, N., Köhler, P. (eds.) 15. gemeinsames kolloquium konstruktionstechnik. interdisziplinäre produktentwicklung, Universität Duisburg-Essen, Essen, pp. 183–192 (2017)
34. Klein, P., van der Vegte, W.F., Hribernik, K., Klaus-Dieter, T.: Towards an approach integrating various levels of data analytics to exploit product-usage information in product development. In: Proceedings of the Design Society: International Conference on Engineering Design, vol. 1, pp. 2627–2636 (2019)

A Semantic Data Model to Represent Building Material Data in AEC Collaborative Workflows

Prathap Valluru[1]([✉]), Janakiram Karlapudi[1], Karsten Menzel[1], Teemu Mätäsniemi[2], and Jari Shemeikka[2]

[1] Institute of Construction Informatics, Technische Universität Dresden, Dresden, Germany
{Prathap.Valluru, Janakiram.Karlapudi, Karsten.Menzel1}@tu-dresden.de
[2] VTT Technical Research Centre of Finland Ltd, Espoo, Finland
{Teemu.Matasniemi, Jari.Shemeikka}@vtt.fi

Abstract. The specification of building material is required in multiple phases of engineering and construction projects towards holistic BIM implementations. Building material information plays a vital role in design decisions by enabling different simulation processes, such as energy, acoustic, lighting, etc. Utilization and sharing of building material information between stakeholders are some of the major influencing factors on the practical implementation of the BIM process. Different meta-data schemas (e.g. IFC) are usually available to represent and share material information amongst partners involved in a construction project. However, these schemas have their own constraints to enable efficient data sharing amongst stakeholders. This paper explains these constraints and proposes a methodological approach for the representation of material data using semantic web concepts aiming to support the sharing of BIM data and interoperability enhancements in collaboration workflows. As a result, the DICBM (https://w3id.org/digitalconstruction/BuildingMaterials) ontology was developed which improves the management of building material information in the BIM-based collaboration process.

Keywords: BIM · Building material ontology · IFC · Linked data · Data sharing

1 Introduction and Background

Over the last two decades, the advancement in Information and Communication Technology (ICT) improved the processing and management of information in the Architecture, Engineering, and Construction (AEC) industries, specifically by adopting Building Information Modeling (BIM) concepts. However, the identification of critical information, its management along with the efficient collaboration, and communication between the participants in the project are some barriers in the traditional building construction process [1, 2]. Research work by L.M. Camarinha-Matos et al. (2007) discussed that Collaborative Networks (CNs) can play a key role in effective

---

The original version of this chapter was revised: the last author's name was corrected. The correction to this chapter is available at https://doi.org/10.1007/978-3-030-62412-5_54

© IFIP International Federation for Information Processing 2020, corrected publication 2021
Published by Springer Nature Switzerland AG 2020
L. M. Camarinha-Matos et al. (Eds.): PRO-VE 2020, IFIP AICT 598, pp. 133–142, 2020.
https://doi.org/10.1007/978-3-030-62412-5_11

knowledge management, and collaboration between teams involved in a project [3]. The different classification of CNs are well described e.g. in research work carried by Camarinha-Matos et al. in (2005), (2010) [4, 5]. The usage of CNs spread to several industries and gained benefits from it.

In recent years, the AEC industry got motivated to use CNs in the project life cycle. As a result, numerous commercial collaboration platforms became available, e.g. BIMCollab[1], BIMcloud[2], A360[3], just to name a few. However, most of these tools utilize proprietary formats for data representation and thus lack in effective integration of Common Data Environments (CDE) [6]. Also, there are still challenges in terms of information sharing and management between the actors in heterogeneous environments [7]. The desire to overcome these challenges gained interest in the BIM4EEB[4] EU project. The project aims to develop (i) a BIM collaborative environment called BIM Management System (BIMMS[5]) with an integrated CDE and web applications and (ii) a linked building data modeling and sharing framework for interoperable communication and data exchange amongst all actors involved in the renovation process. The work presented in this paper focuses on the latter topic namely at ontology models for building material information.

To specify the scope of collaboration activities in AEC researchers of the BIM4EEB project identified approximately 23 stakeholders and close to 200 distinct collaboration scenarios undertaken by the stakeholders in six life cycle stages of a building under renovation [8]. Such a complex collaboration network needs access to all information about the building for each specific activity handled by the stakeholders in flexible, interoperable formats. Information about building materials is one of the important aspects to manage a building holistically and in a sustainable way over all phases of its building life cycle. The assignment of material specifications to building elements and sharing these details between stakeholders involved is a decisive task and influences a project to a great extent. This information associated with different layers of building elements is necessary to perform energy, acoustic, lighting, etc. simulations at different stages of the project. Development and analysis of engineering models of a building from its early stages onwards enable performance evaluations and support informed design decisions based on optimization [9–11]. The efficient data transfer from BIM to analytical models considerably increases the efficiency and reduces the inconsistencies, efforts, and time [12]. Based on previous research on the persistent challenges for data sharing [9, 13–16], this paper introduces a semantic data model to represent building material information in the conversion process of BIM models to analytical models (e.g. Building Energy Model (BEM), Structural Model, MEP Model, etc.). Also, it explores different complexities in present data schemas and explains different constraints imposed by this.

---

[1] https://www.bimcollab.com/.

[2] https://graphisoft.com/support/system_requirements/AC21/bimcloud/.

[3] https://a360.autodesk.com/.

[4] https://www.bim4eeb-project.eu/.

[5] https://bim4eeb.oneteam.it/BIMMS/Default.aspx#.

1.1 Building Information Modeling for Collaboration

Building Information Modeling (BIM) has gained major attention in the AEC industry. The acronym BIM has several definitions developed by the scientific community [17, 18] and is supported by multiple standards [19–21]. However, the common idea of BIM is to represent built assets in a digital format based on reliable, coordinated, and appropriate information throughout the building life cycle. Coordinated information models generated from the BIM process can enable stakeholders to use project information consistently and reliably over different project scopes [22].

The development of the schema of the Industry Foundation Classes (IFC), standardized by ISO 16739 [23], became a major openBIM data model. The IFC allows various actors involved in the project life cycle to represent BIM data uniformly. Apart from the development of BIM models' geometry, the effective usage of it across the different disciplines is still a challenge. The major reason is due to a lack of a collaborative environment and interoperability between the heterogeneous BIM tools. The desire to overcome these constraints gained attention to develop BIM-based collaborative spaces called Common Data Environment (CDE) and the use of semantic web technologies. In such collaborative systems, IFC has been used for model-based collaboration [24]. However, recent research [25, 26] comprehensively explains the constraints of the IFC schema corresponding to extendibility, querying, reasoning, and interoperability. Most of these limitations can be overcome by adopting semantic web technologies.

1.2 Information Management in AEC Using Semantic Web Technologies

The term Semantic Web (SW) was introduced by Tim Berners-Lee in (2001) [27]. The introduction of SW standards allows us to publish data on the web but this data was never linked. By considering this problem, Tim Berners-Lee introduced the Linked Data[6] concept in 2006, to link information across domains. Apart from the technical evaluation of Semantic Web and Linked Data, the need has increased for shared semantics and a web of data and information derived from it [28].

For example, collaborative networks *"consist of a variety of entities that are largely autonomous, geographically distributed, and heterogeneous in terms of their operating environment"* [29]. Such systems require the adoption of ontologies for the integration of data sets and knowledge representation.

Early research efforts [30–33] using ontologies in CNs, created an interest in the AEC industry to use ontologies. Meanwhile, several research efforts [34–38] were carried out in the Architecture, Engineering, Construction, and Facilities Management (AEC/FM) sectors to improve the availability of building data by using Semantic Web technologies and Linked Data approach. The main goal of using SW technologies and the Linked Data approach is to achieve data universality and interlinking of data from different sources. Additionally, the concept of the semantic web enables greater extensibility of information and knowledge modeling according to the domain requirements.

---

[6] https://www.w3.org/DesignIssues/LinkedData.

2 DICBM: Digital Construction Building Material Ontology

2.1 Building Material Data in IFC

The open meta data model IFC is considered as a reference model for material data. In the IFC-based, openBIM meta-data model entities are related to their resources using the concept of objectified relationships. Material specifications of building elements are defined as a resource in the IFC- schema. They are related to respective building elements through the objectified relationship called *'IfcRelAssociatesMaterial'*. Research from [34] proposes a translation of the EXPRESS schema to ifcOWL, i.e. an ontological representation of IFC aiming to achieve improved functionalities and benefitting from linked data concepts. In this case, modeling of material and assignment to building elements uses a similar method, but modeling languages are different. Limitations in terms of extendibility, reasoning, vocabulary, and inference are distinct [39].

To address these issues, various approaches were proposed to reduce these limitations of ifcOWL and to simplify the ontological representation. Some of them are *simpleBIM* [36], *ifcWOD* [39], and *BimSPARQL* [40]. The above-introduced approaches (*ifcWOD, simpleBIM, BimSPARQL*) have the potential to improve the execution of queries. But for real industrial applications, it is necessary to go with a more generic approach using modular ontologies and RDF graphs [26]. The Digital Construction Building Material (DICBM) ontology proposed in this paper is a modular ontology and represents material data effectively.

2.2 Overview of the Building Material Ontology

DICBM contains the required set of terminological axioms and vocabulary to represent construction details and material data along with the analytical parameters for building elements.

Figure 1 provides an overview of classes and object properties defined in DICBM. The prefix and namespace used to refer the material ontology shown below.

@*PREFIX dicbm:* <https://w3id.org/digitalconstruction/BuildingMaterials#>.

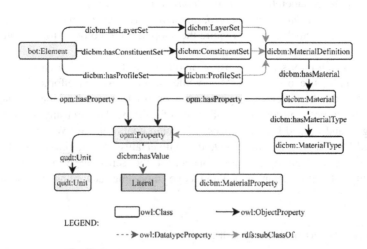

Fig. 1. Overview of building material ontology

2.3 Integration of External Ontology Concepts and Roles

The concept of integration of external ontologies is a process of adoption of other ontologies or ontology concepts within the development of new ontologies [41]. In DICBM, this integration process is carried out for the representation of material definition concepts, properties, and its units. Some information about objects and parameters are already modeled in existing AEC-domain specific or generic ontologies.

Instead of redefining these concepts in DICBM, the classes and object properties from the existing ontologies BOT [35], OPM [37], and QUDT[7] are adopted. This will also allow for alignment between different ontologies, domains and enable extended modelling capabilities and usage of DICBM. The Class *bot:Element* is defined in the DICBM ontology to represent a different kind of building element designed and managed by stakeholders from different engineering disciplines. Similarly, the class *bot:Zone* is used to represent the spatial elements designed by architects, used by tenants, and managed by the owners of the building. The Object Property (OP) *bot: adjacentElement* [35] is used to link the spatial elements with an element that shares part of its boundary.

The Class *opm:Property* [37] is defined to describe the properties of an object in DICBM. The object property *opm:hasProperty* [37] is used in DICBM to maintain properties of the object. This property is treated as the main object property and all other defined properties in DICBM are considered as sub-properties of *opm: hasProperty*. Thus, descriptive information which satisfies the information requirements of different collaborators can be easily linked to building elements and zones. Examples are technical properties, prices, comfort parameters, etc. The class *qudt:Unit* is integrated with DICBM to represent the unit for the material properties and object properties. The OP *qudt:Unit* is used to enable a relationship between *qudt:Unit* and the properties of an element.

2.4 Material Definition

The material data needs to be assigned to building elements on different levels [23]. For example, in IFC material properties are assigned to layer, profile, and constituent. This feature is defined explicitly by grouping using the concept called MaterialDefinition in DICBM. A concept to represent material related information that has material related properties is *dicbm:MaterialDefinition*. Material Definition closely represents the entity IfcMaterialDefinition in IFC. The *dicbm:MaterialDefinition* has six subclasses, which are *dicbm:LayerSet, dicbm:ConstituentSet, dicbm:ProfileSet, dicbm:Layer, dicbm: Constituent,* and *dicbm:Profile*.

Building elements (e.g. wall, roof, etc.) may consist of one or more layers. These layers' information for a specific building element is grouped using the LayerSet concept of the IFC schema. This grouping mechanism automatically separates the repetitive definition of similar layer information in different parts. Furthermore, the concept of LayerSet enables the definition of one single set for a distinct layer to n number of walls (or other elements) based on its category. Additionally, the relative

---

[7] http://www.qudt.org/2.1/catalog/qudt-catalog.html.

positioning of individual layers can be expressed. The object property *dicbm: hasLayerSet* is used to link the element with its layer set. The range of the Object Property (OP) *dicbm:hasLayerSet* is defined explicitly as *dicbm:LayerSet*.

The *dicbm:Layer* is the concept to represent a layer of an element. A layer may be inner or outer layer of a building element based on its placement in the structure. To distinguish between the inner and outer layer of the element, OP *dicbm:InnerLayer, dicbm:OuterLayer* is used to link the source nodes of the element, layer set, and layer. The property chain axioms are defined for *dicbm:hasLayer* to assign the layer to the element. The range of the *dicbm:hasLayer is dicbm:Layer*. The property axiom of *dicbm:hasLayer* is shown in the Fig. 2.

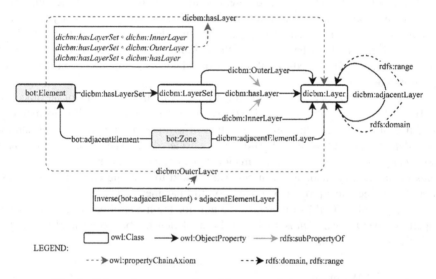

Fig. 2. Schematic representation of layer association with its element

The order and position of layers in the building element is also considered in DICBM. The role called adjacent layer is introduced, which relates layers to each other. This role was inspired by an object property adjacent element in the BOT [35] ontology. Figure 2 shows the link between (building) elements, layer set, and constituent layers.

The OP *dicbm:adjacentLayer* is a symmetric property. To define the layer arrangement explicitly, layer position is described by linking with its adjacent elements. The OP *dicbm:adjacentElementLayer* links topological elements to the element layer sharing its boundary. The outer layer of the wall is explicitly defined by using the property chain axioms. The *dicbm:OuterLayer* is the OP to link a building element to its outer layer.

2.5   Material, Material Type, and Material Property

The *dicbm:Material* is a concept to represent the material. Material type, associated products, properties exist in the context of material data. Material is linked with its objects using the role *dicbm:hasMaterial*. For example, the material of the layer is described as *dicbm:hasMaterial(dicbm:Layer, dicbm:Material)* by using functional syntax. A *dicbm:hasMaterial* is an *owl:ObjectProperty* and range is the concept *dicbm: Material*.

Material property is a characteristic of a material. It holds the data related to different properties of a material. A class *dicbm:MaterialProperty* is defined in the DICBM ontology and it is considered as a subclass of *opm:Property*. This concept represents a characteristic of a material.

2.6   Data Properties in DICBM

Data property *dicbm:Name* is modeled in DICBM to represent the name of objects and material properties. The *dicbm:hasRerence* is a data property used to link property with its source. Figure 3 shows the data properties defined in the DICBM ontology. Value describes the simple, defined, or measured quantity of the property of an object.

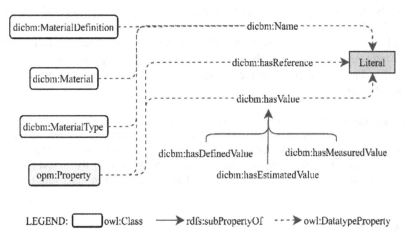

Fig. 3. Data properties in the ontology schema

Stakeholders involved in data acquisition (e.g. surveyors) create measured values and model creation before a renovation starts. Defined values are used by stakeholders from the engineering disciplines. The definition is the outcome of dimensioning activities for which simulations are heavily used. Defined values are used by engineers employed by construction companies. Estimated values are used by quantity surveyors before the procurement activities will be completed.

As one can see, the proposed ontology supports effective data sharing in collaborative networks in the AEC-domain during renovation activities, since property values can be clearly distinguished according to authenticated sources, calculated values, and values from measurement processes.

3   Conclusions

Building material data are important information for the performance evaluation of buildings, including energy simulations, environmental impact studies, structural analysis, or the dimensioning of building elements [42]. Numerous stakeholders must share their expertise during this evaluation process since it is necessary to evaluate building performance holistically, i.e. from a societal, economic, and ecological perspective. In order to support seamless, effective information sharing between different digital building models created by different experts, it is necessary to capture material information of building elements in a generic, easily accessible, transparent, and flexible way. Re-formatting of data, labour-intensive search, and selection activities must be eliminated.

Thus, the Linked Data concept in combination with semantic modelling is one possible solution to address these requirements. Therefore, the authors presented in this paper a semantic model that can capture building material specifications and link those to building elements (layers) and additionally link building elements to zones, which are finally occupied by tenants. The material information data specified and stored using DICBM can be linked to different models within a Common Data Environment. DICBM can be used in combination with a further product, quantity, and property-related information. Therefore, the authors argue that the proposed approach has the potential to become an enabling technology to support collaborative networks in the AEC&FM-sector.

Acknowledgments. This research is carried out as a part of the BIM4EEB project (BIM based fast toolkit for the Efficient rEnovation of Buildings). The BIM4EEB project is supported and funded by the European Union's Horizon 2020 research and innovation program. We would like to show our gratitude to the European Commission for the support of the BIM4EEB project. Finally, we would like to thank all partners in the BIM4EEB project for their valuable inputs.

References

1. Pandey, K.K.: for. In: Munshi, U.M., Verma, N. (eds.) Data Science Landscape. SBD, vol. 38, pp. 151–164. Springer, Singapore (2018). https://doi.org/10.1007/978-981-10-7515-5_11
2. Jiang, J., Chen, J.: Contractual collaboration systems of mega complex construction project organizations. In: ICCREM 2014: Smart Construction and Management in the Context of New Technology (2014)
3. Camarinha-Matos, L.M., Afsarmanesh, H.: Collaborative networks in industry and services: research scope and challenges. IFAC Proc. Vol. **40**, 33–42 (2007)
4. Camarinha-Matos, L.M., Afsarmanesh, H.: Collaborative networks. In: Wang, K., Kovacs, G.L., Wozny, M., Fang, M. (eds.) PROLAMAT 2006. IIFIP, vol. 207, pp. 26–40. Springer, Boston, MA (2006). https://doi.org/10.1007/0-387-34403-9_4

5. Camarinha-Matos, L.M., Afsarmanesh, H.: Classes of collaborative networks. In: IT Outsourcing: Concepts, Methodologies, Tools, and Applications, pp. 364–370. IGI Global (2009)
6. Alreshidi, E., Mourshed, M., Rezgui, Y.: Factors for effective BIM governance. J. Build. Eng. **10**, 89–101 (2017)
7. Sousa, C., Pereira, C.: Sharing through collaborative spaces: enhancing collaborative networks interoperability. In: Camarinha-Matos, L.M., Afsarmanesh, H. (eds.) PRO-VE 2014. IAICT, vol. 434, pp. 481–488. Springer, Heidelberg (2014). https://doi.org/10.1007/978-3-662-44745-1_48
8. BIM4EEB: D2.1 Definition of relevant activities and involved stakeholders in actual and efficient renovation processes (2019). https://www.bim4eeb-project.eu/reports.html
9. Karlapudi, J., Shetty, S.: A methodology to determine and classify data sharing requirements between OpenBIM models and energy simulation models. In: 31. Forum Bauinformatik, Berlin (2019)
10. Yin, H., Stack, P., Menzel, K.: Decision support for building renovation strategies. In: Proceedings of the ASCE-Congress in Computing in Civil Engineering, pp. 834–841 (2011)
11. Cahill, B., Menzel, K., Flynn, D.: BIM as a centre piece for optimised building operation. In: eWork and eBusiness in Architecture, Engineering and Construction, pp. 549–555 (2012)
12. Keller, M., Menzel, K., Scherer, R.J.: Toward a meta-model for collaborative construction project management. In: Proceedings of the Working Conference on Virtual Enterprises, pp. 361–368 (2005)
13. Lilis, G.N., Giannakis, G.I., Rovas, D.V.: Automatic generation of second-level space boundary topology from IFC geometry inputs. Autom. Constr. **76**, 108–124 (2017)
14. Keller, M., Katranuschkov, P., Menzel, K.: Modelling collaborative processes for virtual organisations in the building industry. In: eWork and eBusiness in Architecture, Engineering and Construction, pp. 417–431. Balkema Publishers (2004)
15. Keller, M., Scherer, R.J., Menzel, K., Theling, T.: Support of collaborative business process networks in AEC. IT-Con J. **11**, 449–465 (2006)
16. Karlapudi, J., Menzel, K.: Analysis on automatic generation of BEPS models from BIM model. In: 8th Conference of IBPSA Proceedings of BauSIM 2020, Austria (2020)
17. Chuck, E., Paul, T., Rafael, S., Kathleen, L.: BIM Handbook: A Guide to Building Information Modeling for Owners, Managers, Designers, Engineers and Contractors. Wiley (2011)
18. Bilal, S.: Building information modelling framework: a research and delivery foundation for industry. Autom. Constr. **14**(1), 15–32 (2009)
19. BSI: PAS 1192-2:2013: Specification for information management for the capital/delivery phase of construction projects using building information modelling. BSI Standards Limited (2013)
20. ISO: ISO 29481-1: 2016 (E): Building Information Modeling—Information Delivery Manual—Part 1: Methodology and Format. ISO, Geneva, Switzerland (2016)
21. ISO: EN ISO 19650-1:2018: Organization and digitization of information about, BSI Standards Limited (2018)
22. Nityantoro, E., Scherer, R.J.: Ontology supported recombination of multi-models. In: Camarinha-Matos, L.M., Scherer, R.J. (eds.) PRO-VE 2013. IAICT, vol. 408, pp. 257–264. Springer, Heidelberg (2013). https://doi.org/10.1007/978-3-642-40543-3_28
23. ISO.: ISO 16739: 2013–Industry Foundation Classes (IFC) for data sharing in the construction and facility management industries (2013)
24. Preidel C., Borrmann A., Oberender C., Tretheway M.: Seamless Integration of Common Data Environment Access into BIM (2015)

25. Beetz, J., Van Leeuwen, J., De Vries, B.: IfcOWL: A case of transforming EXPRESS schemas into ontologies. Ai Edam. **23**, 89–101 (2009)
26. Bonduel M., Oraskari J., Pauwels P., Vergauwen M., Klein R.: The IFC to linked building data converter-current status. In: 6th Linked Data in Architecture and Construction Workshop, vol. 2159, pp. 34–43 (2018)
27. Berners-Lee, T., Hendler, J., Lassila, O.: The semantic web. Scientific american, pp. 34–43 (2001)
28. Shadbolt, N., Berners-Lee, T., Hall, W.: The semantic web revisited. IEEE Intell. Syst. **21** (3), 96–101 (2006)
29. Camarinha-Matos, L.M., Afsarmanesh, H.: Collaborative networks: a new scientific. J. Intell. Manuf. **16**, 439–452 (2005)
30. Spoladore, D.: Ontology-based decision support systems for health data management to support collaboration in ambient assisted living and work reintegration. In: Camarinha-Matos, Luis M., Afsarmanesh, H., Fornasiero, R. (eds.) PRO-VE 2017. IAICT, vol. 506, pp. 341–352. Springer, Cham (2017). https://doi.org/10.1007/978-3-319-65151-4_32
31. Pagoropoulos, A., Andersen, J.A.B., Kjær, L.L., Maier, A., McAloone, T.C.: Building an ontology of product/service-systems: using a maritime case study to elicit classifications and characteristics. In: Camarinha-Matos, L.M., Afsarmanesh, H. (eds.) PRO-VE 2014. IAICT, vol. 434, pp. 119–126. Springer, Heidelberg (2014). https://doi.org/10.1007/978-3-662-44745-1_11
32. Antonelli, D., Bruno, G.: Ontology-Based Framework to Design a Collaborative Human-Robotic Workcell. In: Camarinha-Matos, Luis M., Afsarmanesh, H., Fornasiero, R. (eds.) PRO-VE 2017. IAICT, vol. 506, pp. 167–174. Springer, Cham (2017). https://doi.org/10.1007/978-3-319-65151-4_16
33. Rachman, A., Chandima Ratnayake, R.M.: Ontology-based semantic modeling for automated identification of damage mechanisms in process plants. In: Camarinha-Matos, Luis M., Afsarmanesh, H., Rezgui, Y. (eds.) PRO-VE 2018. IAICT, vol. 534, pp. 457–466. Springer, Cham (2018). https://doi.org/10.1007/978-3-319-99127-6_39
34. Pauwels, P., Terkaj, W.: EXPRESS to OWL for construction industry: towards a recommendable and usable ifcOWL ontology. Autom. Constr. **63**, 100–133 (2016)
35. Rasmussen, M.H., Pauwels, P., Lefrançois, M., Schneider, G.F.: Building topology ontology. W3C Draft Community Group Report (2019)
36. Pauwels, P., Roxin, A.: SimpleBIM: from full ifcOWL graphs to simplified building graphs. In: Proceedings of the 11th ECPPM, pp. 11–18 (2016)
37. Rasmussen, M.H., Lefrançois, M., Pauwels, P., Hviid, C.A., Karlshøj, J.: Managing interrelated project information in AEC knowledge graphs. Autom. Constr. **108**, 102956 (2019)
38. Karlapudi, J., Menzel, K., Törmä, S., Hryshchenko, A., Valluru, P.: Enhancement of BIM data representation in product-process modelling for building renovation. In: Proceedings of 17th IFIP International Conference on Product Lifecycle Management. 5–8 July, Rapperswil, Switzerland (2020)
39. De Farias, T.M., Roxin, A., Nicolle, C.: IfcWoD, semantically adapting IFC model relations into OWL properties (2015)
40. Zhang, C., Beetz, J., de Vries, B.: BimSPARQL: domain-specific functional SPARQL extensions for querying RDF building data. Semantic Web **9**, 1–27 (2018)
41. Sofia, P.H., Asuncion, G.-P., Joao, P.M.: Some issues on ontology integration. In: Proceedings of the IJCAI (1999)
42. Ahmed, A., Menzel, K., Ploennigs, J., Cahill, B.: Aspects of multi-dimensional building performance data management. In: Proceeding of EG-ICE, TU Berlin, Germany (2009)

Towards a Framework for Federated Interoperability to Implement an Automated Model Transformation

Mustapha Labreche[1(✉)], Aurélie Montarnal[1], Sébastien Truptil[1],
Xavier Lorca[1], Sébastien Weill[2], and Jean-Pièrre Adi[2]

[1] IMT Mines Albi, 20 Chemin de La Teulière, 81000 Albi, France
{Mustapha.Labreche,Aurelie.Montarnal,
Xavier.Lorca}@mines-albi.fr, Sebastien.Truptil@cea.fr
[2] Sylob, 7 Rue Marcel Dassault, 81990 Cambon, France
Sebastien.Weill@forterro.com, jpa@sylob.com

Abstract. In order to adapt to changes in industrial world (customers and markets) and to competition, to create economic or strategic partnerships with external players or simply to integrate a connector to exchange information between the various services and software of a company, it is essential to have the necessary software tools (by development or deployment) that guarantee effective communication between the various parties, which are often heterogeneous and not known in advance, and overcome certain difficulties such as the multiplicity of information sources and the quality of the data.

In such a context, the exchange or migration of data is a critical step. In order to facilitate the exchange, our approach aims at implementing federated interoperability with automated model transformation, supported by an interoperability evaluation, in order to ensure data retention despite the unforeseen uses (for example, some fields divert or mislabel) and to ensure their consistency during the transformation.

Keywords: Model-driven engineering · Automatic transformation · Federated interoperability · Interoperability evaluation

1 Introduction

Collaborative networks (CN) represent a set of heterogeneous organizations with different services, skills and systems, but who share a common interest [1]. In this context, companies are increasingly turning towards collaborations with an opportunistic dynamic of creation and dismantling in order to benefit from new know-how and to propose new offers [2]. For this, in order to communicate between partners in a CN, it is necessary to be able to quickly and efficiently collaborate. So, a way to translate data on the fly is needed to ensure smooth collaborative workflows.

This observation has repercussions on information systems and more particularly on data exchange. Indeed, information systems must be able to exchange and use information regardless of the data format without requiring laborious human actions.

L. M. Camarinha-Matos et al. (Eds.): PRO-VE 2020, IFIP AICT 598, pp. 143–152, 2020.
https://doi.org/10.1007/978-3-030-62412-5_12

Thus, the issue of interoperability of systems is defined by [3] as «The ability of two or more systems and components to exchange and reuse the information».

However, the implementation of interoperability is not trivial because of the presence of barriers: conceptual barriers (semantic and syntactic incompatibility of information), technological barriers (incompatibility of platforms or architectures), and organizational barriers (incompatibility of structures and management techniques) [4]. Establishing interoperability is therefore about removing barriers, and to this end there are three fundamental approaches to achieving interoperability [4]:

- Integrated approach: the different parties use a common format for the information accepted by all parties.
- Unified approach: the parties define a common format and must then translate their data into the common template before exchanging it.
- Federated approach: in this approach there is no common format. To establish interoperability, the parties must adapt on-the-fly and no party imposes any model or working method and must translate the data received.

The paper proposes an approach to facilitate the exchange or transfer and integration of data from one system to another with different data formats. Therefore, trying a manual solution is error-prone and time-consuming, and is difficult to reproduce in another context (due to the specific rules imposed). The contribution of the paper is a methodology for implementing federated interoperability "on-the-fly" through an automated model transformation, supported by a three-level interoperability assessment model, which will have to answer the following questions:

1. How to ensure federated interoperability?

- How to manage the heterogeneity of systems?
- How to ensure the coherence of transformed data?

2. What are the qualitative or quantitative evaluation criteria for interoperability?

2   Related Works and Technical Recall

Interoperability is a prerequisite to reduce the difficulty of collaboration. The approach presented in the paper deals with federated interoperability with an emphasis on the heterogeneity of information systems. This section will provide an overview of research activities in this field and will outline some models for interoperability assessment, frameworks for developing interoperability, and some methodologies to solving complex interoperability problems [5]:

2.1   Interoperability Assessment

In order to be able to improve interoperability, it is important to be able to evaluate it. For a company, the evaluation will allow it to know its strengths and weaknesses for a partnership with other companies [5]. Interoperability can be measured qualitatively or quantitatively and assessed on three levels [6]: (1) the maturity assessment which aims to evaluate the company's capacity to adapt to possible partnerships, (2) the compatibility assessment which allows to calculate the degree of compatibility between two systems and (3) the performance assessment which evaluates the performances during the partnership.

There are several approaches in the literature, including Level of Information System Interoperability (LISI) [7] which is one of the first maturity models for assessing interoperability between different information systems (Organizational Interoperability Maturity Model (OIMM) extends this approach by including organizational interoperability [8]). Other approaches consider only the assessment of semantic interoperability [9] or conceptual interoperability [10]. While others cover the three interoperability barriers [11] or the three levels of assessment [12].

2.2 Interoperability Frameworks

Interoperability Development for Enterprise Application and Software (IDEAS) [12] is a Framework that proposes to establish interoperability based on three layers: Business, Knowledge and Information and Communications Technology (ICT) by considering the semantic dimension on each of the layers and takes into account other qualitative attributes (security, performance, portability ...) in order to develop a common understanding.

European Interoperability Framework (EIF) [13] proposes a framework that identifies a set of standards and recommendations that guide the way European public services cooperate online by defining three types of interoperability: organizational, semantic and technical.

INTEROP-NoE [14] defines a framework for delivering interoperability solutions within an enterprise based on two dimensions: interoperability barriers and interoperability levels. The barriers (organizational, conceptual and technological) relate to the problems that block the development of interoperability and the levels (business, processes, services and data) represent the different views where interoperability can be implemented. This framework has become a standard (ISO 11354-1) for which several works on interoperability have been based and presented in the literature [15].

2.3 Interoperability Methodology

A methodology is built to analyze and design a system to solve complex problems [5]. Developing a methodology for enterprise interoperability involves efficiently designing, structuring, aligning and implementing a set of methods, models and approaches from several scientific fields [16] to overcome the different barriers and achieve interoperability at each level. In that way, model-driven (MD) approaches are frequently used.

Model-Driven Engineering (MDE) is a high-level abstraction approach that applies the benefits of modeling to software engineering activities and where the notion of *model* is a central concept for which there is no universal definition [17]. In [18] «A Model is a description of a system, where 'system' may include not only software and hardware but organizations and processes. A model is represented by a set of elements that are structurally defined by properties and interrelated by relationships. Thus, the set of model elements conforms to the complete representation of the modeled concerns, a model is said to conform to a *metamodel* that defines both aspects of the model, namely syntax and semantics [19].

A metamodel is therefore an explicit model of the elements and rules needed to build specific models, but like the definition of a model, there are a variety of definitions of metamodel. We can then say that if a metamodel is a model of a *modeling language*, there must be a metamodel describing the metamodel and so on [20].

Several concepts based on MDE have emerged:

– Model-Driven Reverse Engineering (MDRE): allows the obtaining and reuse of representations (e.g. source code or configuration file from legacy system).
– Model-Driven Interoperability (MDI): it aims at defining solutions to achieve interoperability between two or more systems by applying MD techniques.

These concepts use model transformation which aims to make models usable which consists in ensuring the passage from one model to another (from a source model to a target model) sharing the same concepts and using transformation rules implemented by a transformation language [21].

In general, model transformation approaches fall into three categories [22]: (1) model-to-text (M2T) often used in MDRE to transform one or more source models to generate scripts, configuration or documentation files, (2) text-to-model (T2M) which takes a text format as input and transforms it into one or more models, (3) model-to-model (M2M) which transforms one or more source models (conforming to a source metamodel) to one or more target models (conforming to a target metamodel).

Various methodologies using these approaches and their concepts are proposed:

HLA Federated Interoperability Framework [23] is one of the most popular methodology for designing complex systems. It is a methodology for the interoperability of heterogeneous information systems and it synchronizes a high-level architecture with the model-driven approach extended to the Web service.

[24] Interoperability Systems Integration and Re-Engineering (IRIS) is a structured approach that defines the tools to be used in each phase of an enterprise interoperability project taking into account different interoperability views, such as Business, Process Management, Knowledge, Human Resources, ICT and Semantics.

Although each methodology has its advantages and provides good theoretical insights, most of them seem to lack concrete application cases. Moreover, to our knowledge, it appears that no methodology or framework is able to address the problem of federated interoperability on the fly between heterogenous systems. Therefore, the use of MD approaches and graph theory are promising way to address this type of problem. Indeed, model-driven approaches allow to formalize and manipulate different levels of abstraction within the framework of federated interoperability through the use of meta-models and their instances in the form of models, and graph theory allows to represent heterogenous systems on the fly and to provide algorithms for evaluating interoperability. In the following section, this combination approach is discussed in detail.

3 Towards an Approach of Representation and Exploitation by Graphs

The paper presents a global approach for establishing and evaluating federated interoperability between heterogeneous systems using graph theory. Indeed, reasoning on graphs to make transformations, detect conflicts, model relationships, find or compute optimized indicators is interesting since they are on the one hand a mathematical modeling tool presenting a visual aspect of meta-models and their related instances for analysis and on the other hand a tool for evaluating the different connections between data, models, meta-models and heterogeneous systems.

Modeling in the form of graphs is obtained by transforming the elements of a model into a set of nodes and the various links between the elements by edges. Then, the transformation from one graph to another representing the source and target models is done by applying a sequence of conversion and mapping rules based on semantics. Thus, the combination of model transformation and graph transformation technics is beneficial since the former is very practical and the latter is very expressive. The details of the approach will be described in the next sections along 3 stages: (i) the database exploration allows discovering the source and target data models (frequently needed as databases tend to evolve overtime and gradually lose their coherency); then, (ii) the metamodel and model representation as graph can be achieved; finally, (iii) a matching analysis helps define the rules that will be used for the transformation of a source database to the target expected database structure.

3.1 Database Exploration and Model Analysis

This step starts with moving from the database to the models, then in discovering and understanding the model constructed by analyzing the structure in order to identify the components of the system and/or to construct the relationships between these components by creating a representation at a higher level of abstraction.

As an example, the case of two relational databases extracted from the system but deployed in two different software versions. In the case of another type of data, the process remains unchanged, only the metamodels to which the models conform are modified.

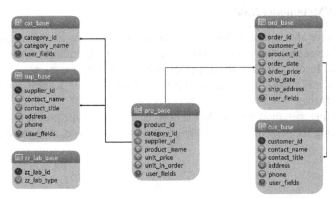

Fig. 1. An example of relational database represented by database scheme (Color figure online)

3.1.1   Database Representation

In a relational database the information is organized in the form of tables (also called relations) where each table is composed of one or more rows representing the records (tuples) and one or more columns listing the attributes that relate to a record.

A key is an attribute (or group of attributes) that uniquely identifies a row in a table. A key is said to be primary and is unique if one of the keys specifies the sequence of data records in the table.

Finally, the relationship between tables can be defined using foreign keys, which is simply a primary key of another table and which also allows correlation between different tables in a database.

An example of such database schema is presented in the Fig. 1, where each table has a set of attributes, a primary key (PK) (red icons) and foreign key(s) (FK) (yellow icons). Some tables have attributes denoted "user_fields" (blue icons) and other tables are prefixed with "zz_.... " which are specific attributes and tables created for customizable use, i.e., created for a specific need. However, they are sometimes diverted from their default function.

3.1.2   Model Analyses

Once the models are built, the next step would be to explore them. In our study this consists of analyzing the input and output models in order to identify and establish relationships at two levels: at the data model level and then at the data level. The linking can be guided by the construction of a weaving model [25] that allows capturing different types of links (semantics, composition, interoperability, data integration, traceability and ontological alignment) [26].

Another step is carried out in order to manage the various conflicts generated by the different information representations between model elements (hierarchization of the same information, aggregation, data types, etc.) [27]. Also, some links can be created and added manually by experts in the field.

At the end of this step, the constructed links allow a better understanding of the heterogeneous parts by exploiting the information specific to each system and between systems. This analysis can be translated into configurations that induce semi-automation/automation of the transformation process.

3.2   Model/Metamodel Modeling

In order to give the approach leverage to adapt to unknown models/metamodels in advance, it is essential to use a solution that allows on-the-fly model transformations to be generated. In other words, the approach must be able to represent different information and apply algorithms in a generic way. This dynamic feature can be offered using graph theory.

To modeling metamodels/models, the class of attributed type graphs is used since it offers modeling formalisms for the different structures (attribute, relation, class, table).

This graph class is characterized by two parts:

1. a part which describes the graph: composed of nodes (graph node) representing tables and edges (graph edge) representing the links between these tables (for example: inheritance or primary keys) and
2. a data description part: composed of nodes (data nodes) representing the data types (string, date…) and edges (node attribute edge) linking the nodes of the graph to the data nodes.

Figure 2 describes simple example of transforming three tables into a graph (Fig. 3). The tables are characterized by and keys (primary and foreign), attributes each having a type (string, date, int,…). The elements of the graph are described in Fig. 4.

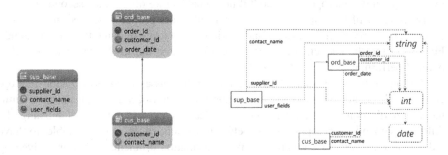

Fig. 2. A simple example of relational database

Fig. 3. Graph representing the database

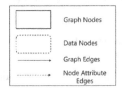

Fig. 4. The description of the different elements of the graph

3.3 Matching and Transformation

Matching is a process that aims to identify and discover correspondences between two or more agents (documents, images, systems…). Matching algorithms are used in several domains and are based on several principles (syntactic, semantic, numerical), which is why various solutions and implementation policies are proposed [28]. The matching ensures a connection (if established) between the agents by means of transformation rules. Thus, matching ensures the interoperability of information systems.

In order to build transformation rules, it is necessary to create a mapping (configuration) between the elements of the metamodels. To do so, we must compute the similarity between the elements (nodes and edges) of the two corresponding graphs using semantic-based matching techniques and algorithms that perform on the graphs.

Once the mapping is done, the final transformation rules are created and defined with the help of the preliminary analysis performed beforehand and some detection measures predefined by experts in the field.

3.4   Interoperability Assessment

From a collaborative perspective, it is important to measure the capacity of collaboration between enterprises by assessing continuously interoperability of (heterogeneous) systems, architectures and services [14] and detect potential problems.

Assessing interoperability will be on three levels: for the first level the objective is to calculate the ability of systems to communicate or exchange and to detect potential problems (can we interoperate or not? If not, what can we do?). In the second level, the measurement will be done continuously on indicators probably defined and fixed in order to detect potential blockages and barriers and try to overcome them (if possible). Finally, in the third level, the objective is to measure the final interoperability (has optimal performance been achieved?)

An approach to assessing interoperability is the assessment of semantic interoperability. The matching approach allows the integration of various measures of similarity and dissimilarity between graphs. Indeed, since we aim at establishing the different semantic correspondences between models, it is quite possible to have redundant, erroneous or incomprehensible information problems which are solved by ontology-based approaches [5]. Calculations using functions based on linguistic and structural similarity [15] and the accuracy or relevance (business aspect) of the information are then proposed as quantitative and qualitative evaluation criteria, that can be in turn used as performance and validation criteria of the proposed methodology.

4   Conclusion and Future Work

The aim of this work is to show that the combined adoption of concepts from graph theory, Model-driven engineering and Model-driven reverse engineering allows both facilitating and establishing on-the-fly federated interoperability and makes the implementation of evaluation mechanisms easier and more uniform between heterogeneous systems.

Such an approach is still in progress and is in development within the framework of a real case study of database transformation relating to the same system, but deployed in two different software versions, with data models that are also different and more or less "customized" by customers. The next steps of the research will thus focus on the implementation of the proposed methodology and its validation thanks to the interoperability assessment criteria.

Finally, this framework can be adapted and applied in the context of a software upgrade, technical migration or implementation of connectors to ensure communication with third-party services.

Acknowledgement. This work is funded by the company Forterro Sylob, which will bring in real case studies.

References

1. Camarinha-Matos, L.M., Fornasiero, R., Afsarmanesh, H.: Collaborative networks as a core enabler of Industry 4.0. In: Camarinha-Matos, L.M., Afsarmanesh, H., Fornasiero, R. (eds.) PRO-VE 2017. IAICT, vol. 506, pp. 3–17. Springer, Cham (2017). https://doi.org/10.1007/978-3-319-65151-4_1
2. Dodgson, M.: Technological Collaboration in Industry: Strategy, Policy and Internationalization in Innovation, vol. 11. Routledge (2018)
3. Standard Computer Dictionary: A Compilation of IEEE Standard Computer Glossaries. IEEE (1990)
4. Chen, D., Doumeingts, G., Vernadat, F.: Architectures for enterprise integration and interoperability: past, present and future. Comput. Ind. **59**(7), 647–659 (2008)
5. Fortineau, V., Paviot, T., Lamouri, S.: Improving the interoperability of industrial information systems with description logic-based models—the state of the art. Comput. Ind. **64**(4), 363–375 (2013)
6. Leal, G.D.S.S., Guédria, W., Panetto, H.: Interoperability assessment: a systematic literature review. Comput. Ind. **106**, 111–132 (2019)
7. DoD, U.S: C4ISR Architecture Working Group (AWG): C4ISR Architecture Framework Version 2.0, Washington DC, December 1997
8. Fewell, S., Clark, T.: Organisational Interoperability: Evaluation and Further Development of the OIM Model. Defence Science and Technology Organisation Edinburgh, Australia (2003)
9. Dibowski, H.: Semantic interoperability evaluation model for devices in automation systems. In: 22nd IEEE International Conference on Emerging Technologies and Factory Automation (ETFA), pp. 1–6. IEEE, September 2017
10. Tolk, A., Muguira, J.A.: The levels of conceptual interoperability model. In: Proceedings of the 2003 Fall Simulation Interoperability Workshop, vol. 7, pp. 1–11. Citeseer (2003)
11. Guédria, W., Naudet, Y., Chen, D.: Maturity model for enterprise interoperability. Enterp. Inf. Syst. **9**(1), 1–28 (2015)
12. IDEAS Consortium: IDEAS Project Deliverables (WP1-WP7). Public Reports (2003)
13. IDABC, Enterprise, and D. G. Industry: European interoperability Framework for pan-European e-government services. European Communities (2004)
14. Panetto, H., Scannapieco, M., Zelm, M.: INTEROP NoE: interoperability research for networked enterprises applications and software. In: Meersman, R., Tari, Z., Corsaro, A. (eds.) OTM 2004. LNCS, vol. 3292, pp. 866–882. Springer, Heidelberg (2004). https://doi.org/10.1007/978-3-540-30470-8_100
15. Neghab, A.P., Etienne, A., Kleiner, M., Roucoules, L.: Performance evaluation of collaboration in the design process: using interoperability measurement. Comput. Ind. **72**, 14–26 (2015)
16. Ensemble, C.: EISB Basic Elements Report. Envisioning, supporting and promoting future internet enterprise systems research through scientific collaboration (FP7-ICT-257548), deliverable D, vol. 2 (2011)
17. Da Silva, A.R.: Model-driven engineering: a survey supported by the unified conceptual model. Comput. Lang. Syst. Struct. **43**, 139–155 (2015)
18. UML, OMG: Unified Modeling Language (OMG UML). Version 2.5. 1 UML (2017)

19. Kleppe, A.: A language description is more than a metamodel. In: Fourth international workshop on software language engineering, vol. 1, megaplanet.org, October 2007
20. OMG: Meta object facility specification. OMG document formal, version 1.4 (2003)
21. Czarnecki, K., Helsen, S.: Feature-based survey of model transformation approaches. IBM Syst. J. **45**(3), 621–645 (2006)
22. Kahani, N., Bagherzadeh, M., Cordy, J.R., Dingel, J., Varró, D.: Survey and classification of model transformation tools. Softw. Syst. Model. **18**(4), 2361–2397 (2018). https://doi.org/10.1007/s10270-018-0665-6
23. Tu, Z., Zacharewicz, G., Chen, D.: Building a high-level architecture federated interoperable framework from legacy information systems. Int. J. Comput. Integr. Manuf. **27**(4), 313–332 (2014)
24. Chalmeta, R., Pazos, V.: A step-by-step methodology for enterprise interoperability projects. Enterp. Inf. Syst. **9**(4), 436–464 (2015)
25. Del Fabro, M.D., Bézivin, J., Valduriez, P.: Weaving models with the eclipse AMW plugin. In: Eclipse Modeling Symposium, Eclipse Summit Europe, vol. 2006, pp. 37–44, October 2006
26. Yie, A.: A non-invasive approach for evolving model transformation chains. Doctoral dissertation, Universidad de Los Andes (2011)
27. Kataria, P.: Resolving semantic conflicts through ontological layering. Doctoral dissertation, University of Westminster (2011)
28. Emmert-Streib, F., Dehmer, M., Shi, Y.: Fifty years of graph matching, network alignment and network comparison. Inf. Sci. **346**, 180–197 (2016)

Blockchain and Knowledge Graphs

Design Principles for Blockchain-Enabled Point Exchange Systems: An Action Design Research on a Polycentric Collaborative Network for Loyalty Programs

Jiaman Chen[1], Wenchi Ying[1]($\boxtimes$), Yonggui Chen[1], and Zupeng Wang[2]

[1] School of Economics and Management,
Beijing Jiaotong University, Beijing, China
{18241270,wcying,16241280}@bjtu.edu.cn
[2] Beijing HuaQi Communication Technology Co Ltd., Beijing, China
wzppatrick@189.cn

Abstract. In order to improve the customer experiences and explore value of loyalty programs, the operators are extending the scope of point redemption through creating a strategic polycentric collaborative network (CN) across multiple LPs. The point exchange is considered as a selectable approach. Because of the complexity, multicurrency and security risk of the CN, the existing process for exchanging points is cumbersome. However, the challenge of corresponding information system (IS) design received few attentions, which is critical for the success of the CN. We fill the gap by introducing blockchain technology and conducting an action design research (ADR). We partnered with a consulting corporate to design blockchain-enabled point exchange systems for the polycentric CN of loyalty programs. Our ADR study is in progress and the preliminary findings of new design principles may contribute to design theory in the blockchain and IS literature, and enrich both research and practice on LP.

Keywords: Loyalty programs · Blockchain · Polycentric collaborative network · Point exchange · SALP

1 Introduction

Loyalty programs (LP) as marketing strategies of corporates are leveraged to encourage customers to continue to shop at or use the services of corporates associated with each program [1] and most of LP offer rewards in the form of points that can be redeemed for goods and services [2]. There are two types of traditional LP including stand-alone loyalty programs (SALP) and multi-vendor loyalty program (MVLP) [3], both of which contain the role of LP operator who issues the points awarded for customers' purchase (see Fig. 1). Thereinto, SALP refers to that the operator is the vendor who provides customers with its own core products at the same time [4], such as airlines or telecom operators. By contrast, MVLP refers to that the operator has no its own products but accumulates other vendors who provide diverse products [5], such as

L. M. Camarinha-Matos et al. (Eds.): PRO-VE 2020, IFIP AICT 598, pp. 155–166, 2020.
https://doi.org/10.1007/978-3-030-62412-5_13

shopping malls or OTA (online travel agency). Traditionally, customers purchase the goods from vendors and collect points rewarded by the operators, as well as can redeem points for new goods or services from operators or vendors.

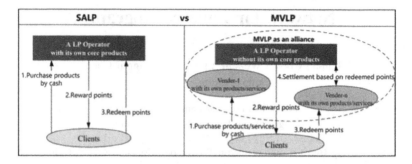

Fig. 1. The Structures of SALP and MVLP

In order to improve the customer experiences and further explore value of loyalty programs, the operators of SALP are expanding the scope of the points redemption, not only introduce more merchants as redeemers instead of vendors [4] (see Fig. 2) but also cooperate to create a strategic collaborative network (CN) of multiple SALPs [6] (see Fig. 3). Thus, the point exchange between SALPs is considered as a selectable approach to strategic CN of multiple SALPs. This is a typical polycentric CN anchored by a consortium of all the participant operators [4, 7].

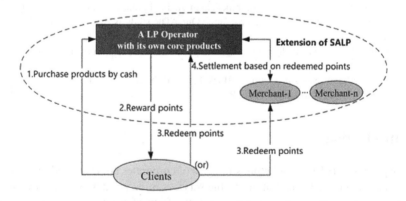

Fig. 2. The Extension of SALP

Because of the complexity, multicurrency and security risk of the collaboration, the existing process for exchanging points among SALPs is cumbersome [4]. However, the challenge of LP system design involving strategic CN received few attentions, which is critical for the success of the CN. Furthermore, the importance of blockchain enabling LP innovation received more attentions [8]. Thus, according to essentials and features

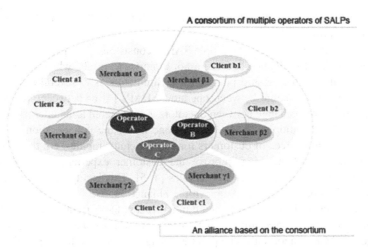

Fig. 3. The Polycentric Collaborative Network of multiple SALPs

of the polycentric CN of multiple SALPs, we introduce blockchain technology to address the challenge and research gap.

We partnered with a consulting corporate and conducted an action design research (ADR) as the method [9] to design a blockchain-enabled system for LP operators.

Thus, we derive our research question: *what are design principles of developing the blockchain-enabled point exchange system for a polycentric CN of multiple SALPs.*

We have completed preliminary findings and are proceeding in summarizing results of the first BIE cycle. In next steps, we will improve and refine the design principles and the system architecture design, and then intervene in development of a prototype of the system based on Oracle blockchain cloud. According to the preliminary findings, our ADR study may contribute to design theory in the blockchain and IS literature, and enrich both research and practice on loyalty programs.

2   Research Background

2.1   Loyalty Programs and a Polycentric CN Based on Point Exchange

Although LP are popularly adopted by the corporates, the customers have become disenchanted with accruing or using loyalty points [10]. The key reasons include a lack of diversity in the range of goods and services that can be redeemed and restrictions on where and when customers can use the points [5], especially in the context of SALP. Thus, the operators of SALP extend the scope of point redemption (see Fig. 2). Specifically, the operators introduce a range of merchants into the LP and consider the points as enterprise currency that can be redeemed across the merchants [4]. The merchants act as redeemers instead of original vendors, the points can be redeemed into vouchers or discount coupon, even into merchants' goods or services directly. Eventually, the settlement, based on the redeemed points, can be reached between the merchants and the operators. Therefore, much of the existing research has focused on

LP design elements, including the financial value of points, reward options, and the rules of redemption [11].

Recently, the strategic CN of multiple SALPs consisting of a operators' consortium and corresponding LP alliance become a hot topic (see Fig. 3), which is viewed as a new opportunity for partnership portfolio [6]. Simultaneously, several studies further examine the point exchange between operators/SLAPs [4] or between customers [5]. Thereinto, the point exchange between operators is considered as an alternative method to strategic CN of multiple SALPs. On the one hand, the collaboration, to a larger extent, can expand sources of customers for each operator rapidly. On the other hand, the corresponding alliance can improve the customer experience through a more diverse range of redeemed goods and services [4, 5]. This is a typical polycentric CN anchored by all operators participating in the alliance [4, 7].

However, due to the complexity and multicurrency, the current process of the point exchanged among SALPs results in that customers are reluctant to use the service of exchange [4]. More importantly, the point exchange system and the consortium model lead to the updating or upgrading of legacy information systems of all the operators, as well as the introduction of an intermediary to operate the exchange business. All above further increase the complexity and security risk of the consortium, which received few attentions in the research fields.

Simultaneously, Breugelmans et al [6] proposed the research agenda to advance LP research and practice, including the challenge of LP designs involving strategic alliance and consortium. Sun et al [8] emphasized the importance of blockchain enabling the LP innovation. According to the features of SALPs alliance as the polycentric CN and the potentials of blockchain in LPs, we introduced blockchain technology to meet the challenge and address the research gap.

2.2   Blockchain's Potentials on a Polycentric CN

Blockchain originates from bitcoin [12], and its applications are already contributing to the remodeling of traditional industries and business models in other areas [13]. Blockchain can be used as an electronic log and smart contracts for transactions and other relevant messages along the commercial activities by enabling secure transfer, reducing fraud, improving proof of tracking, enhancing transparency, reducing cost and increasing efficiency [14].

Wang et al [5] leveraged BubiChain to examine the point exchange activities among customers in the context of MVLP, and further mentioned that future research needed to explore the complicated relationships between blockchain-based LP design and LP engagement. Obviously, the blockchain-based design for the polycentric CN of multiple SALPs and corresponding alliance should be further explored, and the model of consortium (federated) blockchain architecture [13] are suitable for SALPs alliance. Moreover, the point exchange system is leveraged to connect each operator's legacy information systems. Kowalewski et al [4] emphasized that transferability rules, customer information security and unbiasedness of the system were essential. These demonstrate blockchain's potentials on realization of the point exchange system for polycentric CN of multiple SALPs, e.g. customer privacy preservation, unified rules of exchange rate and transferability, transparency and traceability of exchange transactions, as well as settlement based on the consistent ledgers [4, 8]. However, the development of the blockchain-enabled point exchange system for polycentric collaborative network of multiple SALPs has remained at the conceptual level and received few attentions, which is critical for the success of the CN.

2.3   A Socio-Technical Perspective Guiding the System Design

Information systems are the typical socio-technical systems [15]. Socio-technical perspective distinguishes the social entities structures and actors as well as the technical entities tasks and technologies [16, 21]. We adopted the socio-technical perspective as a theoretical lens [17] to guide the ADR. Specifically, structures are characterized by project organizations and institutional arrangements and embodied as the polycentric CN anchored by a consortium of all the participant operators. Actors are characterized by a shared culture and business context and embodied as core operators, complement merchants and all the clients in corresponding LP alliance. Technologies are characterized by technological tools or platforms and embodied as the architecture of blockchain-enabled point exchange systems. Tasks are characterized by the processes which are required to fulfill work or the delivery of functionalities.

Obviously, the system design is reflected in the organizational context related to shaping entities at the structure, actor, and technology levels, while actions at the three levels then lead to design principles at the task level.

3   Research Methodology

3.1   Action Design Research

This study is intended to develop a blockchain-enabled point exchange system for a polycentric CN of multiple SALPs. The design principles will constitute an IS design theory [18], which can reduce developers' uncertainty in implementation of relevant information systems (IS) and increase the chances of IS success [19]. ADR is a form of design research, which combines design science research with action research, and integrates the building and evaluation phases of the design process through organizational intervention [9]. ADR also differs from action research in which the design of an IS-related artifact is not necessarily required [20]. Sein et al [9] establish four phases for ADR: (1) problem formulation; (2) building, intervention and evaluation (the BIE cycles); (3) reflection and learning; (4) formalization of learning.

We chose ADR as the research method for two reasons. First, ADR treats an IS-related artifact as an ensemble artifact, which refers to a bundle of tools or systems (software and/or hardware) and treats the design process as a socio-technical construction that involves both technical and organizational factors [22]. Prior ADR studies have also shown that ADR method allows scholars to gain richer insights about the interactions of technology and organization [23]. Second, thanks to the incorporation of action research and organizational intervention, ADR is a dynamic process between building and evaluation rather than a stage-gate process, like that in other forms of design research. Therefore, ADR allows researchers to respond to unexpected consequences. For example, design research often assumes that problems identified at the beginning of the process will not change, but ADR allows the problems to be modified as the project goes.

3.2 Project Setting

The CU Group (a pseudonym) is the only Chinese telecom operator listed on the stock exchanges of New York, Hong Kong, and Shanghai. It has been a Fortune 500 company for many years and was ranked at No. 262 in Fortune 500 in 2019. The CU Group owns nearly 200 m customers and the business value underlying its LP system has reached the scale of billions of yuan (CNY).

However, the CU Group also encountered the challenges of traditional SALP, such as the lack of diversity of goods and services that can be redeemed. Despite the large scale of financial value in LP, the points for each customer are frequently regarded as 'sunk assets' and eventually expire, and the usage of corresponding funds toward points failed to get the expected effectiveness. Thus, the CU Group, on the one hand, introduced more merchants as point redeemers, on the other hand, sought for cooperation with other operators. Given the risk of peer competition, the CU Group decided to initiate a horizontal alliance with the operators from different business fields, such as airlines and banks. Thereinto, developing a blockchain-based point exchange system was top priority.

The HuaQi Corporate (HuaQi), headquartered in Beijing, had been rooted in consulting business of telecom field and extended its business scope into other fields in recent years. Based on the rich experiences on IT/IS planning and design, the HuaQi has been one of the CU Group certificated partners and undertaken many important consulting projects of the CU Group. However, the HuaQi, in the face of the challenges of emerging technologies, accepted the assignment and recognized difficulties of the tasks. Thus, the HuaQi invited our research team to participate in the design process, perceive the problems and provide the knowledge of theory and technological advances. The process of development includes several IT-dominant BIE cycles, a new set of design principles emerged during the BIE cycles.

4   Research in Progress and Preliminary Findings

Our ADR study is in progress and we have completed the tasks of the problem formulation phase and the first building-intervention-evaluation phase (the first BIE cycle). We are proceeding in the second BIE cycle.

4.1   ADR Problem Formulation

Our research in this phase formulates the problem, which should be an instance of a class of problems. The objectives, challenges and actions during problem formulation phase are depicted in Table 1.

Table 1. Objectives, Challenges and Actions during Problem Formulation Phase

Objectives	Challenges or Actions
Conceptualize the research opportunity	How to develop a point exchange system for a loyalty-program alliance?
Formulate initial research questions	What are design principles of developing the blockchain-enabled point exchange system for a polycentric CN of multiple SALPs?
Cast the problem as an instance of a class of problems	(1) Unified process and security of exchange transferability (2) Transaction traceability and privacy preservation without intermediary (3) Settlement based on consistent rules
Identify contributing theoretical bases and prior technology advances	(1) Originally expected contributions: We focused on leveraging blockchain to manage the whole process of point exchange among operators' systems (2) Unexpected Challenges: Leveraging blockchain to manage the whole process caused that the legacy systems must be upgraded a lot and cost a lot (3) Shifted expected contributions: we derived two basic principles–minimum modification for legacy systems and technology hybridization of blockchain and conventional technologies–to guide new design actions

4.2   First BIE Cycle: Preliminary Design Principles and System Architecture

We originally leveraged blockchain to manage the whole process of point exchange among operators' systems. However, the solution was not accepted by the operators, as an expert of the HuaQi mentioned, "The original solution showed that the legacy systems must be upgraded a lot and cost a lot".

Thus, we analyzed the business process among multiple SALPs again (see Fig. 4) and summarized three core tasks for the system design: 1) Unified process and security of exchange transferability, 2) Transaction traceability and privacy preservation without intermediary, 3) Settlement based on consistent rules.

Simultaneously, we adopted a socio-technical perspective on structure, actors and technologies to identify the design context of polycentric CN of multiple SALPs, and derived two basic principles – minimum modification for legacy systems and technology hybridization of blockchain and conventional technologies, which received recognition of both the HuaQi and the CU Group. Thus, we combined the core tasks and the two basic principles to contribute to the six concrete design principles (see Table 2).

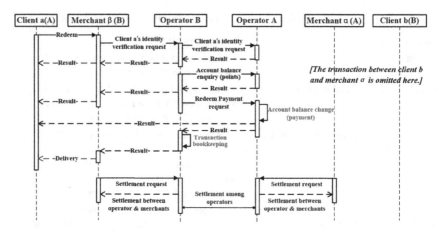

Fig. 4. Business Process Analysis on point exchange among multiple SALPs

Table 2. Preliminary Design Principles (DPs) for a BC-enabled Point Exchange System of Polycentric CN

Basic Principles	Core Tasks		
	Unified process and security of exchange transferability	Transaction traceability and privacy preservation without intermediary	Settlement based on consistent rules
Minimum modification for legacy systems	DP-1: Given technological heterogeneity of different operators' (LP) legacy systems, the operators should provide standard interfaces of legacy systems and the practitioners provide standard interfaces of blockchain, so that all the systems can easily use their functionalities by calling the interfaces	DP-3: Given limited boundaries of each legacy system, each operator only creates a special exchange account in the (LP) system, so that they can record how many points each client exchanges, accumulate exchanged points and avoid double payment	DP-5: Given multicurrency of cross-boundary transactions, operators set a consistent exchange rate according to financial cost of points in their own loyalty programs, so that not only each (LP) legacy system can be stable to keep original settlement rules to merchants and clients, but also the exchange rate can be stable for transactions
Technology hybridization of blockchain and conventional technologies	DP-2: Given complexity of point exchange process, the practitioners manage all the interfaces, integrate them into a set of unified processes and manage permission of process-interface calling through installing smart contracts based on blockchain, so that interactions among operators' legacy systems and blockchain can be well-organized, flexible and secure	DP-4: Given the complexity of cross-system transactions, the practitioners provide distributed ledgers to record cross-system transaction details in the blocks and to bridge the (special) exchange accounts of operators' legacy systems, so that the whole process of transactions is seamless and traceable. Simultaneously, blockchain can be used to ensure feasibility of transactions without sharing of customers' critical information	DP-6: Given the complexity of settlement based on multi-account and multicurrency, the practitioners provide each (LP) legacy system with transparent and reliable ledgers that are ensured by blockchain's consensus mechanism, and provide smart contracts for cross-system settlement, so that settlement between operators and merchants, or among operators, can be executed based on consistent rules

According to the design principles, we further designed the system architecture consisting of application layer, service (interface) layer and blockchain layer (see Fig. 5). The application layer included (LP) legacy systems. We created the service (interface) layer through service-oriented architecture, in order to manage interactions among legacy systems and blockchain. Distributed ledgers and smart contracts were deployed the blockchain layer in order to work with other layers and to ensure reliability of the whole systems.

We have evaluated the preliminary findings through proof of concept (POC). Here we provided an example to show the details of transactions and process (see Fig. 6).

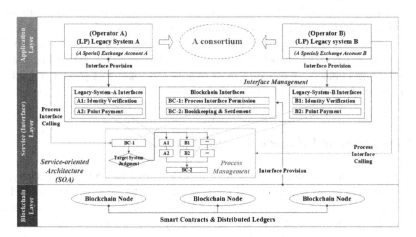

Fig. 5. Architecture for a Blockchain-enabled Point Exchange System of Polycentric CN

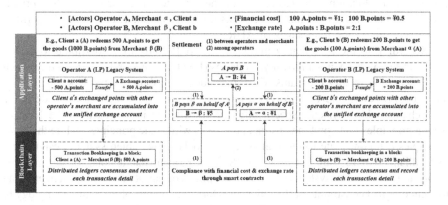

Fig. 6. An example for a Blockchain-enabled Point Exchange System of Polycentric CN

According to the horizontal alliance expected by the CU (as description in the project setting) and the system architecture designed in our research; we simulated the process of exchanging points in real scenarios. In order to simplify the explanation, a simplified example is as follow:

(1) Context setting: Operator A has merchant α & client a, while Operator B has merchant β & client b. A strategic alliance is created by Operator A and Operator B and consists of operators and their own merchants and clients. Operator A sets up a unified exchange account (A-*exchange-account*) in its own (LP) legacy system, similarly, Operator B sets up B-*exchange-account*.

(2) Exchange rate setting: 100 A.*points* are worth \$1, while 100 B.*points* are worth \$0.5. Therefore, the exchange rate between A.points and B.points is 2:1.

(3) Transactions: When a redeems 500 A.*points* to get the goods (equivalent to 1000 B.*points*) from β, a's 500 A.*points* are transferred into A-*exchange-account*, and the corresponding "Transaction Bookkeeping in a block" occurs. Theoretically, β gets the 500 A.*points* in the blockchain. Practically, A collect the 500 A.*points* for β. Similar scenario toward the transaction between b and α.

(4) Settlement: According to distributed ledgers (blockchain), B pays β \$5 on behalf of A, while A pays α \$1 on behalf of B. Finally, A pays B \$4. Eventually, the corresponding points are recalled from A-*exchange-account* by Operator A's (LP) legacy system. Similar scenario toward Operator B.

5 Next Steps and Expected Contributions

We are proceeding in summarizing the feedbacks from the POC. Fortunately, the feedbacks do not seem to disrupt our design principles so far. In next steps, we will first improve and refine the design principles and the system architecture design, and then to intervene in development of a prototype of the system based on Oracle blockchain cloud. Second, we will deeply evaluate the outcomes of the prototype in pilot run to examine the set of design principles. Third, we will summarize the findings in the Reflection and Learning phase, and derive the final design guidelines in the Formalization of Learning phase. Finally, we will summarize the ADR process in the form of table according to the four stages of ADR.

According to the preliminary findings, our ADR study may contribute to design theory in the blockchain and loyalty programs (LP) literature, and enrich both research and practice on loyalty programs. First, our study contributes to the blockchain literature by providing prescriptive design knowledge on how organizations design a blockchain-enabled system. Specifically, the knowledge is proposed in the form of design principles that combine abstract core tasks with basic principles, while the basic principles can contribute to the scalability of blockchain-enabled system design. Second, alliances of LPs are hot topics in IS. The frequent interactions among multiple actors and information systems as well as complicated transactions and settlements lead to technological constraints of the alliances. Our study adopts blockchain technology to mitigate the constraints of the SALP alliance. Obviously, a future research direction is to further explore blockchain applications in other types of LP alliances and more design principles for blockchain-enabled systems.

Acknowledgement. Funding for this research was provided by the Fundamental Research Funds for the Central Universities (2019RCW011) and Beijing Jiaotong University Education Foundation (03060083).

References

1. Sharp, B., Sharp, A.: Loyalty programs and their impact on repeat-purchase loyalty patterns. Int. J. Res. Market. **14**(5), 473–486 (1997)
2. Berry, J.: The 2015 Colloquy Loyalty Census: Big Numbers, Big Hurdles," Colloquy Loyalty Talks, 1 August 2015. https://www.colloquy.com/resources/pdf/reports/2015-loyalty-census.pdf
3. Rese, M., Hundertmark, A., Schimmelpfennig, H., Schons, L.M.: Loyalty program types as drivers of customer retention: a comparison of stand-alone programs and multi-vendor loyalty programs through the lens of transaction cost economics. Int. Rev. Retail Distrib. Consum. Res. **23**(3), 305–323 (2013)
4. Kowalewski, D., McLaughlin, J., Hill, A.: Blockchain will transform customer loyalty programs. Harvard Bus. Rev. **14** (2017)
5. Wang, L., Luo, X.R., Lee, F.: Unveiling the interplay between blockchain and loyalty program participation: a qualitative approach based on BubiChain. Int. J. Inf. Manage. **49**, 397–410 (2019)
6. Breugelmans, E., et al.: Advancing research on loyalty programs: a future research agenda. Marketing Letters **26**(2), 127–139 (2014). https://doi.org/10.1007/s11002-014-9311-4
7. Lubell, M., Berardo, R., Mewhirter, J.: The origins of conflict in polycentric governance systems. Public Admin. Rev. **80**(2), 222–233 (2020)
8. Sun, D., Ying, W., Zhang, X., Feng, L.: Developing a Blockchain-based loyalty programs system to hybridize business and charity: an action design research. In: Fortieth International Conference on Information Systems, Munich (2019)
9. Sein, M.K., Henfridsson, O., Purao, S., Rossi, M., Lindgren, R.: Action design research. MIS Q. **35**(4), 1099–1099 (2011)
10. Alejandro, T.B., Kang, J., Groza, M.D.: Leveraging loyalty programs to build customer–company identification. J. Bus. Res. **69**(3), 1190–1198 (2016)
11. Dorotic, M., Bijmolt, T.H.A., Verhoef, P.C.: Loyalty programmes: current knowledge and research directions. Int. J. Manage. Rev. **14**(3), 217–247 (2012)
12. Nakamoto, S.: Bitcoin: a peer-to-peer electronic cash system (2008)
13. Casino, F., Dasaklis, T.K., Patsakis, C.: A systematic literature review of blockchain-based applications: current status, classification and open issues. Telematics Inform. **36**, 55–81 (2019)
14. Ying, W., Jia, S., Du, W.: Digital enablement of blockchain: evidence from HNA group. Int. J. Inf. Manage. **39**(1), 1–4 (2018)
15. Bygstad, B., Nielsen, P.A., Munkvold, B.E.: Four integration patterns: a socio-technical approach to integration in IS development projects. Inf. Syst. J. **20**(1), 53–80 (2010)
16. Lyytinen, K., Newman, M.: Explaining information systems change: a punctuated socio-technical change model. Eur. J. Inf. Syst. **17**(6), 589–613 (2008)
17. Pan, S.L., Tan, B.: Demystifying case research: a structured–pragmatic–situational (SPS) approach to conducting case studies. Inf. Organ. **21**(3), 161–176 (2001)
18. Gregor, S., Hevner, A.R.: Positioning and presenting design science research for maximum impact. MIS Q. **37**(2), 337–356 (2013)

19. Markus, M.L., Majchrzak, A., Gasser, L.: A design theory for systems that support emergent knowledge processes. MIS Q. **26**(3), 179–212 (2002)
20. Baskerville, R., Myers, M.D.: Special issue on action research in information systems: making IS research relevant to practice: foreword. MIS Q. **28**(3), 329–335 (2004)
21. Dremel, C., Herterich, M.M., Wulf, J., Vom Brocke, J.: Actualizing big data analytics affordances: a revelatory case study. Inf. Manage. **57**(1), 103–121 (2020)
22. Orlikowski, W.J., Iacono, C.S.: Research commentary: desperately seeking the 'IT' in IT research- a call to theorizing the IT artifact. Inf. Syst. Res. **12**(2), 121–134 (2001)
23. Ebel, P., Bretschneider, U., Leimeister, J.M.: Leveraging virtual business model innovation: a framework for designing business model development tools. Inf. Syst. J. **26**(5), 519–550 (2016)

Bitcoin Adoption as a New Technology for Payment Mechanism in a Tourism Collaborative Network

Mehdi Daryaei[1(✉)], Javad Jassbi[2,3], Reza Radfar[4],
and Abbas Khamseh[5]

[1] Department of Technology Management, Faculty of Management
and Economics, Science and Research Branch, Islamic Azad University,
Tehran, Iran
mehdi.daryaei@carleton.ca

[2] Javad Jassbi, Center of Technology and Systems (CTS), UNINOVA,
Department of Mechanical and Industrial Engineering, Faculty of Sciences
and Technology, Nova University of Lisbon, 2829-516 Caparica, Portugal
j.jassbi@uninova.pt, j.jassbi@fct.unl.pt

[3] Department of Industrial Management, Faculty of Management
and Economics, Science and Research Branch, Azad University, Tehran, Iran

[4] Department of Industrial Management, Faculty of Management & Economics,
Science and Research Branch, Islamic Azad University, Tehran, Iran
r.radfar@srbiau.ac.ir

[5] Department of Industrial Management, Karaj Branch, Islamic Azad University,
Karaj, Iran
Abbas.khamseh@kiau.ac.ir

Abstract. Bitcoin is designed to operate as a fine mechanism of Collaborative Network (CN). The Tourism Industry is a particular sector in which this emerging technology, as a new mechanism of payment based on peer to peer and autonomous characteristics, could have a significant impact on growth and helps to reach untapped regions. Given its revolutionary nature, Bitcoin is not yet penetrated in this industry, while the main issue is the number of players who are connected from service providers to tourists, agencies, and suppliers. These heterogeneous players need to use Bitcoin simultaneously when compatibility is the major problem. This means that the Technology Adoption/Acceptance are affected by the behavior of the Tourism Collaborative Network (TCN). The aim of this work is to develop a Technology Acceptance/Adaptation model to evaluate the situation of Bitcoin in TCN and identify factors affecting Bitcoin acceptance/adoption in the context of CN as well.

Keywords: Bitcoin · Digital currency · Cryptocurrencies · Technology adoption · Technology acceptance · Tourism collaborative network

The original version of this chapter was revised: the authors' affiliations were corrected. The correction to this chapter is available at https://doi.org/10.1007/978-3-030-62412-5_54

L. M. Camarinha-Matos et al. (Eds.): PRO-VE 2020, IFIP AICT 598, pp. 167–176, 2020.
https://doi.org/10.1007/978-3-030-62412-5_14

1 Introduction

According to the World Bank [2], nearly 1.7 billion people are globally unbanked, including 225 million people in China, 190 million in India, and so on. Although, one billion have smartphone and nearly 500 million have internet access [24].

Local tourist attractions or people who are living in the countries mentioned above, therefore, suffer from lots of difficulties in terms of currency exchanging or even developing local tourist attractions as well. The statistics [2] also tell us that despite technology's rapid growth and expansion in terms of banking services, the actual customer services were not satisfactory enough in recent years, at least for almost 22% of the world. Other sorts of tourism such as slum tourism, rural tourism, agritourism are another growing niche market built for adventurous travelers eager to place themselves in a different lifestyle [18]. Small island economies (SIE) such as Malta, the Caribbean economies, and others are experiencing massive Correspond Banking Relationships (CBRs) challenges [18, 22] that lead to isolating the trade networks. IMF[1] believes that loss of CBRs "could disrupt financial services" [19]. The tourism ecosystem is vast and heterogeneous in essence. UNWTO[2] defines [21, 22] tourism stakeholders consisted of national and local governments, tourism enterprises, establishments, and institutions that are engaged in financing the related projects. Travelers, all businesses related to traveling and even local people are part of this ecosystem. World Bank and IMF above-mentioned concerns ring the bell that the large parts of the world are still unreachable for the tourism industry only because of the inefficient financial system which imposes many restrictions on travel.

To address the problem, Bitcoin geared with blockchain technology beneath it encourages SIEs and other untapped regions to trigger a new mechanism of currency exchanging, offers a Distributed Ledger Technology that people are able to send money directly [1] in order to overcome the traditional financial system flaws [9]. As a result, financial transactions cannot be overlooked as a big part of the Tourism Collaborative Network (TCN).

The idea of CN was proposed by Camarinha-Matos and Afsarmanesh [12] which is explained as a network consisting of a broad of entities mentioning people and organizations. CNs are heterogeneous regarding their applications, environment, or their operations while they are backed with computer networks, collaborating to accomplish the common goal globally. The collaboration between individuals and their relationships is based on their shared mutual interests, their goals, and the motivations that shape a "professional virtual community" [12]. This network has consisted of groups of functions that collaborate in the specific project with each other and are using their specialties to improve the performance [7].

---

[1] International Monetary Fund.

[2] The world tourism organization.

1.1   Problem Domain and Motivation

The existing financial constraints and limitations contribute to the direct impact on the traveling business and damage the TCN. The intention of employing Bitcoin as a new form of payment channel can be accomplished only by identifying factors affecting the intersection area of TCN and Bitcoin Collaborative Network (BCN), namely End-users and Merchants, to adopt Bitcoin as an innovative fashion. We introduce BCN players including Bitcoin early adopters and acceptances such as miners, traders, herders, merchants, and consumers who are willing to hold or collect Bitcoin or spend their Bitcoin in exchange for valuable services. To deal with our concerned problem, we decided to conduct an innovative way and investigate Technology Acceptance in TCN domain employing CNs Approach. As illustrated in Fig. 1 and based on the UNWTO major role players' definition, we draw a brand-new mesh to explain the relationship between two fragmented ecosystems. It is clear that the intersection as the Joint Spot needs to function properly to put the whole ecosystem to work (see Fig. 1). To bring the Bitcoin payment as a common payment mechanism into the mainstream, the mentioned key users in Joint Spot should accept and adopt Bitcoin as a reliable payment mechanism. Therefore, the research question is "what factors contribute to Bitcoin adoption/acceptance?".

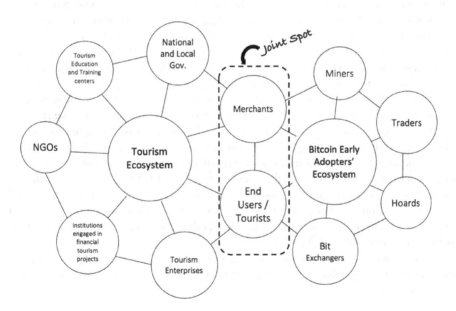

Fig. 1. TCN and BCN in a heterogeneous network context.

2   Foundations and Related Works

Bitcoin is "an open-source" [1] computerized application and digital currency introduced by Satoshi Nakamoto [1]. Using almost a $40 smartphone and an internet connection everyone can perform a transaction [24]. No need to figure out technical details. Having a bitcoin wallet address everyone can send or receive bitcoin [1]. It's sort of like sending out an email. Coins that earned by the merchants can be traded and exchangeable at any online Bit Exchangers, Bit ATMs (BTM) instantly. Since there is no need to have a sophisticated technology to perform a transaction, bitcoin came into existence to cut out transaction costs associated with the intermediaries which are technically trusted provisions in nature [1, 3]. On the other side, it is a young technology then individuals have little information about its core functions. Hence, this foggy environment might negatively affect users' attitudes to adopt/accept Bitcoin on their daily basis transactions. Thus, the economic and business consequences of bitcoin adoption are crucial for the community [8, 11] which is tied to personal characteristics and their attitudes toward use. Valuable research works focusing on peoples' behavior [6, 15] on how to achieve greater acceptance and effective utilization of information systems summarized as follows.

Accepting Bitcoin from a specific party indicates a form of trust relationship [16]. On the other hand, security should be highlighted as the major factor to influence users' decisions toward the e-payment system acceptance, lack of security provisions and become victims of the theft as a result of sensitive account information disclosure is viewed as a major barrier for online users, accordingly [4, 10, 16]. Bitcoin volatility can be addressed as an important risk factor and cause a negative mindset for tourists who intended to use Bitcoin as a payment method [19, 20].

Reference [16] emphasizes that the lack of legal supports leads to negative impacts on users' attitudes. Researchers [8] believe that people who are willing to take risks are among the Bitcoin adopters. Reference [13] stated that all unbaked people can join the global payment system through their private Bitcoin wallet. Studies also emphasized the importance of perceived usefulness, ease of use, and awareness that have a significant positive association, with the intention to use [5, 14, 17]. Thanks to the miners, as the instant electronic payment method, the Bitcoin platform works fast, easy, and well-proven to operate borderless transfers also [1, 14]. To investigate the mentioned factors, we reviewed the most cited previous Technology Acceptance theories which some of them are listed in Table 1.

To our knowledge, this is the first time that we integrate Technology Acceptance theories into CNs in order to explain the best performance out of TCN and for the case of Bitcoin.

Table 1. Review of the most cited Technology Acceptance Models.

Model	Dependent Variable (DV)	Role of * in CN *Volatility *Competitive Advantage *Government Regulatory	Additional independent variable affecting DV	Scholar (s)
Theory of Planned Behavior	Intention, Behavior	None	Subjective norm Perceived behavioral control Attitude	Ajzen (1991)
Unified Theory of Acceptance and Use of Technology UTAUT	Behavioral Intention	None	Performance expectancy Effort expectancy Social influence Facilitating conditions	Venkatesh et al. (2003)
TAM3	Behavioral Intention	None	Subjective norm Image Job relevance Output quality Result demonstrability Computer self-efficacy Perceptions of external control Computer anxiety Computer playfulness Perceived enjoyment Objective usability	Venkatesh & Bala (2008)
UTAUT2	Behavioral Intention Use Behavior	None	Performance expectancy effort expectancy social influence facilitating conditions Hedonic motivation Price value Habit	Venkatesh et al. (2012)

3   Research Question and Methodological Procedures

Identifying factors affecting bitcoin adoption/acceptance would be the scope of the research. In this work and to achieve the goals, the following process shown in Fig. 2 was conducted. To perform an in-depth systematic literature review, some features of PRISMA statement [25] have been adopted. We limited our investigations scope to the factors of acceptance or non-acceptance of bitcoin technology, application of bitcoin in the tourism industry, new form of payment mechanism, use of technology acceptance theories, keywords such as acceptance of bitcoin, application of bitcoin and their security in the tourism industry. After the screening came up with 150 papers nominated and selected.

Then in-line with the literature, we deep interviewed the factors with our 8 professionals with tourism background, either academic, travelers, or agents dealing with the ecosystem actively to obtain a better understanding of the situation. 13 factors discussed and confirmed that have the most effects on adoption/acceptance process.

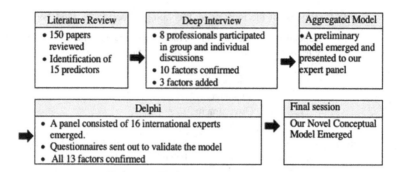

Fig. 2. Methodology process and procedures

Followed our group and individual discussions, our preliminary model has formed. Then, twenty-seven available experts from scholars and market experts contacted and asked to help as Delphi panelists for verifying the initial conceptual model. Structured online and offline open scale (From 0 to 10) questionnaires with an open statement box distributed. At last, sixteen professionals from Iran, Switzerland, Ukraine, Italy, Austria, and Portugal, handed back the questionnaires and engaged as a part of the research. This was followed by analyzing the questionnaires, giving feedback, and conducting several discussion sessions to make sure they are satisfied with the final result to come up with a conceptual model, as an outcome of our deep work.

4   Conceptual Model

Based on the literature review, 15 factors (Computer Playfulness, Facilitating Conditions, Price Value, Loss of Private Key, Victim of Theft, Perceived Usefulness, Computer Anxiety, Trust, Awareness, Job Relevance, Gender Effect, Fast and Cheap, Technological Complexity, Risk Taking Characteristics, and Perceived Compatibility) from previous acceptance models have derived. Five factors (Habit, Computer Playfulness, Price Value, Computer Anxiety, Job Relevance) eliminated and three other factors - Volatility, Government Regulatory and Competitive Advantage - added to preliminary model as a result of the deep interview. Computer Anxiety, Job Relevance, Computer Playfulness, Price Value, and Facilitating conditions; eliminated regarding their unique definition, their scope, narrow focus and constrains on the company and employee relationship side. Volatility, Government Regulatory, and Competitive Advantage added to the model according to the new CNs approach to evaluate the model in the TCN context (see Table 2).

Table 2. Constructs definition in the context of both Technology Acceptance and CN.

Predictors	Definition	Dependent Variable (DV)
Volatility	The degree that an individual perceives trade price variation over time	Tech. Adoption/Acceptance
Competitive advantages	The degree in which an individual perceives that the use of innovation places the business in a superior position	Tech. Adoption/Acceptance
Government regulatory	The degree that an individual perceives that the technology is under the authorities' control	Tech. Adoption/Acceptance

After developing the initial model, questionnaires were sent for our international experts' panel. The result of summarizing the questionnaires, analyzing their feedbacks, and follow-up discussion ended up finalizing the list of most effective factors, presented in Table 3.

Table 3. Experts panel output

Predictors	Mean	Status	Direct effects on Adoption/Acceptance
Government Regulatory	9.4	A & SA	+
Awareness	8.8	A & SA	+
Perceived Compatibility	8.6	A & SA	+
Technology Complexity	8.6	A & SA	−
Perceived Usefulness	8.5	A & SA	+
Competitive Advantages	8.4	A & SA	+
Providing Fast and Cheap Services	8.3	A & SA	+
Volatility	8.1	[a]A & SA	−
Loss of Private Keys & Victim of Theft	8	A & SA	−
Trust	7.8	A & SA	+
Risk Taking Personality	7.8	A & SA	+
Gender Effects	5.3	[b]NAg-NDg	Neutral

[a]Agree & Strongly Agree
[b]Nor Agree nor Disagree

Considering that in the questionnaire, over 7 (the scale is between 0 to 10) is classified as Agree and Strongly Agree, it could be claimed that Government Regulatory leads to an increase in Bitcoin adoption/acceptance. The analysis of the answers to the questions showed that almost 92% Agreed that awareness of the Bitcoin mechanism and its functioning or learning of how to use Bitcoin has a positive effect on the adoption process. More than 88% agreed that Bitcoin integration with other payment systems increases the level of system compatibility. 89% believed that making

Bitcoin wallet more friendly and easy to use makes Bitcoin popular. Therefore, Technology Complexity has a negative effect on the adoption/acceptance process. More than 81% believed that making the technology more usable such as joining more merchants to the ecosystem, increases Perceived Usefulness. 85% of the experts discussed that the possibility of booking services (including flights, hotels, etc.) via Bitcoin, creates a competitive advantage for related businesses leads to improve Bitcoin adoption/acceptance and helps to achieve higher customer satisfaction. The experts also agreed that - almost 86% - the quick and inexpensive nature of Bitcoin transactions enhances Bitcoin adoption special for the merchants. More than 87% of the experts agreed that Volatility has a negative effect on the adoption process and intention to use. Some of the experts mentioned that instant conversion to a defined stable coin reduces the uncertainties. Loss of Private Keys and Victim of Theft are the most mentionable risks that cryptocurrencies adopters may face. Almost 83% stated that it has a negative effect on the intention to use and should be considered as a major uncertainty. Because of the importance of both factors, we open two additional boxes and place it under the Perceived Risk factor in our conceptual model. 77% believed that Trust factor and having confidence in the proper functioning of Bitcoin technology enhances Bitcoin adoption/acceptance. More than 84% agreed that tourists or merchants with Risk Taking personality are more willing to accept Bitcoin. At last, our experts were not agreed or disagreed with the possibility of Bitcoin literacy differences between men and women (Gender Effects). Other valuable comments of our experts were mostly relied on the importance of awareness, allocating bonuses for newcomers, ease of exchange, ease of operation and wide usage, more advertising, and reducing risks.

As a result, Fig. 3 demonstrates a novel model proposed in this work. It reflects the key factors influencing the Bitcoin adoption in TCN, aiming to gain a better understanding of how two heterogeneous systems might function ideally.

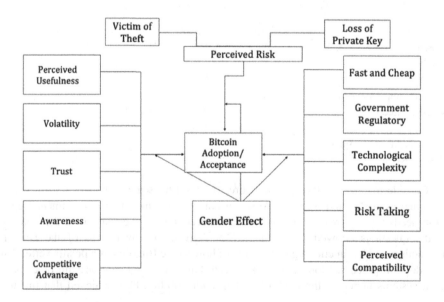

Fig. 3. Conceptual model of factors affecting Bitcoin adoption in a TCN

The proposed conceptual model improves the previous acceptance models considering new components to give us a better and more realistic explanation of TCN players' behaviors in terms of Bitcoin technology in the context of CNs.

5 Conclusion

Global financial inefficiencies and its constraints have caused a lot of inequities in the Tourism Industry to achieve sustainable development. Bitcoin promises to offer a new form of payment channel that could be a solution. To achieve a long-lasting collaboration, heterogeneous players tend to embrace Bitcoin simultaneously as compatibility is the main challenge.

In this paper, it is claimed that a new way of looking to the form of Collaboration between TCN and BCN based on Joint Spot is introduced. To our knowledge, this is the first model that formulated the technology acceptance concept in regard to TCN and BCN ecosystems. The proposed conceptual model adds "Volatility", "Government Regulatory" and "Competitive Advantage" (see Table 2) as three key pillars that are the most important predictors in both supply and demand side in the context of CN. However, further researches are underway to evaluate other related issues. Given the unforeseen nature and special characteristics of Bitcoin as an emerging technology to establish a novel payment mechanism, the conceptual model could be extended to the other ecosystems. The new components of the model are coming from the CN background, such as trust, which could lead to understanding better the challenge of Technology acceptance/adoption in other types of CNs such as supply chains, clusters, and so on dealing with emerging technologies. The focus of this study was limited to Bitcoin acceptance in TCN. In contrast, in further study, the adoption of cryptocurrencies and the role of smart contracts are recommended for a broader range of CNs. Also, quantifying the model and find the weights of criteria and their mutual impact would be interesting subjects for further research.

References

1. Nakamoto, S.: Bitcoin: a peer-to-peer electronic cash system [Pdf], January 2008. https://bitcoin.org/
2. World Bank: The unbanked. Retrieved July 04, 2020, from https://globalfindex.worldbank.org/chapters/unbanked
3. Willie, P.: Can all sectors of the hospitality and tourism industry be influenced by the innovation of Blockchain technology? Worldwide Hosp. Tour. Themes. 11(2), 112–120 (2019)
4. Alshamsi, A., Andras, P.: User perception of Bitcoin usability and security across novice users. Int. J. Human Comput. Stud. 126, 94–110 (2019)
5. Shahzad, F., Xiu, G., Wang, J., Shahbaz, M.: An empirical investigation on the adoption of cryptocurrencies among the people of mainland China. Technol. Soc. 55, 33–40 (2018)
6. Venkatesh, V., Thong, J.Y.L., Xu, X.: Consumer acceptance and use of information technology: extending the unified theory of acceptance and use of technology. MIS Q. 36(1), 157 (2012)

7. Radfar, R., Khamseh, A.: Explanation of research and developments networking effect in the value's improvement of SMES. Roshd-e-fanavari. **14**, 2–12 (2008)
8. Saiedi, E., Broström, A., Ruiz, F.: Global drivers of cryptocurrency infrastructure adoption. Small Bus. Econ. 1–54 (2020). https://doi.org/10.1007/s11187-019-00309-8
9. Fernández-Villaverde, J., Sanches, D., Schilling, L., Uhlig, H.: Central Bank Digital Currency: Central Banking For All? (No. w26753). National Bureau of Economic Research (2020)
10. Oliveira, A.I., Pereira, P., Jassbi, J.: Collaborative safe escape in digital transformation. collaborative networks and digital transformation In: IFIP Advances in Information and Communication Technology, pp. 431–444 (2019)
11. Bystryakov, A., Nenovsky, N., Ponomarenko, E.: The national culture effect on the adoption of the internet-banking. Econ. Stud. **28**(6), 3–18 (2019)
12. Camarinha-Matos, L.M., Afsarmanesh, H.: Some basic concepts. a research agenda for emerging business models. In: Camarinha-Matos, L.M., Afsarmanesh, H. (eds.) Collaborative networked organizations, pp. 7–9. Springer, New York (2004). https://doi.org/10.1007/b116613
13. Bank4you Group: Cryptocurrencies—the perfect solution for unbanked people (2018). Retrieved 03 July 2020. https://medium.com/@Bank4youGroup/cryptocurrencies-the-perfect-solution-for-unbanked-people-55a4baab9bd
14. Baur, A.W., Bühler, J., Bick, M., Bonorden, C.S.: Cryptocurrencies as a disruption? Empirical findings on user adoption and future potential of bitcoin and co. In: Janssen, M., et al. (eds.) I3E 2015. LNCS, vol. 9373, pp. 63–80. Springer, Cham (2015). https://doi.org/10.1007/978-3-319-25013-7_6
15. Davis, F.D.: Perceived usefulness, perceived ease of use, and user acceptance of information technology. MIS Q. **13**(3), 319–340 (1989)
16. Möser, M., Böhme, R., Breuker, D.: Towards risk scoring of Bitcoin transactions. In: International Conference on Financial Cryptography and Data Security (2014)
17. Alaeddin, O., Altounjy, R.: Trust, technology awareness and satisfaction effect into the intention to use cryptocurrency among generation Z in Malaysia. Int. J. Eng. Technol. **7** (4.29), 8–10 (2018)
18. Jayawardena, C.: What are the key innovative strategies needed for future tourism in the world? Worldwide Hosp. Tourism Themes (2019)
19. Sanders, R.: World view: chance for Caribbean 'high risk' banks to challenge CBR ruling (2016). Retrieved 06 July 2020. http://www.tribune242.com/news/2016/sep/26/chance-caribbean-high-risk-banks-challenge-cbr-rul/
20. Walton, A., Johnston, K.: Exploring perceptions of bitcoin adoption: the South African virtual community perspective. Interdiscip. J. Inf. Knowl. Manage. **13**, 165–182 (2018)
21. Rahman, M.: Stakeholders in tourism development, 06 September 2019. Retrieved 04 September 2020. https://www.howandwhat.net/stakeholders-tourism-development/
22. Safe Coastal Tourism. (n.d.): Safecoastaltourism.org, 04 September 2020. https://www.safecoastaltourism.org/article/stakeholders-tourism-development-according-unwto
23. Kwok, A.O.J., Koh, S.G.M.: Is Blockchain technology a watershed for tourism development? Curr. Iss. Tour. **22**(20), 1–6 (2018)
24. Libra White Paper [PDF]: Libra Association Members, Geneva, June 2019
25. Moher, D., Liberati, A., Tetzlaff, J., Altman, D.G.: Prisma group: preferred reporting items for systematic reviews and meta-analyses: the PRISMA statement. PLoS Med. **6**(7), e1000097 (2009)

How to Effectively Make and Use Knowledge Graphs Through Collaborative Activities: A Socio-Technical Perspective

Yanan Gao, Xiyan Lv, and Wenchi Ying[(✉)]

School of Economics and Management, Beijng Jiaotong University,
Beijing, China
{19120605,lvxiyan,wcying}@bjtu.edu.cn

Abstract. Knowledge graphs (KG) as emerging technology contribute to knowledge networking and efficient knowledge collaboration. Sound knowledge about why organizations should develop KGs and how they can make and use KG is the key to success. However, the organized work on the Make and Use of KG can be perceived as another kind of highly collaborative activities between organizations, people, machines and systems, which received few attentions in research. Thus, we adopt socio-technical systems (STS) perspective to review, practice and study how to effectively make and use KGs through collaborative activities. This study reveals a collaborative-activity framework of KG's Make and Use and corresponding collaborative mechanisms, which may contribute to the existing literature of KG/AI, knowledge collaborative networks and STS. Organizations can use this framework to develop their own domain-specific KG and KG-based information.

Keywords: Knowledge graphs (KG) · Make and use · Collaborative activities · Collaborative networks · Socio-technical systems

1 Introduction

Knowledge graphs (KG), first proposed by Google, is an emerging digital technology that can enhance the results of search engines and the effectiveness of cognitive artifact intelligence with information gathered from a variety of sources [1]. The concept of KG was first proposed by Google, where KG is a semantic graph consisting of nodes and edges. The nodes represent entities or concepts, and the edges represent various semantic relationships between entities or concepts [2]. In particular, based on co-occurrence analysis, social network analysis and other basic theory, KG is built to explain the structures of domains [3]. KG was originally intended to enhance the user search experience and later widely used in intelligent question answering, personalized recommendation and other fields, and further in-depth combined with the specific business needs to provide comprehensive knowledge services.

Gartner, the leading research and advisory company, highlights knowledge graphs as an emerging technology with significant impacts on business, society and people [1], which has become a hot topic in academia. Digital technologies, especially in China,

L. M. Camarinha-Matos et al. (Eds.): PRO-VE 2020, IFIP AICT 598, pp. 177–187, 2020.
https://doi.org/10.1007/978-3-030-62412-5_15

has been deeply applied to and influenced many industries. Many enterprises and universities are intended to adopt KG to enhance or transform their information systems (IS) [4]. As the keystone technology of cognitive artificial intelligence, KG enables IS to contribute to knowledge sharing and intelligent collaboration among people from all walks of life, and even enables interactions between humans and machines. Thus, effective KG applications consist of the high-quality KG and the KG-based IS [4]. Obviously, the success of KG applications relies on actions in both the *Make and Use of KG* and collaboration among the actions [5].

Ongoing work on knowledge graphs can be organized in such a way that they are perceived as highly collaborative activities, and thus KGs will be broadly accepted as central knowledge hubs to overcome resistance within an organization against external knowledge [1]. Therefore, the process of KG's Make and Use is a series of interdisciplinary and cross-domain collaborative activities among social and technical entities such as organizations, people, machines, and systems [6]. However, most extant research focused on the general KG (e.g., Wikipedia and Baidu Baike) [7], computer technology level (e.g., modeling and algorithms for KG's fusion and reasoning) [2] or some domain-specific KG applications and results (e.g., specific domains of Medicine, Law and Education) [8]. Because of complexity in, and differentiation among specific domains, the process of KG's Make and Use received few attentions, which leads to the lack of experiences and frameworks to guide reusable actions for development of KG applications.

Thus, we adopt the socio-technical systems (STS) perspective as the guiding theoretical lens to address the gap. STS theory is a well-established perspective in IS research and leveraged to study the phenomena (e.g., KG applications) combining social and technical factors [9], especially technical-induced organizational tasks and actions [10]. Thus, we derive our research question: *How to effectively make and use knowledge graphs through collaborative actions from socio-technical perspective?*

According to reviews on KG literature and our practice on development of KG-based applications in an IT/IS consulting domain. We have completed preliminary findings and propose *a collaborative-activity framework of KG's Make and Use* which combines the socio-technical factors including structures, actors, technologies and tasks. The study identifies two tasks of KG applications – Make and Use, and further reveals collaboration mechanisms regarding socio-technical actions not only within the Make and the Use separately but also between them through three interaction cycles. Thus, our findings may make both important theoretical and practical contributions. First, this study contributes not only to the KG/AI and knowledge collaborative networks literature but also to the STS literature. Second, organizations can use our findings to develop their own domain-specific KG and KG-based IS, and by doing so, increase the success rate of their KG applications.

2   Research Background

2.1   Knowledge Graph (KG) and Collaboration in KG's Make and Use

Data are symbols that represent the properties of objects and events, information consists of processed data, and knowledge is the appropriate collection of information that can answers the *what/how/why* question [11]. Knowledge graph (KG) can link the different data/information streams in an intelligent and dynamic way [1]. KG has the characteristics of huge scale, rich semantics, excellent quality and friendly structure that are different from the traditional semantic network [12]. KG can be used to explicitly capture requirement semantics that are limited towards traditional databases [13]. KG can link the different streams and multimodal data in a structured way. Through in-depth semantic analysis and mining, with the help of powerful semantic processing capabilities and open interconnection capabilities, KG provides users with intelligent search and other services through a visual interface [8]. Thus, KG is an emerging digital technology that can enhance the results of search engines and the effectiveness of domain-specific cognitive AI with information gathered from a variety of sources [12].

As the keystone technology of cognitive artificial intelligence, KG enables IS to contribute to knowledge sharing and intelligent collaboration among people from all walks of life, and even enables interactions between humans and machines. Extant research mainly focused on the general KG [7], computer technology level [2] or some domain-specific KG applications and results [8]. However, research on how to build KG-based applications effectively remain limited. Gartner Hype Cycle shows that KG has still appeared on the stage of "innovation trigger" [14], which means that KG will be affected by uncertain factors on collaborative-network robustness, resource constraints, and actor selection [15] as well as the differentiation of domain-specific scenario and business needs [16]. All above lead to the lack of experiences and frameworks to guide reusable actions for development of effective KG applications. Simultaneously, effective KG applications consist of the high-quality KG and the KG-based IS [4]. Obviously, the success of KG applications relies on actions in both the *Make and Use of KG* and collaboration among the actions [5]. Organizations are eager to explore that how KG is designed and built (the Make of KG), how KG is used and embedded into concrete IS (the Use of KG) and how the Make and Use can be effectively collaborative, and the relevant research gap remains.

Furthermore, Ongoing work on knowledge graphs can be organized in such a way that they are perceived as highly collaborative activities [1], and the complexity of domain-specific KG reflects in collaborative network factors including organizations, people, machines, and systems [6]. Obviously, the process of KG's Make and Use is a series of interdisciplinary and cross-domain collaborative activities whose factors are almost consistent with the social and technical entities of socio-technical perspective [17]. Thus, socio-technical systems (STS) theory provides us with a suitable theoretical lens to address the research gap.

2.2   A Socio-Technical Perspective Toward Collaboration in KG Make and Use

STS theory is a well-established perspective in IS research and leveraged to study the technical-induced organizational tasks and actions [17]. Collaborative activities in KG's Make and Use are a typical IS phenomenon so that the Make and the Use are not only technical tasks but also social tasks [17]. E.g., Andreas Blumauer [1] suggests that KG cannot be Made without support throughout the whole organizations, while new external roles/persons with diverse skills and knowledge should be introduced as well in order to support this transformation. In addition, the Use of KG must also start with planned goals and strategies which requires a series of criteria and mechanisms involving actions on workflow, skills, technological tools or platforms.

STS theory distinguishes the social system and the technical system through four entities [17] that can exactly correspond to the four factors of collaborative networks. The former involves socio-technical entities *structures* and *actors*, while the latter involves socio-technical entities *technologies* and *tasks* (See Fig. 1). Specifically, *structures* refer to the KG's project organizations, institutional arrangements and working criteria; *actors* are the participants of KG projects who have different expertise or capabilities and play different roles in activities; *technologies* refer to the technological tools or platforms involved in the Make or Use of KG; *tasks* are the processes required to achieve goals or provide deliverables.

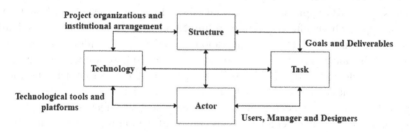

Fig. 1. The socio-technical system model (according to [9])

Obviously, the processes of Make and Use are two typical types of KG tasks that should be supported by actions from other three socio-technical entities. Thus, STS is not static but dynamic. To fulfill the tasks of KG's Make and Use, it is necessary to further identify and leverage structure-level, actor-level and technology-level collaborative actions [10]. More importantly, the interactions between Make and Use concern both rigor and relevance of KG study as well as effectiveness of KG application [5]. Simultaneously, the Make and Use of KG are not achieved at one stroke, while the interactions between the Make and Use of emerging technologies are a long-term process of alignment on adaptation, experimentation and actualization [18]. However, the socio-technical perspective on the Make and Use of emerging digital technologies also received few attentions. Thus, we derive our research question: *How to effectively make and use knowledge graphs through collaborative actions from socio-technical perspective?*

3 Research in Progress and Preliminary Findings

We have systematically reviewed literature on KG's Make and Use. Our KG project that started from 2019 is in progress and supported by HuaQiCT Co. Ltd., a class-A qualification IT/IS consulting company in China.

3.1 Collaborative-Activity Framework of KG's Make and Use

According to reviews on literature and our practice on development of KG-based applications in an IT/IS consulting domain, we have completed preliminary findings and propose *a collaborative-activity framework of KG's Make and Use* (See Fig. 2) which combines the socio-technical factors including structures, actors, technologies and tasks.

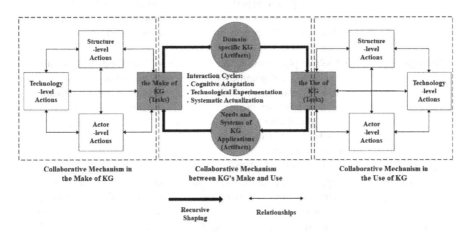

Fig. 2. Collaborative-activity Framework of KG's make and use

The study identifies two tasks of KG applications – Make and Use, and further reveals collaboration mechanisms regarding socio-technical actions not only within the Make and the Use separately but also between them. Thus, the focal components in collaborative-activity framework of KG's Make and Use are showed in Table 1.

3.2 Collaborative Mechanism in the Make of KG

KG-Make Tasks

We classify the KG-Make tasks into the expertise-dominant task and technology-dominant task. Specifically, *the expertise-dominant task* refers to that the experts, according to their expertise on KG and specific domain, make the KG mainly by a manual means. The success of expertise-dominant depends on the experts' knowledge and experiences but is difficult to deal with a large amount of text, where supports of technological tools and platforms are necessary. By contrast, *the technology-dominant*

Table 1. Focal components in collaborative-activity framework of KG's Make and Use

Tasks	The Make of KG • The expertise-dominant task • The technical-dominant task	The Use of KG • The graph-visualization task • The graph-association task
Structures	• Technical-oriented group • professional crowdsourcing community	• Product/application-oriented group • IT/IS-oriented group
Actors	• KG architects with the ambidextrous skills on knowledge management and big data analytics • Technical experts mastering modeling, algorithm and other information technologies of KG • Domain-specific experts familiar with the business context • Domain-specific employees for annotation and labeling	• Product managers (PM)/ Business analysts (BA) • Domain-specific experts familiar with the business context • Technical experts mastering KG-based IT/IS skills • KG consultants with experiences on similar domain or other domain
Technologies	• Tools or platforms of data acquisition and preprocessing • Tools or platforms of KG's representation, extraction, storage and query • Tools or platforms of crowdsourcing	• KG' databases and the suite of model and algorithms • Domain-specific information systems
Collaboration within KG's Make or Use	• Tasks of KG's Make are supported by a series of relevant actions on structure, actor and technology levels	• Tasks of KG's Use are supported by a series of relevant actions on structure, actor and technology levels
Artifacts involving KG	• Domain-specific KG is both the immediate concrete outcomes of the Make of KG and the inputs of the Use of KG • Needs and IS of KG-based applications are separated into the Needs as both the inputs of the Make of KG and the outputs derived from the concrete applications as well as the IS as the outputs of the Use of KG	
Collaborative Interaction between KG's Make and Use	• Interactions between KG's Make and Use are a process of cyclic shaping that contribute to quality and applicability of KG through three cycles • Each cycle involves a collaborative action. The actions includes conceptual adaptation, technological experimentation and systematic actualization	

task refers to that the KG is made automatically through information technology tools or platforms. The task is suitable for textual information extraction but is often lack of relevance and accuracy, where text annotation and labeling are necessary.

KG-Make Actions

A series of KG-Make actions should be taken on the structure, actor, and technology levels in order to improve depth, breath and quality of KG result (See Table 2). This study also combines both the tasks in practice and the bidirectional approach contribute to collaboration between KG's Make and Use (See 3.4).

Table 2. KG-Make actions on the structure, actor and technology levels

Structure level	Actor level	Technology level
• Constructing a technical-oriented group consisting of multi-role actors who can complement each other • Establishing a professional crowdsourcing community for annotation and labeling that are significant parts of KG's Make	• Setting up the role of KG architects owning the ambidextrous skill to coordinate the Make of KG • Accumulating domain-specific experts and technical experts into technical-oriented group and recruiting some experts and employees into crowdsourcing community through unified working criteria	• Acquiring the tools or platforms of data acquisition & preprocessing • KG's representation, reasoning & query and crowdsourcing through cloud computing environments or open-source software • Integrating the tools and platforms through enacting technological criteria

3.3   Collaborative Mechanism in the Use of KG

KG-Use Tasks

We classify the KG-Use tasks into the graph-visualization task and the graph-association task. Specifically, *the graph-visualization task* refers to basic applications of KG, such as retrieval and reasoning. The task also can be combined with concrete business context, but the business context is only based on the data visualization of KG, such as enhanced information index in knowledge service systems (e.g., [19]). By contrast, *the graph-association task* is defined as in-depth applications of KG embedded into concrete business processes or insights, such as personalized search and recommendation, context-based question answering and intelligence prediction (e.g., [20, 21]).

KG-Use Actions

A series of KG-Use actions should be taken on the structure, actor and technology levels in order to explore the business scenario of KG application and to develop KG-based IS (See Table 3). This study also aligns KG-Use tasks and KG-Make tasks in practice (See 3.4).

Table 3. KG-Make actions on the structure, actor, and technology levels

Structure level	Actor level	Technology level
• Constructing a product/application-oriented group who are intended to use KG in IT/IS product/project • Aligning product/application group and IT/IS-oriented group through a digital innovation vision	• Improving KG-related knowledge of PM/BA and experts through a central education program • Recruiting KG consultants from university or professional institute	• Deploying the KG databases in the concrete IS environments • Integrating KG into domain-specific IS trough combination of models and algorithms

3.4   Collaborative Mechanism Between KG's Make and Use

Interactive Action-1: Conceptual Adaptation

The uncertainty of development and utilization of emerging digital technologies [22] deeply affects processes of the Make and Use of KG. At the beginning of technological growth, especially the first two stages of Gartner Hype Cycle [23], the expectations of Makers and Users are different. The differences between KG's Make and Use reveal the intangible boundary [24] that originates from actors' cognitions. Thus, the conceptual adaptation is the first action that span the boundary.

On the one hand, most actors related to KG's Make and Use are different. However, the domain-specific experts should be assigned to participate in each tasks of KG. The experts are familiar with the business needs and responsible for conceptual definitions such as domain-specific entities and relations. The unified and unambiguous criteria of conceptual definitions are the common basis of KG's Make and Use. On the other hand, the Make of KG is subject to the Use of KG, the Use-ends groups may be too aggressive to cause conflicts among different technological groups. Thus, due to their ambidextrous capacities on both knowledge management and big data analytics, the Make-ends KG architects should be assigned to be the boundary spanners. The KG architects should coordinate technological groups at both ends to design the KG's criteria of representation, storage and query, so that the KG outcomes and KG-based IS needs can be in alignment.

Interactive Action-2: Technical Experimentation

Unlike mature technologies, KG as an emerging digital technology does not have any existing use cases in most domains [18]. Moreover, because of domain-specific features, a certain domain-specific KG and its application approach, to a large extent, cannot be reused directly in others, e.g., the use cases of entities and relations in the biomedical domain can be extracted from existing professional database such as Comparative Toxicogenomics Database [25], while management-science domain has no similar database that can offer us unified and unambiguous concepts. That means people should start "from zero to one", where a series of technical experimentations is necessary. The technical experimentation is an heuristic action that explores KG's Use scenarios and typical use cases which will be leveraged to guide a large-scale Make and Use of KG in subsequent IT/IS projects.

The process of technical experimentation should be bidirectional. On the one hand, KG architects and domain-specific experts, in a certain scope of business, work together to build some expertise-dominant instances by KG representation tools. The instances may inspire PM/BA to create use scenarios, e.g., when we build seven KG instances of IS-related theory, the teachers found that KG could be used in MOOC as a graph-visualization task that provided students with knowledge map and index. On the other hand, technology-dominant KG can be extracted and built from high-quality documents by KG extraction tools (e.g., OpenIE, Python or other tools). Meanwhile, according to need description of PM/BA, KG architects and technical experts will improve corresponding algorithms (e.g., syntactic dependency) to optimize KG results at the Make-ends and KG use case at the Use-ends. Furthermore, we found that two types of KG created by the approaches above could be combined again on the semantic level by NLP tools. The overlaps and relevant parts of KG could guide us to further adjust algorithms of KG's Make and needs of KG's Use.

Interactive Action-3: Systematic Actualization

On the basis of the technical experimentation, the systematic actualization is a large-scale action that realizes both the domain-specific KG and the KG-based IS. On the one hand, KG architects and technical experts, according to the results of experimentation, enact criteria for text annotation and labeling and design corresponding tasks and workflow. The employees should be selected or recruited from both domain-specific users and students and conduct the annotation and labeling by the crowdsourcing platform. KG technical experts, according to the results of annotation and labeling, further train the algorithms of KG's Make by machine learning. On the other hand, IS technical experts integrate the KG results from the Make-ends into concrete business system development. Whether the graph-visualization task or the graph-association task, KG architects and PM/BA should evaluate the application results by developing a set of indicators.

Obviously, the process of KG's Make and Use is endless and continuously improved. Thus, all the tasks of KG are application-oriented. The results of KG's Use may not only lead to the adjustment even reset of KG's Make but also contribute to new needs of KG applications. Accordingly, the new needs may be fed back to *the technical experimentation* or to *the conceptual adaptation* due to the unexpected consequences.

4 Conclusion

So far, our KG project is being in the prototype run while we are proceeding in examining theory-evidence-findings alignment. Simultaneously, given both the limited space of this article and the research in progress, we only summarize the preliminary concepts of framework. In the next step, we will describe the details of our action design research and analysis, further refine the explanation to the findings, and derive the final design theory of KG's Make and Use.

Our preliminary findings may unveil *a collaborative-activity framework of KG's Make and Use* which address the research gap regarding the collaborative activities on the Make and Use of KG as an emerging technology. The framework combines the socio-technical factors, identifies two tasks of KG applications – Make and Use, and further reveals collaboration mechanisms regarding socio-technical actions not only within the Make and the Use separately but also between them through three interaction cycles.

Thus, our findings may make both important theoretical and practical contributions. First, this study contributes not only to the KG/AI and knowledge collaborative networks literature but also to the STS literature. Second, organizations can use our findings to develop their own domain-specific KG and KG-based IS, and by doing so, increase the success rate of their KG applications. Furthermore, we hope our findings will have impact on the future applications of KG in diverse domains.

Acknowledgement. Funding for this research was provided by "Research on scene behavior intelligence in collaborative network based on data analysis" (NSFC 61972029), "the Fundamental Research Funds for the Central Universities" (2019RCW011) and "Beijing Jiaotong University Education Foundation" (03060083).

References

1. Andreas, B., Helmut, N.: The Knowledge Graph Cookbook Recipes That Work. Edition mono/monochrom, Vienna (2020)
2. Yan, J., Wang, C., Cheng, W., Gao, M., Zhou, A.: A retrospective of knowledge graphs. Front. Comput. Sci. **12**(1), 55–74 (2018). https://doi.org/10.1007/s11704-016-5228-9
3. Hao-Yu, D., Lan, W.: MOOC instruction optimization in "emergency and first aid"—from the perspective of the knowledge graph. DEStech Trans. Comput. Sci. Eng. (csma) (2017)
4. Xiao, Y.H.: Knowledge graph and cognitive intelligence. Zhangjiang Technol. Rev. **04**, 30–33 (2019). (in Chinese)
5. Chen, G.Q., Wu, G., Gu, Y.D., Lu, B.J., Wei, Q.: The challenges for big data driven research and applications in the context of managerial decision-making: Paradigm shift and research directions. J. Manage. Sci. Chin. **21**(07), 1–10 (2018). (in Chinese)
6. Camarinha-Matos, L., Afsarmanesh, H.: Classes of collaborative networks. In: IT Outsourcing: Concepts, Methodologies, Tools, and Applications, pp 364–370. IGI Global (2010)
7. Chen, X.J., Jia, S.B., Xiang, Y.: A review: knowledge reasoning over knowledge graph. Expert Syst. Appl. **141**, 112948 (2020)
8. Cao, Q., Zhao, Y.M.: The realization process and application of knowledge map. Inf. Studi. Theo. Appl. **38**(12), 127–132 (2015)
9. Lyytinen, K., Newman, M.: Explaining information systems change: a punctuated socio-technical change model. Eur. J. Inf. Syst. **17**(6), 589–613 (2008)
10. Dremel, C., Herterich, M.M., Wulf, J., Vom Brocke, J.: Actualizing big data analytics affordances: a revelatory case study. Inf. Manage. **57**(1), 103121 (2020)
11. Ackoff, R.L.: From data to wisdom. J. Appl. Syst. Anal. **16**(1), 3–9 (1989)
12. Xiao, Y.H., et al.: Knowledge Graph: Concepts and Techniques. Publishing House of Electronics Industry, Beijing (2020). (in Chinese)

13. Miller, J.J.: Graph database applications and concepts with Neo4j. In: Proceedings of the Southern Association for Information Systems Conference, Atlanta, GA, USA, 2013, vol 36 (2013)
14. Linden, A., Fenn, J.: Understanding Gartner's hype cycles. Strategic Analysis Report No R-20-1971 Gartner, Inc., p. 88 (2003)
15. Xu, X.F., Hao, J., Deng, Y.R., Wang, Y.: Design optimization of resource combination for collaborative logistics network under uncertainty. Appl. Soft Comput. **56**, 684–691 (2017)
16. Zhang, G.Q., Shang, J., Li, W.L.: Collaborative production planning of supply chain under price and demand uncertainty. Eur. J. Oper. Res. **215**(3), 590–603 (2011)
17. Wang, H.F., Chen, M.L.: Review for information system sociomateriality. Sci. Technol. Manage. Res. **18**, 153–161 (2017). (in Chinese)
18. Du, W.Y., Pan, S.L., Leidner, D.E., Ying, W.C.: Affordances, experimentation and actualization of FinTech: a blockchain implementation study. J. Strat. Inf. Syst. **28**(1), 50–65 (2019)
19. Dietz, L., Kotov, A., Meij, E.: Utilizing knowledge graphs for text-centric information retrieval. In: The 41st International ACM SIGIR Conference on Research & Development in Information Retrieval, 2018, pp. 1387–1390 (2018)
20. Kumar, A.J., Schmidt, C., Köhler, J.: A knowledge graph based speech interface for question answering systems. Speech Commun. **92**, 1–12 (2017)
21. Zhang, Y.X., Yang, K.L., Du, W., Xu, W.: Predicting stock price movement direction with enterprise knowledge graph. In: PACIS, 2018, p. 237 (2018)
22. Roca, J.B., Vaishnav, P., Morgan, M.G., Mendonça, J., Fuchs, E.: When risks cannot be seen: regulating uncertainty in emerging technologies. Res. Policy **46**(7), 1215–1233 (2017)
23. Kasey, P.: 5 Trends appear on the Gartner hype cycle for emerging technologies (2019). https://www.gartner.com/smarterwithgartner/5-trends-appear-on-the-gartner-hype-cycle-for-emerging-technologies-2019/
24. Du, W.Y., Pan, S.L.: Boundary spanning by design: toward aligning boundary-spanning capacity and strategy in it outsourcing. IEEE Trans. Eng. Manage. **60**(1), 59–76 (2012)
25. Wang, Q.Y., et al.: Paperrobot: incremental draft generation of scientific ideas. arXiv preprint arXiv:190507870 (2019)

Maintenance, Compliance and Liability

Liability in Collaborative Maintenance of Critical System of Systems

A. Luis Osório[1]([⊠]), Luis M. Camarinha-Matos[2],
Hamideh Afsarmanesh[3], and Adam Belloum[3]

[1] ISEL - Instituto Superior de Engenharia de Lisboa, Instituto Politécnico de
Lisboa, and POLITEC&ID, Lisbon, Portugal
lo@isel.ipl.pt
[2] Faculty of Sciences and Technology, NOVA University of Lisbon
and CTS-UNINOVA, Lisbon, Portugal
cam@uninova.pt
[3] University of Amsterdam (UvA), Amsterdam, The Netherlands
{h.afsarmanesh,a.belloum}@uva.nl

Abstract. Our society is facing a growing dependency on services supported
by multiple interconnected computing and cyberphysical artifacts, constituting
complex systems-of-systems. Such dependence means that a web of technology
suppliers and IT departments have the responsibility to guarantee the operational
quality of such systems. In this scenario where dependable services are maintained and evolved by networks of organizations, the question is how to ensure a
liability framework able to reduce or help to solve potential legal conflicts. This
work on liability in Collaborative Maintenance of Critical System of Systems
grounds on previous research on the open Informatics system of systems (ISoS)
framework. It extends the ECoNet collaborative network infrastructure with
facets to support liability and maintenance. We propose and discuss a strategy
for the management of evidence towards a conflictless collaborative context for
the maintenance of critical systems-of-systems.

Keywords: Complex informatics system of systems · Distributed systems ·
Collaborative networks · Dependability

1 Introduction

Achieving reliable complex digital environments requires the management of collaborative maintenance among providers of computing and communication technology
artifacts. The fact that complex digital technology systems (system-of-systems) are of
the responsibility of different stakeholders, and in some cases, share technology elements, the origin of failures is hard to identify. The proper operation of such systems
requires stakeholders to collaborate in the diagnosis and maintenance interventions.
The understanding of interdependencies and the complex interconnections of a network
of systems manifested through shared states are, according to [10], essential to evaluate
associated operational risks.

© IFIP International Federation for Information Processing 2020
Published by Springer Nature Switzerland AG 2020
L. M. Camarinha-Matos et al. (Eds.): PRO-VE 2020, IFIP AICT 598, pp. 191–202, 2020.
https://doi.org/10.1007/978-3-030-62412-5_16

For instance, a helpdesk ticket service integrating fault ticket events from a diversity of sources, either from systems and manual origin, which decides about responses to repair situations, is an example of a complex system of systems. However, the traditional organization of software products lacks preparation from inception for collaborative multi-stakeholder support and maintenance. In many cases, accountability models and intervention plans, answering failure events under automated procedures, are not available. The maintenance of shared products/components requires stakeholders to coordinate maintenance services under complex liability contracts. Collaborative maintenance also needs to be supported by proper interactions among informatics systems from various application domains, e.g., accounting, billing, operational teams scheduling, and negotiation. At a higher abstraction level, business processes need to manage such collaborative liability in a streamlined and efficient way.

Collaborative maintenance of complex systems needs, therefore, the formalization of "responsibility borders" and specific liability-oriented interactions among technology systems, which are currently not adequately addressed by existing products. Despite numerous research contributions to structure computing and communication artifacts, existing products commonly establish isolated islands without formal mechanisms to model dependencies among elements of different suppliers. An adequate liability framework would require a standardization of technology artifacts, data and process models, and interactions between system elements. Towards this aim, in [4], a system concept is proposed as an entity that interacts with others establishing a system boundary. However, a formal model to support the management of such computing entities is still lacking.

This research further discusses an approach for dependability based on previous research on error detection, fault diagnosis, and recovery [3] that seems a crucial contribution to our study. Our paper extends these ideas and our previous research work on formal models for both a collaborative enabled and liability framework, namely by structuring the organization's computing and cyberphysical artifacts based on the ISoS framework [14, 15]. We also consider related research on computing services, guided by the HORUS industry problem [6], to propose a strategy based on the Collaborative Network concepts.

2   Guiding Use Case

In this paper, we analyze the HORUS case study where multiple stakeholders are responsible for subsets of technology artifacts in a forecourt (fueling station). The main problem, in this case, is the lack of systemic model structuring computing and cyberphysical elements and the formalization of a collaboration-enabled framework for technology artifacts and liability framework. Our approach to the HORUS system maintenance considers three cooperating informatics systems: (1) The HORUS core system, responsible for post-payment control, (2) the point of sale (POS) managing payments, and (3) the CCTV, managing the video cameras and video recorders. As such, the technology systems in this fueling station depend on computing and cyberphysical elements under the responsibility of three stakeholders, respectively, company

A (payment enforcement system), company B (fueling payment system), and company C (security and surveillance systems).

The HORUS system is responsible for the payment enforcement, meaning validating a vehicle that requests fueling to be authorized by the Point-of-Sails (POS) system. When a vehicle stops at a fuel station close to a pump, the HORUS system collects its license plate through a License Plate Recognition (LPR) component and the respective video camera. When the POS system (of the responsibility of company B) receives a fueling request from a pump, it asks the HORUS core system (of the responsibility of company A) if the customer has any pending payment. The LPR component, which used to identify vehicles, depends on video cameras that are managed by the CCTV system (of the responsibility of company C).

When a problem exists with a camera, e.g., it tilts down, the operator at the POS console detects a yellow icon, meaning that the HORUS core system did not answer the pending payment validation. In a situation like this, it is common to call all stakeholders to contribute to resolving the problem. Empirical evidence shows that, in most cases, the resolution of the issue would only need a CCTV technician from company C. Furthermore, to guarantee that a POS operator always sees a green or red icon is not trivial. A green icon means the vehicle has no pending payments, while a red one means that a no-payment event exists. When the screen icon is red, the standard procedure is to call the customer to resolve the case before authorizing the vehicle can get fuel. The minimization of occurrences of yellow icons resulting from some failure needs a novel collaborative liability and governance model to improve monitoring and maintenance interventions. The challenge is to restrict requests to those who need to intervene to fix some technology part under their responsibility.

Grounded on previous research on developing an open informatics system of systems (ISoS), the concepts of informatics system (Isystem) and Cooperation Enabled Services (CES), and the Collaborative network infrastructure ECoNet) [17] are now explored and extended to address liability challenge related to the proper operation of technological artifacts.

3   Research Trends and Industry Approaches

The area of systems' maintenance has a long tradition in addressing how to guarantee that manufactured systems work correctly. For instance, in [19], a definition of maintenance is presented as a "*set of activities required to keep physical assets in the desired operating condition or to restore them to this condition.*" We suggest updating the definition by considering a maintenance system like the one guaranteeing that a set of technological artifacts work correctly under the quality of services contract. The difference is in the subject of maintenance.

The need to consider increasing integration requirements establishes a complex web of the interrelated technology artifacts. The growing adoption of smart things in the sense that technology systems more and more incorporate some physical elements with embedded computing and communication capabilities suggests a novel approach to integration. Since technology artifacts are connected things, commonly referred to as Cyber-Physical Systems (CPS)/Internet of things (IoT), they can incorporate a monitoring view by implementing instrumentation services to plug a monitoring infrastructure [5]. Taking our fueling forecourt case and considering that gate locking elements tend to be electronic and somehow integrated, it makes it possible to infer about its proper functioning. Such technology artifacts require monitoring, and there is, therefore, a need to frame them into some novel monitoring framework. The assumption in [19] oriented to technology as physical assets, needs a new abstraction layer to model technology assets as elements of a system composed of independent computational elements. By independent computational elements, we mean artifacts with computing and communication capabilities. Our interest is for independent (smart) elements meaning that our understanding of monitoring refers to technology artifacts led by a computational decision center.

In [19], an overview of the timeline of the maintenance function mentions cooperation. In this timeline, a "cooperative partnership" perspective occurs around 2000. The cooperative and collaborative aspects are explored further in [9] as key aspects of monitoring. In the context of the TEMIC project, the mentioned authors present and discuss a platform to remotely or locally integrate autonomous supervision, monitoring, and maintenance management systems by emphasizing the collaboration perspective.

More recent research confirms the trend towards a collaborative view as technology artifacts are more connected and application domains interleaved, requiring higher integration degrees. The MANTIS project is an example aiming at developing a *"proactive maintenance service platform architecture based on Cyber-Physical Systems"* [13]. In the context of the same project, in [18], the concept of Collaborative Maintenance is motivated by the *"optimum maintenance of assets, different systems, and stakeholders have to share information, resources, and responsibilities, i.e., collaboration is required."*

Collaborative maintenance is also a research topic associated with industry 4.0 [7]. For instance, the research reported in [21] proposes a strategy and a system for the monitoring of a car engine production line aiming at reducing breakdowns of shop-floor machines that typically prevent the lines from operating for hours. As such, the authors proposed a collaborative maintenance strategy through a context-aware system that makes operators aware of the problems. However, in this and other research works, formulated questions are centered on integration without a particular emphasis on responsibility or liability issues. For instance, the research in [21] is, in fact, more concerned with stoppage time and the impact on the production line. No research work, to our knowledge, addresses liability by discussing interdependencies among systems, considering subsets of elements (or systems), under different responsibilities, e.g., maintained by different supplying companies.

4   Adopting the ISoS Systems Modularity Framework

The lack of a well-founded model for the coordination of the participating stakeholders in collaborative maintenance of a critical system of systems (SoS) motivates our research towards a strategy for liability management.

The recent trend to "see" a web of things accessed by the integration of services running on the cloud does not seems to match practical coordination models delimited by restricted contexts (system's responsibility). We can consider a video camera in a fueling forecourt accessed as a thing in the context of some cloud level service (IoT application) [2]. However, a video camera is a thing that is part of some system, the abstraction responsible for its lifecycle management. In the HORUS case, the HORUS informatics system shares access to cameras to identify vehicles positioned for fuelling. However, the camera is of the responsibility of the abstraction that manages the life cycle of video surveillance-related elements, e.g., video cameras, video server recorder, from other subsystems. Figure 1 depicts a simplified view of this scenario, showing three informatics systems (Isystems) that cooperate with the HORUS Isystem.

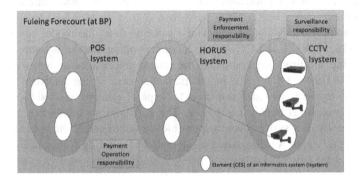

Fig. 1. The primary computational and cyberphysical responsibilities in a forecourt

The adoption of a framework like ISoS by the industry is a complicated, slow, and risky process [8]. In our work, the support of BP Portugal, expressed by the willingness to evolve to a competitive multi-supplier scenario, has been of paramount importance. Being HORUS, an Isystem of our responsibility and the start-up Exploitsys responsible for its support and maintenance, we can influence the validation and adoption of new models. The adoption of ISoS is, however, constrained since it requires changes in the deployed critical system (legacy artifacts). Given the involved costs and operational risks, companies are as conservative as possible. The current implementation of the HORUS Isystem is already monitored by a system that collects (instruments) behavior data from the system's components to infer about their proper functioning. The Exploitsys company adopted the OpenNMS, an open-source system based on the Java technology ecosystem and OSGi specifications and implementations for this purpose. The OpenNMS[1] monitoring system is a paradigmatic example of a product grounded on a project developed under the open-source model since its formation in 2002 [1] and widely adopted by industry and by the research community.

In the following sections, we detail our research strategy to evolve from the current implementation to a collaborative model where monitoring of each informatics system has its monitoring strategy. Such a monitoring process has the additional responsibility

---

[1] https://www.opennms.com/.

to manage functional relationships between elements of different informatics systems prone to generate liability conflicts in establishing which of the system assumes the consequences of failure.

4.1 The Proposed Approach for a Collaborative Monitoring

The proposed strategy is to adopt the ISoS modularity framework as a basis. Instead of taking a monolithic architecture as followed by other works, we intend to preserve the business responsibilities and map them to the Informatics System (Isystem) concept. It means that a hierarchical monitoring framework considering (intra) Isystems decisions replaces the current flat interconnection between elements under different business responsibilities.

While initially validating for the video cameras case, the model considers each Isystem (POS, HORUS, and CCTV) has a corresponding tandem Isystem responsible for monitoring the proper operation of the related informatics system (respectively, POS-M, HORUS-M, CCTV-M). In the particular case of the HORUS Monitoring (HORUS-M) Isystem, the video camera is the type of element selected to validate the proposed approach, as depicted in Fig. 2. The collaborative monitoring involves an additional informatics system class responsible for coordinating the specialized informatics systems, which we designate by Integrated Monitoring (Integrated-M).

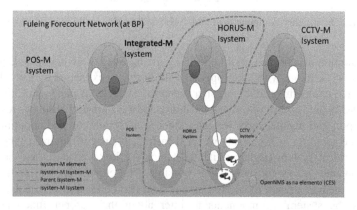

Fig. 2. Proposal of a hierarchical collaborative monitoring context

The region delimited by a dashed line represents the as-is that needs to evolve to the proposed model. Meanwhile, the HORUS-M Isystem directly accesses the video cameras. We expect from Prosegur (a surveillance company) the adherence to the ISoS model to change their management systems to cope with the purposed approach. The plan is to validate the HORUS-M concepts accessing directly through a specific (adapter) element to connect directly to the video cameras using ONVIF[2] protocols.

---

[2] https://www.onvif.org/.

This adapter will evolve later for the service concept in the ISoS model with the adoption of the CCTV-M Isystem.

The apparent throwing out (eventually seen as a demotion) of the OpenNMS informatics system as an element of the suggested Isystem-M might be at first confusing. The idea is to frame the valuable computational responsibilities already offered by OpenNMS into a broader and integrating framework, making explicit the different responsibilities at the organization technology landscape level. Current approaches do not follow formal delimitations of technology artifacts, leading to conflicts when making some suppliers accountable for failures with business costs consequences. Furthermore, our option for OpenNMS considered its open development model and the fact that it grounds on Java/OSGi with an emphasis on the open specifications. While the ISoS deals with technology diversity, the development costs, and the willingness to reduce vendor dependencies suggests a technology convergence strategy to minimize heterogeneity.

Another not trivial aspect is the fact that OpenNMS, by conception, addresses the monitoring of network-level elements primarily. The Simple Network Management Protocol (SNMP) and related concepts like the Management Information Base (MIB) modeling data properties with associated Object Identifiers (OIDs) underly the OpenNMS monitoring system. Any instrumentation variable, e.g., in a trap or other message, has an associated OID [23].

4.2 The Need for Collaborative Monitoring

Although from the conceptual viewpoint, the proposed strategy has a straightforward appearance, when considering legacy systems and elements to evolve, it requires investment and changes in related legacy or new technology systems and processes. As an example, when a problem in a video camera occurs, the HORUS-M receives a trap event, the camera agent triggers (SNMP terminology). However, since the HORUS system supported by Exploitsys is using a camera device of the responsibility of another supplier, in our case, Prosegur, the question is: why not to forward the event directly to the "owner" of the technology element? It is technically possible, however since both companies compete for the best service for the BP Portugal company, why should Exploitsys assume the responsibility to forward trap events? Or should the trap events be managed and sent by an independent coordination system, i.e., collaborative monitoring coordination operationalized by Integration-M, as depicted in Fig. 2?

The HORUS collaborative monitoring case is simple since it does not involve a massive number of technological artifacts. However, at the same time, it is complex enough to validate alternative collaborative monitoring coordination models since it includes at least three independent suppliers. One main challenge here is to establish a collaboration model able to join at some unique decision coordination point the support interventions after a careful and reliable diagnosis process.

In a different application domain (healthcare), the design of an electrocardiogram (ECG) monitoring systems, as presented and discussed in [20], is an example of an integrated monitoring system in a critical application domain. The proposed architecture follows the integration of a diversity of technology artifacts from sensors to computational decision support entities where some are executed on the cloud with the primary concern to guarantee the quality of services considering enforcement, security, and smartness. The introduced smartness is to provide *"flexibility and enable interoperability between a myriad of healthcare monitoring devices."*. The approach, however, shows a monolithic architecture that seems complicated to plug as a subsystem into a broader healthcare collaborative monitoring environment. Each technology artifact being either a cyberphysical element (sensor/actuator) or a pure computational part running somewhere on a computational platform (on-premises, cloud, for), needs to be under an integrated monitoring strategy.

In our ISoS approach [16], each computational responsibility structures as services organized as compositions establishing CES as an element of an informatics system. The informatics system (Isystem) concept determines the computational responsibility commonly attributed to the supplier, the responsible of the Isystem support. Under our ISoS framework, we would consider the Electrocardiogram Informatics System, the ECG Isystem, and an ECG-M, ECG Monitoring Informatics System, as a different system responsible for monitoring the ECG elements, both computational and cyberphysical [20].

Monitoring is of paramount importance to delimit and accurately assign liabilities from the occurrence of any failure. A complex system of systems with system elements shared among different Isystems establishes aggregations that are challenging to maintain and evolve. When a component fails, as possible, the problem shall be detected, diagnosed, and repaired by supporting responsibility at the coordination abstraction layer. In our approach to avoid disturbing Exploitsys (responsible for HORUS Isystem), we proposed that when a video camera in a fueling forecourt fails for some reason, it is of the responsibility of CCTV-M to signal HORUS-M that the problem is under resolution. Furthermore, before the HORUS Isystem detects a problem in a video camera, we expect that the technician from Prosegur is in the process of repairing it. Our proposed separation of concerns, namely: i) operation with the responsibility of the Isystems HORUS and ii) monitoring with the responsibility of the Isystems CCTV, and the accountability of the tandems, HORUS-M and CCTV-M, aims to facilitate the development of intelligent collaborative strategies to diagnose and identify recurrent problems and suggest changes.

5   Liability Managed at Collaborative Networked Level

The experience with the HORUS deployment has been raising new questions, namely the need for some new form of coordination among suppliers of both technology artifacts and services. As prevalent in large organizations, a helpdesk service provider centralizes and coordinates repairing tickets from a diversity of origins, from manual ones to automatically generated in legacy applications (Isystems in our terminology). The emails continue being the preferred support for ticket information exchange, making it challenging to integrate approaches where automatic events integrate partner's maintenance business processes. One important aspect is to establish a governance model for such collaborative maintenance cases. A key research question is how to preserve the liability of each supplier since the proper functioning of business

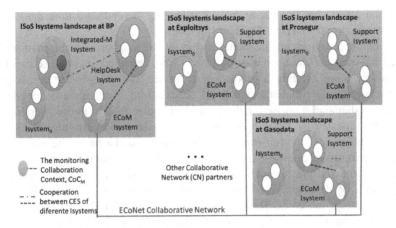

Fig. 3. Adopting ECoNet CN platform to coordinate collaborative maintenance

activities depends on intertwined cooperation relationships among technology systems under different support responsibilities.

Based on the ECoNet research [17], we propose that the second monitoring coordination layer, our Integration-M, takes the responsibility of cooperating with a Helpdesk Isystem that coordinates tickets and maintenance operations through the services of the ECoNet platform as depicted in Fig. 3.

The legacy adapters implementing the exchange of data or control between organizations evolve to adopt the unified Collaborative Context (CoC). In our collaborative monitoring, the strategy is to persuade companies to utilize the open ECoM Isystem. As already discussed, this requires a change to the current approach, where technology artifacts depend on specific architectures. With our approach, by structuring computational responsibilities under the proposed ISoS framework [15], would facilitate technology landscapes with well-defined "responsibility borders", and in this way, enable evolution towards agnostic technology landscapes. However, the problem is much more complicated than the technology diversity. Since a network of stakeholders is involved, where each company has its technology and processes culture, there is a need for a coordination strategy able to minimize interoperability risks. Coordination is a crucial concept for understanding liability and dependability, and it remains recurrent research for decades.

About two decades ago [12] suggested coordination from three perspectives: i) impacts of information technology on persons and markets, ii) design of cooperation tools, and iii) design of distributed and parallel computer systems. Twenty years later, the approach to coordination needs updated terminology and concepts, but the core problem remains. Mapping the proposed perspective to our strategy implies: i) the need to design Isystems answering organization, workers, and market needs, ii) to consider Isystems as automation computing artifacts or implementing functionalities for users (tools) need to answer collaboration needs, and iii) the underlying execution environments on-premises or on the cloud need to be reliable, elastic, secure, in supporting system of Isystems at each networked organization. However, the diversity of legacy models and approaches to systems make challenging the endeavor to design collaborative maintenance to manage the liability properly.

The assumption from our industrial partner of the long-term characteristics of the changes has been of paramount importance. Since suppliers naturally compete for being the only one offering a product or a service, the changes for the necessary preparedness to join a collaborative network needs a third force – the user organization. The Porter's diamond discussed in the context of competition in the software industry [22] slightly updated by changing software by Isystems and changing "Related and Supporting Industries" by user-organizations shows a similar pattern to our proposed strategy. The renewed challenge is how should the holistic solutions cope with market competition to avoid the current vendor-lock-in situation. We argue that by applying our approach of developing an agnostic ISoS framework [15], we achieve added quality and competing costs. There is, however, the need for changing the discourse from software to Isystems, the proposed "systems thinking," leading to integrated collaborative monitoring for the system of systems in a collaborative network context. More than a decade later [11] Porter's diamond is decorated by the *Chance* and *Government* concepts as additional dimensions interpreted as facilitators for competition. The *Government* dimension confirms the need for investment in research and validation through pilots. Public or user organization investment, on the one hand, helps to "impose" the move from the vendor-specific through open standards to the systems thinking where solutions evolve towards agnostic decisions at procurement processes. On the other hand, as a strategy to induce market competition and get products and services at sustainable costs [15].

In our approach, the adoption of the ISoS framework structuring and enhancing the technology infrastructure with four monitoring informatics systems aims to establish an accountability border formed by the respective operational and tandem monitoring Isystems. Each tandem monitoring Isystem has the responsibility of detecting any element malfunction of the respective Isystem. It means that when a video camera shows some king of breakdown, e.g., for some reason, the resolution changed, a trap is generated by the camera's monitoring agent (SNMP agent) to be managed by the CCTV-M Isystem. The CCTV-M Isystem notifies the Integrated-M, that forwards the occurrence to the monitoring tandem of Isystems that depends on the camera of the responsibility of CCTV Isystem, in our case, the HORUS-M. Since the exchange of data to supplier's support Isystems managed by the Helpdesk Isystem in coordination with Integrated-M as depicted in Fig. 3, any delay in repairing the camera is of the responsibility of the CCTV Isystem supplier. Depending on specialized collaborative monitoring processes, the suppliers with interdependent elements are this way able to follow-up mutual maintenance interventions and being aware of potentially related failures in the Isystem(s) they are responsible for supporting.

6   Conclusions and Further Research

This paper presents and discusses ongoing research on liability in Collaborative Maintenance of the Critical System of Systems. The open Informatics system of systems (ISoS) framework and the ECoNet collaborative network infrastructure is adopted to structure a collaborative monitoring strategy for a petroleum distribution company. The approach aims to formalize accountability borders for suppliers of informatics and cyberphysical systems, with share elements. The approach considers that each operational Isystem has a tandem monitoring Isystem responsible for monitoring its proper operation. The model applies to a fueling distribution network and plans to involve three main Isystems (POS, POS-M, HORUS, HORUS-M, and CCTV, CCTV-M) that interact in the context of the fueling management process.

Beyond the need to evolve strategies and models to conciliate de legacy systems and development initiatives as the case of the OpenNMS open-source project, higher-level abstractions need to be designed and validated. An interesting example is to establish liability models to be managed and decided at the Integrated-M level quality of service rates according to the experienced behavior of each Isystem and taking into account interdependencies and proper actions concerning each supplier responsible for the support (maintenance). The liability of suppliers accountable for complex interdependent Isystems and its mapping to an appropriate and fair management of quality of services of each responsibility needs further research.

Acknowledgments. The research conducted by GIATSI/ISEL/IPL develops in collaboration with the SOCOLNET scientific network and its ARCON-ACM initiative. BP Portugal, through the research project HORUS, A-to-Be (Brisa Innovation and Technology) with the research MOBICS/CITS, and FORDESI SITL-IoT through the PT-2020 research project, partially supports the research work. The participation of the start-ups Exploitsys and Makewise has been of paramount importance. Partial support also from the Center of Technology and Systems – UNINOVA, and the Portuguese FCT Foundation (project UIDB/00066/2020), and the European Commission (project DiGiFoF).

References

1. Andreolini, M., Colajanni, M., Pietri, M.: A scalable architecture for real-time monitoring of large information systems. In: 2012 Second Symposium on Network Cloud Computing and Applications, pp. 143–150, December 2012
2. Atlam, H.F., Walters, R.J., Wills, G.B.: Fog computing and the internet of things: a review. Big Data Cogn Comput. **2**(2), 10 (2018)
3. Avižienis, A.: Design of fault-tolerant computers. In: Proceedings of November 14–16, 1967, Fall Joint Computer Conference, AFIPS 1967 (Fall), pp. 733–743. Association for Computing Machinery, New York (1967)
4. Avižienis, A., Laprie, J.-C., Randell, B.: Dependability and its threats: a taxonomy. In: Jacquart, R., (ed.) Building the Information Society, pp. 91–120. Springer, Boston (2004)
5. Calado, J.M.F., Osorio, A.L.: Dynamic integration of mould industry analytics and design forecastings. In: Camarinha-Matos, L., Afsarmanesh, H., Fornasiero, R. (eds.) Collaboration in a Data-Rich World. PRO-VE 2017. IFIP, vol. 506, pp. 649–657. Springer, Cham (2017). https://doi.org/10.1007/978-3-319-65151-4_57
6. Camarinha-Matos, L.M., Afsarmanesh, H., Ermilova, E., Ferrada, F., Klen, A., Jarimo, T.: ARCON reference models for collaborative networks. In: Camarinha-Matos, L.M., Afsarmanesh, H. (ed.) Collaborative Networks: Reference Modeling, pp. 83–112. Springer US (2008). https://doi.org/10.1007/978-0-387-79426-6_8

7. Camarinha-Matos, L.M., Fornasiero, R., Ramezani, J., Ferrada, F.: Collaborative networks: a pillar of digital transformation. Appl. Sci. **9**(24), 5431 (2019)
8. Capodieci, P., et al.: Improving resilience of interdependent critical infrastructures via an online alerting system. In: 2010 Complexity Engineering, pp. 88–90, February 2010
9. Garcia, E., Guyennet, H, Lapayre, J.C., Zerhouni, N.: A new industrial cooperative tele-maintenance platform. Comput. Ind. Eng. **46**(4), 851–864 (2004). Computers and Industrial Engineering Special Issue on Selected papers form the 29th International Conference on Computers and Industrial Engineering
10. Haimes, Y.Y.: Risk modeling of interdependent complex systems of systems: Theory and practice. Risk Anal. **38**(1), 84–98 (2018)
11. Heeks, R.: Using competitive advantage theory to analyze it sectors in developing countries: a software industry case analysis. Inf. Technol. Int. Dev. **3**, 5–34 (2007)
12. Malone, T.W., Crowston, K.: The interdisciplinary study of coordination. ACM Comput. Surv. **26**(1), 87–119 (1994)
13. Ortega, U.Z.: The mantis book. cyber physical system based proactive collaborative maintenance (2019)
14. Osório, A.L., Camarinha-Matos, L.M., Afsarmanesh, H.: Cooperation enabled systems for collaborative networks. In: Camarinha-Matos, L.M., Pereira-Klen, A., Afsarmanesh, H. (eds.) PRO-VE 2011. IFIP AICT, vol. 362, pp. 400–409. Springer, Heidelberg (2011). https://doi.org/10.1007/978-3-642-23330-2_44
15. A. Luis Osorio. *Towards Vendor-Agnostic IT-System of IT-Systems with the CEDE Platform*, pages 494–505. Springer International Publishing, Cham, 2016
16. Osório, A.L., Camarinha-Matos, L.M., Afsarmanesh, H., Belloum, A.: Towards a mobility payment service based on collaborative open systems. In: Camarinha-Matos, L.M., Afsarmanesh, H., Antonelli, D. (eds.) PRO-VE 2019. IFIP AICT, vol. 568, pp. 379–392. Springer, Cham (2019). https://doi.org/10.1007/978-3-030-28464-0_33
17. Osório, L.A., Camarinha-Matos, L.M., Afsarmanesh, H.: ECoNet platform for collaborative logistics and transport. In: Camarinha-Matos, L.M., Bénaben, F., Picard, W. (eds.) PRO-VE 2015. IFIP AICT, vol. 463, pp. 265–276. Springer, Cham (2015). https://doi.org/10.1007/978-3-319-24141-8_24
18. Papa, G., Zurutuza, U., Uribeetxeberria, R.: Cyber physical system based proactive collaborative maintenance. In: 2016 International Conference on Smart Systems and Technologies (SST), pp. 173–178, October 2016
19. Pintelon, L., Parodi-Herz, A.: Maintenance: An Evolutionary Perspective, pp. 21–48. Springer, London (2008)
20. Serhani, M.A., El Kassabi, H.T., Ismail, H., Navaz, A.N.: ECG monitoring systems: Review, architecture, processes, and key challenges. Sensors **20**(6), 1796 (2020)
21. Sipsas, K., Alexopoulos, K., Xanthakis, V., Chryssolouris, G.: Collaborative maintenance in flow-line manufacturing environments: an industry 4.0 approach. Procedia CIRP **55**, 236–241 (2016). 5th CIRP Global Web Conference - Research and Innovation for Future Production (CIRPe 2016)
22. Quintin, M.S.: Competitive advantage in the software industry. WIT Transactions on Information and Communication Technologies (1993)
23. Wang, Z., Wang, Y., Shao, G.: Research and design of network servers monitoring system based on snmp. In: 2009 First International Workshop on Education Technology and Computer Science, vol. 3, pp. 857–860 (2009)

Applying Predictive Maintenance in Flexible Manufacturing

Go Muan Sang[1], Lai Xu[1(✉)], Paul de Vrieze[1], and Yuewei Bai[2]

[1] Faculty of Science and Technology, Bournemouth University,
Poole, Dorset, UK
{gsang,lxu,pdevrieze}@bournemouth.ac.uk
[2] Industry Engineering of Engineering College, Shanghai Polytechnic
University, Shanghai, China
ywbai@sspu.edu.cn

Abstract. In Industry 4.0 context, manufacturing related processes e.g. design processes, maintenance processes are collaboratively processed across different factories and enterprises. The state i.e. operation, failures of production equipment tools could easily impact on the collaboration and related processes. This complex collaboration requires a flexible and extensible system architecture and platform, to support dynamic collaborations with advanced capabilities such as big data analytics for maintenance. As such, this paper looks at how to support data-driven and flexible predictive maintenance in collaboration using FIWARE? Especially, applying big data analytics and data-driven approach for effective maintenance schedule plan, employing FIWARE Framework, which leads to support collaboration among different organizations modularizing of different related functions and security requirements.

Keywords: Collaboration · Predictive maintenance · Maintenance schedule plan · Industry 4.0

1 Introduction

Modern collaborative manufacturing industries are advancing to embrace the concept of Industry 4.0 in achieving high levels of productivity and flexibility. Modular collaboration is essential to enabling the flexibility (pluggable components i.e. processes, machine, devices) for cross-organization to work seamlessly [1]. In this aspect, organizations can establish collaboration by connecting devices with required data to perform business functions, enabling the maximum capacity of establishing instant collaboration among collaborative partners [1]. This however requires the underlying system flexible enough to support the collaborative business process whilst maintaining trust and transparency among partners [2]. Besides, the capability of predictive maintenance with a flexible platform is critically important for supporting the whole production chain in the collaborative manufacturing environment.

In Industry 4.0 manufacturing context, the interaction and data exchange occur in various components e.g. systems, machines, IoT, etc., and this facilitates the underlying business processes across different collaborative domains. These collaborative

L. M. Camarinha-Matos et al. (Eds.): PRO-VE 2020, IFIP AICT 598, pp. 203–212, 2020.
https://doi.org/10.1007/978-3-030-62412-5_17

processes produce a huge amount of data and thereby bring opportunities such as big data driven discoveries such as analytics [1, 3]. However, traditional data processing and tools face huge challenges in dealing with big data, advanced analytics and offering a flexible analytics architecture platform [1, 3].

Besides, effective maintenance is critical to the manufacturing chain as it associates with downtime and faulty product which can affect the collaborations i.e. integrated value and processes [4]. Traditional maintenance approaches such as corrective (re-active), preventive, are not effective for the demand of modern collaborative manu-facturing due to cost and management concerns [5]. Big data analytics with advanced techniques like machine learning offer an opportunity to maximize maintenance capability, namely predictive maintenance [2]. A flexible predictive maintenance solution is needed to provide effective maintenance management, enhancing the whole maintenance, and production process and minimizing downtime and cost.

This paper looks at how to support flexible predictive maintenance platform complying Industry 4.0 standards and Reference Architecture Model Industry (RAMI) 4.0 using FIWARE framework, which leads to support collaboration among different organizations modularizing of related functions. We look at how to support predictive maintenance for flexible manufacturing, which means we are not only looking at how to maintain one machine with different components but a series of machines within a product line. The contributions of this work are: a) to investigate a predictive main-tenance method for supporting multi-machines within a product line, b) to introduce a predictive maintenance method and schedule plan utilizing state-of-the-art approach for supporting flexible manufacturing, and c) using the designed predictive maintenance method to apply to an application case.

2 Related Work

Modern industrial collaborative computing is driven by Industry 4.0 [1]. Industry 4.0 can be realized as a collaborative value-creating network that supports flexibility and application of intelligent machines and processes using advanced technologies such as the internet of things (IoT), Cyber Physical Systems (CPS), big data analytics and cloud [1]. In the case of Industry 4.0 manufacturing, business processes are collaboratively processed across different factories and organizations for effective handling of pro-duction life cycle and demands [1, 6]. This process however is complex and hence entails a modular platform with flexibility and transparency for the data to flow across different collaborative domains [2].

A flexible and modular architecture platform is essential to supporting modern collaborative industry smart systems [4]. RAMI 4.0 simplifies Industry 4.0 with a three-dimensional model; hierarchy levels, functional layers and product lifecycle value stream [2]. RAMI 4.0 offers a simplified coherent view which provides an under-standing of complex systems and processes involved in complex Industry 4.0 [2]. FIWARE, an open source framework exists as a service ecosystem composed of dif-ferent key components called Generic Enablers (GEs). Using these GE components such as IoT/smart devices, services and big data analysis components, smart solutions can be developed for different needs or processes, promoting interoperability and modularity [4, 7]. Our previous work offers FIWARE predictive maintenance however does not cover the aspect of RAMI 4.0 and maintenance schedule plan [4]. Besides, a 5-level CPS architecture is proposed by [8] to support a step by step approach for designing smart manufacturing systems. This approach is based on a sequential manner which can be difficult to deal with the dynamic changes and demands of modern industry.

2.1   Predictive Maintenance Model

Maintenance is becoming essential to modern manufacturing as it impacts on costs which are related with downtime and faulty products [9]. Predictive maintenance is based on data-driven methods and maintenance activity is scheduled in advance and acted before a failure event occurs [9]. Thus, it offers advanced analytics and a cost-effective option [2, 9], compared with traditional approaches such as corrective, pre-ventive maintenance which are costly and complex [5].

Tool condition detection and Remaining Useful Life (RUL) estimation help to manage optimal predictive maintenance [2, 5]. This facilitates producing effective maintenance schedule plan in advance, subsequently minimizing downtime, cost, and unnecessary maintenance, and maintaining effective operating conditions of machine equipment [2, 9]. RUL estimation of a component derives from the present time and the end of its useful life whereas the degradation or health of a component is considered for the tool condition detection [2, 5].

Time series or sequential sensor data such as operational and condition data collected from manufacturing machine/equipment are used for data-driven predictive models such as tool condition detection aspects, RUL [4]. In this process, Long Short-Term Memory Network (LSTM) well suits for the predictive models [4], compared with other widely used techniques such as sequence learning Hidden Markov Model, Recurrent Neural Network which face different challenges such as computational complexity and storage [10, 11].

In the context of collaborative manufacturing, maintenance is complex as it associates with different systems/components e.g. IoT devices, CNC machines, tools, etc. At this stage, different aspects of maintenance such as single-component and limited multi-component systems are predominantly explored in the research community. In the case of conventional maintenance, single-component systems were focused in [12, 13]. These works generally consider for individual equipment or component and ignore other associated components. Subsequently, multi-component systems become the focus of various works [14–16]. In this context, production equipment with a multi-component system was focused. Moreover, additional considerations such as economic (cost related to machine, fixing, downtime), a dynamic group in maintenance are realized by [15] for cost savings.

At this stage, current approaches still lack the attention for Industry 4.0, particularly considering the nature and increasing application of complex systems i.e. multiple machines with multiple components. Traditional maintenance approaches such as corrective, preventive are ineffective, expensive and possibly initiate human error [9]. Our previous works only focus on the aspect of FIWARE [4] but do not consider for schedule plan and RAMI 4.0 architecture [2]. Thus, this demands a new approach which considers complex systems for optimal maintenance schedule plan in flexible predictive maintenance. In addition to complex systems, key factors such as maintenance task, cost, availability, should be considered in deciding optimal maintenance schedule plan.

3 Predictive Maintenance Model for Flexible Manufacturing

We propose the predictive maintenance model described in Fig. 1, which supports the proposed predictive maintenance for flexible manufacturing. The predictive maintenance module takes as inputs of data from machines as well as data related to machines and generates the outcomes of the predictive models that forecast the future machine conditions assisting decision making for optimal maintenance schedule plan.

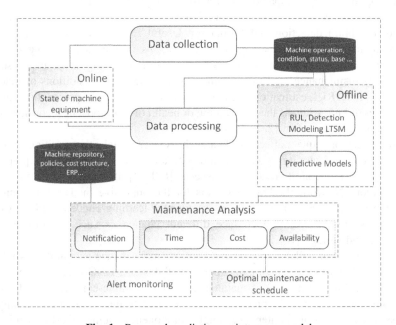

Fig. 1. Proposed predictive maintenance model

There are three main functions in the predictive maintenance model, namely data collection, data processing, and maintenance analysis. The **data collection** in general is online activities related to various data. First data needs to be collected from different machines within a product line of flexible manufacturing; online data collection allows data to be received synchronously from the product line. Secondly, real-time data can better reflect the machines' conditions. In a flexible manufacturing environment, various data such as operation, event and condition data are collected [2]; operation data refers to data about the certain process; event data generally refers to information about what happened to the asset i.e. machine equipment, and which maintenance was applied to it; condition data such as health and measurements of the physical asset.

Moreover, various sensors such as ultrasonic sensors, accelerometers, gyroscopes, etc. are used for dealing with different data signals such as vibrations, pressure, temperature, etc. exist and [17]. Various data storages such as relational database, NoSQL, Hadoop or data lake can be used for different needs i.e. streaming, structured data etc. [3].

The **data processing** concerns with the general operations conducted to producing insight from a large amount of data [18]. Raw data must be converted into information for decision making [18]. Typically, data preprocessing, cleaning and reduction, are carried out [3]. *Data preprocessing* may involve removing redundant or inconsistent data whereas *data cleaning* might deal with missing value, format. *Data reduction* generally deals with transforming data into ordered, meaningful, and simplified forms such as feature or case collection [3]. In the proposed model, data processing also concerns with both online and offline. The online aspect refers to real-time monitoring and alert notification. For this process, the condition and status of the machine equipment or tool of the production system are considered. Typically, the real-time data about status or condition is compared with the threshold of the machine equipment maintained in a database for monitoring and notification.

Regarding the offline aspect, it focuses on the predictive models such as RUL and detection of machine tool wear, derived from LSTM. The trained models are deployed and used for RUL estimation and detection for potential problems arising in production. To facilitate capabilities such as big data analytics of predictive maintenance, various data such as sensors, manufacturer data and machine tool operator data are utilized for predicting the machine condition and RUL [4, 5]. Regarding the machine conditions and RUL, the machine components of the same type with failure data or any event that states the end of the component life [2].

As for the real-time aspect i.e. alert, monitoring in the dashboard, the underlying assets i.e. machine, device, factory, etc. are considered [2]. For online processing in Algorithm 1, real-time operational data derived from the underlying machine/ equipment N is processed and compared with the threshold. When the state i is above the threshold i, the alert i will prompt to perform the executable maintenance task for the qualified item j. In this case, maintenance task such as minor adjustment which can be executed by automation, is considered. If the maintenance task cannot solve the problem, the qualified available maintenance operator k will be required, and the corresponding item of alert i will then also be set to normal. In this case, a database with the maintenance repository is used for storing the key threshold of the asset i.e. machine equipment.

At the **maintenance analysis,** it takes as inputs the outcomes of the predictive models that forecast the future machine conditions assisting decision making for optimal maintenance schedule plan. The result of maintenance analysis both online and offline will be presented in a dashboard. Different notification and the maintenance analysis based on time, cost, and availability are involved in this level. Based on the notification of machine condition of each asset (including its future trend) and RUL, the Maintenance Analysis module provides the probability necessary for computing the weights following Algorithm 2 and 3.

```
Algorithm 1: Online (Real-time) processing
  for each maintenance asset i to N do
      if state(i) < threshold(i) then break end if // exit as not outstanding asset
      set alert(i) = true
      for each maintenance task j of item(i) do
          if task(j) == true then
              do maintenance task (j) // automation maintenance
              waitForTaskExecution()
              if(state(i) < threshold (i)) then
                  set alert(i) = false // set as completed
              else
              for k of operator(i) do
                  if operator (k) == true then
                      do maintenance task (j)
                      set maintenance task (j) = false
                      set alert(i) = false
                  end if
              end for
          end if
          if (alert(i) == false) then break end if
      end for
  end for


  Algorithm 2: Maintenance schedule processing
      Output maintenance schedule plan
      Initialize maintenance schedule = null
      Set cost = 0, time = 0, availability = 0
      maintenanceAssets = Get Maintenance Assets // invoke algorithm 3
      // compute for each maintenance assets
      availability = Compute Maintenance Availability (maintenanceAssets)
      time = Compute Maintenance Time (maintenanceAssets)
      cost = Compute Maintenance Cost (maintenanceAssets)
      // get the optimal schedule by overall minimum cost
      maintenance schedule = min (cost, time, availability)
      return maintenance schedule

  Algorithm 3: Get maintenance assets (multi-machines/components) processing
      Output maintenance assets
      Initialize maintenance_assets = null
      maintenanceAssets = Get Machine Assets // from database for outstanding alerts
      for each m in maintenanceAssets do
          if m is multiple machine or component then
              for each k in m do
                  if k requires maintenance then
                      maintenance_assets += k
                  else
                      break
                  end if
              end for
          else m is single machine or component then
              if m requires maintenance then
                  maintenance_assets += m
              else break end if
          end if
      end for
      return maintenance_assets
```

The Maintenance Analysis module determines the maintenance schedule plan for all the activities that can be computed as the estimated automation task or operator/engineer displacement time from the assets (machine equipment). This also depends on the relative positions of the assets, the displacement time or automation of the repair machine equipment of the completed maintenance activity. The cost associated with the operation, downtimes, repair, etc. to the asset m. Note that, all these costs depend also on the characteristics of the task and operator. The availability is associated with the asset items for maintenance (e.g. work in progress production). The schedule activity is triggered via the Optimal Maintenance Scheduling module, which determines the optimal maintenance schedule by considering the above-determined maintenance constraints such as cost, time, and availability. Subsequently effective maintenance schedule plan can be produced, enabling optimal procedure task.

4   Predictive Maintenance Model Application Case

A flexible manufacturing factory operates with a variety of systems such as processing, logistics, information, machine equipment tools, collaborative processes and data, etc. Figure 2 depicts an example of the flexible factory. In this case, the processing system operates with three robots, 4 sets of machines, AGV trolleys, carrier plates and a warehouse. For operation such as measurement, cleaning and drying the workpiece, machine tools such as coordinate measuring machine, cleaning machine, drying machine are utilized. During operation, these different machines equipment tools generate various data. Besides, collaborative processes or data are processed or accessed across collaborative domains i.e. suppliers, machine manufacturers, insurers, etc.

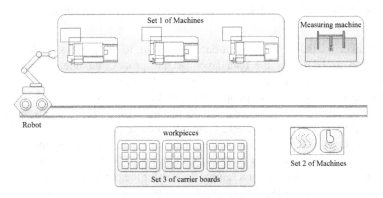

Fig. 2. Flexible manufacturing factory

From our literature review in Sect. 2, it is realized that FIWARE framework with RAMI 4.0 offers the flexibility, modularity and simplified architecture which are critical to the application case to effectively manage dynamic collaborations, productivity, product life cycle and costs. To achieve an optimal solution and satisfy the standards of Industry 4.0, FIWARE framework in the context of RAMI 4.0 and data model from [4] are thus adopted for the proposed predictive maintenance. The proposed predictive maintenance model in Fig. 1 is applied for the application case applying RAMI 4.0 and key components of FIWARE framework in Fig. 3.

At the resource module, the assets i.e. factory machines, robots, etc. represent the asset layer of RAMI 4.0, operate and connect with the Orion context broker, associated processes and data storage via related adapters. In the middleware and data module, it represents the communication and information layer of RAMI 4.0 and using NGSI REST API and PEP Proxy for interaction and security enforcement, the Orion

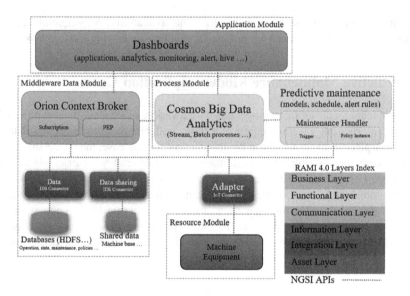

Fig. 3. RAMI 4.0 FIWARE predictive maintenance model for application case

context broker facilitates the context data processing to the process module and data storage such as HDFS as the data layer. At the process module, it represents the functional layer of RAMI 4.0 and Cosmos Big Data analysis enables both batch and stream processing including Hadoop engine, and related predictive models which are connected to the context broker and the application module [7]. Various applications and user interfaces can be integrated as required at the application module, representing the business layer of RAMI 4.0. Moreover, real-time data triggered by the asset can be served by different applications such as QuantumLeap, Grafana, Hive, etc.

An initial result trained from a sample dataset for the predictive model using Keras, TensorFlow backend and the Adam optimizer is presented in Fig. 4. Optimized model learning will be conducted before deployment.

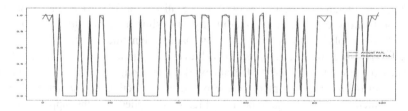

Fig. 4. Initial result from sample flexible manufacturing dataset

The analysis based on the predictive models such as RUL, detection and maintenance analysis information related to maintenance cost, time and availability from the machine repository (machine schedule, availability, design, capabilities, configurations, parameters, etc.) stored in a database using the adopted data model from [4], are available via the dashboards. As a result, the maintenance operators can obtain information about the availability of the resources towards the creation of effective maintenance schedule process plans via the dashboard. Subsequently it will reduce downtimes, cost and enhance the production chain.

A network of collaborations in different processes such as machines, suppliers, machine manufacturers, insurers, customers exists in the case, and this poses challenges such as trust among collaborative partners. To support transparent collaboration, FIWARE's IDS connectors are utilized for accessing and processing collaborative data such as machine base data from manufacturers, machine diagnosis for insurers, and product design data from designers. This facilitates transparent interaction and data exchange across collaborations enabling access usage policy and thus traceability. FIWARE container virtualization is adopted for better scalability of the proposed solution.

5 Conclusion

Modern collaborative manufacturing is complex, face different challenges, and requires a flexible architecture platform that will assist in managing optimal maintenance. We proposed a Predictive Maintenance Model that offers a flexible and modular system using FIWARE and RAMI 4.0 complying Industry 4.0 standards and enabling advanced analytics such as LSTM models. Using a flexible manufacturing case, the proposed model is demonstrated in a way that different systems or processes can be integrated in a modular fashion, and effective maintenance schedule can be planned. Ultimately, it enables effective maintenance management, enhancing the whole production and maintenance process with transparent collaboration, and minimizing downtime and cost. Lastly, optimized predictive and maintenance schedule models with both application case and other use cases across the industry will be performed and evaluated in future work.

Acknowledgments. This research is partially funded by the State Key Research and Development Program of China (2017YFE0118700) and it is part of the FIRST project which has received funding from the European Union's Horizon 2020 research and innovation programme under the Marie Skłodowska-Curie grant agreement No. 734599.

References

1. Thoben, K.D., Wiesner, S.A., Wuest, T.: "Industrie 4.0" and smart manufacturing-a review of research issues and application examples (2017). https://doi.org/10.20965/ijat.2017.p0004
2. Sang, G.M., Xu, L., de Vrieze, P., Bai, Y.: Predictive maintenance in industry 4.0. In: 10th International Conference on Information Systems and Technologies, 4–5 June 2020 (2020)
3. Sang, G.M., Xu, L., de Vrieze, P.: Simplifying big data analytics systems with a reference architecture. In: Camarinha-Matos, L.M., Afsarmanesh, H., Fornasiero, R. (eds.) PRO-VE 2017. IFIP AICT, vol. 506, pp. 242–249. Springer, Cham (2017). https://doi.org/10.1007/978-3-319-65151-4_23

4. Sang, G.M., Xu, L., de Vrieze, P., Bai, Y.: Towards predictive maintenance for flexible manufacturing using FIWARE. In: Dupuy-Chessa, S., Proper, H.A. (eds.) CAiSE 2020. LNBIP, vol. 382, pp. 17–28. Springer, Cham (2020). https://doi.org/10.1007/978-3-030-49165-9_2

5. Tobon-Mejia, D.A., Medjaher, K., Zerhouni, N.: CNC machine tools wear diagnostic and prognostic by using dynamic Bayesian networks. Mech. Syst. Signal Process. (2012). https://doi.org/10.1016/j.ymssp.2011.10.018

6. Debevec, M., Simic, M., Herakovic, N.: Virtual factory as an advanced approach for production process optimization. Int. J. Simul. Model. (2014). https://doi.org/10.2507/IJSIMM13(1)6.260

7. Catalogue, F.: FIWARE Catalogue, https://www.fiware.org/developers/catalogue/. Accessed 30 Mar 2020

8. Lee, J., Bagheri, B., Kao, H.A.: A cyber-physical systems architecture for Industry 4.0-based manufacturing systems. Manuf. Lett. (2015). https://doi.org/10.1016/j.mfglet.2014.12.001

9. Mobley, R.K.: An Introduction to Predictive Maintenance, 2nd edn. (2002). https://doi.org/10.1016/B978-075067531-4/50018-X

10. Baruah, P., Chinnam, R.B.: HMMs for diagnostics and prognostics in machining processes. Int. J. Prod. Res. (2005). https://doi.org/10.1080/00207540412331327727

11. Bengio, Y., Simard, P., Frasconi, P.: Learning long-term dependencies with gradient descent is difficult. IEEE Trans. Neural Networks (1994). https://doi.org/10.1109/72.279181

12. Wang, H.: A survey of maintenance policies of deteriorating systems. Eur. J. Oper. Res. (2002). https://doi.org/10.1016/S0377-2217(01)00197-7

13. Chan, G.K., Asgarpoor, S.: Optimum maintenance policy with Markov processes. Electr. Power Syst. Res. (2006). https://doi.org/10.1016/j.epsr.2005.09.010

14. Nicolai, R.P., Dekker, R.: A review of multi-component maintenance models. In: Proceedings of the European Safety and Reliability Conference 2007, ESREL 2007 - Risk, Reliability and Societal Safety (2007)

15. Dekker, R., Wildeman, R.E., Van Der Duyn Schouten, F.A.: A review of multi-component maintenance models with economic dependence. Math. Methods Oper. Res. (1997). https://doi.org/10.1007/BF01194788

16. Van Horenbeek, A., Pintelon, L.: A dynamic predictive maintenance policy for complex multi-component systems. Reliab. Eng. Syst. Saf. (2013). https://doi.org/10.1016/j.ress.2013.02.029

17. Teti, R., Jemielniak, K., O'Donnell, G., Dornfeld, D.: Advanced monitoring of machining operations. CIRP Ann. Manuf. Technol. (2010). https://doi.org/10.1016/j.cirp.2010.05.010

18. Sang, G.M., Xu, L., de Vrieze, P.: A reference architecture for big data systems. In: SKIMA 2016 - 2016 10th International Conference on Software, Knowledge, Information Management and Applications (2017). https://doi.org/10.1109/SKIMA.2016.7916249

Verification and Compliance in Collaborative Processes

Oyepeju Oyekola[✉] and Lai Xu

Computing and Informatics, Bournemouth University, Poole, BH12 5BB
Bournemouth, UK
{ooyekola,lxu}@bournemouth.ac.uk

Abstract. Evidently, COVID-19 has changed our lives and is likely to make a lasting impact on our economic development and our industry and services. With the ongoing process of digital transformation in industry and services, Collaborative Networks (CNs) is required to be more efficient, productive, flexible, resilient and sustainable according to change of situations and related rules applied afterwards. Although the CN area is relatively young, it requires the previous research to be extended, i.e. business process management from dealing with processes within a single organization into processes across different organizations. In this paper, we review current business process verification and compliance research. Different tools approaches and limitations of them are compared. The further research issues and potential solutions of business process verification and compliance check are discussed in the context of CNs.

Keywords: Collaborative networks · Collaborative business process · Business process verification · Compliance · Change

1 Introduction

The advancement in technology and the development of commercial business models has brought about intensified collaborative network (CN), which presents businesses that operate in a global context. Such collaborative networks bring about growing interconnectivity of all processes in the value chain (Human and machine). During their process life cycle, business processes are subject to change as a result of the emergence of new market needs and ever-changing requirement due to the implementation of new laws, policies and regulations. For instance, the on-going BREXIT in the UK, once finalized can bring about new laws and regulation, which might have a knock-on effect on Collaborative Business Process (CBP) across Europe. Consequently, collaborative business partners are faced with a high level of complexity dealing with these changes and continuously verifying the compliance of their business processes with existing regulations or any changes in the regulatory requirements.

So far, business process verification and compliance have received substantial research attention over the last two decades focusing on checking the complaint behaviour of business processes against several policies and regulations. Most of the reviewed studies mostly focus on the business process within one single organization

© IFIP International Federation for Information Processing 2020
Published by Springer Nature Switzerland AG 2020
L. M. Camarinha-Matos et al. (Eds.): PRO-VE 2020, IFIP AICT 598, pp. 213–223, 2020.
https://doi.org/10.1007/978-3-030-62412-5_18

using different approaches [1]. Compared to the compliance checking of a single business process, achieving compliance of Collaborative Business Process (CBP) is a daunting task as compliance must be achieved not only with the internal regulations but also with different applicable external laws and regulations in place for all partners involved. It, therefore, becomes imperative for organizations to check and verify their process and review internal and external business policies fast enough to match the regulatory demands to avoid fines or litigation. Thus, a knowledge gap exists in automatically verifying the compliance of CBP with existing business processes against amended regulations to avoid starting from scratch, wasting time and resources in creating new processes each time policies or regulations changes.

2   Process Verification vs. Compliance for Collaborative Business Processes

Figure 1 presents a general relationship between collaborative process verification and collaborative process compliance checking. While the process verification is done at the process design stage, the process compliance check is applied for both process design and process running stages. At the process design time, a business process model is designed to comply with different rules, during process running time; the process compliance is monitored and related according to the changed rules.

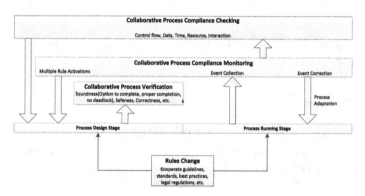

Fig. 1. The relation between verification and compliance

Naturally, process models may exhibit undesired properties in form of error which can prevent successful execution. For instance, in a collaborative business Process involving multiple process partners (i.e. private and public model). If a partner private model is changed uncontrollably, it can bring about the erroneous model to other process partners. It, therefore, becomes crucial to verify the correctness of the collaborative model before implementation as an erroneous model can result in behavioural anomalies within the entire process. The author in [2] describes three levels of correctness in-process model i.e. (i) syntactical correctness – checking the correct use of element (such as tasks, gateways, swim lanes, events), (ii) behavioural correctness (i.e. business process verification) – are the correctness of a model with regards to a set of properties such as deadlock, livelock, or dataflow errors, and (iii) semantics correctness (Business Process Compliance) – checking whether a business process model complies with applicable standards, law and/or regulations. These levels of correctness interlinked with each other and must be considered to fully achieve error-free model.

In this paper, we present the state of the art of CBP verification and business process compliance verification approaches. Complementarily, several open issues will be identified regarding the collaborative process. The rest of the paper is described as follows: Sect. 3 reviewed the state of the art of different process verification approaches in the area of CBP. Section 4 discusses the general view of business process compliance and the different compliance verification approaches. In Sect. 5, we highlight the work being carried out in collaborative process compliance as well as compliance challenges in the context of CN. And lastly, we make conclusions and reveal our ongoing work in CBP in Sect. 6.

3   Collaborative Business Process Verification Approaches

Business process verification is the act of proving the correctness of a model with regards to a set of properties. Presently, several powerful modelling languages have been used in modelling CBP, such as UP-ColBPIP, UMM, IOWF, BPMN 2.0 [3]. Formalizing the execution semantics of such languages enable the definition of formal methods and eliminate language ambiguities. At such, much effort has been devoted to the formalizing the execution semantics of BPMN with some works focusing on the transformation of BPMN elements using an intermediary formal model such as Petri net, process calculi etc. While some works used behavioural anti-patterns, others provide a direct formalization of BPMN semantics. To formally verify the correctness of a model, several verification approaches have been identified in the literature as well as different supporting tools. Preliminary works geared towards the verification of syntactical correctness and behavioural correctness i.e. soundness and weak soundness constraints [4]. To know more about soundness constraints, the reader is referred to [5].

The general approaches of the process verification are based on Petri Net or its variables. Initially, a process model is mapped onto a reset net, and then determines the correctness of the model by analyzing its state-space performances to generate all possible reachable states of a process model [5]. The weak soundness property and the irreducible cancellation regions property have also been determined with the use of backwards coverability notion in reset nets [6].

Aalst [7] described an approach to analyze and model inter-organizational workflows based on synchronous and asynchronous communication. The approach was used to obtain a global workflow modelled using Inter-Organizational Workflow (IOWF), which was then transform into a WF-net and verify its soundness property. Similarly, Jorge Roa et al. [8] propose a verification method - Global Interaction Net (GI-Net) based on Hierarchical and Coloured Petri Net (HCP-Net) to formalize CBP model in UP-ColBPIP, then use CPN tools (Coloured Petri Nets) to verify the Global Interaction soundness property. Their approach was able to support advanced control flow issues like advanced synchronisations, exemption management and cancellation regions, which was not supported in [7]. Roa et al. [8] proposed method is independent of the semantics and can be used with any modelling language for CBP. Though, the model must be structured (i.e. for any other modelling language such as BPMN in a non-structured model, it needs to be converted into a structured model before deriving its corresponding GI-Net). The method is limited to detecting an error in the global view of the interaction of CBPs without considering the private aspects of the collaborative partners. And most importantly the methods rely on state-space exploration, which may harm performance due to the state space explosion problem.

To improve the performance of their verification method, Roa et al. [9] propose a new approach to verify the control flow of CBPs using behavioural anti-patterns and enable the detection of deadlocks in the control flow of CBPs. The approach supports the verification of advanced elements such as exception management, advanced synchronization and multiple instances. Their study reveals that the use of anti-patterns is as accurate as of the use of formal methods, but the latter improves the performance of the verification method [10]. Zhang et al. [11] mapped two formal methods i.e. Petri nets (representing local flow model) and Pi calculus (represent the interaction between model) to model and generate the state graph of CBP using a collaborative reduction tool, then verify the structural soundness of the unified model. In [12], the author models a cross-organisational workflow using Interaction-Oriented Petri Nets (IOPN) then verifies the correctness (soundness and relaxed soundness) of the model based on the invariant analysis. Kheldoun et al. [13] proposed a formal semantics of BPMN using ECARTNets to describe collaborative process then, verify its soundness property using Maude LTL model checker. Their proposed method can formalize BPMN elements like multiple instantiations of subprocesses, cancellation, exception handling while considering the data flow aspect.

In [14], the author proposed a direct formalization for a relevant subset of BPMN for mapping the CBP model in terms of Labeled Transition System (LTS). Then, automatically verify some properties (soundness and safeness) using LTL model checker. Their approach mainly focuses on the control-flow perspective and communication aspects of business processes. Another interesting work is described in [15], they provide a direct formalism of a subset of BPMN semantics using First-Order Logic (FOL) and further develop a verification tool (fbpmn tool) which was implemented in TLA + using TLC model checker. Their approach was able to automatically verify some properties (soundness and safeness).

Overall, most of these studies fail to fully extend the formalism of tricky issues like multiple instances, subprocesses, error handling, loops and data object representation for a CBP. Studies that do not abstract data in verification are either required to state-bound domains which are subject to state-explosion [15] or rely on animation than a complete verification [16], making it difficult to verify a model for any possible initial value of the data [15].

Hence, there is still a need to define a formal semantics which will cover a comprehensive semantics that captures data objects, multi instances, looping and error handling for collaborative business processes. Besides, existing verification approaches for CBPs as review earlier mostly focus on control flow perspectives and communication aspects of business processes, whereby other process perspectives such as data, thermal and resources are abstracted.

Table 1. Comparison of verification approaches in CBP

Approach	Transformation					Anti-patterns		Direct Formalization		
Reference	[10]	[8]	[11]	[12]	[13]	[9]	[10]	[14]	[15]	[37]
Formalism	WF-NET	GI-NET	Petri Net & Pi Calculus	Invariant analysis	ECATNets	Behavioural anti-patterns	Anti-patterns	LTS	FOL	LTS
Tools		CPN				Eclipse plug-in		BProve	tfBPMN	-
Model language	IOWF	UP-ColBPIP	Petri Net & Pi Calculus	IOPN	BPMN	UP-ColBPIP	UP-ColBPIP	BPMN 2.0	BPMN	BPMN
Techniques	-	-	-	-	Maude LTL model checker	-	-	LTL Model checker	TLC Model checker	-
Property verified	Soundness Property	Global soundness	Soundness property	soundness and relaxed soundness	Soundness property	Soundness Property: Deadlock in the control flow of CBP	Soundness Property: Deadlock in the control flow of CBP	Soundness and safeness	Soundness Property	well-structuredness, safeness, and soundness
Sub processes	-	-	-	-	Yes	-	-	-	Yes	Yes
Data	-	-	-	-	-	-	-	-	-	-
Loop	-	-	-	-	Yes	-	-	-	-	-
Multi instance	-	-	-	-	Yes	Yes	Yes	-	-	-
Cancellation regions	-	Yes	-	-	Yes	-	Yes	-	-	-
advanced synchronisations	-	Yes	-	-	-	Yes	Yes	-	-	-
exemption management	-	Yes	-	-	Yes	Yes	Yes	-	-	-

(Left vertical label: *Advance supported elements*)

Table 1 summaries different collaborative business process verification approaches. In general, there are three general types of verification approaches, namely transformation, anti-patterns, and direct formalization which are specified at the top row of the table. Different process verification approaches are also looking at from different aspects, such as which formalism used; properties verified and supported advanced elements of process characteristics, such as supporting sub-process, data flow, etc., which are shown in the first column of the table.

4 Business Process Compliance

While initial works concentrate on the process verification of syntactical correctness and behavioural correctness as mentioned in Sect. 2, recent work addressed issues relating to semantic correctness (processes compliance). Business process compliance denotes checking the compliant behaviour of business processes with applicable corporate guidelines, standards, best practices, legal regulations etc. The regulatory requirements are elicited from the general regulatory document and form constraints that restrict the impermissible behaviour of an organization business process. Though, elicitation of relevant requirement from the source document is not sufficient, as the requirements need to be transformed and translated into a formal form i.e. compliance rules to enable compliance verification over business process models.

It is worth noting that business processes compliance relates to conformance to different process perspective that is different phases of the process life cycles such as control flow, data, time and resources perspectives. The different process perspectives help to establish a relationship which facilitates derivation and categorization of compliance rules from the general policies and regulations. Compliance rules must be comprehensible and at the same time should have a precise semantics to enable automated processing and avoid ambiguities. Hence, several researchers have placed their focus on enabling the specification of compliance rules using different approaches with differences in the level of formalism.

Exiting approaches used in formalizing compliance rules are mostly based on temporal logic and Deontic Logic. Approaches based on temporal logic uses logical language like Computational Tree Logic-CTL [18] and Linear Temporal Logic-LTL [17] to express compliance rules. While approaches based on Deontic logic use languages such as PENELOPE (Process Entailment from the Elicitation of Obligation and Permission) [20] and Formal Contract language (FCL) [19]. As the logic-based approaches are complex and difficult to comprehend for users, and mainly consider the control flow perspectives. Researchers propose a comprehensible pattern and visual-based approaches. The pattern-based approach hides formal details behind the textual description and is limited to a set of predefined compliance rules patterns [21]. The approach addresses control flow, data, thermal and resource perspectives. While the visual languages provide an intuitive way to model compliance rule and hide formal details but are not limited to a predefined set of patterns [22].

4.1 Compliance Verification Approaches

Business Process Compliance involves using different compliance management strategy that is design time and run-time compliance strategy to ensure process compliance [1]. A Design-time strategy is a preventive approach that aims at managing and ensuring the compliance of business processes at the design phase or before execution time [23]. To check business process compliance at design time several approaches have been proposed as well as different verification techniques. In [24], the approaches are categorized based on logic-based, static-based, pattern-based, and query-based approaches. These approaches often propose different languages to support checking in terms of structural behaviour, contractual obligations and security and privacy [25] and address different phases of the process life cycle.

These categorized approaches are based on different underlying techniques in which the common techniques used is model checking. Studies like [18] have reported the use of model checking to verify the compliance of business process addressing different process perspectives. Though model checking techniques can identify the source of error but has its drawback. For instance, since the techniques rely on the exploration of the state space of process model then it can result in a state-space explosion which is a big challenge for practical implementation. Though, the challenges can be mitigated with the application of abstraction methods and techniques [26]. To address these issues, studies like [27, 28] proposed other techniques like graph reduction and sequentialization of parallel workflow and predicate abstractions [29]. While most of these approaches consider the control-flow perspective only, few studied also consider data perspectives and time perspectives.

Furthermore, Business process compliance checking and verification have been well addressed in literature from different angles in terms of privacy and security based on RBAC (Role-Based Access Control model) for access control and authorization based on roles [30], TBAC (Task-Based Access Control) for access control and authorization policies based on task executed in the process [31], ABAC (Attribute-Based Access Control) [32], SecBPMN [33] and STS-ml [34].

Table 2 summarizes some of the state-of-the-art approaches for design-time compliance checking and verification. The approaches are classified based on their underlying techniques that are logic-based, static based, query-based, pattern-based approaches [24] and approaches based on compliance with privacy and security.

Compared to design-time checking (see Fig. 1), run-time compliance strategy involves checking business process compliance during its execution [23]. The reality is that even if a business process has been checked during design-time, there is no certainty that the corresponding running process instance will be compliant as a result of human and machine-related errors. This implies that after designing a process model and the actual execution of a process is initiated, the running process instances need to be constantly monitored to detect any inconsistencies or violations [24]. The run-time approach has been well addressed in the literature and is categorized based on run-time compliance monitoring approach and run-time compliance detection [24]. Both approaches are further classified into monitoring–based approaches, logic-based approaches, and model-based approaches. While the runtime compliance approach is perceived to be flexible and having the ability to handle compliance violations beyond design time; the design time is preferable for being pre-emptive in detecting compliance violations and allowing corrections at an earlier stage during process design.

Table 2. Summary of compliance verification approaches

Formalism		Approach	Applications	Control flow	Data	Resources	Time
Model	CR						
Logic based Approaches							
BCL		Deontic	Design time	x			
FCL		Deontic	Design time	x			x
		Model checking	Design time	x			
PCL		Deontic	Design time	x			
PENELOPE		Deontic	Design time	x			x
NTL-ALC		Model checking	Design time	x			
CRL		Temporal	Design time	x			
Static based compliance approaches							
BPEL -> π-calculus -> FSM	BPSL-LTL	Model checking	Design time	x	x		x
Timed automata	CTL	Model checking	Design time	x			
Pattern/graph based approaches							
PROPOLS - FSA		Pattern-based	Design time	x			x
BPMN-> automata	LTL	Model checking & bi-simulation	Design time	x			
BPEL-> LTS->TDFA	Ontology language	compliance verification approach	Design time	x			
LTL	CRL-LTL	Pattern-based	Design time	x			
Query based Approaches							
BPMN-Q		Graph reduction technique and model checking	Design time	x	x		
Approaches based on compliance with security and privacy							
RBAC		Temporal logic	Design time				
TBAC		Temporal logic	Design time	x	x		x
ABAC		Temporal logic	Design time	x	x		x
SecBPMN		Temporal logic	Design time	x	x		
STS-ml		-	Design time	x	x		

5 Compliance in Collaborative Processes

Collaborative Network (CN) has been the topic of discussion in the literature involving a diverse range of new forms of collaboration i.e. from vertically integrated organizations into a more flexible network organisation such as Virtual Organisations, Virtual Enterprise, chain or enterprise networks. CN involves business integration and collaboration between geographically distributed and heterogeneous organizations to achieve strategic objectives in a timely and cost-effective manner. Such integration and collaboration among the organizations are established and carried out through Collaborative Business Processes (CBP) enabled by advancement in technology. Though, it is accompanied by a high level of complexity in regards to governance and compliance challenges which is yet to be fully explored.

By nature, achieving compliance of CBP in the context of CN is complex and requires unique characteristics and requirements due to its design principles for decentralized decision making. For instance, different partners combine resources and skills to design and execute a business opportunity and at the same time act independently from each other. The fact that each partner is geographically distributed makes them distinct from partners in the same location. In particular, besides the internal policies and external regulations regulating each partner process, their process is also governed by contractual obligations as well as international regulations guiding their overall process operations. Achieving compliance in such a network environment will be challenging and especially when process structure is change by a partner in an uncontrolled manner, or when policy or regulations changes.

Potential changes in process or policies and regulations are inevitable and should be expected either through market expectations and needs, amendment of existing laws or implementation of new laws, policies and regulations. A great example is with the COVID-19, which has made the government around the world to revise and amends regulations in response to the virus outbreak. Most organizations must change and comply with their businesses and services according to the strategies published by the governments of different countries. Collaborative business partners will need to assess and deal with changes in regulatory requirements around the world differently. These changes might have a direct effect on the entire business collaboration and its existing processes resulting in heavy cost as well as causing an organization to modify its entire process or part of it to achieve compliance. Falling to manage or constantly monitor these changes can lead to penalties and potential legal issues.

In reality, compliance can be fulfilled before a change in CBP but this might not remain satisfied after any change occurs. Therefore, after a change has been applied to a process or compliance rules, it is imperative to identify changes in the policy, follow a formal method to re-evaluate the compliance rules, identify the components of the process that are affected by the amendments, and recheck all the three correctness level specifically checking if the existing or redesigned collaborative process still complies with all compliance rules. Though, few works have been done in the literature addressing the impact of change on the compliance of CBP. For instance, the work of [35], analyses how compliance rule and process changes impact on each other, then, further propose an algorithm that deals with the change propagation in CBP. And of recent, Kasse [36], propose a simulation technique to assess the impact of regulatory variations over existing or redesign collaborative business process. Compliance of CBP, however, is yet to be fully investigated or checked after any changes in process or compliance rule.

It is worth noting that despite the overwhelming body of literature addressing the compliance-related problem from a variety of perspectives, it is hard to oversee, compare and make a decision on which of the existing approaches could be utilized to check the compliance of CBP after any changes. Hence we justify the need to optimize different compliance verification approaches and provide an efficient algorithm that will support compliance verification of CBP after any change to keep the CBP model behaviourally and semantically correct both at design time and runtime.

6 Conclusion and Future Research

The paper first provides a clear picture of the relationship between collaborative process verification and collaborative process compliance. Different approaches for collaborative process verification in Sect. 3 and process compliance in Sects. 4 and 5 are summarized. The paper also reviews the different techniques used in the verification and compliance check, i.e. formal methods, model checkers, graph reduction, sequentialization of parallel workflow, and predicate abstractions, etc.

More recently using process traces and process simulation are used to check collaborative process compliance due to the complex nature of collaboration. Traditionally, the properties for process verification or checking are limited. Today collaborative networks are often subject to restrictions that stem from laws, regulations or guidelines which are not just impacting the control flows of the processes, but also data flow, resource flow, and process exceptional handling. The compliance properties thus need to be largely extended not only to cover traditional process properties, but also security and time, etc. COVID-19 has changed our lives and is likely to make a lasting impact on our economic development. All existing CNs are facing some levels' changes. The paper provides the first step forward to the solutions of compliance checking of CNs in dynamic environments.

Acknowledgements. This research is part of the FIRST project which has received funding from the European Union's Horizon 2020 research and innovation programme under the Marie Skłodowska-Curie grant agreement No. 734599.

References

1. El Gammal, A.F.S.A.: Towards a comprehensive framework for business process compliance. Tilburg University, School of Economics and Management (2012)
2. Petersen, S.A., Pourzolfaghar, Z., Alloush, I., Ahlers, D., Krogstie, J., Helfert, M.: Value-added services, virtual enterprises and data spaces inspired enterprise architecture for smart cities. In: Camarinha-Matos, Luis M., Afsarmanesh, H., Antonelli, D. (eds.) PRO-VE 2019. IFIP AICT, vol. 568, pp. 393–402. Springer, Cham (2019). https://doi.org/10.1007/978-3-030-28464-0_34

3. von Rosing, M., et al.: Business Process Model and Notation-BPMN (2015)
4. Knuplesch, D., Reichert, M., Kumar, A.: A framework for visually monitoring business process compliance. Inf. Syst. **64**, 381–409 (2017)
5. Wynn, M.T., et al.: Business process verification–finally a reality! Business Process Management Journal (2009)
6. Finkel, A., Schnoebelen, P.: Well-structured transition systems everywhere! Theoret. Comput. Sci. **256**(1–2), 63–92 (2001)
7. Van Der Aalst, M.: Modeling and analyzing interorganizational workflows. In: Proceedings 1998 International Conference on Application of Concurrency to System Design. IEEE (1998)
8. Roa, J., Chiotti, O., Villarreal, P.: A verification method for collaborative business processes. In: Daniel, F., Barkaoui, K., Dustdar, S. (eds.) BPM 2011. LNBIP, vol. 99, pp. 293–305. Springer, Heidelberg (2012). https://doi.org/10.1007/978-3-642-28108-2_29
9. Roa, J., Chiotti, O.J.A., Villarreal, P.D.: Detection of anti-patterns in the control flow of collaborative business processes. In: Simposio Argentino de Ingeniería de Software (ASSE 2015)-JAIIO 44, Rosario (2015)
10. Roa, J., et al.: Specification of behavioural anti-patterns for the verification of block-structured collaborative business processes. Inf. Softw. Technol. **75**, 148–170 (2016)
11. Zhang, L., Lu, Y., Xu, F.: Unified modelling and analysis of the collaboration business process based on Petri nets and Pi calculus. IET Softw. **4**(5), 303–317 (2010)
12. Ge, J., Hu, H.: A decomposition approach with invariant analysis for workflow coordination. In: Chen, L., Liu, C., Liu, Q., Deng, K. (eds.) DASFAA 2009. LNCS, vol. 5667, pp. 290–302. Springer, Heidelberg (2009). https://doi.org/10.1007/978-3-642-04205-8_25
13. Kheldoun, A., Barkaoui, K., Ioualalen, M.: Formal verification of complex business processes based on high-level Petri nets. J. Inf. Sci. **385**, 39–54 (2017)
14. Corradini, F., et al.: BProVe: a formal verification framework for business process models. In: 32nd IEEE/ACM International Conference on Automated Software Engineering (ASE). IEEE (2017)
15. Houhou, S., Baarir, S., Poizat, P., Quéinnec, P.: A first-order logic semantics for communication-parametric BPMN collaborations. In: Hildebrandt, T., van Dongen, B.F., Röglinger, M., Mendling, J. (eds.) BPM 2019. LNCS, vol. 11675, pp. 52–68. Springer, Cham (2019). https://doi.org/10.1007/978-3-030-26619-6_6
16. Corradini, F., Muzi, C., Re, B., Rossi, L., Tiezzi, F.: Animating Multiple instances in BPMN collaborations: from formal semantics to tool support. In: Weske, M., Montali, M., Weber, I., vom Brocke, J. (eds.) BPM 2018. LNCS, vol. 11080, pp. 83–101. Springer, Cham (2018). https://doi.org/10.1007/978-3-319-98648-7_6
17. Ghose, A., Koliadis, G.: Auditing business process compliance. In: Krämer, Bernd J., Lin, K.-J., Narasimhan, P. (eds.) ICSOC 2007. LNCS, vol. 4749, pp. 169–180. Springer, Heidelberg (2007). https://doi.org/10.1007/978-3-540-74974-5_14
18. Nishizaki, S.-y., Ohata, T.: Real-time model checking for regulatory compliance. In: Das, V. V., Chaba, Y. (eds.) Mobile Communication and Power Engineering. CCIS, vol. 296, pp. 70–77. Springer, Heidelberg (2013). https://doi.org/10.1007/978-3-642-35864-7_10
19. Governatori, G., Rotolo, A.: Norm compliance in business process modeling. In: Dean, M., Hall, J., Rotolo, A., Tabet, S. (eds.) RuleML 2010. LNCS, vol. 6403, pp. 194–209. Springer, Heidelberg (2010). https://doi.org/10.1007/978-3-642-16289-3_17
20. Goedertier, S., Vanthienen, J.: Designing compliant business processes with obligations and permissions. In: International Conference on Business Process Management. Springer (2006)
21. Turetken, O., et al.: Capturing compliance requirements: a pattern-based approach. IEEE Softw. **29**(3), 28–36 (2012). https://doi.org/10.1109/MS.2012.45

22. Knuplesch, D., et al.: Visual modelling of business process compliance rules with the support of multiple perspectives. In: International Conference on Conceptual Modelling. Springer (2013)
23. Fdhila, W., et al.: Change and compliance in collaborative processes. In: IEEE International Conference on Services Computing. IEEE (2015)
24. Hashmi, M., et al.: Are we done with business process compliance: state of the art and challenges ahead. **57**(1), 79–133 (2018)
25. Kasse, J.P., et al.: The need for compliance verification in collaborative business processes. In: Working Conference on Virtual Enterprises. Springer (2018)
26. Frederick, K. Frantz. A: taxonomy of model abstraction techniques. In: Proceedings of the 27th Conference on Winter Simulation, pp. 1413–1420 (1995). https://doi.org/10.1145/224401.224834
27. Awad, A., Sakr, S.: Querying graph-based repositories of business process models. In: Yoshikawa, M., Meng, X., Yumoto, T., Ma, Q., Sun, L., Watanabe, C. (eds.) DASFAA 2010. LNCS, vol. 6193, pp. 33–44. Springer, Heidelberg (2010). https://doi.org/10.1007/978-3-642-14589-6_4
28. Barnawi, A., et al.: An anti-pattern-based runtime business process compliance monitoring framework **7**(2) (2016)
29. Knuplesch, D., Reichert, M.: Ensuring business process compliance along the process life cycle (2012)
30. Combi, C., Viganò, L., Zavatteri, M.: Security constraints in temporal role-based access-controlled workflows. In: Proceedings of the Sixth ACM Conference on Data and Application Security and Privacy (2016)
31. Thomas, R.K., Sandhu, R.S.: Task-based authorization controls (TBAC): a family of models for active and enterprise-oriented authorization management. Database Security XI. IFIP AICT, pp. 166–181. Springer, Boston, MA (1998). https://doi.org/10.1007/978-0-387-35285-5_10
32. Gautam, M., et al.: Poster: Constrained policy mining in attribute-based access control. In: Proceedings of the 22nd ACM on Symposium on Access Control Models and Technologies (2017)
33. Salnitri, M., Dalpiaz, F., Giorgini, P.: Modeling and verifying security policies in business processes. In: Bider, I., Gaaloul, K., Krogstie, J., Nurcan, S., Proper, Henderik A., Schmidt, R., Soffer, P. (eds.) BPMDS/EMMSAD -2014. LNBIP, vol. 175, pp. 200–214. Springer, Heidelberg (2014). https://doi.org/10.1007/978-3-662-43745-2_14
34. Robol, M., Salnitri, M., Giorgini, P.: Toward GDPR-compliant socio-technical systems: modeling language and reasoning framework. In: Poels, G., Gailly, F., Serral Asensio, E., Snoeck, M. (eds.) PoEM 2017. LNBIP, vol. 305, pp. 236–250. Springer, Cham (2017). https://doi.org/10.1007/978-3-319-70241-4_16
35. Knuplesch, D., Fdhila, W., Reichert, M., Rinderle-Ma, S.: Detecting the effects of changes on the compliance of cross-organizational business processes. In: Johannesson, P., Lee, M. L., Liddle, Stephen W., Opdahl, Andreas L., López, Ó.P. (eds.) ER 2015. LNCS, vol. 9381, pp. 94–107. Springer, Cham (2015). https://doi.org/10.1007/978-3-319-25264-3_7
36. Kasse, J.: Supporting Compliance Verification for Collaborative Business Processes. Bournemouth University, UK (2019)
37. Corradini, F., et al.: Well-structuredness, Safeness and Soundness: A Formal Classification of BPMN (Collaborations) (2020)

Digital Transformation

Strategic Target System to Select Digitalization Measures in Manufacturing Companies

Günther Schuh[1]([⊠]), Jan Hicking[1], Felix Jordan[2],
Max-Ferdinand Stroh[1], and Stephan-Andrés Saß[1]

[1] Institute for Industrial Management, FIR at RWTH Aachen University,
Campus Boulevard 55, 52074 Aachen, Germany
{Guenther.Schuh,Jan.Hicking,Max-Ferdinand.Stroh,
Stephan-Andres.Sass}@fir.rwth-aachen.de
[2] Elisa Deutschland GmbH, Campus-Boulevard 57, 52070 Aachen, Germany
Felix.Jordan@elisa.com

Abstract. Manufacturing companies face the challenge of selecting digitalization measures that fit their strategy. Measures that are initiated and not aligned with the company's strategy carry the risk of failing due to lack of relevance. This leads to an ineffective use of scarce human and financial resources. This paper presents a target system to help companies select relevant digitalization measures compliant with their strategy for IT-OT-integration projects. The target system was developed based on literature research and expert interviews, and later validated in two use cases. The target system considers the goals of production companies and combines them with digitalization measures. The measures are classified by different maturity levels required for their realization. Thus, the target system enables manufacturing companies to evaluate digitalization measures with regards to their strategic relevance and the required Industrie 4.0 maturity level for their realization. This ensures an effective use of resources.

Keywords: Industry 4.0 · Digitalization · Strategy · IT-OT-Integration

1 Introduction

Industry 4.0 requires producing companies to transform their technological landscape. One challenge is the integration of Information Technology (IT) and Operational Technology (OT) to achieve the business potentials of Industrie 4.0 [1, 2]. Since many OT-systems were developed to ensure an efficient production, they tend to lack interface standards for IT-systems. This results in technological silos and untapped data sources [3]. With limited digitalisation resources, especially in SMEs, companies need to have a clear understanding of the business case when entering IT-OT-integration projects: What are the expected efforts, and what is the business impact in return.

This paper introduces a target system that reveals the effect of Industrie 4.0 maturity levels on a production system's efficiency. It shall support companies to understand which maturity level has impact on the production system's efficiency. Thus, it sheds light onto the expected business impact of an IT-OT-integration project. The target

© IFIP International Federation for Information Processing 2020
Published by Springer Nature Switzerland AG 2020
L. M. Camarinha-Matos et al. (Eds.): PRO-VE 2020, IFIP AICT 598, pp. 227–236, 2020.
https://doi.org/10.1007/978-3-030-62412-5_19

system is one stream to support companies selecting their Industrie 4.0 projects. The second stream (not part of this paper) is a methodology to assess the technological maturity of OT-systems. This methodology will help estimate the expected efforts to integrate OT-systems. Both streams combined will enable SMEs to quickly define and prioritize their Industrie 4.0 business cases.

This target system focusses on the IT-OT-Integration in a manufacturing environment. It is designed for being used by a company's (production-) management team.

The overall goal of the paper is reflected in the research question: "How must a target system for the selection of digitalization measures in the context of IT-OT integration in a manufacturing environment be designed?"

In the beginning of the paper the target system is derived based on a literature review. The Industrie 4.0 Maturity Index [4] is used to connect the goals with potential measures, the utility potentials. Afterwards, a general IT-OT-Integration methodology is presented, in which the target system can be used. In the end, the target system is applied to two use-cases and the results are discussed briefly.

2 Background

IT-OT-Integration plays a significant role in the implementation of Industry 4.0 [1]. *Information Technology (IT)* is synonymous with the office floor systems, which capture, process, and provide data and information within the enterprise. IT includes ERP (Enterprise Resource Planning) and CRM (Customer Relationship Management) systems and supports the management's decision-making processes [5]. IT systems work with pre-processed data [6].

Operational Technology (OT) compromises of the shop floor systems, that support the physical value adding processes through supervising and controlling hard- and software [7]. Controlling and supervision occurs with OT-systems i.e. MES, SCADA, sensors and actors [5]. To better support and control the operational processes, OT-systems have to be capable of processing real-time data [6].

IT-OT-Integration describes the merging of operational technology with information technology, so that data can effortlessly be transferred between these systems [8].

The challenge of merging IT and OT systems in a manufacturing environment has scarcely been covered by literature. The literature was evaluated based on three selection criteria: 1) Are the challenges of IT-OT-integration addressed in particular, 2) Does the literature provide enough technical depth to derive guidance on how to tackle an integration project, 3) Does the literature consider the business potential of the IT-OT-integration activity?

None of the identified and analyzed literature met the requirements of addressing the issues of IT-OT-integration, while providing enough technical depths to serve as a guideline on how to tackle the integration. Finally, the identified literature lacks the business potential that accompanies the integration.

Only three of the examined papers are focusing on the issue of IT-OT-Integration [9–11]. While all three of them cover business benefits of integration, they maintain a high-level perspective, and do not consider the needs of a manufacturing company.

And only [9] and [10] have at least some technical depth for the reader to assess the technical effort of the integration activity.

Literature that focuses on managing Manufacturing Execution Systems [12] tend to have a very deep technical depth but are lacking the differentiation between IT and OT landscapes and therefore cannot serve as guidelines through the IT-OT-integration.

In addition, literature that focusses the topic of Enterprise Architecture Management was assessed. None of the found pieces differentiated specifically between IT and OT systems, and while some provided some technical depth [13–16], only one stresses the business potentials of the integration [17]. As a result, none of them are suited for the paper's purpose. Furthermore, an analysis of reference architectures in the context of IT-OT convergence was done. Research produced poor results with regards to the technical depth [18, 19]. The reference architectures RAMI 4.0 and Industrial Internet of Things Reference Architecture (IIRA) lacked technical depth on managing IT-OT-landscapes and miss on OT-related business potentials regarding integration [18, 20].

To further individualize the needs of the SMEs, this paper uses utility potentials to closer analyze and identify, which measures must be implemented to achieve the desired sub-, intermediate-, and overall objective. According to SCHUH AND KREUTZER utility is a highly individualized approach to measure the fulfilment of a need [21]. A potential is defined as the opportunity to develop or succeed [22]. In combination, this paper thus defines a utility potential to be the opportunity to successfully fulfil a business need. In the context of the developed target system the utility potential refers to the digitalization measure to be taken and its resulting utility.

3 Description of the Methodology

3.1 Derivation of the Target System

The methodology is supposed to enable producing SMEs to engage in IT-OT-integration projects that fit their company's (digitalisation) strategy. Furthermore, the authors assume that optimising the production system's efficiency is the paramount goal for the production manager. Hence, this generic target system discloses the impact of digitalisation maturity on the production system's efficiency. The target system combines two concepts: ERLACH's work on production system efficiency and its influencing parts [23], and the Industrie 4.0 Maturity Index [24].

ERLACH discusses the effects of a production system's variability, quality, speed, and profitability on its efficiency. A production system consists of input resources that are processed into output in the production system. Accordingly, an increase in production system efficiency is achieved either by increasing the output with the same resource input or by reducing the resource input with the same output [25].

The *variability* of a production indicates the broadness of the production spectrum it can handle and whether it handles customer-specific products [23, 26]. Variability is defined as number of OK parts as output per number of (machine) setups [23]. Increasing the variability therefore has a positive impact on the production system efficiency [27]. The *quality* of a production can be derived from the scrap, the achievable tolerance level of the production processes and the adherence to delivery dates [23, 26]. It is defined that quality is measured by number of OK parts per number of total output. As a result, a higher quality improves the efficiency of a production system [28]. The *speed* of a production is determined by the duration of the value-adding process steps, the associated secondary activities as well as the throughput time [23, 26]. Speed is defined as number of OK parts per time, and thus correlates positively with the production system efficiency [29]. The *profitability* of production refers to productivity, with employee productivity, machine utilisation and material utilisation being the main determination factors [23, 26]. Profitability can be determined as number of OK parts per costs. Hence, a higher profitability indicates an increased production system efficiency

ERLACH states that quality and profitability, as well as variability and speed, are conflicting, while variability and quality do not have a positive effect on each other but may affect one another in a negative way. Only speed and economy show a target compatibility, meaning that the optimization of the one leads to an improvement of the other [23]. These four factors are defined as the intermediate goals for the target system. The sub-objectives and their relations are arranged in the target system of overall and intermediate objectives as shown in Fig. 1.

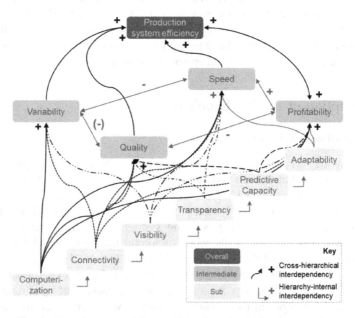

Fig. 1. Target system with overall, intermediate, and sub-objectives

The six maturity levels introduced by the Industrie 4.0 Maturity Index are introduced as sub-objectives: Computerization, Connectivity, Visibility, Transparency, Predictive Capacity, and Adaptability. *Computerization* is implemented when the relevant process steps in the area under consideration are supported or carried out through the (isolated) use of digital technologies [30]. The second level, *connectivity,* is achieved when the isolated digital technologies are integrated horizontally, i.e. have the necessary software interfaces and hardware ports through which they communicate with decentralized IT systems [30]. The *visibility* level means that the digital technologies are vertically connected as data sources, so that data and information about the business processes are available and can be exchanged in real time [30]. The fourth level of maturity, *transparency*, will be achieved by contextualization of data and information. This enables root-cause analyses to support the decision-making [30]. The maturity level *predictive capacity* means that management can reliably project decisions and their effects into the future and thus simulate future scenarios to aid the decision-making process. In addition, the company can anticipate upcoming events and proactively demonstrate response actions to the management to make operations more robust [30]. *Adaptability* is the highest level of the Industry 4.0 Maturity Index and includes the ability to autonomously adapt to changes in the business environment, to make decisions through the IT systems in use and to initiate measures [30].

The paper introduces the maturity levels as sub-objectives. It is defined that there are no direct positive or negative correlations in between the maturity levels. Nevertheless, the preceding maturity levels need to be achieved before it is possible to reach the next maturity level.

Table 1 shows the positive correlations between intermediate and sub objectives with an "x".

Table 1. Influence of the stages of maturity on the intermediate objectives

Maturity Level/Intermediate objective	Variability	Quality	Speed	Profitability	Source
Computerization	×	×	×	×	[31]
Connectivity	×	×	×	×	[32–34]
Visibility	×		×	×	[5, 35–38]
Transparency		×	×		[39]
Predictive Capacity		×		×	[40]
Adaptability			×	×	[32, 41]

A deeper understanding of this paper's results can be gained with Table 2. It shows examples of measures pertaining to each maturity level in increasing order of maturity.

Table 2. Exemplary extract of measures to achieve each Maturity Level

Maturity level	Exemplary measure	Source
Computerization	CNC controls throughout the factory	[4]
Connectivity	Machines are connected to MES	[4]
Visibility	Digital order, asset and material tracking	[42]
Transparency	Realization of a digital production shadow	[43]
Predictive Capacity	Manufacturing process optimization via machine learning	[44]
Adaptability	Adaptive reaction of manufacturing line to errors	[45]

Each exemplary measure represents part of the means to achieving the maturity level it is assigned to. Even though the maturity levels induce each other, they do not affect each other positively or negatively. Combining these measures with consequential utilities describe utility potentials and are subordinate to the maturity levels in the target system and therefore to the intermediate and overall objectives.

3.2 Methodology for the Application of the Target System

The target system's application forms part of a bigger methodology for a goal-oriented IT-OT-Integration process. Figure 2 shows this process. It consists of two general streams, the assessment of IT and OT-Systems as well as the selection of utility potentials. In the end the two streams are combined to match the current IT-OT-Landscape with the selected utility potentials. However, both systems can be applied separately. The selection of utility potentials via the target system, which this paper focuses on, are marked in dashed lines, and are described in this section.

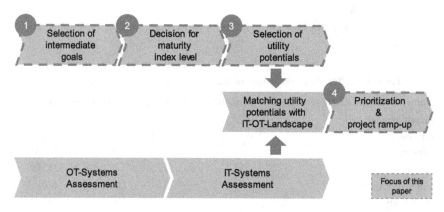

Fig. 2. Methodology for the application of the target system

The first step is the selection of intermediate goals. The overall goal for the target system is production system efficiency to achieve customer value, which is fixed. Generally, the intermediate goals should be selected based on the manufacturing and corporate strategy of the company. In a workshop, the potential benefits of the intermediate goals can be collected and mapped to the company's strategic goals.

Once the intermediate goals are selected, the current maturity level, as well as the aspired maturity level, must be selected.

Based on the selected maturity level the utility potentials are selected. This paper offers an exemplary selection of possible measures to realize the utility potentials. This list will be enhanced in future publications. However, the selected maturity level serves as base and inspiration for defining the concrete utility potentials that shall be taken.

Usually an assessment of a manufacturing facility reveals more than one potential measure or utility potential that can be addressed. Therefore, the last step of the proposed methodology is prioritization and project ramp up. In the beginning of this step the list of selected and identified measures is prioritized. The authors recommend a cost-benefit-analysis by assessing the potential costs in relation to the potential benefits of measures taken. The results can be visualized in a portfolio-matrix, to show cost estimate versus utility estimate.

Once the prioritization is finished, measures are selected and then transferred into individual projects, which can then be ramped up.

4 Discussion of the Target System for Two Industry Use Cases

In this section, the authors present the practical application of the target-system for two industry use-cases. The target system was applied in expert workshops during the meeting of the user-committee of the underlying research project. The chosen targets of the participants have been randomly altered to ensure privacy.

Company 1 is a manufacturer of electronic components for a wide range of international customers. The batch sizes within their production differ from ten to 50,000 pieces.

Company 2 is a prototyping and product development provider. Next to series manufacturing of products for their customers, they are building prototypes from mechanical to mechatronic products. The batch sizes range from one to several hundred products.

Table 3 shows an excerpt from the results of the application of the target system in both companies. Both companies selected a single intermediate goal. During the workshop it became obvious, that the selection of the intermediate goal is challenging and should be done with care. In this case, company 1 focusses on *quality* improvement and company 2 on *speed*.

Table 3. Example results of target system application

Company/selected items	Company 1 (Electronics)	Company 2 (Protoyping)
1. Intermediate goal	Quality	Speed
2. Maturity Level	Transparency	Connectivity
3. Prioritized measures	Realization of a digital shadow	Implementation of ERP-System
	Automated calculation of production KPIs	Connection of existing machines to MES
	...	...

Afterwards, the companies identified their Industrie 4.0 maturity level based on the information provided for the Industrie 4.0 Maturity Index. Both companies identified lower maturity levels for themselves, which represents the current state of the industry [30]. The maturity level reflects the current state of Industry 4.0 in a company.

To advance in their level, industry 4.0 measures need to be applied. Based on the selected maturity level the companies developed potential measures to reach their goals. In the presented use-cases, company 1 mainly focused on the realization of a digital shadow to improve the overall quality in production. Company 2 selected the implementation of an ERP-System as the main goal for improving its production speed.

Generally, the feedback regarding the developed target system was exceedingly positive. This first evaluation confirmed the findings in literature from which the target system was derived. The application was very intuitive and good to explain.

Further improvement can be made on the list of potential measures provided. This will be enhanced within the research-project. Some participants of the workshop also mentioned that some companies' challenges could not be covered directly by the target system. This is because the target system serves as a bridge between the strategical and the practical perspective, focusing on IT-OT-Integration. Therefore, it serves as a means of improvement rather than for troubleshooting. All participants agreed that the system was helpful in aligning current digitalization measures taken in a manufacturing environment with the company's strategy.

Future research will focus on assessing the current IT-OT-Integration level in a manufacturing environment to select measures based on the planned development of a company. This will further improve the application and coverage of the target system.

5 Conclusion

This paper focuses on the development of a target system for selecting digitalization measures in a manufacturing companies. Based on that, a target system linking company goals with Industrie 4.0 maturity levels and utility potentials is presented. Next to that, the paper presents a methodology for the application of the target system. Finally, the methodology is applied to two industry use-cases and evaluated based on the results.

The first applications of the target system show, that it can be used successfully for structuring the digitalization process within a manufacturing company. Once the IT-OT-Assessment stream is added to the methodology it will reach its full potential as the selection of utility potentials can be matched with the current IT-OT-Landscape and vice versa. Both utility potentials as well as the assessment of the IT-OT-Landscape need further development, which will be covered in future publications.

Acknowledgements. The IGF project 20768 BG of the Research Association FIR e. V. at the RWTH Aachen University is funded via the AiF within the framework of the programme for the funding of cooperative industrial research (IGF) by the Federal Ministry of Economics and Energy (BMWi) on the basis of a resolution of the German Bundestag.

References

1. Schlick, C. (ed.): Megatrend Digitalisierung - Potenziale der Arbeits- und Betriebsorganisation. GITO, Berlin (2016)
2. Weber, H., Viehmann, J.: Unternehmens-IT für die Digitalisierung 4.0. Springer Fachmedien Wiesbaden, Wiesbaden (2017)
3. Agarwal, N., Brem, A.: Strategic business transformation through technology convergence. Implications Gen. Electric's Ind. Internet Initiative. IJTM **67**, 196–214 (2015)
4. Schuh, G., Anderl, R., Gausemeier, J., Hompel, M., ten Wahlster, W.: Industrie 4.0 maturity index. Managing the Digital Transformation of Companies, Munich (2017)
5. Noronha, A., Moriarty, R., O'Connell, K., Villa, N.: Attaining IoT value: how to move from connecting things to capturing insights. Gain an Edge by Taking Analytics to the Edge. Hrsg.: Cisco Systems, I. https://www.cisco.com/c/dam/en_us/solutions/trends/iot/docs/iot-data-analytics-white-paper.P
6. Kuusk, A.G., Gao, J.: Consolidating people, process and technology to bridge the great wall of operational and information technologies. In: Tse, P.W., Mathew, J., Wong, K., Lam, R., Ko, C.N. (eds.) Proceedings of the 8th World Congress Engineering Asset Management 2013, pp. 1715–1726. Springer, Cham (2014). https://doi.org/10.1007/978-3-319-09507-3_147
7. Chemudupati, A., et al.: The convergence of IT and Operational Technology (2012)
8. Garimella, P.K.: IT-OT Integration Challenges in Utilities, Kathmandu, Nepal: an IEEE Nepal Sub Section Conference. IEEE, Piscataway, NJ, 25–27 October 2018 (2018)
9. Kuusk, A., Gao, J.: Factors for successfully integrating operational and information technologies. In: 2015 Portland International Conference on Management of Engineering and Technology (PICMET), pp. 1513–1523. IEEE (2015)
10. Verdouw, C.N., Robbemond, R., Kruize, J.W.: Integration of Production Control and Enterprise Management Systems in Horticulture (2015)
11. Lara, P., Sánchez, M., Villalobos, J.: Bridging the IT and OT worlds using an extensible modeling language. In: Comyn-Wattiau, I., Tanaka, K., Song, I.-Y., Yamamoto, S., Saeki, M. (eds.) ER 2016. LNCS, vol. 9974, pp. 122–129. Springer, Cham (2016). https://doi.org/10.1007/978-3-319-46397-1_10
12. Kletti, J.: MES - Manufacturing Execution System. Springer, Heidelberg (2015)
13. Krcmar, H.: Informationsmanagement. Springer Gabler, Wiesbaden (2015)
14. Lehner, F., Scholz, M., Wildner, S.: Wirtschaftsinformatik. Eine Einführung. Hanser, Carl, München (2008)
15. Zimmermann, A., Schmidt, R., Sandkuhl, K., Jugel, D., Möhring, M., Wißotzki, M.: Enterprise architecture management for the Internet of things. Bonn (2015)
16. Tiemeyer, E., Bergmann, R.: Handbuch IT-Management. Konzepte, Methoden, Lösungen und Arbeitshilfen für die Praxis. Hanser, München, München (2015)
17. Matthes, D.: Enterprise Architecture Frameworks Kompendium. Springer, Heidelberg (2011)
18. IIC - Industrial Internet Consortium: The Industrial Internet of Things Volume G1: Reference Architecture (2019)
19. Bassi, A., et al.: Enabling Things to Talk. Springer, Heidelberg (2013)
20. Status Report: Reference Architecture Model Industrie 4.0 (RAMI4.0) (2015)
21. Schuh, G., Kreutzer, R.: Methodology to Assess the Utility Potentials of Cyber-Physical Systems' Field Data. A Literature Review and Rough Solution Concept (2017)
22. Cambridge University Press: POTENTIAL| meaning in the Cambridge English Dictionary. https://dictionary.cambridge.org/dictionary/english/potential
23. Erlach, K.: Wertstromdesign. Der Weg zur schlanken Fabrik. Springer, Berlin (2010)

24. Schuh, G., Anderl, R., Dumitrescu, R., Krüger, A., ten Hompel, M.: Using the Industrie 4.0 Maturity Index in Industry – current challenges, case studies and trends (acatech COOPERATION)
25. Gottmann, J.: Produktionscontrolling. Springer Fachmedien Wiesbaden, Wiesbaden (2016)
26. Pfeffer, M.: Bewertung von Wertströmen. Kosten-Nutzen-Betrachtung von Optimierungsszenarien. Springer Gabler, Wiesbaden (2014)
27. Deuse, J., Lenze, D., Klenner, F., Friedich, T.: Manufacturing Data Analytics zur Identifikation dynamischer Engpässe in Produktionssystemen mit hoher wertschöpfender Variabilität. In: Schlick, C. (ed.) Megatrend Digitalisierung - Potenziale der Arbeits- und Betriebsorganisation, pp. 11–26. GITO, Berlin (2016)
28. Schröder, A.-K., Nebl, T.: Qualität - Einflussfaktor auf die Produktivität. In: Specht, D. (ed.) Weiterentwicklung der Produktion. Tagungsband der Herbsttagung 2008 der Wissenschaftlichen Kommission Produktionswirtschaft im VHB, pp. 117–141. Gabler, Wiesbaden (2009)
29. Adam, D.: Produktionspolitik. Gabler Verlag, Wiesbaden (1976)
30. Schuh, G., Anderl, R. Dumitrescu, R., Krüger, A., ten Hompel, M.: Industrie 4.0 Maturity Index. Managing the Digital Transformation of Companies – UPDATE 2020 – (acatech STUDY)
31. Vajna, S., Weber, C., Zeman, K., Hehenberger, P., Gerhard, D., Wartzack, S. (eds.): CAx für Ingenieure. Eine praxisbezogene Einführung. Springer Vieweg, Berlin, Germany (2018)
32. Bürger, T., Tragl, K.: SPS-Automatisierung mit den Technologien der IT-Welt verbinden. In: Vogel-Heuser, B., Bauernhansl, T., Hompel, M. ten (eds.) Handbuch Industrie 4.0 Bd. 1. Produktion, pp. 207–217. Springer, Berlin (2017)
33. Vajna, S., Weber, C., Schlingensiepen, J., Schlottmann, D.: CAD/CAM für Ingenieure. Hardware, Software, Strategien. Vieweg + Teubner Verlag, Wiesbaden (1994)
34. Mertens, P., Bodendorf, F., König, W., Schumann, M., Hess, T., Buxmann, P.: Grundzüge der Wirtschaftsinformatik. Springer, Heidelberg (2017)
35. Kleinemeier, M.: Von der Automatisierungspyramide zu Unternehmenssteuerungs-Netzwerken. In: Vogel-Heuser, B., Bauernhansl, T., Hompel, M. ten (eds.) Handbuch Industrie 4.0 Bd. 1. Produktion, pp. 219–226. Springer Vieweg, Berlin (2017)
36. Geissbauer, R., Vedso, J., Schrauf, S.: Industry 4.0: Building the digital enterprise. What we mean by Industry 4.0/Survey key findings/Blueprint for digital success
37. Wellenreuther, G., Zastrow, D.: Automatisieren mit SPS. Vieweg + Teubner (2009)
38. The IT/OT integration imperative for utility distribution businesses (2016)
39. Manyika, J., et al.: Big Data: The Next Frontier for Innovation, Comptetition, and Productivity (2011)
40. VDI Verein Deutscher Ingenieure e. V.: Ganzheitliche Produktionssysteme – Grundlagen, Einführung und Bewertung. Beuth Verlag, Berlin 03.100.50 (2012)
41. Reinhart, G., et al.: Strategien zur Transformation der Produktionsumgebung. In: Reinhart, G. (ed.) Handbuch Industrie 4.0. Geschäftsmodelle, Prozesse, Technik, pp. 213–256. Hanser, München (2017)
42. Goto, S., Yoshie, O., Fujimura, S.: Industrial IoT business workshop on smart connected application development for operational technology (OT) system integrator. IEEE IEEM2017, 10–13 December, Singapore. IEEE, Piscataway (2017)
43. Pelino, M., Hewitt, A.: The Forrester Wave™: IoT Software Platforms, Q4 2016. The 11 Providers That Matter Most And How They Stack Up (2016)
44. Global Lighthouse Network: Insights from the Forefront of the Fourth Industrial Revolution (2019)
45. Geleç, E., et al.: Metamorphose zur intelligenten und vernetzen Fabrik. In: Weinert, N., Plank, M., Ullrich, A. (eds.) Metamorphose zur intelligenten und vernetzten Fabrik, pp. 39–120. Springer, Heidelberg (2017). https://doi.org/10.1007/978-3-662-54317-7_3

Fostering Digital Growth in SMEs: Organizational Competence for Digital Transformation

José M. González-Varona[✉], Fernando Acebes, David Poza, and Adolfo López-Paredes

Dpto. de Organización de Empresas y CIM. Escuela de Ingenierías Industriales.
Universidad de Valladolid, C/Paseo del Cauce 59, 47011 Valladolid, Spain
josemanuel.gonzalez.varona@uva.es

Abstract. Digital transformation has become a necessity for SMEs if they want to compete in an increasingly globalized market. The proposed maturity models are not really useful for moving forward, as they have been developed for large companies and are not adapted to the particularities of SMEs. We propose an alternative approach based on individual and organizational skills and capabilities. SMEs have digital transformation capabilities that could become a digital transformation competence. The paper aims to discuss these issues.

Keywords: Digital transformation · Organizational competence · SME

1 Introduction

In recent years, the integration and exploitation of new digital technologies has become one of the greatest challenges faced by organizations. No organization is immune to their effects and their future performance will depend on the success of their assimilation [1–4]. They have the capacity to transform the products, services, operations, and even the business models of organizations, as well as their competitive environment [2, 5–8]. The integration of these technologies is generating an unprecedented and progressive digitalization that encourages innovation and transformation of organizations [3, 9]. It will be necessary to develop a new portfolio of digital transformation capabilities that allows organizations flexibility and responsiveness to the rapid changes required to generate new value propositions for customers and transform operating models [10]. This is especially important since there are many examples throughout the history of organizations that failed in technological advance by focusing their efforts on technologies without investing in organizational capabilities that guarantee their impact [1].

Currently digital technologies are no longer reserved for large companies, but also available to small and medium-sized enterprises (SMEs). SMEs have their own characteristics that make them different from large companies. They have more limited resources and specialization capabilities limited by their size. But SMEs have advantages like a simpler hierarchy level that allows faster decision-making [11]. While the digital transformation (DT) of businesses affects both large and small companies, SMEs are of particular interest in this regard because of their important role in the

L. M. Camarinha-Matos et al. (Eds.): PRO-VE 2020, IFIP AICT 598, pp. 237–248, 2020.
https://doi.org/10.1007/978-3-030-62412-5_20

economy [12], representing more than 99 percent of companies in the European Union [13].

Preparing for digital transformation is not an easy task, it is necessary to develop digital capacities in which the activities, people, culture and structure of the organization are synchronized and aligned with a set of organizational objectives [14].

In this context, we will carry out a review and analysis of the existing literature on DT and organizational competence to understand their relationship and mutual influence; identifying the most relevant digital capabilities to promote the digital transformation of SMEs, we study those research questions:

RQ1 - Can digital transformation capabilities become an organizational competence for digital transformation (OCDT)?

RQ2 - If so, what are the most significant dimensions that would form part of the organizational competence for the digital transformation of SMEs?

The rest of the document has been organized as follows: in Sect. 2, we address the theoretical framework of DT and organizational competence. In Sect. 3, we describe the research work, detailing the process of data collection and analysis. In Sect. 4, we present the results of the study, and we conclude by presenting in Sects. 5 and 6 results and the main conclusions in relation to the two issues that are the object of this research work.

2 Conceptual Framework Development

2.1 Digital Transformation in SMEs

DT is increasingly becoming the generally accepted medium for achieving organizational goals, including transformations of key business operations that affect the organization's products and processes, as well as its structure and concepts of business [2]. In this sense, DT involves the reinvention of the company, as well as the markets and industries in which it operates. A broad definition of DT, is the integration of digital technologies and business processes in a digital economy [15]. Another wide-ranging definition is the one that considers DT as the use of technology to radically improve the performance or reach of organizations [16]. According to this evolution Vial [17] proposes a definition of DT as *"a process that aims to improve an entity by triggering significant changes to its properties through combinations of information, computing, communication, and connectivity technologies"*. The result of the transformation is a conscious and sustainable change in business performance [18].

2.2 Organizational Competence

In 1990 C. K. Prahalad and Gary Hamel [19] first introduced the concept of core competence in their article "The Core Competence of the Corporation" and defined it as *"collective learning in the organization, especially how to coordinate various production skills and integrate multiple systems of technologies"*. A core competence is a harmonized combination of multiple resources and skills that differentiates the organization in the marketplace and therefore forms the basis of the organization's competitiveness. It would be of interest for the future advancement of OCDT's knowledge of SMEs to investigate whether it can become part of the organization's core competence and thus form the basis of the company's competitiveness. During the first years of the 90 s, researchers made efforts to define the competencies of organizations, indicating as key elements of competence the abilities, capacities, knowledge, learning, coordination, organization and relationships [19–21].

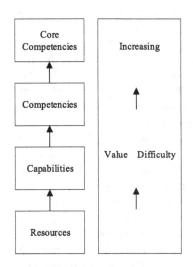

Fig. 1. Hierarchy of competencies. Source: Mansour Javidan

Aaker [22] classifies the production factors of an organization as Assets and Capabilities; Assets are properties that the organization has and are used to generate income. Capabilities are the knowledge, skills, methods, techniques, procedures, processes, and routines used to implement, operate, and coordinate the assets and resources of an organization [23, 24]. Finally, they define "Skills" as special forms of capacity, generally of individuals or teams that are used in special situations or are related to the use of a special asset [25].

We can define organizational competence as *"the ability to maintain the coordinated deployment of assets in a way that helps a company achieve its objectives"* [26]. It is an integrated group of specific assets that includes individuals and groups that can perform distinctive activities that constitute organizational routines/processes [27]. Javidan [28] defined the concepts of core competence, competencies, capabilities and organizational resources to create a universal understanding of these concepts. Several authors propose several models for the development of organizational competences [26, 29, 30] but we have chosen the model proposed by Mansour Javidan for its simplicity and ease of application in SMEs (Fig. 1); in addition to its high use by other authors, with a large number of bibliographic citations.

All organizations have their DT capabilities, skills to exploit their DT resources. They are business processes and routines that manage the interaction between the organization's resources, capabilities have a functional basis. But this does not mean that they will become competencies and even become part of the core competence of the organization.

For a SME digital capacity refers to the organization's willingness to push the digital agenda and become a digital company [31]. SMEs develop digital capabilities is a prerequisite to start and advance towards digital maturity, and therefore it is important to know what are the key dimensions of digital capabilities, how they can be measured and used to support a digital business model [32].

3   Research Design

The research has included a review of the relevant scientific literature and development of a proposed DT competence model, based on the results obtained in case studies and relevant scientific literature models. The stages of model development include the identification of relevant organizational capabilities and skills to develop a DT competence model in SMEs and its grouping into relevant dimensions. Initially we identified the bibliographic databases that best met the requirements of the study. We decided to use the Elsevier Scopus and Web of Science (WoS) databases in combination. These databases are considered benchmarks for demonstrating the quality of scientific publications. WoS and Scopus are the most widespread databases in different scientific fields, and the most frequently used to search scientific literature [33]. The search focused on journal articles and reviews. Therefore, only 'finished' peer-reviewed articles in indexed academic journals were included, professional journals were also excluded. In addition, the search was limited to articles written in English.

The study began by collecting data using a Boolean keyword search of articles in the WoS main collection and Scopus. The descriptors used were "enabler*", "driver*" or "capabilit*" and "digital transformation" and "firm*", "compan*" or "SME*". This search identified 75 papers in WoS and 76 in Scopus that met the established requirements. Those duplicate papers in both databases were eliminated, resulting in a total of 111 different papers that served as the basis for the research. The relevant papers were selected for their content and subject matter by a preliminary reading of the abstract and introduction of all of them, resulting in 39 irrelevant to the research and a total of 72 relevant to our research (Table 1).

Papers identified as relevant were read in full, focusing on the consideration of drivers for DT, as well as the role of drivers for the development of organizational competence. From the reading made, we identi-

Table 1. Research design

Data criteria identification			
Data base	WoS, Scopus	Time Spam	All years
Doc. Types	Academic papers (articles and reviews) Written in English		
Search	STEP 1 - WoS and Scopus Boolean search within title, abstract and keywords - With the descriptors ("enabler*" or "driver*" or "capabilit*") AND "digital transformation" AND ("firm*" OR "compan*" OR "SME*") - 75 articles founded in WoS - 76 articles founded in Scopus		
	STEP 2 - All articles were then reviewed and duplicates were removed. - WoS and Scopus review showed 72 different papers - New search [("enabler*" or "driver*" or "capabil*") and "digital*" and ("estrateg*" or "alignment*")] categories "management" and "Business" and "engineering" and "economics" => Additional 177 articles found		
Final corpus	Corpus of 90 scholarly documents identified publishes between 2003 and 2020		

fied the need for a new additional search, focusing on the keywords detected and not used in the initial search and limiting the search categories to "management", "business", "engineering" and "economics". The search terms used were "enabler*", "driver*" or "capabilit*" and "digital*" and "estrateg*" or "alignment*". This search identified 56 papers in WoS and 121 in Scopus that met the established requirements. All of them were reviewed by eliminating those that were not relevant to the object of study or that were duplicated, resulting in a total of 18 additional documents in the new search. The final corpus covers a period of time between 2003 and 2020.

4 Findings: Organizational Competence Model for Digital Transformation

We conducted an in-depth analysis of the papers to determine how the authors describe the enablers for advancing the digitalization of companies. In this process, the selected papers were used to identify which are the most important digital enablers that allow the development of the necessary capabilities for the development an OCDT, their characteristics and the dimensions that group them. SME's DT is twofold, from an external perspective it affects the relationship with suppliers, competitors, customers and other external stakeholders, and from an internal perspective it affects managers and employees who make decisions on the adoption of new digital technologies, the structure of the company and the way work is done and organized [17]. It is a simultaneous process, internal to the company and external to a wider ecosystem [34]. In our research we will focus on the internal perspective, developing the concept of OCDT. The OCDT model can help SMEs to know their level of digital transformation and therefore establish collaboration models between SMEs with similar levels of digital transformation.

The developed model follows the hierarchy of competencies of Javidan [28] and consists of 5 dimensions or capabilities for the development of a competency that together include the factors that allow success in the DT. These factors are called elements of competence and are made up of the physical, human and organizational resources available to the SME (Fig. 2).

4.1   Governance

Governance is needed at all levels of the organization. In a context of uncertainty, complexity and rapid change, it must be aligned with DT [12] and the redesign of flexible and manageable governance structures to ensure flexibility and control in the SME [29]. Advancing DT will require innovations in SME management, such as building new digital governance capabilities to digitally transform internal collaborative approaches [35, 36].

4.1.1   Vision and Strategy

An OCDT must be specifically aligned with the vision, mission and strategy of the organization. One of the most important decisions to be made by the SME is to establish a common and clear vision throughout the organization, to inform the direction to be taken by all stakeholders and thus ensure the future success of the TD, many authors emphasize this statement [37–39]. In addition, the decisions to be made by management will include how the vision will be established and communicated to

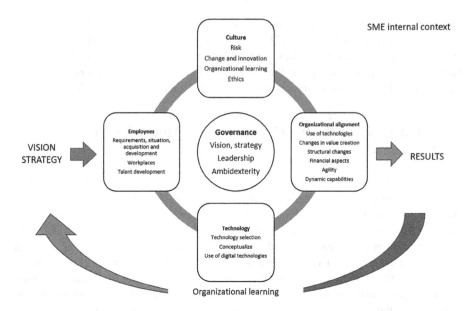

Fig. 2. Organizational Competence for Digital Transformation (OCDT)

the rest of the organization. Adopting a clear digital strategy is key to advancing DT [34]. DT strategy is a plan that helps companies to govern the transformations that arise from the integration of digital technologies, as well as in their operations after a transformation [40].

4.1.2   Leadership

One of the main challenges facing SME leaders is how to optimally integrate business systems and digital technologies into their organizations to maximize their potential [41]. Leaders most likely to succeed will be those who are able to effectively align the business and digital strategy of SMEs [42]. Knowledge sharing and innovation needed to advance DT are effectively stimulated through transformational employee leadership [43]. Leading in a digital economy is about creating the conditions for success, inspiring and engaging people as members of a community of leaders so that everyone can contribute their efforts to achieving the goals set. Building a community of leaders is based on four components: increasing customer value, serving a higher purpose, strengthening connectivity and fostering creativity and continuous innovation [44].

4.1.3   Ambidexterity

Ambidexterity combines two different conceptions of organizational orientation and performance [45, 46]. On the one hand, exploitation focuses on current internal knowledge, capabilities and decision making to maximize short-term performance. On the other hand, exploration, which focuses on learning new knowledge, discovering new capabilities and investigating new ways of doing business, is related to long-term results. The combination of exploitation and exploration activities affects the generation of knowledge and innovation in SMEs [47–49].

4.2   Organizational Alignment

The adoption and integration of new digital technologies in SMEs will influence various business activities, including business models, as new forms of cooperation between companies, new products and services, and changes in the relationship with employees, customers, suppliers and other stakeholders. These changes are also forcing companies to rethink their strategy and look for new business opportunities [14, 50–52]. New operations will be necessary when different technologies are integrated and new ways of creating value will require changes in the organizational configuration, mainly in those digital activities incorporated into the organizational structure; products, processes, or skills will be affected by the changes. DT deployment will require an alignment of four elements of competence: use of technologies, changes in value creation, structural changes and financial aspects [40].

Although SMEs financial resources are limited, they will have to make an effort to redirect their financial investments to support the DT, in accordance with their strategic vision [53]. Agility is essential for SMEs to respond quickly to environmental changes and leverage opportunities advantage, allowing them to implement strategic changes in their structures, processes, products and services to adapt, survive and gain competitive advantage from change [54–57]. As noted above, SMEs have inherent characteristics that place them at an initial disadvantage with respect to large companies, although some studies also point to some advantages in terms of achieving agility. SMEs that have achieved agility have higher profit margins than larger companies, due to the lower cost of transforming their business model [58]. In addition, SMEs are highly influenced by the manager's mentality in order to advance in digitalization and agility, so when managers can articulate their strategies and broaden their viewpoints, they are more open to innovations and changes in processes that generate better performance [59]. Finally, SMEs could take advantage of their external relations to overcome the constraints related to their small size and have access to resources and capabilities not available internally [60–62], such as new opportunities, financial resources, human and technical resources.

4.3   Culture

All SMEs develop their own corporate culture by integrating the visions, values and beliefs shared by all the people involved. Companies have to develop digital capabilities where the culture of a company is synchronized and aligned with the organizational objectives. Companies that mature digitally have organizational cultures that share common characteristics; a greater appetite for risk, rapid experimentation, strong investment in talent and the development of leaders with "soft" skills [14]. Companies at the forefront of their digital transformation have made risk taking like a cultural norm. Development of high performance culture, sustainable over time, that allows leadership based on the values and capacities of the organization, will be of great importance to face the important current challenges [63].

4.4 Technology

SMEs are continuously faced with the decision of selecting the technologies to be incorporated. Determining the most appropriate options is difficult because the number and complexity of available technologies is constantly increasing. However, selecting the right technologies can create significant competitive advantages for an enterprise in a complex business environment. Digital technologies enable the development of new or improved products and services delivered to customers more efficiently. These technologies also enable fundamentally new ways of organizing business [64]. The ability to conceptualize how digital technologies may affect the business model is a missing skill in firms in DT early stage [1]. The use of technology is revealed as one of the key technological skills to be developed in order to advance in DT. Technologies integration to transform the business model and companies operation will determine the success of the DT. The history of technological advancement in business is full of examples of companies that failed to implement because they did not invest in organizational capabilities to ensure impact [1]. The use of technology can develop superior technological capabilities that allow for greater agility in responding to changes in the context in which organizations operate [65, 66].

4.5 Employees

This group includes the personal skills needed in SMEs to develop an OCDT, related to the general objectives of management and their expectations about personal competencies. The DT is carried out by people, to fulfil the vision, mission and strategy of the SME. An essential capability is to train employees for networking, which requires appropriate skills and guidelines based on values rather than rigid rules [10]. Fostering social networking among employees is also important, e.g. by participating in online communities, where the involvement of managers is desirable, new insights can emerge and facilitate innovation and business growth. What differentiates DT from other fields of study is that knowledge acquired by employees is used to improve decision-making skills. DT requires employees to rethink old processes and re-imagine new processes and decisions [67].

5 Conclusion

According to the research carried out, we can answer our research questions in the affirmative. We can develop an OCDT that allows SMEs to be more competitive and better suited to their characteristics. This OCDT model is based on five dimensions, each of which will require the development of digital capabilities. In future researchs we will delve into the relationships between the elements of competence and their influence on the competitiveness of SMEs.

SMEs usually face DT in a different situation than large companies, they are usually less formal and have a smaller organizational structure, they are smaller in size and operate on a smaller scale, and their resources to deal with DT are less [59, 68, 69]. Thus, although they have some advantage over large companies, they usually start out with a disadvantage, which remains over time. DT is a relatively new phenomenon and the end state of a digitally mature organization is not yet clearly defined [1]. The current maturity models have been developed for large companies and their usefulness for SMEs is limited, a different approach would be required using an individual and organizational competence-based approach. The Organizational Competence of Digital Transformation (OCDT) model presented in this paper will help the DT of SMEs with the aim of generating competitive advantages and allowing SMEs to successfully adapt to the new competitive environment generated by digital technologies and characterized by innovation and constant change. A model based on organizational competencies can help SMEs to advance in their digital maturity [70] to refer to the ability to respond to change early way. This study allowed the development of an OCDT that can help SME identify and develop the DT capabilities to advance the DT of their business model.

This model takes into account the specific characteristics of SMEs and is better adapted than other models that allow advancing in digital maturity but were designed to be applied in large companies. In this sense, research results contribute to a better understanding of the role of organizational learning and its relationship to the formation and development of an OCDT. Furthermore, it allows to know which are the digital capabilities and skills that a SME has, to face DT and to plan the actions to be carried out to close detected gaps. In future researchs, we will use other descriptors like the term "organi*" in order to obtain a broader coverage than "compan*".

References

1. Kane, G.C., Palmer, D., Philips, A.N., Kiron, D., Buckley, N.: Strategy, not technology, drives digital transformation. MIT Sloan Manag. Rev. **57181**, 27 (2015)
2. Hess, T., Benlian, A., Matt, C., Wiesböck, F.: Options for formulating a digital transformation strategy. MIS Q. Exec. **15**(2), 103–119 (2016)
3. Legner, C., et al.: Digitalization: opportunity and challenge for the business and information systems engineering community. Bus. Inf. Syst. Eng. **59**(4), 301–308 (2017). https://doi.org/10.1007/s12599-017-0484-2
4. Sebastian, I.M., Ross, J.W., Beath, C., Mocker, M., Moloney, K.G., Fonstad, N.O.: How big old companies navigate digital transformation. MIS Q. Exec. **16**, 1–17 (2017)
5. Fichman, R.G., Dos Santos, B.L., Zheng, Z.: Digital innovation as a fundamental and powerful concept in the information systems curriculum. MIS Q. Manag. Inf. Syst. **38**(2), 329–353 (2014)
6. Lucas Jr., H.C., Agarwal, R., Clemons, E.K., El Sawy, O.A., Weber, B.: Impactful research on transformational information technology: an opportunity to inform new audiences. MIS Q. Manag. Inf. Syst. **37**(2), 371–382 (2013)
7. Yoo, Y., Boland, R., Lyytinen, K., Majchrzak, A.: Organizing for innovation in the digitized world. Organ. Sci. **23**, 1398–1408 (2012)
8. Macchion, L., Marchiori, I., Vinelli, A., Fornasiero, R.: Proposing a Tool for Supply Chain Configuration: An Application to Customised Production. In: Tolio, T., Copani, G., Terkaj, W. (eds.) Factories of the Future, pp. 217–231. Springer, Cham (2019). https://doi.org/10.1007/978-3-319-94358-9_10

9. Macchion, L., Moretto, A.M., Caniato, F., Caridi, M., Danese, P., Vinelli, A.: International e-commerce for fashion products: what is the relationship with performance? Int. J. Retail Distrib. Manag. **45**(9), 1011–1031 (2017)
10. Berman, S.J.: Digital transformation: opportunities to create new business models. Strateg. Leadersh. **40**(2), 16–24 (2012)
11. North, K., Varvakis, G. (eds.): Competitive Strategies for Small and Medium Enterprises. Springer, Cham (2016). https://doi.org/10.1007/978-3-319-27303-7
12. Bharadwaj, A., El Sawy, O., Pavlou, P., Venkatraman, N.: Digital business strategy: toward a next generation of insights. MIS Q. **37**(2), 471–482 (2013)
13. Muller, P., Mattes, A., Klitou, D., Lonkeu, O.,... P. R.-... /LE E. E. U., and U. 2018: Annual report on European SMEs 2017/2018: SMEs growing beyond borders (2018)
14. Kane, G.C., Palmer, D., Phillips, A.N., Kiron, D., Buckley, N.: Aligning the organization for its digital future. MIT Sloan Manag. Rev. (2016)
15. Liu, D.Y., Chen, S.W., Chou, T.C.: Resource fit in digital transformation: lessons learned from the CBC Bank global e-banking project. Manag. Decis. **49**(10), 1728–1742 (2011)
16. Westerman, G., Mcafee, A., Bonnet, D.: Leading Digital: Turning Technology into Business Transformation. Harvard Business Press, Boston (2014)
17. Vial, G.: Understanding digital transformation: a review and a research agenda. J. Strateg. Inf. Syst. (2019)
18. Purchase, V., Parry, G., Valerdi, R., Nightingale, D., Mills, J.: enterprise transformation: why are we interested, what is it, and what are the challenges? J. Enterp. Transform. **1**(1), 14–33 (2011)
19. Prahalad, C.K., Hamel, G.: The core competence of the corporation. Harv. Bus. Rev. **68**(3), 79–91 (1990)
20. Leonard-Barton, D.: Core capabilities and core rigidities: a paradox in managing new product development. Strateg. Manag. J. **13**(S1), 111–125 (1992)
21. Dosi, G., Teece, D.J.: Organizational competencies and the boundaries of the firm. In: Markets and Organization, pp. 281–302. Springer, Heidelberg (1998)
22. Aaker, D.A.: Managing assets and skills: the key to a sustainable competitive advantage. Calif. Manage. Rev. **31**(2), 91–106 (1989)
23. Grant, R.M.: Prospering in dynamically-competitive environments: organizational capability as knowledge integration. Organ. Sci. **7**(4), 375–387 (1996)
24. Amit, R., Schoemaker, P.J.H.: Strategic assets and organizational rent. Strateg. Manag. J. **14**(1), 33–46 (1993)
25. Sanchez, R., Heene, A., Howard, T.: Towards the theory and practice of competence-based competion. Dyn. Competence-based Compet. (1996)
26. Sanchez, R.: Understanding competence-based management - Identifying and managing five modes of competence. J. Bus. Res. **57**(5), 518–532 (2004)
27. Teece, D.J., Pisano, G., Shuen, A.: Dynamic capabilities and strategic management. Strateg. Manag. J. **18**(7), 509–533 (1997)
28. Javidan, M.: Core competence: what does it mean in practice? Long Range Plann. **31**(1), 60–71 (1998)
29. Warner, K.S.R., Wäger, M.: Building dynamic capabilities for digital transformation: an ongoing process of strategic renewal. Long Range Plann. **52**(3), 326–349 (2019)
30. Mills, J., Platts, K., Bourne, M., Richards, H.: Strategy and Performance: Competing through Competences. Cambridge University Press, Cambridge (2002)
31. Uhl, A., Gollenia, L.A.: Digital enterprise transformation: a business-driven approach to leveraging innovative IT. (2016)

32. Ng, H.Y., Tan, P.S., Lim, Y.G.: Methodology for digitalization - a conceptual model. In: IEEE International Conference on Industrial Engineering and Engineering Management, pp. 1269–1273 (2018)
33. Guz, A.N., Rushchitsky, J.J.: Scopus: a system for the evaluation of scientific journals. Int. Appl. Mech. **45**(4), 351–362 (2009)
34. Peter, M.K., Kraft, C., Lindeque, J.: Strategic action fields of digital transformation. An exploration of the strategic action fields of Swiss SMEs and large enterprises. J. Strateg. Manag. **13**(1), 160–180 (2020)
35. Singh, A., Hess, T.: How chief digital officers promote the digital transformation of their companies. MIS Q. Exec. **16**(1), 1–17 (2017)
36. Birkinshaw, J.: What to expect from agile. MIT Sloan Manag. Rev. 59, 39–43 (2018)
37. Fitzgerald, M., Kruschwitz, N., Bonnet, D., Welch, M.: Embracing digital technology a new strategic imperative (2013)
38. Webb, N.: Vodafone puts mobility at the heart of business strategy. Hum. Resour. Manag. Int. Dig. **21**(1), 5–8 (2013)
39. Luftman, J., Brier, T.: Achieving and sustaining business-IT alignment. Calif. Manage. Rev. **1**, 109–122 (1999)
40. Matt, C., Hess, T., Benlian, A.: Digital transformation strategies. Bus. Inf. Syst. Eng. **57**(5), 339–343 (2015). https://doi.org/10.1007/s12599-015-0401-5
41. Ferneley, E., Bell, F.: Using bricolage to integrate business and information technology innovation in SMEs. Technovation **26**(2), 232–241 (2006)
42. Li, W., Liu, K., Belitski, M., Ghobadian, A., O'Regan, N.: e-Leadership through strategic alignment: an empirical study of small- and medium-sized enterprises in the digital age. J. Inf. Technol. **31**(2), 185–206 (2016)
43. Bednall, T.C., Rafferty, A.E., Shipton, H., Sanders, K., Jackson, C.J.: Innovative behaviour: how much transformational leadership do you need? Br. J. Manag. **29**(4), 796–816 (2018)
44. Rogers, D.L.: The Digital Transformation Playbook: Rethink Your Business for the Digital Age, Columbia U. (2016)
45. Dai, Y., Du, K., Byun, G., Zhu, X.: Ambidexterity in new ventures: the impact of new product development alliances and transactive memory systems. J. Bus. Res. **75**, 77–85 (2017)
46. Solano Acosta, A., Herrero Crespo, Á., Collado Agudo, J.: Effect of market orientation, network capability and entrepreneurial orientation on international performance of small and medium enterprises (SMEs). Int. Bus. Rev. **27**(6), 1128–1140 (2018)
47. Chang, Y., Hughes, M., Hotho, S.: Internal and external antecedents of SMEs' innovation ambidexterity outcomes. Manag. Decis. **49**(10), 1658–1676 (2011)
48. Heavey, C., Simsek, Z., Fox, B.C.: Managerial social networks and ambidexterity of SMEs: the moderating role of a proactive commitment to innovation. Hum. Resour. Manage. **54**(S1), s201–s221 (2015)
49. Soto-Acosta, P., Popa, S., Martinez-Conesa, I.: Information technology, knowledge management and environmental dynamism as drivers of innovation ambidexterity: a study in SMEs. J. Knowl. Manag. **22**(4), 824–849 (2018)
50. Rachinger, M., Rauter, R., Müller, C., Vorraber, W., Schirgi, E.: Digitalization and its influence on business model innovation. J. Manuf. Technol. Manag. **30**(8), 1143–1160 (2019)
51. Westerman, G., Bonnet, D.: Revamping your business through digital transformation. MIT Sloan Manag. Rev. **56**, 10–13 (2015)
52. Chanias, S., Myers, M.D., Hess, T.: Digital transformation strategy making in pre-digital organizations: the case of a financial services provider. J. Strateg. Inf. Syst. **28**(1), 17–33 (2019)

53. Gurbaxani, V., Dunkle, D.: Gearing up for successful digital transformation. MIS Q. Exec. **18**(3), 209–220 (2019)
54. Overby, E., Bharadwaj, A., Sambamurthy, V.: Enterprise agility and the enabling role of information technology. Eur. J. Inf. Syst. **15**(2), 120–131 (2006)
55. Roberts, N., Grover, V.: Leveraging information technology infrastructure to facilitate a firm's customer agility and competitive activity: an empirical investigation. J. Manag. Inf. Syst. **28**(4), 231–270 (2012)
56. Sambamurthy, V., Bharadwaj, A., Grover, V.: Shaping agility through digital options: Reconceptualizing the role of information technology in contemporary firms. MIS Q. Manag. Inf. Syst. **27**(2), 237–264 (2003)
57. Sanchez, R.: Strategic flexibility in product competition. Strateg. Manag. J. **16**(1), 135–159 (1995)
58. Neirotti, P., Raguseo, E., Paolucci, E.: Flexible work practices and the firm's need for external orientation: an empirical study of SMEs. J. Enterp. Inf. Manag. **30**(6), 922–943 (2017)
59. Levy, M., Powell, P.: Information systems strategy for small and medium sized enterprises: an organisational perspective. J. Strateg. Inf. Syst. **9**(1), 63–84 (2000)
60. Hite, J.M., Hesterly, W.S.: The evolution of firm networks: from emergence to early growth of the firm. Strateg. Manag. J. **22**(3), 275–286 (2001)
61. Rehm, S.-V., Goel, L.: Using information systems to achieve complementarity in SME innovation networks. Inf. Manag. **54**(4), 438–451 (2017)
62. Rindova, V.P., Yeow, A., Martins, L.L., Faraj, S.: Partnering portfolios, value-creation logics, and growth trajectories: a comparison of Yahoo and Google (1995 to 2007). Strateg. Entrep. J. **6**(2), 133–151 (2012)
63. Quinn, R.E., Thakor, A.V.: Creating a purpose-driven organization. Harv. Bus. Rev. **96**(4), 78–85 (2018)
64. Johnson, M.W., Christensen, C.M., Kagermann, H.: Reinventing your business model. Harv. Bus. Rev. **86**(12), 50–59 (2008)
65. Lu, Y., Ramamurthy, K.: Understanding the link between information technology capability and organizational agility: an empirical examination. MIS Q. **35**(4), 931–954 (2011)
66. González-Varona, J.M., Poza, D., Acebes, F., Villafáñez, F., Pajares, J., López-Paredes, A.: New business models for sustainable spare parts logistics: a case study. Sustainable **12**(8), 3071 (2020)
67. Schallmo, D., Williams, C.A., Boardman, L.: Digital transformation of business models-best practice, enablers, and roadmap. Int. J. Innov. Manag. **21**(8), 1–17 (2017)
68. Meister, D.B.: Entrepreneurial firms and information systems capabilities. In: AMCIS 2017 - America's Conference on Information Systems: A Tradition of Innovation, vol. 2017, August 2017
69. González-Varona, J.M., López-Paredes, A., Pajares, J., Acebes, F., Villafáñez, F.: Aplicabilidad de los Modelos de Madurez de Business Intelligence a PYMES. Dir. y Organ. **71**, 31–45 (2020)
70. Kane, G.C.: Digital maturity, not digital transformation. MIT Sloan Manag. Rev. **56**(4), 37–44 (2017)

Digital Transformation of Virtual Enterprises for Providing Collaborative Services in Smart Cities

Bokolo Anthony Jr.[1(✉)], Sobah Abbas Petersen[1], and Markus Helfert[2]

[1] Department of Computer Science, Norwegian University of Science and Technology, NTNU, 7491 Trondheim, Norway
{anthony.j.bokolo,sobah.a.petersen}@ntnu.no
[2] Innovation Value Institute, School of Business, Maynooth University, Maynooth Co., Kildare, Ireland
markus.helfert@mu.ie

Abstract. Municipalities are digitally transforming urban environment into smarter cities aimed at addressing urban growth and social challenges. This transition of urban space influenced by Information and Communications Technology (ICT) enables novel business models and Virtual Enterprises (VE) processes. Presently, there is need to provide insights into the state-of-the-art of VE and development of digital transformation in order to improve services provided to citizens and stakeholders in smart cities. Therefore, the aim of this study is to employ ArchiMate as the modelling language to demonstrate the digitalization of VE to depict how VE collaborates in smart cities. Evidence from a focus group discussion was modelled in ArchiMate to present findings on how VE can be digitalized to provide collaborative services. Implications from this study provide insights to guide VE to understand the imperative need of digital changes in smart cities.

Keywords: Digital transformation · Virtual Enterprises · Collaborative services · Smart cities · ArchiMate language

1 Introduction

A city is a permanent and large human environment which provides several opportunities and services to its residents [1]. Cities are currently improving performance and quality of urban services by deploying digital, intelligent, and smart approaches [2]. Accordingly, municipalities are exploring solutions to provide services in a sustainable, resourceful, and responsive method for its citizens [3]. Digitalization is pushing municipalities beyond its conventional limits and also providing opportunities to improve services productivity provided to citizens [4]. The concept of smart city aims to deploy digital technologies to support better development and administration within city operations [5]. Digitization refers to the process of adapting analog information into a digital format [6]. Respectively, Digital Transformation (DT) refers to the use of technologies, and its competences to digitize institutional assets [7].

L. M. Camarinha-Matos et al. (Eds.): PRO-VE 2020, IFIP AICT 598, pp. 249–260, 2020.
https://doi.org/10.1007/978-3-030-62412-5_21

DT of enterprises in urban environment support cities in achieving a balanced ecosystem [8]. DT involves changing of an organization or community in delivering better services or products through Information Technology (IT) as the core element. DT promotes better collaboration and communication among Virtual Enterprises (VE) that provide services in smart cities [1]. Since the notion of VE first appeared in late 1980s [9], VE has been distinguished from a simple integration and collaboration of businesses as technology-driven dynamic coalitions formed based on the use of Information Systems (IS) [10]. Presently, urban services are characterized by unanticipated and often dramatic changes. In this challenging and difficult situation, stakeholders and partners must develop and implement innovative and new strategies to provide services to citizens [11]. Amongst the most inventive initiatives being employed by enterprises in cities sphere is the concept of VE [12].

VE refers to a virtual establishment which comprises of independent merchants, competitors, clients involved in a temporary collaboration or network organization using IT to share cost and technology to address current market demand in exploiting specific opportunity [13]. Moreover, VE can be said to be a temporary alliance of organizations with similar capabilities that co-operate in sharing resources and core competencies to respond to business prospects, and whose collaboration is facilitated by Information Communications Technology (ICT) [14]. Additionally, VE is a synergetic combination of dissimilar companies that liaison to realize specific business goal within a specific time at a reduced cost [15]. The physically dispersed organizations work together to fulfil their set goals by exploiting ICT to provide value-added benefits to clients [5]. The success of VE dynamically relies on participation of the members in sharing and creating knowledge across disciplinary, cultural and/or spatial boundaries either in real-time or asynchronously [16].

VE have lately received much attention due to the changing needs of business community and advancement of technological inventions [13]. Therefore, VE has become essential for continuous business survival in emergent business sector to increase competitiveness, optimize resource use, and increase business scale [14]. But, to achieve an interoperability, responsiveness and agility of VE operations [17], in smart city, a method is needed to provide modelling concepts that support the illustration of VE business process across different layers, granularity, abstraction and phases [18]. Currently, there is limited methods that mainly facilitate the modelling of VE business models in a holistic approach [19]. Furthermore, fewer studies have investigated the potential impact of DT of VE on value creation in the smart city context. An appropriate approach is needed to examine VE in providing services in urban domain [20]. Due to disruptions from digital transformation and nature of VEs, it is required to design models to help explore the progression of DT and VE in smart cities [19]. Thus, this research attempts to resolve the following research question:

RQ. How can DT aid in providing collaborative services amongst VE operating in smart city context?

Therefore, this study provides insights into the state-of-the-art of VE and development of DT in order to improve services provided to citizens and stakeholders in smart cities. ArchiMate is employed to model VEs business process in providing collaborative services in smart cities, which is focused on the DT of VE. The remainder of this study is structured as follows. Section 2 is theoretical background. Section 3 presents the methodology. Section 4 is ArchiMate modelling of VE. Section 5 is the discussions and implications. Section 6 is the conclusion.

2 Theoretical Background

This section discusses on the background of smart city, overview of VE, characteristics of VE, life cycle of VE, digital transformation of VE in smart cities, and related works.

2.1 Background of Smart Cities

Cities involve multifaceted systems which comprises of different citizens, stakeholders, housing, physical infrastructure, utilities, economic activities, and services [6]. With approximately four billion people residing in cities presently, an international trend of digital-based growth is taking place [21]. This change is driving policy innovations for novel technological implementations and data-oriented approaches aimed at addressing environmental, social problems and urban growth [4].

Thus, municipalities are working to make their cities smarter. Where a smart city as stated by the United Nations (UN) is an innovative city that deploys ICT and other mediums to enhance the quality of life, productivity of urban amenities, and affordability [5], while confirming that it addresses the requirements of present and generations to come in relation to environmental, economic, and societal aspects [1].

Smart cities can bring about future environmental, financial, and social benefits supported by digital technological innovations [22]. Making city smarter aims to adopt urban polices mostly aligned to resource monitoring, effective administration, strategic design, implementation, and control activities in an urban space to improve liveability, efficiency, and sustainability [3].

2.2 Overview of Virtual Enterprise

The term virtual enterprise is attributed to Mowshowitz [9], who aligned VE with virtual memory used in IT system processing. But, VE gained its current prominence for organizations from Davidow and Malone's study [23]. Also, researchers such as Byrne Week [24] defined VE as a momentary network of independent establishments to share costs, knowledge, and access to members market based on a common business understanding [20]. VE concept has emerged progressed in response to globalization and coming of the digital age. The characteristics of VE that distinguish its formation from traditional businesses are discussed as seen in Table 1.

VE is a predominant area that is usually referred to as an extended enterprise or virtual corporation [19]. Accordingly, VE is a dynamically reconfigurable networked of enterprises that shares information and/or knowledge, resources and processes to meet a fast-changing window of opportunities [10, 12]. Although, VE consists of several enterprises, the service they provide appears as a sole service to the society. Thus, its internal process resembles a decentralized enterprise [11, 20, 25].

Table 1. Characteristics of virtual enterprise

Characteristics	Description
Virtuality	VE deploy ICT that enables geographically dispersed businesses to connect with each other in achieving mutual business goal [14]. ICT is deployed to support the coordination of each members owned assets [12] and decreases transaction costs [11]
Dynamics	VE are mostly dynamic, short lived [12], and all partners have same rights where there is no leading enterprise in the consortium [11]
Flexibility	VE have tactical goals to exploit adaptability towards societal changes [12]. Thus, VE has a flexible logistic structure with rules that renders it to be adaptable. An enterprise can leave or become a member in the network at any time [11]
Autonomy	VE are able to adapt to fast changing environment to support flexibility in achieving an effective business collaboration and information flows to enable an automatic negotiation and decision making system [14]
Heterogeneity and immobility	VE is joined based on the individual resource and skills of different business by sharing different data and competence to achieve viable advantages in a short run [14]
Focus on core competencies	In VE each firm participates with its competence, which is matches up to other businesses' skills. Also, every partner firm backs the VE with its own core resource, thereby enabling excellence products and services [11]
Opportunity driven	In a VE participating businesses work collectively to achieve specific opportunities. This creates a means for innovation which enables VE to respond efficiently and rapidly to changing market demand [11]
Semi stable relationship	A less-formal associations of dependence are formed among the businesses so that they survive in the market without the VE consortium [11].
Trust	A significant feature is the degree of trust among businesses [15]. Trust influence partners intention of sharing information within the strategic alliance network, which also render enterprises to be more interdependent [11, 16]

2.3 Virtual Enterprise Life Cycle

Since the inception of VE there has been much discussion regarding its life cycle which comprises of creation, operation, continuation/reconfiguration, evolution, and dissolution [10–12, 18, 19], as seen in Fig. 1.

Figure 1 depicts VE life cycle, each of the process are discussed below;

The *creation phase* starts when a new business prospect is identified. Thus, it is required to rapidly plan an appropriate virtual firm by identifying associates and establishing cooperative contracts [11]. The creation phase forms a group of partners to achieve a commercial process [12]. The creation phase involves *searching for partners, negotiation, and establishment of legal agreements*. *Searching for partners* involves publishing notice of the specifications of VE`s needs, including all the requirements

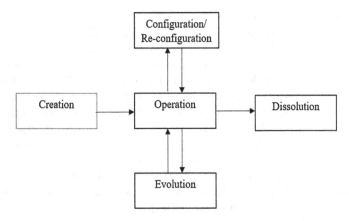

Fig. 1. Virtual enterprise life cycle

such as quality, technical aspects, and inclusion of enterprises who meet the minimum standards stipulated [12]. *Negotiation* is employed to select associates based on a given period, value, and price grounded on a pre-defined objective [12]. *Establishment of legal agreements* involves the signing and legalizing of contract associated with VE consortium to legalize the partner agreements reached [12].

Operation phase is invoked when business members perform business operations in achieving their mutual goal. In this phase the supervision of the project is carried out to resolve issues if any [12]. Additionally, collaborative business processes are employed and continuously monitored for VE to adopt to changes [19]. *Evolution* involves the re-defining of existing applied models to be more effective based on internal situations by optimizing business scenarios [19].

Configuration/re-configuration defines the method utilized to design VE models such as the information, systems, resources, etc. [19]. This phase also involves specifying enterprise processes and scenarios, specifying technologies, systems, and shared resources required to develop VE models [12]. Lastly, the *dissolution phase* begins when VE accomplishes the implementation of its set goals. The dissolution phase aims to dismantle the coalited enterprises [12].

This current study will only consider the creation and operation phase of VE in smart city as seen in Sect. 4.2 of this paper.

2.4 Digital Transformation of Virtual Enterprise in Smart City

According to Oxford dictionary digital refers to digits of "0" or "1" that indicates a data or signal. Digitize is the format of depicting information as "0" or "1" to be utilized by compilers [6]. DT involves conversion of analogue into digital information. It describes the act of converting information from analog to digital which can result to change in business model towards providing novel revenue stream as well as new value suggestions [26]. Presently, the society is experiencing the transformative impacts of digital disruption such as data analytics, machine learning, social media, mobile computing, cloud/fog computing, artificial intelligence, robotic process automation, internet of things, blockchain and other technologies at a highly accelerated pace [8]. DT is an integration of business models and innovation [27].

DT establishes new links inside VEs by streamlining the operations, growing the businesses and supporting customer relationships. There is no doubt that digitalization is here to stay [27], it's no longer an option, but its inevitable [28]. In urban context, DT involves a rudimental change in the way enterprises in cities functions with innovative strategies, to address citizen's needs, who are consumers of the services via wearable technologies, mobile devices, or other devices [27]. Also, enterprises in cities needs to redesign the services by keeping the citizens as the concentration and with detailed strategies towards digitizing the processes that reduces human dependency [26]. Hence, VEs in smart cities are embarking on DT of their business processes to improve profitability and competitiveness by business processes, making information, and product/services available in digital forms [6].

2.5   Related Works

Over the decades a few studies explored VE based on Enterprise Architecture (EA) perspective among these studies Petersen et al. [29] explored on achieving value added services in VE and data based on EA for smart cities. The researchers developed an EA framework to support VE in cities for utilizing data to create value added services. Mouhib et al. [30] suggested adopting EA to improve VE modeling in addressing complexity and uncertainty of VE. Their study identified the requirements of VE modeling. Noran [17] examined how to improve collaborative agile healthcare synergy. The author aimed to improve interoperability and cooperation of participants grounded on collaborative networks and EA life cycle-based paradigm enabled by EA. Kim et al. [19] implemented a modeling approach for interoperable and agile VE to supports all facets of VE modeling in an elegant method to achieve an integrated synergy effects for domain experts.

Perrin and Godart [31] designed a model to enhance collaborative work in VE. The authors aimed to provide adequate information support for cooperation and coordination among VEs. Aerts et al. [32] developed a flexible agent-oriented ICT architecture for VE to improve the requirements for achieving an agile enterprise that utilizes ICT support. Petersen et al. [13] proposed an agent-based approach to model VE, deployed for assisting co-operative work among remote partners. Their study aimed to achieve a standardised modelling during the life cycle of VE. Camarinha-Matos et al. [10] presented an architecture for VE. Among the review studies there is lack of research that employed a modelling approach to demonstrate the digitalization of VE in smart city context to provide collaborative services. Hence, this current study addresses this setback.

3   Methodology

This study employs focus group discussion to collect data for DT of VE in providing collaborative services in smart city. Focus group discussions was used as the primary source of data as it enables researchers to understand participant descriptions and accounts of events and actions [22, 33]. Accordingly, this study collects data from an organization and a municipality in Norway based on the recommendation of Creswell and Poth [34], by employing focus group discussions to improve empirical grounding of the domain investigated.

Before the focus group sessions, the interviewers prepared a model of an architecture similar to Fig. 2 to ensure that all vital issues were discussed during the session. Then after each session, the interviewer's presents models from the discussions. The models for each session were then refined, confirmed and illustrated in ArchiMate (see Sect. 4.2) analogous to prior study [35] to depict DT of VE in smart cities. Besides, this study adheres to Norwegian Centre for Research Data (NSD) ethics guidelines and the names, organization, and current title of contributors is removed in this study, hence all informants are anonymous.

4   ArchiMate Modelling

4.1   Overview of ArchiMate Modelling

In information system enterprise modelling language describes how an enterprise develops and provides value represented from a high abstraction level. Enterprise modelling language defines business operations and illustrates how activities are achieved by deployed systems and technology [36]. Several enterprise modelling languages exist such as 4EM, Unified Modelling Language (UML), semantic object model, integrated enterprise balancing, etc. but are unfeasible. This is because they are inadequate in expressiveness when describing digital enterprise ecosystems. Thus, there is need for an enterprise modelling approaches that can be extended or evolved in order to carter for current and emerging development developments such as DT. Respectively, the ArchiMate modelling language was selected to be employed in this study to model DT of VE in smart cities. Also, ArchiMate is selected in this study as a modelling language because it supports a high-level concept that focuses on business and how it can be aligned and mapped with the IT strategy.

ArchiMate Version 1.0 was first announced on February 2009 by the Technical Standard after it was formally approved by the Open Group. ArchiMate is a modelling method which differentiates between a business layer, an application layer, and technology layer. ArchiMate is an open, free and independent tool for description of enterprise architectures [35]. ArchiMate is designed for modelling enterprise architectures based on 56 different elements and relationships notations in its current version 3.0. ArchiMate supports enterprise architects to examine, define, and visualize the relationships and dependencies among business domains in an explicit way and enables modelling defined by The Open Group Architecture Framework (TOGAF), an established enterprise architecture methodology adopted by leading organizations [37]. ArchiMate is simple but comprehensive in providing a structuring tool for architecture in layers and aspects. The ArchiMate meta-model involves of 3 types of elements which includes active structure elements, behaviour elements, and passive structure elements [35].

4.2   ArchiMate Modelling of VE in Smart Cities

This sub-section depicts the application of ArchiMate to present findings from the focus group discussion on digital transformation of creation and operation phase of VE in providing collaborative services to citizens and stakeholders in smart city as seen in Fig. 2 and 3. Figure 2 illustrates how VE explicitly collaborates in smart cities. Also, Fig. 2 explicitly describes the creation phase of VE illustrating how individual enterprises in VE1 (payment processing company, infrastructure provider company, and Electric Vehicle (EV) charger company) and VE2 (municipality administration, energy company, city bus company, and EV rental company) which collaborates to create and provide services to citizens and stakeholders.

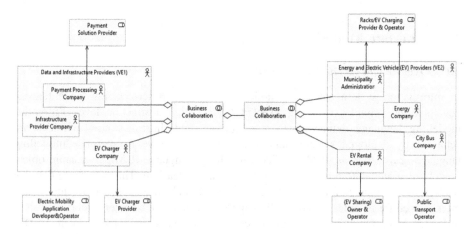

Fig. 2. ArchiMate business layer for creation phase of VE

Furthermore, Fig. 3 depicts the operation of VEs in the business layer in relation to technology, application and motivation layers based on ArchiMate in providing collaborative electric mobility service in smart city. Also, Fig. 3 describes the relationships between business services, applications and technological infrastructure adopted for DT of VE in smart city context structured based on business, application, technology, and motivation layers. Therefore, each layer delivers services that aids the operation of the upper layer [36].

The motivation layer captures the requirement which is to achieve the DT of VEs in proving electric mobility services by various partners. Next, the business layer comprises of the internal and external business operations in providing business products and services (electric mobility service and other digital services) to the city's citizens. These business services as seen in Fig. 3 and 4 are achieved by business operations that utilize and transform each enterprise roles which are executed or assigned by business actors in VE1 (data and infrastructure providers) and VE2 (energy and EV provider).

As seen in Fig. 4 the application layer illustrates the interaction of several business process carried out by VEs supported by system applications. The system applications

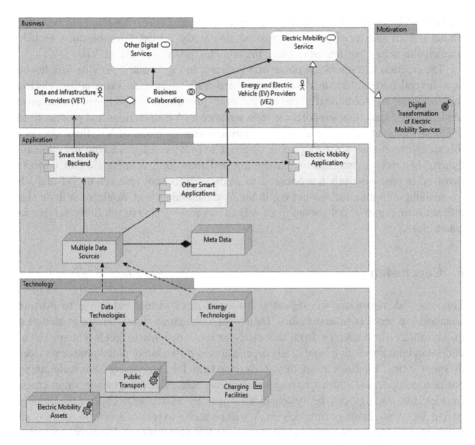

Fig. 3. ArchiMate metamodel view for operation phase of VE

comprise of smart mobility backend, electric mobility application, other smart applications that uses data from multiple data sources. The technological layer describes how the aforementioned applications are supported by data technologies and energy technologies that process, communicate, and store data from electric mobility assets, public transport vehicles, and charging facilities.

5 Discussions and Implications

This study extends the idea of DT by employing enterprise modelling approach to design and manage city components and processes. ArchiMate is employed for modelling VE because it can model enterprise structure within layers, showing all the components and their dependencies, visualize the relations between businesses. ArchiMate is easily understand by both IT/business experts and non-experts, possible to visualize models in views, personalized for specific stakeholders with definite information requirements. Additionally, ArchiMate is adopted in this study to illustrate the DT of VE collaborating in providing services in smart cities. Based on the modelled findings from the focus group discussion this study provides implications to help municipalities and businesses manage the complex process of DT of VE.

The creation and operation phase of VE shown in Fig. 3 and 4 provide insights on how several partners in smart cities can collaborate to provide value added electric mobility services. Additionally, this current study provides a comprehensible enterprise modelling approach that supports the representation of VE operations and process from different views and levels of abstraction during operation phase of VE. Findings from this study presents an abstract graphic language to provide insights to business domain experts or business managers in designing and managing collaboration of partners involved in providing urban services. This study adds to prior research on DT and VE by enabling communications among different stakeholders and would contribute significantly to improve collaboration of VE in improving electric mobility service in smart cities.

6 Conclusion

This study demonstrates the digital transformation of virtual enterprise to provide collaborative services in smart cities. Data from focus group discussions was modelled in ArchiMate. Implications from this study provide insights to guide enterprises to understand the imperative need of digital changes in provision of collaborative services in smart cities. Findings from this study can help for developing and maintaining business components and improving collaborative enterprise processes in smart cities. Besides, the findings can be systematically used by IT/business experts to digitally design VE. Also, findings from this study will be useful to researchers who might want to better understand practical implementation of VE model into real society, economic and social context, focusing on smart cities.

Additionally, DT supports VEs in breaking silos of competences to build new bridges and collaboration taking advantages of digital potential for city development. Although, this study contributes to model the DT of VE in smart cities, it is faced with a few limitations. First, only the creation and operation phase of VE are covered in this study, the configuration/re-configuration, evolution, and dissolution phase are not addressed. Secondly, different modelling languages for describing collaborative services are not compared. Future work will involves investigating the stakeholders such as municipality who drives DT of VE in smart cities and how such transformation relates to other sectors such as the technological sector to the business sector etc. Also, comparison of different modelling languages for describing collaborative services will be carried out. Lastly, other phases of VE will be modelled.

References

1. Salem, F.: A smart city for public value: digital transformation through agile governance-the case of 'smart Dubai'. World Government Summit Publications (2016, Forthcoming)
2. Anthony, B., Petersen, S.A., Ahlers, D., Krogstie, J., Livik, K.: Big data-oriented energy prosumption service in smart community districts: a multi-case study perspective. Energy Inform. 2(1), 1–26 (2019). https://doi.org/10.1186/s42162-019-0101-3
3. Kumar, H., Singh, M.K., Gupta, M.P., Madaan, J.: Moving towards smart cities: solutions that lead to the smart city transformation framework. Technol. Forecast. Soc. Change, 119281 (2018)
4. Anthony Jr., B., Majid, M.A., Romli, A.: A trivial approach for achieving Smart City: a way forward towards a sustainable society. In: 21st Saudi Computer Society National Computer Conference (NCC), pp. 1–6 (2018)
5. Anthony Jr., B., Abbas Petersen, S., Ahlers, D., Krogstie, J.: API deployment for big data management towards sustainable energy prosumption in smart cities-a layered architecture perspective. Int. J. Sustain. Energy 39, 263–289 (2020)
6. Ekman, P., Thilenius, P., Thompson, S., Whitaker, J.: Digital transformation of global business processes: the role of dual embeddedness. Bus. Process Manag. J. 26, 570-592 (2019)
7. Heilig, L., Lalla-Ruiz, E., Voß, S.: Digital transformation in maritime ports: analysis and a game theoretic framework. NETNOMICS: Econ. Res. Electron. Netw. 18(2), 227–254 (2017). https://doi.org/10.1007/s11066-017-9122-x
8. Berman, S., Marshall, A.: The next digital transformation: from an individual-centered to an everyone-to-everyone economy. Strategy Leadersh. 42, 9–17 (2014)
9. Mowshowitz, A.: Social dimensions of office automation. Adv. Comput. 25, 335–404 (1986)
10. Camarinha-Matos, L.M., Afsarmanesh, H., Garita, C., Lima, C.: Towards an architecture for virtual enterprises. J. Intell. Manuf. 9, 189–199 (1998). https://doi.org/10.1023/A: 1008880215595
11. Pires, S.R., Bremer, C.F., De Santa Eulalia, L.A., Goulart, C.P.: Supply chain and virtual enterprises: comparisons, migration and a case study. Int. J. Logist. 4, 297–311 (2001)
12. Brahimi, M.: An agents' model using ontologies and web services for creating and managing virtual enterprises. Int. J. Comput. Digit. Syst. 8, 1–9 (2019)
13. Petersen, S.A., Divitini, M., Matskin, M.: An agent-based approach to modelling virtual enterprises. Prod. Plan. Control 12, 224–233 (2001)
14. Samdantsoodol, A., Cang, S., Yu, H., Eardley, A., Buyantsogt, A.: Predicting the relationships between virtual enterprises and agility in supply chains. Expert Syst. Appl. 84, 58–73 (2017)
15. Sari, B., Sen, T., Kilic, S.E.: Ahp model for the selection of partner companies in virtual enterprises. Int. J. Adv. Manuf. Technol. 38, 367–376 (2008). https://doi.org/10.1007/ s00170-007-1097-6
16. Liu, P., Raahemi, B., Benyoucef, M.: Knowledge sharing in dynamic virtual enterprises: a socio-technological perspective. Knowl.-Based Syst. 24, 427–443 (2011)
17. Noran, O.: Enhancing collaborative healthcare synergy. In: Camarinha-Matos, L.M., Scherer, R.J. (eds.) PRO-VE 2013. IAICT, vol. 408, pp. 459–467. Springer, Heidelberg (2013). https://doi.org/10.1007/978-3-642-40543-3_49
18. Mahmoodpour, M., Mahmood, K., Lobov, A.: IoT-based senses for virtual enterprises. In: IECON, pp. 4181–4186 (2018)
19. Kim, T.Y., Lee, S., Kim, K., Kim, C.H.: A modeling framework for agile and interoperable virtual enterprises. Comput. Ind. 57, 204–217 (2006)

20. Fischer, K., Muller, J.P., Heimig, I., Scheer, A.W.: Intelligent agents in virtual enterprises. In: PAAM 1996, pp. 205–223 (1996)
21. Bokolo, A.J., Petersen, S.A.: A smart city adoption model to improve sustainable living. Norsk konferanse for organisasjoners bruk av informasjonsteknologi (2019)
22. Ekman, P., Röndell, J., Yang, Y.: Exploring smart cities and market transformations from a service-dominant logic perspective. Sustain. Cities Soc. **51**, 101731 (2019)
23. Davidow, W.H.: The virtual corporation: structuring and revitalizing the corporation for the 21st century (1992)
24. Week, B.: The virtual corporation, pp. 98–103 (1993)
25. Browne, J., Zhang, J.: Extended and virtual enterprises–similarities and differences. Int. J. Agile Manag. Syst. **1**, 30–36 (1999)
26. Roedder, N., Dauer, D., Laubis, K., Karaenke, P., Weinhardt, C.: The digital transformation and smart data analytics: an overview of enabling developments and application areas: In: 2016 IEEE International Conference on Big Data (Big Data), pp. 2795–2802 (2016)
27. Mihardjo, L.W.W., Sasmoko, Alamsjah, F., Elidjen: Digital transformation: a transformational performance-based conceptual model through co-creation strategy and business model innovation in the Industry 4.0 in Indonesia. Int. J. Econ. Bus. Res. **18**, 369–386 (2019)
28. Kempegowda, S.M., Chaczko, Z.: Industry 4.0 complemented with EA approach: a proposal for digital transformation success. In: ICSEng, pp. 1–6 (2018)
29. Petersen, S.A., Pourzolfaghar, Z., Alloush, I., Ahlers, D., Krogstie, J., Helfert, M.: Value-added services, virtual enterprises and data spaces inspired enterprise architecture for smart cities. In: Camarinha-Matos, L.M., Afsarmanesh, H., Antonelli, D. (eds.) PRO-VE 2019. IAICT, vol. 568, pp. 393–402. Springer, Cham (2019). https://doi.org/10.1007/978-3-030-28464-0_34
30. Mouhib, N., Bah, S., Berrado, A.: Enterprise architecture improvement for virtual enterprise modeling. In: Proceedings of the International Conference on Industrial Engineering and Operations Management, pp. 11–13 (2017)
31. Perrin, O., Godart, C.: A model to support collaborative work in virtual enterprises. Data Knowl. Eng. **50**, 63–86 (2004)
32. Aerts, A.T.M., Szirbik, N.B., Goossenaerts, J.B.: A flexible, agent-based ICT architecture for virtual enterprises. Comput. Ind. **49**, 311–327 (2002)
33. Yin, R.K.: Case Study Research: Design and Methods (Applied Social Research Methods). Sage Publications, Thousand Oaks (2014)
34. Creswell, J.W., Poth, C.N.: Qualitative Inquiry and Research Design: Choosing Among Five Approaches. Sage Publications, Thousand Oaks (2016)
35. Iacob, M.E., Meertens, L.O., Jonkers, H., Quartel, D.A.C., Nieuwenhuis, L.J.M., van Sinderen, M.J.: From enterprise architecture to business models and back. Softw. Syst. Model. **13**(3), 1059–1083 (2012). https://doi.org/10.1007/s10270-012-0304-6
36. Caetano, A., et al.: Representation and analysis of enterprise models with semantic techniques: an application to ArchiMate, e3value and business model canvas. Knowl. Inf. Syst. **50**(1), 315–346 (2016). https://doi.org/10.1007/s10115-016-0933-0
37. Anthony Jr., B., Abbas Petersen, S., Ahlers, D., Krogstie, J.: Big data driven multi-tier architecture for electric mobility as a service in smart cities: a design science approach. Int. J. Energy Sect. Manag., 1–25 (2020)

Skills for Organizations of the Future

Towards Agile Operation for Small Teams in Knowledge Intensive Organizations: A Collaboration Framework

Qinghua Liu[1], Juanqiong Gou[1(✉)], and Luis M. Camarinha-Matos[2]

[1] School of Economic and Management, Beijing Jiaotong University,
Beijing, China
{18120615, jqgou}@bjtu.edu.cn
[2] School of Science and Technology, NOVA University of Lisbon
and CTS-UNINOVA, Caparica, Portugal
cam@uninova.pt

Abstract. Knowledge Intensive Organizations (KIOs) are of growing importance worldwide. But comparing to other kinds of enterprises, they are challenged by more uncertainty and complex situations. In the context of a KIO, various small teams can be dynamically organized to collaboratively pursue knowledge creation initiatives. As these small teams, which bred from KIOs, often involve activities that cannot be fully predetermined, they need to be supported by related resources and services in a more agile way during their operation and evolution stages. This paper presents a new three-layer collaboration framework for agile operation of small teams on the basis of existing models from the paradigm of Collaborative Networks, with a set of roles and mechanisms proposed in each layer. Considering the framework, related digital platforms and artificial intelligence applications can be developed, giving effective support to small teams' knowledge creation processes. A case study has been developed for a research group to illustrate the proposed framework.

Keywords: Knowledge Intensive Organizations · Agile Operation · Collaborative Networks · Digital platforms

1 Introduction

As the rise of the knowledge economy is having a profound impact in society, Knowledge Intensive Organizations (KIOs) have drawn much attention worldwide during the past years [1]. KIOs were initially defined as "organizations whose primary value-added activities consist of the accumulation, creation, or dissemination of knowledge for the purpose of developing a customized service" [2]. Although an agreement on their definition and typology is unavailable [3], KIOs have common characteristics and face similar challenges. Activities in KIOs are often interdependent and cannot be fully predetermined, as they often entail innovation on the part of the individual and involve further complex tasks [4]. To deal with uncertainty and complexity, effective collaboration among individuals inside KIOs are of growing importance.

© IFIP International Federation for Information Processing 2020
Published by Springer Nature Switzerland AG 2020
L. M. Camarinha-Matos et al. (Eds.): PRO-VE 2020, IFIP AICT 598, pp. 263–272, 2020.
https://doi.org/10.1007/978-3-030-62412-5_22

The paradigm of Collaborative Networks (CNs) has been applied to a great variety of domains, including manufacturing and other industries [5]. As the theoretical models of CNs show good potential to also deal with inner-organization affairs [6], this paper explores their application in KIOs. Collaborative Networks address structuring organizations into two high levels of Collaborative Networked Organizations (CNO) [7], according to which a KIO can be seen as a long-term strategic alliances and small teams inside the KIO as goal-oriented networks [6]. The lifecycle of a CNO consists of the main phases of creation, operation, evolution, metamorphosis and dissolution [8]. While in existing literature long-term strategic alliances are mostly studied in their capacity to enhance dynamic and fluid establishment of goal-oriented networks in their creation phase [9], the operation phase of small teams also needs constant support from their KIO environment. This paper mainly concentrates on the operation stage of the small teams and puts forward the concept of Agile Operation of Small Teams.

If the operation stage of a goal-oriented network can be supported by the long-term strategic alliance in an agile way, we then define this stage as Agile Operation. Considering this context, our work is guided by a main question:

How to effectively support Agile Operation of small teams in Knowledge Intensive Organizations?

The paper is structured as follows: after introducing and contextualizing the research question in Sect. 1, Sect. 2 presents an overview of the main foundations used in this work on Agile Operation in KIOs. Section 3 describes a three-layer collaboration framework, the main idea of which is adding a new Operation Layer to improve interaction between small teams and the KIO. Then Sect. 4 provides a case study to better illustrate the framework. Finally, Sect. 5 presents the conclusion and opportunities for further work.

2 Related Works

2.1 Knowledge Creation in KIOs

As knowledge is the main production factor and the outcome they offer [10], Knowledge creation is one of the most important task for KIOs. In Nonaka and Takeuchi's theory of Organizational Knowledge Creation, the notion of "knowledge conversion", which focuses on how tacit knowledge is converted to explicit knowledge and vice versa, is the cornerstone [11]. While prior literature provided evidence that processes related to knowledge conversion may foster organizational knowledge creation, most knowledge management projects based on Nonaka's SECI model failed [12]. In [13] there is an argument that tacit and explicit knowledge are not the two ends of a continuum but two sides of the same coin, and it makes no sense to talk about two types of knowledge separately or to believe that one is converted into the other.

Actually, the production of knowledge is increasingly collaborative [14]. From the complex responsive processes perspective, Stacey [15] assumes that knowledge is continuously replicated and potentially transformed in the communicative interaction between people. Starting from this assumption, it is crucial to pay particular attention to two aspects. From one side, internal and external connections of KIOs should be established and maintained (somehow related to the open innovation concept). In knowledge creation networks, the strength of connections between individuals has a positive effect on knowledge creation before a certain threshold [16]. Researchers also stressed the importance of the collaboration with external networks for knowledge creation [17]. From another perspective, KIOs need to help individual professionals to better engage in related knowledge creation activities [15]. Fresh forms of interaction are also need to be established for small teams' knowledge creation performance [13].

2.2 Collaborative Networks and Their Operation

CNs consist of sets of entities that collaborate to better achieve common or compatible goals, thus jointly generating value [18]. From the grasping of a collaboration opportunity to a successful collaboration, normally a CN will go through several stages of its lifecycle, which generally include: creation, operation, evolution, metamorphosis and dissolution [8].

By definition, operation is the phase where the network runs, executing the required business processes towards reaching its goals, that is, developing a solution and further maintaining it [8]. In [19] it is stated that operation is the most important stage not only for its longer activity duration comparing to other stages, but also because operation is the phase when a network really offers services and makes business. During operation, goal-oriented networks need to be managed and supported effectively. For instance, [20] introduces a framework in which promises can be made and monitored to make sure that collaborative behaviors will be done in goal-oriented networks. Other works also focus on further support such as risk control mechanisms [21] and performance indicators [19].

Evolution is a phase that may happen when problems take place during the operation phase [8]. As an illustration, [22] presents a comprehensive list of collaborative business processes and base practices, in which the Operation and Evolution phases are organized into the same subcategory. As mentioned before, small teams in KIOs get involved in a lot of unpredictable and complex tasks, so activities in the evolution stage actually happen at a high frequency for them. This is also one of the main reasons why Agile Operation is crucial for these teams. Thus, in this paper, evolution is considered as a part of the operation stage for small teams in KIOs, and the supporting activities for the evolution phase are also considered as a requirement of Agile Operation.

3 An Agile Operation Framework

In the Information System field, agility can be defined as "the continual readiness to rapidly or inherently create change, proactively or reactively embrace change, and learn from change while contributing to perceived customer value, through its collective components and relationships with its environment" [23]. Nevertheless, due to the lack of appropriate principles and methods, supporting goal-oriented networks in an agile way during their operation stage is still challenging.

In a KIO environment, activities in small teams are often interdependent and cannot be fully predetermined. Efficient knowledge creation needs individual professionals to engage in related processes in a more agile way. Thus, small teams need to interact with the KIO environment to quickly fulfill changing demands such as adding a new member, setting a new ICT service, or merely finding an answer for a single question from a professional individual. However, acting as long-term strategic alliances (of people), current KIOs cannot respond quickly enough to those real-time demands in most cases. Although the mission for a long-term strategic alliance is increasing the network's preparedness towards rapid configuration of temporary alliances for potential collaboration [18], managing a large network requires stable and reliable mechanisms and information infrastructures. Once a long-term strategic alliance finishes the creation of a goal-oriented network with configuration of related resources and services, it is hard for such entities to make further changes due to the high time cost and labor cost. The contradiction between fast evolving demands and stable resources is the main challenge for realizing Agile Operation.

For the purpose of improving the interaction efficiency between small teams and their KIO environment, thus supporting Agile Operation, this section suggests a three-layer collaboration framework.

As shown in Fig. 1, the proposed Agile Operation Framework comprises three layers: (1) Small Teams Layer, (2) Operation Layer, and (3) Strategic Alliance Layer, which are further explained below.

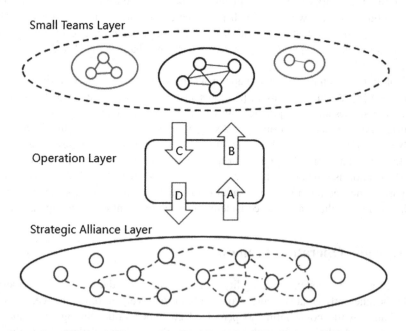

Fig. 1. Agile operation framework for small teams in KIOs

Small Teams Layer: Contains several small teams (goal-oriented networks). Each small team includes a set of participating members as well as related resources and services to support them working on the collaborative goal. In a KIO environment, small teams' knowledge creation activities take place in this layer directly. These activities may involve online and offline communication, training and learning, document writing and processing, etc. [4].

Operation Layer: Aims at fulfilling agile demands from the Small Teams Layer and contains a number of support mechanisms and roles. This layer keeps frequent interaction with both the Small Teams Layer and the Strategic Alliance Layer. Roles in this layer act similarly to "Virtual Organization Brokers" in existing literature [24], but the difference is that they keep close contact with goal-oriented networks during their whole lifecycle, especially during the operation stage.

Strategic Alliance Layer: Composed of members of the KIO, resources, and "connections" in a long-term strategic alliance. The resources may include facilities, information systems and data, financial resources, external relationships, etc. "Connections" generally include agreements, principles, mechanisms that support on-going and future collaboration, as well as relationships between members, and members' access to the resources. The Strategic Alliance Layer aims at increasing members' preparedness towards rapid configuration of temporary networks for collaboration [18] (the Small Teams in this case), as well as providing support during the operation of those temporary networks.

Regarding the Operation Layer, the interaction with the other two layers can comprise four processes. Process A represents the interaction started by the Strategic Alliance Layer. The main aim for this process is the organization of "abilities". An ability is a collection of resources and methods which can be abstractly packaged and integrated to accomplish a certain task. Process B and C are the interaction between the Operation Layer and the Small Teams Layer. Fully acquainted with the abilities, "brokers" in the Operation Layer can quickly develop customized services for the Small Teams in Process B. Process C represents that the Operation Layer getting feedback from the Small Teams Layer. In this process, members of the Small Teams may directly tell "brokers" their demands, or the Operation Layer keeps collecting and analyzing the data from the Small Teams Layer during their operation phase. In this way, Process B and C make a close loop: customized services, feedback, new customized services, new feedback. Finally, the Operation Layer brings collaborative record and experience back to the Strategic Alliance Layer in Process D, which can improve the connections and help the whole KIO better prepared for future collaboration.

With the Operation Layer and namely through its four processes, the operation of small teams can fulfill the demand of agility: rapidly creating changes, proactively embracing changes, and learning from changes.

4   Case Study

To better illustrate how the framework described in Sect. 3 should be applied in real situations, a brief case study was conducted in a research group.

The research group (the KIO, in this case) is based on a university, consisting of 3 faculties and more than 20 graduate students. The research group also maintains continued cooperation with a number of external partners.

WeChat, an online instant messaging application, is used by the team to help with communication, file sharing and other joint work, accompanied by occasional offline meetings. There is a WeChat group for all team members, which can be labeled as "the public group". About 20 smaller groups, each comprising 4-10 members ("small teams"), also exist. These groups are created for certain goals, like working on a given project or discussing an academic topic during a period of time.

The usage of WeChat makes the research group similar to a Professional Virtual Community (PVC), which is a typical long-term strategic alliance in CNs [18], and the smaller groups act as Virtual Teams bred from the PVC. But the difference is that professional individuals are independent in typical PVCs, while members in the public group belong to the same KIO, the research group. The research group has left a history of communication records in both public group and smaller groups in WeChat. Based on these records, as a kind of resource in the Strategic Alliance Layer, the case developed one "ability" and provided some simple agile services to the small teams to simulate the processes in an Operation Layer.

First, as shown in Fig. 2(a), the communication record in WeChat groups was collected and reorganized. A complete conversation for a period of time was defined as a "situation" [25]. Situations were divided into four types: communication, sharing, tasks, and offline meeting notice. In addition to recording the date, time and participants, each type of situation records different additional information, such as filename, sharer, place of an offline meeting, etc.

The organized records extracted from WeChat groups can help in obtaining some preliminary analysis results. It can be assumed that the more situations did a group member participate in, the more active he or she was in the group. Likewise, if two group members participated in the same situations for many times, they tend to have a close connection. Figure 2(b) shows the analysis results in a WeChat group which consists of 7 members. Each circle in this figure represents a member in the group and the number in a circle (proportional to its radius) indicates how many situations did the member participate in. The thickness of a connecting line between two circles represents how many situations include both these two members. Obviously, in the example, Y was the most active member in the group, and he has strong connection with G and Q. Using the same method to analyze all smaller WeChat groups which bred from the public group and superposing their figures, a possible result is shown in Fig. 2(c), which indicates members' activities and connections for the whole research group.

Each smaller WeChat group has its goals or academic topics represented by "keywords". For example, the keywords of the group in Fig. 2(b) are "System Analysis" and "Writing an Article". If a member of the research group participates in many situations in this group, he or she is more likely to have experience and knowledge on

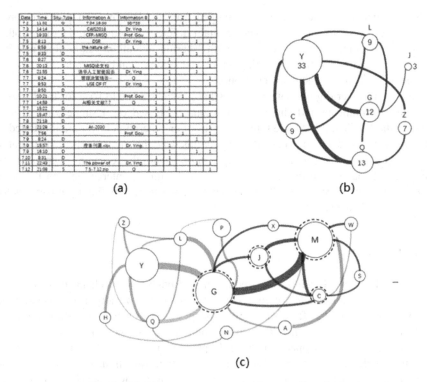

(a)   (b)

(c)

Fig. 2. WeChat group communication record analysis

"System Analysis". In Fig. 2(c), the highlighted circles and the corresponding connecting line represent members who are active on a certain keyword and the connection between them.

The data analysis above can be considered as a part of Process A in Fig. 1 Confirmed the willingness of all members in the research group to provide their help to projects if their professional skills are needed, an "ability" had been developed based on the analysis result: if the knowledge creation processes in a research project needs certain knowledge or professional skills, the right member in the research group will be quickly found.

Then, the other three processes in the Operation Layer can also be developed. Process B in this case can be the developing of a kind of service or AI assistant, to help a small team find and make a quick agreement with "the right member" and then make him or her engaged in the knowledge creation activities. In Process C, a "broker" in the research group will keep hearing the demands from the small teams: what the "keywords" they are working about and what kind of knowledge or skills they probably need. Another possible scenario is that a "broker" or n artificial intelligence agent may find small teams' demands directly from ongoing WeChat interaction or data from other digital platforms. Finally, in Process D, all new interaction records emerged during the small teams' operation, including their interaction with the Operation Layer, will be collected and stored into the Strategic Alliance Layer.

Some other abilities can also be developed from the WeChat group chat records. For instance, as the four situation types contain different information, data from other sources like document profiles (matched with "sharing" situations) and offline meeting records (matched with "offline meeting notice" situations) can be introduced to enrich the Operation Layer of the research group.

Like many other digital platforms, WeChat provides a sound base for the research group to communicate and share digital resources. Based on a single kind of data resource, the WeChat record, the four processes of an Operation Layer are illustrated to fulfill the real-time demands of small teams. In this way, the small teams in the research group can be operated in a more agile way: On one hand, the research group can keep hearing the demand from the small teams and make further interactions; on the other hand, small teams are provided the continual readiness to rapidly find right partners for the emerging changes.

5   Conclusion

Knowledge Intensive Organizations require new models and mechanisms to face the challenge of uncertainties and complexities. Based on the paradigm of Collaborative Networks, this paper put forward a new concept—Agile Operation of Small Teams, which means small teams in KIOs can be continuously supported by their breeding environment during their operation stage. In practice of CNs, goal-oriented networks' interaction with the long-term strategic alliance are mostly limited to their creation stage, so it is hard to provide small teams with constant agile services to embrace changes. This paper proposes a framework for a possible approach to support this Agile Operation.

In the proposed three-layer framework, the Small Teams Layer and Strategic Alliance Layer focus on small teams' agile services and KIOs' resource management separately. As CNs address structuring organizations into two high levels of CNO, the main innovation of this work is adding an Operation Layer to the framework. Acting as a "transmission gear" between the other two layers, the Operation Layer can keep frequent interaction with both resources in KIO environment and KIOs operation through four key processes. A case study was also presented and discussed in the paper to better illustrate the applicability of the framework.

Future work will focus on development methods for related components in the three-layer collaboration framework and intelligent applications for knowledge creation activities in KIOs.

Acknowledgements. The presented research works have been supported by "the National Natural Science Foundation of China" (61972029) and "Science and Technology Development Center, Ministry of Education" (2018A02008). Partial support also from the Portuguese FCT foundation through the program UIDB/00066/2020 and European Commission through the project DiGiFoF (Nr. 601089-EPP-1-2018-1-RO-EPPKA2-KA).

References

1. Millar, C.C.J.M., Lockett, M., Mahon, J.F.: Knowledge intensive organisations: on the frontiers of knowledge management. J. Knowl. Manag. **20**, 845–857 (2016). https://doi.org/10.1108/JKM-07-2016-0296
2. Bettencourt, L., Ostrom, A., Brown, S., Roundtree, R.: Client co-production in knowledge-intensive business services. Calif. Manag. Rev. **44**, 100+ (2002). https://doi.org/10.2307/41166145
3. Makani, J., Taylor, L.: Towards a typology of knowledge-intensive organizations: determinant factors. Knowl. Manag. Res. Pract. **8**, 265–277. https://doi.org/10.1057/kmrp.2010.13
4. Little, T.A., Deokar, A.V.: Understanding knowledge creation in the context of knowledge-intensive business processes. J. Knowl. Manag. **20**, 858–879 (2016). https://doi.org/10.1108/JKM-11-2015-0443
5. Camarinha-Matos, L., Fornasiero, R., Ramezani, J., Ferrada, F.: Collaborative networks: a pillar of digital transformation. Appl. Sci. **9**, 5431 (2019). https://doi.org/10.3390/app9245431
6. Gou, J., Liu, Q., Mu, W., Ying, W., Afsarmanesh, H., Benaben, F.: A digital-enabled framework for intelligent collaboration in small teams. In: Camarinha-Matos, L.M., Afsarmanesh, H., Antonelli, D. (eds.) PRO-VE 2019. IAICT, vol. 568, pp. 193–202. Springer, Cham (2019). https://doi.org/10.1007/978-3-030-28464-0_18
7. Camarinha-Matos, L., Afsarmanesh, H.: Classes of collaborative networks. In: Encyclopedia of Networked and Virtual Organizations, pp. 193–198. IGI Global, New York (2008)
8. Afsarmanesh, H., Camarinha-Matos, L.M.: The ARCON modeling framework. In: Camarinha-Matos, L.M., Afsarmanesh, H. (eds.) Collaborative Networks: Reference Modeling, pp. 67–82. Springer, New York (2008). https://doi.org/10.1007/978-0-387-79426-6_7
9. Afsarmanesh, H., Camarinha-Matos, L.M., Msanjila, S.S.: On management of 2nd generation virtual organizations breeding environments. Ann. Rev. Control **33**, 209–219 (2009). https://doi.org/10.1016/j.arcontrol.2009.05.007
10. Schricke, E., Zenker, A., Stahlecker, T.: Knowledge-intensive (business) services in Europe. European Commission, Brussels (2012). https://doi.org/10.2777/59168
11. Nonaka, I.: A dynamic theory of organizational knowledge creation. Organ. Sci. **5**, 14–37 (1994). https://doi.org/10.1287/orsc.5.1.14
12. Chang, C.-M., Hsu, M.-H., Yen, C.-H.: Factors affecting knowledge management success: the fit perspective. J. Knowl. Manag. **16**, 847–861 (2012). https://doi.org/10.1108/13673271211276155
13. Tsoukas, H.: How should we understand tacit knowledge? A phenomenological view. In: Handbook of Organizational Learning and Knowledge Management, 2nd edn., pp. 453–476. Wiley, Chichester (2015)
14. Adams, J.D., Black, G.C., Clemmons, J.R., Stephan, P.E.: Scientific teams and institutional collaborations: Evidence from US universities, 1981–1999. Res. Policy **34**, 259–285 (2005). https://doi.org/10.1016/j.respol.2005.01.014
15. Stacey, R.D.: Complex responsive processes and the traditional concerns of the strategist. In: Strategic Management and Organisational Dynamics, pp. 404–430. Pearson Education, Harlow (2007)
16. Wang, J.: Knowledge creation in collaboration networks: effects of tie configuration. Res. Policy **45**, 68–80 (2016)

17. Crescenzi, R., Nathan, M., Rodriguez-Pose, A.: Do inventors talk to strangers? On proximity and collaborative knowledge creation. Res. Policy **45**, 177–194 (2016)
18. Camarinha-Matos, L.M., Afsarmanesh, H., Ollus, M.: ECOLEAD and CNO base concepts. In: Camarinha-Matos, L.M., Afsarmanesh, H., Ollus, M. (eds.) Methods and Tools for Collaborative Networked Organizations, pp. 3–32. Springer, Boston (2008). https://doi.org/10.1007/978-0-387-79424-2_1
19. Graça, P., Camarinha-Matos, L.: Performance indicators for collaborative business ecosystems—literature review and trends. Technol. Forecast. Soc. Change **116** (2016). https://doi.org/10.1016/j.techfore.2016.10.012
20. Shadi, M., Afsarmanesh, H.: Behavior modeling in virtual organizations. In: 2013 27th International Conference on Advanced Information Networking and Applications Workshops, pp. 50–55 (2013). https://doi.org/10.1109/WAINA.2013.95
21. Afsarmanesh, H., Shadi, M.: Bayesian network-based risk prediction in virtual organizations. In: Camarinha-Matos, L.M., Bénaben, F., Picard, W. (eds.) PRO-VE 2015. IAICT, vol. 463, pp. 39–52. Springer, Cham (2015). https://doi.org/10.1007/978-3-319-24141-8_4
22. Cancian, M., Rabelo, R., Gresse von Wangenheim, C.: Collaborative business processes for enhancing partnerships among software services providers. Enterp. Inf. Syst. **9**, 1–26 (2015). https://doi.org/10.1080/17517575.2014.985617
23. Conboy, K.: Agility from first principles: reconstructing the concept of agility in information systems development. Inf. Syst. Res. **20**, 329–354 (2009). https://doi.org/10.1287/isre.1090.0236
24. Katzy, B.R., Loeh, H., Zhang, C.: Virtual organising scenarios. In: Camarinha-Matos, L.M., Afsarmanesh, H. (eds.) Collaborative Networked Organizations, pp. 27–40. Springer, Boston (2004). https://doi.org/10.1007/1-4020-7833-1_5
25. Chang, C.K.: Situation analytics—at the dawn of a new software engineering paradigm. Sci. China Inf. Sci. **61**(5), 1–14 (2018). https://doi.org/10.1007/s11432-017-9372-7

OMiLAB: A Smart Innovation Environment for Digital Engineers

Dimitris Karagiannis[1], Robert Andrei Buchmann[2(✉)],
Xavier Boucher[3], Sergio Cavalieri[4], Adrian Florea[5], Dimitris Kiritsis[6],
and Moonkun Lee[7]

[1] Research Group Knowledge Engineering, University of Vienna,
Wahringerstr. 29, 1090 Vienna, Austria
dk@dke.univie.ac.at
[2] Business Informatics Research Center, University Babeș-Bolyai, Str. T. Mihali
58-60, 400591 Cluj Napoca, Romania
robert.buchmann@econ.ubbcluj.ro
[3] Mines Saint-Etienne, Université Clermont Auvergne, CNRS, UMR 6158
LIMOS-Institut Fayol, 158 Cours Fauriel, 42023 Saint-Etienne, France
boucher@emse.fr
[4] CELS Research Group, University of Bergamo, Viale G. Marconi 5, 24044
Bergamo, Dalmine, Italy
sergio.cavalieri@unibg.it
[5] Computer Science and Electrical Engineering Department, Lucian Blaga
University of Sibiu, Str. E. Cioran 4, Sibiu 550025, Romania
adrian.florea@ulbsibiu.ro
[6] ICT4SM Group, SCI-STI-DK, Swiss Federal Institute of Technology
in Lausanne, Station 9, 1015 Lausanne, Switzerland
dimitris.kiritsis@epfl.ch
[7] OMiLAB KOREA Research Center, Chonbuk National University,
567 Baekje-daero, Deokjin-gu, Jeonju 54896, South Korea
moonkun@jbnu.ac.kr

Abstract. This position paper introduces a Smart Innovation Environment for experimentation related to digital transformation projects, for the consolidation of a proposed "Digital Engineer" skill profile (with a business-oriented facet labelled as "Digital Innovator"). In the Internet of Things era, this profile implies the ability to perform both digital design and engineering activities, to semantically bridge multiple layers of abstraction and specificity – from business analysis down to cyber-physical engineering. In the paper's proposal, this integration is enabled by conceptual modelling methods and interoperable modelling tools, tailored to support the creation of Digital Twins for innovative digital business models. The architecture of the proposed environment is guided by a Design Research perspective – i.e., it is a treatment to an education "design problem" regarding the Digital Engineer skill profile in the IoT era. The proposed environment encompasses workspaces and toolkits are currently evaluated in "innovation corners" deployed across the OMiLAB ecosystem.

Keywords: OMiLAB · Digital Twin · Digital Engineer · Digital Innovator · Agile Modelling Method Engineering · Cyber-Physical systems

© IFIP International Federation for Information Processing 2020
Published by Springer Nature Switzerland AG 2020
L. M. Camarinha-Matos et al. (Eds.): PRO-VE 2020, IFIP AICT 598, pp. 273–282, 2020.
https://doi.org/10.1007/978-3-030-62412-5_23

1   Introduction

The growing popularity of the Digital Twin concept and the Internet of Things (IoT) paradigm reclaims new digitalisation skills. This paper proposes an updated vision on the *Digital Engineer* skill profile, with an alternative facet labelled as *Digital Innovator* - where a business analyst view gains priority. These profiles are still to be consolidated in higher education curricula, although they have been present for some time as organisational roles in digital transformation projects. The "Digital Engineer" term has been used as an educational profile since the late 90s [1] – however, in the IoT/Digital Twin era it must be updated, considering that interoperability and integration are rapidly evolving in scope and possibilities.

A challenge arising with this evolution is to set up adequate environments for developing and consolidating the Digital Engineer/Innovator skill profiles – i.e. to answer the questions: *what assets should be made available for an integrated experimentation or learning experience? how can the business view be integrated with conceptual and engineering views in a modular environment - deployed as either a research or didactic laboratory?* In response to this challenge, a Smart Innovation Environment is hereby presented. The environment is designed and tested in the collaboration network of the Open Models Laboratory (OMiLAB) [2] - a digital ecosystem previously presented as a socio-technical ecosystem with a focal point on conceptualisation processes in [3].

This paper isolates one key asset of the ecosystem – the **Smart Innovation Environment** for Digital Engineers, an orchestration of software/hardware resources and workspace configurations articulated in an experimental setup to serve either as a didactic or a research laboratory in OMiLAB "nodes" being set up in partner universities or companies. Specifically, the proposed environment incorporates workspaces for Digital Design Thinking and Digital Twin-based engineering, supported by appropriate integration platforms and interoperability facilitators, employing Conceptual Modelling methods to bridge the semantic gaps between Design Thinking results (of innovation workshops) and feasibility experiments with Digital Twins proofs-of-concept. Demonstration scenarios, reusable components and knowledge assets are being accumulated from the network effect of collaboration between organizations adopting the "OMiLAB node" status [2].

The work at hand is framed from a Design Research perspective [4], as a treatment to an education design problem – the development of the Digital Engineer skill profile. This framing will be outlined in Sect. 2. Section 3 will detail the pillars of the proposed environment and their key assets. Section 4 will comment on related works. The paper ends with a SWOT evaluation.

2   Problem Statement and Requirements

We start by formulating the motivating requirements for which the proposed innovation environment was developed. These requirements originate both in position statements regarding the Digital Engineer skill profile and in the human resource needs of recent research projects running in institutions involved in the OMiLAB collaboration network. According to [5], "the Digital Engineer will be a person with knowledge and skill in the use of engineering and digital technology to enable major process improvements and performance increases in both physical and business operations." The role is intended to accelerate business insight "through more integrated asset management" within "highly instrumented facilities" (comprising enablers such as smart equipment, simulators etc.), with a profile that integrates "historically-disconnected skills".

Additionally, the Conceptual Modelling education "design problem", as framed in [6], inspired this work towards the aim of elevating the value of conceptual modelling from traditional use cases (software design, business process management) to a generalised value proposition, where modelling languages are "knowledge schemas" that can be tailored for any domain and depth of specificity. When this idea is coupled with interoperable modelling environments, it leads to a form of Digital Twin engineering that is *semantics-driven in the centre* (the so-called "next generation Digital Twin" [7]) and *computationally-intensive at the edge* (i.e. computationally-heavy tasks are delegated to cyber-physical systems and edge services). In Table 1 we aggregate a list of "environment requirements" for which this paper's proposal was designed, together with brief suggestions about how they are addressed by the current environment architecture.

Table 1. Requirements for the Smart Innovation Environment

Requirement	How the Smart Innovation Environment addresses the requirement
The Modelling Method Agility requirement. There is a need for conceptual modelling methods that can be tailored for capturing multiple layers of abstraction, specificity and granularity – from high level business insights down to run-time constraints and properties	*Building on the tradition of multi-perspective enterprise modelling, the proposed Smart Innovation Environment employs a generic concept of "modelling method" introduced in [8], whose building blocks can be tailored through metamodelling in order to achieve alignment with a targeted domain, specificity and granularity* *Integration and customisation of modelling languages are thus enabled, making them responsive to explicit "modelling method requirements" (as defined in [9]). An initial toolkit of agile modelling environments is provided*
The **Technology requirement.** There is a need for fast prototyping enablers – both for the agile modelling methods invoked in the previous point and for the cyber-physical counterparts of Digital Twins. Out-of-the box components must support evaluation and interoperability	*The proposed environment is built on three pillars – each with its own toolkits and interoperability features:* *(a) toolkit for Digital Design Thinking to support facilitation workshops and ideation at business scenario level;* *(b) toolkit for Digital Twin modelling and integration;* *(c) toolkit for engineering of Digital Twin-based cyber-physical demonstrators*

(continued)

Table 1. (*continued*)

Requirement	How the Smart Innovation Environment addresses the requirement
The **Openness requirement.** Open platforms and open interfaces are preferred in the choice of technology, to facilitate reuse prototypical building blocks and the accumulation of learned lessons	*The proposed environment includes a Web integration platform [10] and a set of out of the box adaptors/services to facilitate interoperability between modelling environments and external artefacts/systems A free metamodelling platform [11] is employed to ensure that all modelling tools are open to further adaptation or reuse. Openness is the fundamental motivator for the OMiLAB ecosystem and its collaboration network*
The **Digital Integration requirement.** Modelling environments must provide machine-readable semantic mediation from the business insights layer (where business model or product characteristics are co-created) down to the layer of cyber-physical demonstrators	*The modelling method engineering technology builds on the notion of **Smart Models** – i.e. Conceptual Models that have three key qualities: (a) they decompose a socio-technical system across multiple perspectives and levels of detail while preserving semantic links across those perspectives/levels; (b) they make diagrammatic content available to both humans and machines, covering a semantic spectrum ranging from highly abstract business ideas/service designs down to the level of executable artefacts; (c) they interact with other systems through a variety of connectivity options (pushing or querying model content)*
The **Knowledge Ecosystem requirement.** Co-creation requires shared knowledge assets to support knowledge transfer across adopters.	*The proposed environment benefits from being part of the OMiLAB digital ecosystem, whose on-line portal [2] and community events [12] facilitate both knowledge sharing and dissemination, while also enabling a social dimension, thus boosting its value as a collaboration network*

3   The Smart Innovation Environment of OMiLAB

Guided by the requirements summarized in Table 1, the proposed innovation environment was designed as a modular laboratory setup that can be easily packaged and deployed on an existing network infrastructure and a limited physical space of one typical lab room.

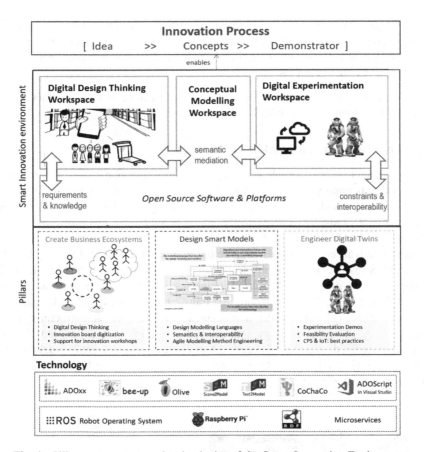

Fig. 1. Pillars, components and technologies of the Smart Innovation Environment

As illustrated in Fig. 1, it is conceptually built on three pillars – each instantiated in an operational workspace and reflecting one of three skill categories:

P1. Creation of Business Ecosystems – currently instantiated in a **Digital Design Thinking** workspace with a toolkit that supports the digitalisation of "innovation boards" that typically emerge during facilitation/innovation workshops.

P2. Smart Modelling – currently instantiated in a **Conceptual Modelling** workspace having at its core the BEE-UP [13, 14] modelling tool, which integrates and extends several established languages: UML, BPMN, EPC, ER, Petri Nets, DMN, Flowcharts. At the same time, to support the "smart model" qualities formulated in Table 1, it provides model interoperability (via HTTP requests or RDF model-to-semantic graph conversion [15]). In addition, the ADOxx metamodelling environment [11] enables further adaptation and extension of modelling tools for the targeted domain-specificity and purpose.

P3. Digital Twin Engineering – currently instantiated in a **Digital Experimentation** workspace that enables the development of cyber-physical demonstrators (Raspberry Pi-based, Robot OS-based) or virtual service demonstrators (e.g. process-aware apps, simulation reports).

In the following, a description of each workspace will be detailed together with the capabilities of their respective toolkits.

3.1   The Digital Design Thinking Workspace

This component supports problem-solving or product development teams that need to perform a participatory analysis of business requirements while co-creating innovative digital business models. The popular approach of Design Thinking [16] captures results in the form of innovation boards where goals, stakeholders, processes and product-service characteristics are pinned, grouped, colour-coded.

In more advanced approaches, graphic figurines can be employed for storyboarding – e.g. SAP Scenes [17]. The hereby proposed environment supports this practice with a toolkit for the digitisation of Design Thinking results – i.e. scene boards are captured by a Webcam and QR code software and transferred in the Scene2Model modelling environment [18, 19] where further annotation and machine-readable structuring can be performed. A mapping ontology maintains the correspondence between the SAP Scenes figurines (identified by QR codes) and concepts in the Scene2Model tool, thus enabling model queries and the semantic enrichment of storyboards with digital modelling means (Fig. 2).

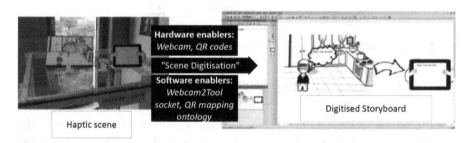

Fig. 2. The principle of Digital Design Thinking (adapted from [18])

3.2   The Conceptual Modelling Workspace

This is the central stage of the entire innovation environment, where co-created ideas are refined into "Smart Models" – i.e. conceptual models that are both human-readable and machine-readable, acting as a semantic and interactive representation of Digital Twins, further enabling model-driven engineering or interoperability with cyber-physical systems in the experimentation workspace. To enable full control on Digital Twin design and an open-endedness of the domain-specificity, the provided toolkit supports both modelling and metamodelling:

- the out-of-the-box BEE-UP tool offers a hybridisation of modelling languages for both engineering and business analysis needs: UML, BPMN, EPC, ER, Petri Nets, Flowcharts and DMN - semantic links across these languages enable a multi-layered description of a System of Systems with adequate granularity;
- the BEE-UP tool can be extended with richer semantics, additional model types or functionality that may be required for a selected domain/purpose; or, novel modelling methods may be developed from scratch with the help of the Agile Modelling Method Engineering methodology [20], applied in tandem with the ADOxx metamodelling platform [11] and the CoChaCo tool for managing the domain analysis and modelling method requirements [9].

In order to establish connectivity with run-time demonstrators, various interoperability channels are provided by both BEE-UP and ADOxx – e.g. HTTP requests can be triggered by model elements; model contents may be exported as RDF graphs to form a "knowledge base" for cyber-physical devices.

3.3   The Digital Experimentation Workspace

This is where software/hardware engineering takes places, taking input from the Smart Models designs and exploiting the model interoperability channels towards the realization of feasibility demonstrators. This streamlining is suggested by Fig. 3. Two categories of artefacts are typically developed:

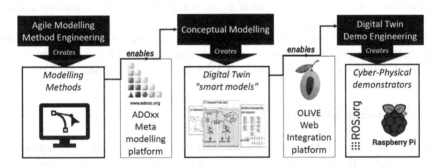

Fig. 3. Streamlined agile engineering activities for Digital Experimentation

- *IoT adaptors and micro-services.* The OLIVE Web integration platform [10] acts as a container for interoperability connectors with external services or physical objects, ensuring that communication between the modelling environment and cyber-physical demonstrators can be achieved (see exemplary service implementations in [21]);
- *Cyber-physical behaviour.* A starter package of robotic and IoT devices (Raspberry Pis or ROS-based), programmable through open interfaces, is provided for the prototyping of cyber-physical demonstrators. Once connected (through the Web integration platform) to the modelling environment, they gain various levels of "model-awareness" – from response-request communication to reasoning on model contents.

4 Related Works

Developing intellectual capital for Industry 4.0 is a major challenge, as digitalisation trends are changing skill profile requirements [22]. Innovation ecosystems can facilitate the creation and multiplication of digital engineering/innovation skills and setting up such environments has become a priority in higher education – see the "microfactory"-centered laboratory described in [23]. The hereby proposed innovation environment does not aim to define a full curriculum, but rather a modular, flexible package of training and experimentation resources that can be adopted for research and education based on innovation processes. Through its distinct but interoperating pillars and a Conceptual Modelling core, it was designed to support study programs in Business Informatics, Computer Science or Industrial Engineering, while encouraging hybrid programs for full benefits. Considerations on Digital Innovation curricula for Information Systems [24] have been taken into account, hence the Business Ecosystem Creation pillar was added as a business analyst-oriented perspective.

The current trends towards digital servitisation open value proposition towards the integration of value-added services associated to product lifecycles, leading to smart Product-Service-Systems (PSS) [25]. Digital engineers should be able to manage digitalisation challenges across multiple levels of smart PSS design – from innovation context analysis [26] to evaluation of alternatives [27].

The current proposal places an explicit focus on knowledge engineering as enabler for Digital Twin and IoT, towards a vision of Smart Systems where not only computational/algorithmic aspects are relevant, but also "by design" semantics that can be consulted at run-time by cyber-physical objects or their driving software agents. The enabled cognition has been detailed technically in works such as [28, 29] – the hereby proposed environment exploits in this sense the semantics component of diagrammatic modelling, which thus becomes a form of knowledge representation.

5 Concluding Evaluation

The paper presents the Smart Innovation Environment of OMiLAB – an operational modular artefact that can be deployed as a research or didactic installation to support Digital Transformation projects. Current deployments take the form of "innovation corners" set up in several universities – e.g., as environments for digital design skill development in the project DIGIFOF [30]. Based on this experience, we conclude with the following SWOT analysis:

- **Strengths:** The three pillars of the proposed environment contribute to developing a cross-disciplinary skill profile based on an "integrated separation" of concerns, covering Design Thinking, Conceptual Modelling and IoT engineering. Each pillar provides toolkits based on platforms with open interfaces. Modularity ensures that the different layers can also be employed independently for limited scopes. Agile Modelling Method Engineering ensures that the conceptualisation of Digital Twins can be tailored to any application domain or virtual enterprise;

- **Weaknesses:** The environment is continuously evolving as new requirements are identified; the current configuration is inherently limited and focused around a selected set of demonstration scenarios (e.g. currently not covering cybersecurity concerns) – however, the reliance on open platforms, open interfaces and general purpose cyber-physical platforms ensures an open-ended evolution;
- **Opportunities:** Both engineering schools and business schools can adopt the proposed environment as either a didactic or research laboratory. Hybrid study programs integrating "historically-disconnected skills" [5] can benefit from the modular yet interoperable proposed environment;
- **Threats:** The viability of the proposed environments depends on the uptake of the Digital Engineer/Innovator skill profiles updated for the IoT era. The Digital Twin notion hereby proposed has a semantic core and a computational flexible edge, which is not necessarily in line with traditional digital engineering tools, but reflects current knowledge-driven IoT deployment strategies.

Acknowledgement. The proposed innovation environment is used by academic as well as industrial partners in the ERASMUS+ KA2 project no. 601089-EPP-1-2018-1-RO-EPPKA2-KA (https://www.digifof.eu/).

References

1. Walczowski, L.T., Dimon, K.R., Waller, W.: A digital engineering curriculum for the new millennium. Int. J. Electr. Eng. Educ. **37**(1), 108–117 (2000)
2. The OMiLAB network nodes. https://www.omilab.org/nodes/nodes.html. Accessed 29 Apr 2020
3. Bork, D., Buchmann, R., Karagiannis, D., Lee, M., Miron, E.T.: An open platform for modeling method conceptualization: the OMiLAB digital ecosystem. Commun. Assoc. Inf. Syst. **44**, 673–697 (2019). https://doi.org/10.17705/1CAIS.04432
4. Wieringa, Roel J.: Design Science Methodology for Information Systems and Software Engineering. Springer, Heidelberg (2014). https://doi.org/10.1007/978-3-662-43839-8
5. Holland, D., Crompton, J.: The Future Belongs to the Digital Engineer. XLIBRIS, Bloomington (2013)
6. Buchmann, R.A., Ghiran, A.M., Döller, V., Karagiannis, D.: Conceptual modeling education as a design problem. Complex Syst. Inform. Model. Q. **21**, 21–33 (2019). https://doi.org/10.7250/csimq.2019-21.02
7. Boschert, S., Heinrich, C., Rosen, R.: Next generation digital twin. In: Proceedings of TMCE 2018, pp. 209–217. TU Delft (2018)
8. Karagiannis, D., Kühn, H.: Metamodelling platforms. In: Bauknecht, K., Tjoa, A.M., Quirchmayr, G. (eds.) EC-Web 2002. LNCS, vol. 2455, p. 182. Springer, Heidelberg (2002). https://doi.org/10.1007/3-540-45705-4_19
9. Karagiannis, D., Burzynski, P., Utz, W., Buchmann, R.: A metamodeling approach to support the engineering of modeling method requirements. In: Proceedings of RE 2019, Jeju Island, Korea, pp. 199–210. IEEE (2019). https://doi.org/10.1109/RE.2019.00030
10. The OLIVE Web integration platform. https://www.adoxx.org/live/olive. Accessed 29 Apr 2020

11. BOC GmbH, The ADOxx metamodelling platform. http://www.adoxx.org. Accessed 29 Apr 2020
12. OMiLAB scientific events. https://austria.omilab.org/psm/events. Accessed 29 Apr 2020
13. The BEE-UP official page. http://austria.omilab.org/psm/content/bee-up/info. Accessed 29 Apr 2020
14. Karagiannis, D., Buchmann, R.A., Burzynski, P., Reimer, U., Walch, M.: Fundamental conceptual modeling languages in OMiLAB. Domain-Specific Conceptual Modeling, pp. 3–30. Springer, Cham (2016). https://doi.org/10.1007/978-3-319-39417-6_1
15. Karagiannis, D., Buchmann, R.A.: Linked open models – extending linked open data with conceptual model information. Inf. Syst. 56, 174–197 (2016). https://doi.org/10.1016/j.is.2015.10.001
16. Institute of Design Stanford, Get started with Design Thinking. https://dschool.stanford.edu/resources/getting-started-with-design-thinking. Accessed 29 Apr 2020
17. SAP SE, SAP Scenes. https://experience.sap.com/designservices/resources/scenes. Accessed 29 Apr 2020
18. Miron, E.-T., Muck, C., Karagiannis, D., Götzinger, D.: Transforming storyboards into diagrammatic models. In: Chapman, P., Stapleton, G., Moktefi, A., Perez-Kriz, S., Bellucci, F. (eds.) Diagrams 2018. LNCS (LNAI), vol. 10871, pp. 770–773. Springer, Cham (2018). https://doi.org/10.1007/978-3-319-91376-6_78
19. The Scene2Model official page. https://austria.omilab.org/psm/content/scene2model/info. Accessed 29 Apr 2020
20. Karagiannis, D.: Conceptual modelling methods: the AMME agile engineering approach. In: Silaghi, G.C., Buchmann, R.A., Boja, C. (eds.) IE 2016. LNBIP, vol. 273, pp. 3–19. Springer, Cham (2018). https://doi.org/10.1007/978-3-319-73459-0_1
21. Walch, M., Karagiannis, D.: How to connect design thinking and cyber-physical systems: the s*IoT conceptual modelling approach. In: Proceedings of HICSS 2019, pp. 7242–7251. University of Hawaii (2019)
22. Nicolaescu, S.S., et al.: Human capital evaluation in knowledge-based organizations based on big data analytics. Future Gener. Comput. Syst. 111, 654–667 (2020)
23. Molina Gutiérrez, A., et al.: Open innovation laboratory for rapid realisation of sensing, smart and sustainable products: motives, concepts and uses in higher education. In: Camarinha-Matos, L.M., Afsarmanesh, H., Rezgui, Y. (eds.) PRO-VE 2018. IAICT, vol. 534, pp. 156–163. Springer, Cham (2018). https://doi.org/10.1007/978-3-319-99127-6_14
24. Fichman, R.G., Dos Santos, B.L., Zheng, Z.: Digital innovation as a fundamental and powerful concept in information systems curricumul. MIS Q. 38(2), 329–353 (2014)
25. Rabe, M., Kühn, A., Dumitrescu, R., Mittag, T., Schneider, M., Gausemeier, J.: Impact of smart services to current value networks. J. Mech. Eng. 13(2), 10–20 (2017)
26. Andriankaja, H., Boucher, X., Medini, K.: Method to design integrated product-service systems based on the extended functional analysis approach. CIRP J. Manuf. Sci. Technol. 21, 120–139 (2018)
27. Osterwalder, A., Pigneur, Y., Bernarda, G., Smith, A.: Value Proposition Design: How to Create Products and Services Customers Want. Wiley, Hoboken (2014)
28. Rozanec, J.M., et al.: Towards actionable cognitive digital twins for manufacturing. In: International Workshop on Semantic Digital Twins, co-located with ESWC 2020, CEUR-WS 2615, paper 5 (2020)
29. Song, J., Choe, Y., Lee, M.: Application of probabilistic process model for smart factory systems. In: Douligeris, C., Karagiannis, D., Apostolou, D. (eds.) KSEM 2019. LNCS (LNAI), vol. 11776, pp. 25–36. Springer, Cham (2019). https://doi.org/10.1007/978-3-030-29563-9_3
30. DIGIFOF project – official page. https://digifof.eu/. Accessed 29 Apr 2020

Improving the Training Methods for Designers of Flexible Production Cells in Factories of the Future

Ion Mironescu[1,2], Daniel-Cristian Crăciunean[1], Adrian Florea[1(✉)], and Ioan Bondrea[3]

[1] Computer Science and Electrical Engineering Department, Lucian Blaga University of Sibiu, Sibiu, Romania
{ion.mironescu, daniel.craciunean, adrian.florea}@ulbsibiu.ro

[2] Agricultural Science and Food Engineering Department, Lucian Blaga University of Sibiu, Sibiu, Romania

[3] Industrial Engineering and Management Department, Lucian Blaga University of Sibiu, Emil Cioran Street 4, 550025 Sibiu, Romania
ioan.bondrea@ulbsibiu.ro

Abstract. This work proposes a design method for flexible manufacturing systems (FMS). The method reduces the learning curve by helping employees to solve problems related to the design and optimization of the layout, operation and control of FMS, avoiding the drawbacks of current tools. The approach uses Domain Specific Modeling Languages (DSML) for specification of FMS. The paper presents the definition of the DSML and the implementation of the graphical modeling and simulation tool bringing important contributions to development of the domain through the use of constructions from categories theory for DSML specifications. This mathematical basis allows the definition of constraints to avoid supplementary costs and eventual damages through incorrect or incomplete specification of the solutions. By interconnecting with ADOxx of the DSML and tool developed, facilitates access to other analysis and simulation tools like Bee-up, Petri net, better exploration of the design space and extended support for the design activity.

Keywords: Modeling · Digitalization · Training · Theory of categories · DSML

1 Introduction

The complexity of manufacturing processes is steadily increasing. The market has a high dynamic in volume and requirements, so that complex manufacturing processes should change in order to respond to the market demands. The trend is the transition from dedicated manufacturing lines (DMLs) to flexible manufacturing systems (FMSs) and reconfigurable manufacturing systems (RMSs) [1]. To obtain and maintain the flexibility, the enterprise need employees trained in system (re)engineering able to

© IFIP International Federation for Information Processing 2020
Published by Springer Nature Switzerland AG 2020
L. M. Camarinha-Matos et al. (Eds.): PRO-VE 2020, IFIP AICT 598, pp. 283–296, 2020.
https://doi.org/10.1007/978-3-030-62412-5_24

design, organize and supervise such systems. They should use the appropriate tools for modeling, simulation and process analysis [2].

There are a variety of tools used for the design and optimization of manufacturing system, which can be positioned between two extremes:

a) Pure modeling and simulation tools like Matlab/Simulink [3], Arena [4], SIMUL8 [5], iGrafx [6] with a higher degree of abstraction of the production processes but more freedom in the choice of simulation methods and in the tuning of simulation parameters. From users, this choice requires more knowledge related to the simulation techniques and the results interpretation.

b) Tools with a more realistically representation of the physical systems modeled and simulated and more integrated with the planning and execution systems of the enterprise like Visual Components[1], ProPlanner [7] and FlexSim [8]. They allow the user to analyze the simulation result in Virtual Reality (VR). FlexSim has complete support for Factory of the Future/Industry 4.0, allowing the implementation of digital twins and the integration of the physical and digital representation through Augmented Reality (AR), co-simulation, virtual PLCs, cloud computing, Big Data Analytics.

The limits between the two extremes are blurring as tools from the first category are starting to be extended with facilities of the second [9, 10].

Although proven by the practice to be very efficient, in specific context all these tools have some limitations:

1) in some cases, the inherent complexity of these programs (a high number of options and libraries with thousands of components) can be overwhelming and counter-productive in a training process;
2) the extensibility of the programs is mostly quantitatively – you can add variation of the same type of component but you cannot define an entirely new type of component;
3) the interoperability with other modeling and simulation tools is limited;
4) there is no possibility to impose constrains at the modeling language level in order to limit the modeling space to feasible/possible solutions.

At least two contexts in which these limitations occur are relevant for our research and teaching activity: the training of manufacturing system design skills and the preliminary design of new manufacturing systems. Therefore, we started the development of a design method and tool that should remove these drawbacks with the trade-off of not having the performances and all the features of the commercial tools.

The paper is structured as follows: Sect. 2 describes the proposed design method with the associated modeling method for manufacturing processes. In Sect. 3 we present the training method that uses the design method. Section 4 presents the results and the discussion. The final section concludes the paper together with the main contributions and further work.

---

[1] https://www.visualcomponents.com.

2 The Proposed Design Method

2.1 Context

As the method is used to design manufacturing system for the Factory of the Future/Industry 4.0 the method will cover some parts of the RAMI 4.0 architecture [11]. Because of its specifying destination – for training and preliminary design, the method will cover only the *Type* range on the *Life Cycle Value Stream* dimension. Only models of the manufacturing system will be created in the development stage and optimized in the maintenance and usage stage. The models will address concepts from the Asset to the Functional layers. The control scheme will include the Hierarchy levels from field devices to station.

2.2 Overview of the Overall Design Method

The design method should guide and support the user to find a solution to a design problem. A design problem is formulated as an assortment of products characterized by type of material and quantity that must be produced under some time and cost constraints. A solution to this problem has two aspects:

- Structural aspect: the components of the production line, their connections and their spatial configuration;
- Organizational aspect: the order and the timing in which the processed parts are entering each component of the production line – the schedule.

The context in which the design process takes place is: a) all the results are virtual/digital design solution and b) no prior experience exists on the problem's systems either because the user doesn't have it or because it is not existing at all (new case). Taking account of the context, the design activity is divided in three sub-activities presented below (A1÷A3).

A1. Layout design - in which the number, types, connections and placement of the components of the line are established. In this phase, the designer evaluates the general capabilities of the resulted solution, in order to assess the capabilities related to the product assortment(s) that it can produce, the maximal and minimal throughput for the line design proposed as solution. The analysis outlines also the design constraints (i.e. critical path, bottleneck components, critical failure points etc.). The assessment serves as a choice criterion for the selection of the design solutions. As a simplifying assumption, each component has the basic control loops for its parameters incorporated.

A2. Operation planning/Scheduling. At this stage, the designer tries to find an optimal schedule of jobs on the manufacturing line designed in A1. The optimization goal refers mostly to the minimization of the completion time, waiting times and/or of the job delays. The result of this activity are optimal or near optimal schedules. This activity has the role of defining the dynamic requirements for the control system which will be designed in the next activity.

A3. Control system design. At this stage, the designer develops the control system that steers the line to automatically perform the operations corresponding to a given schedule. The system should assure that the jobs are executed in the prescribed order and with the prescribed timing and that the concurrent processes are coordinated so that no undesired events occur. It specifies the number and type of control components, the connections between them and with the manufacturing line components and the control algorithms they implement. Given the assumption made for A1, this refer mainly to the supervisory control system.

When starting a solution from scratch (new production line) the order in which these activities are performed in the first cycle is: A1, A2, A3. Every improvement can imply design iteration on one activity and then design iteration on the other activities. Before the system is instantiated (e.g. the real system is built and installed), A2 should be performed sufficient times in order to cover the space of possible schedules. This process results in the design of a controlled system capable to automatically perform the schedules from the space. One application in which our research group is interested is the design of supervisory control for existing manufacturing systems that doesn't have one – and corresponding bringing them to Industry 4.0 standards. This is current in SMEs where traditionally automation/digitalization is absent or is minimal (like food industry). For such systems, the digital representation of the layout is produced through A1 and the digital representation of the current schedules is realised through A2; on the basis of these digital representations, a digital design of the control system is obtained through A3, which can be subsequently implemented.

2.3   Proposed Digital Workflow

The use of the Domain Specific Modeling Languages (DSML) in developing the digital design tools assures that the resulting applications are highly interoperable (they use the same data model) and support collaborative work (they can access a common model repository). In activity A1, the design tool is used to visually compose the layout of the manufacturing line using the graphical representation of the elements of DSML. The result is a model of the manufacturing line, both in its graphical representation (the layout of the manufacturing line) and its internal data structure representation; the last one is used to perform a structural analysis to assess the fitness of the design solution. For extending the range of performed analysis, the model is transformed in other equivalent models for which a wider range of structural analysis tools exists.

In A2 stage, the model is used in conjunction with the defined job configuration, optimization criteria and constraints, to determine the complexity of the corresponding optimization problem. This information is associated to the model in the model repository so that it can be used subsequently by all users with access to repository. The complexity determines the choice of the solving algorithm. The data structure suitable for the chosen algorithm is then generated from the model. By running the algorithm with this data structure, a schedule is obtained. By associating the schedule with the model, simulation cases are obtained; they can be simulated with the internal simulator of the design tool or with an external simulator. The internal simulator is hardcoded and uses the behavior associated to the language components. In an external simulator, different behaviors can be associated to the components, providing some flexibility.

In A3 phase, the model is completed with control elements. In the design tool, the control elements are visually placed and connected to the manufacturing line compo-nents and the control algorithms are defined in the control elements. Flexibility is assured by allowing external programs to interact with the simulation of the model so that more elaborate control strategies can be implemented in this external program. The simulation can interact with cyber physical systems to provide a realistic view.

2.4   Formalizing the Concept of Modeling Method

We implemented our modeling method by following the approach described in [12, 13] for which the ADOxx environment offers full support. We started with the first component of the modeling method, and we defined the modeling language and the modeling procedure. The modeling procedure formalizes the use of the modeling language for the models building. Then, we defined and implemented the second component of the modeling method – the ensemble of the mechanisms & algorithms which can explore and alter the state of the models. The mechanism and algorithms are the basic blocks for building more complex structural analysis and the simulation tools.

We chose to implement our modeling language as a Domain-Specific Language (DSL) [14, 15] in order to facilitate its use by domain experts. The experts will have the possibility to build models for specific domain problems (i.e. the design of a definite manufacturing system) using familiar concepts. We will use the term Domain-Specific Modeling Language (DSML) to designate the developed language. Based on our own domain expertise, we identified the basic concepts and the connections between them. A model of the manufacturing system is built as a graph with instances of the basic concepts as nodes and edges representing connection between instances. We defined a graphical notation for the DSML by assigning visual symbols to each concept. Consequently, the modeling procedure has a substantial visual programming component which is a "de facto" standard for the modern modeling and simulation method and tools. The process will be detailed in the Subsect. 2.5.

We considered the particularities of the manufacturing systems in the development of mechanisms and algorithms complementing the DSML. At structural level, a manufacturing systems can be viewed as a collection of interconnected subsystems, each with its individual state. The state of the manufacturing system at a certain point in time is the global aggregation of the local states of the subsystems. At behavioral level, each subsystem can evolve (i.e. changes its state) concurrently/in parallel to the others. The subsystems exchange information so that they can influence each other local states. Taking into account the assumptions, we considered both formalisms for representation of concurrent systems, namely Petri net [16] and the algebra of communicating systems [17], as the underlying fundament for the development at this stage. In this way, we can exploit both the graph representation of the models which can easily be transformed in other graphs (i.e. Petri net), and the categorical approach to metamodeling [18, 19].

2.5   DSML Definition

The concepts and the design consideration for the proposed DSML named the Modeling Language for Manufacturing Processes (MLMP) are summarized in Table 1. The language is the basis for the categorical modeling method we propose. This is a further development of the work presented in [20]. Our method uses the theory of categories to support the metamodeling activity specific to the modeling and simulation toll development in the ADOxx environment.

Table 1. Modeling language concepts

Concept	Graphical representation
Ports The ports are used to realize connection between the other components modeled as concepts of the language. This connection represents way to transfer mater, information or energy between components. Every port has a type and a direction which indicates what is transferred and in which direction. In this approach, we used M for materials and I for information as such classes.	
Material type port	
Information type port	
Human operator It can be modeled as mobile control components that can attach and detached from information ports and are capable of high level control algorithms.	
Buffer Buffers are components that store material without transform it so they must have all material ports of the same type. Buffers are characterized by their maximal capacity – the number of units of the same type that they can store. The maximal capacity is fixed and can't be extended (constant attribute). Their variable attribute is the current content which can vary between 0 to maxim capacity.	
Machines Are components that transfer material between their input and output ports asa rezult of the commands they receive on the in information port.	
Transport machines Are components that transfer material without transforming it. They only change the position of material from the input buffer to the output buffer.	
Workstation Workstation are components that transform materials from one type to another	
Autonomous guided vehicles (AGV) Are practically mobile buffers having all attributes and behavior of a buffer but can connect and disconnect their ports from the corresponding ports of buffers and can move between preprogramed positions.	
Conveyors, belts, pipes (CBP) They transport only one material so all ports are of the same type and the defining feature is the throughput – number of material units transported in the time unit. This can be variable in some limits, thus the component has a minimal throughput and a maximal throughput as constant attributes and the current throughput as a variable attribute with values in this range.	
Manipulator Is a flexible transporter that can transfer multiple types of materials between different In and Out ports of the same type. The most usual example is an robotic arm that can handle different types of materials moving them between different manufacturing (sub)lines.	
Control component Are components that transfer only information so they have only information ports - not necessarily all of the same information type. They allow the definition of control algorithms that describe what command are transferred to other components on the in ports as the result of the signal received on the in ports.	

2.6   Categorical Specification of MLMP

To give a mathematical foundation to the process of the generating models in the MLMP, firstly each concept corresponding to a component type presented in Table 1 were described using the set theory. On this basis, we then defined the MLMP model as a directed graph with nodes representing the concepts and arcs representing the connections.

We used a categorical sketch as a metamodel for MLMP. The sketch has the property to incorporate beside an exact formal syntax also the semantic of the meta-model. We started from a general sketch [21, 22] (a directed multigraph with loops containing t the MLMP concepts) and added the constraints from above. We defined also the functor that transform a sketch $S=(\mathcal{G}, \mathcal{C}(\mathcal{G}))$ in a static visual model. We added to the sketch S beside the constraints $(\mathcal{G})$ also types, attributes and behavioral rules allowing the definition of the model's behavior. Double pushout graph transformations [23, 24] were used to specify the behavior of model described using the MLMP model. The rigorous mathematical description of the method is beyond the scope of this article and is provided on line[2]. We used the structures and rules to implement the metamodel in the ADOxx environment [15] and we developed a model editor and simulator for MLMP. This was the basic tool used in the training process described in the following section. The ADOxx ecosystem supports the development of collaborative tools based on the same model.

3   Training Method

During the development stages and after the release of the alpha version we have conducted several tests to gather feedback, understand the usability issues and identify how the method is improving the classical approach. The final testing process involved 12 people of different ages, but with the same technical background (engineering students, professors, researchers). The people were grouped in four teams so that each comprised one member which was familiar with the manufacturing process, one familiar with the optimizations methods and one familiar with control problems. The teams took part in Problem Based Learning trainings for manufacturing plant design. The training was divided in four sessions: one preparatory and three following the activities of the design method. In the preparatory session, the team members known each other, the used tools and methodology were presented and used in small didactic examples. In the second session, the teams had to design the layout of manufacturing lines that should produce a given assortment of products with a specified throughput and prove through analysis the capabilities of the designed line. In the third session, they had to find an optimal schedule for the production line designed in the previous session. In the final session, the trainees had to design the control system for the designed plant.

---

[2] https://digifof.eu/sites/default/files/d3.3_design_method_for_the_factory_of_the_future.pdf.

4   Results and Discussions

According to the specialization of the manufacturing engineers involved, two training were performed each with two teams. The use case where provided by the industry. A first step in establishing a collaboration network with the industry based on the design tool was put in place by installing the application at the enterprises witch accepted to offer the cases and connecting it to the shared repository. After a short tutorial, the design engineer where capable of expressing the design problems in the application. The use cases where stored in the repository being so accessible on line to the team participants.

The first training has started with a food industry case – a chocolate manufacturing line. The second training used a case from automotive industry. In each of them, one team used the MLMP modeling as support tool for designing the line layout, the other used only a graphic program (Sketch-up) to draw the layout. The problem settings where exported for them from the collaborative repository. In the next training sessions, the Petri net tool was used for the optimization and controller synthesis. Below we present the use cases:

1. For the first use case, the trainees had to design a manufacturing line that produces chocolate truffles and packages them first in aluminium foil bags and then in cardboard boxes. This case came from a manufacturer of confectionery products which has a high mix low volume manufacturing process with a variable demand in assortment and volume, relatively short production cycle (1 day) and a just-in-time producing policy. The variability is given by both the confectionery assortment and the packaging type.

The position of the raw materials storages, the shape and dimension of the factory floor are given. A design solution expressed in MLMP is presented in Fig. 1.

- AGV1 transports the buckets with chocolate ganache mass (m1) from the buffer B1 to the buffer B3;
- AGV2 transports the cardboard packaging material (m2) from the buffer B2 to the buffer B7;
- On line 1 (L1), the chocolate ganache mass (m1) is taken from B3 by the workstation WS1; inside WS1 chocolate is melted and chocolate truffles (m3) are formed. The product m3 is discharged in the buffer B4 feeding the transport line with freezing areas B11. The chocolate truffles are loaded in the buffer B5, which is feeding WS2. Two processes occur here: the formation of the aluminum bags (material m7, brought from the buffer B12) and the filling of the aluminum bags with chocolate truffles. The product is m4 – an aluminum bag filled with chocolate truffles – and is stored in the buffer B6;
- On line 2 (L2), cardboard packaging material (m2) is transported by AGV2 to the WS3, where the cardboard packaging boxes (m5) are formed; they are loaded in the buffer B8;
- On the assembly line, the Manipulator M1 transfers m4 and m5 products in the feeding buffers B9 and B10 of the WS4, where the aluminum bags with truffles are introduced in the cardboard boxes. The final products m6 (cardboard boxes having aluminum bags with truffles) are sent in B11 buffer.

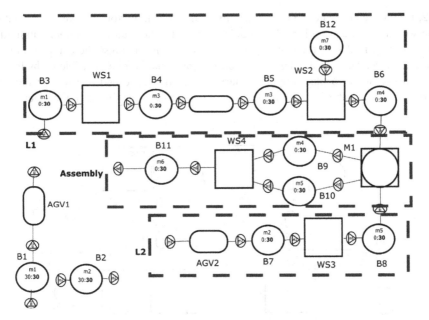

Fig. 1. MLMP model of the chocolate truffle line

For the analysis, the case was transformed to an equivalent timed Petri net. The Petri net was used to check the connectivity of the net, the reachability of the final state (final product in the storage), completion the throughput (number of tokens passing through the net in a given time). In the third training session, the model was asked to optimise a schedule for a number of jobs, each with specific product quantities of products (processing times) and specific deadline. The solution was computed in Matlab and then simulated in the design tool for verification. In the last session, the automatization system was developed by the students through Petri net based controller synthesis. The model of the plant obtained in the session 2 was used to synthesise of a Petri net controller. One particular problem to solve was to force the manipulator M to put alternatively bags and cardboard on the buffers of the WS4 (deadlock danger). The control system was then implemented by that team that used the model in the design tool using the control elements and tested through simulation.

2. The second use case is specific to automotive industry. The analysed case is of a low mix high volume manufacturing line. The business is order based, with an established customers' base of automobile producers with a relatively high and predictable demand.

The setting, presented in Fig. 2, is an assembly line for an optoelectronic part of the automatic breaking system. The components of the part (e. g PCB m1, casing m2, lenses m3) are temporarily stored in buffers along the line. On each component, particular operation (adjusting, heating, welding, testing) are performed on the corresponding workstations (WS1-WS8) and after that they are assembled together. In the original setup, the parts are moved from a station to another by human operators (H1,

H2, H3), which execute the operations, too. The case starts from an existing layout of the workstations and buffers. The problem raised by the industrial partner submitting the case was to design the paths of operators so that to minimise the completion time for one piece. Thus, in the design session the teams had to draw feasible paths for the human operators, to place supplementary buffers if needed and to evaluate the performances. In the third and fourth sessions, the approach was similar to the other cases.

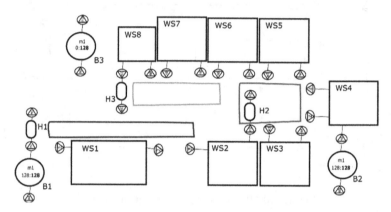

Fig. 2. MLMP model of the automotive assembly line

The comparison between the two teams had revealed the following differences:

- The team that used the design tool has found faster (in shorter time) a functional solution. This had two reasons:
  - The collaboration and communication between the team members was better as the expression of ideas and the comprehension of change proposals was eased by the use of a common graphical language.
  - Although the drawing tool was also collaborative, it distributed only the visual changes of the layout. The team that used the design tool accessed each time the updated model so that the direct analysis was possible.
  - The second team was slower because they were making mistakes which where only late discovered, after the translation to Petri net and structural analysis. The most common mistakes for those that had not used the modeling tools were: forgotten buffers, incorrect connected components and unconnected components. These mistakes were mostly prevented by the modeling tool.
- The translation to the Petri net and back was faster for the team that used the modeling tool because the pattern of transformation were easier to identify for the simplified models as for the real objects.
- The formulation of the optimisation problems was easier as the particularities of the system (number of machines, interdependencies were easier read from model).
- The structure of the real control system was better understood by the users of the modeling tool. They quickly identified patterns for conversion in both directions.

The solutions developed by the team using the collaborative design application were stored in the repository and became immediately accessible to the design engineers from the two enterprises which gave the cases. The engineers took part, virtually, to the assessment of the solutions. They also presented the solution to the management; we received positive feedback. An integration with a collaborative platform for the Knowledge Triangle developed in the frame of the KNOWinFOOD project [25] is in discussion; this integration will allow the solving of tasks given by industry by students and researchers from the high education institutes. Also, the training experience was shared through the repository with the other OMiLAB laboratories.

The training was a real use case of the design method and the associated tool. The use case shoved that both, design method and tool, perform well in the context for which they were developed (meaning the forming of manufacturing system designer skills for employees with absent or less prior experience). The trainees succeeded, with little training, to develop a digital models of two manufacturing lines and to generate the digital artefacts to cover the intended parts of the RAMI 4.0 architecture.

The categorical formulation of the metamodeling language gives a formal definition to the modeling language. This allows: formal analysis of the models; formal specification of constraints that enforce some properties on the models limiting the design space; axiomatic construction of models. The imposing of constraints was used in the application to limit the possibility to generate bad designs with good results. The students produced faster valid designs by exploring only the design space of valid states.

The formal definition of the modeling language is the basis of easy manual or automatic translation to other modeling languages with formal definition, like Petri net, property that was also used by the students. The formal definition allows the axiomatic construction of models. This creates the possibility to extend our tool in the next iteration to support axiomatic design.

Compared to general modeling languages (UML, BPMN, EPC) and similar or derivative languages used in some tools (iGrafx), the DSML we proposed is less abstract. Basic concepts as buffer or transport belts must not be constructed by refining or composing language elements. Compared with the languages of general purpose simulation and modeling tools like Matlab Simulink SIMULA8, our modeling language is better suited for the design of manufacturing system layouts as the geometrical dimensions and position of elements are of relevance and they are neglected in the aforementioned languages. Our language cannot compete in expressive power with the languages of the tools with full-fledged 3D graphical development environments (Arena, AnyLogic, FlexSim) but gains with its ease of use (few components to learn) and support for feasible designs (no incorrect models). Only Flexsim and Anylogic have some shared model repository capabilities due to their web based character. No tool allows the combination of different modeling languages similar to the facilities offered to our developed language by the underlying ADOxx ecosystem.

5 Conclusions and Further Work

This work describes the development of a modeling method and the associated DSML-MLMP to be used as a core element in the design of the digital factory of the future. The mathematical fundamentals of developing the modeling language and methods and arguments sustaining the adequacy of the chosen mathematical instrument (category theory) for this task are presented.

The developed design method and associated DSML and tool where tested in a training for manufacturing system designer skills. The results of the training have shown that they are easy to learn and to use in the context of no or little design experience. Using the OMiLAB ecosystem[3], the tool facilitates the collaboration between the training team members and allows the establishment of collaborative networks on the knowledge triangle [15, 24].

For the future development of the instrument, we plan to introduce the following features:

– Support all activities of the design method with tools integrated through the ADOxx ecosystem. This allows the better interoperability of the tools, reducing the time of switching between the tools and imposing constrains that assures the avoidance of faulty or inconsistent design solution on all levels.
– Formalize the training activities based on further in depth studies with more statistical relevance and build a virtual training environment.
– Use the model to build a digital twin of the factory.

Acknowledgments. This work was partially developed under the ERASMUS+ KA2 project "The FOF-Designer: Digital Design Skills for Factories of the Future", financing contract no. 2018-2553/001-001, project number 601089-EPP-1-2018-1-RO-EPPKA2-KA, web: https://www.digifof.eu/.

References

1. Benyoucef, L.: Introduction. In: Benyoucef, L. (ed.). Reconfigurable Manufacturing Systems: From Design to Implementation. Springer, Heidelberg (2018)
2. Mourtzis, D.: Simulation in the design and operation of manufacturing systems: state of the art and new trends. Int. J. Prod. Res. https://doi.org/10.1080/00207543.2019.1636321
3. Klee, H., Allen, R.: Simulation of Dynamic Systems with MATLAB® and Simulink®, 3rd edn. Taylor & Francis, Abingdon (2018)
4. Rossetti, M.D.: Simulation Modeling and Arena, 2nd edn. Wiley, Hoboken (2015)
5. Fousek, J., Kuncová, M., Fábry, J.: Discrete event simulation - production model in SIMUL8. In: ECMS 2017, pp. 229–234 (2017)
6. Kolinski, A., Sliwczynski, B., Golinska-Dawson, P.: The assessment of the economic efficiency of production process - simulation approach. In: 24th International Conference on Production Research ICPR (2017)

---

[3] https://www.omilab.org/nodes/nodes.html.

7. Sly, D., Schneider, J.: Collaborative process engineering framework for ground vehicle systems manufacturing. In: 2011 NDIA Ground Vehicle Systems Engineering and Technology Symposium, Systems Engineering and Integration (Se)Mini-Symposium, Dearborn, Michigan, PE, 9–11 August 2011 (2011)
8. Pawlewski, P., Hoffa-Dabrowska, P., Golinska-Dawson, P., Werner-Lewandowska, K. (eds.): FlexSim in Academe: Teaching and Research. E. Springer, Cham (2019). https://doi.org/10.1007/978-3-030-04519-7
9. Khaled, N., Pattel, B., Siddiqui, A.: Digital Twin Development and Deployment on the Cloud: Developing Cloud-Friendly Dynamic Models Using Simulink®/SimscapeTM and Amazon AWS. Academic Press, Cambridge (2020)
10. Borshchev, A.: The Big Book of Simulation Modeling Multimethod Modeling with Anylogic 6. AnyLogic North America, Oakbrook Terrace (2013)
11. Lydon, B.: RAMI 4.0 reference architectural model for Industrie 4.0. InTech **66**(2) (2019)
12. Karagiannis, D., Kühn, H.: Metamodelling platforms. In: Bauknecht, K., Tjoa, A.M., Quirchmayr, G. (eds.) EC-Web 2002. LNCS, vol. 2455, p. 182. Springer, Heidelberg (2002). https://doi.org/10.1007/3-540-45705-4_19
13. Bork, D., Buchman, R.A., Karagiannis, D., Lee, M., Miron, E.T.: An open platform for modeling method conceptualization: the OMiLAB digital ecosystem. Commun. Assoc. Inf. Syst. **34**, 555–579 (2019)
14. Fowler, M., Parsons, R.: Domain Specific Languages, 1st edn. Addison-Wesley Longman, Amsterdam (2010)
15. Karagiannis, D., Mayr, H.C., Mylopoulos, J.: Domain-Specific Conceptual Modeling: Concepts, Methods and Tools. Springer, Heidelberg (2016). https://doi.org/10.1007/978-3-319-39417-6
16. Reisig, W.: Understanding Petri Nets: Modeling Techniques, Analysis Methods, Case Studies. Springer, Heidelberg (2019)
17. Fokkink, W.J.: Modelling Distributed Systems. Texts in Theoretical Computer Science. An EATCS Series. Springer, Heidelberg (2007). https://doi.org/10.1007/978-3-540-73938-8
18. Crăciunean, D.-C., Karagiannis, D.: Categorical modeling method of intelligent WorkFlow. In: Groza, A., Prasath, R. (eds.) MIKE 2018. LNCS (LNAI), vol. 11308, pp. 112–126. Springer, Cham (2018). https://doi.org/10.1007/978-3-030-05918-7_11
19. Crăciunean, D.C.: Categorical grammars for processes modeling. Int. J. Adv. Comput. Sci. Appl. (IJACSA) **10**(1) (2019)
20. Mironescu, I.D.: An ADOxx based environment for problem based learning in manufacturing systems design. In: 9th International Conference on Manufacturing Science and Education "Trends in New Industrial Revolution", MATEC Web Conference, vol. 290 (2019)
21. Wolter, U., Diskin, Z.: The Next Hundred Diagrammatic Specification Techniques, A Gentle Introduction to Generalized Sketches, 02 September 2015
22. Diskin, Z., Maibaum, T.: Category theory and model-driven engineering: from formal semantics to design patterns and beyond. In: ACCAT 2012 (2012)
23. Plump, D.: Checking graph-transformation systems for confluence. ECEASST **26** (2010). https://doi.org/10.14279/tuj.eceasst.26.367
24. Ehrig, H., Ermel, C., Golas, U., Hermann, F.: Graph and Model Transformation: General Framework and Applications. Springer, Heidelberg (2015). https://doi.org/10.1007/978-3-662-47980-3

25. Georgescu, C., Mironescu, M., Mironescu, I.D.: The "Knowledge triangle for food innovation by harnessing the tradition and assuring sustainability" KNOWinFOOD Project as a tool to educate students to obtain innovative products incorporating bioactive compounds. Adv. Pharmacol. Clin. Trials **4**(1), 5 (2019). https://medwinpublishers.com/APCT/APCT16000150.pdf
26. Karagiannis, D., Buchmann, R.A., Boucher, X., Cavalieri, S., Florea, A., Kiritsis, D.: OMiLAB: a smart innovation environment for digital engineers. In: Camarinha-Matos, L.M. et al. (eds.) PRO-VE 2020. IFIP AICT, vol. 598, pp. xx–yy. Springer, Heidelberg (2020)

Immersive Systems in Human-Centered Manufacturing: The Informational Dimension

Filipa Rente Ramalho[1,2]([X]), António Lucas Soares[1,2],
and António Henrique Almeida[1]

[1] INESC TEC, Porto, Portugal
{filipa.ramalho,asoares,antonio.h.almeida}@inesctec.pt
[2] University of Porto, Porto, Portugal

Abstract. The rise of smart manufacturing environments, characterized by high quantity of data/information available, contributes to a growing interest and research towards the use of immersive technologies not only in factories but also across entire value chains. New immersive technologies and devices are being developed to improve cooperation within Collaborative Networks (CNs), especially in the human-machine hybrid networks context. The application of these technologies in such complex environments expands substantially the modes how information is delivered and used, which may exacerbate one of the oldest problems of cognitive ergonomics: information overload. Therefore, this work presents applications of immersive technologies in manufacturing into the perspective of "information work" and "immersive human-centered manufacturing systems". A framework is proposed to be developed in a FabLab to understand the worker needs and interactions. This FabLab aims to demonstrate the potential/real application of immersive technologies, towards the enhancement of the human worker cognitive capabilities.

Keywords: Mixed reality · Augmented reality · Virtual reality · Industry 4.0 · Human-worker · Human-centered manufacturing · Information management

1 Introduction

In the context of industry 4.0 (i4.0), "the continuing convergence of the real and the virtual worlds will be the main driver of innovation and change in all sectors of our economy" [1]. This convergence is achieved by creating multiple digital data and information flows between different systems/machines, between those systems and workers, between workers and systems/machines in a kind of human-machine hybrid network. The socio-technical context can be characterized by intra and inter organization's collaboration-intensive processes in a human-machine hybrid network - human-to-machine, machine-to-machine, and human-to-human - requiring operational information as well as codified knowledge for learning. Information can be communicated through different channels, and managed by a variety of systems, both implemented through several technologies like immersive technologies using virtual reality (VR), augmented reality (AR) or mixed reality (MR). Even though only recently have companies and researchers started exploring the practical applications of these

© IFIP International Federation for Information Processing 2020
Published by Springer Nature Switzerland AG 2020
L. M. Camarinha-Matos et al. (Eds.): PRO-VE 2020, IFIP AICT 598, pp. 297–307, 2020.
https://doi.org/10.1007/978-3-030-62412-5_25

technologies in the manufacturing sector, these have been around longer than we might expect [2, 3]. Immersive technologies together with other more mature technologies, when combined with IoT, data analysis and artificial intelligence (AI), enable the creation of tools aimed to help and support workers in their individual and collaborative work [4].

The main contribution of this paper is put the application of immersive technologies in manufacturing into the perspective of "information work" and "immersive human-centered manufacturing systems". A framework to be developed in the context of a FabLab is proposed, using of the concept of information work and information work analysis to understand the worker needs and their interactions with information infrastructures, systems and machines.

The paper starts to review the potential of immersive systems applications in manufacturing. Secondly, it addresses the importance of manufacturing systems centered in the human worker as a context to a perspective of the development and adoption of immersive systems as an informational problem, originated in the informational needs of the worker. Finally, this perspective is used to structure and inform the technological architecture of the Immersive Human-Centered System (IHCs) demo and training approach in a context of a FabLab.

2 Immersive Systems in Manufacturing

The potential of immersive systems can be aggregated in diverse applications typically executed within different teams from different companies working virtually and collaboratively, such as product design and development, operations support, maintenance and remote assistance, inspection and quality, learning, and training.

Product design and development are processes that normally involve a lot of communication and reviews among all stakeholders [5]. Immersive technologies can support these processes by increasing and improving the quality of their tasks, simplifying collaboration, and communication between different parties [5–7]. People involved can interact in collaboration with the process even though they are geographically dispersed [5]. Conventionally, designers use 2D CAD models to test and experiment with mainly 3D products. Physical prototypes are used to test the product design for products that need to be tested in real-time [7]. They are challenging to produce and difficult to redesign for testing and retesting, so this is very expensive and it consumes more time and, in turn, lengthens the Time To Market [7]. Using VR, designers can design products in a 3D space and test them in simulated environments until the design is final and approved. In addition, VR also offers the ability to test products under normal conditions and identify design flaws that cannot be found using conventional testing methods [7]. This ensures that the final products have a higher quality and live up to what was specified, minimizing requests for changes and other complaints from the customer [8].

Regarding operations support, traditionally, work instructions were made available in PDF files printed or displayed on screens [9]. That way, workers always have to look to the side to know what the instruction is or to consult the information and look again at the part/area where they are working. The use of AR allows the information of work instructions to be displayed in real-time and in the workers' field of view [10, 11]. This eliminates the need to consult documents alongside or on other devices outside the human field of view. In the context of collaborative network (CNs), this kind of technology may support the dissemination and communication of best practices and guidelines for manufacturing operations support. This can be essential to guarantee high quality and high-performance of entire value chains.

In maintenance and remote assistance, it is known that equipment or machinery failure is a problem that causes unexpected downtime and requires immediate responses. Sometimes, maintenance teams may not be "close" to solve the problem and restore the equipment, in time to avoid a significant loss of productivity [12]. Viewing data and information regarding the performance of production equipment can allow maintenance teams to identify equipment integrity problems that are often overlooked. The use of immersive technologies, namely AR, to guide workers with less experience in equipment maintenance is a solution that helps solving equipment failure, ensuring that production stops much less time [9, 10, 12]. AR can allow maintenance teams to identify equipment needs and malfunction problems [12], eliminating incorrect assumptions, reducing the risk of breakdowns, and allowing faster and more effective maintenance [9].

Regarding the assistance, technicians can obtain the details of parts of a product during production and after its implementation, connecting the product in a network. This information helps the support engineer to obtain historical product performance data in its context and environment for its configuration [12]. With the use of AR applications, together with videoconferencing and notes recorded in 3D representations, the maintenance task is facilitated reducing the costs of support and assistance [9, 13]. Thus, in the context of CNs, the ability to get knowledge and information from companies with expertise in machine maintenance is essential for a quicker reaction in order to solve problems and reduce downtime. Also, taking advantage of a more digitized manufacturing environment, capable of streamline both vertical and horizontal data integration, it is possible to propagate data related to the product.

While companies are looking to maximize productivity, they are also looking to increase the quality and conformity of their products [14]. To ensure product quality and compliance and to apply automated test methods, technicians need to inspect hundreds of units for defects or non-conformities [14, 15]. Due to human limitations, technicians are unaware of subtle indicators of non-compliance [14]. The use of AR combined with artificial intelligence and sensing technology can support the detection of these subtle deviations, thus increasing the quality of the product [15]. Concerning the quality inspection of materials needed for production, the products can be inspected and compared visually with the information provided by the supplier [14]. All divergences may be highlighted in a way that is overlaid on reality [15]. The information about the product being inspected can be displayed in the operator's field of view. For CNs, immersive technologies can support the inspection and quality analysis of products in which parts and components are manufactured and assembled within a distributed network of companies. Exploring artificial intelligence and these technologies, it is possible to provide an effective way of continuous product inspection to guarantee that product quality is assured along the entire value chain.

Training is vital for production workers to perform their tasks with maximum effectiveness and efficiency [16]. This process takes time, and the allocation of inexperienced people to perform critical operations can compromise the quality of work or even lead to safety problems [17]. Training new workers in a VR environment can allow them to gain experience and proficiency in their tasks without compromising the productivity, quality, and safety [18]. At the same time, proper application of AR means that workers can be trained, protected, and informed without wasting resources because they do not need an experienced worker guiding them [16, 17]. Workers can be conducted step by step, with guidance information overlaid on real and physical world parts and assemblies, in their field of view, thus time needed to improve the worker's skill set is shorter [16–18]. CNs in manufacturing are characterized by a high diversity of products, sometimes customized for a specific customer, with a low quantity of production (single lot size). Therefore, to guarantee the easy dissemination of training material, focused on operators' needs, immersive technologies should be seen essential for virtual and collaborative network performance.

3   Information in Human-Centered Manufacturing Systems

Production focused on the human worker has become increasingly important for organizations and, therefore, sparked research interest in order to achieve more sustainable production [19, 20]. This interest stems from studies suggesting that this approach helps to increase competitiveness, especially taking into account the new social challenges that i4.0 represents. Thus, companies must use new information and production systems to help older workers, with physical difficulties, more experienced, and inexperienced in improving the performance of their tasks in the factory. The new production systems should be characterized by cooperation between machines and human-workers and designed not to replace the skills and abilities of human workers, but to help them to be more efficient considering this cooperation [19]. The design of these systems must be centered on the human worker, going beyond those that are the traditional human factors that focus only on helping organizations to manage the workload healthily and safely. On the contrary, the design should evolve to a higher human level, considering factors such as job satisfaction or the experience and competence of workers [20].

The literature suggests that, to date, most of the research production systems performance is focused on operational functions, disregarding the effect of human factors that can also affect system performance [21]. In fact, more research is needed to develop intelligent and adaptable systems to optimize production systems considering the characteristics of the human worker regarding cognitive issues (in addition to physical ones) such as his subjective impressions, individual needs, skills, abilities, and resilience. Although immersive systems promise to be disrupting in the production industry, research is not completely convincing on the centeredness of the human-worker. If, on the one hand, these systems work as a substantial improvement in the physical ergonomic aspects, on the other hand, it is not so clear how these systems address the aspects related to cognitive ergonomics. One fundamental dimension of cognitive ergonomics in industrial applications is how information is captured, organized, delivered, and used by the human workers. Immersive systems expand substantially the modes how information is delivered and used that, together with the velocity and volume of data creation, may exacerbate one of the oldest problems of cognitive ergonomics: information overload.

As stated in [22], "Identifying and gathering the right data, deploying it for the right purposes and effectively analyzing it will be critical to make the right Industry 4.0 decisions". Therefore, information management is needed to enable the efficiency and effective use of information alongside the value chains' tasks and processes, particularly in the shop-floor applications fostered by immersive systems [23, 24]. Nonetheless, current management and information management tools reside in a logical-physical dichotomy, which prevents the development and use of all the ingenuity, creativity, and know-how by human-workers [25]. Consequently, a socio-technical change is needed in order to consider this problem when designing and implementing immersive systems.

It is a common place to state that for an organization to be successful, it needs to deliver to its workers the necessary information, at the right time and in the right place so they are able to complete their work tasks [26]. The main challenge in solving this issue related to information organization is not in identifying which worker needs information, or what information is necessary to provide or even for which task it is necessary to provide information. The real challenge is to make all these aspects converge productively for the worker and, consequently, for the organization. As a way forward to research this problem, we propose applying the information work analysis approach [26] whose main objective is to analyze in detail the interface between work information and the information infrastructures and systems used to organize knowledge and information. With this approach it is possible to investigate, through work information, human work in context, establishing premises to relate the notion of "information work" and "immersive human centered manufacturing systems" (IHCs). The IHCs act as systems of organization of information and knowledge that will contribute for the task of creating useful information, to be delivered to the right worker and at the right time. Thus, it is important to understand human workers, information work and information systems as components of an inclusive and holistic system of human work, with unique aspects in terms of characteristics and qualities [26]. To understand and develop this holistic system and to make work possible, it is necessary to understand the people (workers), the machines, the information, the interactions and their associated behaviors and the notions of the purpose, meaning and values related to the work [26].

4 Immersive Human-Centered Manufacturing Systems Research in Lab

Understanding the real impact and return of investment of immersive and human-centered technologies is today a complex task for manufacturing companies. Few companies are able to invest significant amounts of money and time to implement and validate a technology within a real industrial scenario. As a consequence, Fab Labs have been designed and developed as a near-real industrial environment where research institutes, universities and industry can work together to implement, test, demonstrate and evaluate innovative and emerging technology. In line with this vision, INESC TEC has been investing and developing a Fab Lab, the iiLAB Industry and Innovation Lab, where different technologies from robotics and flexible logistics, industrial cyber-physical systems (Internet of Things) and new communication technologies (e.g. 5G), to human-centered technologies are combined within an Industry 4.0 compliant architecture. Here it is possible to carry out demonstrations in the form of a showroom, experimentation and prototyping space for technological companies, and to offer advanced training courses for manufacturing companies.

The assets and information system architecture are maintained based on the research work performed by the research center and based on the strategic partnerships with the technology companies. The following image (Fig. 1) provides a high-level vision on the technology and architecture that is being developed in the iiLAB.

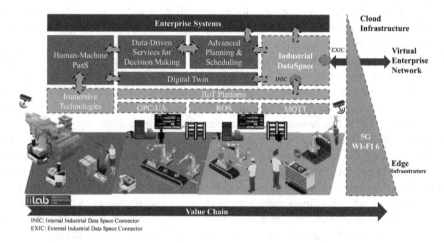

INIC: Internal Industrial Data Space Connector
EXIC: External Industrial Data Space Connector

Fig. 1. iiLab Technology Vision Architecture

The FabLab objective is to represent an industrial infrastructure that belongs to a complex and distributed value chain. Therefore, not only the vertical interoperability is important, but also the capability to share information within the virtual network (horizontal integration). In the shop-floor, different digital technology such as AGVs, robotic arms, conveyors, vertical and automated warehouses, advanced machines (e.g. CNCs) and quality control stations, work in a collaborative way. In order to manage and control such digital technology, cognitive-enhanced operators are considered, exploring human-machine technologies based on immersive reality.

As previously explained, the use of immersive technologies in i4.0 plays a key role in supporting workers throughout their tasks in the plant. Operators become able to use tablets, head-mounted displays and other technology solutions to enrich the reality with information and intelligence that enable them to improve their performance and enhance the overall system performance, as well as directly interact with the production system.

It is therefore essential that these solutions take the production system complexity as a starting point, and focus on the workers' needs, namely by knowing their context and the situations in which their activity takes place (Fig. 2). The context is formed in layers, is dynamic and involves several situations. These layers are composed of various types of data and information, such as environment data; operations data; worker physiological data; and organizational information (e.g. products, process information). On the other hand, a situation fits into a context, as each situation is characterized by a set of contextual factors. A situation can also be considered an action that occurs in a specific time and space, for example, a specific interaction of the worker with a machine. The concept on which this iiLab architecture is based considers the worker as the central element of the production system which, in turn, must not only be able to understand the surrounding context and production environment, but also the situation in which the production operation takes place.

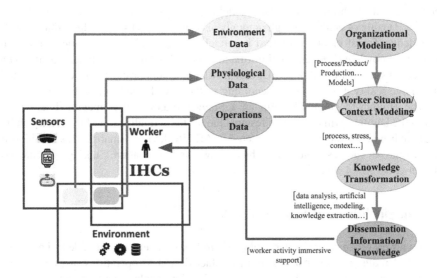

Fig. 2. Immersive Human-Centered System (IHCs) approach

The necessary data and information can be collected by various sensors (which are installed along the factory floor) and wearables (which can be used by operators). In this way, it is considered the sensing of the environment, the sensing of the worker and the sensing of the operations, i.e. the worker's behavior towards the environment and vice-versa. Firstly, it is essential to capture this data as well as the organizational information, namely the information on processes, products and production. Then it is necessary to model both the context and the situation of the worker and its work needs (Worker Situation/Context Modeling). This is a crucial phase and is important to use the information work analysis, previously described, to provide workers with the information needs as presented in this diagram (Dissemination Information/Knowledge) (Fig. 2).

In order to achieve this level of interoperability between machines, assets and operators, the iiLab Technology Vision Architecture (Fig. 1) previously referred was designed, based on the i4.0 framework and standards. In the first level, an Industrial Internet of Things (IIoT) guarantees data interoperability with the shop-floor, with specific customized agents that enable bi-directional communication with every cyber-physical system. In order to have a holistic and integrated vision on the data and information extracted from the shop-floor, as well as guarantee a full and safe integration with external entities of the value chain, an Industrial Data Space infrastructure was adopted. This IDS platform allows the definition of a meta-model for the information management in the iiLab, exploring a federation structure of databases located inside and outside of the institute.

The information based on this meta-model is then used to build a reliable and effective Digital Twin of the FabLab. This modular and flexible Digital Twin provides the necessary structured information to extract knowledge and transform it, through techniques and technologies of data modelling and analysis as well as artificial intelligence, capable of analyzing high amounts of data to extract knowledge, following the Knowledge Transformation referred in model of Fig. 2. Thus, it becomes possible to share this knowledge, generating information that will be made available directly to the worker (Dissemination of Information/Knowledge), supporting their activity through immersive reality environments, according to their needs, and in real time (Fig. 2).

The Human-Machine Platform as a Service (PaaS), fully integrated and fused within the Digital Twin context, is responsible for the virtualization of the reality within a 3D environment, capable to be rendered in AR/VR devices (smartphones & tablets or on AR glasses such as HoloLens, which allow hands-free usage), taking advantage of 5G networks low latency.

5   Conclusions and Future Work

We reviewed how immersive technologies are being developed, suitable to be applied in several industrial applications, from product design to operations instructions and maintenance as well as on training and technical knowledge management and visualization. These technologies are being addressed to empower humans with tools, worker-oriented interfaces, and better working conditions to continue performing accordingly within complex and knowledge-intensive industrial processes. However, some challenges are not being addressed regarding the design, implementation and adoption of these technologies. Manufacturing companies are still not able to understand how these technologies can have a direct impact on their daily business and overall performance. This is a reality, mainly because most of the recent research is focused on technological aspects, leaving behind the information management aspects, fundamental to deal with the organizational context, and for the success and sustainability of the immersive systems applications.

In order to cope with these challenges, this paper proposes the design and development of a digital platform, fully aligned with the Industry 4.0 standards, within a FabLab that represents a near-real complex manufacturing scenario, where massive data can be correctly gathered and handled in order to generate information capable to be correctly modeled and managed to feed the different immersive technologies available. This FabLab will have an important role in demonstrating the potential and the real application of the immersive technologies, towards the enhancement of the human worker cognitive capabilities, with direct impact on the overall production system performance.

As future work, the information system architecture here presented will be installed and validated in the iiLab infrastructure. In parallel, different demonstrators, representative from the opportunities previously identified for immersive technology applications, will be identified, described and implemented. From an information management perspective, models capable to represent and relate the information needed to clearly represent the context and the situation where the demonstration will take place, will be defined. These demonstrators will not only represent internal operations but will also explore the needs for horizontal integration within the entire value chain. This will provide relevant contribution of research in CNs domain, focused on the new generation of networks leveraged on the collaboration between humans and machines/robots. These challenges are already identified in different research papers [27, 28] as significant topics of study and validation for the near future.

Acknowledgments. The first author was funded by the Ph.D. Grant PD/BD/143163/2019 from Portuguese funding agency, FCT - Fundação para a Ciência e a Tecnologia.

References

1. Kagermann, H.: Change through digitization—value creation in the age of Industry 4.0. In: Albach, H., Meffert, H., Pinkwart, A., Reichwald, R. (eds.) Management of Permanent Change, pp. 23–45. Springer, Wiesbaden (2015). https://doi.org/10.1007/978-3-658-05014-6_2
2. Choi, S., Jung, K., Noh, S.: Do: Virtual reality applications in manufacturing industries: Past research, present findings, and future directions. Concurr. Eng. **23**, 40–63 (2015)
3. Ferraguti, F., et al.: Augmented reality based approach for on-line quality assessment of polished surfaces. Robot. Comput. Integr. Manuf. **59**, 158–167 (2019)
4. Thomas, M.D.: Intelligent realities for workers using augmented reality, virtual reality and beyond. IIC J. Innov., 1–18 (2019)
5. Mourtzis, D., Zogopoulos, V., Vlachou, E.: Augmented reality supported product design towards Industry 4.0: a teaching factory paradigm. Procedia Manuf. **23**, 207–212 (2018)
6. Zawadzki, P., Zywicki, K.: Smart product design and production control for effective mass customization in the Industry 4.0 concept. Manag. Prod. Eng. Rev. **7**, 105–112 (2016)
7. Nunes, M.L., Pereira, A.C., Alves, A.C.: Smart products development approaches for Industry 4.0. Procedia Manuf. **13**, 1215–1222 (2017)
8. Prost, S., Mattheiss, E., Tscheligi, M.: From awareness to empowerment: using design fiction to explore paths towards a sustainable energy future. In: 18th ACM International Conference on Computer-Supported Cooperative Work and Social Computing, CSCW 2015, pp. 1649–1658. Association for Computing Machinery, Inc., AIT Austrian Institute of Technology, Vienna (2015)
9. Gattullo, M., Scurati, G.W., Fiorentino, M., Uva, A.E., Ferrise, F., Bordegoni, M.: Towards augmented reality manuals for Industry 4.0: a methodology. Robot. Comput. Integr. Manuf. **56**, 276–286 (2019)

10. Espíndola, D.B., Pereira, C.E., Schneider, E., Ventura, R.: Improving maintenance operations through application of mixed reality systems, vol. 46, p. 11 (2013
11. Mourtzis, D., Zogopoulos, V., Xanthi, F.: Augmented reality application to support the assembly of highly customized products and to adapt to production re-scheduling. Int. J. Adv. Manuf. Technol. **105**(9), 3899–3910 (2019). https://doi.org/10.1007/s00170-019-03941-6
12. Masoni, R., et al.: Supporting remote maintenance in Industry 4.0 through augmented reality. Procedia Manuf. **11**, 1296–1302 (2017)
13. Aschenbrenner, D., Latoschik, M.E., Schillingz, K.: Industrial maintenance with augmented reality: two case studies. In: Proceedings of the ACM Symposium on Virtual Reality Software and Technology VRST, 02–04 November, pp. 341–342 (2016)
14. Lee, J.M., Lee, K.H., Kim, D.S., Kim, C.H.: Active inspection supporting system based on mixed reality after design and manufacture in an offshore structure. J. Mech. Sci. Technol. **24**, 197–202 (2010)
15. Muñoz, A., Mahiques, X., Solanes, J.E., Martí, A., Gracia, L., Tornero, J.: Mixed reality-based user interface for quality control inspection of car body surfaces. J. Manuf. Syst. **53**, 75–92 (2019)
16. Quint, F., Sebastian, K., Gorecky, D.: A mixed-reality learning environment. Procedia Comput. Sci. **75**, 43–48 (2015)
17. Longo, F., Nicoletti, L., Padovano, A.: Smart operators in Industry 4.0: a human-centered approach to enhance operators' capabilities and competencies within the new smart factory context. Comput. Ind. Eng. **113**, 144–159 (2017)
18. Roldán, J.J., Crespo, E., Martín-Barrio, A., Peña-Tapia, E., Barrientos, A.: A training system for Industry 4.0 operators in complex assemblies based on virtual reality and process mining. Robot. Comput. Integr. Manuf. **59**, 305–316 (2019)
19. Romero, D., Noran, O., Stahre, J., Bernus, P., Fast-Berglund, Å.: Towards a human-centred reference architecture for next generation balanced automation systems: human-automation symbiosis. In: Umeda, S., Nakano, M., Mizuyama, H., Hibino, H., Kiritsis, D., von Cieminski, G. (eds.) APMS 2015. IAICT, vol. 460, pp. 556–566. Springer, Cham (2015). https://doi.org/10.1007/978-3-319-22759-7_64
20. Peruzzini, M., Pellicciari, M., Gadaleta, M.: A comparative study on computer-integrated set-ups to design human-centred manufacturing systems. Robot. Comput. Integr. Manuf. **55**, 265–278 (2019)
21. Wang, Q., Abubakar, M.I.: Human factors and their effects on human-centred assembly systems - a literature review-based study. In: IOP Conference Series: Materials Science and Engineering, vol. 239 (2017)
22. Lee, M.-X., Lee, Y.-C., Chou, C.J.: Essential implications of the digital transformation in Industry 4.0. J. Sci. Ind. Res. **76**, 465–467 (2017)
23. Stock, T., Seliger, G.: Opportunities of sustainable manufacturing in Industry 4.0. In: Procedia CIRP, p. 536 (2016)
24. Wan, S., Li, D., Gao, J., Roy, R., Tong, Y.: Process and knowledge management in a collaborative maintenance planning system for high value machine tools. Comput. Ind. **84**, 14 (2017). OP-In
25. Ramalho, F., Soares, A.L.: Augmented reality in complex manufacturing systems as an informational problem: a human-centered approach. In: iConference 2020 Proceedings, Boras, Sweden, pp. 1–7 (2020)
26. Huvila, I.: The Ecology of Information Work (2007)

27. Camarinha-Matos, L.M., Fornasiero, R., Afsarmanesh, H.: Collaborative networks as a core enabler of Industry 4.0. In: Camarinha-Matos, L.M., Afsarmanesh, H., Fornasiero, R. (eds.) PRO-VE 2017. IAICT, vol. 506, pp. 3–17. Springer, Cham (2017). https://doi.org/10.1007/978-3-319-65151-4_1

28. Hernandez, J.E., Kacprzyk, J., Panetto, H., De-angelis, M.: Collaborative networks as a core enabler of industry 4.0. IFIP Int. Fed. Inf. Process. **506**, 761–774 (2017)

Collaboration in Open Innovation

Collaborative Networking to Enable Innovation and Entrepreneurship Through Open Innovation Hubs: The Entrepreneurship Learning Centre of Mexico City

Jhonattan Miranda[1]([⊠]), José Bernardo Rosas-Fernández[2], and Arturo Molina[1]

[1] School of Engineering and Sciences, Tecnologico de Monterrey, Mexico City, Mexico
{jhonattan.miranda, armolina}@tec.mx
[2] Secretary of Education, Science, Technology and Innovation, Government of Mexico City, Mexico City, Mexico
jbrosas@cdmx.gob.mx

Abstract. Collaborative Networks have shown to have a high potential as drivers of value creation; therefore, it is increasingly frequent to observe how organisations and governments are implementing collaborative networking to support their innovation processes and foster entrepreneurship in benefit to society. Consequently, it is observed that these implementations can contribute to accelerating the development of weaker local and regional economies, especially in developing countries. In this paper, it is presented the Open Innovation Hub of México City of the *ECOS Network* and how by applying collaborative networking, it is possible to foster both innovation and entrepreneurship. Also, the Learning Centre for Entrepreneurship in Mexico City as part of this Hub is described. Finally, a case study with an imparted teaching-learning program is presented. And so, there are described how by using the concepts of Open Innovation and Education 4.0 are designed and implemented specific teaching-learning programs to encourage the creation of new enterprises.

Keywords: Collaborative networks · Open innovation · Entrepreneurship · Higher education · Educational innovation · Education 4.0

1 Introduction

In recent years, the economies of many countries have lost dynamism and have been lower than official estimates, especially for developing countries [1–3]. Consequently, many efforts and strategies have emerged to contribute to economic growth. In this context, innovation and entrepreneurship have been found to be excellent engines to achieve economic growth since these activities stimulate regional economies by strengthening the economy and creating jobs [4]. As part of these activities, the design and development of technology-based solutions have shown to have a more significant

L. M. Camarinha-Matos et al. (Eds.): PRO-VE 2020, IFIP AICT 598, pp. 311–323, 2020.
https://doi.org/10.1007/978-3-030-62412-5_26

effect not only to the economic growth of developing countries but also to overcome the gap with technologically advanced countries [5]. Therefore, today developing countries are promoting the development of technology-based products/services and stimulating technology transfer to activate regional economies [6].

In the case of the Greater Mexico City, the biggest in Mexico, this situation is challenging since it is one of the largest metropolitan areas in the world with a population of more than 21 million people [7]. Therefore, the social challenges in this region are enormous. In this sense, in recent years, this region has faced a large scale of social problems such as unemployment, pollution, delinquency, complex mobility, lack of sufficient water supply, and also it is very susceptible to natural disasters such as major earthquakes and sanitary contingencies that origin greater negative effects. This situation provokes severe economic disequilibrium that affects especially vulnerable sectors of society and micro, small and medium-sized enterprises. For these reasons, it is necessary the creation of initiatives that can act and respond in a quick way to these problems. Therefore, it is required to implement strategies that can satisfy the needed demand of the region. As a result, it is needed to build innovation ecosystems as a common link between different organisations to participate in the creation of Collaborative Networks (CNs) to achieve right solutions, since it has been observed that organisations that work independently do not have enough capacities and capabilities to meet the demand that this region requires and current similar systems are not fully effective [8].

In this paper, a strategy to face these issues through the creation of an Open Innovation Hub is presented. Hence, this work presents the five created entities that make up this Hub, (i) The observatory of technology, innovation and development, (ii) The entrepreneurship learning centre, (iii) The intellectual property strategy centre, (iv) The technology transfer and escalation office and the supports for (iv) developing technological road maps and (v) Mentoring from technological experts. The main purpose of this work is to provide an operating reference that can be used and replicated by other regions, especially for cities that have a high concentration of population. Finally, in this paper is presented the Entrepreneurship Learning Centre of Mexico City in order to show how CNs are built to operate this centre and how is carry out a learning-teaching program with the citizen of Mexico City and a Bootcamp for the creation of Sensing, Smart and Sustainable enterprises is presented as a case study.

2   Collaborative Networks and Open Innovation

Today, many organisations of different sectors are adopting strategies and best practices which are based on collaborative and cooperative processes. Then, these organisations are considering the participation of different actors from different sectors and expertise areas to improve their ability to innovate and manage the processes of value co-creation [9]. Therefore, different methodologies, frameworks and concepts have emerged to articulate and manage these activities such as Collaborative Network Organisation (CNO) frameworks and the concept of Open Innovation.

A CNO or simply knows as Collaborative Network (CN) is a network that consists of a variety of entities (e.g. organisations, enterprises, universities, people, among others) that are largely autonomous, geographically distributed, and heterogeneous in their operating environment, culture, social capital and goals that have come together to collaborate in order to better achieve common or compatibles goals, and whose interactions can be supported by computer networks' [10, 11]. In this sense, it has been observed that CNs have been shown a high potential not only as drivers of value co-creation but also as drivers to share knowledge, resources, joining complementary skills and capacities and even risks, which allow them to strengthen their processes and make the most of resources [9, 12]. Also, it has been demonstrated that CNs induce the implementation of Open Innovation processes since it allows the confrontation of internal and external ideas and practices, the combination of resources and technologies and the creation of synergies between different multidisciplinary actors.

On the other hand, Open Innovation is generally seen as a key collaborative strategy. Therefore, organisations are taking advantages of these joint projects to evolve and face in a right way current challenges through the co-development of innovative and disruptive processes, services and products which currently are mainly based on technological solutions (including connectivity, digitalisation, and virtuality). This concept was introduced by H. Chesbrough, and it refers that "Open innovation assumes that firms can and should use external ideas as well as internal ideas, and internal and external paths to market (...). Valuable ideas can come from inside or outside the company and can go to market from inside or outside the company as well" [13]. The keys to open innovation paradigm are openness, collaboration and the search for creativity. Therefore, many organisations have been adopted this way to operate during innovation processes, and they include the participation of not only of internal actors but also the participation of external actors to improve the competitive possibilities of the organisation. In this paper, both terms CNs and Open Innovation are implemented as the main strategy to operate and manage an Open Innovation Hub in Mexico City.

3   The Open Innovation Hub of Mexico City

According to the literature, Innovation Hubs envision a centre of exchange that builds on the foundation of creativity and innovation to create not only new high value-added products (and services), and business/processes that will aid the creation of new business models and enterprises "startups" but also to provide quick solutions to current social problems [8]. In this sense, many Innovation Hubs have been emerged to promote knowledge-sharing and collaborative and cooperative processes to encourage co-designing and co-development of technology-based solutions. Therefore, Innovation Hubs are committed to ensuring the development and implementation of the best technological solutions by taking advantages of diverse resources coming from different places.

More recently, the term Digital Innovation Hubs has been emerged to support companies through the use of information and communication technologies (ICTs) [14]. Hence, these Hubs are not only adopting ICTs, but also they are utilising best practices and activities such as platforms for collaborative networking and services (e.g. online file storage services, communication web-based systems, social networking, and other robust platforms such as enterprise software and PLM systems). Then, nowadays, these terms can be indistinctly used since both of them are powered by the Internet of Things (IoT) and current ICTs.

In this paper, it is presented the Open Innovation Hub of Mexico City. This Hub was created in 2019 as part of the CN called *"Red ECOS"*, which is in charge of coordinating, managing, and funding its sub-networks (e.g. electromobility network, seismology network, bioenergy network, among others) within the Government Program 2019–2024 of the Secretary of Education, Science, and Technology of the Government of Mexico City. The Hub is related to the concept of "strengthening the social economy and entrepreneurship"; likewise, it proposes to coordinate actions to promote the constitution and strengthening of the social and solidarity economy sector. This Hub consists in the participation of different actors to support these initiatives and in this way, promote the co-design and co-development of technology-based solutions that can address current priorities and problems in the region. Therefore, the main objective of this Open Innovation Hub is to foster and strengthen the scientific, technological and digital infrastructure by generating physical and virtual innovation ecosystems that can link and articulate the participation of diverse actors from different sectors both internal (government) and external (e.g. academic, scientific, industrial, entrepreneurs, society and other government areas) to generate joint-projects with the primary purpose of contributing with positive effects to the regional economic development and the social welfare of citizens. In specific, this Hub will support technology-based product development and enterprise creation.

The main defined activities to be performed in this Hub are listed below: (i) Provide right tools and strategic information, (ii) Provide a diagnosis of priorities/problems to be focused, (iii) Provide teaching-learning programs for human resources training, (iv) Provide support for technological solutions by technological experts, (v) Provide support for defining intellectual property strategies and for intellectual property processes and management, and (vi) Provide support for defining best strategies for technology transfer including knowledge transfer, funding, licensing, and project management. Consequently, this Hub will operate by linking actors from different sectors, and there were created different entities as part of this Open Innovation Hub. Figure 1 shows the defined strategies that pursue this Hub, the integrated CN and the created entities.

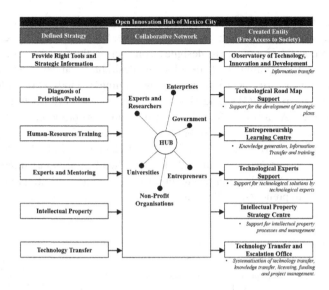

Fig. 1. The Open Innovation Hub of Mexico City – Main Model

4   The Entrepreneurship Learning Centre of Mexico City

Currently, the role of universities in the entrepreneurship context goes far beyond the knowledge-generation/information-transfer to participating in business ecosystems, partnerships and industrial alliances. Therefore, today, it is considered that universities are excellent drivers to achieve innovation and foster entrepreneurship through the implementation of new teaching-learning programs.

In this sense, the term *Education 4.0* has been used to describe how today's teaching-learning programs are being designed and taking advantages of current ICTs and physical infrastructure/facilities. Education 4.0 comes from the well-known concept of *Industry 4.0,* which refers to technological evolution according to the periods of four industrial revolutions that have been experienced in humanity [15]. Therefore, in the case of the education sector, the improvements of pedagogical processes and their relationship with the technological evolution are known today as Education 4.0. In this sense, new learning methods (i.e. problem-based learning (PBL), learning by doing (LBD), challenge-based learning (CBL), among others) and practices that use efficiently new infrastructures/facilities (i.e. collaborative and co-working spaces, maker spaces, specialised labs, among others...), tools and ICTs (i.e. virtual classrooms, Learning Management Systems (LMS), Massive Open Online Courses (MOOCs), AR and VR platforms, among others..) have emerged and considered as part of the design of new teaching-learning programs that will allow participants/students/entrepreneurs acquire and train desirable competencies both soft and hard competencies in this area.

Therefore, the Tecnológico de Monterrey, University in Mexico is participating in the design and operation of the proposed Entrepreneurship Learning Centre of the Open Innovation Hub. The main objective of this learning centre is to stablish an entrepreneurial culture, the training of society, and the support for the development of new products (and services), new business/processes and the creation of new enterprises (startups and spin-offs) through the implementation of teaching-learning programs. The proposed programs are designed considering the four key components of Education 4.0, (i) training and developing desirable competencies in today's students/entrepreneurs, (ii) incorporation of new learning methods, (iii) implementation of current and emerging ICTs, and (iv) use of innovative infrastructure to improve learning processes. As a result, four different programs are proposed to start with the operation of this learning centre, (i) MOOCs, (ii) Face-to-Face Courses and Hybrid Learning Programs, (iii) Personalised Mentoring, and (iv) Talks-Networking with Experts. These programs are aligned to specifically promote three types of entrepreneurship, (i) Social Entrepreneurship, (ii) Technological Entrepreneurship and (iii) Scientific Entrepreneurship. See Fig. 2.

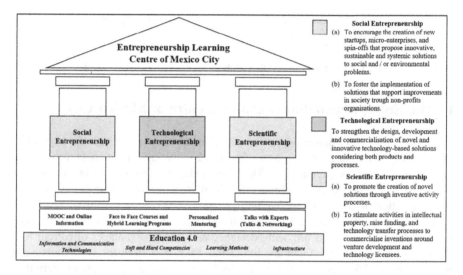

Fig. 2. The Entrepreneurship Learning Centre of Mexico City – Model

Figure 3 shows the generic teaching-learning model used in the design of the proposed programs. This model illustrates what are the main inputs and outputs that were considered in the proposed teaching-learning programs. Also, there are illustrated how these processes will be performed (mechanisms) and the participating actors that will be controlling the processes.

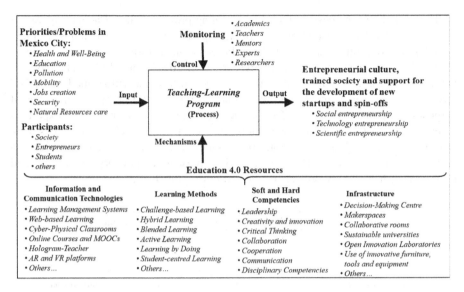

Fig. 3. Proposed Teaching-Learning Model to foster the entrepreneurial culture

5 Case Study: The Sensing, Smart and Sustainable Enterprise Creation Bootcamp – Learning-Teaching Program

In order to show how the proposed Entrepreneurship Learning Centre works, in this section is presented the Sensing, Smart and Sustainable (S^3) Enterprise Creation program that is a designed intensive teaching-learning program in the modality of a bootcamp. The design of this bootcamp also is based on the concepts of CNs and Open Innovation since it adopts active learning dynamics in which the participation of different actors is required. The primary purpose of this teaching-learning program is that participants can learn main processes that are carried out during innovation and entrepreneurship processes by doing specific activities and using specific tools. Therefore, this teaching-learning program was designed under two main frameworks, Education 4.0 and S^3 Enterprise [16, 17].

The framework of S^3 Enterprise tries to encourage entrepreneurs to create highly competitive enterprises through the incorporation of the sensing [18], smart [19, 20], and sustainable [21] characteristics during the enterprise creation process. The main objective of this new generation of enterprises is that they can be able to satisfactorily respond to market uncertainties, improve their processes and optimise the use of their resources. Therefore, new enterprises must adopt new strategies, practices and technologies that allow them to be competitive in the market and respond adequately to customers' demand [22].

To apply these three characteristics, it is necessary to take advantage of both current and emerging technologies (IoT, artificial intelligence, sensing technologies, big data, among others), and collaborative strategies.

Figure 4 shows the designed teaching-learning program called *The Sensing, Smart and Sustainable Enterprise Creation - Bootcamp*. This bootcamp is composed of five modules (i) Conceptualisation, (ii) Value Proposition, (iii) Structuring, (iv) Business model, and (v) Infrastructure that are reviewed over 10 sessions (40 h.). The modules are taught by using new learning methods in face-to-face and virtual modality. Also, this bootcamp considers mentoring, such as key activity since each project has different purposes and creation processes. Then participants can interact with different experts in order to accompany the participants during the enterprise creation process; thus, new enterprises, spin-offs and non-profit organisation can emerge. Table 1 presents a summary of the taught bootcamp and Table 2 presents a summary of the obtained results by each of the six projects developed during this bootcamp.

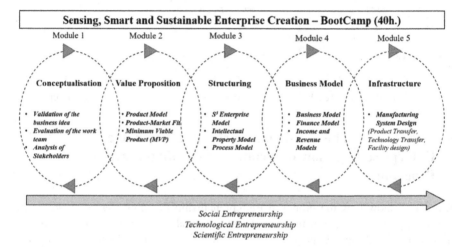

Fig. 4. Designed Teaching-Learning Program – The Sensing, Smart and Sustainable Enterprise Creation in the Bootcamp modality

Table 1. Summarised results of the performed S³ Enterprise Creation Bootcamp

Alternative Credential: S³ Enterprise Creation Bootcamp, Hybrid Learning (Face-to-Face and Virtual Modality).
Duration: 10 sessions, 40 h.
Participant Profile: Junior Entrepreneurs and participants from startups and non-profit organisations
Number of Participants: 20 (6 projects).

Input	Process	Output
1. Conceptualisation Conceptualise a new business idea providing technology-based solutions aligned to the	**Main Learning Method:** *Problem-based learning and Active Learning* **Main Competencies: Soft:** *Critical Thinking, Creativity*	• Validation of the business idea • Definition of new business models/processes

(continued)

Table 1. (*continued*)

Alternative Credential: S³ Enterprise Creation Bootcamp, Hybrid Learning (Face-to-Face and Virtual Modality).
Duration: 10 sessions, 40 h.
Participant Profile: Junior Entrepreneurs and participants from startups and non-profit organisations
Number of Participants: 20 (6 projects).

Input	Process	Output
current priorities/problems of Mexico City.	*and Innovation, Hard: Promote the development of technology-based enterprises/spin-offs* **Main Infrastructure:** *Designing rooms and Gesell chamber* **Main ICT:** *MOOC and Mobile APP* [17]	•Identification of new products (and services) • Creation of new enterprises (startups or spin-offs)
2. Value Proposition Define and validate the value proposition of the product/service/business that will be provided by the conceptualised enterprise.	**Main Learning Method:** *Blended-based Learning and Learning by Doing* **Main Competencies:** *Soft: Collaboration and Cooperation, Hard: Use of Collaborative Virtual Platforms* **Main Infrastructure:** *Designing rooms, Makerspaces and the Decision-Making Centre* **Main ICT:** *MOOC and Online Materials*	• Understanding of the Product, Customer, Sales model • Validation of the Product-Market
3. Structuring State the structure of the defined enterprise considering, purposes, functionalities, processes, and legal aspects.	**Main Learning Method:** *Active Learning and Hybrid Learning* **Main Competencies:** *Soft: Collaboration, Cooperation and Communication, Hard: Virtual and Digital infrastructure* **Main Infrastructure:** *Virtual Classroom, Computational Labs* **Main ICT:** *MOOC and Online Materials*	• Definition of the sensing, smart and sustainable model • Definition of the processes to be performed • Identification of the Intellectual Property strategy

(*continued*)

Table 1. (*continued*)

Alternative Credential: S³ Enterprise Creation Bootcamp, Hybrid Learning (Face-to-Face and Virtual Modality).
Duration: 10 sessions, 40 h.
Participant Profile: Junior Entrepreneurs and participants from startups and non-profit organisations
Number of Participants: 20 (6 projects).

Input	Process	Output
4. Business Model Refine the business idea and build a robust business model.	**Main Learning Method:** *Challenge-based learning and Blended Learning* **Main Competencies:** *Soft: Collaboration and Cooperation, Hard: Use of digital platforms* **Main Infrastructure:** *Virtual Classroom and LMS* **Main ICT:** *MOOC, LMS and Online materials*	• Validation of the Finance, Income and Revenue models • Refinement of the Business Model
5. Infrastructure Define the needed infrastructure or manufacturing system to be implemented.	**Main Learning Method:** *Challenge-based learning and Active Learning* **Main Competencies:** *Soft: Critical Thinking and Communication, Hard: Definition of Virtual and Digital infrastructure* ***Main Infrastructure:*** *Virtual classroom and Decision-Making Centre* **Main ICT:** *MOOC, LMS, and Online materials*	• Definition of the manufacturing system design (product transfer, technology transfer or facility design) strategies • Enterprise Pitch

Table 2. Summary of the obtained results by the participants

Input	Particular process	Improved value
Project 1: Startup in the area of collection and recycling of vegetable oil, and creation of biofuel	Spin-Off strategy process and New Product Development	• Incorporation of new products/services • Definition of its business model • Intellectual property strategy
Project 2: Startup in the area of digital platforms for education	Spin-Off strategy process	• Incorporation of new products • Definition of a product portfolio • Redefinition of its business model

(*continued*)

Table 2. (*continued*)

Input	Particular process	Improved value
Project 3: Startup in the area of communication and streaming services	Enterprise creation	• Definition of a product-service system • Definition of a product/service portfolio • Definition of a business model
Project 4: Startup in the area of waste management and recycling	Spin-Off strategy process	• Development of a minimum viable product • Definition of a shared value strategy • Redefinition of its business model
Project 5: Startup in the area of e-commerce by promoting the exchange of goods and services	Spin-Off strategy process	• Definition of a shared value strategy • Definition of its business model
Project 6: Non-Profit Organisation that support the supply chain process to small producers in the agro industry sector	Sustainable organisation model and validation of technologies	• Definition of a sustainable organisation strategy • Intellectual property strategy

6   Conclusion and Future Work

Dynamic in big cities are complex since it demands the right solutions for many social problems. Therefore, the collaborative and cooperative participation of different actors has shown to be an effective strategy for joint efforts and share resources and responsibilities. In this sense, it can be proved that by applying concepts such as CN and Open Innovation can be structured new initiatives that involve the participation of different actors, both internal and external. Then, innovation processes, development times, communication channels and optimisation of the use of resources are improved.

In the context of innovation and entrepreneurship, it was observed that creating adequate ecosystems such as Innovation Hubs was useful to articulate initiatives to fostering innovation and entrepreneurship in society and promoting the development of technology-based solutions that can be materialised in new product/services and business models. Then, the creation of new startups and spin-offs is promoted. In this sense, it is noted that higher education has had an important role since it is a direct bridge between society-innovation-entrepreneurship. Then, the capacities of universities can be used to train desirable competencies in the profile of current students/professionals/entrepreneurs, both soft and hard.

Future work is related to document an evaluation of the performance of the different created entities of the Hub. Also, currently, it is carried out a bootcamp participants' assessment in order to measure the benefits obtained in the outcomes. Finally, it is in progress the development of an On-Demand virtual platform – MOOC to meet the demand for users that Mexico City requires.

Acknowledgements. This work has been supported by the Government of Mexico City through the project SECTEI/212/2019 – Support for the Operation of the Center for the Learning of Technological and Social Entrepreneurship in Mexico City (Apoyo para la Operación del Centro para el Aprendizaje del Emprendimiento Tecnológico y Social de la Ciudad de México). Also, the authors would like to acknowledge the technical support of WritingLab, TecLabs, Tecnologico de Monterrey, Mexico.

References

1. Fitzgerald, A., Wankerl, A., Schramm, C.: Inside real innovation. How the right approach can move ideas from R&D to market - and get the economy moving. In: World Scientificic Publishing Co., Singapore (2010)
2. Klofsten, M., Fayolle, A., Guerrero, M., Mian, S., Urbano, D., Wright, M.: The entrepreneurial university as driver for economic growth and social change-Key strategic challenges. Technol. Forecast. Soc. Chang. **141**, 149–158 (2019)
3. Pérez, S.: Por qué a México le urgen emprendedores. https://www.fortuneenespanol.com/leadership/emprendedores-emprendimiento-mexico/
4. Farayibi, A.: Entrepreneurship as a driver of economic growth: evidence from enterprise development in Nigeria. In: SSRN 2852865 (2015)
5. Patnaik, J., Bhowmick, B.: Appropriate technology: revisiting the movement in developing countries for sustainability. Int. J. Urban Civ. Eng. **12**(3), 308–312 (2018)
6. Havierniková, K., Okreglicka, M., Kordoš, M.: Selected aspects of risk management in Polish and Slovak SMEs. In: Littera Scripta, vol. 6 (2019)
7. United Nations: The World's Cities in 2018. In: United Nations, p. 6 (2018)
8. Sharma, S.K., Meyer, K.E.: New startup ecosystems and the innovation hub. Industrializing Innovation-the Next Revolution, pp. 87–111. Springer, Cham (2019). https://doi.org/10.1007/978-3-030-12430-4_8
9. Himmelman, A.T.: On coalitions and the transformation of power relations: collaborative betterment and collaborative empowerment. Am. J. Community Psychol. **29**(2), 277–284 (2001)
10. Camarinha-Matos, L.M., Afsarmanesh, H.: Collaborative networks: a new scientific discipline. J. Intell. Manuf. **16**(4–5), 439–452 (2005)
11. Camarinha-Matos, L.M., Afsarmanesh, H.: Collaborative networks. In: Wang, K., Kovacs, G.L., Wozny, M., Fang, M. (eds.) PROLAMAT 2006. IIFIP, vol. 207, pp. 26–40. Springer, Boston, MA (2006). https://doi.org/10.1007/0-387-34403-9_4
12. Romero, D., Molina, A.: Collaborative networked organisations and customer communities: value co-creation and co-innovation in the networking era. Prod. Plan. Control **22**(5–6), 447–472 (2011)
13. Chesbrough, H., Vanhaverbeke, W., West, J.: Open innovation: researching a new paradigm. In: Oxford University Press on Demand (2006)
14. Rissola, G., Sorvik, J.: Dgital innovation hubs in smart spcialisaton strategies. In: JRC Technical Reports (2018)
15. Miranda, J., López, C.S., Navarro, S., Bustamante, M.R., Molina, J.M., Molina, A.: Open innovation laboratories as enabling resources to reach the vision of education 4.0. In: IEEE International Conference on Engineering, Technology and Innovation (ICE/ITMC), pp. 1–7. IEEE (2019)

16. Weichhart, G., Molina, A., Chen, D., Whitman, L.E., Vernadat, F.: Challenges and current developments for sensing, smart and sustainable enterprise systems. Comput. Ind. **79**, 34–46 (2016)
17. Guerrini, F.M., de Sousa, T.B., Yamanari, J.S.: Sensing, smart and sustainable S^3 enterprises: principles, goals and rules. In: Camarinha-Matos, L.M., Afsarmanesh, H., Rezgui, Y. (eds.) PRO-VE 2018. IAICT, vol. 534, pp. 147–155. Springer, Cham (2018). https://doi.org/10.1007/978-3-319-99127-6_13
18. Ferro-Beca, M.D., Sarraipa, J., Agostinho, C., Gigante, F., Jose-Nunez, M., Jardim-Gonçalves, R.: A framework for enterprise context analysis based on semantic principles. Comput. Sci. Inf. Syst. **12**(3), 931–960 (2015)
19. Filos, E.: Smart organisations in the digital age. In: Mezgar, I. (ed.) Integration of ICT in Smart Organisations. Idea Group Publishing, London (2006)
20. Mauricio-Moreno, H., Miranda, J., Chavarría, D., Ramírez-Cadena, M., Molina, A.: Design S3-RF (sustainable x smart x sensing - reference framework) for the future manufacturing enterprise. IFAC-PapersOnLine **48**(3), 58–63 (2015)
21. Chavarría-Barrientos, D., Batres, R., Wright, P.K., Molina, A.: A methodology to create a sensing, smart and sustainable manufacturing enterprise. Int. J. Prod. Res. **56**(1–2), 584–603 (2018)
22. Miranda, J., Pérez-Rodríguez, R., Borja, V., Wright, P.K., Molina, A.: Sensing, smart and sustainable product development (S3 product) reference framework. Int. J. Prod. Res. **57** (14), 4391–4412 (2019). https://doi.org/10.1080/00207543.2017.1401237

A Model to Support OI Collaborative Risks Applying Social Network Analysis

Marco Nunes[1(✉)] and António Abreu[2,3(✉)]

[1] Department of Industrial Engineering,
University of Beira Interior, 6201-001 Covilha, Portugal
marco.nunes@ubi.pt
[2] Department of Mechanical Engineering,
Polytechnic Institute of Lisbon, 1959-007 Lisbon, Portugal
ajfa@dem.isel.ipl.pt
[3] CTS Uninova, 2829-516 Caparica, Portugal

Abstract. Across the literature, is often claimed that the shortage of models to support projects in the collaborative dimension, creates distrust and pushes way organizations from those collaborative initiatives, such as the open innovation (OI). In the present work, a model based on three different scientific fields (Risk Management, Open Innovation, and Social Network Analysis), is introduces, aiming to support the management of OI projects. The model identifies project critical success factors (CSFs) by analysing three distinct collaborative dimensions (3-CD) that usually take place in OI projects - (1) Participation Degree, (2) Communication Degree, and (3) Response Agility Degree – of accomplished projects. Such CSFs can then be used to guide and estimate an outcome likelihood of upcoming or ongoing OI projects.

Keywords: Project management · Risk management · Sustainability · Social network analysis · Open innovation · Critical success factors · Collaborative networks

1 Introduction

The achievement of sustainable competitive advantages in the present complex and unforeseeable business landscape, compels organizations to develop strategies to boost their performance and innovation capacities [1]. Innovation and performance are dependent from factors, such as availability of resources, ability of top management to motivate a team [2], leadership style [3], ability of working in networks of collaboration [4], just to name a few. The last-mentioned factor is pointed as a major predictor of success regarding performance and innovation [5]. However, success is not proportional to the size of a given collaborative network, rather its quality measured in expertise diversity and reach [6]. Usually, most organizations alone do not hold the necessary resources and knowledge to efficiently innovate and perform, therefore they engage in networks of collaboration with business partners, customers, universities, in order to overcome those weaknesses [7]. OI [8], is one of the popular models in which organizations engage to overcome such weaknesses. However, despite the successful cases of the application of OI regarding innovation initiatives and organizational

© IFIP International Federation for Information Processing 2020
Published by Springer Nature Switzerland AG 2020
L. M. Camarinha-Matos et al. (Eds.): PRO-VE 2020, IFIP AICT 598, pp. 324–335, 2020.
https://doi.org/10.1007/978-3-030-62412-5_27

performance [7], organizations are not adopting it in a frequent way. This happens due the lack of existing models to support collaborative networks [8, 9]. Furthermore, OI does not properly work without the co-creation of value. This implies a trustworthy commitment between the different interacting entities, which not always is very easy to achieve. In the present work, a model developed based three different scientific fields (Fig. 1) (Risk Management, Open Innovation, and Social Network Analysis) provides support on the management of OI project's collaborative challenges. The model identifies OI project critical success factors (CSFs) – by analysing three distinct collaborative dimensions (3-CD) that usually take place in OI projects: (1) Participation Degree, (2) Communication Degree, (3) Response Agility Degree – from delivered projects. Such CSFs can then be used to guide and estimate, the outcome likelihood of a given upcoming or ongoing OI projects.

Fig. 1. The three different scientific fields that constitute the basis of the presented model

2 Literature Review

2.1 OI Benefits and Limitations

OI is an innovation model credited to Henry Chesbrough [8] and is considered a driver of organizational innovation [9]. OI can be defined as the use of inflows and outflows of knowledge and resources, to speed up internal organizational innovation [11]. OI states that organizations work together through networks of collaboration, sharing know-how, experiences, ideas, and technologies, to create value that they could not create if they worked in isolation [8]. OI has two different types knowledge and resources flows [8] – (1) outside-in (the most popular), and (2) inside-out. The first, when organizations use knowledge or/ and resources from the external environment. The second, takes place when organizations share their knowledge or/ and resources with the external environment. when both flow types simultaneously take place in an organization, can be called as a coupled flow type. This flow occurs through collaborative partnerships in forms of joint research, consortium, joint ventures, or others. Literature suggests, that OI positively contributes to the social, economic, and environmental sustainability [12]. Contrary to the closed innovation [7], OI enables organizations to increase the learning capacity, reduce costs of innovation, enlarge the diversity of R&D investments, facilitate new market's entrance, share risks with OI partners, create new revenue streams, just to name a few [7, 12]. However, engaging in OI projects, may represent some downsides to organizations, such as higher dependence on external knowledge, less overall control over the innovation process, eminent risk of leak of confidential information and resources, less overall control over intellectual property, and so on [7, 12]. Research shows that, political, and culture issues, are the major constraints to OI [13]. Research identifies three major risk dimensions, that may emerge as organizations engage in OI projects [14]. They are: (1) pure risk or uncertainty (the probability of the occurrence of an event), (2) inherent risk of a innovation project (risks associated with resources, task duration, and costs estimations, political and regulation, risks), and (3) collaborative risks (comprises behavioral risks, task assignment risks to OI partners, and critical enterprises risks). Efficient collaboration is critical for OI projects, and it is critical be aware of the different dimensions that collaboration comprises. Before organizations engage into OI projects, research suggest that four critical dimensions of collaboration should be clearly understood. They are [10]: (1) Networking (comprises communication, information, and experiences exchange, usually without the existence of a common goal or structure to regulate timing and respective individual contribution), (2) Coordination (in addition to networking, comprises the alignment of the different activities, to efficiently achieve results, (3) Cooperation (in addition to networking and coordination, essentially comprises resource sharing, division of labor), and finally (4) Collaboration (in addition to the latest three, it requires trust, engagement, and the sharing of responsibilities and risks).

2.2 Risk Management and CFSs in Project Management

The PMI (Project management institute) defines project management as the application of skills, tools, knowledge, and techniques to project activities or tasks, so that project requirements across a project lifecycle are met [15]. As organizations deliver projects, risks (threats or/ and opportunities) emerge across a project's lifecycle. Such risks (usually threats), if not efficiently managed, will eventually lower the chances of a successful project outcome, which represents the non-alignment with at least one of the following project constraints - scope, cost, quality, schedule, or resources [15]. Project risk management expert [16] argues that here are four types of risks (Table 1) that may occur as projects are delivered, and for each, a proper management approach.

Other authors suggest that project risks, are in fact project critical success factors. Pinto & Slevin, 1988 [17] identified a set of project CSFs that alters their importance function of a given project phase. They are: (1) project mission poorly defined, (2) lack or inefficient top management support, (3) poorly project schedule definition, (4) poor or lack of client consultation, (5) lack of adequate expertise and technology, (6) insufficient team experience and skills, (7) ambiguous client acceptance, (8) inexistent proper project activities monitoring and feedback, (9) poor or inefficient communication, and (10) unable to deal with deviations from planned activities. To efficiently manage project risks, a wide-accepted risk management process is provided by the ISO 31000:2018 [18]. It consists of six well-structured steps, that identify, treat, and monitor risks. They are [18]: (1) establishing scope (clearly define risk management activities scope), defining context (define external and internal contexts) and criteria (define type and amount of risk that an organization is able to accept), (2) identifying risks (uncover and describe risks that may help or threaten organization's objectives),

Table 1. Four types of project risks [16]

Risk types	Characterization	Suggested treatment approach
Event Risk	Also called "stochastic uncertainty", or event risks, related to something that did not happened yet, but if it happens, will affect one or several project objectives	Well-established techniques supported in Risk Management Standards [49, 51]
Variability risk	Also called "aleatoric uncertainty", are several possible known outcomes, but unknowing which one will really take place	Advanced analysis models: Monte Carlo simulation for example
Ambiguity risk	Also called "epistemic uncertainty" or know-how and know-what risks, emerge due the lack of knowledge or understanding. Include the use and application of new technology, competitor capabilities, market conditions, just to name a few	Learning from experience (lessons learned). Simulation and prototyping
Emergent risk	Also called "ontological uncertainty", or "Black Swans", can simply not be seen, because they are outside a human's mindset or experience. Usually arise from game-changers result of disruptive innovations	Contingency planning

(3) analyzing risks (understand nature of uncertainties, risks and risks sources, consequences, events, scenarios, likelihoods, and risk controls), (4) evaluating risks (comparing results between risk analysis reports and defined risk criteria to identify where action is needed), (5) treating risks (define how and what treatment options will be implemented to treat risk, and measure its progress across time), (6) recording and reporting all previous steps (continuously monitor and review evolution of uncovered risks and the efficacy of implemented controlled measures).

2.3   The Application of SNA in Project Management

SNA can be defined as the process of studying and analysing social structures data using variety of metrics based on graph theory, which contributes to understand how social structures emerge and evolve across time, and their impact in the environment where they do exist [19]. SNA plays a critical role in understanding social capital issues and importance and has been adopted into organizational Risk Management Processes (RMPs) as a critical support tool in risk analysis and decision making [20, 21]. SNA studies and analysis talent shortages and retention, unethical behavior, network collaboration, innovation patterns, cultural fit, organizational and individual values, group and individual performance, fraud detection, just to name a few [22]. Although still at a very initial stage, SNA has been gaining huge popularity throughout the latest years, because provides unique insight in understanding the extent people's behaviors and formal and informal relationships influences outcomes, such as performance, innovation, social cohesion, information diffusion, just to name a few [23, 24]. The application of SNA in project management essentially targets the identification of project CSFs regarding the dynamic of formal and informal project's networks. Across literature, there are countless applications of SNA in project management. For example, Krackhardt, 1993 [6] argues that there are at least three critical project networks that are critical for the success of an organization. They are [6]: (1) advice network (uncovers actors to whom other actors go to get help to do their job), (2) trust network (uncovers actors where through sensitive information is exchanged), and (3) communication network (uncovers actors where through work-related information is exchanged). Rob Cross, 2004 [25] identified several unique organizational actors based on their location within a project social structure, which strongly impacts organizational performance and innovation. They are [25]: central connectors (central people where too many rely on for help or advice), boundary spanners (connect different organizational silos or departments), peripheral actors (isolated experts or non-integrated employees) and energizers (people that energize others). Most meaningful metrics used by SNA in organizations are centrality metrics [26]. Network centrality refers to the structural location of a given entity in a network, and measures a person's importance, influence, prestige, and control [25]. Network centrality, in a collaborative social network, is associated with informal power, which may influence decision-making and coordination [27]. Freeman, 1979 [28] defines centrality metrics, such as degree [26]- as an index of a network activity's potential, betweenness [26] - as an index of communication control by connecting two different clusters of an network, and closeness [26] - as an index of independence network control potential. All mentioned metrics, but not only, will have impact in project outcome – successful or unsuccessful outcome [27].

3   Proposed Model Development

The presented model in this work provides support to the collaborative network risk's management, in OI projects. First, the proposed model identifies OI project CSFs, by analysing the 3-CD that usually emerge in delivered OI projects. They are: (1) Participation Degree, (2) Communication Degree, and (3) Response Agility Degree. Second, after CSFs have been identified, these can be used to guide an upcoming or ongoing OI project, by estimating an outcome likelihood. In nutshell, the presented model aims to efficiently answer the following research question: to which extent does the dynamic collaboration of the different organizations that participate in a given OI project across all the distinct phases of a OI project lifecycle, conditions a project outcome? Answering the mentioned research question, is directly addressing the collaborative [14] and ambiguity [16] risk types, as organizations collaborate [10] in an outside-in, inside-out or coupled way [8] to deliver OI projects. The proposed model properly addresses both, collaborative and ambiguity risks types, in four different dimensions. First, the presented model is fully aligned with the suggested treatment approaches illustrated in Table 1 (lessons learned and simulation) for both risks suggested by [14] and [16], as it generates measurable information on how collaboration did occur from delivered OI projects, which in other words can be translated into lessons learned.

Second, estimating a project outcome likelihood, enabled by the comparison between identified CSFs and the actual evolution of an ongoing OI project, is doing a simulation of a possible future event, which as well represents a treatment approach suggested by [14, 16]. Third, the proposed model in this work analysis two (advice and communication networks) of the three organizational critical networks proposed by [6]. Fourth, the presented model applies SNA centrality metrics to identify behaviors associated with success or failure project outcomes, as suggested by [25–28] as being the most efficient and adequate tool to uncover dynamic relationships. The above-mentioned dimensions represent the contributes of both, SNA, and project management scientific fields, in the development of the presented model in this work. In Table 2, is illustrated the contribution of the risk management scientific field in the development of the presented model in this work.

Table 2. Contribution of the risk management process, to the presented model in this work.

Steps [18]	Proposed model corresponding process steps
"scope, context & criteria"	1-Select, collect, and prepare collaborative data (3-CD), from successful, and unsuccessful delivered projects
"risk identification"	2-Identification of unique collaborative behaviors (CBs) associated with successful, and unsuccessful delivered projects
"risk analysis"	3-Define and quantitatively measure project CSFs
"risk evaluation"	4-Quantitatively measure deviation between *actual status* of ongoing project and *desired status* regarding CSFs
"risk treatment"	5-Apply (quantitatively) actions to align ongoing project evolution with identified CSFs
"monitoring, and reviewing"	6-Continuously update the CSFs identification process (*continuous improvement cycle – self learning system*)

3.1 Proposed Model Functioning Principles

First, data from a set of successful (PSO) and failure (PFO) delivered OI project's outcomes is collected according to Table 3. Collected information will be individually (project by project, phase by phase) quantitatively analyzed through the application of a set of SNA techniques & statistics, as illustrated in Table 3 (SNA Metric). Next, two project profiles will be generated. One project success profile (PSP) and one project failure profile (PFP). Both profiles, represent the average results of all individual results from all analyzed project data. In other words, it characterizes all the successful and unsuccessful delivered OI projects, respectively. Second, the proposed model initiates the identification collaborative behaviors (CBs) for both, PSP and PFP. Through a comparative process, each of the calculated metrics, will be analyzed (compared). At this point the model is looking for collaborative behaviors (CBs) that are unique to be observed in each project phase in both, PSP and PFP profiles. Third, if unique CBs are identified, means that OI critical success factors (CSFs) have been uncovered. In other words, the proposed model, has identified different dynamic collaborative behaviors - regarding the 3-CD dimensions - in projects that were successful delivered, from projects that were not delivered with success. It can also be concluded that project outcome (success or failure) is directly influenced by dynamic collaborative behaviors. If CSFs are not identified, then it can be concluded that project outcome is not directly influenced by organizational dynamic collaborative behaviors (CBs). Fourth, once having identified project CSFs, these can be used to guide and estimate the outcome likelihood of a given ongoing OI project. This implies, that for a given ongoing OI project, step 1 of the proposed model (according to Table 2) in this work process must be conducted for the respective time slot that characterizes the actual point (AP) (actual status of a project function of its project lifecycle status) of a given ongoing OI project, at the time of the assessment. In the assessment (according to Table 3) at the ongoing OI project, the same metrics that analyzed the set of delivered projects are to be applied (Table 3) for the respective time slot. For example, if an ongoing project is in the middle of phase 2 (according to the planed project lifecycle), then step 1 of the proposed model is to be conducted from the start of phase 2, until the middle of phase 2. At this point (AP) of the ongoing project, it will be generated an actual point project profile (APPP), which comprises the values of the metrics according to Table 3. Then, the values regarding the three collaborative dimensions (3-CD) of the ongoing project actual point profile (APPP) will be compared with the values of the collaborative dimensions (3-CD) of the PSP and PFP profiles, and the deviation between the actual status and a desired status will be calculated. Fifth, if the results show that the ongoing project results are not aligned with the results of the CSFs, then actions to bring the ongoing project back on track aligned with the values of the CSFs are needed. If the contrary, then the ongoing project - function of the 3-CD – is likely heading towards a successful outcome. The outcome likelihood will be estimated function of the highest percentage of metric-results pointing out towards success or failure outcome, unsuccessful or successful outcome, respectively. Finally, once the ongoing project is finished, undergoes all process previewed in this model for a delivered project, which will contribute to refine the identification of OI project CSFs. This step is representing the continuous improvement cycle, which can be considered an intelligent-learning system.

3.2   Proposed Model Application and Implementation

In Fig. 2, is illustrated the generic project lifecycle of phase pha of an OI project. In this phase participated six different organizations (O1, ..., O6) where each contributed with a competence (a, ..., f) respectively, illustrated at the competencies chart. In this phase, occurred five project meetings (E1, ..., Et).

In each box above each meeting, are illustrated the organizations that participated in each meeting. The lines that link participating organizations, represent relationships degrees, which characterizes the number of times that any two organizations participated in project meetings. For example, O1 and O4, have a degree of 3 at the last project meeting, meaning they were together in three of five project meetings. The upper right box - ($\sum$ Emails) - represents the email communication channels between the organizations throughout all the phase *pha*. For example, applying (1) to O2, and O4, the participation evolution rates are for both negative (Fig. 3). Applying (2) to the email communication network, the density value is 53%, which represents a shared control (*Ds* < 85%) network type (Table 3).

Table 3. 3-CD and respective SNA metrics of the proposed model in this work

3-CD	Proposed model description & metrics
Participation Degree (project meetings)	Objective: Analyze the participation of Key organizations (function of their competencies in the project) in face to face project meetings Required data: In each project meeting across a project phase, all the participating organizations should be record, as well as their competencies in the project SNA Metric: For this collaborative dimension, the centrality metric Total-degree [25] will be used to quantify the project meetings participating rate. For every key organization, a participating evolution rate will be traced with a simple linear regression $$C_{DT}(n_i) = \sum_j x_{ji} \quad (1)$$ Where: C_{DT} = total degree of any given entity in a network (graph) n = total number of entities in a network, for i = 1, ..., n x_{ji} = number of connections (links) from entity j to entity i, where i $\neq$ j, and vice-versa The possible outputs are: 1- Negative slope (evolution): represents a decrease in the participation degree, as a given project phase heads towards the end 2- Positive slope (evolution): represents an increase in the participation degree as a given project phase heads towards the end 3- Neutral slope (evolution): represents a stable (continuously) participation degree as a given project phase heads towards the end
Communication Degree (project emails)	Objective: Analyze the density (reach) of the project email communication network and understand how a given organization holds control over that network. It is related with the importance of the communication network proposed by [6] Required data: All project exchanged emails within a given project phase, must be collected within a given time slot SNA Metric: For this collaborative dimension, the centrality metric Density [25] will be applied to quantify the spread or reach of the project email network in a project phase $$Ds = \frac{N_{LREAL}}{N_{LMAX}} \quad (2)$$ Where: Number of maximum ties = $N_{LMAX} = \frac{n(n-1)}{2} \quad (3)$ n = number of entities within a graph The possible outputs are: a. Total control: ($Ds > 85\%$) one organization completely controls the email communication network throughout a given project phase

(continued)

Table 3. (*continued*)

3-CD	Proposed model description & metrics
	b. Shared control: (*Ds* < 85%) one organization alone does not control, the email communication network throughout a given project phase
Response Agility Degree (project emails)	Objective: Analyze the feedback speed of an answer to an information- seeking sent email, regarding project activities. It is related with the importance of the advice network proposed by [6]
	Required data: All emails sent seeking/providing project data related with the chronologic timeline attached to each email
	SNA Metric: For this collaborative dimension, the centrality metric Reciprocity [25] will be applied to analyze which emails were replied (answered) with information project related, with the associated chronologic timeline to each pair sent/ received
	$R = \frac{L}{|L|}$ (4)
	Where:
	L = Number of connections heading in both directions
	$\|L\|$ = total number of links within a network
	The output for the reciprocity metric is:
	A value in units of hours, that range from "1" (representing an instantaneous answer: < than 1 h period of time) up to "0" (represents the maximum duration of a given project phase in hours, for those cases where feedback is not found throughout the lifetime of a project in the respective email network)

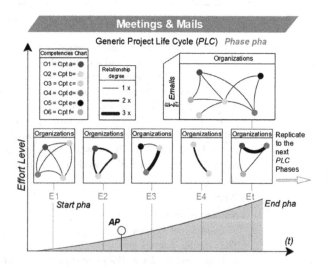

Fig. 2. Application framework of the presented model in this work

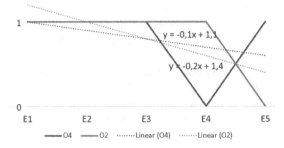

Fig. 3. Participation evolution rate for O2, and O4 according to Fig. 2.

If the project lifecycle of Fig. 2 represented a PSP, then the results regarding (1) and (2), would be CSFs. As conclusion, the participation degree evolution in project meetings of organizations that bring competencies b, and d, for future OI projects in phase *pha*, should follow the evolution (negative) illustrated at Fig. 3. Still, the email network communication, should be of *shared control* type, meaning that no organization holds completely control over it. Finally, for an ongoing project, data until the AP point (Fig. 2) should be collected and analysed. The results should then be compared with the results of the CSFs, and function of the deviation between actual status of ongoing project (AP) and desired status regarding CSFs, corrective measures should, or not be implemented.

4   Conclusions and Further Developments

As demonstrated in 3.2, the proposed model in this work, efficiently answers the research question presented in chapter 3. The proposed model generates valuable insight regarding to how past collaboration occurred (lessons-learned and working culture) between the different organizations that participated together in OI projects that had a successful and failure outcome. This enables organizations to eliminate or minimize behaviors associated with failure project outcome and replicate those associated with success. Quantifying collaborative behaviors, enables organizations to craft more data driven strategies, rather than traditional gute feeling approaches, and a more accurate management of intangible organizational assets. The presented model in this work, quantitatively measures two major risks - collaborative [14], and ambiguity [16] - that threatens the engagement of organizations in OI projects. The model proposed in this work, if efficiently implemented, is also a step forward in the organizational digital transformation strategy once it collects and analysis and interprets data in a fully automated way (self-learning system). Also, the collecting data process is non-invasive, and almost bias-free, by opposition to pulse surveys for example. Still, the proposed model, quantifies how much work is done through the mix of informal and formal networks of collaboration across an OI project. Finally, it contributes to the economic, social, and environmental sustainability by reducing risk associated with collaborative networks in projects, which in turn optimizes resources usage, and turns organization leaner oriented. However, the implementation of the model may be slow at an initial stage. This happens due a necessary change in the working culture of an organization, essentially regarding the data preparation, availability, and collection processes. Project related information that flows across phone calls and corridor chats, are not able to be collected by the model. In part this occurs due legal and ethical constraints, which ultimately can hinder the successful implementation of the proposed model in organizations. Finally, further research regarding the development of SNA metrics is recommended, to enable a deeper understanding to which extent organizational collaborative behaviors influence project outcomes.

References

1. Friar, J.: Competitive advantage through product performance innovation in a competitive market. J. Prod. Innov. Manag. **12**, 33–42 (2003)
2. Hansen, M.: Collaboration: How Leaders Avoid the Traps, Create Unity, and Reap Big Results; Harvard. Business School Press, Cambridge (2009)
3. Lutfihak, A., Evrim, G.: Disruption and ambidexterity: how innovation strategies evolve? Soc. Behav. Sci. **235**, 782–787 (2016)
4. Camarinha-Matos, L., Abreu, A.: Performance Indicators Based on Collaboration Benefits. Prod. Plan. Control **18**, 273–282 (2006)
5. Arena, M.: Adaptive Space: How GM and Other Companies are Positively Disrupting Themselves and Transforming into Agile Organizations. McGraw Hill Education, New York (2018)
6. Krackhardt, D., Hanson, J.: Informal Networks the Company behind the Charts. Harvard College Review, Massachusetts (1993). https://www.andrew.cmu.edu/user/krack/documents/pubs/1993/1993%20Informal%20Networks.pdf. Accessed 5 Mar 2018
7. Ullrich, A., Vladova, G.: Weighing the pros and cons of engaging in open innovation. Technol. Innov. Manag. Rev. **6**, 34–40 (2016)
8. Chesbrough, H.: The era of open innovation. MIT Sloan Manag. Rev. **44**, 35–41 (2003)
9. Santos, R., Abreu, A., Anes, V.: Developing a green product-based in an open innovation environment. case study: electrical vehicle. In: Camarinha-Matos, L.M., Afsarmanesh, H., Antonelli, D. (eds.) PRO-VE 2019. IAICT, vol. 568, pp. 115–127. Springer, Cham (2019). https://doi.org/10.1007/978-3-030-28464-0_11
10. Camarinha-Matos, L.M., Afsarmanesh, H.: Collaborative networks. In: Wang, K., Kovacs, G.L., Wozny, M., Fang, M. (eds.) PROLAMAT 2006. IIFIP, vol. 207, pp. 26–40. Springer, Boston, MA (2006). https://doi.org/10.1007/0-387-34403-9_4
11. Huizingh, E.: Open innovation: state of the art and future perspectives. Technovation **31**, 2–9 (2011)
12. Rauter, R., Globocnik, D., Perl-Vorbach, E., Baumgartner, R.: Open innovation and its effects on economic and sustainability innovation performance. J. Innov. Knowl. 4 (2018)
13. Narsalay, R., Kavathekar, J., Light, D.: A hands-off approach to open innovation doesn't work (2016). https://hbr.org/2016/05/a-hands-off-approach-to-open-innovation-doesnt-work. Accessed 06 Sept 2018
14. Abreu, A., Martins Moleiro, J.D., Calado, J.M.F.: Fuzzy logic model to support risk assessment in innovation ecosystems. In: 2018 13th APCA International Conference on Automatic Control and Soft Computing (CONTROLO), Ponta Delgada, pp. 104–109 (2018)
15. PMI (Project Management Institute) Project Management Body of Knowledge (PMBOK® Guide), 6th edn. Project Management Institute, Inc., Newtown Square (2017)

16. Hillson. D. How to manage the risks you didn't know you were taking. http://riskdoctor. com/docs/NA14MTL02%20Hillson%20paper%20%20How%20to%20manage%20all% 20your%20risks.pdf. Accessed 4 Jan 2020
17. Pinto, J.K., Slevin, D.P.: Critical success factors across the project life cycle: definitions and measurement techniques. Proj. Manag. J. **19**, 67–75 (1988)
18. ISO – The International Organization for Standardization. https://www.iso.org/home.html. Accessed 01 Jan 2019
19. Durland, M., Fredericks, K.: An introduction to social network analysis. New Dir. Eval. **2005**, 5–13 (2006). https://doi.org/10.1002/ev.157
20. Krivkovich, A., Levy, C.: Managing the people side of risk. McKinsey Global Institute (2015).   https://www.mckinsey.com/business-functions/risk/our-insights/managing-the-people-side-of-risk. Accessed 15 Feb 2019
21. Nunes, M., Abreu, A.: Applying social network analysis to identify project critical success factors. Sustainability **12**, 1503 (2020). https://doi.org/10.3390/su12041503
22. Blacker, K., McConnell, P.: People Risk Management: A Practical Approach to Managing the Human Factors That Could Harm Your Business. Kogan Page Publishers, CPI Group (UK) Ltd, Croydon (2015)
23. Borgatti, S.: Introduction to social network analysis stephen, University of Kentucky (2016). https://statisticalhorizons.com/wp-content/uploads/SNA-Sample-Materials.pdf. Accessed 15 Jan 2019
24. Ruan, X., Ochieng, A.: The evaluation of social network analysis application's in the UK construction industry. ARCOM 2011 (2012)
25. Cross, R., Parker, A.: The Hidden Power of Social Networks: Understanding How Work Really Gets Done in Organizations. Harvard Business School Press, Boston (2004)
26. Wasserman, S., Faust, K.: Social network analysis in the social and behavioral sciences. In: Social Network Analysis: Methods and Applications, pp. 1–27. Cambridge University Press; Cambridge (1994). ISBN 9780521387071
27. Liaquat, H., Wu, A., Choi, B.: Measuring coordination through social networks. In: Proceedings of the ICIS 2006 Proceedings, Milwaukee, Wisconsin, USA, 10–13 December 2006
28. Freeman, L.: Centrality in social networks conceptual clarification. Soc. Netw. **1**, 215–239 (1979)

A Framework Based on Fuzzy Logic to Manage Risk in an Open Innovation Context

Ricardo Santos[1,2(✉)], Antonio Abreu[1,3], J. M. F. Calado[1,4],
José Miguel Soares[5], and José Duarte Moleiro Martins[6,7]

[1] ISEL - Instituto Superior de Engenharia de Lisboa,
Instituto Politécnico de Lisboa, Lisbon, Portugal
ricardosimoessantos84@ua.pt
[2] GOVCOPP - University of Aveiro, Aveiro, Portugal
[3] CTS Uninova, Faculdade de Ciências e Tecnologia,
Universidade Nova de Lisboa, Lisbon, Portugal
[4] IDMEC-IST-UL, Lisbon, Portugal
[5] ISEG - Lisbon School of Economics and Management,
Universidade de Lisboa, Lisbon, Portugal
[6] ISCAL - Instituto Superior de Contabilidade e Administração de Lisboa,
Lisbon, Portugal
[7] UNIDE - ISCTE - IUL, Lisbon, Portugal

Abstract. Virtual enterprises (VE), is well-known to make use of open innovation to achieve competitiveness, through innovation on product development.

However, its limited resources, combined with the innovation resulted from the diversity of partners involved, rises some challenges to its management, specifically regarded with risk management. To fulfill these requirements, risk management's models, have been conceived to assist managers, on preventing threats with such risks, although without adequately incorporate the influence of each process domain on product development, as well as the subjectivity regarding human perception. In order to consider these issues, this work presents an approach, supported by fuzzy logic, to assess the risk's level on product development in an open innovation context. The model robustness, will be assessed through a case study, where it will be also discussed the benefits and challenges found.

Keywords: Collaborative networks · Open innovation · New product development · Risk management · Fuzzy logic

1 Introduction

The uncertainty with the economic context, and the market competition as well, have pushed companies to find ways to survive [1]. Based on works, found on literature, innovation should exist on new product development (NPD), so the organizations, can reach competitive advantage in the existed (or even new) markets [2].

In this context, a VE (virtual enterprise) arises as an (temporary) organization's alliance (on collaborative context), with the purpose of sharing different assets, namely

© IFIP International Federation for Information Processing 2020
Published by Springer Nature Switzerland AG 2020
L. M. Camarinha-Matos et al. (Eds.): PRO-VE 2020, IFIP AICT 598, pp. 336–349, 2020.
https://doi.org/10.1007/978-3-030-62412-5_28

resources (e.g. materials, equipment, etc.) and competencies, to develop products that provides a better answer to the opportunities that might appear on market [3].

However, NPD it is not an easy task, especially for VEs, given the existence of several risks, regarding the different processes of each component/phase of the product.

Thus, and to benefit from the collaborative network, it's suggested the use of suitable risk models in an OI (Open Innovation) context, since that OI operates essentially in a collaborative context [4]. However, there is few risk assessments approaches on literature, related to the application in OI's context on behalf of NPD [2, 3].

Furthermore, the choice of the OI's "right" actor/partner, allows the risk's minimization on each product process, and therefore, the minimization of the global risk of the product development, assuming therefore, one of the proposes to develop such approaches. On these context, risk management, could support VEs to mitigate unwanted risks that can jeopardize the success on NPD [5], by using it as a procedure to identify, evaluate, watch and also report, all the risk's involved here, regarding the probabilities of occurrence and also the impact as well. The evaluation and the assessment of each risk, allows the elaboration of a set of procedures to reduce the impact of any negative effects that might appear [4]. Based on common practices, on behalf of project management applications, there are on literature, several risk assessment approaches, that can be identified, namely; DT (Decision Trees), FTA (Fault Tree Analysis) [4], FMEA (Failure Mode Effects Analysis) [5], AHP (Analytic Hierarchy Process) [6] and RDM (Risk Diagnosing Methodology) [7], among others. However, there are works that relates innovation with product development. An example, is found on [3], regarding the development of a risk-based technology management approach, by considering both innovation and product delivery quantitative objectives, with the aim of tracking and the monitoring them, during its life cycle. In [8], are identified some of the risks, commonly appeared on open innovation projects, related to a set of situations, such as the leakage within market information, the external technology dependence, the difficulties arise with the protection of the intellectual property, among others. Still regarding the intellectual property protection, in [9], it is highlighted several factors related to this issue. Among the risk models existed on literature, is the work of [9], with focus on the integration of costumer's risk assessment in NPD, or the work from [10], where it was designed an approach based on an open-source software to provide early warnings, as well as their mitigation.

Despite the existence of several methods found on literature, there are few approaches, related to risk management on VEs, where it's intended to explore a possible existence of influence between the processes involved on the development of the product, by also including at the same time, the human perception on defining each risk based on its probability of occurrence and impact as well [11]. Thus, in this paper, it will be presented an approach to incorporate such issues, where on Sect. 2 it's described the research method, followed by Sect. 3, which describes the validation method of the approach, proposed in this work. Section 4 ends up with the conclusions and some future work recommendations.

2 Research Method

2.1 Proposed Approach

According to what was referred before, it was developed an approach to asses and account, an eventual relationship regarding the risk related to each project (concerning the development of each individual component/system product by considering different domains) and the risk, associated to each VE's domain, as an organization created to develop the product. Based on [2, 3, 5, 11], it's shown on Fig. 1, the risk taxonomy adopted, regarding Process and Product Risk levels.

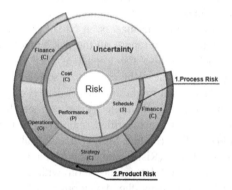

Fig. 1. Adopted risks (adapted from [11])

The execution of a project (with success or not), might have impact on several domains of each organization, in particularly on VE [2, 3, 11]. Considering, that each process, regarding to a product's system component, has a development project involved and therefore a risk associated to it, the correspondent Project Risk Management (PRM), can be considered as part of the VE's Risk Management (VERM), responsible for the NPD (Fig. 2).

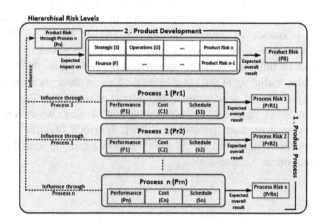

Fig. 2. Hierarchical risk level relationship between PRM and CRM

Furthermore, the Process Risk of a given process n (PrR_n), is obtained by considering the risk achieved on its several domains, such as the C_n (Cost), P_n (Performance), S_n (Schedule), etc. Thus, and by knowing that each PRM, assesses its correspondent process through it's different domains (cost, time and performance), each PRM regarding each process can be linked to the VERM, through the product development, which is considered as the origin of the VE.

Therefore, some studies (e.g. [6, 12]) suggests that a given process's risk, can influence the risk value of the VE's overall PR (Product Risk) on its different domain. Thus, in study we have considered the following ones, namely, S (Strategic), O (Operations) and F (Finance).

The need of qualifying and even quantifying this influence, is to predict a possible effect from a given process n to the VE's behavior, through the transition from a current phase into a new one, which results through its application [5]. The categories of the risk mentioned here, i.e., S (Schedule), P (Performance) and C (Cost), are presented and discussed on [2, 3, 7, 12], as a set of risk elements that normally concerns the project management. Thus, and based on [2, 3, 6, 7], the process risk was defined, as:

- S (Schedule): Accomplishment degree of the timeframe, in order to fulfill the deadlines of the project, according to the initially planned [2].
- P (Performance): Degree of accomplishment, regarding the technical and business goals, related to the project, based on the outputs of the process [6].
- C (Cost): Degree of accomplishment, regarding budget constraints, related to the project [3, 7].

Each project, in this way, can impact the corporate risk of the organization, through their associated domains with it (e.g. O (Operations), S (Schedule), F (Finance), E (Environment) and IS (Information Systems)).

In this case, and as product (VE) domains, it was considered the following ones:

- Strategic risk (S): Related to errors that might be occur, such as a product's technology that might not satisfy the consumer's requirements [3, 7].
- Operational risk (O): Regarding the deployment of the process, which includes some of the problems associated to the distribution and also the procurement (e.g. delay related to the production with the product to be launched on market) [2].
- Financial risk (F): Resulted from the product financing (VE) (e.g. access to working capitals, foreign exchange rates, interest rate risk), liquidity problems (e.g. credit risks), among others [1, 2].

Apart from the domains presented here, this model can be also expanded into other risk categories.

2.2 Model's Architecture

The model presented here, was developed according to the concept of NPD (Fig. 2), and it's based on a single method to include the uncertainty and ambiguity of human perception on risk assessment (Fig. 3) regarding product development.

Therefore, and according to the relation described before (Fig. 2), the method described here, recurs to fuzzy logic to perform an analysis (quantitative and qualitative) of PR's assessment in an OI context. This is performed by integrating process and product development risk levels as unique approach.

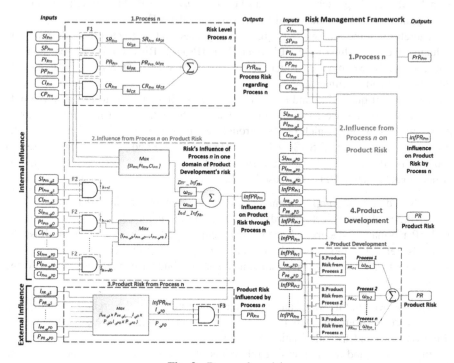

Fig. 3. Proposed model.

The 1st level, has the purpose of assessing the PR_n (process risk by considering a given process n), while the 2nd level, assesses the PR (product risk) level, by considering the $InfPR_{Prn}$ (influence related to each process n) on the PR (product's risk) (Fig. 3).

Regarding each process risk type, considered on Fig. 1 (i.e. S (Schedule), P (Performance) and C (Cost)), there is an individual risk ($^-R_{Prn}$), related to each product's process n, which is obtained from each correspondent $^-I_{Prn}$ (expected impact) and its correspondent $^-P_{Prn}$ (probability of occurrence) considered here (Fig. 3), namely.:

$$SR_{\mathrm{Pr}n} = SP_{\mathrm{Pr}n}.SI_{\mathrm{Pr}n} \tag{1}$$

$$PR_{\mathrm{Pr}n} = PP_{\mathrm{Pr}n}.PI_{\mathrm{Pr}n} \tag{2}$$

$$CR_{\mathrm{Pr}n} = CP_{\mathrm{Pr}n}.CI_{\mathrm{Pr}n} \tag{3}$$

Based on Figs. 2 and 3, the Process Risk (PrR_{Prn}) related to a given process n, is obtained by gathering all of the risk categories referred here, namely:

$$\Pr R_{Pr\,n} = \omega_{SR}.SR_{Pr\,n} + \omega_{PR}.PR_{Pr\,n} + \omega_{CR}.CR_{Pr\,n} \tag{4}$$

Through Fig. 3, there is a set of weights $(\omega_{-R_{Pr\,n}})$ each one corresponded to a process risk category, namely Schedule (S), Performance (P) and Cost (C). Such weights, satisfies the following condition:

$$1 = \omega_{SR_{Pr\,n}} + \omega_{TR_{Pr\,n}} + \omega_{CR_{Pr\,n}} \tag{5}$$

A possible influence, concerning each process risk n (PrR_{Prn}), related to each PD (product development domain), is also accounted in this model by considering the existence of an expected impact variable $(^-I_{Prn \to PD})$, that affects one (can be more) product domains. In this work, we have accounted 3 product development domains, on behalf of the VE considered here, i.e.: S (Strategic), O (Operations) and F (Finance). Based on the risks C (Cost), S (Schedule) and P (Performance), it was obtained a set of values of impact, regarding each product development domain $(^-I_{Prn \to PD})$ considered here. For each product development domain (PD), and based on the risk manager's perception, only one value is selected, among the different values of influence, from each impact value $(^-I_{Prn \to PD})$ for each process domain, namely; Schedule (S), Performance (P) and Cost (C). Thus, and for each product domain, fuzzy logic is used based on a set of qualitative (linguistic) variables and inference rules, in order to achieve the correspondent values of $^-I_{Prn \to PD}$. The variable Ind_Inf_{rn} (indirect influence of a given process n) on each product domain, is obtained by accounting the maximum value of 3 impact values regarding each product domain $(^-I_{Prn \to PD})$, obtained before, i.e.:

$$Ind\_Inf_{PRn} = \max\{SI_{Pr\,n \to S}, PI_{Pr\,n \to S}, CI_{Pr\,n \to S}, \ldots, SI_{Pr\,n \to O}, PI_{Pr\,n \to O}, CI_{Pr\,n \to O}\} \tag{6}$$

The direct influence, resulted from the impact of each process domain, is also considered here, to account the possible impact of the resources used on each process, over the resources applied on the NPD context, in terms of its availability.

Therefore, the process domain that brings more impact, allows the definition of the direct influence, regarding a certain process n (Dir_InfP_{rn}), which is defined, by obtaining the maximum of the 3 values mentioned above, namely:

$$Dir\_Inf_{Pr\,n} = \max\{SI_{Pr\,n}, PI_{Pr\,n}, CI_{Pr\,n}\} \tag{7}$$

Thus, the total influence from a given process n on product development ($InfPR_{Pr\,n}$) will be obtained through the sum of Ind_Inf_{PRn} with the $Dir\_Inf_{Pr\,n}$, i.e.:

$$InfPR_{Pr\,n} = Ind\_Inf_{Pr\,n}.\varpi_{Ind} + Dir\_Inf_{Pr\,n}.\varpi_{Dir.} \tag{8}$$

The weights ω_{Dir} and ω_{Ind}, are corresponded each one, to the direct and indirect influence, with the purpose of ponder the relative importance, defined by the risk manager for each one of the values achieved before. All of these weights, complies with the following expression/condition:

$$1 = \omega_{Dir.} + \omega_{Ind.} \tag{9}$$

Thus, the product development risk for each project n (PR_{Pm}), is resulted from the combination of the $P_{PR \rightarrow PD}$ (probability of occurrence of the event), the $I_{PR \rightarrow PD}$ (expected impact of PR in the organization) and the $InfPR_{Pr\,n}$ (influence from the process n on product development), i.e.:

$$PR_{Pr\,n} = P_{PR \rightarrow PD} \cdot I_{PR \rightarrow PD} \cdot InfPR_{Pr\,n} \tag{10}$$

With $I_{PR \rightarrow PD}$ and $P_{PR \rightarrow PD}$, being the external impact in a given product domain (PD) ($I_{PR \rightarrow PD}$) and the correspondent value of probability of occurrence ($P_{PR \rightarrow PD}$). Both values, results from the selection of the maximum product value, regarding each product domain (PD) considered here (i.e. S (Strategic), F (Finance) and O (Operations)), namely:

$$\langle I_{PR \rightarrow PD}, P_{PR \rightarrow PD} \rangle = \max\{I_{PR \rightarrow S} \times P_{PR \rightarrow S}, I_{PR \rightarrow O} \times P_{PR \rightarrow O}, \ldots, I_{PR \rightarrow PD} \times P_{PR \rightarrow PD}\} \tag{11}$$

The Product Risk (PR), is therefore obtained from the contribution of each Process Risk (PrR_{Pm}) considered, and according to its relative importance (ω_{Pm}), i.e.:

$$PR = \omega_{Pr\,1} \cdot PR_{Pr\,1} + \omega_{Pr\,2} \cdot PR_{Pr\,2} + \omega_{Pr\,n} \cdot PR_{Pr\,n} \tag{12}$$

Where $\omega_{Pr\,1}$, $\omega_{Pr\,2}$ and $\omega_{Pr\,n}$, are weights, used to define the relative importance for the process's 1, 2 and n.

2.3   Fuzzy Deployment

The risk levels, regarding the values of PrR_{Pm} and PR, results from each correspondent FIS (Fuzzy Inference System) (Fig. 3) considered here and following a set of IF-AND-THEN heuristic rules (by impact category). Through Fig. 3 and regarding the Process Risk Level, the FIS F1, follows the (1–3) expressions, related to the inputs $^{-}I_{Prn}$ and $^{-}P_{Prn}$, namely:

$$^{-}R_{Pr\,n} = {}^{-}P_{Pr\,n} \cap {}^{-}I_{Pr\,n} \tag{13}$$

Therefore, the heuristic rules, concerning the FIS F1 (Fig. 4), are defined according to the sentence: "IF $^{-}I_{Prn}$ (Impact) is I AND $^{-}P_{Prn}$ (probability of occurrence) is P, THEN the $^{-}R_{Pm}$ (process risk) is R".

A similar logic, based on (10), can also be performed, for the PR_{Prn} (Product Risk level), although, by also accounting the influence related to process n on product development $(InfPR_{Prn})$, i.e.:

$$PR_{Prn} = P_{PR \to PD} \cap I_{PR \to PD} \cap InfPR_{Prn} \qquad (14)$$

Therefore, the heuristic rules, regarding FIS F3 (Fig. 4), can be stated as: "IF $InfPR_{Prn}$ (Process n Influence on Product) is Inf AND $P_{PR \to PD}$ (probability of occurrence) is P AND $I_{PR \to PD}$ (impact) is I THEN product risk level (PR) is PR (Fig. 3).

The possible influence of the process n, regarding each VE domain, can also be accounted by recurring to FIS F2 (Fig. 3), to perform the follow statement: "IF $CI_{Prm \to PD}$ (impact) is Ic AND $PI_{Prm \to PD}$ (impact) is Ip AND $SI_{Prm \to PD}$ (impact) is, THEN the average value of process n impact over each one of the product domains $^{-}I_{Prm \to PD}$ is Inf".

2.4   Linguistic Variables

Regarding the number of linguistic levels, and according to [11], it's normally advised that this value should not exceed 9 levels, since it represents the limits of human perception in terms of discrimination. Thus, and based on such recommendations, the linguistic variables were established in order to not surpass 5 levels, with each one, having a pertinence function of the triangular type. For all the domains of the process's probability of occurrence $(^{-}P_{Prm})$, on Table 1, are shown the pertinence functions.

Table 1. Pertinence functions, regarding the probability of occurrence (P)

Pertinence Levels	Description	Frequency	Fuzzy Parameters [α, β, γ]
Rare	It is estimated that the event will occur only in exceptional circumstances.	Event has occurred or is expected to occur once in the next 48 months	(0 ,0 ,0.25)
Unlikely	The event is not likely, but it can occur.	Event has occurred or is expected to occur once in the next 24 months	(0 ,0.25,0.50)
Likely	Probable occurrence event	Event has occurred or is expected to occur once in the next 18 months	(0.25,0.50,0.75)
Very Likely	The event will likely occur	Event has occurred or is expected to occur once in the next 12 months	(0.5,0.75,1.0)
Expected	The event is expected to occur	Event has occurred or is expected to occur once in the next 6 months	(0.75, 1, 1)

Similar table was also performed, by considering the probability of occurrence of the product's risk $(P_{PR \to PD})$. The pertinence functions, regarding the different expected impacts, considered for each process n $(^{-}I_{Prm})$, are presented on Table 2.

Table 2. Pertinence functions, for each impact (I) and process domain

Pertinence Levels	Process Domain			Fuzzy Parameters [α, β, γ]
	Schedule (S)	Performance (P)	Cost (C)	
Neglectable	Insignificant impact on the processes required to obtain deliverables. No changes in established activities	Insignificant impact on the initial project budget (<2%)	Timing delay is easily recoverable.	(0,0,2.5)
Low	Prevents the fulfillment of one or more activities established for each project task. No task changes.	Low impact on project budget (2-5%)	Low schedule delay is not recoverable.	(0,2.5, 5.0)
Moderate	Prevents the fulfillment of one or more tasks. No requirement changes.	Moderate impact on the initial project budget (5-10%)	Moderate delay in the completion of the project. Without compromising the project requirements.	(2.5,5.0,7.5)
High	Prevents the fulfillment of one or more project requirements. Scope change required.	High impact on the initial project budget (10-30%)	Acceleration in the fulfillment of tasks with anticipation of the project calendar.	(5.0,7.5,10.0)
Severe	It prevents the fulfillment of the project's objective (s), and it is not possible to achieve it even with changes in scope.	Impact on the initial heavy budget making the project unfeasible (>30%)	Project deadline exceeded making it impossible to complete the project since the project is no longer adequate to the organizational reality.	(7.5,10.0,10.0)

Similar table was also used, related to the correspondent (and also expected) $^{-}I_{Prm \rightarrow PD}$ (impact values regarding each process domain over each product domain) considered in this work. On Table 3, it's presented the pertinence functions, regarding the process risk ($^{-}R_{Prm}$) for each process domain. Similar table was also considered for PR_{Prm}.

Table 3. Pertinence functions, regarding the product risk level

Pertinence Levels	Description	Fuzzy Parameters [α, β, γ]
Very low	Risk can be accepted as it does not pose a threat to the project/organization, it must be monitored to ensure that its level does not change.	(0, 0, 0.25)
Low	Risk can be accepted. Risk control must be carried out based on a cost-benefit analysis	(0 , 0.25, 0.50)
Moderate	Risk must be mitigated; the effectiveness of controls must be monitored.	(0.25, 0.50, 0.75)
High	Efforts should be made to mitigate risk as soon as possible.	(0.50, 0.75,1.0)
Very High	Immediate action must be taken to mitigate the risk.	(0.75, 1.0, 1.0)

2.5   Software Implementation

The inference rules, as well as the definition of the membership functions, was built, by using Matlab® Fuzzy Logic Toolbox™ (version R2016a) software, to develop and assess each FIS (Fuzzy Inference System) behavior.

All the three FIS, considered here (i.e. F1, F2 and F3), were implemented by recurring to Mamdani's inference system (Fig. 4), due to its wide acceptance on literature and better adaptation to human inputs [11].

Regarding the Pr level, F1 has its inputs based on the $^-P_{Prn}$ (Probability of occurrence), and its correspondent $^-I_{Prn}$ (expected impact value), with the output, being the $^-R_{Prn}$ (Process Risk Level) related to each process domain considered. Regarding the implementation of FIS F2, it has on its inputs the expected impact variables $SIP_{m \to PD}$, $PIP_{m \to PD}$ and $CIP_{m \to PD}$, where the output of F2 is $^-IP_{m \to PD}$ (average impact concerning process n, related to each domain of the product).

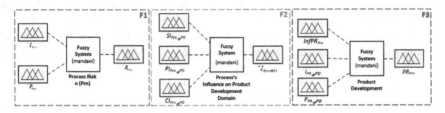

Fig. 4. FIS's deployment on Matlab

The inputs of FIS F3, are the variables $PP_{R \to PD}$, $IP_{R \to PD}$ and $InfPR_{rn}$, while the output consists of the variable product risk level (PR) from Process n (PR_{rn}).

Regarding the available defuzzification approaches, it was used the centroid method, for each FIS proposed in this paper, given its widely application [11].

Regarding the FIS "F1", on Fig. 5, it is presented the surfaces, regarding each risk category (domain) of the process, considered in this work.

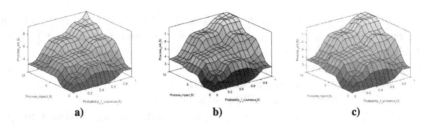

Fig. 5. FIS's surface, for each process level domain (F1) a) Schedule b) Performance c) Cost

The differences achieved with the three obtained surfaces, are mainly resulted from the difference with the inference rules, regarding each domain considered, which allows the achievement of different output combinations regarding the same values of inputs.

3 Case Study

A case study was used to assess the model's robustness, which was based on a VE, established in order to develop an electric vehicle in open innovation context, to achieve different innovations, with one of them related to its autonomy.

This VE, is based on a collaboration network, formed by 14 partners, which involves several industries and 2 research centers, regarding to each car part.

The purpose, was to share the resources, skills, and core competencies among the partners involved in order to obtain a set of innovations around the product development, which includes a better response to the market requirements, the reduce of time to market, and the increase of the credibility of the project to obtain the necessary funds from the European union and private investors.

Other innovations have been achieved within the car and through the development of the different car's components, essential to build the vehicle according to the purposes of the virtual enterprise. From all the processes, involved on VE's product development, we have selected a set of 5 processes, which are presented on Table 4.

Table 4. OI's partners

Pr.	Prod. Ref.	Description	Actors Involved
...	...	...	...
1	K01Pr2	Traction control system	P8,P7
2	K02Pr2	HMI development software	P2,P11
3	K87Pr2	GPS Navigation System	P4
...	...	...	...
4	K02Pr3	Chassis' design	P2,P5,P9
...	...	...	...
5	K01Pr5	New Protocol Communication (car lights, error code diagnosis)	P5, P6
...	...	...	...

As it described on Table 4, each process is related to a given car (product) part, whose responsibility (in some cases), can be shared by more than one OI's partner.

Each process has different risk types, namely the performance (ex.: failure on meeting a set of requirements defined to the traction control system), cost (ex.: unexpectable costs related to the car chassis) and schedule (ex.: non-compliance related to the deadlines with navigation (GPS) system design).

Based on the model, presented on Fig. 3, and regarding its application, a group of risk managers, each one, regarding each network partner (and therefore each process), have assessed the process involved here, on behalf of the 17 variables to use, and regarding the inputs of the model, shown on Fig. 3.

Thus, on Table 5 are described the same inputs, as well as the inputs, regarding the different weights. Such results, presented on Table 5, and based on qualitative (linguistic) values, were further converted into a quantitative ones, by using a series of intervals, to improve the analysis of the obtained results, concerning the 5 project considered here, including the overall product development risk as well.

Table 6, presents the main output values from the model, which includes the weight values (ω_{SRn}, ω_{PRn}, ω_{SRn}), related to the process risk level, the weight values (ω_{Dir}, $\omega_{Ind.}$) related to the influence of each process n and finally, the weight values ω_{Prn}, (regarding the product level) related to each process n.

Table 5. Inputs used and obtained outputs

N.	Pr.	SI_{Prn}	SP_{Prn}	PI_{Prn}	PP_{Prn}	CI_{Prn}	CP_{Prn}	I_{APO}	P_{APO}	$InfPR_{Prn}$
						FIS F1			FIS F3	
	1	Insignificant	Low	Low	Rare	Rare	Unlikely	Insignificant	Insignificant	Insignificant
	2	Low	Moderate	Low	Unlikely	Unlikely	Unlikely	Severe	Moderate	Low
Inputs	3	Insignificant	Low	Moderate	Likely	Likely	Likely	Moderate	Moderate	Moderate
	4	Insignificant	High	Severe	Very Likely	Likely	Unlikely	High	Moderate	High
	5	Low	Moderate	Moderate	Expected	Expected	Expected	Severe	Low	Severe

Pr.	SI_{Prn4S}	PI_{Prn4S}	CI_{Prn4S}	SI_{Prn4O}	PI_{Prn4O}	CI_{Prn4O}	SI_{Prn4F}	PI_{Prn4F}	CI_{Prn4F}
					FIS F2				
1	Insignificant	Insignificant	High	Insignificant	Insignificant	Insignificant	Low	Insignificant	High
2	Low	Moderate	Low	Severe	Moderate	Low	Insignificant	Severe	Low
3	Moderate	Moderate	Moderate	Moderate	Insignificant	Moderate	Moderate	Moderate	Moderate
4	High	Moderate	High	High	Moderate	High	Low	High	High
5	Severe	Severe	Low	Severe	Low	Severe	Low	Severe	Low

Pr.	Pr.	SR_{Prn}	PR_{Prn}	CR_{Prn}	I_{Prn4S}	I_{Prn4O}	I_{Prn4F}	PR_{Prn}	Linguistic	Numeric
		FIS F1			FIS F2			FIS F3	Legend (variable levels)	
	1	Rare	Low	Insignificant	Insignificant	Insignificant	High	Insignificant	Insignificant	[0,2]
	2	Low	Low	Low	Low	Moderate	Low	Low	Low	]2,4]
Outputs	3	Moderate	Insignificant	Moderate	Moderate	Low	Moderate	Moderate	Moderate	]4,6]
	4	High	High	Moderate	High	Moderate	High	Moderate	High	]6,8]
	5	Moderate	Severe	Severe	Moderate	Severe	Low	Moderate	Severe	]8,10]

Table 6. Outputs, regarding the process and product risks

Pr.	SR_{Prn}	PR_{Prn}	CR_{Prn}	ω_{SR}	ω_{PR}	ω_{CR}	$\omega_{Ind.}$	$\omega_{Dir.}$	PrR_{Prn}	PR_{Prn} (1)	ω_{PRn} (2)	(1)·(2)
1	1,75	3,35	7,12	0,27	0,21	0,52	0,62	0,38	4,88	3,80	0,21	0,80
2	3,90	5,62	2,70	0,36	0,14	0,50	0,59	0,41	3,54	5,23	0,19	0,99
3	0,67	3,32	9,72	0,30	0,22	0,48	0,47	0,53	5,60	3,70	0,17	0,63
4	1,12	7,49	5,87	0,39	0,17	0,44	0,57	0,43	4,29	4,95	0,22	1,09
5	3,18	5,20	8,70	0,37	0,13	0,50	0,47	0,53	6,20	6,36	0,21	1,34
Product Risk (PR)												4,85

Based on the results presented on Table 5 and 6, we verify that the process nr. 3, is more likely to violate the initial budget, which brings more risk. However, and given its reduced influence over the product under development, the PR's value from process number 3 (PR_{Pr3}) are small, with the contribution to the product risk, being even smaller, becoming almost neglectable, given the ω_{PRn} (relative importance), defined by the risk manager.

The process that will bring more threats to the NPD's manager is Pr5 (process number 5), due to its high risk's value, which is achieved through PrR_{Pr5}, and also, by its influence over Product Risk, being therefore expressed through the risk on the product from PR_{Pr5} (process number 5). This analysis, also allows to identify the process that has high risk, as well as the cause associated to it, with the purpose of studying new measures/actions to reduce the risk associated, even before the development of the process number 5. Through the results referred above, it can be possible to reorder the 5 process's, by prioritizing them, based on the risks related (PrR_{Prn}). The process with more risk is number. 5 (Pr5), followed by the processes Pr 3, Pr1, Pr 4 and Pr 2.

4 Conclusions of the Work

The aim of this work, was to develop an approach to evaluate the VE's product risk, in an OI context, not only by accounting the different risks related to each process domain of the VE's product, but also, by considering the possible influence regarding each process risk on the VE's overall risk through its different domains.

The obtained results, allows to show the influence that each process can have on each VE's domain, and therefore into its overall risk, being therefore an advantage, when compared to other methods, since it can assess the contribution (in terms of risk) of each process into to the VE's overall risk.

Furthermore, the approach developed in this work, allows the evaluation and prioritization of each process considered here, based on its risk. The method also provides information regarding the source of risk that contributes to the VE's overall risk, allowing therefore to identify the OI's partner that contributes more to the VE's overall risk.

Nevertheless, the deployment of FIS's to evaluate the several risks considered here, have reduced the ambiguity and uncertainty, related with risk analysis.

A future work should also analyze the risk concerning each individual activity associated to each process, by accounting the threats and the opportunities.

Acknowledgements. This work, was in part supported by IPL (Polytechnic Institute of Lisbon) through the IDI&CA (Projects for Research, Development, Innovation and Artistic Creation) context, on behalf of the research and development project ANEEC - Assessment of the level of business efficiency to increase competitiveness, IPL/2020/ANEEC_ISCAL. Partial support also from the Center of Technology and Systems – UNINOVA, and the FCT Foundation (project UIDB/00066/2020).

References

1. Mansor, N., Yahaya, S.N., Okazaki, K.: Risk factors affecting new product development (NPD). Int. J. Recent Res. Appl. Stud. **27**(1), 18–25 (2016)
2. Abreu, A., Martins, J.M., Calado, M.F.J.: A fuzzy reasoning approach to assess innovation risk in ecosystems. Open Eng. **8**, 551–561 (2018)
3. Coras, E.L., Tantau, A.D.: A risk mitigation model in SME's open innovation projects. Manag. Market. **8**(2) (2013)
4. Camarinha-Matos, L.M., Afsarmanesh, H.: A comprehensive modeling framework for collaborative networked organizations. J. Intell. Manuf. **5**(18), 529–542 (2007). https://doi.org/10.1007/s10845-007-0063-3
5. Rosas, J., Macedo, P., Tenera, A., Abreu, A., Urze, P.: Risk assessment in open innovation networks. In: Camarinha-Matos, L.M., Bénaben, F., Picard, W. (eds.) PRO-VE 2015. IAICT, vol. 463, pp. 27–38. Springer, Cham (2015). https://doi.org/10.1007/978-3-319-24141-8_3
6. Kim, Y., Vonortas, N.S.: Managing risk in the formative years: evidence from young enterprises in Europe. Technovation **8**(34), 454–465 (2014)
7. Song, W., Ming, X., Xu, Z.: Risk evaluation of customer integration in new product development under uncertainty. Comput. Ind. Eng. **3**, 402–412 (2013)

8. Xiaoren, Z., Ling, D., Xiangdong, C.: Interaction of open innovation and business ecosystem. Int. J. u e Serv. Sci. Technol. **1**(7), 51–64 (2014)
9. Rossi, B., Russo, B., Succi, G.: Adoption of free/libre open source software in public organizations: factors of impact. Inf. Technol. People **2**(25), 156–187 (2012)
10. Abreu, A., Martins, J., Calado, J.M.F.: Fuzzy logic model to support risk assessment in innovation ecosystems. In: 13th CONTROLO, Ponta Delgada, pp. 104–109 (2018)
11. Meyer, W.G.: Quantifying risk: measuring the invisible. Paper presented at PMI® Global Congress 2015 EMEA, London, England. Newtown Square, PMI (2015)
12. Grace, M.F., Leverty, J.T., Phillips, R.D., Shimpi, P.: The value of investing in enterprise risk management. J. Risk Insur. **2**(82), 289–316 (2015)

Collaboration in Supply Chain

Reshaping Supply Chain Collaboration - The Role of Digital Leadership in a Networked Organization

Marzena Frankowska[✉] and Andrzej Rzeczycki

University of Szczecin, Management Institute,
Cukrowa 8 Street, 71-004 Szczecin, Poland
marzena.frankowska@usz.edu.pl

Abstract. The article presents a case study of Bossard AG, which is an internationally active Swiss fastener technology and logistics company. The example of Bossard AG shows how, by seeking competitive advantage within existing manufacturing supply chains, the traditional meaning of relationships between supply chain participants is changing. In this new model, by simultaneously building a Collaborative Networked Organization and searching for digital competences in the supply chain, there appears a second leader, who is limited to the part of the supply chain for which they are responsible. This results in reshaping the entire supply chain collaboration.

Keywords: Supply chain collaboration · Digital leadership · Digital transformation · Supplier · Collaborative networked organization

1 Introduction

Nowadays, the economy is described as the VUCA world, which is characterized by volatility, uncertainty, complexity, and ambiguity of general conditions and business situations. In order to better understand the opportunities and risks today, organizations are encouraged to shift their focus from competitive rivalry to mutually beneficial relationships and cooperation [1, 2]. In this sense, the partners within supply chains are supported to align their strategy to be more responsive to the environment, and therefore remain competitive [3]. The growing complexity of relationships between chain partners transforms not only the chain's structure but also ways of cooperation. Thus, many researchers are working on developing the concept of a network-based view of supply chains [4, 5]. Networking has become one of the most important characteristics of the modern economy, which is also reflected in the perception of supply chains [1]. Furthermore, in recent years, there has been a significant increase in the number of appearing collaborative networks, which show either a continuous or temporary collaboration, as well as use information technologies to better respond to tougher market challenges [6]. Supply chain collaboration is one of the forms of Collaborative Networked Organization (CNO) [7]. An increase in the use of information technologies and the coordination of activities have been widely discussed by

© IFIP International Federation for Information Processing 2020
Published by Springer Nature Switzerland AG 2020
L. M. Camarinha-Matos et al. (Eds.): PRO-VE 2020, IFIP AICT 598, pp. 353–364, 2020.
https://doi.org/10.1007/978-3-030-62412-5_29

researchers as a means of overcoming the challenge of the complexity of Supply Chain Collaboration [8].

Nowadays, many supply chains are transforming from traditional, structured, and linear supply chains to an interconnected organization that can more readily incorporate ecosystem partners and evolve to react more flexibly [9]. Industry 4.0 concepts and technologies bring a new challenge for incumbent firms to anticipate and implement new business models, which are often offered by emerging actors in the digital ecosystem [10]. However, according to Andersson et al. [11], enhancing the competitive digital positioning of firms does not solely depend on technology nor its processes, but has a high component of leadership deployment.

These challenges affect supply chain collaboration in various areas. So far, both the structure of the supply chain and the prevailing relationships have been determined primarily by the focal company. The technological progress and globalization increase the impact of network and digital transformation on the ability to achieve competitive advantage in supply chains. This creates new opportunities for other supply chain members (suppliers, distributors, etc.) who can provide a new type of added value that is based on digital advantage. However, there arises the question of how this change will affect the structure of collaborative relations in the supply chain, particularly between the focal company and the partner company. As a result of literature analysis, research gaps were identified at the intersection of research on networking, digitization and leadership in supply chains. The indicated areas are characterized by high complexity and dynamics, and their recognition is at an early stage of research development. Therefore, the paper primarily focuses on revealing the multidimensional complexity that occurs under the conditions of supply chain operations understood as CNO. The research aims at assessing the role of digital leadership in supply chains, in the context of how it influences the supply chain collaboration relationship structure. The following research questions were formulated:

- Who is the leader in the supply chain operating as CNO?
- How does the arrangement of inter-organizational relations in the supply chain change as a result of the emergence of a digital leader?

In order to answer the questions, a theoretical review and empirical approach were combined. The research methods used were case study with direct observation, document analysis and testing of digital solutions functioning in the supply network. The empirical research is based on Bossard AG Company, which is a first-tier supplier in a manufacturing supply chain.

The paper is organized as follows. Section 2 presents the theoretical background on the different forms of leadership in supply chains and networks in the context of digital transformation. Section 3 provides the research methodology, as well as case analysis of a supplier that became the digital leader in a collaborative supply chain. In Sect. 4 there is presented a discussion on changing relationship patterns in supply chains. In the last section, the authors present conclusions and remarks.

2 Traditional, Collaborative and Digital Leadership in a Supply Chain

Considerable effort in research and practice is devoted to leadership development. The formal study of leadership, i.e. influencing one or more individuals towards achieving a shared goal, began 150 years ago [12]. Traditional leadership theories are based on the intra-organizational view stating that when someone is in charge, there is a supervisor-subordinate relationship [13]. This perception is quite typical, even for the most recent approaches that focus on cross-organizational leadership. It is assumed that in the supply chain structure, leadership is usually taken by the focal company [14]. Managers in supply chains have to collaborate, given the complex nature of cross-organizational, professional, and geographical environments. The literature suggests that the leadership of the core organization has a positive effect on maintaining the cross-sectoral cooperation as it has a positive impact on information sharing, joint decisions, relationship establishment and maintenance in the cooperative network [15]. It is described as integrative leadership, which applies to the core organization and its cooperative network that has no obvious direct administrative affiliation among enterprises. One sees leadership as part of a set of managerial capabilities at mainly individual, as well as organizational and inter-organizational (network) levels necessary for ensuring supply chain effectiveness and superior performance [8, 16]. From this perspective, it is not limited to coordination, collaboration, and integration alone, but also includes management and control of supply activities, whether it is within individual organizations, internal and external supply chains, or supply chain networks [17].

These characteristics do not fully correspond to the specifics of network collaboration. The traditional use of the terms 'leader' or 'leadership' is not appropriate in collaborative networks as there are no 'followers' or supervisor-subordinate relations within. Instead, there are equal horizontal relationships that are not focused on delivering system changes [13]. In the new approach, the conductor (orchestra leader) is put in opposition to the partner [18]. The difference between management and leadership of a networked organization consists of using the resources of member organizations that do not belong only to the leader [19]. Reconceptualization of the traditional leadership theories into the new leadership paradigm based on the Complexity Leadership Theory [20] directed the research on leadership in the networks. In this paper, network leadership is defined as a process of influencing one or more co-members of a collective to advance towards one or more shared goals [21]. It enables and enhances the emergent collective action that produces learning and adaptive outcomes [22].

There can be observed shifts from the importance of achieving tasks to the importance of being able to reach agreements, take the risks needed to build a new whole and make changes to existing systems [23]. Complexity Leadership Theory, with its focus on actors that interact in networks in ways that produce new patterns of behaviour or new modes of operating, lends itself well to the distributed model of leadership that values communicating with multiple modes through multiple networks [20].

Undoubtedly, this is a significant challenge for collaborative supply chains. Increasing the number of linkages through the distributed model of leadership increases the possibility of a multidimensional change [24]. As leadership in a collaborative network (supply chain) is based on communication and sharing knowledge between actors, it can be said that it is impossible without the use of IT-enabled tools and digital transformation. However, even the biggest organizations lack the power, knowledge, or capability to design or deploy end-to-end information integration through the supply network and manage it themselves [25]. This is the reason why companies collaborate under the concept of the Digital supply chain (DSC).

Nowadays, the context of leadership in collaborative networks became Industry 4.0 environment. Information integration introduces new systemic value elements. In today's connected world, it is not possible to achieve strategic success independently of the business ecosystem [26] and without IT-enabled tools. Enterprises and entire networks are gradually forming digital business ecosystem architecture which is a framework for designing requirements and functionalities for digital supply chain integration [27].

An enterprise that takes the leadership role in a CNO (supply network) must develop digital leadership, which can be described as the capability and capacity to manage the volatility, uncertainty, complexity, and ambiguity (VUCA) in order to create common and dynamic challenges in digital transformation (DT) [28, 29]. The combination of sophisticated connectivity and proficiency in composing with multiple modes promises to be a powerful tool for leadership [24]. However, studies of successful firms indicate that DT does not depend on technology adoption but the leadership mindset and its strategies [30]. The studies conducted among American management professionals prove that the keys to successful digital transformation are more concerned with strategy, culture and talent development than with technology issues [31, 32]. The effect of digital technology challenges requires leaders to proactively respond to the "new normal" [33], where new business environments require a new leadership paradigm that moves from egocentric towards altrocentric leadership [34]. Leadership in the digital era requires the exercise of influence rather than excessive force and power [16].

The above considerations lead to two conclusions. First, a focal company needs to become a digital leader to maintain leadership in its collaborative supply chain. Secondly, it is a very difficult task to perform, as it covers many aspects, which include, among others, developing and implementing a business strategy, business models, enterprise platform or corporate IT function [31]. Therefore, in the period of development of cloud computing, blockchain or IoT technologies and the growth of enterprise maturity, temporary solutions are sought to conduct DT, corresponding to the capabilities of the supply chain partners.

This creates new opportunities for collaboration in supply chains, which are a multi-stakeholder environment involving different needs, goals, and digital capabilities. So far, focal companies have been seen as hub organizations that lead the integration work, along with their main suppliers. Digital technology ecosystems are an open environment used to build and model interoperable system integration. It has been noticed that suppliers (small and medium enterprises) take digital leadership in business process integration. As a result, they can cooperate more and more often with core enterprises and actively create their role as a collaborative network integrator. Questions remain: how will this change the relationship in the supply chain between partners, what benefits will it bring, and will it not cause leadership problems?

3 Methodology and Research Results

The research aims at assessing the role of digital leadership in supply chains, in the context of how it influences the supply chain collaboration relationship structure. The main premise is the necessity to reveal multi-dimensional complexity that occurs under the conditions of supply chain operations, understood as Collaborative Networked Organization. Thus, the choice of research method must take into account high complexity and dynamics of the research area, which is located at the intersection of research on networking, digitization, and leadership in supply chains. Analysis of the literature proves that research in this area is still an initial stage.

The research methods used were case study with direct observation, document analysis and testing of digital solutions functioning in the supply network. According to Yin [35], a case study design should be considered when: (a) the focus of the study is to answer "how" and "why" questions; (b) one cannot manipulate the behaviour of those involved in the study; (c) one wants to cover contextual conditions because one believes they are relevant to the phenomenon under study; or (d) the boundaries are not clear between the phenomenon and context. Following Walsham [36], Siggelkow [37] and Yin [35], a "revelatory" case study founded on the interpretive paradigm has been conducted in Bossard AG company, which is a first-tier supplier in a manufacturing supply chain.

Bossard Group AG is a Swiss company (based in Zug), which was founded as a small hardware store in 1831. Currently, the company is still shaped by members of the founding family, but in the meantime, it has become a global corporation driven by a specific strategy for business development and digital leadership. The beginning of this intensive development took place in the 1950s, as a result of the growing industrial demand for high-quality nuts, bolts and screws. Along with the increase in sales, the company expanded its operations to other parts of Europe, raising additional funds through the Swiss stock exchange. In 1999, Bossard AG entered the Chinese market and opened offices for Bossard Industrial Fasteners International Trading (Shanghai) in several locations, and eventually also established itself on the North American market. At the same time, the company experienced a crisis in the competitiveness of fasteners in both new and current markets. This was the first impulse for reflection on the implementation of a new business strategy based on digital solutions.

Work on the digital transformation strategy in Bossard Group began in 2015. During this period, it was particularly important for the company not to neglect its operations and build on existing strengths while developing additional competences. Developing its digital competences, the company also began to provide engineering and logistics services related to the products delivered, as well as used social media in its operations. These activities are identified with business models for products and services that take advantage of both the physical and digital world as appropriate. The finally adopted and ongoing transformation strategy has been included in the three horizons model, where the company assumed the following goals: extend and defend the core business, build emerging businesses and create viable options [38].

The company has achieved global reach with 80 service locations, 41 warehouses and 14 application engineering laboratories around the world, employing 2,500 employees and becoming the leading supplier in the supply chain of fasteners, which helps manufacturing companies use technological progress in their favour.

The building of digital leadership at Bossard AG was based on a change in the product sales model. Currently, instead of selling fasteners, the company offers a digital solution (ARIMS platform as part of the Smart Factory Logistics solution) that allows improving the supply chain and, at the same time, provides warehouse and transport support for fasteners used by the core company within its production process (last mile management). The platform remains under the management of Bossard AG throughout the entire period of cooperation, the company's employees introduce new suppliers and set system parameters (e.g. in terms of re-ordering points or orders size). As a result, Bossard AG does not lose control over this part of the supply chain regardless of its increasing bargaining power.

The interactive ARIMS platform provides full control over material flow, order tracking, interactive inventory management and access to intelligent analysis. These features improve the predictability and efficiency of the supply chain. It also ensures transparency in terms of information about delivered parts at any time and place. ARIMS is based on a cloud solution with a user-friendly interface and intuitive functions. The digital platform is the foundation of the Bossard Smart Factory Logistics methodology. The ARIMS platform can be integrated with B2B ERP and enables M2M communication.

Bossard AG also offers its customers the Assembly Technology Expert service, under which it supports technical knowledge in the field of fasteners as part of fastener design tool containing engineering applications required by design engineers. Both Bossard AG digital solutions, Assembly Technology Expert and Smart Factory Logistics, allow in particular:

- consolidation of the supplier base, which eliminates discrepancies in the supplier base and fixed costs in the scope of ordering fasteners,
- increasing the quality and reliability of the product, processes and production safety, which translates into a smaller number of shortcomings and complaints, and the number of product recalls to rectify defects,
- globalizing manufacturing operations by introducing a strategic supplier that provides manufacturing sites with consistent global quality and reliable services at the local level,
- saving resources, including time through the use of lean methodology in production management, which allows reducing total production costs,
- providing faster delivery of products to the market ensuring competitive advantage,
- adapting the applied solutions to the client's needs, strengthening competitiveness and innovation,
- providing access to the latest technology and know-how in various fields, thanks to the support of experts in the field of design and logistics of fasteners.

As part of cooperation with clients, the company provides process design and optimization services that focus on increasing production efficiency and lowering the total cost of acquisition (TCO), using value stream analysis. The opportunity to reduce costs and simplify processes is the first impulse to join the Bossard digital strategy, followed by its expansion with the entire supply network. The first incentive to start cooperation is the possibility of using an online calculator estimating the potential profits from running a collaborative chain in the field of fasteners.

The next step in the strengthening position within supply chain collaboration is the currently strongly supported and exposed element of supplier consolidation. As part of this solution, Bossard AG incorporates its client's other suppliers into the digital platform by predefining delivery terms. In practice, the procedure boils down to four main steps:

1. Partially or fully automated intelligent Kanban systems monitor stock levels and trigger replenishment requests.
2. The ARIMS platform that works with them sends orders directly to suppliers or forwards them to ERP system.
3. Suppliers prepare ordered materials and mark individual batches of details with labels of their location.
4. According to predefined arrangements, ordered materials are consolidated into one shipment and delivered either to the dock or directly to the points of consumption.

The solution is an important step in the development of the company as a network integrator, in which the functions of the chain coordinator and cooperation architect are strongly exposed.

Bossard AG supports the digitization strategy with a high-quality product strategy in line with international standards, along with testing and confirmation processes for this quality. It has ten accredited Bossard research laboratories in Europe, America and Asia, thanks to which, together with their equipment for measuring and testing cutting edges, it guarantees reliable quality assurance and the quality of error-free production. This is an additional value that is transmitted along with digital competences, becoming a necessary condition for the success of the entire company strategy.

4   Discussion

The identified requirements for the transformation of digital business systems indicate that the basis for successful implementation of this process is the development of a business model, the use of an information platform, the introduction of business process standards in the field of supply chain connectivity and the introduction of an intermediary in the field of data transfer between actors [25, 31]. These conditions were specifically met by Bossard AG. The business model developed for product development with additional inventory management services and lean processes support was based on a digital platform. The new digital ecosystem uses cloud computing as the leading technology. As a consequence of the gradually introduced changes, Bossard AG achieved the fourth level of digital transformation, referred to as business network redesign [26, 39]. This required the introduction of new processes and combining them with existing ones that resulted in redesigning of the scope of the exchange between Bossard AG and its customers (manufacturing companies). The implemented solutions go beyond the organizational boundaries by leveraging information technology to transform the value activities with external stakeholders to improve firm and supply chain performance.

Bossard AG took over the role of the operator of the services provided, without transferring neither know-how nor control in the operation of the platform. Thus, despite being a supplier of B and C components, it allowed him to maintain the role of a digital leader in a relevant part of the supply chain.

Based on the analysis of the literature and the case of Bossard AG, the key elements in creating the role of a digital leader in supply chain collaboration can be considered:

- network based supply chain view (CNO),
- IT-enabled and digital transformation supporting communication efficiency and interoperable systems integration,
- leadership in implementation of IT-enabled solutions in the supply chain, understood as the ability and capacity to control the introduced solutions, and simultaneously to create a new structure of supply chain relationships.

These statements reveal the difference in supplier and focal company approach to supply chain collaboration within the digital ecosystem (Table 1).

Table 1. Approach to the supply chain collaboration in the perspective of focal company and supplier (Bossard)

	Focal company's perspective	Supplier's perspective
Context	Railway industry, automotive, others with dominant machining and assembly processes	
Supply chain specificity	Supply chains of final goods and type A elements	Supply chains of B and C elements
Collaborative networks	An extensive supplier base	Mainly binary relations with focal company Ultimately integration of the supplier base of the focal company
Digital transformation	Disjoined DT within the supply chain Partial solutions implemented at various levels by the focal company and supply chain partners	Business network redesign Digital platforms supporting supply management processes
Leadership	Focal company is a supply chain leader	The supplier is a digital leader Upstream supply chain integrator

Source: own elaboration.

When analysing the supplier's digital leadership, it can be seen that by responding to the needs of the focal company, the value chain is modified to some extent.

Interestingly, in this case, digital leadership does not mean collaborative leadership. From Bossard AG's perspective, it includes coordination, collaboration, integration, as well as management and control of supply activities, which proves the integrative approach. Therefore, the classic approach to leadership in the supply chain is revealed [17]. As already mentioned, even the biggest organizations lack the power, knowledge, or capability to design or deploy end-to-end information integration through the supply network and manage it themselves [25]. Thus, the focal company adopts the supplier's innovative digital solutions and accepts its leadership in a given part of the supply chain. The example of Bossard AG shows how, by seeking competitive advantage within existing supply chain, the traditional picture of collaborative relationships between supply chain members is changing (Fig. 1). In this approach, there is an interweaving of processes resulting from the desire to gain the advantage of cooperation and digital advantage in the supply chain. They manifest themselves in the form of networking the supply chain (CNO) and its digital transformation. As a result, a second leader in the supply chain appears. Its operation is limited to a specific part of the supply chain. However, thanks to his digital skills and solutions, the efficiency of the entire supply chain increases, which can be described as achieving a digital advantage.

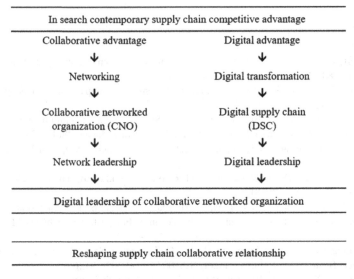

Fig. 1. Reshaping supply chain collaboration due to the construction of the CNO based on digital leadership. Source: own elaboration.

Questions remain, how many leaders can there be in the supply chain, and is there a risk of conflict as a result of a changed relationship structure in supply chain? In fact, in the traditional approach to leadership, there can be just one leader. Contemporary supply chains, on the other hand, are becoming a CNO with a different leadership approach. When looking for competitive advantage, they probably unknowingly implement a model called distributed leadership. It is surprising that the described example of Bossard AG indicates the adaptation of this model by several focal companies. According to the Complexity Leadership Theory, the CNO lends well to the distributed model of leadership, which focuses on actors that interact in networks in ways that produce new patterns of behaviour or new modes of operating [20]. This is a contribution to a better understanding of supply chain collaboration development. Due to the initial nature of the research, it is difficult to determine whether two leaders, i.e. the main leader (focal company) and digital leader (supplier) can be considered a hybrid and temporary solution, or whether the introduced leadership model will be widely used.

Attention should be paid to the limitations of the presented conclusions. This particularly applies to the scope of the study, which covered only one company. The fact is that Bossard AG, being a global supplier of B and C components, is successfully implementing digital leadership in supply chains. Nevertheless, further companies should be included in subsequent studies to deepen the research scope. Although only a single case study was analysed, it can be used for further elaboration of the model of building and maintaining relationships (including leadership) within the supply chain. It would be justified to use game theory as a tool to study the preferences and strengths of individual participants in the supply chain in building a new type of relationship.

References

1. Lambert, D.M., Cooper, M.C.: Issues in supply chain management. Ind. Mark. Manage. 29(1), 65–84 (2000)
2. Wisner, J.D., Tan, K.Ch.: Supply chain management and its impact on purchasing. J. Supply Chain Manag. 36(4), 33–42 (2000)
3. Tarifa-Fernandez, J., de Burgos-Jiménez, J.: Supply chain integration and performance relationship: a moderating effects review. Int. J. Logistics Manag. 28(4), 1243–1271 (2017)
4. Lee, P.D.: Measuring supply chain integration: a social network approach. Supply Chain Forum Int. J. 6(2), 58–67 (2005)
5. Frankowska, M.: Współdziałanie przedsiębiorstw w klastrowych łańcuchach dostaw. CeDeWu, Warszawa (2018)
6. Graça, P., Camarinha-Matos, L.M.: Performance indicators for collaborative business ecosystems—literature review and trends. Technol. Forecast. Soc. Chang. 116, 237–255 (2017)
7. Camarinha-Matos, L.M., Afsarmanesh, H.: Collaborative Networks: Reference Modeling. Springer, Boston (2008). https://doi.org/10.1007/978-0-387-79426-6
8. Cooper, S., Watson, D., Worrall, R.: Managing supply chain networks: a framework for achieving superior performance through leadership capabilities development in supply chain node. In: PMA International Conference 2016 Performance Measurement and Management: New Theories for New Practices, pp. 1–19. Edinburgh, Scotland (2016)
9. Mariani, J., Quasney, E., Raynor, M.E.: Forging links into loops: the Internet of Things' potential to recast supply chain management. Deloitte Rev. (17) (2015). http://dupress.com/articles/internet-of-things-supply-chain-management/
10. Gray, P., et al.: Realizing strategic value through center-edge digital transformation in consumer-centric industries. MIS Q. Executive 12(1), 115–117 (2013)

11. Andersson, P., Movin, S., Mähring, M., Teigland, R., Wennberg, K.: Managing Digital Transformation. SSE Institute for Research, Stockholm (2018)
12. Chen, I.J., Paulraj, A.: Towards a theory of supply chain management: the constructs and measurements. J. Oper. Manag. **22**, 119–150 (2004)
13. Myrna, P., Keast, R.A.: New look in collaborative networks: process catalysts. In: Raffel, J. A., Leisink, P., Middlebrooks, A.E. (eds.) Public Sector Leadership: International Challenges and Perspectives, pp. 163–176. Edward Elgar Publishing (2009)
14. Stock, J.R., Lambert, D.M.: Strategic Logistics Management. McGraw-Hill, Boston (2001)
15. Zhang, D., Sun, X., Liu, Y., Zhou, S., Zhang, H.: The effects of integrative leadership on the enterprise synergy innovation performance in a supply chain cooperative network. Sustainability **10**, 2342 (2018)
16. Bolden, R., Hawkins, B., Gosling, J., Taylor, S.: Exploring Leadership: Individual, Organizational and Societal Perspectives. Oxford University Press, Oxford (2011)
17. Marchese, K., Lam, B.: Supply chain leadership: distinctive approaches to innovation, collaboration and talent alignment. Deloitte, pp. 1–17 (2014)
18. Agranoff, R., McGuire, M.: Collaborative Public Management: New Strategies for Local Governments. Georgetown University Press (2003)
19. Frankowska, M.: The role of cluster manager as the third party action in strengthening cooperation of cluster companies. In: Mesquita, A., Silva, P. (eds.) Proceedings of the 15th European Conference on Management, Leadership and Governance ECMLG 2019, ACPI Reading, pp. 141–149 (2019)
20. Uhl-Bien, M., Marion, R., McKelvey, B.: Complexity Leadership Theory: Shifting Leadership From the Industrial Age to the Knowledge Era. Leadership Institute Faculty Publications (2007)
21. de Vreede, T., Steele, L., de Vreede, G.J., Briggs, R.: LeadLets: towards a pattern language for leadership development of human and AI agents. In: Proceedings of the 53rd Hawaii International Conference on System Sciences, pp. 683–693 (2020)
22. Schreiber, C., Carley, K.M.: Network leadership, leading for learning and adaptability. In: Uhl-Bien, M., Marion, R. (eds.) Complexity Leadership: Part 1: Conceptual Foundations, pp. 291–331. Information Age Publishing (2008)
23. Feyerherm, A.E.: Changing and converging mind-sets of participants during collaborative environmental rule-making: two negotiated regulation case studies. In: Research in Corporate Social Performance and Policy, Supplement 1, pp. 213–257. JAI Press, New York (1995)
24. Murray, J.: Complexity leadership and collective action in the age of networks. Coll. Engl. **79**(5), 512–525 (2017)
25. Korpela, K., Hallikas, J., Dahlberg, T.: Digital supply chain transformation toward blockchain integration. In: Proceedings of the 50th Hawaii International Conference on System Sciences, HICSS, pp. 4182–4192 (2017)
26. Iansiti, M., Levien, R.: Strategy as ecology. Harvard Bus. Rev. (2004)
27. Kagermann, H., Wahlster, W., Helbig, J. Recommendations for implementing the strategic initiative Industrie 4.0: final report of the Industrie 4.0. Working Group (2013)
28. Sasmoko, S., Mihardjo, L.W., Alamsjah, F., Elidjen, D.: Dynamic capability: the effect of digital leadership on fostering innovation capability based on market orientation. Manag. Sci. Lett. **9**, 1633–1644 (2019)
29. Zhu, W., Wang, Z.: The collaborative networks and thematic trends of research on purchasing and supply management for environmental sustainability: a bibliometric review. Sustainability **10**, 1510 (2018)
30. Bonch, M.: How to create an exponential mindset. Harvard Bus. Rev. (2016)

31. El Sawy, O.A., Amsinck, H., Kræmmergaard, P., Vinther, A.L.: How LEGO built the foundations and enterprise capabilities for digital leadership. MIS Q. Executive, 141–166 (2016)
32. Kane, G.C., Palmer, D., Phillips, A.N., Kiron, D.: Is your business ready for a digital future. MIT Sloan Manag. Rev. (2015)
33. Vogel, P., Hultin, G.: Digitalization and why leaders need to take it seriously. In: Thomson, P., Johnson, M., Devlin J.M. (eds.) Conquering Digital Overload, pp. 1–8. Palgrave Macmillan, Cham (2018)
34. Jakubik, M., Berazhny, I.: Rethinking leadership and its practices in the digital Era. In: Management International Conference, Monastier di Treviso, Venice, Italy (2017)
35. Yin, R.K: Case Study Research: Design & Methods. Sage Publications (2009)
36. Walsham, G.: Doing interpretive research. Eur. J. Inf. Syst. **15**, 320–330 (2006)
37. Siggelkow, N.: Persuasion with case studies. Acad. Manag. J. **50**(1), 20–24 (2007)
38. Michel, S.: Digital transformation or strategies for companies (2019). https://namics.com/en/topics-trends/top-topics/business-innovation/smart-business-day-2019-bossard
39. Ismail, M.H., Khater, M., Zaki, M.: Digital business transformation and strategy: what do we know so far? In: Cambridge Service Alliance Working Paper (2017)

Artificial Intelligence in Supply Chain Operations Planning: Collaboration and Digital Perspectives

María Ángeles Rodríguez, M. M. E. Alemany$^{(\boxtimes)}$, Andrés Boza, Llanos Cuenca, and Ángel Ortiz

Research Centre on Production Management and Engineering (CIGIP), Universitat Politècnica de València, Camino de Vera S/N, 46002 València, Spain
{marodsa4,mareva,aboza,llcuenca,aortiz}@cigip.upv.es

Abstract. Digital transformation provide supply chains (SCs) with extensive accurate data that should be combined with analytical techniques to improve their management. Among these techniques Artificial Intelligence (AI) has proved their suitability, memory and ability to manage uncertain and constantly changing information. Despite the fact that a number of AI literature reviews exist, no comprehensive review of reviews for the SC operations planning has yet been conducted. This paper aims to provide a comprehensive review of AI literature reviews in a structured manner to gain insights into their evolution in incorporating new ICTs and collaboration. Results show that hybridization man-machine and collaboration and ethical aspects are understudied.

Keywords: Artificial Intelligence · Supply Chain Operations Planning · Hybridization · Industry 4.0 · Big Data · Internet of Things · Blockchain

1 Introduction

The digital transformation has driven hyper-connected organizations. An example of this is Industry 4.0, which represents a concept of intelligent manufacturing networks in which machines and products interact with each other without human control. In this context, the new Information and Communication Technologies (ICT) allow obtaining precise data in real time [1]. This abundance of data together with the analytical capabilities of techniques such as Big Data Analytics (BDA), Artificial Intelligence (AI) or Operational Research (OR) allow combine multiple independent data analysis models, historical data repositories and real-time data flows, enabling a more intelligent management of supply chains (SCs) including smarter planning and operational decisions in the whole Supply Chain Management (SCM). There is a lack of consensus about the definition of SCM in the literature. Along these lines after a deeper literature review on this concept, [2] propose the following SCM definition: "*The management of a network of relationships within a firm and between interdependent organizations and business units consisting of material suppliers, purchasing, production facilities, logistics, marketing, and related systems that facilitate the forward and reverse flow of materials, services, finances and information from the original producer to final*

© IFIP International Federation for Information Processing 2020
Published by Springer Nature Switzerland AG 2020
L. M. Camarinha-Matos et al. (Eds.): PRO-VE 2020, IFIP AICT 598, pp. 365–378, 2020.
https://doi.org/10.1007/978-3-030-62412-5_30

customer with the benefits of adding value, maximizing profitability through efficiencies, and achieving customer satisfaction".

Since SCM requires the comprehension of complex and interrelated decision-making processes [3], their integration with the above technologies can improve their efficiency, sustainability, flexibility, agility, robustness and resilience. The SC operations planning is crucial for this. However, the increasing uncertainty and the dynamic environment make the synchronized planning necessary. Synchronized planning describes a state in which a constant flow of data from the supply network enables organizations to accurately plan production to match the actual demand. But this new paradigm of SC planning will require transforming data, facilitating real-time decision making using online data, automating decision making and making it smarter, not only for pre-programmed decisions but also with some learning capability. These necessary capabilities can be achieved using techniques that fall within the broad spectrum of AI [4].

Because of the increasing number of AI applications, the main objective of this paper is to conduct a comprehensive review of literature reviews: i.e. analyse in a structured manner previous reviews in the AI field applied to SC operations planning with the aim of discovering the focus of the analysis made and detecting gaps for future studies. Different reviews exist on the topic that either exclusively focus on SC planning or address a broader perspective of SCM dealing with SC planning jointly with other SC decision making processes. However, we have not found any review of reviews that is the scope of this paper and, even less, none review that consider all the structural dimensions of our analysis. These dimensions are defined with the aim of answering the following research questions (RQs):

– **RQ1**. What have been the interest for revising AI applied to SC operations planning over the past two decades and from which perspectives?
– **RQ2**. To what extent has the AI research addressed the SC operations planning alone or jointly with other SC processes taking into account some type of integration or collaboration?
– **RQ3**. What are the most studied AI methods alone or jointly with other techniques and new ICTs (hybridization)?
– **RQ4**. What are the main future research lines identified by existing literature reviews?

To answer these RQs, this paper has been organized as follows. The Sect. 2 describes relevant AI techniques for the purpose of this paper. In Sect. 3, the research methodology followed for the literature review is presented. In Sect. 4, the structural dimensions used for the review are described, meanwhile in Sect. 5 the material evaluation is made based on these structural dimensions. Finally, in Sect. 6 the conclusions and suggestions for future reviews are made.

2 Artificial Intelligence (AI)

There is no commonly accepted definition of AI [5]. In 1956, the father of AI, Dr. Marvin L. Minsky, defined it as *"the science of making machines do things that would require intelligence if done by men"* [6], emphasizing that machines would have reasoning processes like humans. In 1982, the father of Expert Systems Dr. Edward Feigenbaum described AI as *"AI is the part of computer science concerned with designing intelligent computer systems, that is, systems that exhibit the characteristics one associate with intelligence in human behavior"* [7], concretizing the field of science that must be dedicated to developed it, the computer science. Nowadays, the High-Level Expert Group on Artificial Intelligence by European Commission proposes this updated definition: *"AI refers to systems that display intelligent behaviors by analyzing their environment and taking actions – with some degree of autonomy – to achieve specific goals"* [8]. This improved definition adds new components such as the analysis of the environment and the action on it, no longer considers it an isolated system, now it must interact with its environment.

In the AI history, there have been different periods known as "AI winter" and "AI summer" characterized by low and high investment periods in the research field, respectively [9]. The first winter was in the 1970s for the failure with the speech recognition research program, and few years after, in 1980s, the AI summer arrived with the commercialization of expert systems (ES). But in 1984, the ES had many issues and were heavily criticized, and the investment fall down [10]. This is known as the second winter. In late 1990s became a new summer, by IBM's Deep Blue system, which beat the actual chess world champion. Finally, after 2010s the arrival of new technologies like Industry 4.0 drive to an explosive growth that has reached the present day [11]. Since the beginning of AI in 1956, researchers from many disciplines contributed to build this field of knowledge. For this reason, AI must be understood from a multidisciplinary perspective. This has originated some ambiguity in the definition of different AI branches depending on their development discipline creating some confusion due to the lack of consensus. In this context and for the purpose of this paper, the most relevant branches considered are the following:

- *Expert Systems (ES)* contains techniques that simulate knowledge of decision-making human to solve complex problems.
- *Machine Learning (ML)* is based on techniques that learn from the input data. Several types of learning can be distinguished [12]: Supervised Learning, when both input and output data are known; Unsupervised Learning, when only the input data is known; and Reinforcement Learning, when learn from the output data whether it has been a success or a failure.
- *Multi-Agent Systems (MAS)* use a multiple interact intelligent agents. An intelligent agent perceives its environment and acts.
- *Neural Networks (NN)* comprises techniques composed of processing elements or neurons that solve problems together.
- *Fuzzy Logic and Fuzzy Sets (FL/FS)* are based on techniques that deals with imprecise, vague or partial information.

- *Metaheuristics (MH)* comprise techniques to solve hard optimization problems where the value of certain decision variables should be found in order to optimize one or several objectives subject to different constraints.

In situations of large volumes of data provided by new ICTs, AI techniques provide capabilities for [4]:

- *Integrate and Transform Data*: ML can help create value by providing companies with intelligent analysis of big data and capturing structured interpretations of the wide variety of increasingly available unstructured data.
- *Automate decision making*: create a set of intelligent decision making models to collect accurate data; solve the models quickly; and evaluate the results.
- *Real-time decision-making:* ES increase the probability of making right real-time and low-cost decisions at the expert level by non-experts.
- *Learning capability*. AI goes one step further, not only applying pre-programmed decisions, but exhibiting some learning capabilities.

[13] show that the new generation of AI simulates, extends and reinforces human intelligence: AI replaces the need for people to analyze, judge, optimize and make decisions through autonomous perception, autonomous learning, autonomous thinking and intelligent behavior. They identify a new generation of AI originated by the irruption of new technologies they call, **AI 2.0** which includes ML, Natural Processing Learning (NPL), Big Data, Cloud Computing, IoT, etc. Next sections try to find out the application of AI techniques to SC operations planning in the era of digital transformation analysing existing reviews on the topic.

3 Research Methodology

The literature review (LR) is recognized as a valid approach and a necessary step in exploring new research directions guiding the research toward new theoretical development. During this LR, the four-step process proposed by [14] was adopted:

1. *Material collection*: The first step was to define the research scope in which to search for material: in this case, AI applied to the SC operations planning. Since several papers were found dealing with this decision-making process jointly with others in the SC or manufacturing context, they will be also included. The search process was carried out by using the search engine of Web of Knowledge. Publication search was conducted in terms of structured combination of the key words in title, abstract and keywords: ("artificial intelligence" OR "expert system" OR "machine learning" OR "agent" OR "neural networks" OR "fuzzy" OR "meta-heuristics") AND ("review" OR "survey" OR "revision" OR "report" OR "study" OR "state of the art" OR "conceptual framework" OR "conceptual model") AND ("production planning" OR "operations planning" OR "aggregate planning" OR

"tactical planning" OR "master planning" OR "operative planning" OR "network planning" OR "process planning" OR "supply chain management" OR "supply chain processes" OR "supply chain planning" OR "production sequencing" OR "production scheduling" OR "scheduling" OR "timing" OR "planning"). Since one of the main objectives is to analyse the impact of new ICTs on the AI application to SC operations planning, the search was limited to the last two decades. A total of 135 references were found.

2. *Descriptive analysis*: formal aspects of the material were assessed. During the material revision, some references were discarded and other were found of interest and added to our LR. A total of 29 references were finally selected for our LR.

3. *Category selection*: the structural dimensions for analysing the collected material were defined to answer our RQs (see Sect. 4).

4. *Material evaluation*: the material was analysed according to the structural dimensions in Sect. 5. Finally, the identification of relevant issues and the interpretation of the results was performed.

4   Category Selection: Structural Dimensions for the LR Analysis

A final total of 29 publications were considered to fit in our scope. In order to answer the four RQs, the selected papers were systematically analysed based on these structural dimensions: 1) *Year of publication* for identifying research trends over time; 2) *LR Dimensions* being the structural dimensions of previous reviews when analysing papers; 3) *SC decision making processes* addressed and 4) their *decision level* in the strategic, tactical and operational hierarchy; 5) *Collaboration/Integration* to identify if existing LR consider the spatial integration (along the SC members) and/or temporal integration (along the different decision levels); 6) *AI techniques* considered; 7) *Hybridization*: other technologies/techniques addressed in the context of digital transformation, 8) *Sectors* contemplated and 9) LR *Future Research Lines*.

5   Material Evaluation: LR Analysis

To answer the "**RQ1**. *What have been the interest for revising AI applied to SC operations planning over the past two decades and from which perspectives?*" the *Year of publication* (Fig. 1) and the *LR Dimensions* employed to review the literature (Table 1) are analyzed. As can be observed in Fig. 1, the number of LR is uneven over the years, with a clear increase in the last two years which means an increasing interest of researchers focusing on reviewing papers in this area.

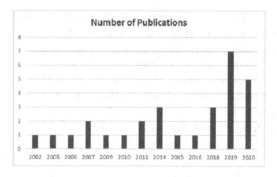

Fig. 1. Number of publications per year on AI applied to SC operations planning.

The most common *LR Dimensions* used to analyse research works (Table 1) are the problem scope (**PS**) (decision-making processes) and/or application area (specific problem to be solved) (65,5%).

Table 1. *Year* and *LR dimensions* used for revising the specific papers on AI applications to SC

Ref	Year	DL	PS	PC	SCS	AIT	AITD	I/C	DS	TE	CO	P/MC
[15]	2002		X			X						
[16]	2005	X						X				
[17]	2006		X			X						
[18]	2007		X			X						
[19]	2007					X	X		X			
[20]	2009		X									
[3]	2010	X	X			X						X
[21]	2011		X			X						
[22]	2011		X			X						
[23]	2014					X	X					
[24]	2014		X			X						
[25]	2014				X							X
[26]	2015		X			X						
[27]	2016		X									
[28]	2018		X					X				
[29]	2018		X				X				X	X
[30]	2018											
[31]	2019		X									
[32]	2019					X			X	X	X	
[33]	2019			X					X			
[34]	2019		X			X						
[35]	2019		X									
[36]	2019				X	X						

(*continued*)

Table 1. (*continued*)

Ref	Year	DL	PS	PC	SCS	AIT	AITD	I/C	DS	TE	CO	P/MC
[37]	2019		X		X							X
[38]	2020		X		X							
[39]	2020			X	X							
[40]	2020		X		X	X		X	X			
[41]	2020		X									X
[42]	2020											
(%)		6,9	65,5	6,9	6,9	58,6	13,8	6,9	10,3	10,3	6,9	17,2

Ref: Reference, **DL:** Decision level, **PS:** Problem scope and/or application area, **PC:** Problem characteristics, **SCS:** SC stages, **AIT:** AI techniques, **AITD:** AI techniques details, **I/C:** Integration/Collaboration, **DS:** Data source, **ICT:** Information and Communication Technologies, **CO:** Country, **P/MC:** Purpose/Main contributions.

It is followed by the AI techniques employed (**AIT**) (58,6%) and specific details on them (**AITD**) (13.8%) such as agent architectures and communication, information model, selection of techniques parameters or attributes and validity methods. Then, the data source (**DS**) used by the AI techniques (10,3%) as regards how the data has been generated (specialist's judgments, based on other studies, case study, historical, simulated, etc.) or its source (management, equipment data, user, product, public or artificial data). In the LRs found, very little attention has been paid to aspects such as the AI application techniques to specific decision level (**DL**) of the hierarchy (strategic, tactical and operational), the number of SC stages covered (**SCS**), the problem characteristics (**PC**) addressed, for instance, related to the structural degree (structural, semi-structural, non-structural) and the environment (deterministic, uncertain, risk). It should be noted that despite the rise of new technologies (**ICT**), not very much attention has been paid to their connection with the AI (10,3%) when revising existing applications. It is worth noting, the even greater scarcity of LRs (6.9%) that analyse papers with AI applications from a collaborative point of view (**I/C**) so important for the SC.

The answer to "*RQ2. To what extent has the AI research addressed the SC operations planning alone or jointly with other SC processes taking into account some type of integration or collaboration?*" can be found by observing the Table 2. Five papers (shaded in grey) have exclusively focused on SC operations planning, 86% on tactical level and 93% on operational level. Many of them include additional SC decision processes and strategic levels. The majority of LR do not focus on specific sectors (**GE**) (62%). The rest have addressed specific sectors such as the fashion and apparel and the mechanical manufacturing (**SP**). Although only two papers (6,9%) has used the integration/collaboration as a dimension for the literature analysis (Table 1), five papers (17%) have reflected on it (**I/C**) (Table 2): more specifically in the integration of tasks at different decision levels [16, 17], enterprise integration [17, 19] e-synchronised SCM [3] and SC collaboration [28].

To answer the "*RQ3. What are the most studied AI methods alone or jointly with other techniques or new ICTs (hybridization)?*" it is necessary to deepen in the study of the Table 3. As can be observed, the most covered AI techniques by the LRs are those

Table 2. SC decision making processes, their decision level and the integration level

Ref	SC Decision-Making Process	Decis Level			IC	Sectors	
		S	T	O		SP	GE
[15]	Scheduling, Process design, Maintenance & repair, Process Select., Facility Layout, Material Select., PP&C, Capacity Planning, Facility Location, Project Management, Tool & Data Selection, Quality Control, Forecasting, Storeroom design, Vendor selection	X	X	X			X
[16]	Low -level (data acquisition, reconciliation, regulatory control), Mid-level (fault detection & diagnosis, supervisory control), High-level tasks (PP&C)			**X**	X	PI	
[17]	Intelligent Manufacturing		**X**	**X**	X		X
[18]	Design, scheduling, Process planning & control, Quality, Maintenance & Fault diagnosis	X	X	X		MM	
[19]	Manufacturing scheduling, Manufacturing control, Enterprise integration, SCM & Process planning	X	X	X	X		X
[20]	Design engineering, Process planning, Assembly line balancing, & Dynamic scheduling.	X	X	X			
[3]	Design, Schedul, PP&C, Quality, Maint & fault diagnosis	X	X	X	X		X
[21]	Operations Management	X	X	X			X
[22]	Apparel design, manufacturing, retailing, and SCM	X	X	X		F&A	
[23]	Manufacturing scheduling			**X**			X
[24]	Design of dedicated & reconfigurable manuf. systems	X					X
[25]	Textile prod., Apparel manufac., Distribution/sales		X	X		F&A	
[26]	General		X	X			X
[27]	Well Planning, Drilling Optimization, Well integrity, Operat. Troubleshooting, Drilling problem detection	X	X	X		DS	
[28]	Inventory Control & Planning, Transportation Network Design, Purchasing & Supply Management, Demand Planning & Forecasting, Order Picking Problems, Customer relationship management, e-synchronised SCM	X	X	X	X		X
[29]	Planning, implementing & controlling		**X**	**X**			X
[30]	Production Management	X	X	X			
[31]	Industrial prognosis	X	X	X			X
[32]	Demand/sales, procurement & supply management, production, inventory & storage, transportation & distribution, SC improvement	X	X	X			X
[33]	Process synthesis & design, PP&C	X	X	X			X
[34]	Exploration & Production operations, drilling and completion, stimulation treatment	X	X	X			
[35]	Wholesaling and retailing in SC		X	X			X
[36]	Design, fabric production, apparel product., & distribution	X	X	X		F&A	
[37]	Manufacturing Planning, Part Variety, Process Planning, Machining, Tool Selection, Welding, Tool Design, Product Development	X	X	X		MM	
[38]	Planning & operations decisions		**X**	**X**		FT	
[39]	Supplier Selection	X					X
[40]	Smart Maintenance, Quality Control, Process Control & Monitoring, Inventory and Distribution Control, Smart Planning & Scheduling, Smart Design of Products and Processes, Time estimation	X	X	X			X
[41]	Marketing, Distributed management, Decision making, Prediction, Efficiency, Security, Classification	X	X	X			X
[42]	Business Management		X	X			X
	Total (%)	69	86	93	17	38	62

S: Strategic, **T**:Tactical, **O**:Operat, **I/C**:Integrat/Collaborat, **SP**:Specific, **GE**:General, **PI**:Process Industries, **MM**:Mechanical Manufacturing, **F&A**:Fashion & Apparel, **DS**:Drilling Sector, **FT**:Freight Transportation,

Table 3. AI Techniques and their hybridization with other Techniques & Technologies

Ref	AI Branches						Hybridization: Techniques & Technologies						
	ES	ML	MAS	NN	FL/FS	MH	OR	BD	IoT	BC	RFID	EC & CC	I4.0
[15]	X						X						
[16]	X		X										
[17]			X										
[18]	X	X		X	X	X	X						
[19]		X											
[20]	X	X	X	X	X	X	X						
[3]	X	X	X	X	X	X							
[21]	X	X		X	X	X							
[22]	X	X	X	X	X	X							
[23]	X	X		X	X	X							
[24]				X	X		X						
[25]	X	X		X	X	X							
[26]	X		X	X	X								
[27]	X	X		X	X	X							
[28]			X										
[29]		X			X		X						
[30]	X	X	X	X	X	X		X					
[31]	X	X		X	X		X					X	X
[32]		X		X									
[33]		X		X			X						
[34]					X		X						
[35]													
[36]	X	X	X	X	X	X		X					
[37]	X												
[38]		X		X			X						
[39]	X	X	X	X			X	X					
[40]		X		X							X		X
[41]		X		X	X				X	X		X	
[42]		X		X	X	X		X					
Total (%)	55,2	65,5	34,5	72,4	58,6	41,4	31,1	10,3	6,9	3,4	3,4	6,9	6,9

Ref: Reference, **ES**: Expert Systems, **ML**: Machine Learning, **MAS**: Multi-Agent Systems, **NN**: Neural Networks, **FL/FS**: Fuzzy Logic/Fuzzy Sets, **MH**: Metaheuristics, **OR**: Operational Research, **BD**: Big Data, **IoT**: Internet of Things, **BC**: Blockchain, **RFID**: Radio Frequency Identification, **EC&CC**: Edge Computing and Cloud Computing, **I4.0**: Industry 4.0.

belonging to the Neural Network (**NN**) (72,4%) and Machine Learning (**ML**) (65,5%), followed by Fuzzy Logic/Fuzzy Sets (**FL/FS**) (58,6%), Expert Systems (**ES**) (55,2%) and Metaheuristics (**MH**) (41,4%), being the least reviewed Multi-Agent Systems (**MAS**) (34,5%). The rise of Big Data in the context of Industry 4.0 which uses ML and NN Algorithms to build models to analyse the data can explain the above figures. Artificial NN has the advantage also of execution speed, once the network has been trained with data sets, rather than having to write programs, becoming more cost effective and convenient in a dynamic environment. As regards the hybridization of AI tools, the majority considers the combination with more traditional techniques such as Operational Research (**OR**) (31.1%). It is noteworthy that despite the growing interest in new technologies, AI literature reviews have not analysed in depth the integration of AI techniques with them: only 10.3% have studied it in a Big Data (**BD**) context, 6.9% with **IoT**, 3.4% with Blockchain (**BC**), 3.4% with **RFID**, 6,9% with Edge Computing and Cloud Computing (**EC&CC**) and 6,9% with **I4.0**. Therefore, it is necessary to incorporate this new dimension in the analysis of IA techniques applied to SC operations planning.

Finally, with the aim of answering the "*RQ4. What are the main future research lines identified by existing literature reviews?*" we have carefully analysed the future research lines and grouped them into seven main blocks (Fig. 2). It can be observed that nearly one third of the papers (31,03%) identify the **hybridization** as one of the main future research areas. This hybridization includes mostly approaches taking advantage of the strengths of the different AI techniques, with other classical methods like operations research and less on integration in software packages.

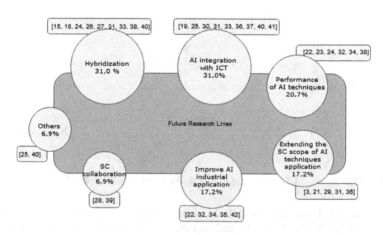

Fig. 2. Future research lines identified in the LR revised

Also, the 31,03% of papers, being relatively recent, highlighted the necessity of **integrating AI with other technologies** such as RFID, mobile computing, IoT, Blockchain, Big Data for data-driven optimization and on-line learning for reducing uncertainty. More specifically, in the field of SC operations planning, different authors point out the necessity of new models that are capable of representing a more cyber-centric Production Environment [30]; integrating their business with cloud-based technologies like Microsoft Azure, Amazon web services, IBM Watson, etc., and parallel computing tools for big data analytics like Hadoop and Hive [36]; the fusion of KBS into web environment can ensure the benefits of KBS to the remote environment [37], to reinforce the role of IoT in ML-PPC [40] and to address challenges to combine Blockchain and AI such as scalability, lack of standards, issues in consensus protocols [41].

The 20.69% of the publications devise as future research directions the study of the **performance of** different **AI techniques** and its comparison among different AI methods in order to justify the choice of some parameters and/or an algorithm rather than another for a given problem or data set, ensuring more objectivity, variety and robustness. The 17.24% identify as new research lines **extending the SC scope of AI Techniques** applied in **some SC problems to other ones**. Also, the 17.24% of the papers pointed out the necessity of **improving AI industrial application in SCM:** the oversimplification of decision-making problems hinders their application in industrial practice.

Although **SC collaboration** is recognized as one pillar of improving SC performance, only two papers that represent the 10.34% of the total address collaboration as a future research line: collaboration dynamics by using Agents, [28], group and negotiation process [39]. Other research lines (6,89%) include to seek the use AI technologies to enhance their efforts to 'go green' [25]; improve the integration between the PPC, logistics, design and the customer and set human interaction and environmental aspect as priorities to ensure the development of ethical manufacturing in I4.0 [40].

6   Conclusions and Suggestions for Future Reviews

Based on the analysis of the previous sections, we propose in the following some guidelines for future literature reviews and AI applications in SC itself. In this regard, more attention should be paid on the following aspects in order to detect potential gaps and boost the real applicability of AI in SC. The temporal integration across decision levels (i.e. tactical and operational plans) and on the spatial integration/collaboration (i.e. across different plans of SC stages and/or stakeholders) requires more attention specially in a real-time environment. The connection between AI and ICT should be better analyzed by future literature reviews in the specific papers in order to identify gaps and increase the use of AI in the context of Industry 4.0.

To improve AI industrial applications, it will be helpful for practitioners more literature reviews focused on specific sectors instead of addressing them in a general way. Besides, although all the literature reviews focus on the different AI techniques applied, the objectives pursued by them are not analyzed, even less from the SC sustainable point of view (economical, environmental and social). To focus on these aspects can support a better assessment of the improvements achieved by the AI implementation on these three different dimensions.

For the social dimension of sustainability, it is very important that future AI techniques and LRs incorporate the hybridization (networks consisting of organizations, people, machines and intelligent systems), collaboration between humans and intelligent autonomous systems with the ethical aspects in order to design and implement responsible AI systems. To achieve this, next AI projects are encouraged to report the way in which they have achieved the FAST Track Principles [43]: Fairness, Accountability, Sustainability, and Transparency.

Finally, the role of the AI systems in pandemic situations such as COVID-19 are fundamental to provide robust and resilient SC models [44]. Besides to assess the robustness of existing or future SC plans against these type outbreaks and the risk propagation should require to combine AI with simulation. This shows the necessity of including simulation techniques in the AI hybridization.

Acknowledgments. This research has been funded by the project entitled NIOTOME (Ref. RTI2018-102020-B-I00) (MCI/AEI/FEDER, UE). The first author was supported by the Generalitat Valenciana (Conselleria de Educación, Investigación, Cultura y Deporte) under Grant ACIF/2019/021.

References

1. Lezoche, M., Hernandez, J.E., del Mar, M., Díaz, E.A., Panetto, H., Kacprzyk, J.: Agri-food 4.0: a survey of the supply chains and technologies for the future agriculture. Comput. Ind. **117**, 103–187 (2020)
2. Stock, J.R., Boyer, S.L.: Developing a consensus definition of supply chain management: a qualitative study. Int. J. Phys. Distrib. Logistics Manag. **39**(8), 690–711 (2009)
3. Min, H.: Artificial intelligence in supply chain management: theory and applications. Int. J. Logistics Res. Appl. **13**(1), 13–39 (2010). https://doi.org/10.1080/13675560902736537
4. Hariri, R.H., Fredericks, E.M., Bowers, K.M.: Uncertainty in big data analytics: survey, opportunities, and challenges. J. Big Data **6**(1), 1–16 (2019). https://doi.org/10.1186/s40537-019-0206-3
5. Duan, Y., Edwards, J.S., Dwivedi, Y.K.: Artificial intelligence for decision making in the era of Big Data – evolution, challenges and research agenda. Int. J. Inf. Manage. **48**(2019), 63–71 (2019). https://doi.org/10.1016/j.ijinfomgt.2019.01.021
6. McCarthy, J., Minsky, M.L., Rochester, N., Shannon, C.E.: A proposal for the dartmouth summer research project on artificial intelligence. AI Mag. **27**(4), 12–14 (2006)
7. Barr, A., Feigenbaum, E.A.: The Handbook of Artificial Intelligence, vol. 2. Heuristech: William Kaufmann, Pitman (1982)
8. High-Level Expert Group on Artificial Intelligence, European Commission. A definition of AI: main capabilities and disciplines (2019)
9. Cioffi, R., Travaglioni, M., Piscitelli, G., Petrillo, A., De Felice, F.: Artificial intelligence and machine learning applications in smart production: progress, trends, and directions. Sustainability (Switzerland) **12**(2) (2020). https://doi.org/10.3390/su12020492
10. Cheng, L., Yu, T.: A new generation of AI: a review and perspective on machine learning technologies applied to smart energy and electric power systems. Int. J. Energy Res. **43**(6), 1928–1973 (2019). https://doi.org/10.1002/er.4333
11. Duan, Y., Edwards, J.S., Dwivedi, Y.K.: Artificial intelligence for decision-making in the era of big data. Evolution, challenges and research agenda. Int. J. Inf. Manag. **48**, 63–71 (2019)
12. Varshney, S., Jigyasu, R., Sharma, A., Mathew, L.: Review of various artificial intelligence techniques and its applications. IOP Conf. Ser. Mater. Sci. Eng. **594**(1) (2019)

13. Cheng, L., Yu, T.: A new generation of AI: a review and perspective on machine learning technologies applied to smart energy and electric power systems. Int. J. Energy Res. **43**, 1928–1973 (2019)

14. Seuring, S., Müller, M.: From a literature review to a conceptual framework for sustainable supply chain management. J. Clean. Prod. **16**(15), 1699–1710 (2008). https://doi.org/10.1016/j.jclepro.2008.04.020

15. Metaxiotis, K.S., Askounis, D., Psarras, J.: Expert Systems In Production Planning And Scheduling: A State-Of-The-Art Survey. J. Intell. Manuf. **13**(4), 253–260 (2002). https://doi.org/10.1023/A:1016064126976

16. Power, Y., Bahri, P.A.: Integration techniques in intelligent operational management: a review. Knowl. Based Syst. **18**(2–3), 89–97 (2005). https://doi.org/10.1016/j.knosys.2004.04.009

17. Shen, W., Hao, Q., Yoon, H.J., Norrie, D.H.: Applications of agent-based systems in intelligent manufacturing: an updated review. Adv. Eng. Inform. **20**(4), 415–431 (2006). https://doi.org/10.1016/j.aei.2006.05.004

18. Kobbacy, K.A.H., Vadera, S., Rasmy, M.H.: AI and OR in management of operations: history and trends. J. Oper. Res. Soc. **58**(1), 10–28 (2007). https://doi.org/10.1057/palgrave.jors.2602132

19. Zhang, W.J., Xie, S.Q.: Agent technology for collaborative process planning: a review. Int. J. Adv. Manuf. Technol. **32**(3), 315–325 (2007). https://doi.org/10.1007/s00170-005-0345-x

20. Ibáñez, O., Cordón, O., Damas, S., Magdalena, L.: A review on the application of hybrid artificial intelligence systems to optimization problems in operations management. In: Corchado, E., Wu, X., Oja, E., Herrero, Á., Baruque, B. (eds.) HAIS 2009. LNCS (LNAI), vol. 5572, pp. 360–367. Springer, Heidelberg (2009). https://doi.org/10.1007/978-3-642-02319-4_43

21. Kobbacy, K.A.H., Vadera, S.: A survey of AI in operations management from 2005 to 2009. J. Manuf. Technol. Manag. **22**(6), 706–733 (2011). https://doi.org/10.1108/17410381111149602

22. Guo, Z.X., Wong, W.K., Leung, S.Y.S., Li, M.: Applications of artificial intelligence in the apparel industry: a review. Text. Res. J. **81**(18), 1871–1892 (2011). https://doi.org/10.1177/0040517511411968

23. Priore, P., Gómez, A., Pino, R., Rosillo, R.: Dynamic scheduling of manufacturing systems using machine learning: an updated review. Artif. Intell. Eng. Des. Anal. Manuf. AIEDAM **28**(1), 83–97 (2014). https://doi.org/10.1017/S0890060413000516

24. Renzi, C., Leali, F., Cavazzuti, M., Andrisano, A.: A review on artificial intelligence applications to the optimal design of dedicated and reconfigurable manufacturing systems. Int. J. Adv. Manuf. Technol. **72**(1–4), 403–418 (2014). https://doi.org/10.1007/s00170-014-5674-1

25. Ngai, E.W.T., Peng, S., Alexander, P., Moon, K.K.L.: Decision support and intelligent systems in the textile and apparel supply chain: an academic review of research articles. Expert Syst. Appl. **41**(1), 81–91 (2014). https://doi.org/10.1016/j.eswa.2013.07.013

26. Rooh, U.A., Li, A., Ali, M.M.: Fuzzy, neural network and expert systems methodologies and applications - a review. J. Mob. Multimedia **11**, 157–176 (2015)

27. Bello, O., Teodoriu, C., Yaqoob, T., Oppelt, J., Holzmann, J., Obiwanne, A.: Application of artificial intelligence techniques in drilling system design and operations: a state of the art review and future research pathways. In: Society of Petroleum Engineers - SPE Nigeria Annual International Conference and Exhibition (2016)

28. Arvitrida, N.I.: A review of agent-based modeling approach in the supply chain collaboration context. IOP Conf. Ser. Mater. Sci. Eng. **337**(1) (2018). https://doi.org/10.1088/1757-899x/337/1/012015

29. Zanon, L.G., Carpinetti, L.C.R.: Fuzzy cognitive maps and grey systems theory in the supply chain management context: a literature review and a research proposal. In: IEEE International Conference on Fuzzy Systems, July 2018, pp. 1–8 (2018). https://doi.org/10.1109/fuzz-ieee.2018.8491473

30. Burggräf, P., Wagner, J., Koke, B.: Artificial intelligence in production management: a review of the current state of affairs and research trends in academia. In: 2018 International Conference on Information Management and Processing, ICIMP 2018, January 2018, pp. 82–88 (2018). https://doi.org/10.1109/icimp1.2018.8325846

31. Diez-Olivan, A., Del Ser, J., Galar, D., Sierra, B.: Data fusion and machine learning for industrial prognosis: trends and perspectives towards Industry 4.0. Inf. Fusion 50, 92–111 (2019). https://doi.org/10.1016/j.inffus.2018.10.005

32. Ni, D., Xiao, Z., Lim, M.K.: A systematic review of the research trends of machine learning in supply chain management. Int. J. Mach. Learn. Cybernet. 11(7), 1463–1482 (2019). https://doi.org/10.1007/s13042-019-01050-0

33. Ning, C., You, F.: Optimization under uncertainty in the era of big data and deep learning: when machine learning meets mathematical programming. Comput. Chem. Eng. 125, 434–448 (2019). https://doi.org/10.1016/j.compchemeng.2019.03.034

34. Okwu, M.O., Nwachukwu, A.N.: A review of fuzzy logic applications in petroleum exploration, production and distribution operations. J. Petrol. Explor. Prod. Technol. 9(2), 1555–1568 (2018). https://doi.org/10.1007/s13202-018-0560-2

35. Weber, F.D., Schütte, R.: State-of-the-art and adoption of artificial intelligence in retailing. Digit. Policy Regul. Gov. 21(3), 264–279 (2019). https://doi.org/10.1108/DPRG-09-2018-0050

36. Giri, C., Jain, S., Zeng, X., Bruniaux, P.: A detailed review of artificial intelligence applied in the fashion and apparel industry. IEEE Access 7, 95376–95396 (2019). https://doi.org/10.1109/ACCESS.2019.2928979

37. Leo Kumar, S.P.: Knowledge-based expert system in manufacturing planning: State-of-the-art review. Int. J. Prod. Res. 57(15–16), 4766–4790 (2019). https://doi.org/10.1080/00207543.2018.1424372

38. Barua, L., Zou, B., Zhou, Y.: Machine learning for international freight transportation management: a comprehensive review. Res. Transp. Bus. Manag. (2020). https://doi.org/10.1016/j.rtbm.2020.100453

39. Chai, J., Ngai, E.W.T.: Decision-making techniques in supplier selection: recent accomplishments and what lies ahead. Expert Syst. Appl. 140 (2020). https://doi.org/10.1016/j.eswa.2019.112903

40. Usuga Cadavid, J.P., Lamouri, S., Grabot, B., Pellerin, R., Fortin, A.: Machine learning applied in production planning and control: a state-of-the-art in the era of industry 4.0. J. Intell. Manuf. 31(6), 1531–1558 (2020). https://doi.org/10.1007/s10845-019-01531-7

41. Ekramifard, A., Amintoosi, H., Seno, A.H., Dehghantanha, A., Parizi, R.M.: A systematic literature review of integration of blockchain and artificial intelligence. In: Choo, K.-K.R., Dehghantanha, A., Parizi, R.M. (eds.) Blockchain Cybersecurity, Trust and Privacy. AIS, vol. 79, pp. 147–160. Springer, Cham (2020). https://doi.org/10.1007/978-3-030-38181-3_8

42. Vrbka, J., Rowland, Z.: Using artificial intelligence in company management. In: Ashmarina, S.I., Vochozka, M., Mantulenko, V.V. (eds.) ISCDTE 2019. LNNS, vol. 84, pp. 422–429. Springer, Cham (2020). https://doi.org/10.1007/978-3-030-27015-5_51

43. Leslie, D.: Understanding artificial intelligence ethics and safety: a guide for the responsible design and implementation of AI systems in the public sector. The Alan Turing Institute (2019)

44. Queiroz, M.M., Ivanov, D., Dolgui, A., et al.: Impacts of epidemic outbreaks on supply chains: mapping a research agenda amid the COVID-19 pandemic through a structured literature review. Ann Oper Res (2020). https://doi.org/10.1007/s10479-020-03685-7

Toward Physical Internet-Enabled Supply Chain and Logistics Networks in Developing Countries

Sam Ban[1], Matthieu Lauras[1(✉)], and Sarot Srang[2]

[1] Industrial Engineering Department, University of Toulouse – IMT Mines Albi,
Campus Jarlard, 81013 Albi CT Cedex 09, France
{sam.ban,matthieu.lauras}@mines-albi.fr
[2] Industrial and Mechanical Engineering Department,
Institute of Technology of Cambodia, Russian Federation Blvd,
P.O. Box 86, Tuol Kouk, Phnom Penh, Cambodia
srangsarot@itc.edu.kh

Abstract. Developing countries have numerous challenges to manage in terms of supply chain and logistics networks such as safety, corruption, pollution, congestion, old and/or unsuitable vehicles, long lead times, economy, wastes and of course poor infrastructures and so on. While developed countries have started to change their mindset and toolboxes for managing their material flows all along their logistics networks, it is not yet the case for developing countries. This research work intends to study potentials benefit for these countries if there are drastic changes of the way physical of material flows are managed. In such a context, Physical Internet paradigm is considered as an interesting avenue for improvement. The objective of this paper is to draft an options that would be necessary to assess and to design the associated research methodology. Insights regarding an ongoing field-oriented research work in Cambodia are developed to highlight the potential.

Keywords: Physical Internet · Supply chain · Logistics · Networks · Developing countries · Cambodia

1 Introduction

Studies like [1] demonstrated that supply chain and logistics play an important role and contribute significantly to economic growth and competitiveness of a country. However, many developing countries have issues and challenges such as corruption and informal payments, lack of institutional capacity and coordination, poor infrastructure and low-quality transportations, weak urban-rural and cross-border transportation networks, restricted participation of the private sector, lack of skilled human resources, and low public and private investments. As mentioned by [2], identifying and solving supply chain and logistics networks problems like these are the key issues of developing countries. Despite efforts and investments that are made to improve the supply chain and logistics networks means of these countries, the problems remain critical. Basically, these countries must cope with numerous supply chain and logistics

© IFIP International Federation for Information Processing 2020
Published by Springer Nature Switzerland AG 2020
L. M. Camarinha-Matos et al. (Eds.): PRO-VE 2020, IFIP AICT 598, pp. 379–389, 2020.
https://doi.org/10.1007/978-3-030-62412-5_31

networks problems such as safety, corruption, pollution, congestion, old and/or unsuitable vehicles, long lead times, wastes and of course poor infrastructures. Therefore, developing countries have a major crisis on their hands [2] if they want to sustainably support their economy. This is particularly true for countries like Cambodia whose economy is mainly based on agricultural productions and distribution of imported materials. In such a context, supply chain and logistics networks must be transformed into a more efficient and effective way. In parallel, we have to consider that the supply chain and logistics networks are running to the industry 4.0 era [3]. This new time is composed of technologies such as advanced robotics, artificial intelligence (AI), blockchain, autonomous vehicles, drones or Internet of Things (IoT) for instance, and of new supply chain and logistics paradigms such as Servitization [4] or Physical Internet (PI) [5]. If most of the developed countries are involved in enhancing their supply chain and logistics networks through these approaches and technologies, developing countries are not outdone. However, there are still tons of questions about how to benefit from these new approaches and technologies in developing countries which have major issues such as poor infrastructures, transportations networks, less-trusted logistics services, information of technology, etc. The current research work is studying this issue by investigating the potentiality of implementing PI paradigm to developing countries in order to enhance their supply chain and logistics networks capabilities. This work is divided into three sections. First section discusses some key points on the literature which focus on the latest research works. Based on author knowledge, this new idea has not been conducted yet in developing countries. The second section develops avenues for implementing PI to supply chain and logistics networks in developing countries. It also suggests a framework able to objectively assess the potential benefits and limits of them and gives some insights regarding an ongoing Cambodian case study. The last section is about conclusion and future work.

2 Literature Review and Research Statement

2.1 Developing Countries Supply Chain and Logistics Networks Features

Some research works like [6, 7] or [8] studied the consequences of low performance supply chain and logistics networks in developing countries. They highlighted that the main issues came from weak capabilities regarding both human and machine means, poor track & trace systems and poor innovative and collaborative approaches. Another report by [9] indicates that the most important factor affecting the international logistics process of African countries was limited information integration, poor infrastructures, and specific local country risks such as corruption. As shown by [10], around 98% of material flows in developing countries like Malaysia highly depend on the road while infrastructures are generally not good. On their side, [11] revealed that the port of developing countries such as Sri Lanka was lower performance of transshipment hub ports comparing to developed countries like Singapore or Netherlands. All these situations caused several issues by leading to increase cost of logistics, CO_2 emission and transport time and to decrease service quality to end-customers [10]. To conclude, developing countries supply chain and logistics networks do not seem to be effective.

Additionally, other studies demonstrated that developing countries have some issues regarding the efficiency of their supply chain and logistics networks. For instance, [12] introduced the top three factors impacting warehousing process efficiency which were labor productivity, warehouse utilization and inventory space utilization. Most of the time, logistics plants (i.e. warehouses or distribution centers) in developing countries are under-used. In parallel, [13] pointed out that the position of the country's ranking for Vietnam in the LPI fell from 48 in 2014 to 64 in 2016 due to higher logistics costs. As a result, they noted that one might pay more attentions to the efficiency of logistics service providers (LSPs) and technologies in developing countries. The increase in volume of both people and material flows in developing countries implied critical stakes regarding last-mile deliveries and urban logistics [14]. These growing processes can cause a major problem not only for the cities, but also for the countries. Inappropriate material flows and lack of supply chain and logistics networks strategies will cause an increase in the final cost of products and traffic flow deterioration. These will affect to the GDP of both developed and developing countries. Last but not least, researchers such as [15] showed that most of the developing countries did not yet adopt supply chain and logistics networks technologies like Intelligent Packaging (IP) or Internet of Thing (IoT). They found that cost and lack of knowledge were the main barriers. This is a questionable situation considering that at the same time people in developing countries are more and more used to live with connected devices such as smartphones.

2.2 The Physical Internet Opportunity

The original manifesto of PI consists in changing the manner in which physical items are managed, delivered, transported, stored, realized, supplied and used to achieve global logistics efficiency and sustainability [5]. In practice, PI is an emergent and innovative concept of interconnected logistics networks capitalizing on the opportunity of sharing assets and capabilities. PI totally challenges in the supply chain foundations. Nowadays, companies are part of a specific and stable network and possess their warehouses, manufacturing plants or fleets. PI takes the opposite of this view and induces that assets should be shared between all the stakeholders part of this global network and used on a need basis.

PI has now been used for many research-works to improve supply chain and logistics networks. However, most of the researches on PI have been being conducted in developed countries like Canada, USA, China, France and some other countries in Europe while developing countries have probably their own issues and challenges regarding PI implementation. [16] showed that supply chains and logistics networks are more and more intensely interconnected on multiple layers, ultimately anytime, anywhere. The interconnectivity layers notably include digital, physical, operational, business, legal and personal layers. They name this new state "hyperconnectivity".

In practice, PI paradigm already implies several innovative proposals and demonstrated its potential benefits. For instance, in the specific context of logistics and transportation in urban environment, [17] showed that the PI initiative enables hyperconnected logistics which is capable of transforming the freight transport fragmentation, logistics and distribution industries into a single manufacturing. Goods would be encapsulated and designed in standard for logistics that are modular, smart and reusable PI-containers, all size (from small cases up to the cases of cargo containers). [17] indicated also that these smart containers (PI container) can be routed from end to end through open hubs by developing real-time identification, tracking, and communication systems. Also, PI containers can store data or information required during different operations in terms of handling and transportation.

On their side, [18] introduced semantic technology for enabled innovative supply chain and logistics networks as adaptive synchromodal planning by improving visibility and consequently predictability of turnaround times at container terminals. The study intended to address the notion of synchromodal transport and the PI. In another research work, [19] investigated the issue of urban transportation in a PI-enabled setting by applying multiple types of vehicles. They found that PI interconnectivity and extra hubs could improve urban transport planning regarding to routing efficiency and postponed services. [20] studied the comparison of PI performance and conventional logistics system to measure the advantages and disadvantages of PI. The analysis show that PI could reduce truck driving distances, times, cost and carbon emission. Instead, it increased the number of PI-container transfers within the PI logistics centers. Inspired by PI concepts, [21] exploited the extra loading capacity of taxis to collect the reverse flows of goods in the city using simulation modelling method. Although the solution resulted in greater distances and higher lead times for the return flows compared to an ideal case. With these results, they highlighted that it was hard to directly compare between real world cases and the proposed solution of the model. The actual cases had very different selection strategies. However, they still claimed that their proposed model was more feasible in the following aspects. With another perspective, [22] introduced the mitigation of supply chain networks disruptions on hubs and factory plants and investigated the inventory model resilience through the PI framework of interconnected logistics services. They wanted to introduce PI disruption mitigation strategies by using simulation modelling technique when plants, warehouses, hubs and distribution centers became unserviceable for a period of time. The results of this technique helped to deal with disruptions in terms of penalty, transport and total costs.

2.3   Research Statement Formulation

The current research wants to use the concepts and technologies of the PI initiative imagined few years ago. Basically, one goal of our research is to demonstrate the potential benefits of PI in the context of developing country (economic, social and environmental dimensions) of physical object mobility.

The main idea of this research is finally to demonstrate (i) the benefits of managing transportation activities through a "connected" approach in developing countries and (ii) the feasibility of such an evolution on one hand, and in developing (iii) the first decision support tools that will allow concretizing this on the other hand.

This research has the following concrete objectives for a developing country: (i) reduce transportation lead times; (ii) improve on-time delivery ratio; (iii) avoid useless travelled distance; (iv) limit waste of goods due to bad transportation; (v) improve carriers' profitability; (vi) allow transportation multimodality; (vii) allow real time tracking of goods; (viii) optimize transportation costs; and (ix) reduce carbon footprint impact of transportation.

It is important to notice here that the current research work did not focus on the technological dimensions of the PI (devices and connected assets, etc.). The research work only focuses on the use of the PI paradigm to better manage the material flows in a specific context of developing countries.

3 Proposal

As the objective is to improve both efficiency and effectiveness of supply chain and logistics networks in developing countries, there is one obvious option that consists drastically in modernizing the infrastructures (roads, buildings, etc.) and the logistics means which are used (vehicles, IT systems, machines, etc.). But building new and modern infrastructures (underground, bridge, highway, flyover) or investing in new transportation means for instance is a very expensive and time-consuming step. Within an opposite view, our suggestion involves in thinking about potential evolutions that might be implemented now, on the basis of existing or accessible means. In the following we first suggest some recommendations for looking for such an improvement inspired by the PI paradigm. Second, we develop a methodological approach allowing us to assess the potential impacts of these different recommendations. Third, we will draft the field-research application which is ongoing in Cambodia and its expected results.

3.1 Putting PI into Practice for Developing Countries

Nowadays, developing countries (like other countries) are using connected devices such as smartphones boosting the network sharing through Internet connectivity. But these technologies are not used or used inappropriately on supply chain and logistics activities while it could be very useful for them. Within an hyperconnected perspective, all the supply chain and logistics networks stakeholders (suppliers, shippers, carriers, customers, etc.) could be connected altogether and allow a set of PI levers that should be implemented in developing countries.

Open-Hubs Initiatives
In the current state of supply chain and logistics networks in developing countries, the product flows are formed by suppliers (mostly from oversea), warehouses and retailers or wholesalers, market and supermarket... As normal, the physical flow goes from one actor to another directly, on a one-to-one basis and through ownership assets. Hyperconnected supply chain and logistics networks will allow more collaboration by means of multiple open hubs in different places. All of these open hubs are composed of a network and would connect each other. It will be possible for any company to access to these open hubs on demand without agreeing for a long period. This consists in applying the concept of SaaS (Software as a Service) to the supply chain and logistics networks assets. As a result, the flow of products would transit much more efficiently and effectively from one hub to another before reaching its customers, and

benefits from mutualization of means all along the value chain. Through the web open hubs strategy, products are not committed as a priori to one plant, the products are consolidated from different sources by multiple carriers and moving toward the same direction to final customers as shown in Fig. 1. This Figure shows the comparison between a simple delivery without PI (Fig. 1(a)) and with PI (Fig. 1(b)). Basically, Fig. 1(b) considers shared warehouses, transportation assets and hyperconnected flows. Each color of the Figure represents different destinations of delivery. As a result, Fig. 1 (b) with hyperconnected could save more times and costs by reducing travel distances and maximizing utilization rate of assets. In such a context, it has been demonstrated that PI can reduce, in developed countries situation, logistics costs by about 75%, carbon emission by 60% and travelled distance by 15% [17]. The remaining question is what we can expect in the context of developing countries?

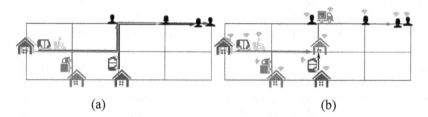

(a)   (b)

Fig. 1. Simple one-to-one flows (a) vs hyperconnected and web open hubs (b).

Dynamic Transportation Chartering and Use

As considering on the supply chains in developing countries, most of shippers and carriers are chartering dedicated vehicles which could be for material and/or people moving, for shipments from one company to another. Within a PI perspective, transportation means (such as motorcycle taxi, bajaj, tuk-tuks, taxis, vans, etc.) might be connected to a common platform in real time. Then, it would be possible to charter dynamically this or this vehicle for a delivery based on geo-localization opportunities or capacity opportunities. Additionally, deliveries might be organized as a relay race between the source and the delivery point in order to accelerate the flow, to limit the cost and better use the available capacities. As a consequence, quality improvement and cost reduction in transport seem to be possible by using modern IT systems able to support the hyperconnectivity concept. Then, an efficient combination of transport modes/vehicles can be optimized by route-planning to guarantee an efficient use of the available resources and by bundling transport streams at certain points to minimize the frequency of transports (especially in cities). Combining different transport modes (multimodal transport) could be useful for transport-quality improvement and cost reduction. The concept of synchromodality can also be seen as a first step towards the PI, synchromodality aims to create a flexible and cooperative transport network by using the different available transport resources. As a consequence, reliability, robustness and resilience of the transport network should be increased by introducing real-time monitoring of the transport chains and real-time mode and route choice. For the connection between the actors, the infrastructure and the different transport modes are essential for the PI and lead to a comprehensive interconnectivity. Sharing all relevant information and guaranteeing the topicality of the data in a real-time manner are also crucial elements for the concept of the PI.

Dynamic Planning and Scheduling

Within a hyperconnected perspective, we could monitor and predict all aspects in real time where the goods are, what the available vehicles are and what the current disruptions are that exist on the infrastructures. This would allow managing the material flows from suppliers to customers much more efficiently and effectively than today. In addition to this kind of behavior, one can also plan proactive measures by considering seasonality or expected or unexpected events. For instance, considering that typhoon season will start in few weeks and that this road might be flooded, then we can prepare in advance some rerouting plans or transportation mode changes. Also, we can avoid road congestion dynamically accordingly to some real-time event management. In such a context, managers would have access to a centralized transportation planning and scheduling system (see Fig. 2). Such a system could estimate their needs, by geographical zone, in terms of transportation, inventory and maybe production for the next periods. First, this would mean that decision makers will have the opportunity to negotiate capacities on-demand and on-the-fly with their providers to avoid shortage situations or brutal increase of unitary costs for instance. Second, this would mean that managers will have the possibility to assess different alternatives a priori to fit supply chain and logistics decisions with established demands and opportunities.

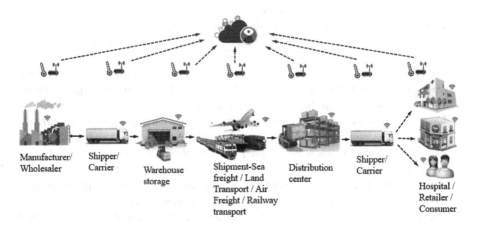

Fig. 2. PI-oriented supply chain and logistics networks for developing countries

Pick-Up and Asynchronous Deliveries

Additionally, in developing countries, majority of the material flows are home delivery. This implies important difficulties as delays and hazards are frequent. In a PI perspective, the supply chain and logistics networks might organize deliveries close to end-customers instead of parcel handed personally to increase the quality of service. Generalization of solutions such as lockers, permanent pick up points and/or temporary pick up points would be a significant change that would have to be assessed.

Obviously, it would be hard to involve all these factors into a general supply chain model applicable for every developing country. In the following of this research, we will have to focus on a specific use case, such as Cambodia, before extending to other clusters of developing countries.

3.2   Performance Assessment Framework

Our suggested methodology framework is broken down into four phases:

1. Phase one is data gathering. As our research work is field-oriented, a concrete dataset is needed and has to be extracted from a real network in order to have a clear vision about the business processes and the material flows of a real system. Obviously, this step can be difficult in the context of networks that might have limited maturity in terms of legacy IT systems. Typically, the dataset that has to be gathered is composed of the following elements:
   a. General features about the network and its environment: it might include information about the business model of the company, business perspectives, market positioning, etc.
   b. Static features about assets which are involving in the considered Supply Chain: it might include information about vehicles, warehouses, items description, supplier description, customer descriptions, etc.
   c. Dynamic features about material flows which are managed by the considered Supply Chain: it might include information about the customer orders, inventories, supplier orders, transportation orders, etc.
2. Phase two consists in analyzing the dataset to transform it into knowledge, to set the problem formulation and to build the model conceptualization. As an output of this step, we should get an accurate and exhaustive map of the studied network.
3. Phase three is related to the design of potential solutions inspired by the PI paradigm and the modelling of them onto a dynamic model able to assess quantitatively the impacts of them on the supply chain and logistics networks. In our case, we have chosen to work through a discrete event simulation approach that is currently ongoing. Basically, this phase will include modelling simulation and validation by experimen. The experiment will consist in defining scenarios that correspond to the AS-IS situation of the material flow management in a developing country use case, and to define a set of TO-BE scenarios representative of PI paradigms in order to assess potential benefits and limits of evolving in that direction.
4. Phase four consists in exploiting the simulation results obtained from the previous phase to make concrete recommendations in terms of organization for developing countries supply chain and logistics networks. Obviously, these recommendations will be made by considering both the assumptions made and the sensitivity of the used model.

3.3   Ongoing Field-Oriented Research

Based on the previous framework, we are working on a Cambodian e-commerce supply chain and logistics network case. This company is located in Phnom Penh and offers apparel, footwear, bags, accessories, electronics, books, automotive, baby, kid toy, and beauty and health products. Consumers can also directly buy products from this company in 3 different stores located in Phnom Penh. The delivery services of products are made by their own employees for Phnom Penh and through 3rd Party Logistics Providers for provinces and countryside. Customers order products every day. The delivery services are shipped these items to customer's home every day. Most of the times, the company manages the delivery services by its own employees. Currently, the company has 200 employees in total and 30 employees for delivery purpose of products to end-customers in Phnom Penh. Currently, the majority of products in warehouses and showrooms are imported from different sources of different suppliers located in Thailand, Vietnam and China. Until now there are over 100,000 items in the warehouses and shops, there are more than 1000 customer orders per day with different items of products each time. The majority of products are clothes which is 80% of the products of selling. Until now, the supply chain provides about 70% of product sales to customers in Phnom Penh and 30% at province of Cambodia. The studied supply chain is represented on the following Fig. 3.

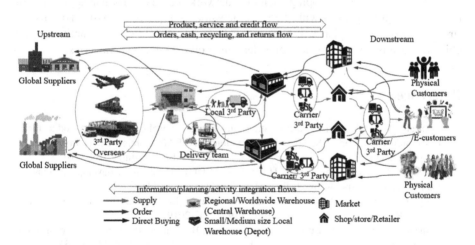

Fig. 3. Supply Chain flow map in Cambodia

At the starting point of the study, this supply chain and logistics network might be considered as very representative of a developing country's economy stakeholder. They noticed poor effectiveness of the means and resources involved in their network on one hand, and a poor efficiency of their network (numerous shortages, low quality of service, long lead-time…) on the other hand. In the following months, the current research work will intend to study the implementation of PI solutions described previously and to objectively assess the expected impacts for this network in terms of both effectiveness and efficiency. Significant improvements are expected.

4 Conclusion and Research Perspectives

While the current research work is in its infancy, we have demonstrated in this paper that developing countries supply chain and logistics networks have great stakes regarding both efficiency and effectiveness. We made the assumption that applying Physical Internet paradigm to this specific context will be useful and bring more benefits for supply chain and logistics in Cambodia. Within this objective, we suggested in this paper a set of concrete options to activate in developing countries and set the basis to make in a near future a concrete and objective assessment of them. A very first draft of an ongoing- field-oriented approach is also mentioned in this paper. Obviously, numerous research perspectives arise from this starting research work. The next steps will consist of finalizing the data gathering process with the Cambodian company in order to feed our future simulation model. Then the development of a discrete event simulation model able to mimic the existing supply chain and logistics network behaviors and to envisage the future ones, based on a PI approach, will be continued. The objective of this model will be to compare the results in terms of Supply Chain performance of developing countries' networks based on classical approaches of material flow management with the same networks running on PI basis. To do so, a structured experiment plan will have to be designed and run to get quantitative and objective results allowing us to make clear and complete recommendations.

References

1. Chheang, V.: FDI, services liberalisation, and logistics development in Cambodia. ERIA Discussion Paper Series, Services Liberalization in ASEAN: Foreign Direct Investment in Logistics Sector, 15–16 November 2016, ISEAS-Yusof Ishak Institute, 268 (2017)
2. Masood, M.T., Khan, A., Naqvi, H.A.: Transportation problems in developing countries Pakistan: a case-in-point. Int. J. Bus. Manag. 6(11), 256 (2011)
3. Tang, C.S., Veelenturf, L.P.: The strategic role of logistics in the industry 4.0 era. Transp. Res. Part E Logist. Transp. Rev. 129, 1–11 (2019)
4. Baines, T., Bigdeli, A.Z., Bustinza, O.F., Shi, V.G., Baldwin, J., Ridgway, K.: Servitization: revisiting the state-of-the-art and research priorities. Int. J. Oper. Prod. Manag. 37(2), 256–278 (2017)
5. Montreuil, B., Meller, R.D., Ballot, E.: Physical internet foundations. In: Borangiu, T., Thomas, A., Trentesaux, D. (eds.) Service Orientation in Holonic and Multi Agent Manufacturing and Robotics. Studies in Computational Intelligence, vol. 472, pp. 151–166. Springer, Heidelberg (2013). https://doi.org/10.1007/978-3-642-35852-4_10
6. Ul-Hameed, W., Shabbir, M., Imran, M., Raza, A., Salman, R.: Remedies of low performance among Pakistani e-logistic companies: the role of firm's IT capability and information communication technology (ICT). Uncertain Supply Chain Manag. 7(2), 369–380 (2019)

7. MahbubulHye, A.K., Miraz, M.H., Sharif, K.I.M., Hassan, M.G.: Factors affecting on e-logistic: mediating role of ICT & technology integration in retail supply chain in Malaysia. TEST Eng. Manag. **82**, 3234–3243 (2020). ISSN 0193-4120

8. Liu, Y.: A study on the factors affecting e-logistics system in Chinese logistics industry. In: 2017 2nd International Conference on Automation, Mechanical Control and Computational Engineering (AMCCE 2017). Advances in Engineering Research, vol. 118, pp: 981–984. Atlantis Press (2017)

9. Yang, C.C., Chang, Y.K.: Crucial factors influencing international logistics operations for African landlocked countries. Marit. Policy Manag. **46**(8), 939–956 (2019)

10. Chen, S.L., Jeevan, J., Cahoon, S.: Malaysian container seaport-hinterland connectivity: status, challenges and strategies. Asian J. Shipping Logist. **32**(3), 127–138 (2016)

11. Kavirathna, C.A., Kawasaki, T., Hanaoka, S.: Transshipment hub port competitiveness of the port of Colombo against the major Southeast Asian hub ports. Asian J. Shipping Logist. **34**(2), 71–82 (2018)

12. Karim, N.H., Rahman, N.S.F.A., Shah, S.F.S.S.J.: Empirical evidence on failure factors of warehouse productivity in Malaysian logistic service sector. Asian J. Shipping Logist. **34**(2), 151–160 (2018)

13. Dang, V.L., Yeo, G.T.: Weighing the key factors to improve Vietnam's logistics system. Asian J. Shipping Logist. **34**(4), 308–316 (2018)

14. Rossolov, A., Lobashov, O., Kopytkov, D., Botsman, A., Lyfenko, S.: A two-echelon green supply chain for urban delivery. Sci. Tech. **18**(6), 495–503 (2019)

15. Noletto, A.P.R., Loureiro, S.A., Castro, R.B., Júnior, O.F.L.: Intelligent packaging and the Internet of Things in Brazilian food supply chains: the current state and challenges. In: Freitag, M., Kotzab, H., Pannek, J. (eds.) Dynamics in Logistics. LNL, pp. 173–183. Springer, Cham (2017). https://doi.org/10.1007/978-3-319-45117-6_16

16. Montreuil, B., Ballot, E., Tremblay, W.: Modular design of physical internet transport, handling and packaging containers. In: Progress in Material Handling Research: 2014, 13th MHI, 2015, International Material Handling Research Colloquium (2015). 978-1-882780-18-3. hal-01487239

17. Crainic, T.G., Montreuil, B.: Physical internet enabled hyperconnected city logistics. Transp. Res. Procedia **12**, 383–398 (2016)

18. Hofman, W., Punter, M., Bastiaansen, H., Cornelisse, E., Dalmolen, S.: Semantic technology for enabling logistics innovations–towards intelligent Cargo in the physical internet. Int. J. Adv. Logist. **5**(2), 58–69 (2016)

19. Ben Mohamed, I., Klibi, W., Labarthe, O., Deschamps, J.C., Babai, M.Z.: Modelling and solution approaches for the interconnected city logistics. Int. J. Prod. Res. **55**(9), 2664–2684 (2017)

20. Fazili, M., Venkatadri, U., Cyrus, P., Tajbakhsh, M.: Physical Internet, conventional and hybrid logistic systems: a routing optimisation-based comparison using the Eastern Canada road network case study. Int. J. Prod. Res. **55**(9), 2703–2730 (2017)

21. Chen, C., Pan, S., Wang, Z., Zhong, R.Y.: Using taxis to collect citywide E-commerce reverse flows: a crowdsourcing solution. Int. J. Prod. Res. **55**(7), 1833–1844 (2017)

22. Yang, Y., Pan, S., Ballot, E.: Mitigating supply chain disruptions through interconnected logistics services in the physical internet. Int. J. Prod. Res. **55**(14), 3970–3983 (2017)

Simulation and Analysis
in Collaborative Systems

A Collaborative Approach to Demand Side Energy Management

Kankam O. Adu-Kankam[1,2(✉)] and Luis M. Camarinha-Matos[1(✉)]

[1] Faculty of Sciences and Technology and UNINOVA - CTS, Nova University of Lisbon, Campus de Caparica, 2829-516 Monte Caparica, Portugal
kankamadu@gmail.com, cam@uninova.pt
[2] School of Engineering, University of Energy and Natural Resources (UENR), P.O. Box 214, Sunyani, Ghana

Abstract. Integrating the idea of collaborations into the energy domain appears a promising feat, although, relatively contemporary and uncommon. In this study, we implement a Demand Side Management strategy using the concept of Collaborative Virtual Power Plant Ecosystem as a digital representation of an Energy Community. The community uses a sharing platform to share experience, technical and professional knowledge, facilitating members ambition to change their energy use behaviours. Members of the community are represented as software agents. Behaviours in the adopted model are arranged in a framework of tasks and goals for agents to accomplish. Agents join the ecosystem under deterministic and stochastic conditions. A multi-method modelling approach is used. This study revealed that through collaboration, agents are able to accomplish set tasks faster, thus reducing their chances of frustration and subsequent exit from the ecosystem. This approach helps to influence member's behaviour and increases membership fluidity, facilitating community stability and sustainability.

Keywords: Collaborative Networks · Virtual power pants · Incentivization · Goal setting · Demand Side Management

1 Introduction

According to the European Commission, buildings are responsible for approximately 40% of the EU's energy consumption and 36% of the CO_2 emissions in Europe [1]. This, therefore, makes buildings the single largest energy consumer in Europe. A claim by [2] disclosed that developed countries could reduce energy demand by up to 20% in the short term and by up to 50% of present levels by mid-century through lifestyle and behavioural changes. These facts therefore reveal the significant role households play towards GHG emissions globally, and also unveil its potential contribution towards mitigation. Some published suggestions in this context include: the deployment of energy-efficient appliances [3], consumer behavioural change [4], and Net Zero Energy Building [5], amongst many. However, amongst the prevailing options, consumer behaviour change is said to offer the lowest cost and fastest switching option for Demand Side Management (DSM) as compared to the others [6].

© IFIP International Federation for Information Processing 2020
Published by Springer Nature Switzerland AG 2020
L. M. Camarinha-Matos et al. (Eds.): PRO-VE 2020, IFIP AICT 598, pp. 393–405, 2020.
https://doi.org/10.1007/978-3-030-62412-5_32

In this simulation study, we approach DSM using a collaborative approach. Our primary objective is to influence ecosystem members to delegate their deferrable loads such as washing machines, dishwashers and tumble dryers to the ecosystem manager for collective control. However, we precede this action with some antecedent interventions in the forms of goals and tasks, to help facilitate the delegation process. The essence of the intervention is to induce or inculcate some fundamental energy use behaviours amongst members in the community. This could help to create a sense of energy conservation awareness within the community before finally introducing delegation. Furthermore, we will also consider how collaborations can also enhance the membership fluidity of the ecosystem. Ensuing from the above our study will be guided by the following research problems (R-P) and research questions (RQ).

RP-1. Delegation of deferrable loads are action that solely depend on the willingness of consumers to engage in. It is therefore envisaged that by introducing this action as a direct and standalone activity in a community, the perceived inconvenience and discomfort may instil anxiety in members, and could make the idea unattractive, resulting in less patronage. We therefore hypnotise that by introducing a set of antecedent interventions, it may be possible to alter the behaviours of consumers towards the enhancement of the delegation process. *RQ1. How can collaborations and antecedent interventions enhance the behaviour of consumers towards the delegation of deferrable loads within an energy ecosystem?*

RP-2. A common problem associated with communities are issues of instability caused by low membership fluidity (LMF). A LMF results in a weak, unstable, and unsustainable community. We further hypnotise that a high membership fluidity could promote a stranger, stable, and sustainable community. *RQ2. How can collaboration through the sharing of experience and knowledge (technical and professional) enhance membership fluidity in an energy ecosystem.*

We consider two scenarios. Scenarios 1: A non-fluid community membership with (a) collaborations, and (b) without collaborations. Scenario 2: A fluid community membership with (a) collaborations, and (b) without collaborations. The selection of these scenarios was based on [7, 8]. According to [8], the ability to attract and retain membership enhances the long term survivability of a community. We adopted a hybrid modelling approach which incorporates a combination of System dynamics, Discrete event and Agent-based technology, using the Anylogic platform [9].

2   Related Works and Theoretical Framework

The emergence of works conducted in the area of DSM and goal setting are currently on the rise. Some of these include works such as [10], where personal goal setting as a way of reducing residential electricity were studied. Another dimension of goal setting was presented in a multidisciplinary study conducted in [11], where a combination of interventions including individual and group goals were studied. An experimental study to compare two groups in terms of their energy conservation behaviour, in combination with energy feedback was also conducted in [12]. A systematic literature review of four behavioural interventions towards residential energy conservation was also conducted in [13].

This study presents a multidisciplinary and interdisciplinary approach to DSM using a combination of concepts borrowed from diverse scientific disciplines. Out of these multiple concepts, a couple has been identified as the core tenet in which this work is grounded. These concepts are briefly explained below.

i. **The CVPP-E concept.** This concept derives its source from the merger of principles and concepts from the disciplines of Collaborative Networks (CNs) and Virtual Power Plants (VPP). At the heart of the concept is the idea of collaborations, which is central to the discipline of Collaborative Networks. CNs represents a rich plethora of knowledge-base and sets of principles that facilitate collaborations in diverse forms as seen in [14–16]. A VPP on the other hand is a virtual entity involving multiple stakeholders and comprising decentralized multi-site heterogeneous technologies, formed by aggregating dispatchable and non-dispatchable distributed energy sources [17]. The synergy of these two concepts led to a hybrid concept called the Collaborative Virtual Power Plant Ecosystem (CVPP-E) introduced in [17, 18]. The CVPP-E can be used to represent a renewable energy community such as in [19]. The CVPP-E depicts a business ecosystem and a community of practice where members approach energy generation, consumption, and conservation from a collaborative approach. The governing structure is polycentric and decentralized with a manager who plays a coordinating role and promotes collaborative behaviours.

ii. **Goal-setting theory.** Theory is summarized in [20], It claims that one's conscious goals affect their achievements. Specific goals improve a person's performance towards the achievement of that goal. Furthermore, it postulates that people with specific goals often perform better than those with vague or no goals. When a goal is met or exceeded, satisfaction increases and vice versa. A goal can instil purpose, challenge, and meaning into what one perceives as a difficult task. Goals can motivate people to develop strategies that will enable them to perform better. In a group context, tasks and information sharing may enhance group performance [21].

3   Modelling Framework

In this section, we describe the building blocks, functions, assumptions and parameters used to develop the model. We propose a sharing platform as the sharing interface for the ecosystem. Membership fluidity is based solely on interest in pro-environmental behaviours. Individuals who are willing to voluntarily make some minor adjustments to their energy use behaviours may join. Members may exit the platform when they persistently fail to accomplish any single task and become frustrated as a result.

3.1   Modelling of Households

In the developed model, households are modelled as software agents. These agents are modelled according to scenarios of behaviour change as described in the Transtheoretical model (TT-M) [22]. We assume that agents have passed the pre-contemplation, contemplation and preparation stages of the TT-M and therefore, we focus attention on the action and maintenance stages only (Fig. 1). We also model all households as having the same schematic behaviour. Households in the ecosystem can only share experiences. We occasionally introduce special agents called technical and professional agents. The population of these special agents is always 5% of the total agent population. Special agents provide only technical and professional knowledge to the community. They do not undergo the behaviour change process.

Fig. 1. Sages of change as described by the TT-M model

3.2   Antecedent Interventions and Delegation of Deferable Loads

A goal is represented by a collection of tasks. The number and types of tasks in a particular goal may vary per model, depending on the objectives. In this instance, we have defined three goals. The first two are antecedent intervention goals, modelled to precede a third and the main goal, which is the delegation of deferrable loads. The rationale behind the interventions is to subtly induce a sense of energy conservation and also introduce a wholistic conservation approach in agents. More details as follows:

Goal 1: Reduce energy waste through prudent energy use practices.
Task 1: Learn the habit of switching off lights in rooms when not in use.
Task 2: Unlearn the habit of overcharging smart devices.
Task 3: Do household chores at night-time.
Goal 2. Adapt basic and low-cost energy-efficient technologies.
Task 1: Use LED/CFL lightbulbs for the household.
Task 2: Use timers for your lighting.
Goal 3. Delegation of deferrable loads.
Task 1: Delegate all deferable loads to CVPP-E manager.

An agent can be said to have accomplished a goal when they complete all tasks associated with that particularly goal. All goals are not attempted at the same time. Agents must complete goal 1 before they progress to attempt goal 2 and finally goal 3. On the contrary, all tasks in a particular goal are attempted at the same time.

3.3   Modelling of Tasks

Let us now analyse in more detail the tasks:

i. Task framework and technical description

Figure 2 shows the framework of a task. Each task is represented by one of these frameworks. The framework is composed of state charts. A state chart is a visual construct that enables the modeller to define event and time-driven behaviours. State charts are usually constituted of different kinds of states and their corresponding transitions. A task framework is composed of 9 simple states, 3 composite states and 15 transitions, labelled as T1 to T15. Out of the 15 transitions, 3 (T1, T10, T11) are triggered by messages. Another set of 3 (T2, T12, T14) are also triggered as rates. 4 (T4, T13, T15) are triggered by conditions, and finally 6 (T3, T5, T6, T7, T8, T9) are triggered as timeouts. A task is modelled through a series of four interconnected blocks namely, task completed block, task processing block, frustrated agent block, and feedback block. These blocks and their related algorithms are described below.

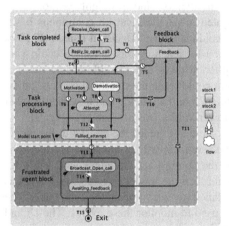

Fig. 2. Framework of a task.

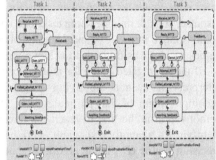

Fig. 3. Model of a goal with three tasks. (E.g. goal 1)

ii. Functions of the various blocks in a task

a. Task processing block (TPB): This is where the agent begins the execution of a task. The sequence of operations starts with T12. T12 is a rate transition and is defined as *the number of attempts per task per day (N_{aT})*. This is used to model the number of times an agent attempts a particular task per day. For instance, the number of times one may attempt to unlearn the habit of turning off the lights after leaving a room, may occur serval times in a day. On the other hand, attempting to unlearn the habit of overcharging smart devices could happen perhaps once, twice or at most three times in a day. These number of attempts could recur for several days, weeks, or even months until the habit is finally unlearned. This suggests that N_{aT} for every task may vary depending on the nature and kind of the task. Nonetheless, we may have to define some tentative boundaries to represent the possible minimum and maximum number of attempts per day. In this model, N_{aT} is modelled using a *uniform discrete distribution (X, Y)* where X is the minimum number of occurrences per day and Y is the maximum number of occurrences per day. For instance, considering goal 1, the following parameters are defined:

Task1 – (N_{aT1}) = *Uniform discrete distribution (0, 10)*; Task 2 –(N_{aT2}) = *Uniform discrete distribution (0, 3)*; Task 3 – (N_{aT3}) = *Uniform discrete distribution (0, 1)*.

At every instance of T12, the states indicated as "motivation" and "demotivation" are activated. These states are used to model the outcome of each attempted task. The possible outcomes are: (i) Positive experience, resulting in a motivation (through T7), or (ii) Negative experience, resulting in a demotivation (through T8). T7 and T8 are random transitions with equal probability of occurrence. This therefore helps to create equal probability for both motivation and demotivation occurring at every iteration. The model assigns a weight $+K$ for every motivation and a weight $-K$ for every demotivation. These two values are aggregated in parallel, and on continuous basis, until one of them reaches a predefined threshold called the "**Decision constant**" (Dc). Since these are stochastic actions, the duration for reaching this threshold could vary from days to weeks or even months for different tasks and for different agents. For instance, considering the same task, one agent could reach the threshold in days, others could achieve it in weeks and for some others, in months. The Dc can be varied. Higher values make tasks difficult to achieve and lower values, easy to achieve (Fig. 3).

If the aggregated value for motivations is the first to reach the threshold, the model interprets this event as signifying an agent with sufficiently high motivation to merit the accomplishment of that particular task. On the contrary, if the aggregated value for demotivation is the first to reach the threshold then the model interprets this event as signifying a demotivated agent who has failed to accomplish the said task. The **Decision factor** (Df) is the algorithm that is used to monitor these events. The Df and the Dc work together to decide whether a task has been completed or otherwise.

For example, considering the scenario of unlearning the habit of turning off the lights after leaving a room. Assuming it took the agent three days to overcome this habit. On the first day, the agent entered the room 10 times (N_{aT} = 10) and out of the 10 events, the agent remembered to turn off the light on 4 occasion (M_1 = 4) but forgot to turn it off on 6 occasions (D_1 = 6). On the second day, the agent entered the room on 12 occasions (N_{aT} = 12) and remembered to turn off the lights on 8 occasions (M_2 = 8) and forgot on 4 occasions (D_2 = 4). On the third day, the agent entered the room 8 times (N_{aT} = 8) and remembered to turn off the light on 8 occasion (M_3 = 8) and forgot none (D_3 = 0). Assuming that a weight $K = 1$ is assigned every time, the agent remembers to turn off the lights (motivation) and weight $-K = -1$ is assigned every time the agents forgot to turn off the lights (demotivation). Then the Df and the Dc will decide based on the following algorithms:

$$Df_{motivation} = [(K * M_1) + (K * M_2) + (K * M_3)] + \ldots\ldots\ldots\ldots\ldots(K * M_N)]$$
$$Df_{demotivation} = [(-K * D_1) + (-K * D_2) + (-K * D_3)] + \ldots\ldots\ldots(-K * D_N)]$$

Considering the scenario described above,

$$Df_{motivation} \, after \, 3 \, days = (1 * 4) + (1 * 8) + (1 * 8)]$$
$$= 4 + 8 + 8 = 20$$

$$Df_{demotivation} \text{ after } 3 \text{ days} = [(-1 * 6) + (-1 * 4) + (-1 * 0)]$$
$$= (-6) + (-4) + (0) = -10$$

Assuming we defined a threshold (Dc) of say: $X_1 = 15$ to represent highly motivated and $X_2 = -15$ to represent highly demotivated, then: When $Df_{motivation} \geq X_1$, the task is said to be completed, and the model transitions to the task completed block. When $Df_{demotivation} \leq X_2$, the task has failed and the model transitions to the "frustrated block. Therefore, considering the scenario above, the condition for $Df_{motivation}$ is true $(20 > 15)$, and the condition for $Df_{demotivation}$ is false $(-10 \not< -15)$. Hence a transition into the task completed block. Parameters defined for this model are: $K = 1$, $-K = -1$, M and D = Random events, $X_1 = 10$, $X_2 = -10$.

> b. **Task completed block** (*TCB*): Transition into this block is facilitated by the $DF_{motivation}$ and the Dc (X_1) and is activated through T4. A task in this state is considered to be completed. When all other tasks in that particular goal have also transitioned into their respective TCBs it can be inferred that the related agent has completed all tasks for that particular goal, therefore the goal has been achieved.
> c. **Frustrated state block** (*FSB*). Transition into this block is facilitated by the $DF_{demotivation}$) and the Dc (X_2) and is activated through T13. Tasks in this state are time dependent. The time of entry into this block is captured as T_1. Agents are modelled to remain in this state for a limited length of time, denoted as T_2. When T_2 expires whilst the agent is still in this state, the agent will exit the platform. At the instance of entering the FSB, the agent broadcasts an open call.

Open calls are modelled to mimic scenarios of agents sharing their problems with the entire ecosystem. When an open call is broadcasted, all ecosystem members will receive a copy, however, only agents who have completed similar task, and special agents can provide feedbacks. After broadcasting an open call, the agent transition internally into the "awaiting feedback state" through T14. If the agent does not receive a feedback in the form of a message, before T_2 elapses, the task will expire, and the agent will abandon all other goals related to that tasks and exits the platform. On the contrary, when the agent receives a feedback before T_2 elapses, the model transitions into the feedback block through T11, where the agent is afforded another opportunity to either attempt the task again or accomplish the task. This will depend on the kind of feedback that is received. The condition for exiting is modelled as a *uniform discrete distribution between* (T_1, T_2). Where $T_1 = $ time of entry (in days), and T_2 is random between 30 to 60 days from time of entry. Furthermore, open call broadcasts are modelled as a rate (R_{fb}) which is a *uniform discrete distribution* (X, Y) where $X = 0$, $Y = 3$ per day.

> d. **Feedback block**. The impact of a feedback on the agent can result in one of two actions: (1) If the feedback is helpful to the agent, the task will transition through T3 to the task completed block to complete the task; else (2) the agent will transition through T5 back to the task procession block to repeat the cycle again. T3 or T5 are modelled as stochastic events with equal probability of occurrence. Which means a received feedback has equal probability to facilitating task completion or otherwise.

3.4   Modelling Feedback

Feedbacks is represented by a "variable rate". This rate can be varied. Rates defined for this model are in the range *rate (0, 10) per day*, which means that the rate of feedback could vary from 0 times per day to 10 times per day. This value could be used to indicate the rate at which the agents responds to feedback per day.

In Fig. 4, we illustrate the exchange of open calls and feedbacks to represent the aspects of collaborations in the model. These information items (open call and feedbacks) are modelled as messages which can be sent from one transition to another. Transitions T1a, T1b, T1c and T11, are message receiving transitions and are triggered by the reception of a message(s). On the contrary, transition T2a, T2b, T2c and T14 send out a message(s) anytime they receive a trigger signal. In Fig. 4, these information exchanges are shown using 4 different agents who are at various stages in their respective tasks. These are: experienced agent-1 (EA1), task currently in the frustrated block. Experienced agent-2 (EA2), task currently in task completed block. Experienced agent 3 (EA3), task currently in task completed block, and a technical agent (TA).

a. **Sending open calls.** When T14 of EA1 receives a trigger signal, it gets triggered and, in the process, broadcasts open calls to all agents on the platform. It then transition from *broadcast_ open_call* state into *awaiting_feedback* state.

b. **Receiving open calls.** TA, EA2 and EA3 will each receive a copy of the open call broadcasted by EA1. The open call will be received by transitions T1a, T1b and T1c of TA, EA2 and EA3 respectively. The receipt of the open call message will trigger these transitions from their respective *receive_open_calls* state into their various *reply_to_open_call* states. In this current state, there is a delay which is modelled as a random distribution in hours, i.e. *random () per hour*. This random-delay function is used to prevents all the agents from triggering their respective T2s at the same time. The rationale behind this delay is to prevent all the agents from responding to the open call at the same time. This therefore helps to spread or distribute the feedbacks over the course of the day.

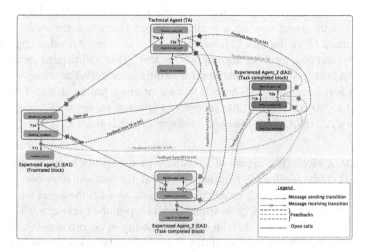

Fig. 4. Illustration of open calls and feedback.

c. **Responding to open calls (feedback).** The delay will elapse at different times for TA, EA2, EA3 and cause transitions T2a, T2b and T2c to be triggered respectively. This causes the various tasks to transition from their respective *reply_to_open_call* state back into the *receive open_call_*state. The triggering of T2a, T2b, and T2c causes three different feedbacks messages to be sent out to the whole community including the specific agent who sent the open call. Although all agents in the community will receive copies of the feedbacks, they are of no relevance to agents who are already in the task completed block, therefore, only agents in the frustrated block can consume such messages. In this scenario, only EA1 can consume these feedbacks. The three feedbacks will be received by T11 of EA1, however, out of the three, only one will be chosen at random to trigger T11, and cause it to transition the task1 out of the frustrated block.

4 Modelling Outcome and Discussion

In the context of this study, a collaborative community is achieved through a network of interconnected agents who share diverse kinds of information through a common sharing platform. It is perceived that the diversity of the shared information is a key element in this kind of collaborations. Using this approach, agents can share their various challenges which made specific task difficult or easy for them to accomplish. Just like real life scenarios, different people will encounter different challenges when attempting to solve the same problem. Therefore, the approach to solving one problem may vary from one person to the other. Consequently, creating a platform where it is possible to share such personal experiences, techniques and skills could help generate a pool of ideas, techniques, skills and experiences that could help others solve the same problem, however, from diverse perspectives. This collaborative idea is what the model under consideration seeks to achieve.

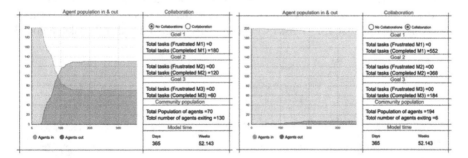

Fig. 5. a. Fixed number of agents with no collaboration b. Fixed number of agents with collaborations

Scenario1. Non-fluid membership with (a) No collaboration, and (b) with collaboration. Figure 5 represents the outcome of the model using a fixed number of agent population consisting of 200 agents in the non-collaboration scenario. It can be seen that 130 agents exited the community due to the absence of feedbacks to help address agent's frustrations. Only 70 out of 200 agents were retained after 365 days representing a scenario of low membership fluidity. In terms of tasks completed, goal 1, recorded 180 completed tasks, goal 2 recorded 120 completed tasks and goal 3, 60 tasks. No task pileups were recorded. On the contrary Fig. 5b is the outcome of the same model, however, with collaboration introduced. It can be seen that 194 out of 200 agents were retained after a period of 356 days. This outcome shows a scenario of high membership fluidity. Only 6 agents exited the community. In terms of tasks, 552 tasks were completed in goal 1, 368 tasks were completed in goal 2, and 184 tasks were completed in goal 3. No task pileups were recorded. By comparing the outcomes of gaol 3 for both scenarios, it can be inferred that the combination of collaborations and antecedent interventions significantly enhanced the delegation of deferrable loads.

Scenario 2. Fluid membership (a) No collaboration, and (b) with collaboration. Figure 6a and 6b shows the outcome of the model with membership fluidity modelled on a weekly basis. The level of fluidity is modelled as a *random function (X, Y) where X* = 0 members per week and *Y* = 5 members per week. Figure 6a shows the instance of the model with no collaboration. The outcome shows that, a total of 222 (152 + 70) agents joined the platform over a period of 365 days, considering there were zero agents at the start of the model. It can also be observed that a total number of 152 agents out of 222 were retained in the community at the end of the model year. Furthermore, 70 agents exited the community. This represent a scenario of low membership fluidity. Figure 6a further revealed that 337 tasks were completed in goal 1, 169 tasks were completed in goal 2 and 78 tasks were completed in goal 3. Furthermore, it can be seen that, at the end of the model run, there was 7 tasks pileups in goal 1, 32 tasks pileups in goal 2 and 53 tasks pileups in goal 3. By comparing Figs. 6a with 6b we notice a significant improvement in the model performance. This is because Fig. 6b represents the scenario with collaborations. In this scenario, we noticed that a total number of 215 (206 + 9) agents joined the community over the model year. Out of this number, the community retained 206 agents and lost only 9 agents. This represent a scenario of high membership fluidity. In terms of tasks management, 511 tasks were completed in goal 1, 294 tasks were completed in goal 2 and, 139 tasks in goal 3.

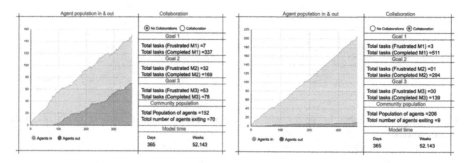

Fig. 6. a. Stochastic addition of agent with no collaboration b. Stochastic addition of agent with collaborations

Task pileups in goal 1, was 3, in goal 2 was 1 and 0 in goal 3. A general conclusion can therefore be drawn that the model performed better under collaborating conditions than otherwise.

One relevant aspect of the ongoing research on CVPP-E, hinges around Delegation of Deferrable Loads (DLs) to the ecosystem manager for collective management. The manager is able to shift the use of these loads to different times of the day to reduce peak demands on the power grid. DLs can also be shifted strategically to utilize renewable energy when generation is high, and curtailed their use when generation is low. These techniques are called "load shifting" and "peak shaving" under DSM.

Although the ultimate goal of the ecosystem is goal 3, which is to influence agents to delegate their deferable loads, we envisage that by introducing this action as a direct and standalone activity, the perceived inconvenience and discomfort to agents could make the idea unattractive, and will result in less patronage. However, we anticipate that through antecedent interventions such as introduced in goal 1 and goal 2, we may be able to take the agent through a journey of small changes preceding the major change. This, we expect, could help to inculcate the necessary discipline and sense of energy conservation, collaborations and community consciousness in the agents before they are due to attempt delegation.

5 Conclusion and Future Work

This study has shown how a combination of collaboration and antecedent interventions could enable some form of behaviour change towards delegation of DLs. It has also been shown that the process could facilitate the achievements of community goals and its subsequent contribution to DSM in general. The study has further shown that when community members are provided with the needed support, in line with community objectives, in a timely manner, using collaborative techniques, they could contribute significantly to the achievement of community gaols. Similarly, efforts at influencing behavioural change could also deliver a promising outcome when implemented within a collaborative environment where members can share relevant and diverse kinds of experiences and knowledge which may not freely be available in a non-collaborating environment. After all, one size does not fit all when it comes to behavioural change approaches. Furthermore, membership fluidity has also been shown to have a significant influence on an ecosystem.

Regarding the ongoing research on CVPP-E and related future works, we intend to model a scenario where the community is constituted of different categories of households. We will consider households with single pensioner, households with multiple pensioners, households with children, households without children and households with single non-pensioner. This categorization and related energy use data is inspired by [23]. In each type of household, we will model different task dynamics to represent the schematic behaviour of each household as they attempt a change in behaviour. For instance, households with children or households with pensioners could be modelled in a way such that they may exhibit different behaviours, which could affect the model outcome significantly. we also intend to advance this study by integrating or coupling each household's energy consumption so that it is possible to visualize how these behaviours impact on the global community's energy use.

Acknowledgement. The authors acknowledge the contributions of the PTDC/EEI-AUT/32410/2017 – Project CESME (Collaborative & Evolvable Smart Manufacturing Ecosystem and the Portuguese FCT program UIDB/00066/2020 for providing financial support for this work. Furthermore, we extend our appreciations to Ghana Educational Trust Fund (GETFund), the University of Energy and Natural Resources and UNINOVA CTS for supporting this work with their research facilities and resources.

References

1. European Commission: Energy performance of buildings directive (2019). https://ec.europa.eu/energy/topics/energy-efficiency/energy-efficient-buildings/energy-performance-buildings-directive_en. Accessed 28 Mar 2020
2. Edenhofer, O., Pichs-Madruga, R., Sokona, Y., Agrawala, S.: Summary for policymakers, New York, NY, USA (2014)
3. Diawuo, F.A., Pina, A., Baptista, P.C., Silva, C.A.: Energy efficiency deployment: a pathway to sustainable electrification in Ghana. J. Clean. Prod. **186**, 544–557 (2018)
4. Adu-Kankam, K.O., Camarinha-Matos, L.M.: A framework for behavioural change through incentivization in a collaborative virtual power plant ecosystem. In: Camarinha-Matos, L.M., Farhadi, N., Lopes, F., Pereira, H. (eds.) DoCEIS 2020. IAICT, vol. 577, pp. 31–40. Springer, Cham (2020). https://doi.org/10.1007/978-3-030-45124-0_3
5. Lopes, R.A., Martins, J., Aelenei, D., Lima, C.P.: A cooperative net zero energy community to improve load matching. Renew. Energy **93**, 1–13 (2016)
6. Abrahamse, W., Steg, L., Vlek, C., Rothengatter, T.: A review of intervention studies aimed at household energy conservation. J. Environ. Psychol. **25**, 273–291 (2005)
7. Wheatley, M., Frieze, D.: Lifecycle of Emergence Using Emergence to Take Social Innovations to Scale. Lifecycle of Emergence. http://www.berkana.org/articles/lifecycle.htm. Accessed 04 Aug 2020
8. Butler, B.S.: Membership size, communication activity, and sustainability: a resource-based model of online social structures. Inf. Syst. Res. **12**(4), 346–362 (2001)
9. AnyLogic: AnyLogic: Simulation Modeling Software (2018). https://www.anylogic.com/. Accessed 13 Feb 2020
10. Harding, M., Hsiaw, A.: Goal setting and energy conservation. J. Econ. Behav. Organ. **107** (PA), 209–227 (2014)
11. Abrahamse, W., Steg, L., Vlek, C., Rothengatter, T.: The effect of tailored information, goal setting, and tailored feedback on household energy use, energy-related behaviors, and behavioral antecedents. J. Environ. Psychol. **27**(4), 265–276 (2007)
12. McCalley, L.T., Midden, C.J.H.: Energy conservation through product-integrated feedback: the roles of goal-setting and social orientation. J. Econ. Psychol. **23**, 589–603 (2002)
13. Andor, M.A., Fels, K.M.: Behavioral economics and energy conservation – a systematic review of non-price interventions and their causal effects. Ecol. Econ. **148**, 178–210 (2018)
14. Ferrada, F., Camarinha-Matos, L.M.: A modelling framework for collaborative network emotions. Enterp. Inf. Syst. **13**(7–8), 1164–1194 (2019)

15. Graça, P., Camarinha-Matos, L.M., Ferrada, F.: A model to assess collaboration performance in a collaborative business ecosystem. In: Camarinha-Matos, L.M., Almeida, R., Oliveira, J. (eds.) DoCEIS 2019. IAICT, vol. 553, pp. 3–13. Springer, Cham (2019). https://doi.org/10.1007/978-3-030-17771-3_1

16. Camarinha-Matos, L.M., Fornasiero, R., Ramezani, J., Ferrada, F.: Collaborative networks: a pillar of digital transformation. Appl. Sci. 9(5431), 1–33 (2019)

17. Adu-Kankam, K.O., Camarinha-Matos, L.M.: Towards collaborative virtual power plants: trends and convergence. Sustain. Energy Grids Netw. 16, 217–230 (2018)

18. Adu-Kankam, K.O., Camarinha-Matos, L.M.: Towards collaborative virtual power plants. In: Camarinha-Matos, L.M., Adu-Kankam, K.O., Julashokri, M. (eds.) DoCEIS 2018. IAICT, vol. 521, pp. 28–39. Springer, Cham (2018). https://doi.org/10.1007/978-3-319-78574-5_3

19. Adu-Kankam, K.O., Camarinha-Matos, L.M.: Emerging community energy ecosystems: analysis of organizational and governance structures of selected representative cases. In: Camarinha-Matos, L.M., Almeida, R., Oliveira, J. (eds.) DoCEIS 2019. IAICT, vol. 553, pp. 24–40. Springer, Cham (2019). https://doi.org/10.1007/978-3-030-17771-3_3

20. Latham, G.P.: The motivational benefits of goal-setting. Acad. Manag. Exec. 18(4), 126–129 (2004)

21. Locke, E.A., Latham, G.P.: New directions in goal-setting theory new directions in goal-setting theory. Psychol. Sci. 15(5), 265–268 (2006)

22. Prochaska, J.O., Diclemente, C.: Transtheoretical therapy: toward a more integrative model of change. Psychother. Theory Res. Pract. 19(3), 276–288 (1982)

23. Zimmermann, J.-P., et al.: Household Electricity Survey: A study of domestic electrical product usage. Milton Keynes (2012)

Analysis of Productivity and Profitability of a SME Through Collaborative Networks Using Discrete Event Simulation Tool: An Automotive Case Study

Emigdio Martínez[1]([⊠]), Daniel Cortés[2], José Ramírez[2],
María Guadalupe Obregón[1], and Arturo Molina[2]

[1] Instituto Politécnico Nacional, UPIICSA, 08400 Mexico City, Mexico
emigdiomartinez22@gmail.com, nathauo@hotmail.com
[2] School of Engineering and Sciences, Tecnologico de Monterrey,
14380 Mexico City, Mexico
{a01655708,a00995924}@itesm.mx, armolina@tec.mx

Abstract. Most companies seek sustainability and competitive advantage for optimal problem solving and value creation. Medium-sized companies that account for more than 90% of the world's total companies with a low research & development, tend to search for alternatives within the private and educational sector that allow them to increase their productivity without having to compromise their competitive activity in their sector. Collaboration with external actors represents an opportunity for organizations as it broadens their development of the productive system and their organizational behaviour. This interaction is known as Open Innovation. This concept has dismantled the traditional organizational archetype enabling universities to link the academy's work into the industrial sector. One-part of the academy, in collaboration with them, is the use of emerging technologies and digital tools that lead into a decision-making efficient process incorporating industry 4.0. A useful technology for this purpose is Discrete Event Simulation, a tool for system analysis, characterized by modifying variables without compromising the current productivity of the company. This document explains through a case study, the use of simulation in an enterprise of the automotive sector through the tool, in the lamination process of production line. The contribution of this paper is generating alternatives for the decision-making process in a real scenario, using the tool to achieve results in collaboration within the industry sector. The analysis shows the improvement, analyzing the productivity and choices, that increase in the profitability of the enterprise.

Keywords: Discrete event simulation · Industry 4.0 · Value creation · Collaborative networks · Making-decision · SME · Automotive industry

© IFIP International Federation for Information Processing 2020
Published by Springer Nature Switzerland AG 2020
L. M. Camarinha-Matos et al. (Eds.): PRO-VE 2020, IFIP AICT 598, pp. 406–417, 2020.
https://doi.org/10.1007/978-3-030-62412-5_33

1 Introduction

Nowadays, Industry 4.0 plays an important role in competitive advantage for many enterprises. All the phases of the industrial revolutions have led great changes to industries and part of their supply chains [1], considering the three key concepts to increase competitiveness advantage: cost leadership strategy, differentiation strategy and focus strategy [2]. To this regard, competitiveness on the manufacturing level has been based on core technologies and tools inherent to the fourth revolution which has impacted positively the economy axis of most enterprises. At present, most of the enterprises worldwide that seek innovation and competitiveness represent more than 90% medium-sized enterprise (SME). With the adoption of industry 4.0 in large enterprises and SME working as intermediaries, there has arisen the interest in adopting new technologies and methodologies for the purpose of competing and innovating their products. In the growth model [3], there is considered technological progress as an important factor in worker's productivity and consequently, in production processes. In recent years, the new technologies introduced by industry 4.0 have intensified changes in the economy of industry. In a study, it explains that the fourth industrial revolution will influence the condition of world industry, depending on the level of industrialization, the condition will be different in each country [4]. Increasing adoption of technologies has had a positive effect on the growth and development of SMEs. Nowadays, innovation in the most highly developed countries has had growth and development. On the other hand, developing countries have sought economic performance and competitive advantage. In 2019, Mexico ranked 51st related to competitive advantage [5]. This represents, approximately 4.1 million by national SMEs [6]. However, in the literature review, there are shown common factors that limit the investing of novel technologies and methodologies related to Industry 4.0, [7–12]. This problem is due to the lack of effective decision-making when designing, evaluating, analysing and modifying strategies and changes to the product or operating process in an SME. Notwithstanding, the low R&D level influences the decision-making of necessary tools, new knowledge and technologies to achieve innovation of the SME. Therefore, considering their limited financial resources, they are forced to look for alternatives with external agents such as universities. Collaboration with universities represents an opportunity for SMES's because of their key role within industry 4.0. One role of the university is the use of emerging technologies and digital tools to propose alternatives to SMEs. An emergent technology that has reached maturity is Discrete Event Simulation (DES) for the decision-making process. DES has demonstrated the feasibility of improving production processes characterized by parametrizing multiple scenarios for analysis and evaluation of either production line or productive system. Furthermore, this tool is characterized by modifying factors in the simulation without compromising the physical design and productivity of the SME. These simulations are achieved using computational resources that work with existing information and allow modifications without modifying the physical system. Given the context described, this paper aims to show how SME's profitability is improved directly from the decision-making process using a DES tool. Nonetheless, this work could not be done without the Collaborative Networks (CN) that arose with the university and industrial sector. The structure of the paper states as follows: In Sect. 2 there is described the collaboration with universities through the Open Innovation Laboratories (OIL), an alternative in which the SMEs can increase their R&D to improve their processes. Section 3 explains the use of the DES tool, how it works, its contributions and the impact of this tool for enterprises, as well as the simulation model that was used in this paper. In Sect. 4 shows the proposal, the analysis and evaluation for decision-making by using DES in collaboration with the SME case study and the university OIL, as well as the methodology to be used. In Sect. 5 describes the case study in the automotive sector, the development of the simulation according to the proposed methodology and the results found by each scenario. In Sect. 6, the conclusions and contributions of this paper.

2   Collaborative Networks

SMEs don't have all the necessary capabilities and infrastructure [13], with limited knowledge in decision-making [14]. Justifying the collaboration with the universities previously, besides being entities that generate knowledge daily, originates a CN with the SME. The CN works with external actors to ensure that new knowledge and technology comes not only from within the organisation but also to outside, this interaction is known as Open Innovation (OI) and has dismantled enterprise's traditional innovation. Therefore, CN with universities helps to promote the generation of new ideas from different parts and the creation of new knowledge. The CN with university allows generating a horizontal integration because they're dedicated to carrying out research and development activities with the SME, improving the processes and the innovation of the products. Likewise, the SME is vertically integrated by increasing the efficiency of all its resources through technology and new knowledge with the university. In some universities, the collaboration with enterprises is carried through an OIL.

2.1   Open Innovation Laboratories

Nowadays, SMEs are seeking the adoption of the OI despite the application of methodologies and mechanisms that they have implemented by their organization [15, 16]. OI has been defined by many authors as a process where flows coordinated knowledge [16, 17], a support in organizations and in the industries [18]; implementing the concept. The OI model also suggests that enterprises should combine external and internal ideas and technologies like effective channels as technologies are advanced [19, 20]. A part of the universities devotes itself to the collaboration with enterprises, these spaces are known as OILs. OIL is a resource leader of the universities that performs many functions, including collaboration with enterprises of different sizes and types of business activities. OIL has a significant impact on innovation, being a paradigm that focuses on the enterprise with the exploitation of external knowledge to improve the innovation of the internal process [21], (e.g. problem-solving by leveraging decision-making and praxis of innovation management [15]), as well as R&D and strategy projects. The OIL has a platform with technologies developed by researchers and students of the same university like methods, methodologies and on the other hand, a series of modern software and hardware and emerging technologies (simulation, big data, printing 3D, among others). For collaboration between university-industry in OI, some authors [13] have selected some main keys that should be considered. In business model is proposed [13] for collaboration between universities and enterprises through the OI. Universities in different countries have implemented the OIL concept, in different ways, some CN collaborate from virtual spaces and the most are face-to-face. Some most well-known terms that have been dealt for OIL are Makerspaces, High Tech Lab, Learning Rooms and Fabs Labs [22].

3   Discrete Event Simulation

The university through its OIL are offering resources to the enterprises with the purpose of generating product innovation and the improving of their processes. In view of this rapid technological evolution, OILs have also been updated through the adoption of emerging tools and technologies. One of the most used tools for decision-making is simulation. Used in the production area, logistics, industrial engineering, among others, it corresponds to a pillar of Industry 4.0. Enterprises react ahead of time using DES cost-effectively and efficiently, allowing decision-makers to have a full perception of the design of the process or product. The results obtained by DES have ensured useful information for speeding up decision-making. So, focusing on DES as CN support for SME-OIL, it is possible to define as one of the useful tools in the CN to represent the real processes in a digital model [23], designing, analyzing and evaluating multiple scenarios and multi-criteria in the decision-making. DES efficiency has been proved by different case studies, [24–29].

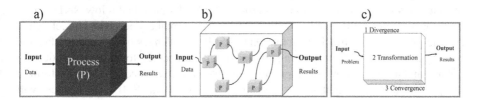

Fig. 1. Simulation models types. (a) Input-Output or Black Box, (b) Glass Box, (c) Three-Stage Process.

Nevertheless, the efficiency of DES depends highly on the availability, quantity and quality of information introduced to the models. There are three types of models according with their application and robustness: Black Box, [30, 31] or also called "input-output", the Glass Box or also known as white box [30, 32] and the Three-Stage Process [30] (See Fig. 1).

4 Use of DES as Support for Effective Decision Making in Analysis and Evaluation of Operative Processes

This section describes and illustrates procedure proposed for simulation using Act Research-Cycle (ARC). Finally, proposal for decision-making in the analysis and evaluation of operational processes an SME is described and illustrated.

4.1 Proceeding Simulation Using Act Research Cycle

Although, simulation is an efficient tool, there is needed techniques or methodology support in the simulation models design. Bangsow [23] proposes VDI 3633 procedure which it's a methodology focused on simulation design and elaboration. Chavarria-Barrientos et al. [33], proposes a continuous improvement technique known as ARC. It's used for each VDI 3633 procedure stage (See Fig. 2). Methodology development provides precise information for results securing of simulation design.

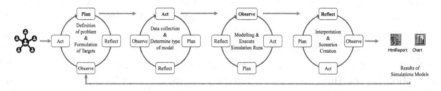

Fig. 2. Steps for development of Simulation models. Propose technique based on ARC

4.2 Proposal

According Schwab K. [34], productivity in processes and enterprises growth are related to Industry 4.0. Nevertheless, most enterprises by SMEs have had a low R&D due to lack tools, technologies and practices necessary to make decisions correct when solving-problems in a timely manner. One of SMEs challenges have faced in effective making-decisions is the improving of operational processes to increase production volume and minimize downtime, giving to understand these processes that transform to the product and give sight to the customer [2]. At present, SME are engaged with universities that enable them to achieve their productive objectives through appropriate technologies and tools for decision-making. CN creation is put into practice between SME-University, but with the purpose of the major cohesion exists, some universities have an OIL, to collaborate, offering technologies, knowledge and tools necessary. Through CN, there arises the exchange and generation of information between SME-OIL, to generate an effective decision-making bearing in mind the limitation and management of the financial resources of the SME. This interaction generating collaborative innovation in the SME. CN proposes DES, a tool that allows to design, analyze and evaluate the operative process through creation of different scenarios, without compromising the financial investment, without changes in the design or the expense of the resources of the SMEs. Therefore, CN generates value creation by using DES, generating accurate and reliable results for decision-making. The simulation procedure [23] for generating results report is based on the ARC strategy, in order to make a cyclically compliant marked steps of DES (See Fig. 3).

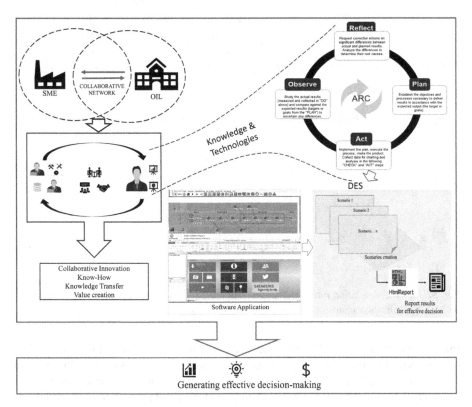

Fig. 3. Proposed framework for effective decision-making in CN for SME-University

5 Case Study

It was developed in a mexican SME in the automotive sector, under the Make To Order (MTO) segment, whose manufacturing business is semi-urban and urban passenger buses. It practices traditional manufacturing, furthermore, has little experience in manufacturing processes. The SME's local market includes large enterprises that offer a diverse product range, whereupon keep motivates to continue improving his operations and minimize costs. This paper was in collaboration with a SME to increase productivity and profitability of production line, specifically in lamination area. This area has different activities: grinding, assemblies of various metal parts, lamination of the chassis structure, fibber-glass molds, among others. In order to improve the productivity area real process, it proposed give alternatives to the SME for process decision-making in collaboration with Tecnologico de Monterrey's OIL through DES tool. Likewise, White Box Model (See Fig. 5a) and Three-Strategy-Process (See Fig. 4), simulated in scenarios different. The applied ARC presented:

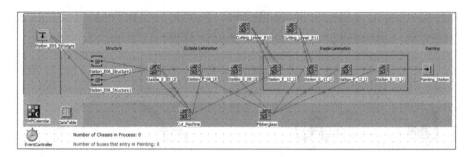

Fig. 4. Simulation lamination area in Tecnomatix by Siemens based in three-stage process

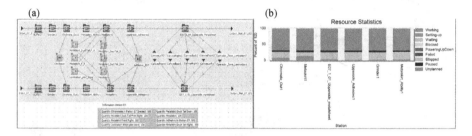

Fig. 5. Execute simulation runs on different stations. (a) Simulation of framework of Station E-07-LE, (b) Utilization chart for station E-07-LE.

Plan. Problem definition: The SME has need to increase its productivity, however, bad management has been detected generating bottlenecks in workstations in the area lamination as well as processing times of activities have a long times and generation of waste has been very high. Formulation of Target: Compare the traditional lamination process area with different in each scenario simulated by DES tool in order to generating effective alternatives for SME decision-making process. The feasible scenarios were evaluated through the productivity generated by processing times and energy consumption of workstations.

Act. Data collection: The data was collected using a VSM. such as the processing times (including movement times), set-up time, recovery time, cycle time, availability and MTTR for each activity. Determine Model Type: White box model [30, 32] was chosen for the 7 workstations of real process (See Fig. 1b). Only considered processing times and failures, amount materials used (See Fig. 6). General model used was the Three-Stages-Process (See Fig. 1c) due to the overall robustness of the simulation data quantities that make up the lamination area. Daily production scheme consists a 10 h workday and 142.24 min time-out, operates for only five days. Model was developed and evaluated in Plant Simulation Tecnomatix by Siemens.

a)   b)

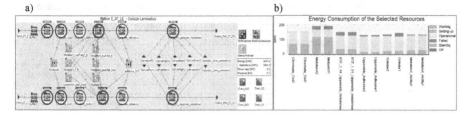

Fig. 6. Energy consumption of tools and equipment in real situation - Station E-07-LE. (a) Energy consumption visualization (b) Energy consumption chart.

Observe. Modelling Simulation: Simulation was developed representing the "structures" area, "lamination area" of the station 7 to 13 (for example E-07-LE, See Fig. 5a) and the "painting" area (See Fig. 4). Execute Simulation Runs: It was run for 37 days to calculate the estimated monthly production without non-working days. The downtime, break time, paused time, unplanned time and failure time, are shown graphically (See Fig. 5b). Therefore, with the SME's time of experience and the simulation results (See Table 1) and the ARC [33], it's determined that the process is in the "introduction of the quality" according to the model of Integration and Modernisatión of Small and Medium Mexicans Enterprise (IMMPAC) [35].

Reflect (Restart the Cycle). Three different scenarios were executed with the DES tool based on the ARC and the objective is also contemplated. Through the results report by Plan Simulation, OIL proposed three scenarios in collaboration with SME to improve the simulation as well as to achieve profitability. In each scenario, the process improved by demonstrating positive results in productivity by eliminating failures, reducing downtimes and personnel management in the software. This gives an anticipation of the application of different proposed improvements, for example, IMMPAC good practices [35] and/or technologies application to reduce time. Scenario 1 (Quality Stage); was associated with orders compliance and addition of continuous production flow. Scenario 2 (Reliability), was designed with two 8-h shift per day, reducing lead time and quantity to meet commitment to the painting area. Finally, scenario 3 (Profitability), involves three 8-h shift per day, with development of cost indicators and time reduction by simulating the application of new technologies based on the criteria of the SME.

5.1   Results

OIL presents the results below: The real situation productivity (84 units monthly) is low compared to the SME target (100 per monthly). On the other hand, scenarios 1, 2 & 3 increase productivity due to the time of each proposed Takt Time and reduction of downtimes, such as planning time, machine start-up time, time to go to the bathroom, meal time, among others. There are chassis that are in lamination process, however, the 3 proposed scenarios decrease or eliminate the bottlenecks. There is a gradual increase

Table 1. Results obtained for Plant Simulation (one month). Comparison real vs scenarios.

Scenario	Station	Available time (daily)	Scrap laminate (pieces/month)	Consumption energy (kWh/month)	Volume (buses/month)
Real situation (quality: in process)	E-07-LE	27,466 s	46	1084.3	84 buses laminated & (16 chassis in process)
	E-08-LE		28	129.2	
	E-09-LE		–	381.3	
	E-10-LI		–	607.3	
	E-11-LI		38	926.0	
	E-12-LI		–	890.7	
	E-13-LI		–	601.8	
Scenario 1 (quality)	E-07-LE	31,200 s	22	1157.8	91 buses laminated & (17 chassis in process)
	E-08-LE		12	209.0	
	E-09-LE		–	417.0	
	E-10-LI		–	632.3	
	E-11-LI		20	1004.2	
	E-12-LI		–	992.2	
	E-13-LI		–	648.5	
Scenario 2 (reliability)	E-07-LE	51,000 s	43	1976.0	148 buses laminated & (16 chassis in process)
	E-08-LE		43	352.9	
	E-09-LE		–	704.0	
	E-10-LI		–	1065.4	
	E-11-LI		28	1696.9	
	E-12-LI		–	1673.1	
	E-13-LI		–	1088.2	
Scenario 3 (profitability)	E-07-LE	51,000 s	33	2019.2	152 buses laminated & (12 chassis in process)
	E-08-LE		44	352.5	
	E-09-LE		–	716.3	
	E-10-LI		–	1063.7	
	E-11-LI		17	1788.7	
	E-12-LI		–	1666.2	
	E-13-LI		–	1085.8	

estimated for each simulated scenario in chasis volume production. The sheet scrap quantities are shown monthly with a normal distribution, declaring to the software a 5% pieces scrap of total produced. For scenarios 1, 2 and 3 was declared a scrap an estimated 4%, 3% and 2% respectively. The scrap generation is with respect to the engineering bill of materials. For the supply voltage, it was determined by the standard average through management by the software (Input: 1 kW of working, 1 kW of setting-up, 0.5 kW Operational, 0.5 kW Failed and 0.1 kW standby), multiplied by processing time of each activities (where the electrical equipment is used) and finally, by the number of chassis that move on to the next activity. The estimated productivity improvements for scenarios 1, 2, and 3 are 8.33%; 76.19% and 89.9% of productivity with respect to the simulated real situation.

6 Conclusions

The CN for this article is comprised of a private SME, academic reasearchers who have functioned as an interest between the two sides, creating OI for the SME and new knowledge and practices for University where the innovation emerging in the face of problem solving. The results, were evaluated considering economic and technological aspects and factors and restrictions provided by the OIL with the support of SME to improve its process. With DES tool and academy knowledge it was determined that the SME has a loss of 16 units in sales due to lack of productive time in its lamination process. This affects the SME's pocket money, in addition to the waste generated in the cuts management in the lamination. The energy use cost will depend on the decisions by the SME when making a proposed scenario to modernize or not equipment and tools. Thanks to CN, the information obtained by use of DES with the support of ARC and VDI 3633 by OIL has led to the value creation and viable alternatives creation in the future for the SME, impacting on profitability. Likewise, it's concluded that by working with DES in the CN, time and costs can be reduced, regardless of business type or process/producto type. For future work, it's intended to use DES for all the processes of production line in enterprise.

Acknowledgments. Special thanks to Instituto Politécnico Nacional and the Unidad Profesional Interdisciplinaria de Ingeniería y Ciencias Sociales y Administrativas (UPIICSA) for academic training. This paper has been partially supported by CONACyT. A special mention is made to the Tecnologico de Monterrey for allowing it to do this work for computing time.

References

1. Bal, H.Ç., Erkan, Ç.: Industry 4.0 and competitiveness. Procedia Comput. Sci. **158**, 625–631 (2019)
2. Porter, M.: Competitive Advantage Creating and Sustaining Superior Performance. Free Press, New York (1985)
3. Solow, R.M.: A contribution to the theory of economic growth. Q. J. Econ. **70**(1), 65–94 (2010). http://www.jstor.org/stable/1884513
4. Upadhyyaya, S.: Country grouping in UNIDO statistics, Vienna, Austria (2014)
5. IMD World Competitiveness ranking. https://www.imd.org/worldcompetitiveness-ranking-2019/
6. Instituto Nacional de Geografía y Estadística (INEGI) (2018). https://www.inegi.org.mx/ENAPROCE
7. Dyerson, R., Spinelli, R.: Revisiting IT readiness: an approach for small firms. Ind. Manag. Data Syst. **116**, 546–563 (2016)
8. Kennedy, J., Hyland, P.: A comparison of manufacturing technology adoption in SMEs and large companies, October 2003
9. Terziovski, M.: Innovation practice and its performance implications in small and medium enterprises (SMEs) in the manufacturing sector: a resource - based view. Strateg. Manag. J. **31**, 892–902 (2010)
10. Vasudevan, H., Chawan, A.: Demystifying knowledge management in Indian manufacturing SMEs. Procedia Eng. **97**, 1724–1734 (2014)

11. Müller, J.M., Voigt, K.-I.: Industry 4.0 - integration strategies for small and medium-sized enterprises. In: International Association for Management of Technology, May 2017, pp. 1–15 (2017)
12. Mittal, S., et al.: A critical review of smart manufacturing & Industry 4.0 maturity models: implications for small and medium-sized enterprises (SMEs). J. Manuf. Syst. **49**, 194–214 (2018)
13. Ivascu, L., Cirjaliu, B., Draghici, A.: Business model for the university-industry collaboration in open innovation. Procedia Econ. Financ. **39**, 674–678 (2016)
14. Simon, H.: Bounded rationality and organizational learning. Organ. Sci. **2**, 125–134 (1991)
15. Chesbrough, H.: Chez Panisse: building an open innovation ecosystem. Calif. Manag. Rev. **56**(4), 144–171 (2014)
16. Leckel, A., et al.: Local open innovation: a means for public policy to increase collaboration for innovation in SMEs. Technol. Forecast. Soc. Change **153**(119891), 20 (2020)
17. Chesbrough, H., Bogers, M.: Explicating open innovation: clarifying an emerging paradigm for understanding innovation keywords, pp. 1–37 (2014)
18. Brunswicker, S., Chesbrough, H.: The adoption of open innovation in large firms. Res. Technol. Manag. **61**, 35–45 (2018)
19. Wynarczyk, P., Piperopoulos, P., Mcadam, M.: Open innovation in small and medium-sized enterprises: an overview. Int. Small Bus. J. **31**, 240–255 (2013)
20. Draghici, A., et al.: A knowledge management approach for the university-industry collaboration in open innovation. Procedia Econ. Financ. **23**, 23–32 (2015)
21. Piller, F.T., West, J.: Firms, users, and innovation: an interactive model of coupled open innovation. In: New Frontiers in Open Innovation, pp. 29–49 (2014)
22. Agyapong, D., Brautlacht, R., Owino, J.: University collaboration - research collaboration and teaching collaboration. In: Handbook of Applied Teaching and Learning, pp. 46–65 (2018)
23. Bangsow, S.: Manufacturing Simulation with Plant Simulation and SimTalk. Usage and Programming with Examples and Solutions. Springer, Heidelberg (2010). https://doi.org/10.1007/978-3-642-05074-9
24. Barrera-Diaz, C.A., et al.: Discrete event simulation output data-handling system in an automotive manufacturing automotive plant. Procedia Manuf. **25**, 23–30 (2018)
25. Siderska, J.: Application of tecnomatix plant simulation for modeling production and logistics processes. Bus. Manag. Educ. **14**(1), 64–73 (2016)
26. Fil'o, M., et al.: PLM systems and tecnomatix plant simulation, a description of the environment, control elements, creation simulations and models. Am. J. Mech. Eng. **1**(7), 165–168 (2013)
27. Villagomez, L.E., et al.: Discrete event simulation as a support in the decision making to improve product and process in the automotive industry - a fuel pump component case study. In: Camarinha-Matos, L.M., Afsarmanesh, H., Antonelli, D. (eds.) PRO-VE 2019. IAICT, vol. 568, pp. 572–581. Springer, Cham (2019). https://doi.org/10.1007/978-3-030-28464-0_50
28. Kostrzewski, M.: Simulation research of order-picking processes high-bay warehouses. Logist. Transp. **20**, 5–12 (2013)
29. Borojevic, S., Jovisevic, V.: Modeling, simulation and optimization of process planning. J. Prod. Eng. **12**(1), 87–90 (2009)
30. Jones, J.C.: Design Methods. Wiley, London (1972)
31. Pidd, M.: Computer Simulation in Management Science, 5th edn. Wiley, Hoboken (2004)
32. Sametinger, J.: Software Engineering with Reusable Components. Springer, Heidelberg (1997). https://doi.org/10.1007/978-3-662-03345-6

33. Chavarría-Barrientos, D., et al.: Methodology to support manufacturing system design using digital models and simulations: an automotive supplier case study. IFAC-Pap. **51**, 1598–1603 (2018)
34. Schwab, K.: The fourth industrial revolution. In: World Economic Forum (2016)
35. Molina, A., Gonzales, D.: IMMPAC - a methodology for the implementation of enterprise integration programs in Mexican SMEs. In: Kosanke, K., Nell, J.G. (eds.) Enterprise Engineering and Integration. Research Reports Esprit, pp. 431–438. Springer, Heidelberg (1997). https://doi.org/10.1007/978-3-642-60889-6_46

A Physics-Based Approach for Managing Supply Chain Risks and Opportunities Within Its Performance Framework

Thibaut Cerabona[1(✉)], Matthieu Lauras[1], Louis Faugère[2],
Jean-Philippe Gitto[3], Benoit Montreuil[2], and Frederick Benaben[1]

[1] Centre Génie Industriel, IMT Mines Albi,
Campus Jarlard, 81013 Albi CT Cedex 09, France
{thibaut.cerabona,matthieu.lauras,
frederick.benaben}@mines-albi.fr
[2] ISyE, H Milton Steward School of Industrial and Systems Engineering,
755 Ferst Drive, Atlanta, GA 30332, USA
{louis.faugere,benoit.montreuil}@isye.gatech.edu
[3] Scalian, 17 Avenue Didier Daurat, Batiment Pythagore,
31700 Blagnac, France
Jean-Philippe.GITTO@scalian.com

Abstract. Managing a Collaborative Network (such as a supply chain) requires setting and pursuing objectives. These can be represented and evaluated by formal Key Performance Indicators (KPIs). Managing a supply chain aims to stretch its KPIs towards target values. Therefore, any Collaborative Network's goal is to monitor its trajectory within the framework of its KPIs. Currently potentiality (risk or opportunity) management is based on the capacity of managers to analyze increasingly complex situations. The new approach presented in this paper opens the door to a new methodology for supply chain potentiality management. It offers an innovative data-driven approach that takes data as input and applies physical principles for supporting decision-making processes to monitor supply chain's performance. With that approach, potentialities are seen as forces that push or pull the network within its multidimensional KPI space.

Keywords: Risk Management · Opportunity Management · Supply Chain Management · Physics

1 Introduction

A Collaborative Network, as defined by [1], is a network of diverse entities (organizations or people) that are autonomous, geographically dispersed and heterogeneous in terms of their operating environment, culture and goals, but willing to collaborate together by exchanging information, resources and responsibilities in order to more easily achieve common goals. Moreover, [2] defines a supply chain as a network of organizations interlinking suppliers, manufacturers and distributors in different activities and processes in order to produce products and services delivered to the final

© IFIP International Federation for Information Processing 2020
Published by Springer Nature Switzerland AG 2020
L. M. Camarinha-Matos et al. (Eds.): PRO-VE 2020, IFIP AICT 598, pp. 418–427, 2020.
https://doi.org/10.1007/978-3-030-62412-5_34

customer. Considering these two definitions, a supply chain can easily be seen and described as a Collaborative Network.

Today's managers are faced with increasingly complex situations in an uncertain environment, especially in the management of risks and opportunities. Although there are already many tools at their disposal, most of them only allow them to visualize and format data related to potential risks and opportunities. The processing of the results provided by these tools is essentially based on the knowledge, experience and understanding of the tool by managers. Is this enough to manage a supply chain in an increasingly competitive market?

This paper claims that (i) the identification of objectives and metrics, and (ii) an intuitive tool to support decision-making are essential for managing efficiently a supply chain. These decisions make it possible to seize opportunities or keep out of risks in order to reach the targeted values of its objectives. This paper answers the following question: *"how to improve the management of a supply chain by piloting its trajectory in its performance framework where risks and opportunities are modelled by physical forces deviating it from its target trajectory?"*. This paper is organized according to the following structure: Sect. 2 provides an overview of existing research works and scientific contributions relating to performance management and the management of elements disrupting the achievement of performance targets. Section 3 describes our physics based approach. Finally, Sect. 4 mentions some perspectives.

2 Background

2.1 Performance Management

In today's world, supply chain management is essential for increasing organizational efficiency and achieving organizational goals such as improving competitiveness, profitability and customer service [4]. Performance measurement is a process that quantifies the effectiveness and efficiency of an action [5]. This process maintains various metrics (like KPIs) that are used to support decision making and management. Indeed, it is not possible to manage an organization without any measures [6]. Measurement is one of the most important activities in management. Most of the studies argue that performance metrics should be composed with financial and non-financial KPIs [6]. Some performance frameworks have been proposed such as: the balanced scorecard of Kaplan and Norton [6], activity-based costing of Anderson and Young [7], Neely's performance prism [8] and the Supply Chain Operations Reference (SCOR) developed by the Supply Chain Council [9].

Therefore, the management of a supply chain involves shaping and pursuit goals and objectives evaluated by formal KPIs. Evaluating supply chain performance is complex due to its multidisciplinary field and the number of actors with different perspectives that create many barriers such as: decentralized data, little cohesion in the chosen indicators, poor communication and no common decision [10]. [4] identified and suggested three levels of performance measurement according to decision making process: operational, tactical and strategic. In a synthetic study that reviewed the literature, [11] identified 27 key performance indicators for the supply chain. 50% of these performance metrics are linked to the internal business of the supply chain. The other 50% are related to the final customer.

2.2 Supply Chain Risk and Opportunity Management

Supply chain is impacted by predictable or unexpected events that threaten the achievement of its performance targets [12]. According to [13], there are a lot of source of risks (which originate from the operational part of a company or from the uncertainty of its external business environment). Moreover, due to the increasing complexity of manufacturing systems and the evolution of legal context which enforces companies to improve their maturity in this domain (for example the ISO 9001), risks management becomes a huge challenge [14]. Therefore, supply chain management needs to deal with them.

In this section the concept of risk and opportunity will be studied from the literature to deliver guidelines for their characterization. First of all, as described in [15], risk management process is divided in four steps:

- Risk identification: detection of risks by studying an organization and its environment with techniques and methodologies such as SWOT analysis or force field analysis [16].
- Risk Assessment: evaluation of the impact of the risk on the organization, it is divided in two parts: qualitative and quantitative analysis.
- Risk Response Strategies: avoidance, sharing, mitigation and acceptance.
- Risk Monitoring and Control: monitor the status of identified risks.

According to [16], the existing results and methods on the domain of risk management can be extended to the question of opportunity management. Thus opportunity management process can be divided in four steps:

- Opportunity identification: does not require any changes to the risk identification step, the same methodologies can be used. In the SWOT analysis, opportunities are taken into account. The force field analysis is a technique widely used in strategic decision-making to identify positive (opportunity) and negative (risk) influences in the achievement of goals [16].
- Opportunity Assessment:
    O A common quantitative analysis can be used to take both the positive and negative effects of uncertainty into account.
    O In [17], risk is defined as a combination of its impact on the organization and its probability of occurrence. So, this very used two-dimension framework can be used for the common qualitative analysis (Fig. 1).

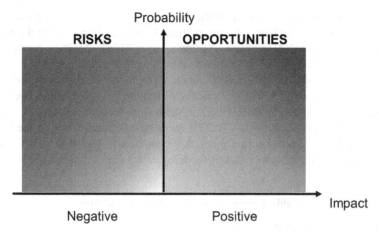

Fig. 1. Two-dimension framework for Risks and Opportunities analysis adapted from [18].

- Opportunity Response Strategies:
    - ○ exploitation: this strategy is symmetrical to "avoidance" strategy, whereas "avoidance" seeks to decrease the probability of occurrence of a risk to 0%, "exploitation" seeks to increase this probability to 100% for an opportunity,
    - ○ sharing: transfers a risk or an opportunity to another member of the network which is abler to deal with it,
    - ○ enhancing: increases the probability and/or the impact in order to maximize the benefit of an opportunity (inversely, "mitigation" seeks to reduce the degree of exposure to a risk),
    - ○ acceptance: no active measure to deal with a risk or an opportunity.
- Opportunity Monitoring and Control: do not require any changes to the risk monitoring and control step, the same methodologies can be used. It aims is to monitor the status of identified risks and opportunities, to identity new risks and opportunities, to ensure the proper implementation of the corrective actions put in place and to review their effectiveness [16].

As discussed in [19] risks and opportunities are very close. The existing research results on the field of risk management can be symmetrically extended to opportunity management. From our vision, both together are considered as potentiality management.

[20] advises managers to focus on two major activities of this four steps process: potentiality assessment and monitoring. Potentiality assessment is a critical and complex step because of the complexity of the models required and the subjective nature of the data available to conduct the analysis [21]. In the literature, many methods have been developed in order to assess and prioritize potentialities. According to [22], the top six of risk assessment tools in automotive supply chains are: cost/benefit analysis, business impact analysis, scenario analysis, environmental risk assessment, FMEA and cause and consequence analysis.

The necessity to rank many quantitative and qualitative conflicting criteria of a finite number of potentialities imposes to regard this problem as a multi attributes decision making (MADM) problem. According to ([20, 21, 23–26]), Analytic Hierarchy Process (AHP), Analytic Network Process (ANP), Technique for Order of Preference by Similarity to Ideal Solution (TOPSIS), Elimination and Choice Expressing Reality (ELECTRE), Preference Ranking Organization Method for Enrichment Evaluations (PROMETHEE) or Measuring Attractiveness by a Categorical Based Evaluation Technique (MACBETH) are MADMs largely used in the literature (see Table 1 for a short description of these methods). The ISO 31000 standard identifies more than thirty tools and methodologies for risk assessment [22].

Table 1. Short description of these MADMs:

MADM	Description
AHP	Technique which can combine qualitative and quantitative factors for prioritizing, evaluating and ranking alternatives
ANP	A broader form of AHP, structures a decision problem as a network.
TOPSIS	A compensatory aggregation method that compares a set of alternatives by calculating the geometric distance between each alternative and the ideal alternative
ELECTRE	Used to reject some alternatives to a multi-criteria problem
PROMETHEE	Allows to establish a ranking between alternatives based on a comparison pair per pair of possible decisions along each criterion [25]
MACBETH	The approach, based on the additive value model, requires only qualitative judgments about differences of value [26]

3   Proposal: A Supply Chain Management Physics-Based Approach

The new approach presented in this paper offers a new and original method for supply chain management. This approach takes data as input and applies physical principles for supporting decision-making processes to control a supply chain's trajectory within multi-dimensional KPI space. This performance space (Fig. 2) allows to locate the considered supply chain in terms of its KPIs and is composed of:

- the performance of the considered supply chain: its current performance according to selected KPIs (orange sphere),
- the target zone: a part of the performance space reflecting the current target of the considered supply chain in terms of KPIs (green sphere),
- the forces: these are the forces to model in the performance space in order to control supply chain performance (color vectors).

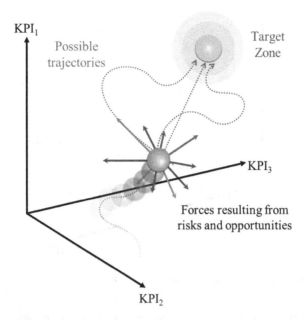

KPI₁

Possible
trajectories

Target
Zone

KPI₃

Forces resulting from
risks and opportunities

KPI₂

Fig. 2. Definition of target zone within the performance framework (Color figure online)

The evolution of KPIs and therefore the evolution of the supply chain's position in its performance space are due to the occurrences of risks or opportunities, when they become actualities. Basically, a risk (a hurricane for example) will move the supply chain away from its objectives, while an opportunity (a new cheaper supplier for example) will bring the supply chain closer to them. Indeed, in the Fig. 3 example, the fictitious considered supply chain is represented in the following performance framework: profit, lead time and product quality (respectively KPI_1, KPI_2 and KPI_3). Some of its suppliers are located in the Gulf of Mexico. They are therefore subject to a high hurricane risk. If its suppliers are hit by a hurricane, it is easy to imagine that the performance of this supply chain will be strongly impacted and degraded: profits will decrease and lead times will strongly increase due to impassable roads, damaged infrastructures and warehouses (violet sphere in Fig. 3 represents its new position in its performance framework). Conversely, if this supply chain seizes the opportunity to source from a new cheaper Asian supplier but with a lower quality, the supply chain will thus move in its performance framework (green sphere in Fig. 3). Its performance in terms of profit will be improved, while the quality of its products decreases.

Thus with that new approach, potentialities can be seen as forces that push and pull the system within its KPIs framework. Indeed, each force reflects the probable consequences of each identified potentiality. The obtained forces, in addition to their direction and intensity (given by the framework of the KPIs dimensions), are different types (please see [18], if you want more information about the four types of forces: internal, external, collaboration and gravity).

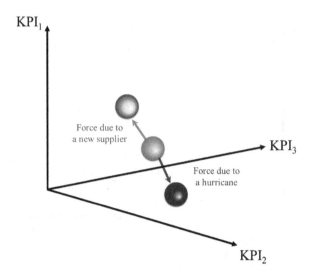

Fig. 3. Fictitious considered supply chain within its KPIs framework (Color figure online)

In order to realize links between KPIs and forces and to be able to observe the impact of forces on the KPI values, forces and KPIs will be modeled by functions of attributes. These attributes characterize and describe the supply chain. They are divided into three categories:

- Internal: attributes that characterize the company we are focusing on (capacity, number of employees, …),
- External: business environment-related and location-related attributes (new laws, environmental hazard, …),
- Interface: attributes that characterize the different partnerships of the considered organization (customer demand, lead time of suppliers, …).

Moreover, this framework can be seen as a decision framework and used to define target zone. An in-depth analysis of the attributes impacted by the identified forces will make it possible to define the lever attributes for decision-making. And thus, find the best possible strategies to reach the target zone. This target zone corresponds to the area of the KPI target value space. The requirements and objectives of the various stakeholders will take into account in this zone. By the intensity of the identified forces, one can study how to define the best compromise between the best combination of potentialities and the required effort to join the target zone (possible trajectories in Fig. 2). Indeed, the intensity of the forces will modify over time the values of the attributes, thus modifying the value of the considered KPIs.

4   Perspectives and Conclusion

The presented approach opens the door to an innovative vision for supply chain management and decision making. The following list is the roadmap to turn that approach into a workable practice:

- In the short term, the bulk of the work is to design and to develop the fictitious supply chain simulation model of a famous commercial aircraft manufacturer using Anylogic software. The goal is to perform multiple simulations of the various potentialities (risks and opportunities) that the aircraft manufacturer's logistics network may face. Indeed, for example, rising and falling demand or stopping the manufacture of a model, which offer the possibility to study their impacts on its supply chain and its performance. In addition, as defined in the article [18], there are four types of forces. Therefore, in a first step, the impacts of the potentialities modelled by each type of force will be studied separately. After multiple simulations of the model, regressions will be performed on the obtained KPIs values. These regressions aim at identifying the impacts on the KPIs of these macro events (potentialities) represented by specific micro-consequences (for example: *"between 20% and 30% of the delivery trucks will face a 2 to 3 h' delay"* [18]). And thus, subsequently be able to study the movement and trajectory of the considered supply chain in its performance framework. The last step will consist in repeating this process, but simultaneously simulating all the considered potentialities. This last series of simulations will enable us to answer the two following points.
- The study of independence or not of the forces in order to determine accessible KPI space areas and efforts to join these areas (analogies with the work of a force and kinetic energy could be exploited).
- How to characterize a force and a decision in terms of time (i.e. over what period of time this strength applies, how much time a manager has to take a decision in order to avoid a risk or to seize an opportunity, what is the time frame to implement a decision, …), costs, reversibility, confidence and type (impulse, progressive, continue, …).
- Taking into account the notions of robustness and resilience of the supply chain in decision making. As defined in [27], supply chain robustness "refers to the ability of a supply chain to withstand disruption and continue operating" and supply chain resilience "references the ability of a supply chain to bounce back from disruption".
- The objective is to develop with this new approach an intuitive and dynamic decision support system where managers are able to pilot the trajectory of the supply chain in its performance framework. So, to be able to observe and visualize the supply chain within its multidimensional KPI space is already a hard challenge. Indeed, its performance framework will surely consist of more than three dimensions. Therefore, we need to find a visualization system: allowing us to abstract ourselves from this problem of representing an n-dimensional space and that is dynamic and intuitive. Thus, Virtual Reality is considered a potent medium for supporting such visualization.

References

1. Camarinha-Matos, L.M., Afsarmanesh, H.: Collaborative networks. In: Wang, K., Kovacs, G.L., Wozny, M., Fang, M. (eds.) PROLAMAT 2006. IIFIP, vol. 207, pp. 26–40. Springer, Boston, MA (2006). https://doi.org/10.1007/0-387-34403-9_4
2. Christopher, M.: Logistics & Supply Chain Management. Financial Times Prentice Hall, Harlow (2011)
3. Taleb, N.N.: The Impact of the Highly Improbable. Random House (2007)
4. Gunasekaran, A., Patel, C., Tirtiroglu, E.: Performance measures and metrics in a supply chain environment. Int. J. Oper. Prod. Manag. **21**, 71–87 (2001)
5. Neely, A., Gregory, M., Platts, K.: Performance measurement system design: a literature review and research agenda. Int. J. Oper. Prod. Manag. **15**, 80–116 (1995). https://doi.org/10.1108/01443579510083622
6. Kaplan, R.S., Norton, D.P.: Putting the balanced scorecard to work. In: The Economic Impact of Knowledge, pp. 315–324. Elsevier (1998). https://doi.org/10.1016/B978-0-7506-7009-8.50023-9
7. Anderson, S.W., Young, S.M.: The impact of contextual and process factors on the evaluation of activity-based costing systems. Acc. Organ. Soc. **24**, 525–559 (1999). https://doi.org/10.1016/S0361-3682(99)00018-5
8. Neely, P.A.: Perspectives on Performance: The Performance Prism. The Evolution of Business Performance Measurement Systems, 8
9. Stewart, G.: Supply-chain operations reference model (SCOR): the first cross-industry framework for integrated supply-chain management. Logist. Inf. Manag. **10**, 62–67 (1997). https://doi.org/10.1108/09576059710815716
10. Lima-Junior, F.R., Carpinetti, L.C.R.: Quantitative models for supply chain performance evaluation: a literature review. Comput. Ind. Eng. **113**, 333–346 (2017). https://doi.org/10.1016/j.cie.2017.09.022
11. Gunasekaran, A., Kobu, B.: Performance measures and metrics in logistics and supply chain management: a review of recent literature (1995–2004) for research and applications. Int. J. Prod. Res. **45**, 2819–2840 (2007). https://doi.org/10.1080/00207540600806513
12. Wagner, S.M., Bode, C.: An empirical investigation into supply chain vulnerability. J. Purchasing Supply Manag. **12**, 301–312 (2006). https://doi.org/10.1016/j.pursup.2007.01.004
13. Colicchia, C., Strozzi, F.: Supply chain risk management: a new methodology for a systematic literature review. Supply Chain Manag. **17**, 403–418 (2012). https://doi.org/10.1108/13598541211246558
14. Gorecki, S., Ribault, J., Zacharewicz, G., Ducq, Y., Perry, N.: Risk management and distributed simulation in Papyrus tool for decision making in industrial context. Comput. Ind. Eng. **137**, 106039 (2019). https://doi.org/10.1016/j.cie.2019.106039
15. Tummala, R., Schoenherr, T.: Assessing and managing risks using the Supply Chain Risk Management Process (SCRMP). Supply Chain Manag. **16**, 474–483 (2011). https://doi.org/10.1108/13598541111171165
16. Hillson, D.: Extending the risk process to manage opportunities. Int. J. Project Manag. **20**, 235–240 (2002). https://doi.org/10.1016/S0263-7863(01)00074-6
17. Edwards, P.J., Bowen, P.A.: Risk Management in Project Organisations. Elsevier, Amsterdam (2005)
18. Benaben, F., Lauras, M., Montreuil, B., Faugère, L., Gou, J., Mu, W.: A physics-based theory to navigate across risks and opportunities in the performance space: application to crisis management. Presented at the Hawaii International Conference on System Sciences (2020)

19. Olsson, R.: In search of opportunity management: is the risk management process enough? Int. J. Project Manag. **25**, 745–752 (2007). https://doi.org/10.1016/j.ijproman.2007.03.005
20. Eren-Dogu, Z.F., Celikoglu, C.C.: Information security risk assessment: Bayesian prioritization for AHP group decision making. Int. J. Innov. Comput. Inf. Control **8**, 8019–8032 (2011)
21. Arikan, R., Dağdeviren, M., Kurt, M.: A fuzzy multi-attribute decision making model for strategic risk assessment. Int. J. Comput. Intell. Syst. **6**, 487–502 (2013). https://doi.org/10. 1080/18756891.2013.781334
22. de Oliveira, U.R., Marins, F.A.S., Rocha, H.M., Salomon, V.A.P.: The ISO 31000 standard in supply chain risk management. J. Clean. Prod. **151**, 616–633 (2017). https://doi.org/10. 1016/j.jclepro.2017.03.054
23. Khemiri, R., Elbedoui-Maktouf, K., Grabot, B., Zouari, B.: A fuzzy multi-criteria decision-making approach for managing performance and risk in integrated procurement–production planning. Int. J. Prod. Res. **55**, 5305–5329 (2017). https://doi.org/10.1080/00207543.2017. 1308575
24. Mojtahedi, S.M.H., Mousavi, S.M., Makui, A.: Project risk identification and assessment simultaneously using multi-attribute group decision making technique. Saf. Sci. **48**, 499–507 (2010). https://doi.org/10.1016/j.ssci.2009.12.016
25. Taillandier, P., Stinckwich, S.: Using the PROMETHEE multi-criteria decision making method to define new exploration strategies for rescue robots. In: 2011 IEEE International Symposium on Safety, Security, and Rescue Robotics, Kyoto, Japan, pp. 321–326. IEEE (2011). https://doi.org/10.1109/SSRR.2011.6106747
26. Bana e Costa, C.A, De Corte, J.M., Vansnick, J.C.: Macbeth. Int. J. Inf. Technol. Decis. Making **11**, 359–387 (2003)
27. Clément, A., Marmier, F., Kamissoko, D., Gourc, D., Wioland, L.: Robustesse, résilience: une brève synthèse des définitions au travers d'une analyse structurée de la littérature. In: MOSIM 2018 - 12ème Conférence internationale de Modélisation, Optimisation et SIMulation (2018)

Product and Service Systems

Value Proposition in Smart PSS Engineering: Case Study in the Residential Heating Appliance Industry

Camilo Murillo Coba[1,2(✉)], Xavier Boucher[1], François Vuillaume[2],
Alexandre Gay[2], and Jesus Gonzalez-Feliu[3]

[1] Mines Saint-Etienne, Université Clermont Auvergne, CNRS, UMR 6158,
LIMOS-Institut Fayol, 158 Cours Fauriel, 42023 Saint-Etienne, France
camilo.murillo@emse.fr,
xavier.boucher@mines-stetienne.fr
[2] e.l.m. Leblanc SAS, 126 rue de Stalingrad, 93 705 Drancy, France
[3] Excelia Group La Rochelle Business School, Centre de Recherche en
Intelligence et Innovation Managériales, 102 rue Coureilles - Les Minimes,
17024 La Rochelle, France

Abstract. This paper explains the first steps of a smart PSS engineering approach, aimed at eliciting stakeholder needs, prototyping the value proposition, representing how the Original Equipment Manufacturer (OEM) will capture value and share it with a collaborative network of stakeholders while identifying and prioritizing risks from the value proposition. The approach addresses two gaps in the field of smart PSS design: (i) the need of visualizing solutions to support the transformation of value propositions for the stakeholders into a contract mechanism supporting value capture by the offering company and (ii) the importance of integrating risk management during the design of Smart PSS value proposition

Keywords: Smart PSS · PSS design · Value proposition · Risk review

1 Introduction and Scientific Positioning

Long-term strategies of manufacturing companies are dependent on their adoption of new Business Models (BM). The commoditization of products and digital development have posed an opportunity for manufacturing companies to transform their current business models into a digital service-oriented business model, in which value-in-use plays a major role. Since value proposition describes the benefits that customers can expect from the solution proposed by a firm [1], a clear design of this proposition seems vital to its market success. However, the formulation of a new value proposition implies several challenges. Among others, a large number of collaborative stakeholders, with distinct non-convergent needs and value expectations requires to be carefully considered during the whole process of solution design. Besides, a new value proposition may create value for several stakeholders (notably customers) but not necessarily generate value for the provider. In order to ensure the capture of value for the provider, a value proposition must be easily replicable in the form of a contract

© IFIP International Federation for Information Processing 2020
Published by Springer Nature Switzerland AG 2020
L. M. Camarinha-Matos et al. (Eds.): PRO-VE 2020, IFIP AICT 598, pp. 431–439, 2020.
https://doi.org/10.1007/978-3-030-62412-5_35

leading to a steady source of revenues. Therefore, design needs adapted mechanisms for economic value capture.

These challenges take special importance in the field of Product-Service Systems (PSS), particularly in 'Smart PSS' defined as "A digital-based ecosystem of value creation characterized by high complexity, dynamics and interconnectedness among stakeholders." [2]. *Value proposition representation* and *stakeholder mapping*, seen as key elements required to build a pertinent usual PSS solution [3], play an essential role in Smart PSS engineering. A well-defined value proposition is crucial to develop long-lasting relationships with users and its relevance should be maintained over time [4]. Although value-based guidance and evidence of risk-based decisions are highly advisable in the design of a complex system [5], scientific literature lacks guidelines on how to identify and evaluate risks during the phase of Smart PSS value proposition design. For a larger state-of-the-art in the field of value proposition design in PSS, the reader can refer to [6].

Aiming at increasing the industrial applicability of Smart PSS design, this research is developed as a collaborative work with the company Elm Leblanc. Thus, the paper deals with the operationalization of methods for smart PSS value proposition building. More precisely, this paper presents a value proposition design approach complementing current frameworks with the following two specific added values:

- The development of an iterative, multi-stakeholder value proposition building approach based on the mapping and visualization of the value creation for each involved stakeholder via a modelling and visualization tool (PS3M) to support the collaborative process [7].
- The inclusion of risk identification and evaluation in an early stage of the value proposition building processes, to mitigate and monitor them during the whole Smart PSS engineering process.

Thus, this paper presents a structured approach to assist Original Equipment Manufacturers (OEMs) in the definition of solution-oriented value propositions for smart PSS. This approach allows to (i) identify key stakeholders for the Smart PSS, (ii) collect key stakeholder needs, (iii) ideate functionalities to satisfy these needs, (iv) define alternative value propositions, (v) identify value capture mechanisms for the solution provider, and (vi) identify the key risks affecting the solution. A case study in the field of the thermo-technology industry (Elm Leblanc) illustrates the approach.

The structure of this paper is as follows. Section 2 describes the approach for designing and prototyping value propositions for Smart PSS. Section 3 illustrates the application to an industrial case. Finally, we present conclusions and perspectives.

2   Value Proposition Prototyping in Smart PSS Engineering

As collaborative research with Elm Leblanc, the authors propose to build the approach based on the scientific gaps already mentioned and the feedback from practitioners of Smart PSS engineering. This approach (Fig. 1) presented in this paper, provides an operational guide for the activities required for defining and prototyping the value proposition for a Smart PSS solution. This approach is part of an extended Smart PSS

Engineering framework presented in [8]. This Smart PSS Engineering framework results from the study of PSS design literature, agile approaches for smart PSS, Value proposition design methods [1, 9], and Risk management [10]. Thus, the approach described below follows an iterative logic inspired by [5]. This logic facilitates to react to the different types of risks during the whole engineering process.

Fig. 1. Overall view of the prototyping approach.

This smart PSS value proposition design includes advances on the two gaps mentioned above, visualization and risks, within various engineering steps. The activities that contribute to risk identification along the whole approach are listed in Table 1. These activities are associated with some of the framework stages presented in this paper. The identified risks are recorded in a *design risk register*, with their corresponding assessments of the probability of occurrence and potential impacts. The design team should come up with monitoring strategies to track the high-impact risks. A graphical decision-based computer tool, PS3M [7], allows capturing visually all useful elements and knowledge contributing to value proposition definition, supporting knowledge sharing among stakeholders along the design process. Hence, PS3M is used to represent graphically the components of the Smart PSS value proposition. It proposes a set of modelling views presenting complementary aspects of the ongoing value proposition, gathering a shared design knowledge base.

Table 1. Activities contributing to risk identification during value proposition design

Stage of the approach	Activities for risk identification
Strategic contextualization	PEST and SWOT analyses, Ecosystem mapping
Collection of stakeholders' needs	Potential market estimation
Value proposition prototyping	Service catalog representation on PS3M, Value model proposition Model-Clash Spider Web [5]

The 'Strategic contextualization' step provides the initial inputs with the identification of key stakeholders, key risks, and a representation of an Ecosystem map within PS3M. This step will not be detailed here, since it is considered as an input of subsequent steps explained below.

2.1   Collection of Stakeholder Needs

After the 'Strategic contextualisation' step, the challenges of design team are to create value in this existing ecosystem, then to estimate the potential market.

The Collection of Value Expectations of Key Stakeholders is made via Design Thinking [9], then integrated with both the visualization and risk approach proposed below. Contextual and in-depth interviews with the key stakeholders are necessary to elicit stakeholders' expectations and problems to be solved. The analysis of these interviews leads to the creation of customer profiles defined in terms of customer jobs, gains, and pains [1]. In addition, expectations are classified into five dimensions of value creation, providing a classification of value expectations to support value proposition building: economical, environmental, social, relational, and functional. These analyses help in understanding the different usage contexts linked to the expectations of each key stakeholder. Finally, current customer experiences are mapped as 'customer journeys' to highlight opportunities to improve the value-in-use experience. All these elements of information can be stored and shared within the design team through the PS3M Ecosystem map to ensure that the value proposition devised from expectations analysis will have high desirability.

The Estimation of Value Potential for the OEM is necessary to ensure the incorporation of the value proposition in a profitable business model. Overall estimation of the potential market becomes imperative before further developing the value proposition. This estimation is a qualitative characterization of the market into distinct customer classes together with a quantitative estimation of the market share in the short and middle term. PS3M proposes a specific 'Demand view' to visualize suitable markets along with potential customer classes with their associated use profiles in a shared project knowledge base. These potential market estimations are used as a source to identify risks affecting provider value capture: the risk register is updated.

2.2   Value Proposition Prototyping

Expectations identified in the previous step are a prior requirement for the ideation phase. Consequently, the design team must prioritize the jobs, pains, and gains of key stakeholders, considering their importance for each stakeholder [1]. Then, the ideation phase consists of a brainstorming session aimed at defining a general value proposition statement, and the functionalities that the solution will offer. These functionalities are captured and represented in the PS3M modeling tool via the combination of two views: the 'product view" depicts tangible and digital elements of the solution in terms of product options and the 'service view" contains intangible elements in terms of service packages. These representations ease risk identification based on of the capabilities required to deliver the services included in the value proposition. The risk register is updated accordingly.

The general value proposition statement has then to be refined to make explicit how physical, digital, and intangible elements generate value for the stakeholders. To support this activity, we propose the use of Value maps [1], which efficiency in Smart Services' design is proven: iteratively, a value map is developed for each key stakeholder separately, resulting in several alternative value propositions for each. These alternative value propositions are structured and formulated as 'service packages' targeted at different customer classes. Then, referring to all previous design knowledge already gathered, the design team defines decision criteria leading to choose the most appropriate value proposition for each key stakeholder, considering OEM's value expectations. At this point in the engineering process, validation of the chosen value propositions is conducted with OEM's internal actors that are in close contact with customers. This validation aims at examining the feasibility of the value proposition, from both a technical and market viability points of view.

Finally, the success conditions of key stakeholders are identified, then displayed in a diagram and registered in the PS3M tool. This representation allows identifying risks related to the potential incompatibilities amongst the success models of each key stakeholder [5], since neglecting them may lead to the failure of the system delivering the PSS solution. These risks are recorded in the Smart PSS design risk register.

2.3   Value Capture Mechanism Design

Designing a value proposition requires presenting evidence of the profitability and scalability of the economic model associated with the value proposition [1]. Since previous research has little addressed this aspect, either for traditional [11], or Smart PSS design [12, 13], it is important to define, at early stage design, the roles of the contract's owner, the revenue mechanism and the possible penalties when the expected functionalities and/or outcomes of the contract are badly delivered. A very clear definition of the contract helps to avoid any failure in value delivery [14].

In this step, the design team explores the different economic models associated with a Smart PSS value proposition, namely, product-oriented, use-oriented, and result-oriented. Aiming at addressing the gap mentioned in the previous paragraph, we propose to draft the Smart PSS contract via the PS3M's specific 'Offer view'. This representation aims at visualizing the alternative paths to deliver the Smart PSS solution, in commercial terms: (i) type of selling contracts, (ii) content of the contracts in terms of products, digital components, and services, (iii) demand forecasting, (iv) characteristics of the customers that are likely to sign the drafted contract. This representation leads to a first global definition of the cost and revenue structures associated with the Smart PSS value proposition.

2.4   Risk Review

The risk register contains the list of all risks identified and assessed through the process of design and prototyping of the value proposition. The classical stages of risk management, namely, identification, evaluation, and prioritization of risks are performed. If after having executed these stages, the OEM finds an acceptable level of risk, it will pursue the engineering process while monitoring and applying such mitigation strategies. On the contrary, if the OEM concludes that the risk level is too high, it will decide to reevaluate the value proposition, target another customer segment, or address other stakeholder jobs, pains, and gains, avoiding in this way to pursue efforts that might compromise the OEM's financial health.

3   Case Study

We illustrate the application of our value proposition prototyping framework via a deductive case study [15] starting from the evolution of a solution developed by a fabricant of gas boilers (the OEM) mainly addressed to social housing. The OEM also performs the maintenance of its products as part of its current service catalog. Converting the current product and service offering into a Smart PSS solution would enable the target customer and maintenance companies to monitor and operate a fleet of gas boilers. To assess the potential of this change, the proposed approach is applied by modelling suitable Smart PSS configurations using the PS3M toolkit: a focus group (design group) within the company was consulted and both primary and secondary data were collected and structured as follows.

3.1   Collection of Stakeholder Needs

Firstly, the design group elaborated a mapping of the current business ecosystem associated with the selling and maintenance of gas boilers, for the target customer. This mapping enabled the OEM to identify several key stakeholders, including end-users of the products, maintenance firms, and energy companies among others. Different risks were identified and recorded in a risk register. The design team identified the stages of the activity cycle of the target customer, namely configuration of the thermal system, installation, commissioning, operation, monitoring, maintenance, repair, and scraping. The OEM decided that the Smart PSS solution would be aimed at the operation and monitoring stage.

In-depth interviews were conducted with social landlords, tenants of the social housing units, and maintenance companies, with the objective to identify their needs. From the interviews' analysis, *customer personas* were created for end-users and maintenance staff personnel. Next, a list of customer jobs, pains, and gains are associated with each customer profile. These insights were categorized into value dimensions, e.g., unnecessary technical interventions impacting the monetary value dimension of the maintenance provider. Then, customer journeys were mapped based on the identified customer pains. These mappings were focused on depicting certain aspects of the user experience concerning the preventive and curative maintenance of the gas boilers, the gas boiler fleet management, the installation of the boiler, among others. The insights obtained with these mappings were used to formulate the potential functionalities of the Smart PSS solution. In parallel, an estimation of the potential market targeted at social landlords was conducted and then represented on the PS3M toolkit.

3.2 Value Proposition Prototyping

The needs of key stakeholders captured in the previous stage and expressed in user stories are used to carry out a creativity workshop. At the end of this workshop, the main functionality of the Smart PSS solution was defined, along with a catalog of services included in the solution. This catalog, modelled via PS3M, was used to identify risks concerning the deployment of the digital services. The most important risks associated with the deployment of these services concern data security, data storage, and data processing in real-time.

The design team linked gain creators and pain relievers to each of the envisioned services, by using PS3M (Fig. 2). Each of these services is related to the key stakeholders that will benefit from the service. Then, a discussion on the usage contexts of the solution helped to define service packages that addressed the different usage contexts of the customers, the social landlords, and the maintenance providers.

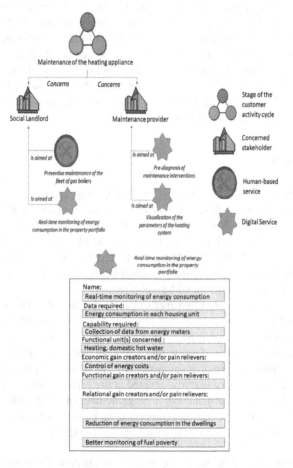

Fig. 2. Value proposition representation on PS3M.

3.3 Value Capture Mechanism

In order to structure the content and terms of the contract, the design team used the PS3M tool to represent visually the components of the contract. The design team decided to sell the hardware and to offer a service contract to either the maintenance provider or the social landlord. This service contract offers a range of smart services, namely, breakdown prediction, remote control of the fleet of gas boilers, energy consumption monitoring, and remote optimization of the settings of the thermal system. This visual representation triggered the discussion within the design about the conditions of the contract, such as the billing plan deadlines and the terms of payment.

3.4 Risk Review

Throughout this value proposition design process, the most important identified risk concerned the identification of the key stakeholders to commercialize the Smart PSS solution. A previous project of the OEM, related to a similar remote-monitoring solution, showed that assuming the wrong stakeholder as a client led to the commercial failure of the Smart PSS solution. In that case, the end-user of the boiler was defined as the client of the solution. However, end-users were not interested in acquiring a solution to identify breakdowns of the product, as they expected the product to work properly all the time: a specific manner to control such a risk had to be devised. Other key risks detected during the next steps of the engineering process dealt with data theft and potential external sabotage of the system.

4   Conclusions

This paper proposed a Value Proposition Prototyping approach aimed at assisting OEMs in the definition of digital service-oriented value propositions. The main contributions of the research dealt with the development of a multi-stakeholder collaborative prototyping approach based on a graphical modelling tool (PS3M) together with the inclusion of risk detection and review linked to value creation. A case study illustrates the approach and underlines the complexity of transforming a usual product-based business model into a smart PSS solution.

The application of the proposed methodology remains at a preliminary level and needs more in-depth developments but already shows the potential of the proposed approach. Further work is required to include a method to evaluate the value proposition(s) that results from the ideation and selection stages. A quantitative risk evaluation may be appropriate in this context. The approach proposed in this paper is expected to be applied in a case study targeted at the private housing market. This new case study involves the participation of a larger number of stakeholders. Therefore, the complexity of the value proposition prototyping tasks increases, making it possible to test the capacity of this work to deal with higher complexity.

Acknowledgments. Part of this work supported by EU DIGIFoF Erasmus+ Project.

References

1. Osterwalder, A., Pigneur, Y., Bernarda, G., Smith, A.: Value Proposition Design: How to Create Products and Services Customers Want. Wiley, Hoboken (2014)
2. Kuhlenkötter, B., et al.: New perspectives for generating smart PSS solutions–life cycle, methodologies and transformation. Procedia CIRP **64**(1), 217–222 (2017)
3. Ilg, J., Wuttke, C.C., Siefert, A.: Systematic prototyping of product-service systems. Procedia CIRP **73**, 50–55 (2018)
4. Valencia Cardona, A.M., Mugge, R., Schoormans, J.P., Schifferstein, H.N.: Challenges in the design of smart product-service systems (PSSs): experiences from practitioners. In: Proceedings of the 19th DMI: Academic Design Management Conference. Design Management in an Era of Disruption, London, UK, 2–4 September 2014. Design Management Institute (2014)
5. Boehm, B., Lane, J.A., Koolmanojwong, S., Turner, R.: The Incremental Commitment Spiral Model: Principles and Practices for Successful Systems and Software. Addison-Wesley Professional, Boston (2014)
6. da Costa Fernandes, S., Pigosso, D.C.A., McAloone, T.C., Rozenfeld, H.: Towards product-service system oriented to circular economy: a systematic review of value proposition design approaches. J. Clean. Prod. **257**, 120507 (2020)
7. Medini, K., Boucher, X.: Specifying a modelling language for PSS engineering–a development method and an operational tool. Comput. Ind. **108**, 89–103 (2019)
8. Murillo Coba, C., Boucher, X., Gonzalez-Feliu, J., Vuillaume, F., Gay, A.: Towards a risk-oriented smart PSS engineering framework. In: CIRP CMS 2020, Chicago, USA, 1–3 July 2020 (2020)
9. Lewrick, M., Link, P., Leifer, L.: The Design Thinking Playbook: Mindful Digital Transformation of Teams, Products, Services, Businesses and Ecosystems. Wiley, Hoboken (2018)
10. Dahmani, S., Boucher, X., Gourc, D., Peillon, S., Marmier, F.: Integrated approach for risk management in servitization decision-making process. Bus. Process Manag. J. (2020). https://doi.org/10.1108/BPMJ-07-2019-0279
11. Fernandes, S., Martins, L.D., Campese, C., Rozenfeld, H.: Representing the value proposition of Product-Service Systems (PSS) in a value-based perspective. In: DS 94: Proceedings of the Design Society: 22nd International Conference on Engineering Design (ICED 2019) (2019)
12. Neuhüttler, J., Woyke, I.C., Ganz, W.: Applying value proposition design for developing smart service business models in manufacturing firms. In: Freund, L.E., Cellary, W. (eds.) AHFE 2017. AISC, vol. 601, pp. 103–114. Springer, Cham (2018). https://doi.org/10.1007/978-3-319-60486-2_10
13. Liu, Z., Ming, X., Song, W.: A framework integrating interval-valued hesitant fuzzy DEMATEL method to capture and evaluate co-creative value propositions for smart PSS. J. Clean. Prod. **215**, 611–625 (2019)
14. Reim, W., Parida, V., Lindström, J.: Risks for functional products–Empirical insights from two Swedish manufacturing companies. Procedia CIRP **11**, 340–345 (2013)
15. Bitektine, A.: Prospective case study design: qualitative method for deductive theory testing. Organ. Res. Methods **11**(1), 160–180 (2008)

Collaborative Product and Service Customization in Fashion Companies

Elena Pessot[1(✉)], Laura Macchion[2], Irene Marchiori[1],
Rosanna Fornasiero[1], Pedro Senna[3,4], and Andrea Vinelli[2]

[1] Institute of Intelligent Industrial Technologies and Systems for Advanced
Manufacturing, National Research Council of Italy,
Via Alfonso Corti 12, 20133 Milan, Italy
{elena.pessot,irene.marchiori,
rosanna.fornasiero}@stiima.cnr.it
[2] Department of Management and Engineering,
University of Padova, Vicenza, Italy
{laura.macchion,andrea.vinelli}@unipd.it
[3] INESC TEC - Campus Da FEUP,
Rua Dr. Roberto Frias, 4200-465 Porto, Portugal
pedro.senna@inesctec.pt
[4] FEUP - Faculdade de Engenharia Da Universidade Do Porto,
Rua Dr. Roberto Frias, Porto 4200-465, Portugal

Abstract. This paper focuses on the identification of collaborative strategies
and practices adopted by companies of the fashion industry in the management
of customized offerings (both products and services) along their supply chain
(SC). A multiple case study approach is applied and four companies (both
medium and large) were interviewed. The cross-case analysis enabled mapping
the cases following two dimensions: type of market asking for the customization
(B2B vs. B2C) and scope of customization (products vs. services). The analysis
highlights the practices and processes related to the customization, the enabling
technologies adopted, and the actors involved by a focal company in the collaboration (both in upstream and downstream networks) to offer the product or
service that meet customer needs.

Keywords: Product customization · Service customization · Personalization ·
Collaboration · Fashion · Supply chain

1 Introduction

Nowadays, fashion industry is characterized by the growing demand for personalized
products and services according to clients' preferences and opinions [1]. Fashion
products are characterized by short life cycles, high volatility in demand, and
increasing variety with low predictability [2]. The fashion industry has a significant
relevance worldwide, and it is fragmented, extremely competitive and globalized [3].

The ability of accurately understanding the customer's personal demand, and the
consequent adoption of appropriate practices, is fundamental to improve the companies' core competitiveness and the customer satisfaction and loyalty [4]. Fashion

© IFIP International Federation for Information Processing 2020
Published by Springer Nature Switzerland AG 2020
L. M. Camarinha-Matos et al. (Eds.): PRO-VE 2020, IFIP AICT 598, pp. 440–449, 2020.
https://doi.org/10.1007/978-3-030-62412-5_36

companies willing to focus on customization should consider the full implementation of collaborative production network as a key issue to respond to ever-changing consumers' demand [4].

Previous literature on customization strategies in the fashion industry has mainly focused on specific activities of supply network management, such as: i) the downstream network, by debating the importance of the SC to respond promptly to the changing demand (e.g. [3]), ii) the upstream network by discussing, for example, the design phase [5, 6]; and, iii) the production process of personalized products (e.g. [7]) or services (such as distributed 3D printing services [8]).

In this sense, a comprehensive study considering the implications on supply network from both product and service perspectives, and the collaborative practices along the overall SC (integrating i, ii and iii), is still missing. This study aims to investigate strategies and practices carried out by companies of the fashion industry in the management of customized goods and services along their SC. To accomplish this goal, a multiple case study methodology is used to highlight different customization strategies and to identify the collaborative practices within the fashion network considering the actors involved (other businesses or final customers).

2 Theoretical Background

Customization represents a relevant opportunity for value creation, but it also remains a key challenge, especially for fashion industry. This industrial sector is characterized by high levels of complexity in terms of products and manufacturing processes, as well as a high number of SC partners [4]. The successful implementation of customization relies on important factors, such as: understanding the market needs, postpone the variety until real demand arises, and establish flexible production processes [9]. Therefore, collaborative and adaptive customization practices are important for the alignment between the market demands, the design of a product and the effective setup of production [10]. From the one side, the co-creation of value represent a benefit both for company, which can adjust the offer, and for customers who have the confidence to obtain the best alternative that meet their needs [11]. From the other side, customization enables producers to integrate with suppliers, as it facilitates the cooperation in the decision making process [12].

To manufacture a personalized product, new technologies can be supportive for the design (e.g. virtual reality) and manufacturing activities (e.g. reconfigurable production system, and additive manufacturing). The design phase for a personalized product is supported by product configurator systems, which ensure to tailor a product according to the specific needs of the customers [5]. Other important tools for the design are the 3D scanner, to acquire data [6], and the CAD 3D tools and 3D printing for the creation of personalized prototypes [13]. 3D printing represents an alternative for customized production because of its ability to produce objects with almost any shape or geometry [8]. Moreover, personalized products require large amount of flexibility, with reconfigurable, on-demand manufacturing systems [14].

In the last years, customization has not been limited only to the development of unique products for the customers, but also to the personalization of the services offered to customer as a strategy to lock them into long-term relationships [15]. A few examples of this strategy are [16]: (i) sale of redesigned clothing (consumers purchase clothing that has been redesigned from old clothing items); (ii) clothing repair/alteration service (consumers are provided with repair services to maintain their clothes); (iii) clothing renting (consumers acquire a certain number of items to be used for a short time period); and (iv) style consultancy service (providing customers with a style consulting, in-store or online, on how to use their clothes or to create new looks). The personalization of services consists of modifying certain components of the service offering, including service delivery, service products and service environments, based on personal profiles [17]. This means that customers are allowed to be involved in the purchase transaction so that their specific needs can be met, e.g. in terms of different delivery options [18]. The service personalization has been mainly analyzed in service marketing theories that debate the greater customer satisfaction, customer shopping experience, service quality, and customer loyalty that can be achieved by adding personalized services to fashion products [18, 19]. In the last years, research has focused on services developed for online purchase and personalization services [19] (i.e. options for personalizing lists, options to save preferences' information, personalized product selection aids). The delivery services offered by e-retailers have become one of the fundamental factors influencing an online shopper's decision [20]. In [18] in fact, it is suggested for the online retailers to improve their abilities in logistics service quality control and establish joint-venture logistics service providers, or build their own logistics network.

Companies can offer the product or service personalization at different levels of the SC, meaning that collaboration is established with the final customer or other business. The theme of product customization has always been closely connected to the Business-to-Consumer (B2C) sales channel [21] to collect personalization requests and needs directly in brick-and-mortar, as well as in online shops. In the Business-to-Business (B2B) world, the personalization is often offered as a combination of customized product and service [22]. Product customization has been a fundamental pillar of the B2C market, often exploited to increase revenues and maintain loyal customers. Conversely, it is still difficult to implement a well-defined customization strategy in the B2B context, even if the growing theme of personalization of services seems to be very supportive for companies to offer other companies a combined customized product and service [22]. The B2C and B2C market segments are radically different, thus, current personalization discussions should also consider customization options that pertain these market segments' peculiarities.

Summing up, few studies investigated the collaborative practices carried out by companies of the fashion industry to support the customization strategies (both at product and service level) and their implications at different SC echelons. Moreover, several technologies were identified to support customization, but they weren't analyzed as enabling the collaborative relationship between the actors in the fashion network. In order to build a complete framework and therefore analyse the practices implemented by fashion companies for customization, two dimensions should be considered: the scope of personalization (i.e. services vs products) and the type of market to whom offer the personalization (i.e. B2B vs B2C).

3 Methodology

Aiming to integrate different perspectives in the investigation of practices and strategies for customization along the SC of the fashion industry, we adopted a multiple case study approach [23]. We selected four companies, creating a sufficiently heterogeneous sample in terms of: dimensions, main business activity (they belong to different SC echelons) and SC processes involved in customization (from sourcing to selling and distribution). According to [23] the number of case studies is sufficient to obtain relevant results since the in-depth case studies allow to gather a large variety of relevant information. An overview of selected cases is shown in Table 1 (data on employees and turnover refer to end of year 2018).

Table 1. Sample of cases from fashion industry.

Company	Employees	Turnover	Fashion sector	Main activity
Case A	96	280 M €	Fashion accessories	Management of design and production of multi-brand accessories
Case B	100	53 M €	Eyewear	Production and delivery of finished and semi-finished lenses (recently also frames)
Case C	3.200	543 M €	High-luxury fashion	E-commerce business platform for selling and retailing luxury fashion items
Case D	80	25 M €	Sportswear (especially footwear)	Design and production of sports shoes and clothes, especially for cycling and snowboarding

Data collection was based on both primary and secondary data, also for triangulation purposes [23]). Primary data sources were semi-structured interviews, based on a common interview protocol. The research protocol was organized to collect data of each company on:

- SC structure and customization strategies;
- Level of collaboration and integration with other SC actors;
- Challenges and enabling technologies in collaborative customization.

A total of 8 interviews (2 per each case) were performed between May and October 2019 by multiple investigators at company site or via Skype call with key roles involved in SC and customization management including CEOs, product owners, SC managers and operations managers. The interviews were recorded and transcribed, and then triangulated with secondary data from annual reports, company websites and press releases of each company.

Data analysis involved two phases: a within-case analysis and a cross-case analysis [24]. In the first phase, data from each company was organized to identify main practices for customizing products and/or services in different SC dimensions, and the qualitative analysis (coding) was mainly aimed at identifying the ones involving collaboration at different SC echelons. In the second phase, the cross-case analysis allowed to extract common and diverse patterns of practices, informed by literature on customization of products and services, and involved channels or SC actors. This step resulted in the classification of the cases along the relevant perspectives to be considered in the customization of products and services in the fashion industry.

4   Case Studies in Fashion Industry

The current section briefly presents the findings of the multiple case study conducted in companies of the fashion industry.

Case A. Company A is the leather goods and footwear division of an international fashion group that includes several brands. The company is based in Italy and manages the design and production of all the shoes and bags of the brands belonging to the group. Based on the type of product, different production channels are used: the luxury segment shoes are made in Italy, while the mass-market segment finds its production in China, guaranteeing the manufacturing of standard products at low costs. Each brand is characterized by its own style and the company is able to guarantee the uniqueness of the products and customize them. The company also manages the distribution of the products towards the brands' retailers and shops in the world. It strictly collaborates with the designers of each luxury brand to carry out the design and the industrialization of the new shoes and accessories collections (more than 100 per year). The collaborative design of fashion collections is supported by the development of the 3D models and prototypes.

Case B. Company B is an Italian medium enterprise of the eyewear industry producing and marketing finished and semi-finished lenses (and recently also frames). The company serves daily more than 600 wholesalers and optical laboratories across the world. Company B relies on collaborative relationships and coordination mechanisms built on trust, mutual economic advantage and technological support to manage the long and globally distributed SC. Collaborative practices mainly focus on the coordinated planning of worldwide deliveries, tailored to customer requests, and personalized packaging. A trade-off between efficiency and flexibility is reached thanks to a balanced level of automation for both production and outbound logistics, the adoption of optimization models for inventory and transportation loading, and a strategy of stock sharing with customers with the support of an on-line platform constantly updated.

Case C. Company C is an English high luxury fashion online retailer. It created a digital marketplace with over 2.900 brands ranging from heritage brands to emerging designers. The company connects creators, curators and consumers, creating a global business ecosystem which enables the matching between the customer requests for high luxury goods and the offer/availability of boutiques around the world. To allow for customization in terms of procurement and distribution in a global SC, the company makes use of digital technologies and a strong collaboration among their distribution delivery carries allow to send products in 190 countries in 3–4 days (in average). Customers can choose between different personalized delivery options: from standard and premium delivery, and click and collect, to same-day delivery in 19 major global cities and store to door in 90 min. The company also offers data-driven services for its customers based on information management tools (i.e. big data analytics and API designs), to provide targeted advertising and customer support, and personalize the shopping experience.

Case D. Company D is an Italian company, specialized in the production of sportswear (especially cycling and snowboarding). Standard products are produced in Asia, while the top-of-the-line items are developed at the Italian headquarter, with selected materials exclusively from "Made in Italy" artisans. The downstream network is divided into a direct (for Italy and Germany) and an indirect market, with several distribution companies worldwide. The customized products are based on specific requirements of customers, with development of ad-hoc prototypes of new models of shoes and clothing, influencing also all the decisions regarding sourcing and production. The customer experience ranges from the selection of materials to the personalized distribution and the after-sale services that guarantee the replacement/repair of products during the use. The collaborative process is supported by 3D modelling on shoes for personalized fit and 3D printing systems.

5   Discussion

According to the collected data and information, the cross-case analysis was organized to map strategies and practices for customization in fashion companies differentiated according to two dimensions, defining the matrix shown in Fig. 1:

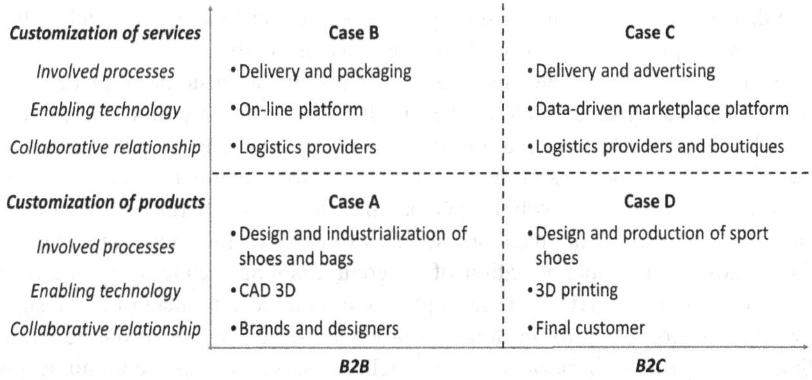

Customization of services	**Case B**	**Case C**
Involved processes	• Delivery and packaging	• Delivery and advertising
Enabling technology	• On-line platform	• Data-driven marketplace platform
Collaborative relationship	• Logistics providers	• Logistics providers and boutiques
Customization of products	**Case A**	**Case D**
Involved processes	• Design and industrialization of shoes and bags	• Design and production of sport shoes
Enabling technology	• CAD 3D	• 3D printing
Collaborative relationship	• Brands and designers	• Final customer
	B2B	*B2C*

Fig. 1. Results of customization strategies and practices in fashion industry.

– Scope of customization: product (Case A and D) versus service (Case B and C);
– Type of market asking for the customization: company on the SC (Case A and B), versus final customer (Case C and D).

By crossing the two dimensions, the practices for customization identified in the cases where studied in terms of:

- Involved processes;
- Enabling technology;
- Collaborative relationships.

On the one hand, product customization mainly relies on the direct involvement of customers (both final customer and brands), and requires the adoption of technologies such as 3D tools, product configurators and 3D printing, to support design and production of prototypes and final goods. In Case A, the collaboration between focal company and designers allows for the realization of product ideas requested by brands into product features on the 3D models to produce. In case D, the use of 3D printing is aimed to realize the prototype of the shoes in strict collaboration with the final customer to satisfy their need of high performance product for sport activities. Each order implies specific materials and components into "customized projects" that need to be coordinated with collaborative work between designers and production managers.

On the other hand, service customization is based on a stronger collaboration with other actors of the downstream network (i.e. intermediaries, retailers, logistic providers), enabled by cloud platforms, to provide a customized service that fulfills the final requirements. Case B offers to its business clients (retailers) the customization of logistics activities (according to single packaging and delivery needs or constraints) through an online platform and the adoption of optimization algorithms for inventory and transportation loading. Company B is able to manage a high variety of packaging solutions and it leads the delivery tasks for the clients collaborating also with other logistics providers to ensure a high level service. The use of an online platform that supports collaborative practices for customized services is present in Case C, which offers several delivery options and targeted advertising to the final customers. To ensure these kinds of service, Company C has to strictly collaborate (also through offer of data-driven services) with logistics providers and the boutiques, which sell their products on the platform, ensuring the availability of goods.

The matrix shows that the involved processes in the customization of products mainly refer to the upstream side of the SC. It focuses on the design and production both for B2C and B2B markets to ensure the best products that fit with the requested characteristics. The processes of the downstream network are mainly addressed for the customization of services, involving personalized logistics (offering different delivery options) and targeted communications services to enhance the shopping experience.

This leads to the implementation of different enabling technologies: the additive manufacturing and the CAD 3D tools support the rapid development of the design and the creation of prototypes for customized products, while the use of online platforms facilitates the sharing of information during delivery services and the communication of personalized advertising to increase customer loyalty.

Focusing on the actors to be involved in a collaborative relationship along the fashion SC, the case studies show there are two main practices to be established. It is clear that, in case of collaboration with logistics providers, designers and other business, it is necessary to establish long-term strategic networks with framework agreements for answering to punctual requests (both form B2B market and B2C). In case of collaboration with final customer, it is necessary to define frameworks for goal-oriented networks with the possibility to have one-to-one formal collaboration.

Therefore, case studies show that is crucial for companies to decide the scope of customization, in terms of involved processes, enabling technologies and actors involved in collaborative relationships, in relation to the reference market. At the same time, the level of collaboration within supply networks is a key point: the cited cases show that collaboration between the SC partners becomes the only way to effectively achieve the objectives of customization. For example, in the cases of 3D CAD and online customization platforms it is evident that the rapid exchange of information between the company and its suppliers can be a critical success factor in order to create exactly the personalized product or service requested by customers.

6 Conclusion

Considering the high importance of the collaboration in the nowadays fashion market, this paper contributes to the debate by deepening how the theme of customization should be developed in accordance with the specific reference market. This work aims to contribute to the debate on customization in fashion industry by a cross-case analysis that highlights the collaborative practices and enabling technologies adopted by companies to offer customized product or services to B2B or B2C markets.

The paper is therefore part of a rapidly growing field of research (i.e. product customization), highlighting how appropriate study of the reference market and of the relations between supply network partners are also absolutely relevant aspects for defining a customization strategy. To this end, the paper considers how a company interfaces within the supply network for the development of customized products and services. The link between personalization, market and supply network relationships represents an interesting research area and new works are encouraged in this line.

Results show that companies should directly collaborate with final customers, and actors of the upstream network (e.g. designers), relying on tools of 3D modelling and 3D printing, to realize virtual models and prototypes aimed at realizing customize products. In case of customized services, focal companies need to collaborate not only with their clients (other businesses or final customers), but also with other actors of the downstream network (e.g. logistics providers). This collaboration, enabled by digital technologies as cloud platforms, improves the service level (e.g. delivery) and meets customers' needs.

The main constraints of the study concern the qualitative design and the limitation to a single industrial sector (fashion industry). Nevertheless, obtained results could be extended to companies of other industries in terms of dimensions that are judged as strategic for customization purposes. Additionally, future works can extent further the impacts of using enabling technologies for collaboration purposes, as well as their role in decision-making that has implications throughout multiple SC echelons.

Future investigations of these studies may bring interesting insights considering, for example, the reference market of companies offering customization in order to analyze in which contexts a personalized product is most appreciated. At the same time, a reasoning on the structure of the supply network will allow to combine a business development plan from the point of view of customization to the feasibility at the supply network level.

Acknowledgments. This research has been conducted as part of the NEXT-NET project, which has received funding from the European Union's Horizon 2020 Research and Innovation Programme under the Grant Agreement n°768884.

References

1. Deloitte: The Deloitte Consumer Review. Make-to-order: the rise of mass personalization (2015). https://www2.deloitte.com/content/dam/Deloitte/ch/Documents/consumer-business/ch-en-consumer-business-made-to-orderconsumer-review.pdf
2. Christopher, M., Lowson, R., Peck, H.: Creating agile supply chains in the fashion industry. Int. J. Retail. Distrib. Manag. **32**(8), 367–376 (2004)
3. Chan, A.T.L., Ngai, E.W.T., Moon, K.K.L.: The effects of strategic and manufacturing flexibilities and supply chain agility on firm performance in the fashion industry. Eur. J. Oper. Res. **259**(2), 486–499 (2017)
4. Macchion, L., Marchiori, I., Vinelli, A., Fornasiero, R.: Proposing a tool for supply chain configuration: an application to customised production. In: Tolio, T., Copani, G., Terkaj, W. (eds.) Factories of the Future, pp. 217–231. Springer, Cham (2019). https://doi.org/10.1007/978-3-319-94358-9_10
5. Zheng, P., Xu, X., Yu, S., Liu, C.: Personalized product configuration framework in an adaptable open architecture product platform. J. Manuf. Syst. **43**, 422–435 (2017)
6. Chu, C.H., Wang, I.J., Wang, J.B., Luh, Y.P.: 3D parametric human face modeling for personalized product design: eyeglasses frame design case. Adv. Eng. Inform. **32**, 202–223 (2017)
7. Macchion, L., Danese, P., Fornasiero, R., Vinelli, A.: Personalisation management in supply networks: an empirical study within the footwear industry. Int. J. Manuf. Technol. Manag. **31**(4), 362–386 (2017)
8. Mai, J., Zhang, L., Tao, F., Ren, L.: Customized production based on distributed 3D printing services in cloud manufacturing. Int. J. Adv. Manuf. Technol. **84**(1), 71–83 (2015). https://doi.org/10.1007/s00170-015-7871-y
9. Joergensen, S.N., Hvilshøj, M., Madsen, O.: Designing modular manufacturing systems using mass customisation theories and methods. Int. J. Mass Custom **4**(3–4), 171–194 (2012)
10. Elgammal, A., Papazoglou, M., Krämer, B., Constantinescu, C.: Design for customization: a new paradigm for product-service system development. Proc. CIRP **64**, 345–350 (2017)
11. Levesque, N., Boeck, H.: Proximity marketing as an enabler of mass customization and personalization in a customer service experience. In: Bellemare, J., Carrier, S., Nielsen, K., Piller, F.T. (eds.) Managing Complexity. SPBE, pp. 405–420. Springer, Cham (2017). https://doi.org/10.1007/978-3-319-29058-4_32
12. Zhang, M., Guo, H., Huo, B., Zhao, X., Huang, J.: Linking supply chain quality integration with mass customization and product modularity. Int. J. Prod. Econ. **207**, 227–235 (2019)
13. Zhang, Y., Kwok, T.H.: An interactive product customization framework for freeform shapes. Rapid Prototyp. J. (2017)
14. Rewers, P., Karwasz, A., Żywicki, K.: A comparative analysis of various production organisation forms on the basis of customised manufacturing. In: Hamrol, A., Kujawińska, A., Barraza, M.F.S. (eds.) MANUFACTURING 2019. LNME, pp. 26–35. Springer, Cham (2019). https://doi.org/10.1007/978-3-030-18789-7_3
15. Chiu, M.C., Tsai, C.H.: Design a personalised product service system utilising a multi-agent system. Adv. Eng. Inform. **43**, 101036 (2020)

16. Lang, C., Armstrong, C.M.J.: Fashion leadership and intention toward clothing product-service retail models. J. Fash. Mark. Manag. **22**(4), 571–587 (2018)
17. Piccoli, G., Lui, T.W., Grün, B.: The impact of IT-enabled customer service systems on service personalization, customer service perceptions, and hotel performance. Tour. Manag. **59**, 349–362 (2017)
18. Hu, M., Huang, F., Hou, H., Chen, Y., Bulysheva, L.: Customized logistics service and online shoppers' satisfaction: an empirical study. Internet Res. **26**(2), 484–497 (2016)
19. Lee, E.J., Park, J.K.: Online service personalization for apparel shopping. J. Retail. Consum. Serv. **16**(2), 83–91 (2009)
20. Morganti, E., Seidel, S., Blanquart, C., Dablanc, L., Lenz, B.: The impact of e-commerce on final deliveries: alternative parcel delivery services in France and Germany. Transp. Res. Proced. **4**(4), 178–190 (2014)
21. Grafmüller, L.K., Habicht, H.: Current challenges for mass customization on B2B markets. In: Bellemare, J., Carrier, S., Nielsen, K., Piller, F.T. (eds.) Managing Complexity. SPBE, pp. 269–279. Springer, Cham (2017). https://doi.org/10.1007/978-3-319-29058-4_21
22. Koutsabasis, P., Stavrakis, M., Viorres, N., Darzentas, J.S., Spyrou, T., Darzentas, J.: A descriptive reference framework for the personalisation of e-business applications. Electron. Commer. Res. **8**(3), 173 (2008)
23. Yin, R.K.: Case Study Research: Design and Methods, 5th edn. SAGE Publications, Thousand Oaks (2013)
24. Eisenhardt, K.M.: Building theories from case study research. Acad. Manag. Rev. **14**(4), 532–550 (1989)

The Digital Twin as a Knowledge-Based Engineering Enabler for Product Development

Miguel Azevedo[1]([⊠]), Sérgio Tavares[2], and António Lucas Soares[3]

[1] University of Porto-Faculty of Engineering, Porto, Portugal
miguel.a.azevedo@inesctec.pt
[2] Efacec SA, Moreira, Portugal
sergio.tavares@efacec.com
[3] INESCTEC, Porto, Portugal
als@fe.up.pt

Abstract. Industry 4.0 encompasses technologies that generate valuable insights from large data exchange networks. This, along with the growing digitalization of organizational information and knowledge, turns these assets into a valuable resource for product and process improvement and optimization. In this context, Knowledge-based Engineering (KBE) is presented as a way to efficiently capture and reuse organizational knowledge. As such, this work conceptualizes the Digital Twin, emerging technology as a KBE enabling application that employs organizational knowledge as the driving force behind product development. To this end, power transformer development is used as a case study.

Keywords: Information management · Knowledge management · Knowledge-based engineering · Digital twin · Power transformer development

1 Introduction

Industry 4.0 has made it possible for information and knowledge to become the most valuable resource in an organization, as the integration of Information and Communication Technologies with physical devices through cyber-physical systems and the Internet of Things results in the creation of large data exchange networks that generate valuable insights for product development and for product life-cycle management.

Moreover, the growing volume, variety and velocity of the information generated during the product lifecycle, which includes product requirements and specifications, design models and data related to product calculation and testing, production and operation, can be an important knowledge base for an organization, assisting design teams and managers in decision-making, which in turn improves product design, reduces lead time and decreases monetary costs.

Consequently, the more efficient and effective planning of strategies and instruments that make the capture, description, organization, and retrieval of information generated during the lifecycle of a product, is a crucial factor to obtain benefits from organizational knowledge.

© IFIP International Federation for Information Processing 2020
Published by Springer Nature Switzerland AG 2020
L. M. Camarinha-Matos et al. (Eds.): PRO-VE 2020, IFIP AICT 598, pp. 450–459, 2020.
https://doi.org/10.1007/978-3-030-62412-5_37

This can be achieved by implementing Knowledge-based engineering (KBE) in product development processes. KBE refers to the knowledge management (KM) tasks of capturing, storing, modeling, and sharing of organizational knowledge, both in explicit form (such as documents or models) and in tacit form (present in the minds of employees and materialized in e.g. collaborative work). This knowledge can then be coded in computational systems, enabling the automation of repetitive design tasks [1].

The concept of KBE was first introduced in the 1980s as part of a new set of software applications called Knowledge-based Engineering Systems. These systems, which are generally integrated with CAD software, capture organizational knowledge, and encourage its reuse, allowing for the automatization of routine design tasks [1]. Thus, Knowledge-based Engineering is the implementation of knowledge management methods and instruments, which support computational systems that make organizational knowledge the centerpiece of engineering design.

KBE is frequently applied in product design, especially in the automotive and aerospace industry. It has yielded results in the reduction of lead time, with implementation cases achieving results of up to 75% reduction in process duration [2]. Furthermore, developed KBE systems also significantly decrease costs and improve employee satisfaction, by providing features that automate design tasks, and consequently, allow for engineers to use their time in creative tasks, instead of repetitive ones [3].

Additionally, benefits related to the quality and validity of product design have also been identified, due to the ability of KBE systems to autonomously validate the design according to product restrictions and requirements, allowing for optimized products that comply with user and client requirements, to be developed faster [4].

The technological advances that characterize Industry 4.0 have also made possible the implementation of new applications that use product lifecycle information to streamline product development and improve product design. This is the case with the Digital Twin (DT), an emerging concept that virtually mirrors a physical product lifecycle, simulating its visual aspect and behavior based on bidirectional data transmission between the physical and the digital space.

In this context, this work explores the applicability of the Digital Twin concept in product development, specifically as a KBE enabling application. As a result, functionalities that employ organizational knowledge to streamline and improve product design are proposed, using power transformer (PT) development, which is characterized by intensive engineering processes that require multidisciplinary teams and expert knowledge [12], as a case study.

2 Digital Twin in Product Development

The Digital Twin is an emerging concept that was first proposed in 2002 as a conceptual model of product lifecycle management that includes a physical system and a virtual system that contains all the information related to it. Because of this, all the information generated since the creation, manufacture, operation, and disposal of the physical product also exists in its virtual copy [5].

Further definitions appear to present different points of view based on the core purpose of the DT. On one hand, some authors propose the DT as a simulation technology that can replicate all possible behaviors of a given machine or product. This perspective [6–8] appears to be attributed mainly to production line DT's, which simulate the behavior of machines on the shop floor. On the other hand, others build on the vision proposed by Grieves, specifically of the DT as an informational entity that maps the entire lifecycle of a product through the capture of virtual and physical data [9, 10].

In product development, academic literature envisions the DT as a linking element that correlates customer preferences and habits, with product design, using virtualization, simulation, and Big data captured during operation, to achieve the goal of optimizing design.

Proposed functionalities include the capability of inferring desirable design characteristics through the capture of online client feedback and information about user habits when interacting with a product. It is argued that this information can also be used by the Digital Twin to define functional requirements and synthesize design restrictions such as weight and height. Moreover, it is suggested that Digital Twin may allow the analysis of user interaction with a product through technologies such as Virtual Reality, eliminating the need for costly ethnographic observations [9].

As engineering design is carried out, the DT guarantees that the design is logically viable, functionally simple, and physically correct. The DT accomplishes this by analyzing data captured during the development process and by sensors to identify and assess the severity of design contradictions. Crucially, it is claimed that Digital Twin can help create the conceptual design itself, by allowing engineers to use contextual usage data, such as physical measured data, to compare virtual and real contexts and understand the ideal conditions for product operation.

In design validation, the Digital Twin is proposed to verify and simulate all aspects of the design, using historical and real-time data to improve virtual models progressively and iteratively. As a result, the production of a small amount of product for testing is no longer necessary, reducing financial and time costs [10].

Additionally, the Digital Twin is also seen as a potential repository of information captured and produced in all phases of the product lifecycle, because it possesses the ability to store, link and make data and information available. This streamlines design process and interconnects various areas of knowledge [11]. This idea is expanded to include data related to the customer, such as their satisfaction and feedback, and about the company, like the number of sales of each product [8].

3 Methodological Approach

The work carried out had the overall goal of developing a Digital Twin concept that employs organizational knowledge to streamline product development tasks, thus adapting development processes into a Knowledge-based engineering paradigm that is supported by the DT. This goal was achieved using the development of power transformers as a case study, specifically in a Portuguese company that operates in the energy and mobility sectors.

The methodology approach to this work was composed of 3 main steps, starting with the analysis of current Power Transformer (PT) development processes through semi-structured interviews with relevant development stakeholders, followed by the contextualization of identified bottlenecks with proposed DT features in academic literature, and finally, the definition of KBE supporting DT functionalities that address IM and KM issues that current processes exhibit.

4 Analysis of the Power Transformer Development Process

4.1 Development Stages

Through the analysis of the case study organization, 4 different stages of power transformer development could be discerned, based on product development steps defined by [9]. Each step has a set of core objectives:

Task Clarification: Identify and validate transformer requirements, as well as allocate the necessary monetary and human resources, to correspond to the customer's expectations in terms of the quality of the design, deadlines, and costs.

Engineering Design: Through engineering calculus and mechanical design, a set of electrical and mechanical specifications are developed. Engineering calculus specifies parameters such as number of coil turns and electromagnetic induction values, while mechanical design, which uses Computer Aided Design (CAD) and Computer Aided Engineering (CAE) tools, develops aspects related to the dimensions, shape, and positioning of PT components.

Virtual Verification: Design testing and validation is accomplished through a set of simulations based on computational tools (such as Finite Element Method and Computational Fluid Dynamics), techniques that assess the behavior and structural integrity of the machine, under different operating conditions. This results in a report containing recommendations for the design of the transformer, which are then followed during production.

Production: Production processes convert models created during development, into an operational machine. Production is done gradually, and after each stage, encountered problems are reported to the product development team, who adapt the PT design based on them.

4.2 Information and Knowledge Management Bottlenecks

From an information and knowledge management point of view, several bottlenecks that negatively impact PT development were identified, while other discerned issues represent missed opportunities in the employment of organizational knowledge to improve power transformer development and design. The critical issues were:

- Data generated during PT operation is not captured in a structured way.
- The search of some instructional documentation such as manuals is not possible, as this information is not fully indexed, and no metadata is associated with it.
- Sharing of acquired organizational knowledge such as lessons learned is mostly done through personalization strategies, and as such, this knowledge is not adequately formalized in any means.

Current design processes are not supported by operational data, as this data is managed mostly by the entities who control its operation. As such, the opportunity to create an important knowledge source for continuous improvement of PT design, should be exploited.

Another potential improvement in PT development can be achieved by providing a mechanism to retrieve manuals and other instructional documentation in an effortless way. Currently, this information is only accessible in design software, as a pop-up window that opens after a "Help" button is clicked.

Finally, currently implemented knowledge management instruments are focused on the sharing of knowledge through in-person interactions between engineers, and the formalization of this knowledge is not a formalized practice. The codification of this knowledge in document format could allow engineers to quickly search organizational knowledge, enabling more frequent and efficient knowledge sharing.

5 Applying the Digital Twin Concept to Power Transformer Development

The development of the DT concept resulted in a set of DT functionalities that not only help resolve bottlenecks in current processes, but also fundamentally adapt them to answer the challenges and opportunities brought by Industry 4.0.

Two types of DT features are proposed, namely those whose main purpose is to use organizational knowledge to improve PT development and operation, and those that focus on capturing and disseminating knowledge, and as such, can be seen as Knowledge Management instruments supported by the DT. The first type effectively resolves the bottleneck related to the misuse of operational sensor data, as it employs it to optimize PT design and streamline development processes, while also solving issues arising from lack of query mechanisms, by providing a centralized information base that users can use for information retrieval.

An overview of proposed DT functionalities is presented in the figure below (Fig. 1).

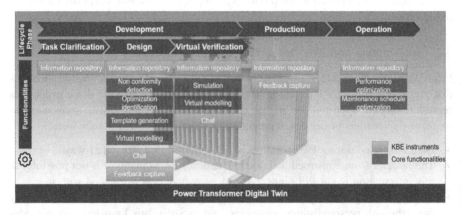

Fig. 1. Overview of the proposed Digital Twin functionalities

5.1   Design Template Generation

Several PT development processes are routine regardless of project characteristics, as although no PT conceptions are the same, machine specifications generally lead to similar designs. Because of this, historical data can be employed to automate and streamline PT development tasks.

The benefits of this opportunity can be materialized through a DT supported design workflow, composed of 4 main tasks:

1. Designers perform engineering calculus;
2. Based on calculus specifications, the DT automatically lists previous PT development projects, according to similarity;
3. Designers select a previous design to serve as a template for the current project; *and*
4. Designers adapt and refine the final solution accordingly to the specific requirements.

This process allows teams to quickly reach an initial PT design, ultimately freeing them to focus on customized design features, specific to the current project. To achieve this, the DT requires Artificial Intelligence algorithms to recognize similarities between PT specifications, and previous PT designs.

5.2   Design Nonconformity and Optimization Detection

In the previously described workflow, DT generated design templates will usually have minor inconsistencies with current project specifications, and thus, the DT should also be able to identify and correct potential mistakes, inaccuracies, or nonconformities in PT design, with the following workflow:

1. DT detects design inconsistency;
2. DT alerts user; *and*
3. User manually adapts the design or commands the DT to autonomously do so.

In this point of view, the DT analyzes the PT design and checks for compliance with rules and requirements coded in the application. When a conflict is detected, the DT informs the user with the type of problem encountered, the components that are affected involved, and the norms or rules that are being infringed. Lastly, the user can opt to manually change the design or command the DT to autonomously do so.

The same process can also be employed for design optimization. To this end, sensor data, which is not useful by itself, can be captured and analyzed by the DT and integrated with other PT lifecycle information, resulting in insights regarding the optimized design of each component of the machine.

5.3   The Digital Twin as an Information Repository

Power transformer development processes involve decision making moments that require stakeholders to have access to the appropriate information that enables them to make the right decisions, especially during design. Because of this, having access to project information that influences design specifications, is crucial.

Moreover, additional decision-making support can be found in design artefacts created in previous PT development projects, as engineers can compare current project specifications with previous ones and draw insights from them.

Consequently, it is proposed that the Digital Twin include an information repository that stores all information captured in external sources, or generated by the DT, during the entire PT lifecycle. This grants to the design team a centralized information base that expands along the development and operation of the power transformer and facilitates the use of information as a major supporting tool for engineering design.

This feature has already been proposed in academic literature in works such as [9] and [11], although these authors limit the scope of DT captured information to design artefacts and other information useful for design tasks.

This work assesses the Digital Twin as an informational entity that replicates the entirety of the PT's lifecycle, and consequently, the information stored in this platform is not restricted to the development phase, instead encompassing all phases, from task clarification to disposal. As such, the DT information repository should include all information created and captured from the ideation to disposal of the power transformer.

5.4   Digital Twin Interactive Feedback

Most of the knowledge acquired in each PT development project is present solely in designers' minds, as opposed to being formalized in a physical or digital document. This entails problems such as loss of organizational knowledge due to employees leaving the organization, as well as a difficulty in identifying stakeholders who possess potentially relevant knowledge for a given design task.

Because of the DT's capability of capturing, organizing and storing PT lifecycle information, this application can also be a crucial instrument to create documents that formalize organizational knowledge and make them available to engineers during PT development.

Over the course of design tasks, product engineers often use their experience and tacit knowledge to support their decision making, with the goal of achieving a design that satisfies project requirements. As a result, the formalization of the thought process behind PT design decisions can be extremely valuable for future projects, allowing engineers to use those knowledge assets to support their own decision making, and ultimately, optimize PT design.

Considering this, it is proposed that the DT include a feature that enables both product and process engineers to leave comments regarding different aspects of PT design. In this perspective, product designers and engineers will formalize their thought process according to these steps:

1. User performs PT design;
2. User selects PT component; *and*
3. User completes *Insight* form.

Ultimately, this DT feature promotes knowledge sharing between product engineers during TP design, and between product and process engineers, during PT production.

6 The Digital Twin Information Architecture

The functionalities proposed for the power transformer Digital Twin require it to capture and generate a large amount of information over the course of the PT lifecycle. This elevates the concept of the Digital Twin as an informational entity, as it does not solely capture information that describes the physical properties of the product, but also captures every other artifact that relates to it, regardless of lifecycle phase.

As such, it is appropriate to conceptualize the Digital Twin information architecture, based on the concept developed for power transformer development.

Given the applications and functionalities attributed to the Digital Twin in the previous chapter, this platform will capture and generate information with different sources, formats, and purposes, during the power transformer lifecycle.

This information is stored and made available, not only as a way to enable PT functionalities to autonomously improve or correct non conformities in the design, but also to provide engineers with a searchable knowledge base that they can use to support and justify their decision making. Consequently, organizational knowledge becomes the foundation of the power transformer design process, thus achieving the primary goal of Knowledge-based Engineering.

The figure below presents an overview of DT information architecture (Fig. 2).

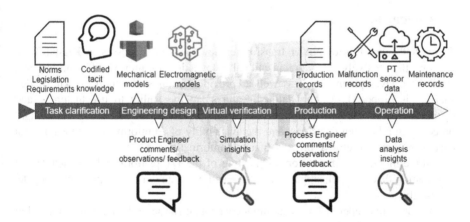

Fig. 2. Overview of the Digital Twin information architecture

6.1 DT Captured Information

The information captured by the Digital Twin originates in the task clarification, engineering design, production, and operation stages of the PT lifecycle.

During task clarification, the DT captures information that restricts PT design, such as normative and legislative rules, as well as client requirements. Furthermore, tacit knowledge present in engineers' minds is also extracted and codified in the DT platform.

In the design phase, models created in the engineering calculus and drawing tasks are captured by the DT, moreover, as the client is regularly sent design models to keep him informed of the progress of the project, his feedback is also stored in the DT. Accordingly, during the design and production phases, the feedback of product and process engineers is also captured.

Finally, as PT operation begins, so does the capture of sensor data by the Digital Twin, which stores it through data warehouse technology and analyzes it with data analysis algorithms and artificial intelligence.

6.2   DT Generated Information

Digital Twin generated information refers to all information that is autonomously created by DT functionalities and tools, instead of being captured in external sources, or created by stakeholder feedback. This type of information is mostly generated by the data analysis and simulation features of the DT, and as such, it involves the virtual verification and operation lifecycle stages.

In the virtual verification stage, the DT produces insights regarding the performance of each component when it is tested in several working conditions and parameters, and during operation, further insights are generated from sensor data analysis.

7   Conclusion

Through the analysis of power transformer development processes, a Digital Twin concept that actively uses organizational knowledge to improve PT design and streamline development tasks, as well as provides features that motivate knowledge sharing, is proposed. Among defined features are the ability to use historical and operational data to create design templates, the possibility of describing the thought process behind design decisions, and the availability of an information repository that users can query to retrieve product lifecycle information.

Furthermore, the information architecture of the DT platform, which includes all information that the application will capture and generate during the product lifecycle, is described.

As such, this paper provides an initial conceptualization of the DT when applied to PT development. Further work is necessary in the areas of requirements elicitation, KM, and software development, to achieve a fully operational DT.

Acknowledgements. The project TRF4p0 - Transformer 4.0 leading to this work is co-financed by the European Regional Development Fund - ERDF, through COMPETE - Operational Program Competitiveness and Internationalization (POCI) and by the Foundation for Science and Technology under the MIT Portugal Program under POCI-01-0247-FEDER-045926.

References

1. Reddy, E.J., Sridhar, C.N.V., Rangadu, V.P.: Knowledge based engineering: notion, approaches and future trends. Am. J. Intell. Syst. **5**(1), 1–17 (2015). https://doi.org/10.5923/j.ajis.20150501.01
2. Emberey, C.L., et al.: Application of knowledge engineering methodologies to support engineering design application development in aerospace. In: Collection of Technical Papers - 7th AIAA Aviation Technology, Integration, and Operations Conference 1 (September), pp. 83–95 (2007). https://doi.org/10.2514/6.2007-7708
3. Lin, B.T., Chan, C.K., Wang, J.C.: A knowledge-based parametric design system for drawing dies. Int. J. Adv. Manuf. Technol. **36**(7–8), 671–680 (2008). https://doi.org/10.1007/s00170-006-0882-y
4. Curran, R., Verhagen, W.J.C., Van Tooren, M.J.L., Van Der Laan, T.H.: A multidisciplinary implementation methodology for knowledge based engineering: KNOMAD. Expert Syst. Appl. **37**(11), 7336–7350 (2010). https://doi.org/10.1016/j.eswa.2010.04.027
5. Grieves, M., Vickers, J.: Digital twin: mitigating unpredictable, undesirable emergent behavior in complex systems. In: Kahlen, F.J., Flumerfelt, S., Alves, A. (eds.) Transdisciplinary Perspectives on Complex Systems, pp. 85–113. Springer, Cham (2017). https://doi.org/10.1007/978-3-319-38756-7_4
6. Gabor, T., Kiermeier, M., Beck, M.T., Neitz, A.: A simulation-based architecture for smart cyber-physical systems. IEEE Int. Conf. Auton. Comput. (ICAC) **2016**, 374–379 (2016). https://doi.org/10.1109/ICAC.2016.29
7. Weyer, S., et al.: Future modeling and simulation of CPS-based factories: an example from the automotive industry. IFAC PapersOnLine **49**(31), 97–102 (2016). https://doi.org/10.1016/j.ifacol.2016.12.168
8. Glaessgen, E.H., Stargel, D.S.: The digital twin paradigm for future NASA and US air force vehicles. In: pp. 1–14 (2012)
9. Tao, F., Cheng, J., Qi, Q., Zhang, M., Zhang, H., Sui, F.: Digital twin-driven product design, manufacturing and service with big data. Int. J. Adv. Manuf. Technol. **94**(9), 3563–3576 (2017). https://doi.org/10.1007/s00170-017-0233-1
10. Tao, F., et al.: Digital twin-driven product design framework. Int. J. Prod. Res. **7543**, 1–19 (2019). https://doi.org/10.1080/00207543.2018.1443229
11. Bradley, D., Hehenberger, P.: Mechatronic futures. In: Hehenberger, P., Bradley, D. (eds.) Mechatronic Futures, pp. 1–15. Springer, Cham (2016). https://doi.org/10.1007/978-3-319-32156-1_1
12. Mendes, H., et al.: Smart design and manufacturing of power transformers tanks. In: 2019 IEEE Industrial and Commercial Power Systems Europe (2019). https://doi.org/10.1109/EEEIC.2019.8783902

Collaboration Impacts

Building Business Impacts of an Industry 4.0 Ecosystem Through Collaborative Network Settings Between IT and Forest Companies

Katri Valkokari$^{(\boxtimes)}$, Pasi Valkokari, Helena Kortelainen, and Jutta Nyblom

VTT, Technical Research Centre of Finland, PL1306, 33101 Tampere, Finland
{Katri.Valkokari, Pasi.Valkokari, HelenaKortelainen, JuttaNyblom}@vtt.fi

Abstract. The paper provides on empirical example of co-innovation process within an Industry 4.0 ecosystem between Finnish IT sector, service designers, researchers and the forest industry companies. Based on empirical evidence the paper summarizes some of key challenges in building business impact from digitalization.

Keywords: Business impact · Ecosystem · Collaborative networks · Industry 4.0 · Co-innovation · Design science · Service design

1 Introduction

In this century, data may become the most important form of capital [1]. Currently, a significant part of the data collected by industrial IT systems is not being used, and therefore, the full potential of the business impacts of Industry 4.0 is not being realised. Old industrial plants have a plethora of data sources documenting their design and behaviour, ranging from diagrams and software to spreadsheets and text documents. Digital strategies in forerunner organisations go beyond technologies. They target improvements in innovation and decision-making [2], i.e. their aim is to build business impacts for an Industry 4.0.

Therefore, digitalisation and data represent significant drivers of change and new business potential in today's business environment. Understanding the systemic change required for Industry 4.0 is at the same time a fascinating academic research question and a practical challenge for all actors within manufacturing industries. This transformation requires novel competencies, solutions and collaboration between companies. Companies aspire to different roles in an ecosystem, and they may also update and upgrade their role over time [3]. In this study, the growth opportunities enabled by digitalisation are examined from the perspective of the business impacts within an ecosystem consisting of IT and forest companies. Thus, this ecosystem can be considered a breeding environment [4] for several collaborative networks constituted around the so-called use cases. Since the area of collaborative networks (CN) is by nature multi-disciplinary as well as interdisciplinary, it can enhance a more holistic

© IFIP International Federation for Information Processing 2020
Published by Springer Nature Switzerland AG 2020
L. M. Camarinha-Matos et al. (Eds.): PRO-VE 2020, IFIP AICT 598, pp. 463–474, 2020.
https://doi.org/10.1007/978-3-030-62412-5_38

understanding of the technology diffusion at stake, as pointed out by Camarinha-Matos et al. 2017 [5].

There is widespread consensus among both academics and practitioners that innovation is the main driver of productivity, economic growth and job creation. Thus, there is huge potential in combining the digital competences of the IT sector with the manufacturing industry to drive future success as well as create new novel business opportunities for the IT sector itself. A prerequisite for enhancing digitalisation is an active, open ecosystemic innovation platform that fosters dynamic collaborative networking. In other words, this innovation platform could be called a breeding environment [4], which enables the preparedness of its members to quickly become engaged in collaboration and co-innovation processes. The full potential of digitalisation in the platform economy cannot be achieved in closed business networks. This premise is the driving force for our study on building business impacts in an Industry 4.0 ecosystem consisting of solution providers (mainly IT companies) and end customers in the manufacturing sector (forest industry companies).

The studied Industry 4.0 ecosystem aims to generate new types of networks of collaborative innovation activities (i.e. interactive networks of multiple CNs in line with the concept of Collaborative Networks 3.0). The networks are built around so-called 'use cases' originating from the operational needs of forest industry companies and among which IT companies have identified their own business opportunities. The members of the SEED ecosystem[1] developed together digital solutions that will improve the international competitiveness of all participants. In addition to three forest companies, two equipment manufacturers and 13 IT supplier (i.e. solution providers and integrators) companies, the case includes three service design companies and three research organisations (as described in more detail in Table 2). Thus, identifying business benefits of such collaboration from the perspective of all actors is one of the key success factors of the ecosystem, one that requires transparent management of intellectual property between the ecosystem actors [6].

2   Building Constructs for a Joint Research Process

2.1   Data Business and Platform Economy

Companies offering IoT platforms as marketplaces are highly valued in B2C products [7], and there are multiple examples of large-scale platform enterprises engaged in consumer business. It is more than likely that the same phenomena will occur in the B2B sector as well. B2B platforms are still rare, and the development trend seems to be more based on a decentralised model with interconnected platforms than on platform monopolies [8]. The forest industry has not shown a great interest in platform economy development for various reasons, one of them being vendor lock-ins. Large design and engineering solution providers offer integrated solutions that tie end-user companies into a solution from one vendor. This so-called vendor-locking situation may be a risk for the end-user company. It increases the dependency of the solution provider, as the

---

[1] www.seedecosystem.fi.

data content is tied to a specific solution [9]. In some cases, even the ownership of data collected by a forest company during its operations is limited to an equipment or a software provider. However, significant value capture as a result of implementing Industry 4.0 solutions to improve competitiveness calls for knowledge sharing and collaboration in the networks and ecosystems. Collecting and integrating the data from various sources, and refining the data into knowledge, can support different user needs and boost the creation of new business [3, 10].

The emerging Industry 4.0 ecosystems requires focal companies to invite other stakeholders to add value to the common platform so that the ecosystem can co-evolve [11]. Thus, in addition to the forest industry companies, a focal company in a collaborative network may be either an equipment or software company, i.e. there is a need to bring together all key players in order to ingrate different data and knowledge sources. However, within the same the ecosystem players must assure each other that the information content is not tied to specific tools and can be processed and utilised with any standard compliant tool so as not to create novel vendor lock-ins [9]. Competences, skills and models for ecosystem orchestration and good practical examples are needed to solve systemic challenges [12]. The value potential of the platform economy and ways to enhance it need to be presented. Successful ecosystems are founded on common platforms consisting of services, tools or technologies, which the members of the ecosystem are able to use to enhance their own performance [13].

2.2 Ecosystems and Collaborative Networking

Global competition has shifted from taking place between individual companies to competition between business networks or, as the increasing interest in sustainability and industrial ecology suggests, between industrial ecosystems [14]. In the current networked business environment, cooperative actions and decisions are not being made in a centralised manner [15]. Therefore, the full potential of a data-based business and platform economy can be captured in collaboration with a variety of external actors, i.e. ecosystems or collaborative networks (CN) and their breeding environments, as access to and integration of third-party data sources is required to explore changes in the current business environment [16].

An ecosystemic way of co-creation requires going beyond the hub-spoke model of network roles [17]. Hence, we aimed to consider the strategic intentions, business undertakings and processes by which an actor engages in building the systemic solutions for an ecosystem [18], and in this way, define actor roles in ecosystems when analysing of the actors' willingness to contribute to the shared agenda of an ecosystem. Accordingly, we have identified four categories for ecosystem actors with specific interests in the results of co-creation. First, the customers of the co-created systemic solutions, i.e. the companies, with the aim being for the ecosystem to look for new solutions to the challenges faced by customers. Second, the actors include solution developers and providers, meaning firms developing new solution to be integrated into the systemic solution of an ecosystem or firms offering an almost ready and generic solution as part of the systemic solution for an ecosystem. Third, the actors should include solution integrators, which are firms aiming to bring the systemic solution for an ecosystem to the marketplace. Finally, the fourth category is innovation intermediaries, research institutes and designers offering special expertise needed to boost the innovation and development work within an ecosystem.

2.3   Looking for Business Potential and Impact

The importance of the forest industry and its supplier network is significant for the Finnish economy. Both the forest industry and the machinery manufacturing industry produce products representing 20% of Finnish exports, with the pulp and paper industry's share alone being 15% (National Board of Customs, 2017, based on CN classification). The overall trend towards servitisation has also changed the nature of Finnish exports, and during the last two decades the share of services in Finnish exports has doubled. In 2017, the value of service exports exceeded that of pulp and paper products.[2] IT-related services alone accounted for 11.4% of the domestic added value in Finland. However, the significance of service innovations is much higher than the figures indicate, as services are also consumed by the export industry and are also included in the value of goods exports (Haaparanta et al., 2017). According to European Commission DESI 2018 research, Finland has one of the most advanced digital economies and strongest digital assets in the EU.[3]

The competitiveness of Finnish forest industry companies was one of the driving forces in the SEED ecosystem. The use case companies in the forest industry expect that SEED will have a positive impact on business profitability, machine runnability, end-product quality and investments. This in turn is expected to have an impact on several hundred million euros worth of revenues in each use case company. Furthermore, in the longer run the companies also expect the ecosystem be able to boost a new kind of a culture to share and utilise data, and thus, build the first steps towards a platform economy and new kinds of digital services in the industry. On the other hand, the solution provider companies, highlighting new type of business development, improve their understanding of specific forest sector needs when collaborating in the SEED ecosystem, which will help them develop novel or extended service offerings for the growing global bio-based product market. It has been estimated that this growth opportunity will account for 10 to 25% of current revenues in the next 3 to 10 years in large and midcap IT companies, but significantly larger growth expectations were mentioned for smaller companies.

3   Research Approach — Enabling Co-learning Between Ecosystem Actors

In-depth empirical research on building business impacts through multiple collaborative networks is still scarce [10], although the vast opportunities and competition between ecosystems instead between companies have been emphasised for Industry 4.0

---

[2] Kansantalouden tilinpidon laskelmat 2000–2018, Tilastokeskus (in Finnish). https://www.stat.fi/tietotrendit/artikkelit/2019/tavaroista-palveluihin-viemme-nyt-enemman-suomalaista-tyota-kuin-ennen/.

[3] See https://ec.europa.eu/digital-single-market/en/des.

ecosystems. Design science was, therefore, a natural choice for the research approach of our study. Using a design science approach [19], we explored the business impacts expected from the shared innovation processes within a hybrid collaborative network setting. The main research questions were as follows: *What could be the benefits of the platform economy as a source of productivity, renewal and growth in the forest industry? How do the roles of various ecosystem actors influence their willingness to contribute to the shared agenda of ecosystems?*

In accordance with design studies, the relevance of the research results and the quality of the research were evaluated against the practices of 24 companies partici-pating in building our Industry 4.0 ecosystem, called SEED, and the coexisting research and innovation processes. Especially the different collaboration and con-tracting practices were studied in order to assess the ecosystem's co-development path on a deeper level.

Figure 1 presents the SEED ecosystem companies and their roles in shared problem solving within the ecosystem.

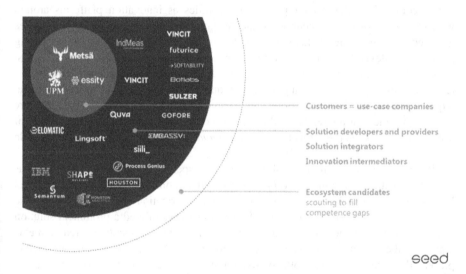

Fig. 1. Three layers of SEED ecosystem

In our study, the forest industry covers mills in the pulp, paper, tissue and board production sectors, i.e. the sawmill industry was not included in this phase. Many forest industry companies, including the companies involved in the studied ecosystem, have initiated their own business ecosystem programmes to boost collaboration with tech-nology providers, and therefore SEED provided a new type of setting for problem solving at the level of an Industry 4.0 ecosystem, one connecting the needs of three forest industry companies. In addition, the SEED ecosystem connects the competences of technology (especially IT) companies and design thinking. Table 1 summarises the roles of the involved ecosystem actors (the roles are defined in Sect. 2.2).

Table 1. Ecosystem actors involved in the study.

Role in ecosystem	Industry	Size	Number of actors
Use case owners	Forest industry companies	3 large	3
Solution providers and developers	Equipment Manufacturing	1 large, 1 small	2
	ICT	6 large, 6 small	12
Solution integrators	ICT	1 large	1
Innovation Intermediaries	Designers	1 large, 2 small	3
	Researchers	2 univ., 1 RTO	3

4 Findings

4.1 The Co-innovation Process

Forest companies offered their production facilities as innovation platforms around which the participating IT, technology and design companies and the research institutes gathered to resolve the challenges presented by the forest companies. As a starting point, actors devised together a two-phase process for joint problem solving. The first phase focused on building deeper *insight*, i.e. framing the problem, defining the research questions and identifying business requirements (viability) as well as technical requirements (feasibility). Therefore, end users, researchers and designers built the core team during the first phase. Then, during the second phase multidisciplinary teams of ecosystem actors worked together to *conceptualise and demonstrate* the possible solutions.

Regarding the joint problem-solving effort, the specific challenge in this study was the prerequisite to combine a diversity of theoretical concepts — as well as practical know-how — from business management and information technology. Here, the design thinking and especially service design approaches offered a prominent solution to involve actors in the joint research process. Thus, the confidentiality requirements regarding the sharing of use-case-specific information between the ecosystem actors presented a bottleneck to the collaborative innovation process for the ecosystem, as the discussions about different collaboration strategies and expectations for ecosystem-level creation required clarification. Therefore, use-case-specific non-disclosure agreements (NDAs) were utilised to enhance knowledge and data sharing between the problem owners (forest companies) and solvers. Table 2 summarises the inputs of actors in different roles and their expectations for collaboration in the network(s).

Table 2. Key activities of ecosystem actors involved in the study.

Role in ecosystem	Industry	Input into the process	Expectation for collaboration
Use case owners	Forest industry companies	Use case requirements, co-innovation platform (factories)	Co-learning for novel solutions, closed own development (other use case owners not included)
Solution providers and developers	Equipment Manufacturing	Existing solutions and knowledge for building novel solutions	Closed own (R&D) development, co-learning for novel solutions
	ICT	Existing solutions and knowledge for building novel PoCs	Closed own (R&D) development Learning by doing and building reference cases
Solution integrators	ICT	Customer requirements, need for solution bundles	Networking and solution integration, models for licencing
Innovation Intermediaries	Designers	User requirements, Design thinking	Networking and building reference cases, competences and tools for co-innovation
	Researchers	Research knowledge and results, design science approach	Enabling co-learning, disseminating research results. ensuring generalisability (comparison between use cases)

4.2 Roles and Collaboration Models

During the development process, the ecosystem actors identified different collaboration models for building business impacts through solutions to be identified and conceptualised together. The models were based on: i) traditional bilateral supplier–customer relationships, ii) system integration and iii) multi-actor solutions based on open boundaries of the digital platform. Figure 2 presents the possible models. Each of the models contain both weaknesses and strengths. The traditional bilateral supplier–customer relationships ensure effective co-operation between the parties because the roles, rights and responsibilities can be formally agreed upon. Thus, the customer has the major responsibility for integrating different solutions, meaning that suppliers have a limited view on customer needs at the system level. The second model, joint offerings, enhances the possibility to integrate the different technological solutions with fluently operating digital tools. Finally, the multi-actor platform model could boost novel business models, such as data-based service offerings. It could also improve the modularity and scalability of solutions, which may require open boundaries and practices for data sharing. Furthermore, the multi-actor model has the potential for solving the challenge regarding vendor lock-ins (see Sect. 2.1).

Although the jointly agreed upon ecosystem agenda emphasised systemic solutions, most of the solution provider companies in this study noted that they prefer traditional

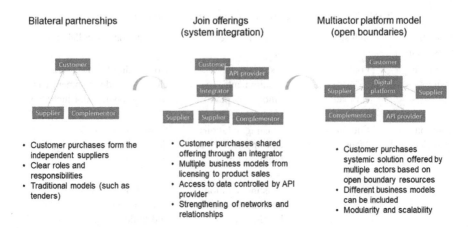

Bilateral partnerships	Join offerings (system integration)	Multiactor platform model (open boundaries)
• Customer purchases form the independent suppliers • Clear roles and responsibilities • Traditional models (such as tenders)	• Customer purchases shared offering through an integrator • Multiple business models from licensing to product sales • Access to data controlled by API provider • Strengthening of networks and relationships	• Customer purchases systemic solution offered by multiple actors based on open boundary resources • Different business models can be included • Modularity and scalability

Fig. 2. Three identified collaboration models.

bilateral partnerships with their potential customers. Therefore, it was realised that the benefits and costs, as well as rights and responsibilities, of these models need to be further analysed. For instance, the governance and need for boundary resources and system integration were recognised by all as important factors that need to be defined.

4.3   Data and Knowledge Sharing

The insight phase led to the acknowledgement that industrial sites have stored huge amounts of data in the various ICT and automation systems during their operations. The challenge here is that the data is not being used to its full potential and no business models exist for utilising the data optimally. Partially, this is due to vendor lock-ins, i.e. to the fact that some of the machinery providers in the forest industry sector are able to control access to the production data of plants. The use case companies estimated that productivity can be increased by several percentage points with new smart solutions and business concepts. In addition, the lack of industrial data format standards hampers the use of data in this domain. Furthermore, the companies lack formal models for sharing and integrating data. Thus, the main obstacle to data sharing often is that companies have not considered their data strategy, i.e. what data could be shared, with whom and what are rules for utilising data. Additionally, making use of the full potential of data requires that the data be further processed as information and knowledge; such a process requires multiple competences from different ecosystem actors. The different dimensions of translating raw data into knowledge require different mechanisms for sharing and protection. The required mechanism will have an impact on possible collaboration models (Sect. 4.2) as well as contracting practices (Sect. 4.4).

Table 3 summarises the key aspects and strategic thinking of the different ecosystem actors with respect to knowledge and data sharing. The forest industry companies are the use case owners; they offered their factories as innovation platforms. For them, it was important to be able to control the ecosystem actors' participation in their use cases. On the other hand, they also wanted to have the possibility to consider knowledge sharing between the use cases. The solution providers (both equipment manufacturers and IT companies) highlighted the need to utilise the improved understanding of customer needs in their own R&D work. In addition, especially the smaller companies emphasised the possibility to demonstrate their competences and build references in a real-world environment. The designer companies and research institutes, which operated as intermediators, especially in first phase, i.e. the insight-building phase of the collaborative process, pointed out the opportunity to gain an understanding of the ecosystem actors' practical problems, conduct research on the co-innovation practices enabling digital transformation and develop novel tools for such processes.

Table 3. Knowledge sharing strategies of ecosystem actors involved in the study.

Role in ecosystem	Industry	Key aspects	Strategies
Use case owners	Forest industry companies	Need to control use case participation, knowledge protection between use case owners (due to competition law)	Acquired knowledge and IP by contractual transaction (sub-contracting solutions developed)
Solution providers and developers	Equipment Manufacturing	Need to utilise the knowledge in own R&D work	Acquired knowledge and IP by contractual transaction
	ICT	Ownership and utilisation of co-developed IP (PoCs) also with other customers	Agreement on ownership of co-developed results
Solution integrators	ICT	Ownership and utilisation of co-developed IP (PoCs) also with other customers	Acquired knowledge and IP by contractual transaction (such as licencing)
Innovation Intermediaries	Designers	Customer references, ownership of novel tools and methods	Participation tools and methods utilised openly (often publicly shared), but their use typically controlled
	Researchers	Possibility to utilise data for research (anonymised)	Public research

During the co-innovation process, it was realised that service design approaches, such as more detailed studies of different user profiles regarding digital solutions, bring benefits to lifetime performance improvement endeavours within the use cases. At the forest industry companies, the user profiles cover the whole range of activities from the shop-floor work to planning and long-term decision making. For instance, if more relevant status and alarm information systems and equipment-level condition monitoring would be available, then additional support for fault identification could be offered.

4.4   Contracting Practices

During the first phases of contract negations between the ecosystem actors, a need arose to clearly define the contracting structure and links between the contracts, i.e. the ecosystem had a consortium agreement and there was a need for an additional use-case-specific non-disclosure agreement (NDA). Furthermore, the ecosystem work received public funding, which introduced some special requirements to contracting. At any rate, the challenge of aligning the dynamic, evolving ecosystem and 'stable' contracts was obvious. It was especially realised that an ecosystem's contact persons should be better involved in contract negotiations, as there still was the tendency to outsource the subject to lawyers.

The level of impacts in a business ecosystem mainly depends on the business needs that the companies were solving, ranging from the effects of conventional process improvement to the effects in emerging ecosystems. Additionally, the potential is not similar for all players in the same collaborative network, which reveals changes in the roles of solution providers. Here, the right to utilise the results was identified as one of the key success factors, i.e. how the actors were able to agree on the rights to utilise the results, such as the technological PoCs tested in collaborative efforts, was crucial (see Table 3). If the customer companies demand an exclusive right to solutions, then the solution providers and integrators have only a limited potential to broaden their business. On the other hand, the availability of technology as well as company resources to grow or gain access to international markets were identified as other important factors.

5   Conclusions

The Finnish forest industry is known for its extremely high level of technology and competence. It has a long history and established development practices; therefore, collaboration with more agile companies could offer them significant potential. For the traditional industry to take the next big step in terms of competitiveness and productivity, the opportunities offered through the digital solutions of Industry 4.0 need to be carefully considered. In addition to technology, novel practices, products and services, business models and networks need to also be developed. Identifying and exploiting the opportunities of Industry 4.0 requires close cooperation with IT companies and challenging existing ways of working. Thus, it was recognised that one of the first tasks is to find a common language between actors coming from different industrial sectors and backgrounds in order to enable them to work together as an ecosystem.

The network actors in our case study worked together to discover the types of tasks and processes to which Industry 4.0 tools could be applied in forest industry processes, as well as how they could be applied. Such applications included, for example, service and maintenance tasks as well as the exchange of information between shifts and plants. The aim of the two-step process was to proceed as quickly as possible to make the concepts and demos generated from ideas available to end users for testing and also to get the resulting solutions to the marketplace.

The managerial implications of this study consist of the practices involved in a co-innovation process within a hybrid collaborative network and a deeper understanding of the business potential from the perspectives of different ecosystem actors. The theoretical contributions indicate that the design science approach is a suitable method for addressing the ill-structured managerial problems of implementing Industry 4.0 tools and requiring constant learning by the actors.

References

1. Harari, Y.: 21 Lessons for the 21st Century. Spiegel & Grau, New York (2018)
2. Kane, G., Palmer, D., Phillips, A., Kiron, D., Buckley, N.: Strategy, not technology, drives digital transformation. MIT Sloan Manag. Rev. July 2015
3. Kortelainen, H., Happonen, A., Hanski, J.: From asset provider to knowledge company—transformation in the digital era. In: Mathew, J., Lim, C.W., Ma, L., Sands, D., Cholette, M. E., Borghesani, P. (eds.) Asset Intelligence Through Integration and Interoperability and Contemporary Vibration Engineering Technologies, pp. 333–341. Springer, Berlin (2019). https://doi.org/10.1007/978-3-319-95711-1_33
4. Afsarmanesh, H., Camarinha-Matos, L.M.: A framework for management of virtual organization breeding environments. Proceedings of PRO-VE, Collaborative Networks and Their Breeding Environments, pp. 35–48. Springer, Valencia (2005). https://doi.org/10.1007/0-387-29360-4_4
5. Camarinha-Matos, L.M., Fornasiero, R., Afsarmanesh, H.: Collaborative networks as a core enabler of industry 4.0. In: Camarinha-Matos, L.M., Afsarmanesh, H., Fornasiero, R. (eds.) PRO-VE 2017. IAICT, vol. 506, pp. 3–17. Springer, Cham (2017). https://doi.org/10.1007/978-3-319-65151-4_1
6. Paasi, J., Valkokari, K., Rusanen, H., Hannu, M., Laiho, T.: Paradox of openness : knowledge sharing-protection tension in ecosystems. In: Ispim 2020, The Conference, Innovation Proceedings, Event Scientific, L U T Publications, June 2020
7. Parker, G.G., Van Alstyne, M.W., Choudary, S.P.: Platform Revolution : How Networked Markets are Transforming The Economy and How to Make Them Work for You, 1st edn. W. W. Norton & Company, New York (2016)
8. Kortelainen, H., et al.: Beyond IoT Business (2019). https://doi.org/10.32040/whitepaper.2019.beyondiot
9. Kortelainen, H., et al.: Data typology in manufacturing industries (2019)
10. Valkokari, K., Rantala, T., Alamäki, A., Palomäki, K.: Business impacts of technology disruption - a design science approach to cognitive systems' adoption within collaborative networks. Collaborative Networks of Cognitive Systems, pp. 333–349. Springer, Berlin (2018). https://doi.org/10.1007/978-3-319-99127-6_29
11. Rong, K., Hu, G., Lin, Y., Shi, Y., Guo, L.: Understanding business ecosystem using a 6C framework in Internet-of-Things-based sectors. Int. J. Prod. Econ. **159**, 41–55 (2015)
12. Nuutinen, M., Valkokari, K., Malmelin, N., Nyblom, J.: Beyond Industry 4.0 - seeking for the philosopher's stone. In: Naples Forum of Service: Theory and Service Science: Integrating Three Perspectives for a New Service Agenda. (2019)
13. Iansiti, M., Levien, R.: The Keystone Advantage: What the New Dynamics of Business Ecosystems Mean for Strategy, Innovation, and Sustainability. Harvard Business School Press, Boston (2004)
14. Ashton, W.S.: The structure, function, and evolution of a regional industrial ecosystem. J. Ind. Ecol. **13**(2), 228–246 (2009)

15. Bernus, P., Noran, O.: Data rich - but information poor. In: IFIP Advances in Information and Communication Technology, vol. 506, pp. 215–2xx (2017)

16. Paajanen, S., Valkokari, K., Aminoff, A.: The opportunities of big data analytics in supply market intelligence. In: Camarinha-Matos, L.M., Afsarmanesh, H., Fornasiero, R. (eds.) PRO-VE 2017. IAICT, vol. 506, pp. 194–205. Springer, Cham (2017). https://doi.org/10.1007/978-3-319-65151-4_19

17. Doz, Y.: Clubs, clans and caravans: the dynamics of alliance membership and governance. In: Trick, M., Ed. Growing the International Firm: Success in Mergers, Acquisitions, Networks and Alliances, Berlin: Carnegie Mellon University Press (2001)

18. Valkokari, K., Seppänen, M., Mäntylä, M., Jylhä-Ollila, S.: Orchestrating innovation ecosystems: a qualitative analysis of ecosystem positioning strategies. Technol. Innov. Manag. Rev. 7(3), 12–24 (2017)

19. March, S.T., Smith, G.F.: Design and natural science research on information technology. Decis. Support Syst. 15(4), 251–266 (1995). https://doi.org/10.1016/0167-9236(94)00041-2

The Role of Collaboration for Sustainable and Efficient Urban Logistics

Leandro Carvalho$^{(\boxtimes)}$, Jorge Freire de Sousa,
and Jorge Pinho de Sousa

Faculty of Engineering, University of Porto/INESC TEC,
Rua Dr. Roberto Frias, 4200-265 Porto, Portugal
{up200301226, jfsousa}@fe.up.pt,
jorge.p.sousa@inesctc.up.pt

Abstract. The scarcity of resources is one of the main concerns for the present and the future of the environment and society. The "load factor" in logistic transport has a great potential for improvement, especially in the *last-mile* deliveries, as the transport of goods is largely fragmented between several small companies using small vehicles. This paper investigates the potential for collaboration to increase efficiency in urban logistics. Based on an overview of the concepts and initiatives regarding vertical and horizontal collaboration, a research agenda is proposed.

Keywords: Urban logistics · Collaboration · Sustainability · Last-mile

1 Introduction

Efficient logistic networks have a determinant role in the economic development of countries, regions, and cities. However, in urban areas, freight transport can have very significant negative impacts in terms of traffic, air and sound pollution, and the safety of the citizens.

According to the European Technology Platform ALICE [1], Eurostat surveys estimate that, for long-distances, 24% of vehicles transporting goods in the European Union (EU) are running empty. In comparison, the average loading of the other freight vehicles is 57%, yielding an overall efficiency of 43%. Flow imbalances can explain only half of this loss. The opportunity is estimated as representing 160 billion Euros and a reduction of 1.3% of $CO2$ emissions.

Urban areas present a higher potential for improvement. The *last-mile* delivery is, in general, performed through a fragmented market. In Europe, 85% of freight companies dedicated to short distance deliveries have less than 5 employees [2]. They often work as subcontractors for large companies, but integration between services is not always achieved. These small companies perform the deliveries in the urban areas often using small trucks or vans. In this context, features such as the lack of standardization of packages, the deadline for deliveries, that is usually very short, and the difficulty of adapting the routes to multiple destinations can significantly reduce the load factor (the relation between the real and the potential loading weight) [3].

© IFIP International Federation for Information Processing 2020
Published by Springer Nature Switzerland AG 2020
L. M. Camarinha-Matos et al. (Eds.): PRO-VE 2020, IFIP AICT 598, pp. 475–484, 2020.
https://doi.org/10.1007/978-3-030-62412-5_39

Resource sharing between stakeholders can improve efficiency in the transport of goods, becoming financially attractive to logistics operators, and bringing benefits for the society and the environment. Despite the increased interest in transport collaboration in the literature, preliminary research suggests a lack of consensus on a *typology* for collaborative logistics in urban areas. This paper is a brief overview of collaboration in urban logistics, more specifically in the *last-mile* delivery, and presents some ongoing initiatives in this sector. Moreover, this work seeks to develop a preliminary research agenda for collaboration in logistics, focusing on resource utilization and social impact.

The paper is structured as follows. The next section details the main stakeholders in collaborative transport and their interests. Then, an overview of collaboration in logistics is given, describing its different types, and presenting practical experiences as examples. Afterwards, a research agenda is presented, entailing the research gaps and opportunities in practice. Finally, we provide the conclusions of this preliminary research.

2   Stakeholders in Logistic Collaboration

Assessing the different types of partnerships in collaborative logistics is a necessary step to describe stakeholders and understand their needs. The overall cost of the supply network activities can be reduced through collaborative agreements between urban logistics stakeholders [4]. [5] classify the different stakeholders of urban transport according to the different land-uses, divided into three main categories: generators of transport demand, transport operators, and interface roles. Residents in the city and the main activities that generate trips (economic, leisure, and others) form the first group. The second category represents providers for the transport of goods and passengers. Finally, the last set includes the public authorities and professional bodies, responsible for planning and organizing the urban space. New solutions are dependent on local authorities' decisions, while the other stakeholders react to those choices.

[6] view the carriers, the authorities, the receivers, and the end consumers as the main stakeholders in urban freight. For these direct participants in the logistics chain, the main benefits of collaboration may be an increase in the load factor (and consequently a cost reduction), increased service capacity, reduced delivery time and, ultimately, increased customer satisfaction and improved image for the companies involved.

However, to this group of stakeholders, we need to add the actors indirectly affected by the urban supply chain, such as the city inhabitants, both users or non-users of public or private transport, and the environment. Therefore, our analysis encompasses the sustainability of the operation, adding the social and environmental goals to the economic standpoint. These three perspectives are often described in the literature as the three P's: People, Planet, and Profit, to which recently a fourth dimension was added, Policy [7].

For both public and private transport users, the reduction of trucks and vans naturally has a direct impact on traffic reduction and congestion. Moreover, the traffic reduction of trucks and vans in urban areas may lead to a significant decrease in the number of accidents involving cyclists and pedestrians. In London, between 2008 and 2012, 53% of cyclist deaths involved heavy goods vehicles [1].

Additionally, the EU has set a target for 2030 of *zero emissions* from logistics operations in the major urban centres. As stated by the European Horizon 2020 innovation programme [8], this target can be achieved through actions that produce new solutions and practices for enhanced collaboration between suppliers, transporters, and public decision-makers in urban regions. The resulting reduction in air and noise pollution would be beneficial to the environment, and thus to citizens in general.

3 Collaboration in Urban Freight Transport

3.1 Vertical and Horizontal Collaboration

To reduce the environmental and social impact of freight transport, regional authorities often implement restricting land-use measures, such as limiting the size of vehicles, reducing parking places, and limiting access to urban centres during specific periods of the day. [9] argue that the negative consequences of these initiatives in terms of efficiency for logistics operators encourage companies to collaborate and share resources, in order to reduce the kilometres driven with empty vehicles. [10] argue that logistic companies look for collaboration as an opportunity to reduce costs, increase productivity, improve customer service, and expand geographical coverage. In the context of supply chain management, [11] states that transport should not be planned only as an operational activity since a collaborative approach can improve the performance of companies. These arguments reinforce the importance of collaboration for the urban logistic stakeholders, and the need to understand the emerging initiatives in the sector.

According to the literature, collaboration in logistics can be *vertical* or *horizontal*. "For vertical collaboration, transport is often organized along modes and service operators. In horizontal collaboration, multiple providers work together in the same section of the transport chain, potentially sharing orders and infrastructure" [12].

Vertical collaboration is part of the essence of logistics, since cooperation between stakeholders will always be necessary, whether at the level of Logistic Service Providers (LSP) complementing their operations (maritime, air and land), or at the level of producers, receivers or final customers, or even between existing platforms and carriers. [11] identifies different relationship degrees in vertical collaboration, that range from pure negotiation on prices to a closer and more integrated relationship composed of joint planning and information systems sharing.

[5] identify three main approaches for vertical collaboration: Efficient Consumer Response (ECR), which promotes automatic procedures to deal with supply chain links; Vendor Management Inventory (VMI), where the supplier is jointly responsible for warehousing; and Shared VMI approaches, with a consortium of producers and/or grouped distribution stakeholders. [13] argues that although initiatives such as ECR and Collaborative Planning, Forecasting, and Replenishment (CPFR) are well known in terms of logistics, the best results of vertical collaboration arise from broad-based strategic collaboration towards a more partnering approach.

Horizontal collaboration is not new in logistics either. However, technological developments, in terms of Information and Communication Technologies (ICT) and Intelligent Transport Systems (ITS), have fostered the creation of new possibilities of collaboration for companies, therefore stimulating a growing interest by researchers. The first works on horizontal collaboration [10, 14, 15] were often based on empirical studies, developed from the management and logistics principles available at the time, based on interviews with managers in the area, and also on comparisons with existing alliances in the air and maritime sectors.

We can find features from both horizontal and vertical collaboration in part of the initiatives implemented by enterprises on logistics. Although, by definition, horizontal collaboration initiatives generate more opportunities to harness idle resources. According to [16], collaboration in transport can take different forms and can be developed at different levels: transactional, informational, and decisional. The transactional level is, in general, vertical, and the other levels can be vertical or horizontal. In the next sections, we will further explore some of these alternatives for collaboration.

3.2   Freight Transportation by Customers

As in other fields of society, in recent years, several resource sharing initiatives have emerged in the logistics sector, as forms of the so-called *sharing economy*. Leveraged by the dissemination of internet and mobile technologies, logistics companies are stimulating the participation of citizens as occasional or, sometimes, regular service providers in the supply chain. [17] describe the example of the *pick-up* point networks, where the stores make the products available in a mid-location, such as locker boxes or fuel stations, and the final customers collect the goods themselves, performing the last-mile transportation to their homes or work. In other cases, these customers can make other deliveries in the neighbourhood. These are typical cases of vertical collaboration, in which the last leg of the transportation is not made by trucks or vans, but by the customers. Streetspotr and Task Rabbit are technological ventures in which persons can execute housework tasks to other people, including collecting and delivering goods [18].

Crowdsourcing in the last-mile is based on the same principles, with people being responsible for the final leg in the delivery, but, in this case, the customer takes advantage of a previously planned trip to transport the goods [19]. Crowdsourcing enables more efficient utilization of existing capacity, reduces transportation costs, and builds customer networks and local communities [18]. This type of service can enhance the urban mobility of both people and freight when the delivery route is integrated into an existing journey [20]. Indeed, detours from the planned journey or dedicated trips will most probably increase vehicle circulation in cities, as few packages are loaded on each delivery service. Several start-ups such as Walmart to go, MyWays from DHL, and Deliv, are investing in business solutions based on benefiting from unused loaded space [21].

3.3   Urban Consolidation Centres

Urban Consolidation Centres (UCCs) are a successful way to reduce the number of large trucks circulating in city centres, quite often with a low load factor. [22] define an urban consolidation centre as "a logistic facility that is situated relatively close to the geographical area that serves the city centre, an entire city, or a specific place for which consolidated deliveries are made". Companies consolidate cargo at UCCs by sharing warehouses, vehicles, human resources, and ICT to reduce trips within cities. Due to these efforts to share goods and infrastructure, UCCs can be analysed from a horizontal or vertical collaboration perspective [12].

[23] lists several examples of joint delivery centres developed in Japan in the last decades, with a particular reference to the project in Yokohama. In this project, 17 companies shared the same UCC (Motomachi) and jointly organized and distributed their products using trucks with the initiative's brand, resulting in a reduction in the number of vehicles from 100 to 29, in the ten days of the project. [24] proposes, for Singapore, a solution of consolidated warehouses and synchronized last-mile, as an alternative to manage the scarcity of resources. Although experiences indicate a positive impact on environmental and social terms, most of these initiatives do not last long [25]. In terms of resource utilization, UCCs increase the load factor in the last-mile, but, on the other hand, they require high investments in infrastructure and ICT. Furthermore, this type of initiative raises costs and delivery times by introducing additional transhipment, often creating a heavy reliance on government subsidies that target social and environmental benefits [26].

3.4   Using Passengers Transport Resources for the Transport of Goods

A well-known collaboration strategy consists in sharing the city's passenger transport infrastructure with the urban logistics network. In many periods of the day, the capacity of urban public transport is under-utilized, thus creating the opportunity to plan the transport of passengers and goods as a single system [6]. [12] presents an overview of the leading research on the use of taxis, buses, and light rail systems to transport both passengers and goods. [27] describe some initiatives of this type, such as the Dabbawala System in India, that uses public trains for the transport of lunch boxes, or the Bussgods Service in Sweden and the Cargo Hitching in the Netherlands, both using bus services to transport parcels. [28] analyse the impact of product distribution through an intercity passenger transport network in Ceará, Brazil.

In similar initiatives, in which passengers and goods share the same infrastructure, logistics providers use the rail structure to transport products [29]. In Dresden, Cargo Tram transports car components to the Volkswagen plant, together with passengers, in the same tram service. Other projects in Zurich, Amsterdam, and Vienna were created based on the German experience.

3.5   Freight Pooling

Horizontal collaboration can be implemented by sharing different tangible and/or intangible assets, alone or in combination [14], such as logistics facilities, skills, and information systems. An example of this type of collaboration occurs when logistic service providers share the freight. In a conventional vertical approach, different operators perform each *distribution leg*, for example, when delivery has road, maritime and last-mile shipments. In this type of collaboration, increasing efficiency may involve better synchronization between partners or a reduction of the total routing cost [30]. Moreover, environmental-friendly initiatives have been launched for the last delivery leg in urban areas, using electric vehicles or bicycles [4], for example.

In another approach, the freight is shared, and each vehicle carries goods from different logistic operators simultaneously. *Freight transport pooling* can be defined "as the use of residual capacities of an already planned vehicle to include more goods" [5]. This type of horizontal collaboration can offer these companies benefits such as a reduction in the transportation costs, an increase of the service levels, handling costs decrease, and brand improvement, among others [31]. Moreover, freight pooling has the purpose of increasing load factors and decrease the number of trucks and vans in urban areas, thus reducing the social and environmental negative impacts of logistics.

Bilateral cooperations are usually based on flexible short-term arrangements, where purchase orders and packages are exchanged promptly to reduce inefficient routes [32]. In multilateral collaborations, agreements or contracts are formalized to define the governance strategy of the partnership, since companies have to control the degree to which structures, information, or purchase orders are shared. For example, in a case where companies are competitors in one market and collaborate in another market, limitations in these sharing schemes would be necessary [10].

For companies to participate in collaboration, there must be a fair distribution of the costs and benefits of the partnership. There is an extensive literature on cost allocation in vertical and horizontal collaboration. Proportional allocation is a simple approach based on the overall volume or weight of the goods. However, more often, these analyses are made using the principles based on game theory [33]. [31] applied the concepts of cooperative game theory in a horizontal collaboration between three companies in Belgium: the partnership improved the efficiency between 10% and 30%, concluding that flexibility, in terms of a time window for deliveries and split of orders, offers better results.

The mistrust between collaboration participants to share orders and information is another potential barrier for the creation of freight poolings. To assure their interests within a collaborative initiative, companies define a limited liability company (LLC) as an impartial entity, responsible for the central management of the alliance [34]. In autocratic alliances, the LLC centralizes decision power; in more participative alliances, the LLC acts as a moderator.

Another issue often studied in horizontal collaborative transport is the method to exchange requests. For this purpose, two main mechanisms can be found in the literature: the capacity exchange price, that defines a fixed rate for extra-capacity available, and auctions, formed by a bidding price-setting problem and a winner determination problem [32].

Companies currently use pooling as an alternative to UCCs, with digital platforms replacing the physical location for the exchange. In a more traditional business model, companies, producers, or receivers can use the internet to simulate, compare, and negotiate the complete supply chain for deliveries. Companies such as MCU Cargo and

Transfix act as facilitators, offering platforms where companies can negotiate the freight, seeking for a simpler and faster transport process. Other business models offer logistic providers the opportunity to share the goods and available space on trucks, in a horizontal collaborative perspective. Truckpad and Bizzcargo are examples of this type of platform. UFreight is a mobile platform, in the prototype phase, for freight pooling integrating cargo bikes, where constant updates on requests, compatible with routes and capacities, improve the load factor and avoid empty return trips [35].

4   Research Agenda

While vertical collaboration has already been widely addressed in the literature, horizontal collaboration, and all its opportunities, has only recently become a subject of research. Although vertical collaboration is inherent to the logistics processes and has the potential to improve the performance of those entities involved in the supply chain, in this paper we claim that horizontal collaboration is more promising in creating new business models that emphasize sustainability in logistics and promote the *best use of resources already available.*

This research also indicates that, in some sense, existing business collaborative initiatives outweigh the knowledge accumulated in many years of research. Companies are overcoming the barriers mentioned above, and are investing and developing *new business models* to collaborate. This opens the opportunity to investigate, through studies in the field, how this evolution is taking place, and which may be the drivers for innovative forms of more sustainable collaboration in urban logistics.

The financial perspective in the decision-making processes of logistic partnerships seems to be predominant. Several scientific studies investigate the costs and benefits of partnerships in an exclusively financial way. But the overall aspects of these operations, which impact multiple stakeholders, should also be explicitly considered. This means *social and environmental issues need to be taken into account,* this being, therefore, a topic with great research potential.

Starting with the identification of the main drivers guiding the research agenda in this area, we first propose the *development of a typology* offering a new way of viewing collaboration. Such a contribution is needed since there is no comprehensive classification (typology) of the different forms of collaboration in logistics, accepted by the academic community and capable of synthesizing the existing terminology and concepts and aggregating the various initiatives that exist in the business world. In this context, this paper aims at contributing to the creation of such a typology.

This new perspective should go beyond the traditional categorizations, by emphasizing a better use of resources, and the consequent social and environmental impacts. Such an analysis should allow the assessment of the potential for optimization of each type of collaboration, its effects on the different stakeholders, and its potential viability as a lasting solution for urban areas.

5 Conclusion

Partially loaded or empty trucks circulating through cities have, for many years, been considered as an intrinsic issue of urban logistics operations. If, in the past, these inefficiencies were somehow tolerated, today's awareness of the limitation and scarcity of resources, coupled with the increasing demand for sustainable operations, creates the right environment for the development of innovative, integrated and more sustainable solutions. In this way, collaboration in logistics emerges as an essential alternative to improve the use of resources.

However, aspects such as the fierce rivalry between companies, whose competitiveness is often based on price, resistance to sharing information, and strict cost-benefit analysis by participants, are obstacles to these new initiatives and often result in failed forms of collaboration. Therefore, the identification of criteria to guide the creation of new business models for companies willing to participate in horizontal collaboration initiatives, possibly triggered by the development of new technologies, will be of interest, not only for these companies but to public authorities that plan and regulate urban mobility.

In order to develop a research agenda for logistics collaboration, which involves the development of a typology for the subject, this paper analysed some critical concepts and components of different types of collaboration, aiming to develop more efficient logistics distribution solutions. The focus was put on the potential of logistic providers to create sustainable alternatives for sharing resources with their customers, with other modes of transport, or among themselves, or for taking advantage of private and public under-utilized infrastructure. This preliminary research agenda should cover the design of a typology on logistics collaboration for urban logistics, the analysis of existing business models for horizontal collaboration, and the mechanisms for a fair distribution of costs and benefits in more sustainable partnerships.

Acknowledgements. This work of the first author is funded by Fundação para a Ciência e Tecnologia (FCT), Portugal, through grant PD/BD/142906/2018.

References

1. European Commission: Urban Freight: Research & Innovation Roadmap, European Technology Platform ALICE (2015)
2. European Commission: A Truly Integrated Transport System For Sustainable and Efficient Logistics, European Technology Platform ALICE (2017)
3. Duarte, A.L.d.C.M., Macau, F., Flores e Silva, C., Sanches, L.M.: Last mile delivery to the bottom of the pyramid in Brazilian slums. Int. J. Phys. Distrib. Logistics Manage **49**(5), 473–491 (2019)
4. Perboli, G., Rosano, M.: Parcel delivery in urban areas: opportunities and threats for the mix of traditional and green business models. Transp. Res. Part C Emerg. Technol. **99**, 19–36 (2019)
5. Gonzalez-Feliu, J., Morana, J., Grau, J.M.S., Ma, T.Y.: Design and scenario assessment for collaborative logistics and freight transport systems. Int. J. Transp. Econ. **40**(2), 207–240 (2013)

6. Bjørgen, A., Seter, H., Kristensen, T., Pitera, K.: The potential for coordinated logistics planning at the local level: a Norwegian in-depth study of public and private stakeholders. J. Transp. Geogr. **76**, 34–41 (2019)

7. Sousa, J.F., Mendes-Moreira, J.: Urban logistic integrated in a multimodal mobility system. In: Proceedings of 18th IEEE International Conference on Intelligent Transportation Systems (ITSC), Las Palmas, Gran Canaria, Spain, pp. 89–94. IEEE Press (2015)

8. European Commission: Work Program 2018–2020 – Smart, Green and integrated transport. HORIZON 2020 (2019)

9. Awasthi, A., Adetiloye, T., Crainic, T.G.: Collaboration partner selection for city logistics planning under municipal freight regulations. Appl. Math. Modell. **40**(1), 510–525 (2016)

10. Cruijssen, F., Cools, M., Dullaert, W.: Horizontal cooperation in logistics: opportunities and impediments. Transp. Res. Part E Logist. Transp. Rev. **43**(2), 129–142 (2007)

11. Mason, R., Lalwani, C., Boughton, R.: Combining vertical and horizontal collaboration for transport optimization. Supply Chain Manage. **12**(3), 187–199 (2007)

12. Cleophas, C., Cottrill, C., Ehmke, J.F., Tierney, K.: Collaborative urban transportation: recent advances in theory and practice. Eur. J. Oper. Res. **273**(3), 801–816 (2018)

13. Renko, S.: Vertical collaboration in the supply chain. In: Renko, S. (ed.) Supply Chain Management-New Perspectives, pp. 183–198. IntechOpen (2011)

14. Verstrepen, S., Cools, M., Cruijssen, F., Dullaert, W.: A dynamic framework for managing horizontal cooperation in logistics. Int. J. Logistics Syst. Manage. **5**(3–4), 228–248 (2009)

15. Cruijssen, F., Salomon, M.: Empirical study: order sharing between transportation companies may result in cost reductions between 5 to 15 percent. CentER Discussion Paper No. 2004–80 (2004)

16. Gonzalez-Feliu, J., Pronello, C., Grau, J.M.S.: Multi-stakeholder collaboration in urban transport: state-of-the-art and research opportunities. Transport **33**(4), 1079–1094 (2018)

17. Savelsbergh, M., Van Woensel, T.: 50th anniversary invited article—city logistics: challenges and opportunities. Transp. Sci. **50**(2), 579–590 (2016)

18. Mladenow, A., Bauer, C., Strauss, C.: "Crowd logistics": the contribution of social crowds in logistics activities. Int. J. Web Inf. Syst. **12**(3), 379–396 (2016)

19. Castillo, V.E., Bell, J.E., Rose, W.J., Rodrigues, A.M.: Crowdsourcing last mile delivery: strategic implications and future research directions. J. Bus. Logistics **39**(1), 7–25 (2018)

20. Rai, H.B., Verlinde, S., Merckx, J., Macharis, C.: Crowd logistics: an opportunity for more sustainable urban freight transport. Eur. Transp. Res. Rev. **9**, 39 (2017)

21. Rougès, J.-F., Montreuil, B.: Crowdsourcing delivery: new interconnected business models to reinvent delivery. In: Proceedings of 1st International Physical Internet Conference, Québec City, Canada (2016)

22. Browne, M., Sweet, M., Woodburn, A., Allen, J.: Urban freight consolidation centres final report. Edited by University of Westminster Transport Studies Group, London (2005)

23. Taniguchi, E.: Concepts of city logistics for sustainable and liveable cities. Procedia Soc. Behav. Sci. **151**, 310–317 (2014)

24. de Souza, R., Xing, Z., Goh, M.: Supply Chain and logistics challenges and opportunities in Asia: innovative urban logistics concept, pp. 2907–2916. In: Proceedings of International Conference on Industrial Engineering and Operations Management, Bali, Indonesia (2014)

25. Lindawati, V.S.J., Goh, M., de Souza, R.: Collaboration in urban logistics: motivations and barriers. International Journal of Urban Sciences. **18**(2), 278–290 (2014)

26. Verlinde, S., Macharis, C., Witlox, F.: How to consolidate urban flows of goods without setting up an urban consolidation centre? Procedia Soc. Behav. Sci. **39**, 687–701 (2012)

27. Van Duin, R., Wiegmans, B., Tavasszy, L., Hendriks, B., He, Y.: Evaluating new participative city logistics concepts: the case of cargo hitching. Transp. Res. Procedia **39**, 565–575 (2019)

28. Guimarães, L.R., Athayde Prata, B., de Sousa, J.P.: Models and algorithms for network design in urban freight distribution systems. Transp. Res. Procedia **47**, 291–298 (2020)

29. Trentini, A., Malhene, N.: Flow management of passengers and goods coexisting in the urban environment: conceptual and operational points of view. Procedia Soc. Behav. Sci. **39**, 807–817 (2012)

30. Montoya-Torres, J.R., Muñoz-Villamizar, A., Vega-Mejía, C.A.: On the impact of collaborative strategies for goods delivery in city logistics. Prod. Plann. Control **27**(6), 443–455 (2016)

31. Vanovermeire, C., Sörensen, K., Van Breedam, A., Vannieuwenhuyse, B., Verstrepen, S.: Horizontal logistics collaboration: Decreasing costs through flexibility and an adequate cost allocation strategy. Int. J. Logistics Res. Appl. **17**(4), 339–355 (2014)

32. Pan, S., Trentesaux, D., Ballot, E., Huang, G.Q.: Horizontal collaborative transport: survey of solutions and practical implementation issues. Int. J. Prod. Res. **57**(15–16), 5340–5361 (2019)

33. Guajardo, M., Rönnqvist, M.: A review on cost allocation methods in collaborative transportation. Int. Trans. Oper. Res. **23**(3), 371–392 (2016)

34. Albers, S., Klaas-Wissing, T.: Organisation of multilateral LTL alliances. Int. J. Logistics Res. Appl. **15**(3), 181–198 (2012)

35. Rosano, M., Demartini, C.G., Lamberti, F., Perboli, G.: A mobile platform for collaborative urban freight transportation. Transp. Res. Procedia **30**, 14–22 (2018)

A Balanced Sociotechnical Framework for Collaborative Networks 4.0

Paula Urze[1(✉)], A. Luis Osório[2], Hamideh Afsarmanesh[3],
and Luis M. Camarinha-Matos[4]

[1] Faculty of Sciences and Technology, NOVA University of Lisbon
and CIUHCT, Lisbon, Portugal
pcu@fct.unl.pt
[2] ISEL - Instituto Superior de Engenharia de Lisboa, Instituto Politécnico de
Lisboa and POLITEC &ID, Lisbon, Portugal
lo@isel.ipl.pt
[3] University of Amsterdam (UvA), Amsterdam, The Netherlands
h.afsarmanesh@uva.nl
[4] Faculty of Sciences and Technology, NOVA University of Lisbon
and CTS-UNINOVA, Lisbon, Portugal
cam@uninova.pt

Abstract. Our research question focusses on the complex networks of organizations of business partners that by exchanging data and sharing control
collaborate for typical business or social objectives. We revisit such networks of
organizations studied under the collaborative networks research area in a multidisciplinary attempt to construct a common balanced sociotechnical framework
based on the interactions between social and engineering sciences. Our proposal
discusses the collaborative network under the 4.0 following industry time frame
classification, considering momentous evolution steps towards the digital. This
paper presents and discusses research towards balanced sociotechnical concepts
and definitions founded on previous studies with a recognized influence from
social science and engineering systems. The paper further points out a strategy
to validate the research in a Robotic Process Automation (RPA) case and, in the
context of the HORUS project with BP Portugal.

Keywords: Sociotechnical systems · Collaborative networks 4.0 ·
Sociotechnical framework

1 Introduction

Industry 4.0 represents an evolving paradigm of manufacturing systems as growing
adoption of automation artifacts towards digitization, as discussed in [24]. In essence,
the corresponding advancements are motivated by the aim of producing maximum
output with minimum resources. The fast-growing adoption by industry of digital
technologies such as cyber-physical systems (CPS), Internet of things (IoT), and cloud
computing [24], have been a significant research and development driver.

Although over the last few decades, the technological evolution progressed at a
pace of growth not uniformly followed by all research areas since the creation of

© IFIP International Federation for Information Processing 2020
Published by Springer Nature Switzerland AG 2020
L. M. Camarinha-Matos et al. (Eds.): PRO-VE 2020, IFIP AICT 598, pp. 485–498, 2020.
https://doi.org/10.1007/978-3-030-62412-5_40

common understandings between different scientific disciplines takes time. The endogeneization of technology advances has been, for a long time, a concern of social science researchers [21]. The Tavistock Institute in London pioneered the concept of sociotechnical systems by the end of the 1960s, to understand the symbiosis between workers and the manufacturing processes and technology.

The more recent decades have also seen the emergence of collaboration in industry and services, raising research questions such as how to best support the interactions between humans and intelligent autonomous systems. Further to the traditional partnership among people and organizations, the concept is now also relating to the growing integration of independent, smart computing elements where the necessarily evolving role of workers needs to be studied. When researching the non-technical challenges of Industry 4.0 [10], it is imperative to discuss the social consequences and context implications from a generalized adoption of digitalization.

Trends to increase control by intelligent autonomous systems, in most cases associated with marketing pressure, need to be carefully studied. A typical result is that the work usually performed by people replaced by computing systems, which raises the question of rethinking an alternative role for human workers. One example of such a fast move is the adoption of software robots to substitute personal interaction with office-like informatics systems by mimicking web interface interactions. Such autonomous computing systems, sometimes identified as Robotic Process Automation (RPA) components [13], constitute a new family of technology artifacts. A simple example of applying the RPA strategy is to imagine a mobile application that, from an authenticated voice order, e.g., "*Please transfer fifty euros from my expenses account to X's allowance account*," automatically transfers the amount from one account to another. Such an intelligent computational agent, activated by voice orders, translates the request into the equivalent interactions with the respective mobile banking app. This trend is getting momentum since the approach does not require complicated and costly changes to the organization's informatics systems. A programmer can simply develop the robotic computational element to install in a mobile or a web browser, e.g., the money transfer between bank accounts. No changes are necessary to the home banking interface, the RPA element just impersonates user interactions, from authentication to filling the proper form fields in the same way the user does to interact with the home banking App.

While simple and with potential value for businesses and people in a diversity of application domains, the RPA technology raises several questions both at the organization level and from the perspective of a collaborative network's organization. Collaborative Networks (CN) [3] and, in particular, what is proposed in [8] as emerging Collaborative Networks 4.0, consider a wide adoption of advanced digital collaboration forms. Taking our simple RPA example, the question is how the adoption of robotic process automation in organizations influences attitudes from an ethical point of view and how we can prevent social disruptions. We mean by social disruptions situations leading to drastic changes in workforces, e.g., the drastic reduction of the workforce without a strategy to establish paths able to integrate workers in alternative functions through training plans or other social or management strategies.

Adopting a balanced approach to the research of the sociotechnical dimensions in CN4.0 is needed to contribute to an equilibrium between social and information sciences, and technical realizations and engineering perspectives. The aim of achieving such balance is a not novel idea, as evidenced by earlier research on balanced automation, namely the introduction of the anthropocentric manufacturing concept centered on people [7]. Despite such more initial contributions, a shared understanding and a clear identity for the sociotechnical system remains an open research question, which we address in this work.

The remaining of this paper organizes as follows: Sect. 2 presents and discusses related research from the social sciences, management, informatics, and engineering fields, establishing the ground for a balance developing twined perspective among social sciences and technical achievements, leading to a sociotechnical understanding of the next generation of collaborative networks or CN 4.0. In Sect. 3, based on related research, we present and discuss a sociotechnical framework to structure and propose guidelines and rules contributing to a balanced, collaborative network under the CN 4.0 vision. Section 4 introduces two ongoing projects grounding the strategy for the validation of the proposed sociotechnical framework. Finally, in Sect. 5, we present conclusions and directions for further research towards a balanced CN 4.0 sociotechnical framework.

2   Sociotechnical Research Approach

The sociotechnical research dates back to the 1950s emerged as a paradigm shift in the way of thinking and managing organizations. The sociotechnical thought roots from the social sciences, and sociotechnical thinking [24], coined in Great Britain from the coal mines case. This research showed that early in 1949, workers had found a way to regain group cohesion and self-regulation, increasing their power, and participate in decisions regarding the organization of their work, albeit with more advanced mechanization. Against the mainstream of Taylorism and bureaucratic principles, the sociotechnical theory claimed an "organizational choice" conducted by the Tavistock Institute of Human Relations in London led by Eric Trist.

Since the edition *of Organizational Choice* in the 1960s [26], a group of social scientists relied on the thesis that organization of work could shape almost independently from technological constraints - there would always be room for an "organizational choice" [5]. Nowadays, the increasing trend for the immateriality of technology makes it possible to consider more design alternatives for production systems that better correspond to the potential of the human user, namely to individual and collective autonomy and cooperation, which in turn increases the organization's effectiveness and efficiency. An essential insight into the approach of sociotechnical systems involves social and technical elements, being the two systems intertwined in a complex network of mutual causality. In other words, the social and technological aspects of organizational systems feed on each other, as new technologies open up new possibilities for work and, in turn, new ways of working open the way for technological change [27]. In reacting to technocentric thought, researchers rooted in the sociotechnical systems (STS) perspective argue that better results are achieved if people, machines, and context meet together [30].

The open system concept is of paramount importance for sociotechnical systems since the worker is, according to [19], a complex, dynamic, stochastic, nonlinear, nonsteady, and self-organizing system. The concept of an open system grounds on the definition proposed by Bertalanffy [30] for living organisms and their interaction with the environment defined by the steady-state theory, according to which an open system is characterized by a steady-state achieved by some stimulus after a disturbance. A sociotechnical system embodies workers as open, living systems interacting in contexts, influencing, and conditioning the technical systems. The sociotechnical discourse is strongly influenced by the open system concept, as formulated by Bertalanffy [30]. As such, the sociotechnical theory has developed the notion of the "interaction of social and technical elements," an essential dimension for studying the performance of systems. The interactions between workers and technology artifacts encompass linear cause and effect relationships when planned, and generally estimated as nonlinear relationships, complex and even unpredictable if unexpected [31]. The resulting interleaved socio and technical elements have different forms of behaving when compared with the technological artifacts, establishing that people are not equipment. Furthermore, with the increasing systems' complexity and interdependencies, technology can demonstrate nonlinear behavior as well. The linear and nonlinear types of interaction arise when a sociotechnical system enters into operation. The mutual adjustment is identified in [28] as the "joint optimization" of two subsystems. Based on these contributions we can summarize sociotechnical systems as showing the following main characteristics as discussed in [4]: i) systems must have interdependent parts; ii) systems have separate but interdependent technical and social subsystems; iii) systems' goals are reached by more than one way (there are always design choices made during the process of development); iv) systems' performance relies on the joint optimization of the technical and social subsystems. Two foundational principles embed early sociotechnical studies, namely: (i) a systems approach, and (ii) emphasis on the interaction between the social and the technological parts.

From our perspective, we need some equilibrium between the sociotechnical and the more technical discourse, i.e., what we call a balanced approach. One paradigmatic example is the innovation in user data entering as materialized by the Robotic Process Automation (RPA) concept. In a simple definition, "*RPA is an umbrella term for tools that operate on the user interface of other computer systems in the way a human would do*" [29]. This view focuses on the innovation aspect but does not address any social concern. However, the mentioned article touches, in fact, social issues when the authors state that "*work that can only be done by humans*." Thus, despite not directly related to social studies, that research shows some social concerns. In [13], while not following a sociotechnical discourse, the social skills and other human competencies like creative thinking or intellectual judgment are used to delimit the intervention domain for the discussed computing software-based robots, the RPA.

Another example of related research develops a framework for intelligent monitoring of a multi-agent system seen as a sociotechnical system [11]. In this case, the advanced concepts to approach a social discourse is a sociotechnical system, including the interplay between humans, organizations, and technical systems. The organizational aspect is not, however, explored or even related to the proposed monitoring system; it diagnoses merely, reconciles, and compensates the technical system. In what seems a complementary approach, a theoretical model for the integration of Industry 4.0 with sociotechnical centers puts the discourse at the organizational level [24]. Despite the formulation of a digitalization strategy to optimize the organization, the sociotechnical language differs. The idea of tandem, establishing a worker-technology tight symbiosis, the proposed six principles—people, infrastructure, technology, processes, culture, and goals—grouped into three perspectives - vertical integration, horizontal integration, and end-to-end integration - are contributions for the sociotechnical (re)construction.

The concept of virtual organizations' breeding environment (VBE), offering a preparedness condition for the creation of dynamic virtual organizations, associates the notion of prestige as a social recognition to measure value related to collaborative networks [1]. The social nature is also associated with the creation of knowledge and knowledge exchange as a core process in knowledge creation and, therefore, a fundamental contribution to trust management. The social perspective is explored further in the classification of VBEs by associating social prestige and considering formal or social orientation in finding social values [2]. This research founds the need to develop a framework where persons and technology somehow framed in organizations and networks cooperate under complex interaction mechanisms.

3   A Sociotechnical Framework for Collaborative Networks 4.0

Future Collaborative Networks is, in our research, understood as featuring entities that interact mostly based on digital mechanisms and structured collaboration concepts. Regarding the digital artifacts, we are thinking of intelligent computational elements (smart technology artifacts), which have the potential of replacing workers and becoming a kind of "digital worker," e.g., the RPA case [15, 29]. Structured collaboration concepts defined as business and social processes join persons or workers. Workers interact employing digital mechanisms, e.g., create a group, invite partners or friends, cowrite a report, establish privacy rules, subscribe to events, from many other daily life activities. Another example requiring research on social aspects when moving towards digitalization is the case of using robots in healthcare to attend patients, in which it is crucial to consider the impact on them [6]. However, from the existing literature, it is difficult to get a common rationale to establish a minimal consensus or a common framework sustaining the discourse and facilitating specialized mappings to each of the participating knowledge domains.

Two approaches can be used as a starting basis in designing such a common understanding:

The modeling of sociotechnical systems, as presented in [22], can be founded on socio-semantic frameworks establishing a hierarchical approach based on three classes of models: i) micro-level, ii) meso-level, and iii) macro-level dynamics. The idea is to build a model based on the study of terms or *n-grams* to identify semantic patterns and, in this way, establish clusterings of related concepts. This research argues about the proximity of understanding social networks of a sociotechnical system where the approach hereby adopted can help to understand semantic interactions in social systems. The proposed agent-nodes and concepts establish complex graphs where contents are exchanged and mediated by technical solutions. Nevertheless, the approach lacks the main concern associated with the symbiosis between technology artifacts and workers.

The second case is derived from the Information Systems perspective and was carried out in a scholarly context, leading to the proposal of the Neo-STS neo-sociotechnical framework. The Neo-STS framework aims at information systems scholars to understand work trends and technology enablers [32]. This research defines a working system as a symbiosis of mutually-shaping social and technology systems. It also proposes a set of axioms to help to structure sociotechnical work organization through the concepts of containment and nested-ness: i) *premise 1* - sociotechnical systems encapsulate work systems, ii) *premise 2* - work systems are a composite of social or technical elements, iii) *premise 3* - composing elements make work systems to derive purpose, meaning, and structure from the multiplicity of contexts, and iv) *premise 4* - work systems are the support of work performance, and goals and values alignment.

The discussed sociotechnical, and related research cases focus on partial perspectives. To our knowledge, no generic reference model exists framing the core concepts under a unified model and considering both the social and engineering sciences and technology bodies of knowledge. The need for a unified model motivates the proposal of what we designate by Sociotechnical System Collaborative Network (STS-CN). This STS-CN framework is a Sociotechnical System (STS) made of STS nodes. An STS node is a sociotechnical system, as depicted in Fig. 1, which can be a composite of other sociotechnical systems (subsystems) or units. A unit is a terminal concept since it can not further decompose into sub-elements. We adopt the concept of system as discussed and defined in the context of INCOSE[1] under an attempt to unify an important concept for both the engineering body of knowledge and other disciplines such as the social sciences [12, 23]. Any system, both real and abstract, is defined as "*A complex whole, whose properties are due to its constituent parts, as well as to relationships among the parts*," which we graphically map into the abstraction presented in Fig. 1, where the whole is the sociotechnical system delimited by some particular context or application domain. The parts that we refer to as elements are called Units if not decomposable into other elements.

The Unit concept represents a single entity such as a worker or a technology artifact in the context of a sociotechnical system. By adopting standard "system concepts" to our proposed balanced approach, we delve into concepts which, in most cases, come from the social sciences to establish a unified discourse for the proposed complex sociotechnical CN 4.0 system. We further incorporate the simple Conceptual Modeling language also used in [20] to model sociotechnical critical air traffic management systems with a focus on workers' (air traffic operators) interactions with system user interfaces. We define a sociotechnical system as a concept inheriting the INCOSE systems definition, as depicted in Fig. 2, formalized using the CmapTools [9]. We adopt a slightly different vocabulary, e.g., instead of a part to identify a leaf or terminal non-decomposable element commonly used in mechanical engineering, we choose the

---

[1] The International Council on Systems Engineering - https://www.incose.org/.

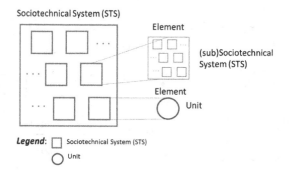

Fig. 1. The abstract representation of a Sociotechnical System

term *Unit,* meaning a terminal concept. A Unit does not decompose into other (sub) units. The Unit is a terminal concept referring to a tangible or conceptual thing.

A Unit can be a Worker or a Technology Artifact, seen as a single entity. By Technology Artifact, we mean an informatics system (Isystem) [17, 18], offering some form of interaction with workers, e.g., a web browser of a mobile application. Both Workers and Information System carry out activities which we do not detail further since they can involve a complex sequence of atomic operations guided by some execution logic established by a program. If a Unit is a Worker, the actions follow a manual procedure, and if the Unit is an Isystem, the instructions follow some computer programming language and computing mechanisms. The sociotechnical dimension of the Technology Artifact is represented by the *"must-consider"* that associates it with its *"Social Aspect."* The Social Aspect decomposes further into a set of sub-aspects, associated with it through the *is-a* relationship in Fig. 2, including *Responsibility*, *Competence*, *Training*, or *Vocational Aptitude*, as essential features to be considered in the design of the respective Isystem. The proposed features are not complete and need to be further detailed. They incorporate Isystem development tools, e.g., a validation mechanism based on some questionnaires for users to feedback valuable suggestions to improve the technological artifact.

In the proposed balanced sociotechnical framework for CN 4.0, the *Sociotechnical System* concept justifies the specialization concerning the *system* since it is *"enhanced-with"* specifying its *"Social Attribute."* In other words, a Sociotechnical System needs to show its *Social Value, Worker Based Decision, Adaptability, Usability*, and *Configurability*. The proposed features summarize what seems a consensus in the sociotechnical systems research community. Still, our purpose is not to formulate the set of concepts as final but rather to contribute to an accurate and consensual definition. Moreover, our concern is related to the balanced perspective since the consensus needs to go beyond the social sciences and also embrace related research areas from engineering sciences.

One interesting question is how to establish a metric for the Social Value of a sociotechnical system. The EU 7th FP research project entitled Theoretical, Empirical and Policy Foundations for Building Social Innovation in Europe (TEPSIE) defines social value as *"the kind of value that innovation is expected to deliver: a value that is*

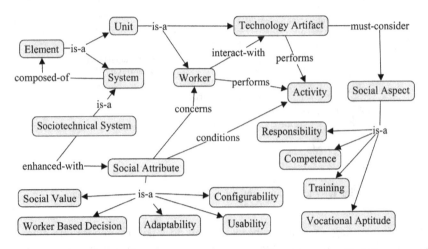

Fig. 2. Relating concepts of a Sociotechnical System in a Concept Map

less concerned with profit and more with issues such as quality of life, solidarity, and well-being" [25]. On the other hand, another research developed at Standford considers that *"Social value is not an objective fact. Instead, it emerges from the interaction of supply and demand and, therefore, may change across time, people, places, and situations"* [16]. Another proposal to rethink value is focused on monetary value contribution and proposes a theoretical framework for the definition of value in social contexts [14].

In our sociotechnical framework, it means that workers or people in a collaborative network shall experience the necessary mechanisms that make them develop their work. A worker negotiating some product development with one or more partners, for instance, in the context of a collaborative network, shall have the means to discuss the terms of the contract, and suggest and accept changes. Furthermore, after achieved an agreement, to close the negotiation, the worker shall have the means to digitally sign it and, this way, commit the negotiation process. If a series of technology artifacts were to offer such expectations, they should perform reliably, be complete for the mission and let all participants be confident in their performance. One main open question is how to embed social values into the design, development, and validation of such technology systems. The clarification of concepts hereby presented expects to help better understanding how the development of technology systems can incorporate sociotechnical attributes from their conception. Since different background knowledge participates in the events of sociotechnical systems, having a common framework seems to be of paramount importance.

The other attributes follow the same rationale since they aim to underlie our framework, and with the validation strategy discussed later in Sect. 4, they expect to provide further understanding. **Social Values**, such as fairness, customer benefits, and work organization models, among others, are embedded by technologists in shaping technological choices of systems design. The ***Worker Based Decision*** feature means that the user of the technology artifact can make the changes, namely withdraw previous decisions, which she/he considers necessary for the execution of the underlying activity. The worker based decision also implies that a technology artifact reliably logs all the decisions and modifications to produce pieces of evidence protecting the user in case of some auditing process. The *Adaptability* feature means that the technology artifact adapts interface mechanisms according to user needs. An example is a keen awareness of different languages and time zones of workers collaborating on different continents in the context of a collaborative network. When collaboration involves workers with language restrictions, the participating technology artifacts shall introduce some translation services. By *Usability,* we mean the design of user interfaces that maximize user accessibility, safety, and simple access mechanisms to needed interface elements. Again, the usability feature relates to competencies or specialized bodies of knowledge, such as e.g., the Interaction Design Foundation[2], a research source for this specific domain. The last concept, *Configurability*, is defined in [11], in the context of a sociotechnical system as *"... self-reconfigurable, i.e., capable of switching autonomously from one configuration to a better one ..."*. The mentioned research proposes to incorporate a *Reconcile* mechanism to find a better configuration capable of better fulfilling user objectives and a *Compensation* mechanism to make the changes effective. We consider Configurability reflected in the capabilities of a technology artifact to change behaviors under the user's control to improve execution quality and performance.

Finally, we discuss the projection of the proposed sociotechnical thoughts to the collaborative network context. In particular, we envisage an integrated digital network of sociotechnical systems, as depicted in Fig. 3. One central aspect is the unified sociotechnical thinking across Collaborative Networks (CN).

Following the definition of a sociotechnical system depicted in Fig. 1, a collaborative network connects instances of those systems that interact to do business and play as a social actor. Our objective is, in a first approach, to clarify and if possible formalize the intrinsic behavior of a sociotechnical system in a network context as a strategy to help to develop a better, more efficient, and "learning" technical system for users at this level considering the system of systems CN. A straightforward example can be an administration employee going to a healthcare service to check the refund of his expenses without the need to scan an invoice and check in the email messages reporting steps of its processing. If a CN 4.0 environment exists involving the (smart) systems of the administration, the healthcare, the laboratory of medical tests, and other involved stakeholders, the user, in the example a public servant, is expected to access a unique employee management interface and access to relevant information on collaborative business processes executed in the background. The simple example offers users the best automation services to make them transparent concerning the number of document exchanges that the organizations are required to carry out. The scenario is possible but still difficult to implement since different organizations with different socio-organizational cultures need to put their technology artifacts in cooperation. However, our research concern in this work is not the technical feasibility but rather to get insights on how to conceive sociotechnical systems, framed by the discussed framework.

---

[2] Interaction Design Foundation - https://www.interaction-design.org/literature

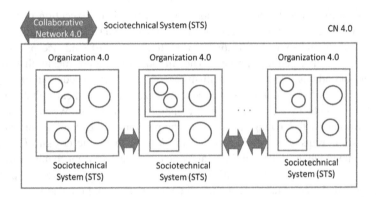

Fig. 3. Collaborative Networks 4.0 as a Sociotechnical System

One interesting aspect that derives from different roles of a public servant and of a user of a healthcare system is considering the following case: i) a servant as a user of the healthcare system, and ii) the servant as an employee of the Public Administration. In both servant and user roles, the expectation is that services integrate, e.g., reimbursement of healthcare expenses shall automatically resolve. We think that a systemic approach to Collaborative Networks 4.0 makes the research challenging since it has to incorporate many views to make services integration more useful and comprehensive.

4   Exploratory Strategy for Validation Case Studies

We discuss two ongoing projects aiming to play as validation case studies for the proposed framework: i) the implementation of robotic process automation (RPA) system from the perspective of a consulting company implementing RPA solutions and, ii) in the HORUS project to rethink the automation of support and maintenance services in a forecourt fueling network. The HORUS project we discuss as a second case aims to develop a technical system to control post-payments in a forecourt fueling station. The post-payment models may lead to situations where drivers leave the forecourt without payment, the motivation for an open standard to automatically manage fueling authorizations accepted at the Point of Sale (POS) technical system.

The RPA case bases on the experience of the private consulting company BTEN in developing processes automation projects for both public and private organizations. From an initial interview with BTEN CEO and partners responsible for RPA projects and based on an anonymous and abstract analysis of deployment projects, the following analytical framework was agreed:

- Motivations for an RPA, to be generalized for any process/technology innovation project;
  - *Socio-Organisational*, e.g., task content; characteristics of operations; organization of work, skills requirements;
  - *Socio-Economical* e.g., productivity; wages; labor costs.

- *SocioTechnical*, e.g., quality of tasks, processes coordination; integration of servives; person/technology interactions.
- Achievements considering sociotechnical changes:
  - *Worker inclusion*, e.g., workers adapting to RPA configuration and operation needs, including training and moving to new functions;
  - *User satisfaction*, e.g., new and integrated, services for citizens or customers.

The proposed framework founds on past and ongoing project cases where the proposed analytical dimensions bases on preliminary observations. As an example, a six months project involving six experts among architects and developers in a public organization was motivated by the need to solve pending delayed processes. One considered aspect we classify as a *SocioTechnical* issue driving the adoption of RPA was the *quality of tasks,* identifying repetitive operations that could be automated. Another aspect considered by the project was *worker inclusion,* realized through training activities and development of new skills. The *user satisfaction* (relating to citizens in the case) has also been a primary driver for the project, addressed by solving delayed processes. Figure 4 depicts the proposed Balanced Sociotechnical Analytical (BSAF) framework shaped as a concept map.

The intention is to extend the application of this framework to new cases of BTEN and also to apply a similar approach directly to customers that agree to participate in the study. The purpose is to consolidate the analytical framework aiming to help both consulting companies to address new customers and also customers themselves, as an approach to better comprehend the founded mechanisms for a win-win implementation of RPA.

The HORUS case has a distinctive nature since the approach is not RPA but rather the automation of the maintenance of technical systems in a fueling forecourt of a fuel distribution network. In this case, workers from the fuel company have to coordinate problem solving actions with workers from suppliers responsible for groups of technical systems. In this case, the challenge is intrinsically collaborative since three independent suppliers are required to coordinate the support and maintenance of the technological systems under their responsibility. Beyond the technical elements establishing how technological systems organize and interact, the relevance for our research is how workers from the collaborating partners and users/customers *perceive* the changes. A critical change of the collaborative maintenance process and technology framework is the possibility of workers from the fuel company and competing suppliers with interdependent technical systems to follow any failure of any computational or cyberphysical system event and its resolution. It means that workers with coordination or operation roles from different organizations develop contributions under an enhanced, mutually "observed" collaborative digital environment. Therefore, our purpose here is not to discuss the technological approach but rather to understand the needed changes as a sociotechnical system. Following the technical and organizational innovation, our main objective is to apply the framework to diagnose the automation achievements under the proposed balanced sociotechnical framework for collaborative networks 4.0.

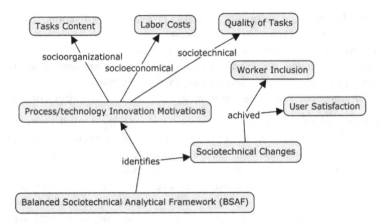

Fig. 4. Concept map of the Balanced Sociotechnical Analytical (BSAF) framework

5 Conclusions and Further Research

In this paper, we propose and discuss a balanced sociotechnical framework for collaborative networks 4.0. The proposed analytical framework is presented and discussed in the context of two exploratory cases, one considering a research partnership with BTEN consulting and the second one, the HORUS research project with BP Portugal, to rethink the processes and the technology system used in a fueling distribution network.

One primary purpose is to understand the motivation for adopting collaborative automation processes from a socio-organizational, socioeconomic, sociotechnical analytical framework. As a complementary analytic dimension, we purpose to include both worker inclusion and user satisfaction. We assume the proposed analytical dimensions as a first attempt, which, based on further data, will probably evidence the need for additional accurate criteria.

In particular, the collaborative network 4.0 context raises additional research questions. Workers are supposed to join more extensive organizational settings making decisions on pressing a button in a desktop, laptop, or mobile interface with an impact on networked business partners. Such challenging collaborative scenarios where workers are accountable under risky decision processes need to be further studied. A balanced sociotechnical CN 4.0 means each networked business partner adopts a whole digital integrated working setup getting workers and clients/customers, respectively, to adapt and to perceive learning experiences.

Acknowledgments. This research develops in the context of the SOCOLNET scientific network and its ARCON-ACM initiative. The research project HORUS sponsored by BP Portugal has partially funded this work. Research has the participation of the consulting company BTEN offering UiPath solutions, as a validation case for the RPA technology. This work has also been partially funded by the Center of Technology and Systems – UNINOVA, and the Portuguese FCT Foundation project UIDB/00066/2020, and by Interuniversity Center for the History of Science and Technology – CIUHCT- and the Portuguese FCT Foundation project UIDB/00286/2020.

References

1. Afsarmanesh, H., Camarinha-Matos, L.M.: A framework for management of virtual organization breeding environments. In: Camarinha-Matos, L.M., Afsarmanesh, H., Ortiz, A. (eds.) PRO-VE 2005. ITIFIP, vol. 186, pp. 35–48. Springer, Boston, MA (2005). https://doi.org/10.1007/0-387-29360-4_4

2. Afsarmanesh, H., Camarinha-Matos, L.M., Ermilova, E.: Vbe reference framework. In: Methods and Tools for Collaborative Networked Organizations, pp. 35–68. Springer, US (2008). https://doi.org/10.1007/978-0-387-79424-2_2

3. Afsarmanesh, H., Ermilova, E., Msanjila, S.S., Camarinha-Matos, L.M.: Modeling and management of information supporting functional dimension of collaborative networks. In: Hameurlain, A., Küng, J., Wagner, R. (eds.) Transactions on Large-Scale Data- and Knowledge-Centered Systems I. LNCS, vol. 5740, pp. 1–37. Springer, Heidelberg (2009). https://doi.org/10.1007/978-3-642-03722-1_1

4. Baxter, G., Sommerville, I.: Sociotechnical systems: from design methods to systems engineering. Interact. Comput. 23(1), 4–17 (2010)

5. Berggren, C.: Alternatives to Lean Production. Cornell University Press, Ithaca (2019)

6. Broadbent, E., Kuo, I.H., Lee, Y.I., Rabindran, J., Kerse, N., Stafford, R., MacDonald, B.A.: Attitudes and reactions to a healthcare robot. Telemed. J. e-Health Off. J. Am. Telemed. Assoc. 16, 608–613 (2010)

7. Camarinha-Matos, L., Rabelo, R., Osorio, L.: Balanced automation. In: Tzafestas, S.G. (eds) Computer-Assisted Management and Control of Manufacturing Systems. Advanced Manufacturing. Springer, London. https://doi.org/10.1007/978-1-4471-0959-4_14

8. Camarinha-Matos, L.M., Fornasiero, R., Ramezani, J., Ferrada, F.: Collaborative networks: a pillar of digital transformation. Appl. Sci. 9(24) (2019)

9. Cañas, A.J., et al.: Cmaptools: a knowledge modeling and sharing environment (2004)

10. Cellary, Wojciech: Non-technical Challenges of Industry 4.0. In: Camarinha-Matos, Luis M., Afsarmanesh, Hamideh, Antonelli, Dario (eds.) PRO-VE 2019. IFIP AICT, vol. 568, pp. 3–10. Springer, Cham (2019). https://doi.org/10.1007/978-3-030-28464-0_1

11. Dalpiaz, F., Giorgini, P., Mylopoulos, J.: Adaptive sociotechnical systems: a requirements-based approach. Requir. Eng. 18(1), 1–24 (2013)

12. Dori, D., et al.: System definition, system worldviews, and systemness characteristics. IEEE Syst. J. 14(2), 1538–1548 (2020)

13. Hofmann, P., Samp, C., Urbach, N.: Robotic process automation. Electron. Markets 30(1), 99–106 (2019). https://doi.org/10.1007/s12525-019-00365-8

14. Kato, S., Ashley, S.R., Weaver, R.L.: Insights for measuring social value: classification of measures related to the capabilities approach. VOLUNTAS: Int. J. Voluntary Nonprofit Organ. 29(3), 558–573 (2018)

15. Madakam, S., Holmukhe, R., Jaiswal, D.: The future digital work force: robotic process automation (rpa). 16, 01 (2019)

16. Mulgan, G.: Measuring social value. Stanford Social Innovation Review (2010)

17. Osório, A.L., Belloum, A., Afsarmanesh, H., Camarinha-Matos, L.M.: Agnostic informatics system of systems: the open ISoS services framework. In: Camarinha-Matos, L.M., Afsarmanesh, H., Fornasiero, R. (eds.) PRO-VE 2017. IAICT, vol. 506, pp. 407–420. Springer, Cham (2017). https://doi.org/10.1007/978-3-319-65151-4_37

18. Osório, A.L.: Towards vendor-agnostic IT-system of IT-systems with the CEDE platform. In: 17th Working Conference on Virtual Enterprises (PRO-VE), vol. 480. AICT of Collaboration in a Hyperconnected World, pp. 494–505, Porto, Portugal, October 2016

19. Petukhov, I., Steshina, L.: Decision-making problems in sociotechnical systems. In: Pomffyova, M. (ed.) Management of Information Systems, chapter 8. IntechOpen, Rijeka (2018)

20. Ragosta, M., Martinie, C., Palanque, P., Navarre, D., Sujan, M.A.: Concept maps for integrating modeling techniques for the analysis and re-design of partly-autonomous interactive systems. In: Proceedings of the 5th International Conference on Application and Theory of Automation in Command and Control Systems, ATACCS 2015, pp. 41–52. Association for Computing Machinery, New York (2015)

21. Ropohl, G.: Philosophy of sociotechnical systems. Techné: Res. Philos. Technol. **4**, 186–194 (1999)

22. Roth, C.: Socio-semantic frameworks. Advances in Complex Systems, World Scientific, 16 (ffhalshs-00927322), pp. 1350013 (2013)

23. Sillitto, H., et al.: Defining "system": a comprehensive approach, July 2017

24. Sony, M., Naik, S.: Industry 4.0 integration with sociotechnical systems theory: a systematic review and proposed theoretical model. Technol. Soc. **61**, 101248 (2020)

25. tepsie. Social innovation theory and research: a guide for researchers. Technical report, TEPSIE EU FP7 Project (2014)

26. EL Trist. *Organizational Choice*. Continuity in Administrative Science and Ancestral Books in the Management of Organizations. Garland, 1963

27. Trist, E.L.: The Evolution of Socio-technical Systems: A Conceptual Framework and an Action Research Program. Issues in the quality of working life: a series of occasional papers. Ontario Ministry of Labour, Ontario Quality of Working Life Centre (1981)

28. Urze, P., Machado, T.: On the assembly line: a view from industrial sociology. In: Information Technology for Balanced Manufacturing Systems, pp. 291–300. Springer, Boston (2006)

29. Wil, M.P., van der Aalst, Bichler, M., Heinzl, A.: Robotic process automation. Bus. Inf. Syst. Eng. **60**(4), 269–272 (2018)

30. von Bertalanffy, L.: The theory of open systems in physics and biology. Science **111**(2872), 23–29 (1950)

31. Walker, G.H., Stanton, N.A., Salmon, P.M., Jenkins, D.P.: A review of sociotechnical systems theory: a classic concept for new command and control paradigms. Theor. Issues Ergon. Sci. **9**(6), 479–499 (2008)

32. Winter, S., Berente, N., Howison, J., Butler, B.: Beyond the organizational 'container': conceptualizing 21st century sociotechnical work. Inf. Organ. **24**(4), 250–269 (2014)

Boosting Sustainability Through Collaboration in Agri-food 4.0

Assessing and Selecting Sustainable and Resilient Suppliers in Agri-Food Supply Chains Using Artificial Intelligence: A Short Review

Antonio Zavala-Alcívar[1], María-José Verdecho[2(✉)],
and Juan-José Alfaro-Saiz[2]

[1] Faculty of Industrial Engineering, Universidad Laica Eloy Alfaro de Manabí,
Manta 130214, Ecuador
antonio.zavala@uleam.edu.ec
[2] Research Centre on Production Management and Engineering (CIGIP),
Universitat Politècnica de València, Camino de Vera S/N, 46022 Valencia, Spain
{mverdecho,jalfaro}@cigip.upv.es

Abstract. The supplier evaluation and selection process is critical to increase the sustainability and resilience of the agri-food supply chain. Therefore, in this sector, it is necessary to consider sustainability and resilience criteria in the supplier evaluation and selection process. The use of artificial intelligence techniques allows managing of a lot of information and the reduction of uncertainty for decision making. The objective of this article is to analyze articles that address the selection of suppliers in agrifood supply chains that pursue to increase their sustainability and resilience by using artificial intelligence techniques to analyze the techniques and criteria used and draw conclusions.

Keywords: Artificial intelligence · Supplier selection · Sustainability · Resilience · Agri-food supply chains

1 Introduction

The supplier evaluation and selection process is one of the fundamental processes in supply chain management. In global markets, there are multiple characteristics that make this process complex such as a greater number of potential suppliers, changing procurement regulations, modification of social policies, constant change in customer preferences, complex decision making when operating in the scope of the supply chain, etc. These characteristics imply that decision making must be quick, adaptive, and complex due to the consideration of uncertainty and, multiple criteria and stakeholders to be satisfied [1].

The criteria generally demanded to suppliers are quality, price, delivery time, and service [2]. In addition, if supply chains are to be resilient and sustainable, it is necessary to consider those criteria that allow increasing business continuity in the face of an interruption in operations [3] and, in turn, increase the sustainability of the chain [4, 5].

© IFIP International Federation for Information Processing 2020
Published by Springer Nature Switzerland AG 2020
L. M. Camarinha-Matos et al. (Eds.): PRO-VE 2020, IFIP AICT 598, pp. 501–510, 2020.
https://doi.org/10.1007/978-3-030-62412-5_41

This challenge is greater in some types of supply chains, for example, in agri-food supply chains, where their characteristics, including the management of perishable products [6], require, among others, rapid and efficient decision-making. Therefore, the evaluation and selection criteria for suppliers must reflect these needs and techniques must be used that allow managing of a lot of information and the reduction of uncertainty [7], which is why artificial intelligence techniques are appropriate.

The objective of this paper is to analyze articles that discuss models regarding the sustainable and resilient supplier selection process in agrifood supply chains using artificial intelligence techniques.

The structure of this paper is as follows. First, the parameters of the search are defined. Then, the analysis of the articles is performed in three points: evolution over time, artificial intelligence techniques and supplier selection criteria. Finally, conclusions are exposed.

2 Literature Review

Supplier evaluation and selection research started in the early 1960s [8] and remains a topic of high-interest today because of its impact on supply chain management. In the current context, it is necessary to include in this process criteria that increase the sustainability and resilience of the supply chain. Several articles have analyzed the main criteria [7] and the main methods and techniques applied in the literature for the evaluation and selection of suppliers. The research [9] analyses 170 articles and concludes that the main techniques for supplier selection are multi-criteria techniques (MCDM), mathematical programming, and artificial intelligence techniques. An analysis of the main MCDM methods used for the process is provided in [10–12] Recent studies have examined hybrid techniques and methods to provide evaluation and selection with more specific criteria [13].

[11] indicate that the focus of supplier evaluation and selection has been extended to a scenario where qualitative, economic, and environmental performance are optimized. Sustainability criteria are structured in three dimensions: economic, environmental, and social. Resilient supply chain criteria can be grouped into four types [14, 15]: supply chain re-engineering, collaboration, agility, and culture. Although recent studies incorporate a greater number and variety of criteria to assess the sustainability of suppliers [3, 4, 13, 16], there are few studies dedicated to the assessment and selection of suppliers jointly with resilience criteria [4].

The applications of artificial intelligence have been a growing topic of interest in the last years. Factors such as managing of large amounts of data shared information, and data processing and predicting for effective decision-making by all members, make the application of artificial intelligence increasingly used [17]. Besides, characteristics such as perishability, seasonality, and changing weather conditions in the agri-food sector [6], make this sector a field for the implementation of artificial intelligence techniques.

2.1 Search Criteria

This article has developed the methodological approach of the Systematic Literature Review (SLR) proposed by [18], which aims to evaluate and interpret available and relevant research on a research question, thematic area, or phenomenon of interest. This approach starts with the formulation of research questions, literature location, selection, analysis and synthesis of papers, and the reporting of results.

Given the objective of this work, the following research question is addressed: *What artificial intelligence techniques and criteria have been used for the evaluation and selection of sustainable and resilient suppliers in the agri-food supply chain?*

Several studies have classified the main artificial intelligence techniques for supplier evaluation and selection. In this article, based on the classifications proposed by [9, 12, 13, 19], the following techniques are considered: Genetic Algorithm (GA), Neural Networks (NN), Case-based reasoning (CBR), Grey system theory (GST), Rough set theory (RST), Fuzzy Logic (FL), Bayesian Networks (BN), Differential Evolution (DE), Particle Swarm Optimization (PSO).

Due to the variety of artificial intelligence techniques, several search keywords were established by changing the artificial intelligence technique used. For genetic algorithms the search string was: *("partner" OR "supplier" OR "vendor") AND ("selection" OR "evaluation" OR "performance" OR "monitoring" OR "development" OR "assessment" OR "approaches") AND ("agri-food" OR "food" OR "agriculture*" OR "agribusiness") AND ("genetic algorithm").*

The database used for the search was Scopus. Initially, 24 articles were obtained. Then, the results were filtered using the following criteria: English language, peer-reviewed indexed journals, and time range from the year 2000. This produced 11 articles, which are analyzed below.

2.2 Result and Discussion

2.2.1 Temporal Analysis

From the results obtained, it can be observed that the topic is a field of recent research, with increasing interest. The first articles were published in 2010, in which two articles were published (Table 1). So far, in 2020, the largest number of articles have been published, 4 articles, which reflects a recent interest in incorporating artificial intelligence techniques for the selection of suppliers in the agri-food sector.

2.2.2 Artificial Intelligence Techniques Analysis

Table 1 presents the main artificial intelligence techniques used in the articles as well as whether only one technique is applied in the solution (Single), several techniques (Hybrid), and whether the study makes a comparison between techniques (Single comparative). The table also presents the uncertainty mitigation approaches applied in the papers analyzed. For this purpose, the proposal by Hamdi et al. (2018) was considered, establishing three approaches to model risk and uncertainty for supplier selection: fuzzy, stochastic and others [20]. The percentage values are presented at the bottom of the table.

It should be noted that no articles were found that used the Case-based Reasoning and Differential Evolution techniques, although they have been used in other sectors [21–23]. The main techniques used are Fuzzy Logic, Genetic Algorithm, and Rough Set Theory. Most of the articles combine two or more artificial intelligence techniques, i.e. the use of hybrid techniques is extended to provide the advantages of different techniques in the proposed solution.

Table 1. Principal artificial intelligence techniques in supplier evaluation and selection for agri-food supply chains.

Paper	Year	Artificial Intelligence Techniques							Application type			Uncertainty		
		GA	NN	GST	RST	FL	BN	PSO	Single	Hybrid	Single Comparative	Fuzzy	Stochastic	Others
[24]	2010				✓				✓					✓
[25]	2010		✓		✓					✓				✓
[26]	2013			✓	✓					✓		✓		
[27]	2015					✓			✓			✓		
[28]	2017	✓							✓				✓	
[29]	2018	✓				✓		✓		✓	✓	✓	✓	
[30]	2019	✓					✓			✓		✓		
[31]	2020					✓			✓			✓		
[32]	2020					✓			✓			✓		
[33]	2020					✓	✓			✓		✓	✓	
[34]	2020	✓						✓		✓	✓	✓		
Total		4	1	1	3	5	2	2	5	6	2	7	4	2
%		36,7	9,09	9,09	27,3	45,5	18,2	18,2	45,5	54,5	18,2	63,6	36,7	18,2

The most used technique is FL (5 articles). Articles [27, 29, 31–33] apply the FL technique to set the level of importance or weight of the criteria for supplier evaluation and selection. This allows them to incorporate uncertainty in the criteria to improve efficiency in the selection of suppliers. Secondly, AG is used in four articles: [28–30, 34]. AG facilitates selection by generating multiple solutions and adapting decision-makers' assessments to changing environments.

Thirdly, the RST technique is used in 3 articles [24–26] characterized by analyzing information acquired basically by experience in an objective way. This technique was the first to be used, but, since 2013, no publications were found in the agri-food sector. BN and PSO have been used in two articles. Studies using BN techniques [30, 33] organize the criteria for evaluating and selecting suppliers into a set of variables and the inter-dependency relationships between them. This technique allows us to establish the probability of unknown variables based on known ones. The PSO articles [29, 34] make it possible to develop a simple interaction between the agents (supplier-manufacturer relationship) by allowing them to interact and adapting their behavior. This characteristic allows PSO techniques to be used not only for supplier evaluation and selection but also for order allocation in changing environments. These two techniques (BN and PSO) have been used in conjunction with other techniques. The GST and NN techniques are used in one article. [25] uses the GST technique because it allows problems to be solved under uncertainty with discrete data and incomplete information. The research considers the advantage of the method that it does not require knowledge of the distribution of parameters or complex intermediate models. [26] applies the NN technique that allows it to estimate or approximate functions that may depend on a large number of inputs. These techniques are also used in conjunction with other techniques to improve their effectiveness.

The main feature of the articles analyzed is the combination of different artificial intelligence techniques to reduce uncertainty and improve efficiency in decision making. Six articles consider a hybrid model and, two articles carry out comparative studies and five articles use a simple technique. The temporal evolution in the application of the techniques can also be analyzed. RST was the first to be applied individually, then in hybrid models together with GST and NN. The FL and GA techniques are applied in many cases jointly. Finally, the BN and PSO techniques have been applied recently.

Two papers develop a comparison between techniques [29, 34]. [29] concludes that the analysis of statistical and unidirectional variance and hypothesis testing show that both algorithms are relatively equal, and the results of the two algorithms do not differ significantly. [34] concludes that the techniques used generated a near-optimal solution in a very short time that did not differ from each other, even when considering multiple agents in several periods.

Considering the approaches to model risk and uncertainty for supplier selection, seven papers employ fuzzy set theory to incorporate inherent uncertainty into the decision model [26, 27, 29–33]. Within these papers, techniques such as fuzzy analytical hierarchy process, fuzzy multi-objective mathematical programming [27] or fuzzy DEMATEL [32] are used. Four papers apply stochastic modelling [28, 29, 33, 34] based on scenario analysis. This approach accepts randomness and uses stochastic problem parameters to reduce uncertainty. Two papers belong to the Others class. In this case, quantitative risk measures are used to mitigate uncertainty [24, 25]. Finally, two papers apply the fuzzy and stochastic approaches to reduce uncertainty, generating comparisons in their applied artificial intelligence techniques [29, 33].

2.2.3 Criteria for Supplier Evaluation and Selection

In the supplier evaluation and selection process, there has been a change in the criteria used to face new requirements. The first works only considered classic business criteria such as cost, quality, etc. The complexity of decision making within the supply chain demanded the introduction of other types of criteria [25] that consider collaboration, working together towards sustainability, and generating resilience in the face of disruptive events. The importance of the criteria lies in their joint and interrelated analysis that allows for the generation of a supplier evaluation and selection process following the strategic objectives and supply chain performance [5].

Considering the analysis of the articles and the criteria for the evaluation and selection of suppliers for sustainable and resilient supply chains established by [4, 13, 16, 35, 36], a classification of criteria into four groups is proposed: business, collaboration, sustainability and resilience. The business criteria are those traditionally used in the supplier evaluation and selection process and cover the criteria: cost/price (C/P), quality (Q), flexibility (F), delivery (D), financial situation (FS) and product characteristics (PC). Collaboration criteria are criteria that have recently been used to measure the degree of coherence between different organizations working or wishing to work collaboratively [37]. These criteria include [4, 14, 38]: technology capability (TC), information shared (IS), process/strategic alignment (PA), culture (C), trust (T). The sustainability criteria cover two (environmental and social) of the three dimensions of sustainability (economic, environmental and social) as economic criteria have been classically considered in the supplier evaluation and selection literature and already appear within the business criteria. The sustainability criteria therefore comprise [4, 13, 16, 39]: pollution practices (PP), employment practices (EP), reputation (R), health and safety practices (HSP) and stakeholder's involvement (SKI). Finally, resilience criteria measure the aspects that impact on improving the resilience of supply chains and include [4, 5, 36]: responsiveness/velocity (RV), geographic segregation (GS), redundancy (surplus inventory) (RSI), rerouting (RE), risk reduction plan (RRP), customization (C), visibility (V), and market adaptation (MA). It has to be noted that criteria are inter-related. For example, the criteria classified in the collaborative group allow an increase in the resilience and sustainability of the supply chain. However, this type of analysis is out of the scope of this paper. Table 2 shows the distribution of the articles in each group.

Table 2. Principal criteria for supplier evaluation and selection in the agri-food supply chain

Paper	Business						Collaboration					Sustainable			Resilient			
	C/P	Q	D	F	FS	PC	TC	IS	PA	C	T	PP	EP	HSP	RV	GS	RSI	RE
[24]	✓	✓	✓	✓		✓				✓		✓			✓	✓		
[25]	✓	✓	✓		✓					✓		✓	✓	✓				
[26]	✓	✓	✓	✓	✓	✓		✓		✓		✓	✓	✓	✓		✓	✓
[27]	✓	✓	✓	✓		✓	✓			✓		✓	✓	✓				
[28]		✓							✓			✓		✓	✓		✓	
[29]	✓	✓	✓		✓	✓											✓	
[30]	✓	✓	✓	✓	✓	✓	✓	✓		✓		✓			✓	✓	✓	✓
[31]	✓	✓	✓				✓				✓				✓			✓
[32]	✓			✓						✓		✓	✓	✓	✓		✓	✓
[33]			✓	✓	✓	✓												
[34]	✓	✓																

The criteria mostly used for supplier evaluation and selection are those belonging to the business criteria group, being the main criteria price, quality, delivery and flexibility. It should be noted that the financial situation is the criterion least often considered for the selection of suppliers, despite its relevance. In the group of collaboration criteria, the main criterion is culture and to a lesser extent the criteria: technological capacity, information shared, trust and strategic alignment. Lack of considering these criteria reduces the supply chain's capability to integrate business objectives and coordinate the way actions are implemented throughout the system [11].

Concerning sustainability criteria, the three criteria that have been used in agri-food chains are: pollution practices, employment practices, and health and safety practices [24–27, 32]. On the other hand, the criteria of reputation and stakeholder's involvement have not been used. The last group concerns resilience criteria. The main criteria analyzed focus on the efficient response and opportunity of the supplier (responsiveness/velocity, redundancy, rerouting) in a reactive sense and allowing an efficient and fast response when a disruptive event in the supply chain is generated. Other criteria that promote prevention capacity in the supply chain [15, 16]: risk reduction plan, customization, visibility, and market adaptation were not considered by the articles despite their relevance, especially in the agri-food sector where their characteristics generate a lot of uncertainty in operations [26].

Comparing the papers in Table 1 and Table 2, several points can be observed. In general, the articles using FL have considered business and sustainability criteria in their analysis. However, there is not a single paper that integrates all business and sustainability criteria into its analysis. Collaboration and resilience criteria are little considered in FL models. In addition, information shared, process/strategic alignment and geographic segregation have not been considered in these papers [27, 29, 31–33]. Articles using RST do not consider all the criteria for collaboration and sustainability. Their analysis overlooks technology capability, process/strategic alignment, trust and geographic segregation [24–26]. The supplier assessment and selection process using a GA integrates most criteria, except trust and employment practices [28–30, 34]. Papers using BN integrate all business and resilience criteria, but exclude from the analysis the criteria of process/strategic alignment, trust, employment practices, reputation, health and safety practices [30, 33]. Collaboration criteria are the least considered when using the NN technique. It has not been considered technology capability, process/strategic alignment, trust and geographic segregation [26]. The articles with PSO and GST are the ones that integrate the least number of criteria. PSO does not consider any of the collaboration and sustainability criteria, and only considers redundancy (surplus inventory) within the resilience criteria [29, 34]. GST does not consider resilience criteria and only considers culture of the collaboration criteria [25].

Papers using fuzzy set theory have considered most of the criteria in their analysis. [26, 27, 29–33]. By contrast, articles using stochastic modeling have focused only on business criteria. They have not considered technology capability, information shared, culture, trust, employment practices and responsiveness/velocity [28, 29, 33, 34]. Finally, papers with quantitative risk measures to mitigate uncertainty do not integrate the collaboration and resilience criteria as technology capability, information shared, process/strategic alignment, trust, geographic segregation and rerouting [29, 33].

3 Conclusion

Supplier assessment and selection is a key process to increase agri-food supply chain sustainability and resilience. In the literature, although few applications use artificial intelligence techniques to support this process, most applications are published recently showing an increasing interest in the last years. The artificial techniques most used are fuzzy logic and genetic algorithms, being hybrid techniques the most used. Some papers also deal with the comparison of two single techniques.

The analysis of literature reviews in supplier selection uses different types of criteria that in this paper are grouped with four types: business, collaboration, sustainability and resilience criteria. When analyzing the papers, it is observed that business criteria are most used, but collaboration, sustainability and resilience criteria should be further considered if agri-food supply chains desire to increase their competitiveness. The papers reviewed use some of the criteria but do not integrate in their models the different types of criteria within each group. Thus, more applications are needed that cover a wide selection of criteria so that the supplier assessment and selection process can be enhanced.

Artificial intelligence techniques are used for different purposes in agri-food supply chains. The process of supplier assessment and selection is one of the applications. More applications are needed that increase the development of suppliers over time. Thus, the supplier assessment and selection process can be extended in a dynamic manner incorporating the performance evaluation, segmentation and improvement of suppliers over time. For that purpose, artificial intelligence techniques could be used for example to classify and forecast future performance of suppliers.

Acknowledgements. Authors of this publication acknowledge the contribution of the Project 691249, RUC-APS "Enhancing and implementing Knowledge based ICT solutions within high Risk and Uncertain Conditions for Agriculture Production Systems" (www.ruc-aps.eu), funded by the European Union under their funding scheme H2020-MSCA-RISE-2015.

References

1. Brandenburg, M., Govindan, K., Sarkis, J., Seuring, S.: Quantitative models for sustainable supply chain management: developments and directions. Eur. J. Oper. Res. **233**, 299–312 (2014)
2. Ocampo, L.A., Abad, G.K.M., Cabusas, K.G.L., Padon, M.L.A., Sevilla, N.C.: Recent approaches to supplier selection: a review of literature within 2006–2016. Int. J. Integr. Supply Manage. **12**, 22–68 (2018)
3. Valipour, S., Safaei, A.: A resilience approach for supplier selection: using Fuzzy analytic network process and grey VIKOR techniques. J. Clean. Prod. **161**, 431–451 (2017)
4. Amindoust, A.: A resilient-sustainable based supplier selection model using a hybrid intelligent method. Comput. Ind. Eng. **126**, 122–135 (2018)
5. Zavala-Alcívar, A., Verdecho, M.-J., Alfaro-Saiz, J.-J.: A conceptual framework to manage resilience and increase sustainability in the supply chain. Sustainability **12**(16), 6300 (2020)

6. Villalobos, J.R., Soto-Silva, W.E., González-Araya, M.C., González-Ramirez, R.G.: Research directions in technology development to support real-time decisions of fresh produce logistics: A review and research agenda. Comput. Electron. Agric. **167**, 105092 (2019)

7. Ristono, A., Santoso, P.B., Tama, I.P.: A literature review of design of criteria for supplier selection. J. Ind. Eng. Manage. **11**, 680–696 (2018)

8. Torres-Ruiz, A., Ravindran, A.R.: Multiple criteria framework for the sustainability risk assessment of a supplier portfolio. J. Clean. Prod. **172**, 4478–4493 (2018)

9. Setak, M., Sharifi, S., Alimohammadian, A.: Supplier selection and order allocation models in supply chain management: a review. World Appl. Sci. J. **18**, 55–72 (2012)

10. Ravindran, A.R., Warsing, D.P.: Supplier selection models and methods. In: Supply Chain Engineering: Models and Applications. Taylor and Francis Group, Boca Raton, Florida (2013)

11. De Boer, L., Labro, E., Morlacchi, P.: A review of methods supporting supplier selection. Eur. J. Purch. Supply Manage. **7**, 75–89 (2011)

12. De Felice, F., Deldoost, M.H., Faizollahi, M., Petrillo, A.: Performance measurement model for the supplier selection based on AHP. Int. J. Eng. Bus. Manag. **7**, 1–13 (2015)

13. Zimmer, K., Fröhling, M., Schultmann, F.: Sustainable supplier management – a review of models supporting sustainable supplier selection, monitoring and development. Int. J. Prod. Res. **54**, 1412–1442 (2016)

14. Christopher, M., Peck, H.: Building the resilient supply chain. Int. J. Logist. Manag. **15**, 1–14 (2014)

15. Ali, A., Mahfouz, A., Arisha, A.: Analysing supply chain resilience: integrating the constructs in a concept mapping framework via a systematic literature review. Supply Chain Manage. **22**, 16–39 (2017)

16. Verdecho, M., Alarcón-Valero, F., Pérez-Perales, D., et al.: A methodology to select suppliers to increase sustainability within supply chains. Cent. Eur. J. Oper. Res. (2020). https://doi.org/10.1007/s10100-019-00668-3

17. Rabelo, L., Bhide, S., Gutierrez, E.: Artificial Intelligence: Advances in Research and Applications. Nova Science Publishers, Inc., Department of Industrial Engineering and Management Systems, University of Central Florida, Orlando, FL, United States (2017)

18. Denyer, D., Tranfield, D.: Producing a systematic review. In: The Sage Handbook of Organizational Research Methods. SAGE Publications Ltd., pp. 671–689 (2019)

19. Chen, Y.-J.: Structured methodology for supplier selection and evaluation in a supply chain. Inf. Sci. (Ny) **181**, 1651–1670 (2011)

20. Hamdi, F., Ghorbel, A., Masmoudi, F., Dupont, L.: Optimization of a supply portfolio in the context of supply chain risk management: literature review. J. Intell. Manuf. **29**(4), 763–788 (2015). https://doi.org/10.1007/s10845-015-1128-3

21. Kumar, V., Srinivasan, S., Das, S.: Optimal solution for supplier selection based on SMART fuzzy case base approach. In: 2014 Joint 7th International Conference on Soft Computing and Intelligent Systems. SCIS 2014 and 15th International Symposium on Advanced Intelligent Systems. ISIS 2014, Institute of Electrical and Electronics Engineers Inc., Department of Computer Science, IISJ Yokohama, Tokai Chiba, Japan, pp. 386–391 (2014)

22. Jahani, A., Murad, M.A.A., bin Sulaiman, M.N., Selamat, M.H.: An agent-based supplier selection framework: Fuzzy case-based reasoning perspective. Strateg. Outsourcing **8**, 180–205 (2015)

23. Wang, Q.: Hybrid knowledge-based flexible supplier selection. In: 8th International Conference on Management of e-Commerce and e-Government. ICMeCG 2014. Institute of Electrical and Electronics Engineers Inc., Department of Information Management, Shanghai Finance University, Shanghai, China, pp. 235–239 (2014)

24. Bai, C., Sarkis, J.: Green supplier development: analytical evaluation using rough set theory. J. Clean. Prod. **18**, 1200–1210 (2010)

25. Bai, C., Sarkis, J.: Integrating sustainability into supplier selection with grey system and rough set methodologies. Int. J. Prod. Econ. **124**, 252–264 (2010)

26. Guo, F., Lu, Q.: Partner selection optimization model of agricultural enterprises in supply chain. Adv. J. Food Sci. Technol. **5**, 1285–1291 (2013)

27. Azadnia, A.H., Saman, M.Z.M., Wong, K.Y.: Sustainable supplier selection and order lot-sizing: an integrated multi-objective decision-making process. Int. J. Prod. Res. **53**, 383–408 (2015)

28. Miranda-Ackerman, M.A., Azzaro-Pantel, C., Aguilar-Lasserre, A.A.: A green supply chain network design framework for the processed food industry: application to the orange juice agrofood cluster. Comput. Ind. Eng. **109**, 369–389 (2017)

29. Hajikhani, A., Khalilzadeh, M., Sadjadi, S.J.: A fuzzy multi-objective multi-product supplier selection and order-allocation problem in supply chain under coverage and price considerations: an urban agricultural case study. Sci. Iran. **25**, 431–449 (2018)

30. Zhang, H., Cui, Y.: A model combining a Bayesian network with a modified genetic algorithm for green supplier selection. Simulation **95**, 1165–1183 (2019)

31. Yadav, S., Garg, D., Luthra, S.: Selection of third-party logistics services for internet of things-based agriculture supply chain management. Int. J. Logist. Syst. Manage. **35**, 204–230 (2020)

32. Yazdani, M., Wang, Z.X., Chan, F.T.S.: A decision support model based on the combined structure of DEMATEL, QFD and fuzzy values. Soft. Comput. **24**(16), 12449–12468 (2020). https://doi.org/10.1007/s00500-020-04685-2

33. Zhang, H., Feng, H., Cui, Y., Wang, Y.: A fuzzy Bayesian network model for quality control in O2O e-commerce. Int. J. Comput. Commun. Control **15**(1), (2020). article number 1003. https://doi.org/10.15837/ijccc.2020.1.3783

34. Amiri, S.A.H.S., Zahedi, A., Kazemi, M., Soroor, J., Hajiaghaei-Keshteli, M.: Determination of the optimal sales level of perishable goods in a two-echelon supply chain network. Comput. Ind. Eng. **139**, 106156 (2020)

35. Roy, S., et al.: A framework for sustainable supplier selection with transportation criteria. Int. J. Sustain. Eng. **13**(2), 77–92 (2020)

36. Parkouhi, S.V., Ghadikolaei, A.S., Lajimi, H.F.: Resilient supplier selection and segmentation in grey environment. J. Clean. Prod. **207**, 1123–1137 (2019)

37. Camarinha-Matos, L.M., Afsarmanesh, H., Galeano, N., Molina, A.: Collaborative networked organizations – concepts and practice in manufacturing enterprises. Comput. Ind. Eng. **57**, 46–60 (2009)

38. Lezoche, M., Panetto, H., Kacprzyk, J., Hernandez, J., Díaz, M.A.: Agri-food 4.0: a survey of the supply chains and technologies for the future agriculture. Comput. Ind. **117**, 103187 (2020)

39. Alikhani, R., Torabi, S., Altay, N.: Strategic supplier selection under sustainability and risk criteria. Int. J. Prod. Econ. **208**, 69–82 (2019)

Assessing the Impact of Pumpkins Plantation, Harvest and Storage Decisions on a Collaborative Supply Chain with Data Analysis Tools

David Pérez[1($\boxtimes$)], Maria de los Ángeles Rodríguez[1], Ángel Ortiz[1], and Cècile Guyon[2]

[1] Research Centre on Production Management and Engineering (CIGIP), Universitat Politècnica de València, Camino de Vera S/N, 46022 València, Spain
{dapepe,marodriguez,aortiz}@cigip.uvp.es
[2] Bretagne Développement Innovation, 1bis Route de Fougères, 35510 Cesson-Sévigne, France
c.guyon@bdi.fr

Abstract. Successful pumpkins production requires the use of varieties that jointly with other factors yield well and produce pumpkins of the size, shape, color, and quality demanded by the market. But not only these issues are important. The perishable nature of pumpkins makes other issues such as how to prevent deterioration after harvest to become also relevant. In this paper the pumpkins plantation, harvest and storage (PHS) process is described and how some decisions affect certain goals, such as yield or conservation time. Additionally, some decision-making insights in a supply chain collaborative scenario made up of two stages: plantation/harvest and storage are given, where yield and conservation time trade-offs are outlined to develop win-win strategies. A real case using data analysis tools is analyzed. Results provide guidelines not only to make decisions independently on each stage but also to collaboratively work.

Keywords: Pumpkins · Plantation harvest and storage process · Collaborative decision-making · Yield-conservation time tradeoff · Data analysis tools

1 Introduction

The term agri-food supply chain (ASC) has been associated to describe the activities from production to distribution that bring agricultural or horticultural products from the farm to the folk [1]. One of these ASC′s is the pumpkins SC. Different activities throughout this SC are carried out by different actors (producers, processors and distributors) from upstream to downstream.

This paper focuses on upstream the pumpkins SC and particularly in the plantation, harvest and storage (PHP) process. Later, pumpkins would be processed or just distributed to the market.

PHP decision-making is not an easy task, since some peculiar issues (that differentiate it from other types of SC′s) must be considered [2] such as the limited

© IFIP International Federation for Information Processing 2020
Published by Springer Nature Switzerland AG 2020
L. M. Camarinha-Matos et al. (Eds.): PRO-VE 2020, IFIP AICT 598, pp. 511–523, 2020.
https://doi.org/10.1007/978-3-030-62412-5_42

pumpkins shelf-life and the importance that consumers give to aspects such as quality, size and health.

Other inherent characteristics are the high levels of uncertainty these ASC should face mainly due to weather unexpected variations [3].

PHP decision-making aims, among others, to optimize different objectives such as the optimization of production yield [4], some physical characteristics or some nutrients level [5]. Another important objective is the maximization of the conservation time while keeping certain levels of the former characteristics and nutrients during storage (either in a warehouse or stored when transported) [6].

Many producers only focus on maximizing yield. This may in turn have consequences not only in terms of environmental or social impacts [7], but also downstream the pumpkins SC, since conservation time during storage can be affected, especially when the time to market is high.

Literature lacks works where the compatibility of yield and conservation time maximizing strategies is analyzed [8]. While yield-maximizing policies result in higher benefits from producers side, they are not optimal in a multi-objective context where other objectives such as conservation time after must be taken into account.

This paper makes then two main contributions:

First, the pumpkins plantation, harvest and storage (PHS) process is characterized, describing the decisions that are made as well as how they affect certain objectives, such as yield or conservation time.

Secondly, some decision-making insights in a supply chain collaborative scenario made up of two stages: plantation/harvest and storage are given, where yield and conservation time trade-offs are outlined to develop win-win strategies. A real case using data analysis tools is analysed. Results provide guidelines not only to make decisions independently on each stage but also to collaboratively work.

The paper is structured as follows: In Chapter 2, a review about the main decisions, objectives and uncertainty sources that characterize the pumpkins PHS process is conducted. Chapter 3 analyzes the PHS decision-making process and how certain decisions can affect various objectives such as yield or conservation time, either from an independent or collaborative perspective, by also reviewing some works. In Chapter 4 a real two-stage SC is analysed by assessing the impact of certain specific PHS decisions on each stage and the whole SC by means of data analysis tools. Finally, in Chapter 5 some conclusions are drawn.

2   Pumpkins Plantation, Harvest and Storage (PHS) Process

This paper aims first to characterize the PHS decision-making process. A literature review was first conducted.

Among others, some of the consulted works were [9–13].

Tables 1, 2, 3 and 4 show what are the main decisions that are made throughout the PHS process as well as their scope, that is, which are their usual values ranges.

The PHP process was splitted into four sub-processes: pre-plantation (Table 1), plantation (Table 2), harvest (Table 3) and storage (Table 4).

Table 1. Main pre-plantation decisions types & scopes in the pumpkins PHS process

Decision types	Decision scope
Place	Pumpkin plants grow faster in hot climates than cold ones
Date	Between late may and mid of July
Crop type	Very rich soils with good drainage and not too soggy and with a lot of space for sprawling vines
Crop temperature	Before sowing seeds the plant soil must be at least 70 °F
Seeds variety	It is important to choose the right pumpkin seeds. There are many different varieties of pumpkins and each of them have different characteristics
Method	Seeds planted directly in the ground or transplanted
Compost use	It is advisable to dig large holes and fill them with a compost mixture one week before planting

Table 2. Main plantation decisions types and scopes in the pumpkins PHS process

Decision types	Decision scope
Mulching	Row covers of different materials to protect plants and to prevent insect problems must be used. They must be removed before flowering to allow pollination
Fertilization	Pumpkins must be fertilized regularly. Adding fertilizer encourages healthy plant growth. A high in nitrogen formula could be used just before vines begin to run and a high in phosphorous one just before the blooming period
Irrigation	Pumpkins need lots of water (at least one inch per week). The amount of water must be decreased when the pumpkins begin to grow and turn orange. Besides, watering must be removed about a week before the planned harvest
Protection	If insecticides, fungicides, or herbicides must be applied against pests, it must be taken into account that bees are essential for pollination and can be killed. If necessary, an organic pesticide to rid the plants out of pests must be used
Pruning	Pruning the vines may help with space and allow the plant's energy to be focused on the other vines and fruits
Fruit Turning	As the fruit develops, they should be turned (with great care not to hurt the vine) to encourage an even shape. A thin board or heavy cardboard under ripening pumpkins must be placed to avoid decay and insect damage

Table 3. Main harvest decisions types and scopes in the pumpkins PHS process

Decision types	Decision scope
Date	Pumpkins must be harvested when they are mature. It typically takes 95 to 120 days. The measurement of some inputs may indicate the ripening degree: dry matter, firmness, peduncle characteristics, colour and quantity of sugar.
Method	The fruit must be cut off the vine carefully, without tearing. A liberal amount of stem will increase the pumpkin's keeping time and prevent early rotting.
Curing period	In normal conditions, pumpkins should be cured in the sun for about a week to toughen the skin. Early frost and cold rainy weather call for early harvest. If so, pumpkins must be cured for 10 days in an area with T^a between 27–29 C.

Table 4. Main storage decisions types and scopes in the pumpkins PHS process

Decision types	Decision scope
Washing/Brushing	Pumpkins are usually washed and kept dry before being stored. A good practice consists in wipening them down with a weak bleach solution to discourage rot
Storage conditions	Pumpkins must be stored in a cool and dry place. They must be kept away from humidity, damp, and direct sunlight. No refrigeration is needed. Temperatures between 10 and 16 °C are ideal
Storage type	The pumpkins can be set in a single layer on bales of hay, cardboard or wooden shelves. They can also be hanged in mesh produce sacks. They must not be stored on concrete since it leads to rot
Rot checking	Soft spots or other signs of rot must be checked from time to time. Rotting pumpkins must be thrown away, or cut and added to the compost pile

The main objectives to be optimized (maximized or minimized) and the uncertainty sources were also analysed [14]:

- *Objectives*: no. of fruits per seed, weight, firmness, colour, dry matter, sugar level, no. of non-sold fruits, conservation time, incomes, costs, benefits.
- *Uncertainty sources*: seeds quality, temperature, rainfall, humity, solar radiation, atmospheric CO2 concentration, soil evaporation, wind, weeds, pests, fire or flood disasters, diseases, effects of fertilization, ripening pace, agricultural machinery breakdowns, rot rate, customer demand, competitors influence.

3 Pumpkins PHS Decision-Making Process in a Collaborative Context

Many works in the literature analyse how different goals values may considerably vary depending on the decisions made throughout the PHS process.

However, most of them face it from a non-collaborative perspective, considering two independent stages.

On the one hand a first stage made up of pre-plantation, plantation and harvest sub-processes where the main goal is to maximize yield [15–17]. Other goals are the optimization (max or min) of certain physical–chemical properties [18–19].

On the other hand a second stage made up of the storage sub-process where the conservation time (while maintaining acceptable levels of certain important properties over time) becomes the most relevant goal to be maximized ([20–27].

Collaborative perspective in which optimal strategies may involve a trade-off between yield and conservation time is rarely discussed [8]. Nevertheless, other trade-offs have extensively analyzed in the literature, mainly those between the yield and some environmental and social impacts (nutrient cycling, water quality, carbon emissions, soil degradation, labor workload, etc.) [28–30].

In this paper an approach based on data analysis tools to support decision-making in the pumpkins PHS process is developed. The obtained results will provide guidelines to make decisions in a collaborative scenario in a two-stage SC (pre-plantation, plantation and harvest sub-processes & storage sub-process) where different trade-offs between yield and conservation time will be outlined.

4   Real Case Study

4.1   Study Area and Experiments Development

The study was carried out in South Britanny (France). Neighboring parcels divided into blocks were selected. Only one type of pumpkin was chosen: the orange summer, an uchiki kuri variety that has been breeded to a hybrid one to be more productive and resistant.

The different experiments were carried out in each block then, assuming almost constant soil characteristics. Besides, only 15 seeds were planted in each block.

The selected decision variables and their specific values concerning to each of the different PHS sub-processes are as follows:

1. *Pre-plantation*: date (21st week; 24th week)
2. *Plantation*: mulching types (plastic; biodegradable)
3. *Harvest*: state based on maturation degree (under maturity; optimum; controlled; over maturity), brushing (yes; no)
4. *Storage*: storage conditions (hangar; controlled conditions/fridge with a temperature of 14 °C, a humidity rate by 60–75% and regular ventilation)

All the other potential variables throughout the different PHS sub-processes (expressed at the beginning of the paper) were assumed to remain constant or not subject to significant variability between the different experiments.

In a first stage, different performance parameters/characteristics of the pumpkins were analyzed after production (pre-plantation, plantation and harvest sub-processes), before being stored (storage sub-process).

- *Yield parameters*: number of commercial fruits/seed planted; Marketable weight/seed planted
- *Physical characteristics*: weight; color; stem stage; hardness with or without skin.
- *Biochemical characteristics*: sugar level; dry matter level.

Different experiments were carried out by crossing the different agreed values for the three decision variables: planting date, mulching type and harvesting state.

It must be remarked that once the seeds are planted, it is relatively easy to guess the maturation degree and therefore the harvesting date from the follow-up of some factors such as temperature or rain (until the flowering) or with the simple visualization of some physical characteristics.

In a second stage, it was aimed to analyze the performance measure "conservation time".

This was done by storing some samples between 20–30 pumpkins from each modality, that is, considering the planting date, mulching type and the harvesting state based on the maturation degree, under two different storage types: hangar and controlled conditions (fridge). A weekly tracking allowed to analyze the pumpkins conservation time for each modality and therefore the losses (rotten pumpkins) over time of each modality.

4.2   Data Collecting and Processing

The study data was collected either in a traditional manual way or with the help of new technologies such as internet of things sensors. Then, the data was stored in several excel spreadsheet for its analysis.

The excel spreadsheets were loaded in a dataset. For that, it was previously necessary to perform a data cleaning (data conversion, missing values correction, etc.) in order to obtain a consistent dataset. Then, a dataframe was created from the dataset.

4.3   Experiments Development and Results

Regarding the first stage (pre-plantation, plantation and harvest sub-processes) it must be noted that due to a lack of data, mulching factor was kept constant (plastic). Therefore eight experiments were carried out (2 levels for "planting date" factor * 4 levels for "harvesting state" factor), resulting in eight different modalities of pumpkins. Different performance parameters/characteristics (dependent variables) were analyzed.

More specifically, a two-factor ANOVA statistic analysis (2*4) with various samples per modality was performed for each dependent variable: weight, fruits per seed, sugar, dry matter and firmness (skinless and with skin).

ANOVA analysis (99% confidence level) based on F ratio performed for each one of the previous dependent variables indicated that there were significant differences between the means obtained for the 2 levels of the "planting date" factor.

There were also significant differences between the means of the 4 levels of the "harvesting state" factor except for the dependent variable "fruits per seed". Finally, only a significant interaction between the factors was found for the dependent variable firmness.

Further analysis based on Tukey's HSD (honestly significant difference) test was performed to find which means were significantly different from each other for the 4 levels factor "harvesting state".

Table 5 shows the mean, standard deviation and 99% confidence levels after ANOVA analysis. Only the dependent variables with no interaction between the factors are shown since the firmness (skinless and with skin) would require more precise analysis.

Table 5. Statistic parameters (mean, standard deviation and 99% confidence levels limits) after ANOVA analysis of some of the different dependent variables measured after production

DEPENDENT VARIABLES	Factors	Levels	Statistic parameters		99% confidence level limits	
			Mean	Standard deviation	Lower limit	Upper limit
WEIGHT (g)	Planting Date	21st week	1468	181,4712399	1333,062002	1602,937998
		24th week	1293,222222	124,6775504	1200,514755	1385,92969
	Harvesting State	Under maturity	1304,222222	139,1170932	1200,77783	1407,666614
		Optimum	1534,611111	252,9806437	1346,500303	1722,72192
		Controlled	1291,488889	102,4285608	1215,325278	1367,6525
		Over maturity	1392,122222	65,63812465	1343,315165	1440,929279
FRUITS PER SEED (nº)	Planting Date	21st week	2,655555556	0,390631018	2,365090975	2,946020137
		24th week	1,083333333	0,256038192	0,892949	1,273717667
SUGAR (ºbrix)	Planting Date	21st week	7,6	1,544491679	6,866631577	8,333368423
		24th week	10,58333333	1,062159036	10,07899012	11,08767655
	Harvesting State	Under maturity	7,566666667	2,525162261	5,870998287	9,262335047
		Optimum	9,133333333	1,724077853	7,975600088	10,29106658
		Controlled	9,244444444	1,200493726	8,438302486	10,0505864
		Over maturity	10,42222222	1,635531401	9,323948688	11,52049576
DRY MATTER (%)	Planting Date	21st week	11,83333333	2,223156369	10,18024345	13,48642321
		24th week	18,18333333	2,763671252	16,12832855	20,23833812
	Harvesting State	Under maturity	15,56666667	4,830596927	11,97474169	19,15859164
		Optimum	17,78333333	3,307214336	15,32416194	20,24250473
		Controlled	13,7	4,097316195	10,65332635	16,74667365
		Over maturity	12,98333333	2,900632115	10,82648748	15,14017919

The main insights were the following:

- F ratio from ANOVA indicated that planting date has an influence over the weight, fruits per seed, sugar and dry matter. But this influence is greater for the last three dependent variables and not as much for the weight. For example the yield (fruits per seed) of planting at 21st week (start of june) rather than at 24th (end of june) results in a mean deviation of 1.5 fruits per seed aprox.
- F ratio from ANOVA indicated that harvesting state has an influence over the weight, sugar and dry matter. Further Tukey's test indicates that: for the weight there is a slight significant variation between the means of the levels "optimum" and "controlled" (250 g. aprox.); for the sugar there is a significant variation between the means of the level "under maturity" with respect "optimum", "controlled" and "over maturity" (2º brix aprox.); for the dry matter there is a significant variation between the means of the level "optimum" with respect "controlled" and "over maturity" (4,5% aprox.).

Regarding the second stage (storage sub-process) it must be also noted that, similarly to the first stage, a lack of data led to not to consider the brushing variable. This simplification led to just check the storage conditions (hangar, controlled conditions/fridge) over the former 8 modalities. A weekly tracking allowed to analyze the "conservation time" of the different samples of pumpkins.

As in the first stage, a two-factor ANOVA analysis (8*2) with various samples per group was performed for the dependent variable conservation time. ANOVA analysis (99% confidence level) based on F ratio indicated that there were significant differences either between some of the means obtained for the 8 levels of the "modality" factor or the means for the 2 levels of the "storage conditions" factor. But in this case, a significant interaction between the factors existed.

It led to separately analyze the simple effects in an attempt to maintain the essential structure of the interaction effect. The approach consisted in breaking the interaction effect into component parts and then tested the separate parts for significance (Tables 6 to 7). Since multiple test were performed, some significance level adjustments were applied, dividing the current one (0,01%) by the number of simple effects tests performed within each factor [31].

Table 6. Statistic parameters (mean and standard deviation) after ANOVA analysis to test effect of storage conditions over each modality.

DEPENDENT VARIABLE	Modality factor	Storage Conditions factor	Statistic parameters	
			Mean	Standard deviation
CONSERVATION TIME (weeks)	21st week -under maturity	hangar	18,6	2,357672727
		fridge	31,7	8,116182218
	21st week -optimum	hangar	19,4	4,404543109
		fridge	29,06666667	5,391351098
	21st week -controlled	hangar	16,06666667	3,321127076
		fridge	18,3	4,526930908
	21st week -over maturity	hangar	13,4	3,317664322
		fridge	15,2	5,155512617
	24th week-optimum	hangar	19,86666667	3,540244813
		fridge	25,4	5,424084223
	24th week-optimum	hangar	20,33333333	5,208304598
		fridge	22,4	4,406891155
	24th week-controlled	hangar	15,83333333	4,698373404
		fridge	17,66666667	5,83292281
	24th week-over maturity	hangar	15,23333333	4,352433591
		fridge	14,7	4,340268544

Table 7. Statistic parameters (mean and standard deviation) after ANOVA analysis to test effect of modality over each storage condition.

DEPENDENT VARIABLE	Storage Conditions factor	Modality factor	Statistic parameters	
			Mean	Standard deviation
CONSERVATION TIME (weeks)	hangar	21st week -under maturity	18,6	2,357672727
		21st week -optimum	19,4	3,74718285
		21st week -controlled	16,06666667	3,321127076
		21st week -over maturity	13,4	3,317664322
		24th week-under maturity	19,86666667	3,540244813
		24th week-optimum	20,33333333	5,208304598
		24th week-controlled	15,83333333	4,698373404
		24th week-over maturity	15,23333333	4,352433591
	fridge	21st week -under maturity	31,7	8,116182218
		21st week -optimum	29,06666667	6,736075463
		21st week -controlled	18,3	4,526930908
		21st week -over maturity	15,2	5,155512617
		24th week-under maturity	25,4	5,424084223
		24th week-optimum	22,4	4,406891155
		24th week-controlled	17,66666667	5,83292281
		24th week-over maturity	14,7	4,340268544

The main insights were the following:

- F-ratio from the various ANOVA analysis to separately test the effect of storage conditions over the different modality levels resulted in significant mean variations only for the modalities 21st week-under maturity, 21st week-optimum and 24th week-under maturity, and mainly the first one (13 weeks gap aprox.)
- F-ratio from the various ANOVA analysis to separately test the effect of modality over the different storage conditions levels resulted in significant mean variations either for the hangar or fridge levels. Further analysis based on Tukey's HSD test was performed to find which means were significantly different from each other for the 8 modality levels.
- HSD scored 3,562 for the case of hangar level, so that significant mean variations were found between:
  - 24th week-optimum with respect to 21st week-controlled, 21st week-over maturity, 24th week-controlled and 24th week-over maturity.
  - 24th week-under maturity with respect to 21st week-controlled, 21st week-over maturity, 24th week-controlled and 24th week-over maturity.
  - 21st week-optimum with respect to 21st week-over maturity, 24th week-controlled and 24th week-over maturity.
  - 21st week-under maturity with respect to 21st week- over maturity
- HSD scored 5,194 for the case of fridge level, so that significant mean variations were found between:
  - 21st week-under maturity with respect to 21st week-controlled, 21st week-over maturity, 24th week-under maturity, 24th week-optimum, 24th week-controlled and 24th week-over maturity.
  - 21st week-optimum with respect to 21st week-controlled, 21st week-over maturity, 24th week-under maturity, 24th week-optimum, 24th week-controlled and 24th week-over maturity.
  - 24th week-under maturity with respect to 21st week-controlled, 21st week-over maturity, 24th week-optimum, 24th week-controlled and 24th week-over maturity.
  - 24th week-optimum with respect to 21st week-over maturity and 24th week-over maturity.

This statistic analysis in both stages can be used as an aid for SC collaborative decision-making, so that different trade-offs between yield and conservation time can be easily computed and therefore implemented (see Fig. 1 and Table 8).

Figure 1 depicts how the losses were over time for the various modalities under different storage conditions. Only the first 28 weeks were represented.

Table 8 shows the different trade-offs for the various modalities. Each modality has a different yield (only dependent of the planting date) and a loss percentage (25%, 50%, 75% and 100%) over time depending on the storage conditions: hangar or fridge. It must be noted that some modalities under certain storage conditions were not completely lost over the 28 weeks tracking time, so that only the loss percentage at that time is indicated.

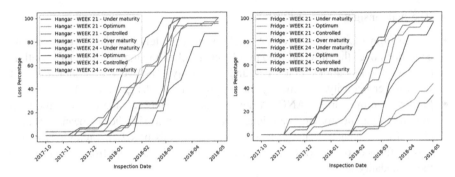

Fig. 1. Loss percentage over time of the different "modalities" varying storage conditions

Table 8. Yield and conservation time (% losses over time) of the various modalities

1st stage (pre-plantation,plantation, harvest)		2nd stage (storage)							
Modalities	YIELD	% LOSSES OVER TIME (weeks) - Hangar				% LOSSES OVER TIME (weeks) - Fridge			
	(no.fruits per seed)	25%	50%	75%	100%	25%	50%	75%	100%
WEEK 21-Under Maturity	2,65	15	19	20	22	27	28 (30%)		
WEEK 21-Optimum		15,5	19,5	21	28 (95%)	24	28 (40%)		
WEEK 21-Controlled		13	15	19	20,5	15	19	21	28
WEEK 21-Over Maturity		10,5	12	15	18,5	11,5	16	18	28 (95%)
WEEK 24-Under Maturity	1,08	20	21	22	28 (93%)	20	22,5	28 (65%)	
WEEK 24-Optimum		13,5	23	24	28 (85%)	18	21,5	23	28 (95%)
WEEK 24-Controlled		10,5	16	20,5	28	10	18	22	26,5
WEEK 24-Over Maturity		12	17,5	21	22	10	16	18	22,5

Some insights from Fig. 1 and Table 8 could be drawn:

- Harvesting states "under maturity" and "optimum" had a reasonable conservation time for storage condition "hangar". However those whose planting date was in the week 24 (higher yields) had even higher conservation times.
- Losses over time, as it could be predicted, were lower for storage condition "fridge". However the maximum variation between "hangar" and "fridge" is given for those whose planting date was in the week 21, mainly for harvesting states "under maturity" and "optimum". No rotten pumpkin after 24–27 weeks stored and 60–70% marketable after 28 weeks.

Different trade-offs between yield and conservation are then outlined. Decision-making in a collaborative scenario will select the most profitable for the SC as a whole. Nevertheless, other factors will have to be considered such as time to market after harvest, targeted quality of pumpkins, sustainable issues (environmental and social impacts) as well as the cost of implementing the different decisions.

It must be finally noted the absence in this paper of knowing how certain relevant characteristics (biochemical or physical) evolve during storage, and therefore meet the customers quality requirements when marketed. This would require a more precise analysis.

5 Conclusions

Two main contributions are made in this paper:

First, the pumpkins plantation, harvest and storage (PHS) process was characterized, describing the decisions and their usual scopes in each of the different sub-processes. Later, with the use of data analysis tools, the effect of some of these decisions (with specific scopes) over certain objectives throughout the PHS process such as physical and biochemical characteristics, yield or conservation time was checked.

Secondly, and taking advantage of the first contribution, some decision-making insights in a collaborative real two-stage pumpkins SC were pointed out. Some trade-offs were outlined between the yield (plantation and harvest 1st stage) and conservation time (storage 2nd stage) to develop win-win strategies.

Acknowledgments. The authors acknowledge the support of the project 691249, RUCAPS: "Enhancing and implementing knowledge based ICT solutions within high risk and uncertain conditions for agriculture production systems", funded by the European Union's research and innovation programme under the H2020 Marie Skłodowska-Curie Actions.

References

1. Prima, W.A., Xing, K., Amer, Y.: Collaboration and sustainable agri-food supply chain: a literature review. MATEC, 5802004 (2016)
2. Pérez Perales, D., Alarcón Valero, F., Drummond, C., Ortiz, Á.: Towards a sustainable agri-food supply chain model. the case of LEAF. In: Ortiz, Á., Andrés Romano, C., Poler, R., García-Sabater, J.-P. (eds.) Engineering Digital Transformation. LNMIE, pp. 333–341. Springer, Cham (2019). https://doi.org/10.1007/978-3-319-96005-0_40
3. Esteso, A., Alemany, M.M.E., Ortiz, A.: Conceptual framework for designing agri-food supply chains under uncertainty by mathematical programming models. Int. J. Prod. Res. **56** (13), 4418–4446 (2018)
4. Bahrami, R., Khodadadi, M., Piry, S., Hassanpanah, D.: The effects of planting methods and head pruning on seed yield and yield components of medicinal pumpkin (Cucurbita Pepo Subsp. Pepo Convar. Pepo Var. Styriaca) at low temperature areas. Pak. J. Bio. Sci. **12**(6), 538–541 (2009)
5. Tarus, W.J., Ochuodho, J.O., Rop, N.K.: Influence of harvesting stage on seed quality aspects of pumpkin (Cucurbita Pepo L.). J. Exp. Agr. **18**(2), 1–9 (2017)
6. Amodio, M.L., Rinaldi, R., Colell, G.: Extending shelf life of fresh-cut pumpkin (Cucurbita Maxima): effect of pre-treatments and storage conditions. Acta Hortic. **876**, 333–340 (2010)
7. Pimentel, D., et al.: Annual vs perennial grain production. Agric. Ecosyst. Environ. **161**, 1–9 (2012)
8. Biesiada, A., Nawirska, A., Kucharska, A., Sokół-Łętowska, A.: The effect of nitrogen fertilization methods on yield and chemical composition of pumpkin (Cucurbita maxima) fruits before and after storage. Veg. Crops. Res. B. **70**, 203–211 (2009)
9. Gwenael, J., Paul, Ch., Sau, I., Saurabh, S., Thomasse, S.: Hitting and harvesting pumpkins. Siam. J. Discrete. Math. **28**(3), 1363–1390 (2014)
10. Oluoch, M.O.: Production practices of pumpkins for improved productivity. Scripta. Hort. **15**, 181–189 (2012)

11. Ondigi, A., Toili, W., Ijani, A., Omuterema, S.: Comparative analysis of production practices and utilization of pumpkins (Cucurbita Pepo and Cucurbita Maxima) by smallholder farmers in the lake victoria basin, East Africa. Afr. J. Environ. Sci. Tech. **2** (9), 296–304 (2008)

12. Naik, M.L., Prasad, V.M., Raya, L.P.: A study on character association and path analysis in pumpkin (Cucurbita Moschata Duch. Ex Poir.). Int. J. Adv. Res. **3**(1), 1030–1034 (2015)

13. Nerson, H., Paris, H.S., Paris, E.P.: Fruit shape, size and seed yield in Cucurbita Pepo. Acta Hort. **510**, 227–230 (2000)

14. Ortiz, A., Alarcón, F., Pérez, D., Alemany, M.M.E.: Identifying the main uncertainties in the agri-food supply chain. In: Mula, J., Barbastefano, R., Díaz-Madroñero, M., Poler, R. (eds.) New global perspectives on industrial engineering and management. LNMIE, pp. 221–229. Springer, Cham (2019). https://doi.org/10.1007/978-3-319-93488-4_25

15. Khalid, E., Mohammed, E.: Dependence of pumpkin yield on plant density and variety. Am. J. Plant. Sci. **2**, 636–643 (2011)

16. Jakop, M., et al.: Yield performance and agronomic efficiency in oil pumpkins (Cucurbita Pepo L. Group Pepo) depending on production systems and varieties. Agr. **14**(1), 25–36 (2017)

17. Ahmed, B., Masud, M.A.T., Zakaria, M., Hossain, M.M., Mian, M.A.K.: Evaluation of pumpkin (Cucurbita Moschata Duch. Ex Poir.) for yield and other characters. Bangl. J. Agr. Res. **42**(1), 1–11 (2017)

18. Zhao, J., et al.: Physicochemical and antioxidant properties of different pumpkin cultivars grown in China. Food Sci. Technol. **9**(4), 308–316 (2015)

19. Zhou, C., et al.: The effect of high hydrostatic pressure on the microbiological quality and physical–chemical characteristics of pumpkin (Cucurbita Maxima Duch.) during refrigerated storage. Innov. Food. Sci. Emerg. **21**, 24–34 (2014)

20. Loy, J.B.: Harvest period and storage affect biomass partitioning and attributes of eating quality in acorn squash (Cucurbita Pepo), Présenté à Cucurbitaceae, Asheville, North Carolina, USA, pp. 568–577 (2006)

21. Nagao, A., Indou, T., Dohi, H.: Effects of curing condition and storage temperature on postharvest quality of squash fruit. J. Jpn. Soc. Hort. Sci. **60**(1), 175–181 (1991)

22. Habibunnisa, R., Prasad, R., Shivaiah, K.M.: Storage behaviour of minimally processed pumpkin (Cucurbita Maxima) under modified atmosphere packaging conditions. Eur. Food Res. Technol. **212**(2), 165–169 (2001)

23. Sharrock, K.R., Parkes, S.L.: Physiological changes during development and storage of fruit of buttercup squash in relation to their susceptibility to Rot. New. Zeal. J. Crop. Hort. **18**(4), 185–196 (1990)

24. Muzzaffar, S., Baba, W.N., Nazir, N., Masoodi, F.A., Bhat, M.M., Bazaz, R.: Effect of storage on physicochemical, microbial and antioxidant properties of pumpkin (Cucurbita Moschata) candy. Cog. Food. Agr. **2**(1), 1163650 (2016)

25. Rahman, M.A., Miaruddin, M., Khan, M.H.H., Masud, M.A.T., Begum, M.M.: Effect of storage periods on postharvest quality of pumpkin. Bangl. J. Agr. Res. **38**(2), 247–255 (2013)

26. Song, J., Wei, Q., Wang, X., Li, D., Liu, C., Zhang, M., Meng, L.: Degradation of carotenoids in dehydrated pumpkins as affected by different storage conditions. Food. Res. Int. **107**, 130–136 (2018)

27. Matová, A.: the influence of genotype and storage condition on the content of selected bioactive substances in the fruit of pumpkin (Cucurbita Moschata Duch.). J. Microbiol. Bioech. Food. Sci. **9**(2), 288–292 (2019)

28. Tilman, D., Balzer, C., Hill, J., Befort, B.L.: Global food demand and the sustainable intensification of agricultura. Proc. Natl. Acad. Sci. U. S. A. **108**, 20260–20264 (2011)

29. Wang, W., et al.: Multiple trade-offs between maximizing yield and minimizing greenhouse gas production in Chinese rice croplands. Land. Degrad. Dev. (2020)
30. Pleijel, H., Uddling, J.: Yield vs. quality trade-offs for wheat in response to carbon dioxide and ozone. Glob. Change. Biol. 18(2), 596–n/a (2011)
31. Pedhazur, E.J., Schmelkin, L.P.: Measurement, Design, and Analysis: an Integrated Approach. Lawrence Erlbaum Associates, Hillsdale (1991)

Impact Analysis of Industrial Standards on Blockchains for Food Supply Chains

Themo Voswinckel[1(✉)], Dino Hardjosuwito[1], Torben Gehring[1],
Ralph Siruet[2], and Andreas Fuessler[2]

[1] Institute for Industrial Management (FIR) at RWTH Aachen University,
Campus-Boulevard 55, Aachen, Germany
info@fir.rwth-aachen.de
[2] GS1 Germany GmbH, Maarweg 133, Cologne, Germany
service@gsl-germany.de

Abstract. One of the major challenges for the use of the Blockchain technology in industrial applications is the lack of existing standards. They ensure the interoperability of sensors, machines and the data-sharing between stakeholders within a food supply chain. Existing Blockchain-independent implementations of technologies for increasing transparency in supply chains use communication standards whose transferability to Blockchain applications has not yet been analysed sufficiently. This publication analyses the suitability of established standards regarding their use in Blockchains. In this context, the requirements for the distributed database and for the protection of sensitive company data must be considered. Therefore an analysis of eventually necessary changes is executed for the adoption of standards and how they could be implemented.

Keywords: Food chain · Supply chain management · Blockchain · Standards

1 Introduction

1.1 The Need for New Solutions in Food Supply Chains

The continuing emergence of scandals within the food industry causes increasing uncertainties among consumers regarding the quality of their daily shopping. One example is the fipronil scandal in Europe in 2017, where an insecticide was discovered in chicken eggs. The total number of the affected eggs only in Germany was estimated to be between 10.7 Million and 35.5 Million [1]. Another example is a meat scandal concerning the German meat producer Wilke in 2019, where Listeria germs were discovered in meat products, which caused three deaths and 37 cases of strong illness [2]. These are only two examples of many in the food industry, which follows as an industry with dynamic company interactions big challenges for the network [3]. Reinforced by several crises, the demand for transparency in supply chains, as a question of risk prevention and consumer protection, has become a general demand for improved access to information in order to regain consumer confidence in food [4]. Through an open-accessible database for value-creating partners, public authorities and

© IFIP International Federation for Information Processing 2020
Published by Springer Nature Switzerland AG 2020
L. M. Camarinha-Matos et al. (Eds.): PRO-VE 2020, IFIP AICT 598, pp. 524–533, 2020.
https://doi.org/10.1007/978-3-030-62412-5_43

end consumers, the chance to detect problems such as the named ones in a faster way can be realized and all concerned supply chain participants can be informed immediately [5].

The degree of trust directly determines the success potential within company-wide networks. This trust can be provided by secure and independent technologies, which therefore can perceive as a promoter for trust and supporter for the success of collaborative networks. [6] A determining factor is the latency between the steps of detecting an event and initiating countermeasures. By applying the Blockchain technology, it is possible to reduce latencies and the impact of an event on the entire supply chain up until the end consumers [7]. Due to the diverse information system architectures of the interacting parties, sensors, machines and products generally do not speak the same "language" today. [8] What's more, companies use different methods to gather, aggregate and exchange data. By using common dictionaries, models and communication standards, companies can facilitate data sharing and accelerate data aggregation and analysis. Companies or their service providers can define proprietary structures for each data-sharing project or they can select from among widely accepted reference architectures and standards. [8] However, there are currently no standards for the use of Blockchain technology [9].

Several organizations address this problem, aiming to facilitate interoperability in Blockchain solutions. Standardization institutions, such as the International Organization for Standardization (ISO), developed standards to increase transparency and harmonization within Blockchain solutions. The standard ISO 20614, for instance, is a data exchange protocol with a focus on interoperability and preservation. Furthermore the member-driven standard organization Enterprise Ethereum Alliance focusses on open Blockchain specifications, which should lead to interoperability and harmonization within Blockchain solutions. There is also GS1, which is a network of not-for-profit organizations that develops and maintain standards to identify products unambiguously. Using these unique identification numbers, companies are able to connect different Blockchain solutions [8].

The described problem is analyzed and outlined in the following chapters. The main focus is on the conceptual comparison of existing traceability processes with Blockchain-based processes. By using established GS1 standards, such as Electronic Product Code Information Services (EPCIS) or Core Business Vocabularies (CBV), an analysis of the transferability takes place.

1.2   The Research Project "SiLKe" Addresses the Needs of New Data Exchange Solutions

The project with the name "SiLKe", which is funded by the German Federal Office for Education and Research (BMBF), takes up the possibility of using the Blockchain technology in supply chain management and investigates a possible implementation of such a solution for food supply chains. The project addresses the requirements on a technical solution from the perspective of the different supply chain stakeholders, transfers these requirements as challenges for the use of a Blockchain and develops a practicable application. One of these challenges, which will be addressed within this paper, is the lack of industry standards for applying a Blockchain solution within an industrial supply chain under consideration of the existing individual IT-infrastructure of each integrated company [9].

2 Applying Standards for Data Management in Blockchain Applications

As the base for a qualified evaluation regarding the implication of applying a Blockchain on the compatibility of industrial cross-company process standards, the first step is to understand the high number of necessary standards which are required for different business processes. The following Fig. 1 gives an overview about the industrial standards established by GS1, which will we considered as a reference within the following analysis.

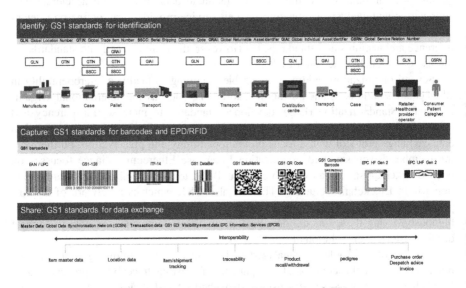

Fig. 1. Overview of industrial standards of GS1

In the following, especially the data management is considered as one of the main aspects to be addressed in the context of Blockchain applications. The focus here is on looking at the different types of data, how this data is generated, stored, backed up and exchanged. These topics are enriched, ensuring appropriate data quality and compliance with data protection. By describing the relevant aspects as they are handled today without the use of Blockchain technology, a comparison is thus made between three different technological approaches (traditional, i.e. without Blockchain, with a Permissioned Blockchain and with a Public Blockchain).

2.1   Data Type

In the context of production networks, the three different kinds of data types, master data, transaction data and event data exist for tracking and tracing information along a supply chain [10]. In the following, they will be presented and evaluated with regard to their usability in a Blockchain solution.

Master Data. Master data is the source of common business data that is used for all systems, applications and processes of an entire company. A further distinction is made between static master data, which is largely unchangeable over time, and relationship master data, which represents data of customers and suppliers. Hereby the identification of a unique designation of e.g. companies, products and locations is necessary [10].

Both kinds of master data can also be exchanged or retrieved via a Blockchain since there is no technical difference between the data and both can be recorded in a Blockchain. Therefore no adjustments are necessary on the technical side. In the case that not all master data is available in the same format for each ecosystem stakeholder, general regulations for the exchange of master data must first be formulated.

Transaction Data. Transaction data is recorded as a result of business transactions, e.g. at the conclusion of a transfer of ownership (e.g. purchase orders, invoices) or the transfer of custody of goods (e.g. transport advice, proof of delivery) [10]. Hereby the identification system serves as an access key to more detailed information as used in the exchange of transaction data [11]. All relevant event data related to business processes from ordering to invoicing can be exchanged via standardized electronic message types. Transaction data can also be exchanged or accessed via a Blockchain. The question arises whether the transaction data itself should be stored in the Blockchain or whether the visible events that triggered transaction data transmission (e.g. a shipping notification) should be recorded in the Blockchain and should be made retrievable.

In the first case, the existing processes for transaction data have to be transferred to the Blockchain. To do this, generally valid regulations and recommendations for the exchange of transaction data by Blockchain would have to be developed first, since these do not exist today with regard to the Blockchain technology. This requires corresponding standardization efforts. A sender and a recipient of a shipping notification, for example, have an essential interest in not giving third parties (such as competitors) any insight into the flows of goods and quantities that can be read from shipping notification data. This goes beyond pure data content and also includes access rights and encryption issues. The development of a proprietary solution for this would be an obstacle to scalability. [11] In the latter case, new event data would be added to the Blockchain, which would be redundant to conventional process data. It is the same process as if the sender and recipient apply the classic EDI message (such as a shipping notification) and get automatically informed of an event [11].

Event Data. Event data are records of the completion of business process steps in which physical or digital entities are handled. Each event records which objects participated in the process, when the process took place, where the objects were and will be located afterwards and in what business context the process took place [10].

Event data represents the category of data types that receives most attention within a Blockchain application for supply chain use cases. One of the core aspects of the SiLKe-project is to exchange this data between the partners by means of a Blockchain. Visible event data does not initially have any influence on the process comparison (with or without Blockchain) [11].

2.2   Data Generation

Before storing data in a Blockchain it is necessary to generate the data. For the first step of data generation, the identification of the respective objects requires special identification keys that enable the differentiation between the different types of objects which are shown in Fig. 1. These are for instance identities for products, for companies and locations, for logistic units and for returnable assets such as vehicles or transport equipment [10]. For the next step, the capture of the data, standardized data carriers are required. Examples are Barcodes as well as RFID-Transponders [10]. With these data carriers it is possible to identify objects by their specific product identification number.

The data generation is one of the upstream processes of the Blockchain and can be realized identically as without a Blockchain. By standardizing the codes and the data carrier, it is possible for each member of the supply chain to read and generate the data for tracking information. The same technology can be used for generating data in a Blockchain solution because the generation is independent of the storage of the data. Here it is important that the data carrier is readable. Nevertheless, a change from bilateral to multilateral data exchange within a Blockchain may change the situation of data access (scope) and the way the generated data is presented (e.g. data encryption or provision of references where data can be found) [11].

2.3   Data Storage

Another important aspect in the context of data management is the storage of data. In currently existing standardization systems, the storage of data is managed depending on the data type. In the case of GS1, the company issuing these Global Location Numbers (GLN) is responsible for keeping business partners informed of all GLNs related to their trading relationship. In contrast, the visible event data is stored in a decentralized way. The companies have their own repository where they save their generated data. Such a repository has an acquisition interface for storing and a query interface for requesting event data. Each entity stores the event data relevant to them and exchanges relevant entries with business partners [12].

In the case of applying a Blockchain, it should represent the repositories and act as a distributed storage network with all the typical technological benefits of a Blockchain. As a consequence, the individual repositories must back up much more extensive data, as they back up the replicated content holistically, which means that scaling problems must be taken into account. In Fig. 2 a possible realization of an integration of a Blockchain in the supply chain is shown. Every company generates its data on its own and represents a node in the Blockchain network. Regarding the requirements of the different types of data, a related storage strategy is applied and only the event data is stored in the Blockchain.

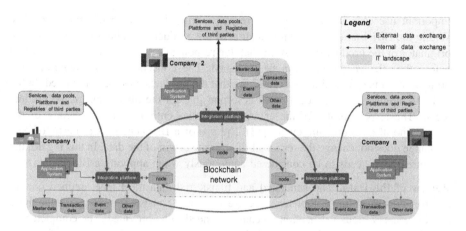

Fig. 2. Transfer of existing traceability processes into a Blockchain application [11]

Due to the fact, that the Blockchain is transparent and every node has access to the data, the question arises how the event data is stored in the Blockchain. There are several ways to store the data. First, the data can be stored completely unencrypted and is only signed cryptographically. The second option is to store only the cryptographic hash value of the data and link the address of the unencrypted data's storage location, which would not be stored in the Blockchain itself. Another option is a combination of these two ways to store the data. In this case, it should be evaluated which option is the most suitable for a food supply chain due to companies' business secrets and the Blockchain scalability. [11] Within the framework of the research project a combination of unencrypted and encrypted data will be used. This is because business secrets are important for companies and not every event data has to be shared with every network member.

2.4   Data Quality

In addition to the generation and storage of the data, the data quality plays a significant role in the context of industrial standards and depends on several factors. In the context of data quality, the aspects of data responsibility, conformity with relevant data as well as the checking of data for completeness, correctness and consistency are dealt with below.

Responsibilities. An important element to be taken into account with regard to the requirements for a traceability system are regulations on the responsibilities for data management. In dependence of the kind of asset to be managed, different roles are accountable for the generation of those assets. The right for the allocation of item identifiers is in the case of GS1 managed by the manufacturers themselves. The interacting parties are responsible for their personal representation. The pallet identification number is either created by the logistics company or to be conveyed by the manufacturer of the goods [10]. Each participant involved in one of the business processes is responsible for the collection, recording and distribution of event data. An important use case in the context of responsibilities is the case of product recalls. Within the GS1 framework, the notification of the product recall has to be made by the originator of the product recall. After that, the responsible authority has to be identified before the affected partners can be informed. The concerned person regarding the product recall is responsible for confirming that the products have been removed. In the end, the initiator of the product recall is responsible for the final report of the product recall. The responsibility for the created events lies entirely with the creator of the event, who also secures the event. [13] The use of a Blockchain as a means of data exchange does not change the responsibility for the origin of the data. In this regard, the structure above needs to be considered analogously when applying a Blockchain.

Review of the Data. The generated and transferred data must meet defined quality requirements regarding completeness, correctness and consistency. To guarantee these requirements, various verification mechanisms need to be provided. The completeness of the data can be ensured by the predefined length of identification numbers (for those with fixed lengths). Since they are composed of different contextual elements, all of them have to be filled with information. [11] More challenging is the review of data regarding correctness. The use of automated data collection technologies increases the safety of reading data correctly. Especially the dimensions "what", "where" and "when" can benefit from that. In this case, the "what", i.e. the object of detection, is usually recorded automatically. This happens by using standardized identifiers on the object and by using a corresponding reader for the identifiers. The "where" can be captured in the same way by scanning a barcode or transponder of the corresponding location. In case of a predefined location such as a warehouse gate, the dimension "where" can be registered in the system, whereby every scanned product can be allocated with the ID of this location. The "when" can be automatically tracked in the moment of the query [11].

This standardized data checking procedure can also be transferred to a Blockchain application. Event data can be checked regarding completeness in the same way and data can be captured automatically with the reading standards and technology. Due to the opportunities offered by the Blockchain technology, Smart Contracts can be used for automated reviewing processes. In addition, they offer further opportunities for the automation of data acquisition. Human sources of error can mostly be eliminated by this automation. In this context, it must be examined which existing verification mechanisms are better (more effective, simpler, less expensive) for Smart Contracts and which verification mechanisms should be replaced by them [11].

Updating and Correction of Data. The last topic in the context of data quality focusses on the aspect of updating or correcting data which has already been saved and shared within a company ecosystem. Due to the tracing of all events during the value creation of an object, it is possible to reconstruct the whole supply chain history. Status updates from objects are generated by creating a new event. It would work in the same way in a Blockchain solution. New events would be stored in the Blockchain and the tracing of all events successively builds up a production history [11].

However, it cannot be ensured that faulty data doesn't get into the Blockchain. In such a case, the data cannot be simply deleted or overwritten. Within the GS1 standard, a subsequent correction event is generated, that corrects a wrong event. [12] The application of a Blockchain and the previously described approach have in common that no faulty block can be simply deleted or replaced. Instead, a new block entry must be entered into the Blockchain containing the corrected information. The correction event could most likely be adopted in a Blockchain solution. Within a consensus method, it is mandatory, that the participants decide if the corrective transaction should be added. This raises the question of whether other participants even have the knowledge to decide on the correctness of other participants' data. At this point, Smart Contracts could again play a supporting role [11].

2.5 Data Exchange

Another aspect which has to be considered is the data exchange, which needs to get realized with different interfaces. Within the GS1 standard, three different interfaces exist [14]. The first interface is the data acquisition interface, which offers the possibility to share data via a website and to send conforming messages to the company IT infrastructure. [11] The second interface is a query control interface, which has two different modes. In the on-demand mode the service-requesting device makes a request and receives an immediate response. In the standing-request mode, the service-requesting device subscribes to a periodically recurring query [14]. The third interface is a query callback interface. Whenever a query service is executed, its results are passed on at the same time [14].

The data exchange itself can be structured architecturally in various ways. In the simplest case, the centralized repository is shared with all value-adding partners [12]. In the case of distributed push choreography, each entity in the supply chain keeps the collected data in its own EPCIS repository. If necessary, each partner can receive and forward it to every partner in the supply chain. No EPCIS queries are involved since the exchange of all events is triggered directly [12]. In the third case of the distributed query choreography, each party in the value chain keeps the collected data in its own local repository. Any party that needs data from another party has to request it [12].

In principle, all three described architectures can also be theoretically realized using Blockchain technology. In an independent architecture, none of the participants would represent a data-holding node and the Blockchain would be the data-providing system. This would mean a complete externalization of the data holding. With the distributed push choreography, the data would be cumulated in the Blockchain, so that the result would be a significant amount of redundant data in the Blockchain. Of the three choreographies, the distributed query choreography has the greatest proximity to a Blockchain, in which the query is regulated via rights management. So this rights management can be used as a guideline for a Blockchain solution [11].

2.6 Privacy

With regard to data protection, the question of how personal data can be protected against misuse must be investigated. With applying non-speaking identities as randomized events and article numbers, conclusions about the underlying products or identities are excluded. A conclusion on the context is only revealed with the respective access rights. Identities should have the aim to identify objects in an economic context and not the involved individuals. The tracked "who" entity within an event is always a company or a company section but never the acting person behind it. In addition, each application should have a reliable system of rights indicating which subscriber can view which information [11].

The described approach above can also be applied to a Blockchain. To ensure that only permitted entities get access, a clear role and right management is necessary. It has to be clearly defined who may read what kind of data from which network partner. Therefore, it is necessary to make use of appropriate encryption methods. At the same time, it must be ensured on the process side that, even with a high level of transparency, no conclusions can be drawn about the persons who are connected with the data [11].

3 Conclusion and Outlook

The assurance of standards for the system-wide exchange of information in business relationships is an essential cornerstone for a functioning supply chain. As we have seen there are a lot of existing company-wide process standards that can be projected onto a Blockchain solution, which was validated within the reseach project consortium. The unique identification through the identities enables the non-overlapping recording of object-related data. The storage of the data in the form of events can also be used in a Blockchain solution. In this case, it is necessary to define what data and what information should be captured and stored. A standardized data carrier for an automatic and fast identification of objects plays an important role in the data generation. Updating or adding information as the production progresses can be carried out seamlessly by applying a Blockchain.

The use of Smart Contracts offers the opportunity to automate specific processes and to check data regarding its completeness and correctness. For this, it is necessary to map the relevant business logic in the corresponding Smart Contracts. Within the framework of the research project SiLKe a Smart Contracts library will therefore be defined and evaluated. Another important point is the management of roles and rights. It has to be clearly defined which member of the network is allowed to write and read transactions. It must be taken into account that even with absolute transparency within the entire supply chain, no business secrets must be derivable from that. This has to be already considered during the development of a Blockchain solution for food supply chains. In this case, sensitive data of companies must be protected. The big challenge is to find a practicable solution for ensuring a safe, unchangeable and transparent food supply chain while guaranteeing a high level of safety of personal and sensitive company data. This is also an important part of the current development in the SiLKe project and will continue to be one of the key issues in the future when industry standards need to be implemented into a Blockchain solution.

References

1. European Comission: Fipronil in eggs. Factsheet. http://publications.jrc.ec.europa.eu/repository/bitstream/JRC110632/jrc110632_final.pdf

2. Hellner, C.: Verkeimt, verkauft, versagt. https://www.zeit.de/wissen/2019-11/rueckrufe-leb ensmittel-wurst-milch-verbraucherschutz-qualitaet

3. Camarinha-Matos, L.M., Afsarmanesh, H.: Collaborative networks in industry and services: research scope and challenges. In: IFAC Proceedings, Nantes, vol. 40, pp. 33–42 (2007)

4. Frentrup, M., Theuvsen, L.: Transparency in supply chains: is trust a limiting factor? In: European Association of Agricultural Economists (ed.) 99th EAAE Seminar 'Trust and Risk in Business Networks. EAAE, pp. 64–74(2006)

5. Abeyratne, S.A., Monfared, R.P.: Blockchain ready manufacturing supply chain using distributed ledger. Int. J. Res. Eng. Technol. **5**, 1–10 (2016)

6. Camarinha-Matos, Luis M., Pereira-Klen, A., Afsarmanesh, H. (eds.): PRO-VE 2011. IAICT, vol. 362. Springer, Heidelberg (2011). https://doi.org/10.1007/978-3-642-23330-2

7. Schuh, G., Anderl, R., Dumitrescu, R., Krüger, A., ten Hompel, M.: Industrie 4.0 maturity index. Managing Digital Transform. Co. (2020)

8. Betti, F., Bezamat, F., Fendri, M., Fernandez, B., Küpper, D., Okur, A.: Share to Gain: Unlocking Data Value in Manufacturing (2020)

9. Herweijer, C., Waghray, D., Warren, S.: Building Block(chain)s for a Better Planet (2018)

10. Janssen, C., et al.: GS1 Global traceability standard. GS1's framework for the design of interoperable traceability systems for supply chains (2017)

11. Füßler, A., Siruet, R.: Konzeptionelle Übertragung bestehender Traceability-Prozesse auf Distributed-Ledger-basierte Anwendungsumgebungen. Entscheidungshilfe für die Umsetzung im Forschungsprojekt SiLKe (2020)

12. Kennedy, A., Troeger, R., Morgan, G., Traub, K., Allgaier, P., Arguin, P.: EPCIS and CBV implementation guideline using EPCIS and CBV standards to gain visibility of business processes (2017)

13. Dabydeen, A., Laur, R.: Product Recall in Multiple Recall Jurisdictions Implementation Guideline (2012)

14. Kennedy, A., et al.: EPC Information Services (EPCIS) Standard (2016)

A Decision Support Tool for the Selection of Promoting Actions to Encourage Collaboration in Projects for the Agriculture Sector

M. M. E. Alemany[1(✉)], F. Alarcón[1], D. Pérez[1], and C. Guyon[2]

[1] Research Centre on Production Management and Engineering (CIGIP),
Universitat Politècnica de València, Camino de Vera S/N, 46022 València, Spain
{mareva, faualva, dapep}@cigip.uvp.es
[2] Bretagne Development Innovation,
1bis Route de Fougères, 35510 Cesson-Sévigne, France
c.guyon@bdi.fr

Abstract. Development and innovation agencies promote consortiums of agricultural stakeholders to collaborate in the proposal of projects for public calls. To achieve this partnerships, these agencies should select between different promoting actions to be performed with two objectives: maximize the number of project proposals presented and minimize the resources invested. To support agencies with these decisions, a computer tool based on a multi-objective integer linear programming model is proposed. To deal with the two objectives the weighting sum method is implemented. The model is validated in different scenarios by means a realistic case of an agency in Brittany (France). The results show the conflict between the two objectives considered and the dependency of the solutions on the scenarios defined. As a conclusion it can be stated that: 1) decision-makers should be careful in defining the weights of each objective and 2) the impact of the different promoting actions on the level of stakeholders' participation should be precisely estimated.

Keywords: Decision support · Optimization · Collaboration · Project proposals · Agriculture

1 Introduction

Many EU-funded research and innovation programmes have been developed since 1990, such as INTERREG, H2020, Intelligent Energy Europe, LIFE, etc. Others, such as Europe-Horizon (2021–2027) are coming soon. Not only EU-funded but also a high number of national and regional programmes have been launched in the last three decades. These programmes aim to drive economic growth and create jobs. They do special emphasis on excellent science, industrial leadership and tackling societal challenges. The goal is to ensure Europe produces world-class science, removes barriers to innovation and makes it easier for the public and private sectors to work together in delivering innovation and collaborative work.

© IFIP International Federation for Information Processing 2020
Published by Springer Nature Switzerland AG 2020
L. M. Camarinha-Matos et al. (Eds.): PRO-VE 2020, IFIP AICT 598, pp. 534–545, 2020.
https://doi.org/10.1007/978-3-030-62412-5_44

At the operational side, these EU, national or regional programmes may comprise one or more thematic sections, which, in turn, describe their overall objectives, the respective calls for proposals, and the topics within each call. Besides, some general annexes describing general rules such as standard admissibility conditions and eligibility criteria, selection and award criteria are presented [1].

One of the problems that some entities face is deciding on which topic or topics from a certain call to make project proposals, since a multitude of them can be presented in each topic. Besides, these entities are often engaged in several programmes, what increases the number of calls and makes the decision-making process more complex due to the limited resources. These entities must assess then what are the inputs (resources, costs...) and outputs (benefits) of presenting projects proposals in different topics of each program call.

Among other data, they must account for the planned start and end dates of the projects (in case they are approved), some strict requirements about the number and type of partners that can participate as well as their objectives or budget.

Finally, these entities, taking into consideration all the previous issues, decide to present a certain number of project proposals, of which only some of them will be approved. These approved proposals will become firm projects and be developed within the defined terms and conditions.

The described problem may be included within what is well known in the literature as project selection problem, considered as the first essential part of project portfolio management. It consists in selecting from a large set of projects, a subset of projects to be undertaken [2].

A large amount of methods for project selection are presented in the literature, basically divided into two categories.

First ones, are based on the multi-objective nature (basically return and risk) of the problem [3]. Different techniques (quantitative and qualitative) to select projects according to these multi-objective criteria are proposed in deterministic and uncertain environments. Regarding deterministic techniques, three are considered as the most popular: analytic hierarchy process (AHP), analytic network process (ANP) and order of preference by similarity to ideal solution (TOPSIS). In stochastic scenarios researchers usually consider uncertainty in the form of fuzzy or interval data and proposed more sophisticated method for ranking projects.

Second ones are based on optimization models, based on operation research tools. Some form of mathematical programming is used to select a set of projects which deliver the maximum benefit represented by an objective function subjected to a series of constraints. They consider relationships between projects and other factors that first ones do not consider [4]. Among the major deterministic optimization models are linear and non-linear programming, integer algorithms, dynamic programming and goal programming [5]. The inclusion of the uncertainty is well described in [6], where a brief review of fuzzy mathematical programming and a comparison with stochastic programming in portfolio selection problem is conducted.

Nevertheless, most of the reviewed works only deal with R&D projects conducted by companies from different sectors or industries to innovate and introduce new products and services or to improve their existing offerings. Typical sectors that invest the most are technological [7], construction [8], energy [9, 10], etc.

Only a few works address the project selection problem as described at the beginning of this introduction, and if so, it is usually done from the perspective of the institution that launches the calls for projects [11, 12], as they must select, once received the project proposals from the different entities, which projects to finance or co-finance with public or private aid.

The literature lacks work in which the project selection is made from the perspective of the agencies whose business is based on disseminating the data and interest of different calls and to encourage the creation of consortia among different partners for the development of projects proposals of which they previously know the selection procedure and criteria. The creation of consortia involves the choice of partners to carry out the projects in a collaborative network context. Selecting partner(s) for collaborative projects is the main challenge that organizations face before they can attain the advantages of collaboration [13]. Collaboration is defined in [14] as process in which entities share information, resources and responsibilities to jointly plan, implement, and evaluate a program of activities to achieve a common goal. In this task of boosting collaborative networks for projects development, even less, research has been done to support these agencies to decide about what types of actions to be done in order to promote project proposals of different partners.

Partially related to this, only a research stream that addresses the partners' selection problem have been found in the literature. [15] develop a conceptual model indicating how an organization should choose the right partners for a set of projects. [16] present an explorative empirical study that shows the steps in the partner selection process. [17] formulates a multicriteria best value source selection methodology for public-private partnerships projects. But these studies neither include optimization models based on mathematical programming nor with the characteristics addressed in the problem under study.

To fill the above gap, in this paper a multi-objective integer linear programming (ILP) model for project selection in this specific scenario is proposed. The main contribution of this paper is to address the project selection problem not from the perspective of the institution that launches the calls for projects but from the perspective of agencies boosting the creation of collaborative networks. These agencies should select the investment in promoting actions to establish consortia among supply chain stakeholders for project proposals. Additionally, the selection of stakeholders (partners) at each supply chain stage to create collaborative networks to participate in different projects proposals presented at each call should be made. In doing so, it is necessary to consider different constraints related to the potential participation of stakeholders in calls based on their previous knowledge and expertise, the maximum number of projects in which each stakeholder can simultaneously participate at each period and the available capacity of the resources to carry out the marketing actions by the agency. In doing so, besides the traditional objective of maximizing the number of projects proposals presented, the resources allocated by the agency to the promoting actions is aimed also to be minimized. These marketing actions are crucial to encourage different companies to be engaged in different partnerships and therefore presenting project proposals.

The rest of the paper is arranged as follows. Section 2 describes the problem being studied, as is the case of an agency that supports and encourages the implementation of projects of different nature. In Sect. 3, a deterministic ILP model to solve the problem is presented. Section 4 reports its application to a realistic case based on different scenarios that validate the model. Finally, some conclusions and future research lines are drawn in Sect. 5.

2 Problem Description

The configuration of the agricultural supply chain under study is assumed to be composed by three stages (see Fig. 1):

- The stage 1 corresponds to the experimental laboratories that test and evaluate the technology developed by the technology manufacturers.
- The stage 2 is integrated by manufacturers of the technology for the agricultural companies
- The stage 3 makes reference to the agricultural companies.

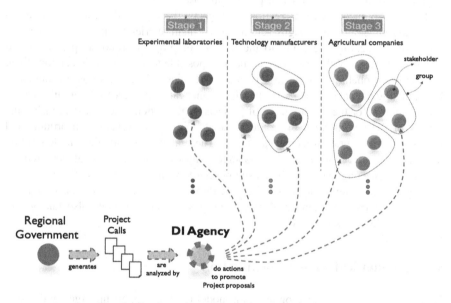

Fig. 1. Configuration of the agricultural supply chain.

In addition, there is an agency dedicated to promote development and innovation projects in the region. This agency, usually of governmental character, promotes collaboration among stakeholders of the different stages to encourage the consortia development to present as many project proposals as possible. These projects respond to regional calls that specify:

- A start and end date for the presentation of project proposals,
- A topic, which may generate more or less interest among stakeholders of different stages of the supply chain and fit in a lesser or greater extent the skills and previous experiences of the stakeholders,
- Economic endowment, which make the call for companies more or less attractive.

Due to the budget limitations, for each call a limited number of projects can be presented. To ensure that a project proposal has some possibility of being accepted in a specific call a minimum number of stakeholders of the different stages is required. Besides, a maximum number is desirable in order to apply for several projects in the same call. Indeed, the consortia for each project can be made up of any number of companies at the third stage, combined or not with suppliers at the first or second stage. Nevertheless, if there are stakeholders at the first stage in the consortium, there may also be a variable number of stakeholders belonging to the second stage. Stakeholders of the same stage that are interested in the same project calls will integrate a group of interest. Because regional calls can be overlapped during different time periods along the year, it is assumed that each group of stakeholders can work simultaneously in the preparation of a limited number of project proposals.

In order to encourage the creation of projects, the agency dedicated to the innovation and development, designs actions, plans them, carries them out, evaluates the results of the actions according to the number of projects proposals presented and calculates the costs of these actions so that it is possible to know in which actions there is a greater probability of success in relation to costs. These actions are aimed at disseminating the data and interest of each regional call and at encouraging the creation of consortiums for the development of projects. If the actions succeed in arousing the interest of the stakeholders these are associated in one or several consortiums and propose one or several projects respectively. These actions include the simple sending of an e-mail (low consumption of resources) until the organization of conferences, stakeholder meeting days (high consumption of resources), etc. So the agency is interested in knowing the actions to be done during each period of the year in order to achieve the maximum number of project proposal presented while also taking into account the resources invested.

3   Mathematical Model Formulation

The notation of the integer programming model used to support the Agency decision about the number of action types to be performed on each group of stakeholders belonging to the different stages for each project call is presented in Tables 1, 2 and 3.

Different objectives are pursued when assigning the number of each action type to the different projects. The first one aims to maximize the number of projects proposals presented for all the project calls triggered during the horizon (1). The second one, aims to minimize the quantity of resources invested in these actions (2).

Table 1. Nomenclature: indexes and sets.

Indexes		Sets	
s	Stage of the agriculture supply chain	G_s	Group of stakeholders g in stage s
g	Group of stakeholders with the same interests		
j	Project call	J_g	Projects calls j of interest for a group of stakeholders g
p	Proposal of projects to be presented		
a	Promotion action type of the agency		
t	Time period	P_j	Group of projects p that can be proposed in a project call j
r	Resource type of the agency		

Table 2. Nomenclature: parameters

Parameters	
ns_g	Number of stakeholders belonging to group g
nj_g	Number of projects in which the stakeholders of group g can simultaneously work
$nsmin_{js}$	Minimum number of stakeholders of stage s required to participate in a project call j
$nsmax_{js}$	Maximum number of stakeholders of stage s allowed to participate in a project call j
$npmax_j$	Maximum number of projects that can be presented for the project call j
ia_{agj}	Impact of one action type a on a group of stakeholders g expressed as the percentage of the number of stakeholders in the group g that will be interested in participating in the project call j.
$cons_{rajt}$	Consumption of resource type r of the agency in doing action type a for the project call j in t
cap_{rt}	Available capacity of resource r during the time period t
δ_{jt}	Parameter with a value of 1 if the time period for presenting proposals to project call j include period t and 0 otherwise

Table 3. Nomenclature: decision variables

Decision variables	
N_{sgjp}	Number of stakeholders in stage s of group g participating in project p of call j
Y_{sjp}	Binary variable with a value of 1 if some stakeholder of stage s participate in project p of call j
YP_{jp}	Binary variable with a value of 1 if project p is presented in project call j and 0 otherwise
YA_{asgj}	Binary variable with a value of 1 if action type a is performed in the group of stakeholders g of stage s for the project call j and 0 otherwise
YAT_a	Total number of type action a carried out by the agency

$$Max[Z1] = \sum_{j} \sum_{p \in P_j} YP_{jp} \tag{1}$$

$$Min[Z2] = \sum_{r} \sum_{a} \sum_{s} \sum_{g \in G_s} \sum_{j \in J_g} \sum_{t \in T_j} cons_{rajt} YA_{asgj} \tag{2}$$

Both objectives are combined by means of the weighting sum method. In order to scale these objectives, each one is divided by their maximum value. This ensures that they both move in the range [0, 1]. The maximum value can be obtained by maximizing only one objective at a time. The weights $w1$ and $w2$ represent the importance provided by the decision-maker to each objective in such a way that the more important the objective, the greater the weight assigned. It is noteworthy that the following relationship always apply: $w1 + w2 = 1$.

$$Max[Z] = w1 \frac{Z1}{Z1max} - w2 \frac{Z2}{Z2max} \tag{3}$$

The following constraints should be respected. Each project proposal p of a certain call j requires a minimum (4) and a maximum (5) number of stakeholders of each stage in case this project is finally presented.

$$nsmin_{js} \cdot YP_{jp} \leq \sum_{g \in G_s} N_{sgjp} \qquad \forall s, j, p \in P_j \tag{4}$$

$$\sum_{g \in G_s} N_{sgjp} \leq nsmax_{js} \cdot YP_{jp} \qquad \forall s, j, p \in P_j \tag{5}$$

The total number of stakeholders of each group at each stage participating in a specific call j should be no higher than the expected impact on each group of stakeholders produced by the action carried out (6).

$$\sum_{p \in P_j} N_{sgpj} \leq \sum_{a} \left(ia_{agj} \cdot ns_g \cdot YA_{asgj} \right) \qquad \forall s, g \in G_s, j \in J_g \tag{6}$$

Constraints (7) calculate the total number of each type action a to be performed by the agency.

$$YAT_a = \sum_{s} \sum_{g \in G_s} \sum_{j \in J_g} YA_{asgj} \qquad \forall a \tag{7}$$

Constraints (8) and (9) establish the relationship between the number of stakeholders interested to participate in a project p of a certain call j and the binary variable indicating if some stakeholder of stage s participate in the corresponding project p.

$$\sum_{g \in G_s} N_{sgjp} \leq M \cdot Y_{sjp} \qquad\qquad \forall s,j,p \in P_j \qquad (8)$$

$$Y_{sjp} \leq \sum_{g \in G_s} N_{sgjp} \qquad\qquad \forall s,j,p \in P_j \qquad (9)$$

Constraints (10) and (11) ensure that a project proposal p should be presented only if there are stakeholders interested on it. Through constraints (12) the maximum number of project proposals that can be presented in a call is respected.

$$Y_{sjp} \leq YP_{jp} \qquad\qquad \forall s,j,p \in P_j \qquad (10)$$

$$YP_{jp} \leq \sum_{s} Y_{sjp} \qquad\qquad \forall j,p \in P_j \qquad (11)$$

$$\sum_{p \in P_j} YP_{jp} \leq npmax_j \qquad\qquad \forall j \qquad (12)$$

It has no sense that stakeholders of the first stage participate in a project proposal if there are no stakeholders of the second stage. Because the laboratories participation only has sense if there are some technological stakeholder that need to do experimentation with the technology. Constraints (13) ensure this aspect.

$$Y_{1jp} \leq Y_{2jp} \qquad\qquad \forall j,p \in P_j \qquad (13)$$

Through constraints (14) it is not allowed to exceed the number of simultaneous projects that one stakeholder of a group is able to attend.

$$\sum_{j} \sum_{p \in P_j} N_{sgjp} \cdot \delta_{jt} \leq nj_g \cdot ns_g \qquad\qquad \forall s, g \in G_s, t \qquad (14)$$

At each time period, the consumed quantity of each resource by all the promoting actions implemented should not be greater than the available capacity of this resource in this time period (15).

$$\sum_{a} \sum_{j} cons_{raj} \cdot \delta_{jt} \cdot YA_{aj} \leq cap_{rt} \qquad\qquad \forall r,t \qquad (15)$$

The nature of the different decision variables is declared by means of the constraints (16).

$$\begin{aligned} N_{sgjp}, \ YAT_a \geq 0, & \qquad\qquad \textit{Integer} \\ Y_{sjp}, \ YP_{jp}, \ YA_{asgj} & \qquad\qquad \textit{Binary} \end{aligned} \qquad (16)$$

4   Implementation and Validation: Application to a Development and Innovation Agency in Brittany

The model was implemented in MPL® 5.0.8 and solved by using the solver Gurobi™ 8.1.1 in a computer with an Intel® Xeon® CPU E5-1620 v2(C) @3.70 GHz processor, with an installed capacity of 35 GB and a 64-bits operating system. Microsoft Access Database was used to store input data and results.

The above MILP model has been validated through a data set inspired in the case of a Development and Innovation Agency in Brittany that interact with stakeholders of the three stages indicated in Fig. 1. It is assumed to be 15 groups of stakeholders: 5 groups in stage 1 with 10 members each one, 4 groups in stage 2 with 10 members each one, and 6 groups in stage 3 with 30 members each. The number of projects in which stakeholders can be simultaneously working are 3 for group 1, 5 for group 2 and 6 for group 3. It is assumed to be 7 project calls with a maximum of 4 projects to be presented per call. The open period for presenting each project call expressed in months can be seen in Fig. 2 from which the δ_{jt} arameter can be defined. The minimum and maximum number of stakeholders for each stage and project call are: for stage 1, 0 and 7, for stage 2, 2 and 12 and for stage 3, 15 and 40, respectively.

It is assumed the Agency has 2 limited resources: money and personnel time work. The agency can implement 5 types of actions: 1) send an e-mail with information about the project call, 2) to send a triptych, 3) to make a call phone, 4) to develop a stakeholder meeting days and 5) to visit the stakeholders. Each action type consumes a different quantity of both types of resources and has a certain impact as regards the stakeholders attracted to participate in different project call. They are defined in a way that the greater the impact of an action type the greater the resources consumption.

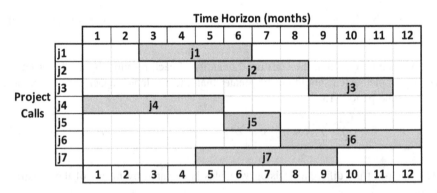

Fig. 2. Time period for presenting project proposals of each call (months).

In order to validate the MILP model proposed, we have assigned different weights to each objective function. This allows us to analyze the impact of these weights on the solutions obtained. In this case, only the money has been considered as the resource to be minimized (Z2) and only the personnel time work has been considered in constraints

(14). Besides in order to analyze the model sensitivity to the impact of each action type ia_{agj} three scenarios have been defined (Table 4).

Table 4. Value of the action impact (ia_{agj}) per action type and scenario.

Action type	Base scenario	Scenario 1	Scenario 2
1	0,025	0,030	0,020
2	0,030	0,035	0,030
3	0,040	0,045	0,100
4	0,850	0,800	0,900
5	0,600	0,400	0,300

Results of the different weights combination as regards the two objective function can be consulted in (Fig. 3) for the three scenarios defined. As it can be observed in all three scenarios the number of projects presented and the investment diminish when the weight assigned to the Z1 decreases showing they are in conflict. It can be seen that to provide some weight to the Z2 ($w2$) inside the interval [0.1, 0.3] considerably decreases the amount of money invested by the Agency, while the number of projects presented practically remains the same. On the opposite, if the weight assigned to Z2 is higher than 0.6 ($w2 > = 0.6$) the number of projects presented considerably decreases being practically null in the interval $0.7 <= w2 <=1$, as it was expected.

Fig. 3. Value of Z1 and Z2 for each scenario under different weights for the objective functions.

It is noteworthy that for each scenario there is a critical combination of weights around in the middle (w1 = 0.5 and w2 = 0.5) where a little variation of weights originates high differences in the projects presented. Therefore, this aspect should be taken into account when defining the weights of each objective. From the different type of actions selected in each scenario, it can be deduced the importance of properly estimating the value of the impact of each action type (ia_{agj}) (Table 5).

Table 5. Nº of each action type for different objective function weights and scenario

w1	w2	BASE SCENARIO					SCENARIO 1					SCENARIO 2				
		YAT(1)	YAT(2)	YAT(3)	YAT(4)	YAT(5)	YAT(1)	YAT(2)	YAT(3)	YAT(4)	YAT(5)	YAT(1)	YAT(2)	YAT(3)	YAT(4)	YAT(5)
1,00	0,00	43	29	47	5	18	42	32	46	14	6	9	7	51	17	5
0,90	0,10	36	22	50	1	21	39	14	43	14	4	0	0	40	15	0
0,80	0,20	36	22	50	1	21	39	14	43	14	4	0	0	40	15	0
0,70	0,30	36	22	50	1	21	39	14	43	14	4	0	0	40	15	0
0,60	0,40	31	13	40	1	21	20	0	28	14	6	0	0	57	11	3
0,50	0,50	17	6	34	2	16	20	0	28	14	6	0	0	52	6	1
0,45	0,55	16	0	21	0	10	10	0	14	8	4	4	4	60	1	0
0,40	0,60	12	0	16	0	7	18	5	22	0	0	4	4	60	1	0
0,38	0,62	21	3	21	0	5	18	5	22	0	0	4	4	60	1	0
0,35	0,65	6	1	6	0	0	5	1	7	0	0	4	4	60	1	0
0,30	0,70	6	1	6	0	0	5	1	7	0	0	0	0	52	1	0
0,20	0,80	0	0	0	0	0	0	0	0	0	0	0	0	48	0	0
0,10	0,90	0	0	0	0	0	0	0	0	0	0	0	0	5	0	0
0,00	1,00	0	0	0	0	0	0	0	0	0	0	0	0	0	0	0

5 Conclusions and Future Research Lines

In this paper a decision support tool based on an ILP model has been developed to assist innovation agencies in deciding the type of actions to promote project proposals in the agricultural sector. The model has been validated through its application to a realistic case inspired on a Development and Innovation Agency in Brittany. From the results obtained it can be concluded that the two objectives considered in the model are in conflict. Therefore, it seems to be reasonable consider both them. Even more, for all scenarios, it is observed that assign even a low weight to the second objective can substantially diminish the money investment with a very small variation in the number of project proposals. Therefore, it is recommended to follow this practice. On the other hand, the results of the model are highly dependent on the impact of each action type, so this parameter should be defined as precisely as possible. Along these lines, future research lines are devised to include the modelling of uncertainty in some parameters such as the impact of action types.

Acknowledgments. The authors acknowledge the support of the project 691249, RUCAPS: "Enhancing and implementing knowledge based ICT solutions within high risk and uncertain conditions for agriculture production systems", funded by the European Union's research and innovation programme under the H2020 Marie Skłodowska-Curie Actions.

References

1. European Comission Funded Programs. https://ec.europa.eu/programmes/horizon2020
2. Zoie, C., Radulescu, M.: Decision analysis for the project selection problem under risk. IFAC Proc. **34**(8), 445–450 (2001)
3. Sadi-Nezhad, S.: A state-of-art survey on project selection using MCDM techniques. J. Project Manage. **2**, 1–10 (2017)

4. Caballero, H.C., Chopra, S., Schmidt, E.K.: Project portfolio selection using mathematical programming and optimization methods. In: Paper presented at PMI® Global Congress 2012–North America, Vancouver, British Columbia, Canada, Newtown Square, PA, Project Management Institute (2012)

5. Ahmad, B., Haq, I.: Project selection techniques, relevance and applications in Pakistan. Int. J. Technol. Res. **4**, 52–60 (2016)

6. Inuiguchi, M., Ramík, J.: Possibilistic linear programming: a brief review of fuzzy mathematical programming and a comparison with stochastic programming in portfolio selection problem. Fuzzy Sets Syst. **111**(1), 3–28 (2000)

7. Stewart, R., Mohamed, S.: IT/IS projects selection using multi-criteria utility theory. Log. Inf. Manage. **15**(4), 254–270 (2002)

8. Alzober, W., Yaakub, A.R.: Integrated model for MCDM: selection contractor in Malaysian construction industry. In: Applied Mechanics and Materials 548, pp. 1587–1595. Trans Tech Publications (2014)

9. Adhikary, P., Roy, P.K., Mazumdar, A.: Optimal renewable energy project selection: a multi-criteria optimization technique approach. Global J. Pure Appl. Math. **11**(5), 3319–3329 (2015)

10. Strang, K.D.: Portfolio selection methodology for a nuclear project. Project Manage. J. **42**(2), 81–93 (2011)

11. Benjamin, C.O.: A linear goal-programming model for public-sector project selection. J. Oper. Res. Soc. **36**(1), 13–23 (1985)

12. Coronado, J.R., Pardo-Mora, E.M., Valero, M.: A multi-objective model for selection of projects to finance new enterprise SMEs in Colombia. J. Ind. Eng. Manage. **4**(3), 407–417 (2011)

13. Mat, N.A.C., Cheung, Y.: Partner selection: criteria for successful collaborative network. In: 20th Australian Conference on Information Systems, pp. 631–641 (2009)

14. Camarinha-Matos, L.M., Afsarmanesh, H.: Collaborative Networks. In: Wang, K., Kovacs, G.L., Wozny, M., Fang, M. (eds.) PROLAMAT 2006. IIFIP, vol. 207, pp. 26–40. Springer, Boston, MA (2006). https://doi.org/10.1007/0-387-34403-9_4

15. Paixão, M., Sbragia, R., Kruglianskas, I.: Factors for selecting partners in innovation projects–evidences from alliances in the Brazilian petrochemical leader. Rev. Admin. Innov. São Paulo **11**(2), 241–272 (2014)

16. Duisters, D., Duysters, G., de Man, A.P.: The partner selection process: steps, effectiveness, governance. Ann. Hematol. **2**, 7–25 (2011)

17. Zhang, X.: Criteria for selecting the private-sector partner in public-private partnerships. J. Constr. Eng. Manage. **131**(6), 631–644 (2005)

Optimization Models to Improve First Quality Agricultural Production Through a Collaboration Program in Different Scenarios

Ana Esteso[1(✉)], M. M. E. Alemany[1], Ángel Ortiz[1],
and Pascale Zaraté[2]

[1] Research Centre on Production Management and Engineering (CIGIP),
Universitat Politècnica de València, Camino de Vera S/N, 46022 València, Spain
{aesteso,mareva,aortiz}@cigip.uvp.es
[2] IRIT, Toulouse University, Toulouse, France
zarate@irit.fr

Abstract. Consumers increasingly require products with higher qualities, leading to loss units not meeting these requirements. Collaboration can be used to increase first quality products production and reduce waste generated along the chain. A collaboration program consisting in a system of investments made by retailers to cooperatives to improve the skills of farms is proposed for this aim. The novelty of this paper is threefold: 1) the business model considered in which cooperatives distribute funds among farms, 2) the inclusion of the dynamic state of products, modelling the quality variation timewise, and 3) the mathematical modelling of five scenarios with different criteria for allocating funds to farms. Results are analyzed and compared for the three aspects of sustainability concluding that: 1) the collaboration program increases the quality of products sold, and 2) interesting tradeoffs occur among the sustainability dimensions, enabling the reduction of unfairness among farms by slightly worsening economic aspects.

Keywords: Agri-food · Collaboration · Quality · Unfairness · Optimization

Nomenclature

Parameters

s_i^{vt}	Quantity of vegetable v harvested in farm i at period t.
a_i	Area of farm i.
g_i^t	Proportion of product of first quality obtained by farm i at period t.
r_i^{vt}	Unitary cost for producing vegetable v at farm i at period t.
sp_j^{vct}	Unitary income for vegetable v with quality c sold to cooperative j at period t.
dij_{ij}^{vt}	Unitary cost for transporting vegetable v from farm i to cooperative j at period t.
djk_{jk}^{vt}	Unitary cost for transporting vegetable v from cooperative j to retailer k at period t.
dkm_{km}^{vt}	Unitary cost for transporting vegetable v from retailer k to market m at period t.

© IFIP International Federation for Information Processing 2020
Published by Springer Nature Switzerland AG 2020
L. M. Camarinha-Matos et al. (Eds.): PRO-VE 2020, IFIP AICT 598, pp. 546–559, 2020.
https://doi.org/10.1007/978-3-030-62412-5_45

djm_{jm}^{vt} Unitary cost for transporting vegetable v from cooperative j to market m at period t.

p_m^{vct} Unitary price of vegetable v with quality c sold at market m at period t.

pc^{vt} Unitary penalty cost for wasting or rejecting demand of vegetable v at period t.

d_m^{vct} Demand of vegetable v with quality c in market m at period t.

l_i Initial skill level of farm i.

L Number of skill levels at the CP.

h Cost of increasing one skill level at the CP.

β Improvement of the first quality product proportion per skill level.

b_k Budget available at retailer k for investments in the CP.

Decision variables

QH_i^{vct} Quantity of vegetable v with quality c harvested in farm i at period t.

I_i^{vct} Quantity of vegetable v with quality c stored in farm i at period t.

W_i^{vct} Quantity of vegetable v with quality c wasted at farm i at period t.

QJ_{ij}^{vct} Quantity of vegetable v with quality c transported from farm i to cooperative j at t.

QK_{jk}^{vct} Quantity of vegetable v with quality c transported from cooperative j to retailer k at t.

QM_{jm}^{vct} Quantity of vegetable v with quality c transported from cooperative j to market m at t.

Q_{km}^{vct} Quantity of vegetable v with quality c transported from retailer k to market m at t.

RD_m^{vt} Quantity of vegetable v demand rejected in market m at period t.

SL_i Current skill level of farm i.

FI_{ik} Number of investments made by retailer k to farm i.

D_i Economic unfairness for farm i.

X_i Unfairness in the allocation of investments for farm i.

1 Introduction

Society is increasingly requiring products with higher qualities, what leads to the waste of products not reaching the required quality. At present, this entails wasting one third of the global harvest [1]. According to the FAO [2], these waste have to be reduced by 60% by 2050 to ensure the sustainability of the agri-food sector.

As a solution, different authors [3–9] implement a collaboration program (CP) among the members of agricultural supply chains to increase the proportion of high quality products to be obtained from the same land. This CP consists in a system of investments made by retailers to small farms (less than 2 ha) that allows them to acquire new technologies, machineries and/or training [3]. It is remarkable that research on agri-food supply chain collaboration particularly focusing on small-scale farmers is in its early development [10, 11]. The main characteristics of the CP contemplated in these studies are displayed in Table 1, in which CP proposed in this paper is also characterized to establish its differences from existing literature.

Table 1. Literature review

Reference	CP participants			Type of funding distribution		Main criteria for funding distribution		
	F	C	MR	S	M	SCP	UFD	UID
Esteso et al. [3]	X		X	X		X		
Sutopo et al. [4]	X		X	X		X		
Sutopo et al. [5]	X		X	X		X		
Sutopo et al. [6]	X		X	X		X		
Sutopo et al. [7]	X		X	X		X		
Sutopo et al. [8]	X		X	X		X		
Wahyudin et al. [9]	X		X	X		X		
This paper	X	X	X	X	X	X	X	X

F: Small farm, C: Cooperative, MR: Modern retailer, S: Single criteria, M: Multiple criteria; SCP: Supply chain profits, UFD: Unfairness in funds distribution, UIC: Unfairness in incomes distribution

The analyzed papers [3–9] do not take into account the cooperatives in the CP. However, a cooperative is an aggrupation of farms that assists its members to facilitate the commercialization of products and provide them resources for the improvement of products [9]. Therefore, it makes sense to think that cooperatives should be responsible of distributing investments made by retailers among their members. On the other hand, analyzed CP decided how to distribute funds among farmers only attending to economic reasons. However, when centrally optimize the entire SC profits leads to inequalities in the profits obtained by the SC members, creating an unfairness concern among them [12] and the unwillingness to collaborate in the implementation of decisions [13].

To fill this gap in literature, this paper adapts the model proposed in [3] to this new business model. In this novel environment, it is necessary to consider the cooperative role when selecting possible ways of distributing funds among farms, what defines different collaboration scenarios. Collaboration arises from the agreements and trust mechanisms accepted and adopted by members from a SC [14]. Collaboration plays an important role in this problem since decisions are made in a synchronized way to obtain better solutions for the entire supply chain (SC) and an incentive alignment is made by distributing the investments among farms [15]. Five different mathematical models are developed for each collaboration scenario. Besides, all models include the transformation of 1st quality product into 2nd quality over time due to the perishability of the agricultural products.

The rest of the paper is structured as follows. Section 2 describes the problem under study and the collaboration scenarios identified in the agri-food sector. Section 3 presents the MILP models developed for the defined scenarios. Section 4 implements the models and evaluate the solutions for different indicators related to the triple bottom line. Finally, Sect. 5 outlines conclusions and future research lines.

2 Problem and Collaboration Scenarios Description

The SC under study commercializes vegetables with limited shelf-life. It is composed by small farms, cooperatives, modern retailers, and consumer markets. Small farms are responsible for the cultivating and harvest of vegetables, their classification into 1st and 2nd quality products and their transport to cooperatives. Cooperatives transport 1st quality products to retailers who commercialize them to consumer markets, and 2nd quality product directly to consumer markets where are sold at a very low price. Due to the perishability of vegetables, 1st quality products become 2nd quality products if they are not sold in the same period of their harvest. In addition, 2nd quality products become uneatable from one period to the next, what leads to the waste of unsold units.

A CP is implemented to increase the quantity of 1st quality products to be obtained from harvest and to reduce the waste generated along the chain. It consists on a system of investments made by retailers to cooperatives, who share the collected investments among the farm members. The CP defines three farming skill levels related to the proportion of 1st quality product obtained from harvest. Each fund allows farms to improve the 1st quality proportion and move up from one skill level to another. The budget for the CP is limited as well as the number of funds that each farm can receive. Different scenarios for the distribution of funds among farms are analyzed (Fig. 1).

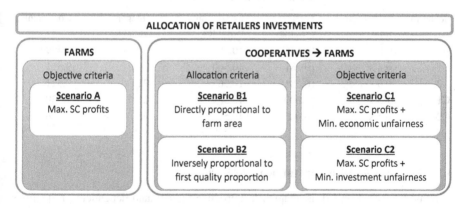

Fig. 1. Scenarios for funding allocation

In Scenario A retailers directly invest on those farms that maximize the SC profits such as in [3]. In the rest of scenarios, retailers invest in cooperatives that share funds among their members. In Scenarios B, cooperatives distribute the funds according to a fixed allocation criterion while in Scenarios C, cooperatives allocate the funds to farms by optimizing two SC objectives. More specifically, in Scenario B1, cooperatives distribute the funds in a way proportional to the farms area (biggest farms obtain more funds) while in Scenario B2, cooperatives distribute the funds in an inversely proportional way to the mean 1st quality proportion of farms (farms with lower proportion of 1st quality product would receive more funds). In case of Scenario C1, cooperatives allocate the funds to farms by maximizing the SC profits and minimizing the unfairness in the incomes received by farms. Finally, in Scenario C2, the funds distribution is made by maximizing the SC profits and minimizing the unfairness in the distribution of funds among farms. One MILP model is proposed for each of the Scenarios. It is noteworthy that the resulting MILP models for the scenarios C1 and C2 are multi-objective.

3 Mathematical Programming Models Formulation

The nomenclature employed to formulate the MILP models aligned to the proposed scenarios is exposed in Table 2, where v refers to vegetables, c to the quality of vegetables, i to small farms, j to cooperatives, k to modern retailers, m to consumer markets, t to the period of time, FC_i to the set of small farms that belong to the cooperative j, and IJ_j to the cooperative to which farm i belongs.

Table 2. Computational efficiency

Scenario	Resolution time	Total variables	Continuous variables	Integer variables	Constraints
A	0.5 s	10,578	10,560	18	9,499
B1	0.4 s	10,581	10,560	21	9,511
B2	0.6 s	10,581	10,560	21	9,511
C1	1.3 s	10,600	10,579	21	9,530
C2	0.5 s	10,600	10,560	40	9,530

3.1 Scenario A: Direct Investments to Farms

This model, based on [3], is adapted to introduce the demand dependent on qualities and the evolution of qualities with time. It maximizes the SC profits composed by the incomes per sales of vegetables, production and transport costs, penalty costs related to waste and unmet demand, and the investments made within the CP (1).

$$
\max Z_A = \sum_v \sum_c \sum_t \left(\sum_k \sum_m Q_{km}^{vct} \cdot p_m^{vct} + \sum_j \sum_m QM_{jm}^{vct} \cdot p_m^{vct} - \sum_i QH_i^{vct} \cdot r_i^{vct} \right.
$$
$$
- \sum_i \sum_{j \in FC_i} QJ_{ij}^{vct} \cdot dij_{ij}^{vt} - \sum_j \sum_k QK_{jk}^{vct} \cdot djk_{jk}^{vt}
$$
$$
- \sum_j \sum_m QM_{jm}^{vct} \cdot djm_{jm}^{vt} - \sum_k \sum_m Q_{km}^{vct} \cdot dkm_{km}^{vt}
$$
$$
\left. - \sum_i W_i^{vct} \cdot pc^{vt} - \sum_m RD_m^{vct} \cdot pc^{vt} \right) - \sum_i \sum_k F_{ik} \cdot h
$$

$$(1)$$

The model is subjected to the following constraints. All product ready for harvest in one period is harvested by farmers (2) and classified into 1st quality and 2nd quality products.

$$
s_i^{vt} = \sum_c QH_i^{vct} \qquad \forall v, t, i \tag{2}
$$

To determine the quantity of 1st quality products, the total quantity to be harvested is multiplied by the initial proportion of 1st quality products at the farm in this period plus the improvement of such proportion thanks to the CP (3). The rest of harvested product is classified as 2nd quality products (4).

$$
QH_i^{vct} = s_i^{vt} \cdot \left(g_i^t + \beta \cdot SL_i \right) \qquad \forall v, c = 1, t, i \tag{3}
$$

$$
QH_i^{vct} = s_i^{vt} \cdot \left(1 - g_i^t - \beta \cdot SL_i \right) \qquad \forall v, c = 2, t, i \tag{4}
$$

Once harvested, the 1st quality product can be transported to the cooperative, stored at the farming location until the following period, or wasted (5). In case a 1st quality product is stored, it is transformed into 2nd quality product in the following period (6).

$$
QH_i^{vct} = \sum_{j \in FC_i} QJ_{ij}^{vct} + W_i^{vct} + I_i^{vct} \qquad \forall v, c = 1, t, i \tag{5}
$$

$$
I_i^{v1t} = I_i^{v2t+1} \qquad \forall v, t, i \tag{6}
$$

On the other hand, the 2nd quality product harvested, and the 2nd quality product originated from 1st quality product transformation can be transported to cooperatives or wasted (7). Note that 2nd quality product cannot be stored from one period to the following due to perishability and quality loss reasons.

$$
QH_i^{vct} + I_i^{vct} = \sum_{j \in FC_i} QJ_{ij}^{vct} + W_i^{vct} \qquad \forall v, c = 2, t, i \tag{7}
$$

Once 1ˢᵗ and 2ⁿᵈ quality products arrive to the cooperative, 1ˢᵗ quality products are transported to modern retailers (8) while 2ⁿᵈ quality products are directly transported to consumer markets (10). Therefore, it is not allowed to transport 1ˢᵗ quality products from cooperatives to consumer markets (9) and 2ⁿᵈ quality products from cooperatives to modern retailers (11).

$$\sum_i QJ_{ij}^{vct} = \sum_k QK_{jk}^{vct} \qquad \forall v, c = 1, t, j \qquad (8)$$

$$QM_{jm}^{vct} = 0 \qquad \forall v, c = 1, t, j \qquad (9)$$

$$\sum_i QJ_{ij}^{vct} = \sum_m QM_{jm}^{vct} \qquad \forall v, c = 2, t, j \qquad (10)$$

$$QK_{jk}^{vct} = 0 \qquad \forall v, c = 2, t, j \qquad (11)$$

On their part, modern retailers are responsible of transporting the received 1ˢᵗ quality products to the consumer markets (12).

$$\sum_j QK_{jk}^{vct} = \sum_m Q_{km}^{vct} \qquad \forall v, c, t, k \qquad (12)$$

Finally, the demand for each product and quality is met at consumer markets. In case there is not enough product to meet the demand, unmet demand is calculated (13).

$$\sum_k Q_{km}^{vct} + \sum_j QM_{jm}^{vct} + RD_m^{vct} = d_m^{vct} \quad \forall v, c, t, m \qquad (13)$$

Regarding the CP, it is ensured that the proportion of first quality product obtained at each farm is lower or equal to the unit (14).

$$g_i^t + \beta \cdot SL_i \leq 1 \qquad \forall i, t \qquad (14)$$

The skill level of each farm is limited by the quantity of skill levels defined in the CP (15). In addition, the skill level of each farm depends on their initial skill level and the number of investments received from retailers, in a way that one received investment switches the farm to the next skill level (16).

$$SL_i \leq L \qquad \forall i \qquad (15)$$

$$SL_i = l_i + \sum_k FI_{ik} \qquad \forall i \qquad (16)$$

The quantity of investments made by a retailer is limited by their budget for the CP (17).

$$\sum_i FI_{ik} \cdot h \le b_k \qquad \forall k \qquad (17)$$

Finally, the nature of variables is defined in (18).

$$\begin{array}{ll} QH_i^{vct}, QJ_{ij}^{vct}, W_i^{vct}, I_i^{vct}, QK_{jk}^{vct}, QM_{jm}^{vct}, Q_{km}^{vct}, RD_m^{vct} & CONTINUOUS \\ FI_{ik}, SL_i & INTEGER \end{array} \qquad (18)$$

3.2 Scenarios B: Investments to Cooperatives – Allocation Criteria

In Scenarios B, retailers invest on cooperatives that share the funds among their members according to different allocation criteria. Scenario B1 allocates the funds to farms in a proportional way to their areas while Scenario B2 allocated them in an inversely proportional way to the initial proportion of 1st quality production per farm.

The MILP model of Scenario A is adapted to Scenarios B by changing constraints related to the distribution of funds (16–17), and adding two new decision variables: FJ_{jk} reflecting the investments made by retailer k to cooperative j, and Inv_i referring to the number of funds received by farm i. Both scenarios pursue the maximization of the SC profits that is reformulated as in Eq. (19).

$$\begin{aligned} \max Z_B = \sum_v \sum_c \sum_t \Bigg(& \sum_k \sum_m Q_{km}^{vct} \cdot p_m^{vct} + \sum_j \sum_m QM_{jm}^{vct} \cdot p_m^{vct} - \sum_i QH_i^{vct} \cdot r_i^{vct} \\ & - \sum_i \sum_{j \in FC_i} QJ_{ij}^{vct} \cdot dij_{ij}^{vt} - \sum_j \sum_k QK_{jk}^{vct} \cdot djk_{jk}^{vt} \\ & - \sum_j \sum_m QM_{jm}^{vct} \cdot djm_{jm}^{vt} - \sum_k \sum_m Q_{km}^{vct} \cdot dkm_{km}^{vt} \\ & - \sum_i W_i^{vct} \cdot pc^{vt} - \sum_m RD_m^{vct} \cdot pc^{vt} \Bigg) - \sum_j \sum_k FJ_{jk} \cdot h \end{aligned}$$

$$(19)$$

Scenario B1. It allocates funds to farms in a proportional way to the farms' areas (the greater the area, more funds) and is formulated as follows.

$$\max Z_B$$

Subject to:
(2)–(15)

$$\sum_j FJ_{jk} \cdot h \le b_k \qquad \forall k \qquad (20)$$

$$\sum_k FJ_{jk} = \sum_{i \in IJ_j} Inv_i \qquad \forall j \qquad (21)$$

$$SL_i = l_i + Inv_i \qquad \forall i \qquad (22)$$

$$Inv_i \le \sum_{j \in FC_i} \sum_k \frac{FJ_{jk} \cdot a_i}{\sum_{i_2 \in IJ_j} a_{i_2}} + 0.5 \qquad \forall i \qquad (23)$$

$$FJ_{jk}, Inv_i \qquad INTEGER \qquad (24)$$

New constraints indicate that the number of investments made by retailers is limited by their budget (20), the number of funds received by a cooperative should be distributed between the farms of such cooperative (21). Each fund increases the farm skill level in one level (22). Finally, the allocation of funds to farms is made in a way directly proportional to the area of the farm (23). Since Inv_i is an integer variable, an 0.5 is added to (23) to round the obtained continuous value to the closer integer (and not the immediately inferior one).

Scenario B2. It allocates funds to farms in an inversely proportional way to the proportion of 1st quality products obtained by farms (the lower the proportion of 1st quality products, more funds) and is formulated as follows.

$$\max Z_B$$

Subject to:
(2)–(15), (20)–(22), (24)

$$Inv_i \le \sum_{j \in FC_i} \sum_k \frac{FJ_{jk} \cdot \frac{1}{g_i}}{\sum_{i_2 \in IJ_j} \frac{1}{g_{i_2}}} + 0.5 \qquad \forall i \qquad (25)$$

The model for Scenario B2 is formulated similarly to the Scenario B1 model by changing the way of allocating funds to farms. In this case, the number of funds received by each farm of a cooperative is inversely proportional to the initial proportion of 1st quality product obtained from harvest. In other words, more funds are allocated to farms with lower initial proportion of 1st quality product (25).

3.3   Scenarios C: Investments to Cooperatives–Objectives Criteria

In Scenarios C, retailers invest on cooperatives who share such funds among farms that compose them by optimizing more than one SC objective. A global objective is created by combining the objectives by means of the weighted sum method [16].

Scenario C1. It Scenario C1 maximizes the profits for the SC (Z_B) (19) and minimizes the economic unfairness among farmers (Z_u) (26). Therefore, this model decides the distribution of funds among farmers while finding a trade-off between the supply chain profits and the unfairness in the distribution of farmers' incomes.

The economic unfairness is calculated as the absolute difference between the incomes per hectare of each farm and the mean income per hectare for all farms belonging to the SC (27). So, the lowest unfairness is, the most equitable will be the share of incomes among farms. To solve the non-linearity of (27), it is transformed into linear Eqs. (28)–(30).

$$\max Z = w_1 \cdot \frac{Z_B}{Z_{B_{max}}} - w_2 \cdot \frac{Z_u}{Z_{umax}} \tag{26}$$

$$Z_u = \sum_i \left| \frac{\sum_{j \in IJ_i} \sum_v \sum_c \sum_t QJ_{ij}^{vct} \cdot sp_j^{vct}}{a_i} - \sum_{i'} \frac{\sum_{j \in IJ_{i'}} \sum_v \sum_c \sum_t QJ_{i'j}^{vct} \cdot sp_j^{vct}}{a_i} \right| \tag{27}$$

$$Z_u = \sum_i D_i \tag{28}$$

$$D_i \geq \frac{\sum_{j \in IJ_i} \sum_v \sum_c \sum_t QJ_{ij}^{vct} \cdot sp_j^{vct}}{a_i} - \sum_{i'} \frac{\sum_{j \in IJ_{i'}} \sum_v \sum_c \sum_t QJ_{i'j}^{vct} \cdot sp_j^{vct}}{a_i} \forall i \tag{29}$$

$$D_i \geq \sum_{i'} \frac{\sum_{j \in IJ_{i'}} \sum_v \sum_c \sum_t QJ_{i'j}^{vct} \cdot sp_j^{vct}}{a_i} - \frac{\sum_{j \in IJ_i} \sum_v \sum_c \sum_t QJ_{ij}^{vct} \cdot sp_j^{vct}}{a_i} \forall i \tag{30}$$

Subject to:
(2)–(15), (20)–(22), (24)

Scenario C2. It maximizes the profits for the SC (Z_B) (19) and minimizes the unfairness in the distribution of funds to farms (Z_I) (31). Therefore, the model decides the distribution of funds among farmers while finding a trade-off between the supply chain profits and the unfairness in the funds' distribution.

The unfairness objective is calculated as the absolute difference between the number of funds received per farm and the funds received by all farms of the SC (32). To solve the non-linearity of (32), it is transformed into (33)–(35).

$$\max Z = w_1 \cdot \frac{Z_B}{Z_{B_{max}}} - w_2 \cdot \frac{Z_I}{Z_{Imax}} \tag{31}$$

$$Z_I = \sum_i \left| Inv_i - \frac{\sum_{i'} Inv_{i'}}{I} \right| \tag{32}$$

$$Z_I = \sum_i X_i \tag{33}$$

$$X_i \geq Inv_i - \frac{\sum_{i'} Inv_{i'}}{I} \forall i \tag{34}$$

$$X_i \geq \frac{\sum_{i'} Inv_{i'}}{I} - Inv_i \forall i \qquad (35)$$

Subject to:
(2)–(15), (20)–(22), (24)

4   Implementation and Evaluation of Results

The proposed models were implemented in the optimization software MPL® 5.0.6.114 and solved with the solver Gurobi^{TM} 8.1.1. Microsoft Access Databases were used to import input data and to collect the obtained values for decision variables. The computer used to solve the model had an Intel® Xeon® CPU E5-2640 v2 with two 2.00 GHz processors, with an installed memory RAM of 32.0 GB and a 64-bits operating system.

Data used to solve the models was extracted from [3] in which a 120 daily periods horizon (4 months) was considered with some modifications. Demand data is modified by multiplying it by a random value between 80 and 120% to create an imbalance between supply and demand. In addition, it is considered that 80% of demand is for 1st quality vegetables while the rest represents the demand for 2nd quality vegetables. It is also considered that vegetables have limited shelf-life since 1st quality products become 2nd quality in one period, and products of 2nd quality become uneatable in one period.

Four evaluation parameters aligned to the three aspects of sustainability are defined to compare results obtained by the proposed scenarios and a scenario not considering the CP (No CP scenario): i) SC profits (economic), ii) proportion of harvest wasted (environmental), iii) unfairness in terms of incomes per hectare perceived by farms (social), and iv) unfairness in the allocation of funds to farms (social). The percentage of unmet demand and the total harvest for both qualities are also analyzed. The results obtained for proposed scenarios are shown in Fig. 2.

The Scenario No CP obtains the worst SC profits and the highest 2nd quality products waste and 1st quality products unmet demand. This means that imbalances between supply and demand, produce oversupply of 2nd quality products and undersupply of 1st quality products. All these indicators are highly improved when considering the CP.

Scenario A is considered as the benchmark for the SC as it obtains the best values for the SC profit, the proportion of harvest wasted, and the percentage of unmet demand for 1st quality vegetables. However, it leads to the highest unmet demand for 2nd quality products and to high unfairness in terms of income per hectare and distribution of funds.

Scenarios considering the business model where cooperatives act as intermediaries deciding how to distribute funds among farms (B1, B2, C1, C2), worsen the SC profits in Scenario A by 16–19%. However, all of them triplicate the SC profits obtained when no considering the CP. In addition, these scenarios are fairer in terms of incomes and

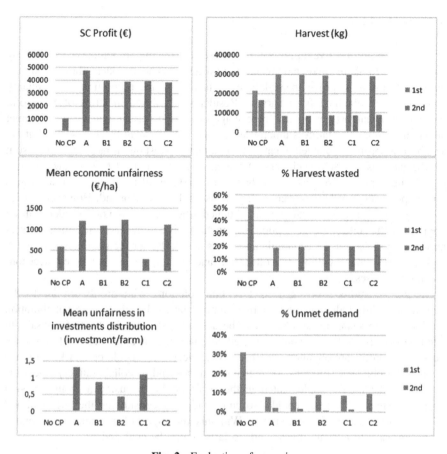

Fig. 2. Evaluation of scenarios

number of funds received by farms. This feeling of justice makes farms more willing to collaborate with the rest of actors of the SC.

It is remarkable that by considering objectives related to the unfairness perception by farms (Scenarios C1 and C2), the unfairness indicators can be highly reduced while the rest of indicators remain with similar results. These scenarios could be then used by cooperatives in cases in which farmers are very reluctant to collaborate and participate in a centralized decision-making approach.

The resolution time as well as the number of variables and constraints of solved models are displayed in Table 2 showing that proposed models solve immediately for the considered instance of data, and the size of the problem increases when investing in the cooperatives and when considering multiple objectives.

5 Conclusions

This paper proposes five optimization models considering different ways used by cooperatives to share funds among farms in a new business model. These funds are used by farms to improve their skill level, increasing the proportion of 1st quality products to be obtained from harvest. Results are analysed in terms of SC profit, percentage of harvest per quality, percentage of harvest wasted, percentage of unmet demand, economic unfairness among farms, and unfairness in the funds distribution. The best SC profit is obtained when retailers directly invest on farms (Scenario A) so it can be used as the SC benchmark. Although scenarios related to the new business model obtain profits 16–19% fewer than benchmark, all of them show similar results for the percentage of harvest per quality, waste and unmet demand. However, implementing the CP triples the SC profits obtained when the CP is not considered in all scenarios. The unfairness perception among farms is highly decreased in these scenarios (up to 75% for the economic unfairness and 100% for the unfairness in funds), making farms more willing to collaborate and participate in centralized decision-making processes.

Therefore, more effort is needed to find solutions with profits similar to the benchmark while reducing the unfairness among farms. For that, more collaboration mechanisms to share investments could be defined and tested in future proposals. In addition, the Nash theory could be used to share the incomes among farms once benchmark profits are obtained. Another future research line could be to ask real farms to rank the obtained solutions for defined scenarios and to collaboratively select the solution to be finally implemented in the agri-food SC by using a group decision support system. This study could also be extended by considering the uncertain and fuzzy nature of the models' parameters. With this, the impact of such uncertainty on the proposed ways to allocate investments to farms could be analyzed.

Acknowledgments. The authors acknowledge the partial support of Project 691249, "RUC-APS: Enhancing and implementing Knowledge based ICT solutions within high Risk and Uncertain Conditions for Agriculture Production Systems", funded by the EU under its funding scheme H2020-MCSA-RISE-2015.

References

1. Azevedo, S., Silva, M., Matias, J., Dias, G.: The influence of collaboration initiatives on the sustainability of the cashew supply chain. Sustainability **10**, 2075 (2018). https://doi.org/10.3390/su10062075
2. FAO: The future of food and agriculture - Trends and challenges, Rome (2017)
3. Esteso, A., del Mar E. Alemany, M., Ortiz, Á., Guyon, C.: A collaborative model to improve farmers' skill level by investments in an uncertain context. In: Camarinha-Matos, L.M., Afsarmanesh, H., Rezgui, Y. (eds.) PRO-VE 2018. IAICT, vol. 534, pp. 590–598. Springer, Cham (2018). https://doi.org/10.1007/978-3-319-99127-6_51

4. Sutopo, W., Hisjam, M., Yuniaristanto: An agri-food supply chain model to empower farmers for supplying deteriorated product to modern retailer. In: Yang, G.-C., Ao, S.-I., Huang, X., Castillo, O. (eds.), IAENG Transaction Engineering Technologies, Special Issue International MultiConference of Engineering and Computer Science 2012. Springer, Netherlands, Dordrecht, pp. 189–202 (2013). https://doi.org/10.1007/978-94-007-5651-9_14

5. Sutopo, W., Hisjam, M., Yuniaristanto, Kurniawan, B.: A goal programming approach for assessing the financial risk of corporate social responsibility programs in agri-food supply chain network. In: Proceeding of the World Congress on Engineering 2013, vol. I, pp. 732–736 (2013)

6. Sutopo, W., Hisjam, M., Yuniaristanto, : An agri-food supply chain model for cultivating the capabilities of farmers accessing market using social responsibility program. Int. Sch. Sci. Res. Innov. 5, 1588–1592 (2011)

7. Sutopo, W., Hisjam, M., Yuniaristanto, : An agri-food supply chain model to enhance the business skills of small-scale farmers using corporate social responsibility. Makara, Teknol. 16, 43–50 (2012)

8. Sutopo, W., Hisjam, M., Yuniaristanto: Developing an agri-food supply chain application for determining the priority of CSR program to empower farmers as a qualified supplier of modern retailer. In: 2013 World Congress Engineering and Computer Science WCECS 2013, vol. 2, pp. 1180–1184 (2013)

9. Wahyudin, R.S., Sutopo, W., Hisjam, M., Yuniaristanto, Kurniawan, B.: An agri-food supply chain model for cultivating the capabilities of farmers in accessing capital using corporate social responsibility program. In: Proceeding of the International MultiConference of Engineering and Computer Science, vol II, pp. 877–882 (2015)

10. Plà, L.M., Sandars, D.L., Higgins, A.J.: A perspective on operational research prospects for agriculture. J. Oper. Res. Soc. 65, 1078–1089 (2014). https://doi.org/10.1057/jors.2013.45

11. Handayati, Y., Simatupang, T.M., Perdana, T.: Agri-food supply chain coordination: the state-of-the-art and recent developments. Logistics Res. 8(1), 1–15 (2015). https://doi.org/10.1007/s12159-015-0125-4

12. Moon, I., Jeong, Y.J., Saha, S.: Investment and coordination decisions in a supply chain of fresh agricultural products. Oper. Res. 20, 1–25. (2018). https://doi.org/10.1007/s12351-018-0411-4

13. Stadtler, H.: A framework for collaborative planning and state-of-the-art. OR Spectr. 31, 5–30 (2009). https://doi.org/10.1007/s00291-007-0104-5

14. Hernández, J.E., Lyons, A.C., Poler, R., Mula, J., Goncalves, R.: A reference architecture for the collaborative planning modelling process in multi-tier supply chain networks: a Zachman-based approach. Prod. Plan. Control. 25, 1118–1134 (2014). https://doi.org/10.1080/09537287.2013.808842

15. Esteso, A., Alemany, M.M.E., Ortiz, A.: Conceptual framework for managing uncertainty in a collaborative agri-food supply chain context. In: Camarinha-Matos, L.M., Afsarmanesh, H., Fornasiero, R. (eds.) PRO-VE 2017. IAICT, vol. 506, pp. 715–724. Springer, Cham (2017). https://doi.org/10.1007/978-3-319-65151-4_64

16. Esteso, A., Alemany, M.M.E., Ortiz, Á., Peidro, D.: A multi-objective model for inventory and planned production reassignment to committed orders with homogeneity requirements. Comput. Ind. Eng. 124, 180–194 (2018). https://doi.org/10.1016/j.cie.2018.07.025

Resilient Strategies and Sustainability in Agri-Food Supply Chains in the Face of High-Risk Events

Antonio Zavala-Alcívar[1], María-José Verdecho[2(✉)], and Juan-José Alfaro-Saiz[2]

[1] Faculty of Industrial Engineering, Universidad Laica Eloy Alfaro de Manabí, Manta 130214, Ecuador
antonio.zavala@uleam.edu.ec
[2] Research Centre on Production Management and Engineering (CIGIP), Universitat Politècnica de València, Camino de Vera S/N, Valencia 46022, Spain
{mverdecho,jalfaro}@cigip.upv.es

Abstract. Agri-food supply chains (AFSCs) are very vulnerable to high risks such as pandemics, causing economic and social impacts mainly on the most vulnerable population. Thus, it is a priority to implement resilient strategies that enable AFSCs to resist, respond and adapt to new market challenges. At the same time, implementing resilient strategies impact on the social, economic and environmental dimensions of sustainability. The objective of this paper is twofold: analyze resilient strategies on AFSCs in the literature and identify how these resilient strategies applied in the face of high risks affect the achievement of sustainability dimensions. The analysis of the articles is carried out in three points: consequences faced by agri-food supply chains due to high risks, strategies applicable in AFSCs, and relationship between resilient strategies and the achievement of sustainability dimensions.

Keywords: Agri-food supply chain · Sustainability · Resilience · High-risk events · COVID-19

1 Introduction

Throughout history, humanity has been challenged by disease outbreaks that have had unprecedented negative consequences on society, severely affecting and modifying common behavior and habits. The response of the countries affected by the COVID-19 pandemic is focused on rules such as movement restriction, social distancing, and border closures [1], generating deep and severe economic implications that affect the operations of the supply chains [2].

The agri-food supply chain (AFSC) is critical to the economic, environmental and social development of countries, and its disruption minimizes the achievement of food security, affecting mainly the most vulnerable populations [3]. Currently, it is one of the chains most affected by the COVID-19 pandemic due to the adaptive strategies to the interruptions it has experienced: panic buying, changes in food purchasing patterns, labor shortages due to social distancing and interruptions in transportation and

© IFIP International Federation for Information Processing 2020
Published by Springer Nature Switzerland AG 2020
L. M. Camarinha-Matos et al. (Eds.): PRO-VE 2020, IFIP AICT 598, pp. 560–570, 2020.
https://doi.org/10.1007/978-3-030-62412-5_46

supplies [2]. The severe effects of this challenge require different strategies and actions, including robust resilience strategies that minimize the ripple effect in the supply chain [4]. These applicable resilient strategies can affect the achievement of sustainability dimensions within supply chains [5].

The literature presents some studies that deal with the supply chain under high risks: influenza [6–9], Ebola [10], cholera [11–13]. These studies have focused mainly on the health sector, considering the analysis of types of procurement policies, limited resource allocation, distribution of medicines to vulnerable areas, and hospital and health facility responses [2]. In other words, actions taken concurrently with the interruption that mainly allow the primary care system to remain operational. Similarly, considering COVID-19 pandemic, research has been conducted to estimate the risks and possible effects on supply chains [2, 5, 14]. The analysis of resilient actions applicable in conjunction with sustainability objectives has been considered by [15]. However, this research does not generate an analysis specific to AFSCs.

Within the agri-food area, [16] focuses its analysis on supply chains under high risk from logistics management. [17, 18] analyze the AFSCs as a mechanism to minimize the spread of disease. However, these studies do not respond to a global analysis of resilient supply chain actions that should be applied when disruption occur and how they affect sustainability objectives. The purpose of this paper is to address this research gap. Then, the objective of this paper is twofold: analyze resilient strategies on AFSCs in the literature and identify how these resilient strategies applied in the face of high risks affect the achievement of sustainability dimensions.

The structure of this paper is as follows. First, the search parameters are defined. Then, the analysis of the articles is carried out in three points: consequences faced by AFSCs due to high risks, strategies applicable in AFSCs, and relationships between resilient strategies and the achievement of sustainability dimensions. Finally, conclusions are drawn.

2 Literature Review

2.1 Search Criteria

The methodological approach applied in this research is the Systematic Literature Review (SLR) proposed by [19]. The procedure applied consists of formulation of research questions; location of literature; selection; analysis and synthesis, and report of results. Considering the objective of this research, the following questions serve as a starting point: *What resilient strategies have AFSCs applied to address high risks such as pandemics? How do resilient strategies applied by AFSCs affect the achievement of their sustainability objectives?* The keyword used were: "resilience management", "high risk" and "agri-food supply chain". This allowed the structuring of search strings with these keywords, for example: ("outbreak*" OR "pandemic*" OR "epidemic*" OR "disease*") AND ("resilien*") AND ("supply chain") AND ("agri-food" OR "food" OR "agriculture*" OR "agribusiness"). The database used was Scopus. Initially, 75 articles were obtained. Later, results were filtered using the following criteria: English language, peer-reviewed indexed journals and time interval from 2000. This resulted in 25 articles, which are discussed below.

2.2 Results and Discussion

2.2.1 Consequences of High-Risk Events in AFSCs

In daily operations, members of supply chains suffer disruptive events that affect their normal operation and cause unforeseen changes and impacts on other members [20, 21]. The level of vulnerability of the supply chain and the type of risk that occurs has to be considered to analyze the level of impact [22]. Pandemics are classified as low probability events with high consequences (LPHC), and therefore have a higher level of impact on supply chains [23, 24]. The lack of capacity in the chain to anticipate or foresee the occurrence of disruption makes their consequences of high impact and even decisive for the continuity of the business [25].

The agri-food supply chain is highly vulnerable, having to adapt quickly to a disruptive event [1] to ensure food security [3]. While the COVID-19 pandemic is deploying, AFSCs have shown this capacity to recover and adapt to disruptive events on the demand and supply side.

The restrictions applied by the states to deal with the COVID-19 pandemic and the disorder in the purchasing attitude of consumers, drastically affected the operations of AFSCs. In the early stage of the social distancing applied in most countries [1], it caused a short-term shortage of supplies mainly due to consumer hoarding [3, 26]. This was exacerbated for perishable items where the food distribution system is based on just-in-time manufacturing and delivery to ensure consumption [27].

Labor shortages due to worker illness, self-isolation, or movement restrictions lead to supply-side disruption. Companies adapt their production system using alternatives such as half shifts, temporary employees, temporary closures of their manufacturing lines, or modification of their products to fit the market [28]. The closure of non-essential businesses during the disruption creates a pool of unemployed labor, which is mainly transferred to essential activities such as food distribution tasks [3]. The closure of borders increased the pressure for shortages, with supply chains having to adapt to new relocation protocols and creating unavoidable delays [1], although the food relocation system is guaranteed.

The consequences of disruption are also reflected in the medium and long term, where there is a growth in the online grocery delivery sector and a prioritization of local food supply chains [27]. AFSCs must adapt to these new consumer requirements.

2.2.2 Resilient Strategies Applied in AFSCs Affected by High-Risk Events

It is of utmost importance for the recovery of normality in a supply chain to establish the appropriate resilient strategies to deal with serious disruptive events. Strategies can be divided into three types: (1) proactive, (2) concurrent and (3) reactive depending on the phase of the disruption [29].

Proactive strategies are developed in the stage before the occurrence of the disruptive event and enable the prevention capability of the supply chain to be activated. To establish preventive strategies, it is necessary to consider the stakeholders, the risks, the vulnerability of the nodes and the possible results of the disturbances [30].

Concurrent strategies allow for resistance and rapid response when the interruption occurs [31]. Their main objective is to provide continuity of supply chain operations, although in many cases, the consequences of disruption make business continuity impossible. And reactive strategies correspond to strategies after surviving the disruptive event, i.e., they include recovery, learning, continuous improvement and adaptation to the new market reality, i.e., returning to the original state of the supply chain or moving to a better state [32, 33]. Table 1 shows the main strategies applied in the articles analyzed. The strategies are classified according to the stage of implementation (proactive (P), concurrent (C) or reactive (R)) and the type of risk category (supply (S) or demand (D)) in the supply chain.

Table 1. Principal strategies depending on the implementation stage and risk category.

Strategies	Articles	Implementation stage			Risk category	
		P	C	R	S	D
1) Policies for stock security, redundancy, and diversification in the stocking of raw materials	[33–36]	✓			✓	
2) Select flexible and agile suppliers with product support capabilities and geographic dispersion.	[27, 33–39]	✓			✓	
3) Implementation of special supplier contracting methodology for critical suppliers, multiple suppliers and substitute suppliers.	[27, 33–35, 37]	✓	✓		✓	
4) Fortification strategies in supply chain design allowing for production flexibility and reprogramming of production	[37, 38, 40, 41]	✓	✓	✓		✓
5) Increase robustness by introducing redundancy in production, excessive inventories and safety stocks	[42]		✓		✓	
6) Establishment of multiple supply and delivery routes; dual supply. Direct distribution to the customer	[26, 37, 39, 43]		✓	✓	✓	✓
7) Integration of logistics capabilities with those of its strategic supply chain local partners	[1, 26, 38, 42–44]		✓	✓	✓	
8) Multiple methods for collaborative forecasting, customer data collection and immediate information exchange.	[35, 36, 41]		✓	✓		✓
9) Interoperability of information systems; visibility and shared information for effective collaborative relationships and shared decision making.	[35, 36, 38–41, 43–46]	✓	✓	✓	✓	✓
10) Contingency plan and business reactivation; insurance and public-private strategic collaboration.	[26, 36, 39, 45]	✓	✓	✓	✓	✓
11) Redesigning the supply chain towards market adaptation	[36, 37, 39, 41, 43, 45]			✓	✓	✓

P: proactive; C: concurrent; R: reactive; S: supply; D: demand

Considering the supplier-manufacturer relationship to be paramount, strategies of stock security, redundancy, and diversification in the stocking of raw materials [33–36], select flexible and agile suppliers with product support capabilities and geographic dispersion [27, 33–39] and implementation of special supplier contracting methodology for critical suppliers, multiple suppliers and substitute suppliers [27, 33–35, 37]. These strategies should be implemented at the prevention stage considering the vulnerability of the focal company and its suppliers [21].

Considering the focal company, fortification strategies in supply chain design that allow for production flexibility and production rescheduling [37, 38, 40, 41] and that increase robustness by introducing production redundancy, excessive inventories and security stocks [42] are proposed. These strategies allow supporting the disruptive event and keeping the productive process adapted to the new reality. These operations depend on the level of connection and flexible commitment of the suppliers.

In the supplier-manufacturer-distributor relationships, the literature analyze strategies of establishment of multiple supply and delivery routes, dual supply, direct distribution to the customer [26, 37, 39, 43] and integration of logistics capabilities with those of its strategic supply chain local partners [1, 26, 38, 42–44]. A relevant characteristic is the use of local companies for the supply of products.

The customer is also considered in resilient strategies when disruptive events occur. Research proposes to establish multiple methods for collaborative forecasting, customer data collection and immediate information exchange [35, 36, 41]. These strategies are applicable in the concurrent and reactive stage of the interruption, considering the survival level of the supply chain. Another strategy of great interest is the interoperability of information systems for efficient, timely and joint decision-making by members of the supply chain [35, 36, 38–41, 43–46]. The adaptation to the new market requirements is applied as a reactive strategy considering a restructuring of the value chain to meet the new consumer requirements [36, 37, 39, 41, 43, 45]. This adaptation depends on the contingency plan and the reactivation of the business, with the public-private strategic partnership being essential to guarantee the continuity of the business [26, 36, 39, 45].

Some strategies remain active during all stages of the disruptive event, generating a continuous improvement cycle in the companies [4]. That is the reason why they are classified in the three stages. The strategies planned in the proactive stage can be implemented in this same stage or when a disruptive event occurs, and it is necessary to monitor their results in the concurrent and reactive stage to generate improvement during and after the disruptive event [30]. These strategies should be considered as interrelated actions, since the consequences of one type of strategy can also impact on the strengthening of others [41, 47].

It should be noted that the consequences of the disruption analyzed envisage a partial continuity of supply chain operations and do not encompass simultaneous interruptions on the supply and demand side for an indefinite period.

2.2.3 Relationships Between Strategies to Increase Resilience and Sustainability Dimensions

Resilient strategies applied when serious disruptive events occur, affects in greater proportion the achievement of the sustainability dimensions. Also, there are situations where sustainability strategies influence the ability of the supply chain to address unplanned disruptions [41], although this last issue is not analyzed in this paper.

Increasing supply chain sustainability imply pursuing three types of sustainability dimensions: economic, environmental and social. The economic dimension is extended in some works, e.g. [48–50], to include other classical business criteria conforming the economic-business dimension. Thus, this dimension focuses on criteria such as organization and strategy (OS), financial situation (FS), technological integration (TI) and product quality (PQ). The environmental dimension refers to criteria such as the rational consumption of resources (RCR), pollution control (PC) and waste management (WM). The social dimension considers stakeholder participation (SP), occupational health and safety (OHS), staff training and satisfaction (STS), and community commitment and support (CCS) [51–53].

Table 2 present a summary of the relationship between strategies to increase resilience and sustainability dimensions. Relationships can be positive when applying the strategy produces a positive impact on the sustainability dimension or negative when applying the strategy produces a negative impact on the sustainability dimension. Resilient strategies analyzed mainly affect the economic-business and environmental dimensions although they also impact the social dimension. In the economic-business dimension, the increase in costs translates into a negative impact on the financial situation of the company. In the environmental dimension, resilient strategies have the greatest impact on increasing resource use and waste management in the supply, production and distribution process. In the social dimension, the stakeholder participation is the subdimension that gets the most number of impacts.

Table 2. Relationships between strategies to increase resilience and the sustainability dimensions.

Strategies	Economic-Business				Environmental			Social			
	OS	FS	TI	PQ	RCR	PC	WM	SP	OHS	STS	CCS
1)	X	X		X	X		X				
2)		X	X	X		X	X				X
3)		X	X	X			X				
4)		X	X	X	X	X			X	X	
5)		X	X	X	X	X			X	X	
6)		X		X	X		X				
7)		X					X	✓		✓	
8)		X	✓				✓				
9)		X	✓	✓	✓		✓	✓			
10)	✓	X	✓					✓	✓	✓	✓
11)	✓	X						✓	✓	✓	✓

✓: positive; X: negative

Strategies 1, 2, 3, 6, and 7 characterized by flexibility, redundancy, and robustness of the supply and distribution process, increase the use of resources within the supply chain. Maintaining inventories to cope with disruptive events generates increased costs, and might reduce product quality due to expiration and increased stock management. Furthermore, AFSCs have a high rate of deterioration, especially of perishable products, and together with uncertain demand and transportation problems, this results in a percentage of items that cannot reach consumers and become waste [54]. If the product is not delivered to customers in time, it is no longer valuable and its subsequent disposal causes contamination. This also affects the social side of sustainability because it reduces the principle of food security for stakeholders, affecting mainly the most vulnerable population.

Sustainable procurement imply the need to evaluate suppliers and work with those with the best sustainable performance [55]. This strategy may generate an unintended inability to change between suppliers where the supply chain tries to ensure continuity, being a constraint. Applying the resilient strategy of maintaining geographically dispersed suppliers and flexible contracting policies affects the social dimension because the company will not contract exclusively with local suppliers. This situation is to be analyzed, given that if in the initial stage of the disruption total closure of borders occurs, it will affect the continuity of geographically dispersed supply.

Strategies 4 and 5 that establish flexibility, redundancy, robustness and reprogramming of production generate increased costs, greater pollution, and waste management. These strategies considered not clean, allow to face the interruption and respond immediately to the new market requirements. In applying these strategies, supply chains must take measures to ensure the safety and health of workers [28, 41], by prevention training and adapting jobs to biosafety needs. This changes the criteria for OHS and STS.

It is important to analyze the evolution of consumers, as established in strategy 8, mainly in the consumer confidence that allows to include safe redundant strategies in points close to customers and avoid increased costs and waste. This increases costs in the company because of the technological level required to implement it.

Some strategies do not conflict with sustainable criteria. Interoperability of information systems, visibility, and information sharing for effective collaboration and joint decision making (strategy 9), business and contingency planning (strategy 10), and subsequent redesign of the supply chain (strategy 11) are necessary to maintain continuity of operations and market adaptability [14, 15]. These strategies, although they generate associated costs, generate a positive relationship with the social criteria of sustainability, because of the use of local labor. It is necessary to strengthen public-private relations to guarantee the continuity of food security, mainly with the supply of the most vulnerable.

The strategies 6, 7, 8 and 9, of balancing global supply with local supply and the adaptation of technological strategies to maintain contact with the client allow social criteria of sustainability to be achieved. These strategies allow supply chains to have a more direct link with stakeholders and promote community engagement and support. These practices benefit the resilient and sustainable criteria of supply chains. It is necessary to increase the culture of development and dynamic capacities of workers as a multifunctional workforce and the formation of interdisciplinary groups to identify vulnerable processes in the supply chain [28, 56].

3 Conclusion

AFSC is being severely affected by the consequences of the COVID-19 pandemic, mainly in the supply of basic food items generating economic-business, environmental and social impacts in society. AFSC is vulnerable because of the high rate of deterioration of its products, its priority in society, the uncertainty of demand and distribution problems. It must generate resilient responses to face this type of interruptions that allow it to resist the disruptive event and continue with its operations adapted to the requirements of the market.

Previous literature develops an analysis of resilient strategies applicable when a serious disruptive event occurs in AFSCs but it overlooks to analyze the impact of these strategies on the sustainability dimensions. This analysis is essential for establishing business designs and policies that include both aspects and allow for business continuity.

This paper analyzes the pandemic risk in AFSCs, its consequences, the applicable strategies depending on the stage of implementation and supply/demand side. It also establishes the main relationships between the strategies to increase resilience and the dimensions of sustainability. The analysis showed a greater impact on the economic-business and environmental dimensions of sustainability, characterized by the flexibility, redundancy, and robustness of resilient strategies. AFSCs must redesign and adapt their value chain with short-term priorities such as adapting the production, distribution, and movement of their workers. Short food supply chains and local productions generate a rapid response to the presented disruption and approach to the consumer. In the long term, strategies that encourage digital preparedness and data sharing must be included. Digitization of the supply chain, building contingency plans and strategic public-private partnerships improve the quality of response to disruptions related to major disruptions without diminishing the achievement of sustainable dimensions.

Further research comprises the simulation of the application of the resilient strategies found in the literature that will allow to analyze their impacts on the economic-business, social and environmental dimensions of sustainability in a more specific way. In addition, human talent management during major disruptions such as pandemics has not been addressed in the AFSC literature. Strategies should be established to promote the development and dynamic capabilities of workers to increase their multi-functionality to cope with, for example, reduced working hours.

Acknowledgements. Authors of this publication acknowledge the contribution of the Project 691249, RUC-APS "Enhancing and implementing Knowledge based ICT solutions within high Risk and Uncertain Conditions for Agriculture Production Systems" (www.ruc-aps.eu), funded by the European Union under their funding scheme H2020-MSCA-RISE-2015.

References

1. Gray, R.: Agriculture, transportation, and the COVID-19 crisis. Can. J. Agric. Econ. **68**, 239–243 (2020)
2. Queiroz, M.M., Ivanov, D., Dolgui, A., Fosso Wamba, S.: Impacts of epidemic outbreaks on supply chains: mapping a research agenda amid the COVID-19 pandemic through a structured literature review. Ann. Oper. Res. (2020). https://doi.org/10.1007/s10479-020-03685-7
3. Hobbs, J.: Food supply chains during the COVID-19 pandemic. Can. J. Agric. Econ. **68**, 171–176 (2020)
4. Shashi, P., Centobelli, P., Cerchione, R., Ertz, M.: Managing supply chain resilience to pursue business and environmental strategies. Bus. Strateg. Environ. **29**(3), 1215–1246 (2019)
5. Ivanov, D.: Predicting the impacts of epidemic outbreaks on global supply chains: a simulation-based analysis on the coronavirus outbreak (COVID-19/SARS-CoV-2) case. Transp. Res. Part E Logist. Transp. Rev. **136**, 101922 (2020)
6. Mamani, H., Chick, S.E., Simchi-Levi, D.: A game-theoretic model of international influenza vaccination coordination. Manage. Sci. **59**(7), 1650–1670 (2013)
7. Liu, M., Zhang, D.: A dynamic logistics model for medical resources allocation in an epidemic control with demand forecast updating. J. Oper. Res. Soc. **67**, 841–852 (2016)
8. Hessel, L.: Pandemic influenza vaccines: meeting the supply, distribution and deployment challenges. Influenza Other Respir. Viruses **3**, 165–170 (2009)
9. Orenstein, W., Schaffner, W.: Lessons learned: role of influenza vaccine production, distribution, supply, and demand—what it means for the provider. Am. J. Med. **121**, S22–S27 (2008)
10. Büyüktahtakın, I., Des-Bordes, E., Kıbış, E.: A new epidemics–logistics model: Insights into controlling the Ebola virus disease in West Africa. Eur. J. Oper. Res. **26**, 1046–1063 (2018)
11. Anparasan, A., Lejeune, M.: Analyzing the response to epidemics: concept of evidence-based Haddon matrix. J. Humanit. Logist. Supply Chain Manag. **7**, 266–283 (2017)
12. Anparasan, A.A., Lejeune, M.A.: Data laboratory for supply chain response models during epidemic outbreaks. Ann. Oper. Res. **270**, 53–64 (2018). https://doi.org/10.1007/s10479-017-2462-y
13. Anparasan, A., Lejeune, M.: Resource deployment and donation allocation for epidemic outbreaks. Ann. Oper. Res. **283**, 9–32 (2019). https://doi.org/10.1007/s10479-016-2392-0
14. Ivanov, D., Dolgui, A.: Viability of intertwined supply networks: extending the supply chain resilience angles towards survivability. A position paper motivated by COVID-19 outbreak. Int. J. Prod. Res. **58**, 2904–2915 (2020)
15. Ivanov, D.: Viable supply chain model: integrating agility, resilience and sustainability perspectives—lessons from and thinking beyond the COVID-19 pandemic. Ann. Oper. Res. (2020). https://doi.org/10.1007/s10479-020-03640-6
16. Ekici, A., Keskinocak, P., Swann, J.: Modeling influenza pandemic and planning food distribution. Manuf. Serv. Oper. Manag. **16**, 11–27 (2014)
17. Miranda, R., Schaffner, D.: Virus risk in the food supply chain. Curr. Op. Food Sci. **30**, 43–48 (2019)
18. Magalhães, A., Rossi, A., Zattar, I., Marques, M., Seleme, R.: Food traceability technologies and foodborne outbreak occurrences. Br. Food J. **121**, 3362–3379 (2019)
19. Denyer, D., Tranfield, D.: Producing a systematic review. In: Buchanan, D., Bryman, A. (eds.) The Sage Handbook of Organizational Research Methods, pp. 671–689. SAGE Publications Ltd., London (2009)

20. Christopher, M., Peck, H.: Building the resilient supply chain. Int. J. Logist. Manag. **15**, 1–14 (2004)
21. Dolgui, A., Ivanov, D., Sokolov, B.: Ripple effect in the supply chain: an analysis and recent literature. Int. J. Prod. Res. **56**, 414–430 (2018)
22. Jüttner, U., Peck, H., Christopher, M.: Supply chain risk management: outlining an agenda for future research. Int. J. Logist. Res. **6**, 197–210 (2003)
23. Behzadi, G., O'Sullivan, M., Olsen, T., Zhang, A.: Agribusiness supply chain risk management: a review of quantitative decision models. Omega (United Kingdom) **79**, 21–42 (2018)
24. Kleindorfer, P., Saad, G.: Managing disruption risks in supply chains. Pr. Op. Man. **14**, 53–68 (2005)
25. Vishnu, C., Sridharan, R., Gunasekaran, A., Ram Kumar, P.: Strategic capabilities for managing risks in supply chains: current state and research futurities. J. Adv. Manag. Res. **17** (2), 173–211 (2019)
26. Deaton, B., Deaton, B.: Food security and Canada's agricultural system challenged by COVID-19. Can. J. Agric. Econ. **68**(2), 143–149 (2020)
27. Richards, T., Rickard, B.: COVID-19 impact on fruit and vegetable markets. C. J. Ag. Ec. **68** (2), 189–194 (2020)
28. Larue, B.: Labor issues and COVID-19. Can. J. Agric. Econ. Can. d'agroeconomie (2020). https://doi.org/10.1111/cjag.12233
29. Hollnagel, E.: Epilogue: RAG: the resilience analysis grid. In: Hollnagel, E., Paries, J., Woods, D., Wreathall, J. (eds.) Resilience Engineering in Practice: A Guidebook. Ashgate Pr., pp. 275–296 (2011)
30. Ponomarov, S., Holcomb, M.: Understanding the concept of supply chain resilience. Int. J. Logist. Manag. **20**, 124–143 (2009)
31. Wu, T., Huang, S., Blackhurst, J., Zhang, X., Wang, S.: Supply chain risk management: an agent-based simulation to study the impact of retail stockouts. IEEE Trans. Eng. Manag. **60**, 676–686 (2013)
32. Schmitt, A., Singh, M.: A quantitative analysis of disruption risk in a multi-echelon supply chain. Int. J. Prod. Econ. **139**, 22–32 (2012)
33. Vroegindewey, R., Hodbod, J.: Resilience of agricultural value chains in developing country contexts: a framework and assessment approach. Sustainability **10**, 916 (2018)
34. Behzadi, G., O'Sullivan, M., Olsen, T., Scrimgeour, F., Zhang, A.: Robust and resilient strategies for managing supply disruptions in an agribusiness supply chain. Int. J. Prod. Econ. **191**, 207–220 (2017)
35. Bottani, E., Murino, T., Schiavo, M., Akkerman, R.: Resilient food supply chain design: modelling framework and metaheuristic solution approach. Comput. Ind. Eng. **135**, 177–198 (2019)
36. Meuwissen, M., et al.: A framework to assess the resilience of farming systems. Agric. Syst. **176**, 102656 (2019)
37. Dutta, P., Shrivastava, H.: The design and planning of an integrated supply chain for perishable products under uncertainties: a case study in milk industry. J. Model. Manag. (2020). https://doi.org/10.1108/JM2-03-2019-0071
38. Aboah, J., Wilson, M., Rich, M., Lyne, M.: Operationalising resilience in tropical agricultural value chains. Supply Chain Manag. **24**, 271–300 (2019)
39. Ravulakollu, A., Urciuoli, L., Rukanova, B., Tan, Y., Hakvoort, R.: Risk based framework for assessing resilience in a complex multi-actor supply chain domain. Supply Chain Forum **19**, 266–281 (2018)
40. Das, K.: Integrating lean, green, and resilience criteria in designing a sustainable food supply chain. Proc. Int. Conf. Ind. Eng. Oper. Manag. **2018**, 462–473 (2018)

41. Zhu, Q., Krikke, H.: Managing a sustainable and resilient perishable food supply chain (PFSC) after an outbreak. Sustainability **12**, 5004 (2020)

42. Rozhkov, M., Ivanov, D.: Contingency production-inventory control policy for capacity disruptions in the retail supply chain with perishable products. IFAC-PapersOnLine **51**, 1448–1452 (2018)

43. Yavari, M., Zaker, H.: Designing a resilient-green closed loop supply chain network for perishable products by considering disruption in both supply chain and power networks. Comput. Chem. Eng. **134**, 106680 (2020)

44. Ye, F., Hou, G., Li, Y., Fu, S.: Managing bioethanol supply chain resiliency: a risk-sharing model to mitigate yield uncertainty risk. Ind. Manag. Data Syst. **118**, 1510–1527 (2018)

45. Jabbarzadeh, A., Fahimnia, B., Sheu, J., Moghadam, H.: Designing a supply chain resilient to major disruptions and supply/demand interruptions. Transp. Res. Part B Methodol. **94**, 121–149 (2016)

46. O'Leary, D.: Evolving information systems and technology research issues for COVID-19 and other pandemics. J. Organ. Comput. Electron. Commer. **30**, 1–8 (2020)

47. Zavala-Alcívar, A., Verdecho, M.-J., Alfaro-Saiz, J.-J.: A conceptual framework to manage resilience and increase sustainability in the supply chain. Sustainability **12**(16), 6300 (2020)

48. Fahimni, B., Jabbarzadeh, A.: Marrying supply chain sustainability and resilience: a match made in heaven. Transp. Res. Part E Logist. Transp. Rev. **91**, 306–324 (2016)

49. Verdecho, M.-J., Alarcón-Valero, F., Pérez-Perales, D., Alfaro-Saiz, J.-J., Rodríguez-Rodríguez, R.: A methodology to select suppliers to increase sustainability within supply chains. CEJOR (2020). https://doi.org/10.1007/s10100-019-00668-3

50. Bai, C., Sarkis, J.: Integrating sustainability into supplier selection with grey system and rough set methodologies. Int. J. Prod. Econ. **124**(1), 252–264 (2010)

51. Bai, C., Sarkis, J.: Green supplier development: analytical evaluation using rough set theory. J. Clean. Prod. **18**, 1200–1210 (2010)

52. Valipour, S., Safaei, A., Fallah, H.: Resilient supplier selection and segmentation in grey environment. J. Clean. Prod. **207**, 1123–1137 (2019)

53. Zimmer, K., Fröhling, M., Schultmann, F.: Sustainable supplier management – a review of models supporting sustainable supplier selection, monitoring and development. Int. J. Prod. Res. **54**, 1412–1442 (2016)

54. Yang, S., Xiao, Y., Kuo, Y.: The supply chain design for perishable food with stochastic demand. Sustainability **9**, 1195 (2017)

55. Zahiri, B., Zhuang, J., Mohammadi, M.: Toward an integrated sustainable-resilient supply chain: a pharmaceutical case study. Transp. Res. Part E Logist. Transp. Rev. **103**, 109–142 (2017)

56. Duong, L., Chong, J.: Supply chain collaboration in the presence of disruptions: a literature review. Int. J. Prod. Res. **58**, 3488–3507 (2020)

Digital Innovation Hubs for Digitalising European Industry

Cobotic Assembly Line Design Problem with Ergonomics

Mohammed-Amine Abdous[1,2(✉)], Xavier Delorme[1],
and Daria Battini[2]

[1] Mines Saint-Etienne, Univ Clermont Auvergne, CNRS, UMR 6158 LIMOS,
Institut Henri Fayol, 42023 Saint-Etienne, France
`mohammed.abdous@emse.fr`
[2] Department of Management and Engineering,
University of Padova, Vicenza, Italy

Abstract. Demands for smaller lot sizes of mass-customized products increased the need for flexibility and adaptability in production lines. Semi-automatic manufacturing systems that involve human operators as well as technological equipment increase the flexibility of manufacturing systems. Such systems combine the benefits of human flexibility and new industrial and assistive technology. The key combinatorial problem to solve in the design of semi-automatic manufacturing lines is the assembly line balancing problem with the selection of equipment. An efficient and sustainable line design requires a cost-effective choice of equipment, and the presence of human increase the importance of ergonomics. In this work, we propose a Multi-objective Mixed-Integer Nonlinear Programming (MO-MINLP) for the design of semi-automated assembly lines. The objectives are the optimization of the design cost and the ergonomics level, modeled with the fatigue and recovery of workers. We propose to solve the problem with a bi-objective local search algorithm, based on the Iterative Local Search metaheuristic. We apply the algorithm on a case study to illustrate the originality of the problem and the solving algorithm.

Keywords: Semi-automated manufacturing systems · Assembly Line Design Problem · Ergonomics · Human-machine collaboration · Industry 4.0

1 Introduction

The current industrial context is characterized by more and more demand for mass-customized products through high agility and flexibility of manufacturing systems. Flexibility and quick changes have become a critical factor in the design of manufacturing systems to adapt to the highly competitive global competition and changing demands. One of the factors that favorite the flexibility of manufacturing systems is the association of human and machine, with an adequate Level of Automation (LoA).

There are three types of manufacturing systems: manual; automated; and semi-automated systems. Even if a manual system is highly flexible and offers a better ability for complex parts assembly, the repetitive aspect of work and the manipulation of loads and heavy tools exposes industrial workers to work-related musculoskeletal disorders

© IFIP International Federation for Information Processing 2020
Published by Springer Nature Switzerland AG 2020
L. M. Camarinha-Matos et al. (Eds.): PRO-VE 2020, IFIP AICT 598, pp. 573–582, 2020.
https://doi.org/10.1007/978-3-030-62412-5_47

(MSDs). Hence, manual lines require a high level of ergonomics and safety. On the other hand, an automated production system provides advantages such as work without break and systems without ergonomic risks, but automatic system flexibility is low due to programming issues, and difficulty in assembling complex and small parts, furthermore, a full level of automation investment cost is high compared to manual systems. Semi-automatic systems benefit from the advantages and strengths of both parts but require an adequate Human-Machine collaboration.

The interaction between humans and machines in semi-automated systems improves complex assembly processes, especially when a machine or equipment provides power assistance to the worker [1]. With the ongoing process of digital transformation in Industry 4.0, there is more and more technological support to enhance the hybridization of collaboration between humans and machines in manufacturing systems. Among the technological equipment used in industry, e.g.: the intelligent automation devices, touch-based admittance control of the robot, collaborative robot (cobot), and assistive exoskeleton technology. There is also an emerging concept of Operator 4.0 [2], this concept within the framework of Industry 4.0 push towards better Human-Machine work for better ergonomics and sustainability of manufacturing systems.

The combinatorial problem associated with the sustainable design of semi-automatic manufacturing lines is the Assembly Line Design Problem with the assignment of operations and the selection of adequate collaborative equipment. This is a strategic problem that involves substantial costs, that contain costs related to the purchase and maintenance of equipment, spare parts, and workers' training. On the other hand, equipment affects the level of ergonomics and productivity of the line through their effect on the physical load of operations and their processing times. Since the design of semi-automatic assembly lines involves conflicting objectives, a multi-objective trade-off between cost and ergonomics could assist decision-makers to choose the most suitable design configuration of the line, from a set of trade-offs between the cost and the ergonomics.

In this article, we propose a bi-objective approach for the Assembly Line Design Problem for semi-automated assembly lines. The first objective is the total design cost, and the second is an ergonomics criterion that considers the fatigue and recovery of workers. In the sequel, the next Section presents a brief literature review of the existing literature related to our work and open research questions. In Sect. 3, we present the problem description and formulation. In Sect. 4, we describe a bi-objective algorithm proposed to obtain potentially non-dominated points. Section 5 presents a didactical example to illustrate the novelty of the approach and its potential. Finally, the conclusion and perspectives in Sect. 6.

2 Literature Review

Assembly lines are manufacturing systems designed for the final assembly of products. This mode of production is suitable for mass production, or mass customization. Several decisions have to be made in the design of assembly lines, including the combinatorial optimization problem of assigning different operations to be performed for each workstation, denoted the Assembly Line Balancing Problem (ALBP). The problem raise interest in the literature, research has been made on different variants of ALBP and solutions approaches [3, 4]. The ALBP becomes more complicated with equipment selection that considers the assignment of operations and the selection of equipment for each workstation referred to as the Assembly Line Design Problem (ALDP) [5]. In the literature, several works have focused on the ALDP and the introduction of ergonomics into the assembly systems. In the next Subsection, we present some related works regarding the ALDP while in Subsect. 2.2, we present works that integrate ergonomics into the assembly lines.

2.1 Assembly Line Design Problem

The articles that investigate the ALDP mainly consider the optimization of criteria related to the costs, such as in [6, 7]. Another related problem is the so-called Robotic Assembly Line Balancing Problem (RALBP), that extends the ALBP with the additional assignment of robots as workstations equipment [8, 9]. Other optimization problems that consider equipment selection are the transfer line balancing problem, these types of lines are fully automated in the majority of cases. In transfer lines, a machining tool (multi-spindle) performs machining operations by block [10, 11].

Since the ALDP present conflicting objectives, the problem was considered in a multi-objective approach, we refer particularly to the work of [12–15]. The literature review in [16] presents a more detailed review of cost and profit assembly line design and balancing problems.

Although the literature presents works that study the modeling and the resolution of the ALDP, usually, these works consider only automatic systems, without mention of human presence and consideration of ergonomics.

2.2 Assembly Lines with Ergonomics

MSDs are a significant source of disease and absenteeism, affecting the economics of the production system and resulting in high compensation and absenteeism costs [17], with a decrease in the overall system productivity and quality performance. Furthermore, the aging workforce aggravates the problem related to ergonomics, with two-third of the European Union workforce aged over 50 years old [14].

In the last decades, some works attempt to include ergonomics into the ALBP to mitigate the risks and reduce MSDs, but mainly focusing on manual assembly lines. Most articles in the literature consider the ergonomics with a risk assessment criteria, such as in [18, 19].

Quantitative and biomechanical models are used in some articles, e.g., in the work of [20] with the quantification of fatigue and recovery of workers in assembly lines. Energy expenditure and rest allowance models as quantitative criteria were used in the articles [21, 22], and the equipment vibration was considered recently in ALDP [23]. We refer for more details, to a recent literature review [24].

Contribution including the safety of workers and ergonomics are recent, and they are not numerous. Furthermore, they only focus on fully manual assembly lines. New advanced equipment and intelligent assistive tools, allow introducing the human-machine collaboration in the design of semi-automatic assembly lines. In this work, we aim to include ergonomics in the challenging assembly line design problem.

3 Problem Description and Formulation

An assembly line is composed of a set of workstations arranged in a linear form, and connected by a material handling device such as conveyor that transport parts between workstations at the end of takt time. The takt time denoted T represents the maximal amount of time sub-assembly products should be processed at a given workstation, often defined by customer demand. The assembly lines are paced without buffer, and the takt time or production rate ($\frac{1}{T}$) defines the pace of the line.

We consider the hypothesis of ALDP (cf. [5]). The decisions are the assignment of operations and the assignment of a unique set of equipment to each workstation. We consider semi-automatic assembly lines, with the presence of a worker in each workstation.

We suppose that equipment is composed of one or many components (e.g. basic manual tool and an exoskeleton). All operations could be executed with all equipment, and only one equipment could be assigned to each workstation. A given set of equipment could influence the physical load of operations and/or the processing time. Each set of equipment has an associated cost. The equipment influences the productivity and the level of ergonomics of a workstation.

The binary decision variable $x_{j,k}$ is used for the assignment of the operation $j \in V$ to a workstation $k \in W$, with $V = \{1,..,n\}$ the set of operations and $W = \{1,..,m\}$ the set of workstations. The binary decision variable $y_{i,k}$ is used for the assignment of an equipment $i \in E$ to workstation k, with $E = \{1,..,r\}$ the set of equipment. C_i represents the cost of equipment $i \in E$.

Equipment i influences the deterministic processing time $t_{i,j}$ of operation j and/or the physical load, defined with $Fload_{i,j}$. Operation time or processing time $t_{i,j}$ set the standard time in which a worker should complete a given operation j when executed with the equipment i. $Fload_{i,j}$ represents the physical load of operation j when executed with the equipment i. The assignment of operations to workstations must respect the takt time T.

3.1 Ergonomics Level

We use the fatigue and recovery model developed by [25] as a criterion for assessing the ergonomics level in a workstation k. The ergonomics level (i.e., the fatigue and recovery criterion) after one takt time in a given workstation is represented with the ALDP notations as in the following equation:

$$F_k = 1 + \left(e^{-K(\sum_{i\in E}\sum_{j\in V}\int_0^{t_{i,j}} Fload_{i,j}(u).x_{j,k}.y_{i,k}du)} - 1 \right) e^{-R.(T-\sum_{i\in E}\sum_{j\in V} t_{i,j}.x_{j,k}.y_{i,k})} \quad \forall k \in W$$

$$(1)$$

$F_k \in [0, 1]$ represents the level of ergonomics in workstation k after one takt time T, depending on a load of operation and the equipment assigned to that workstation. K and R are constant values, representing the worker's capabilities, which are considered as constant representing an average worker. We refer to the work of [20] and [26] for more details on the ergonomics model and its use in assembly lines, and on the assessment of ergonomics load of operations.

3.2 Multi-objective Mixed-Integer Nonlinear Programming

We present in the following the Multi-objective Mixed-Integer Nonlinear Programming (MO-MINLP). To include the ergonomics level in the ALDP.

$$OF1: Maximize\{Min_{k \in W}\{F_k\}\}; OF2: Minimize\left\{\sum_{i \in E} \sum_{k \in W} C_i \cdot y_{i,k}\right\} \quad (2)$$

$$\sum_{k \in W} x_{j,k} = 1 \quad \forall j \in V \quad (3)$$

$$\sum_{i \in E} y_{i,k} = 1 \quad \forall k \in W \quad (4)$$

$$\sum_{i \in E} \sum_{j \in V} t_{i,j} \cdot x_{j,k} \cdot y_{i,k} \leq T \quad \forall k \in W \quad (5)$$

$$\sum_{k \in W} k.x_{h,k} \leq \sum_{k \in W} k.x_{g,k} \quad \forall (h, g) \in P \quad (6)$$

$$x_{j,k}, y_{i,k} \in \{0, 1\} \quad (7)$$

The Objective Function (OF1) maximizes the ergonomics level at the most charged workstation (i.e., workstation k where the worker presents the lowest level of ergonomics: $Min_{k \in W}\{F_k\}$), while the OF2 minimizes the design cost of the assembly line. Constraint (3) assigns each operation to one workstation. Constraint (4) ensures that no more than one equipment can be assigned to the same workstation. Constraint (5) ensures the respect of takt time in each workstation. The respect of precedence constraints, defined with the set of precedence couple P is ensured with the constraint (6). Finally, decision variables are binaries (7).

The MO-MINLP defined with the set of constraints {(2) to (7)} is non-linear due to the OF1 and the product of the two decision variables $x_{j,k}.y_{i,k}$. The problem is denoted Cobotic Assembly Line Design Problem (CALDP) to refer to the specificities of semi-automated assembly lines proposed in this paper.

4 Multi-objective Iterative Local Search

ALDP is an NP-Hard combinatorial problem [5], in addition to the combinatorial aspects of the problem, the MO-MINLP, denoted CALDP in Sect. 3 presents also conflicting objectives, which are the investment cost and the level of ergonomics. It is important to define a compromise between the two objectives and to offer a quick solution to decision-makers. We propose to solve the problem with a metaheuristic.

The metaheuristic does not guarantee optimality but can achieve acceptable results in a reasonable computational time.

We propose a multi-objective metaheuristic, based on the well-known framework of Iterative Local Search (ILS) (cf. [27] for more details). ILS is a multi-start based metaheuristic that iterates a specific local search procedure from different starting solutions to sample various regions of the pool of solutions and avoid local optimum. We chose ILS to take advantage of the Cplex's built-in one-tree algorithm, details about the algorithm and its implementation are discussed in [28]. The one-three algorithm allows us to generate quickly multiple feasible solutions to the Robotic Assembly Line Balancing Problem or RALBP (i.e., a feasible balancing solution with operations and equipment assignment defined with a linear formulation from the literature [8]), all multiples solutions are stored in a set or pool of solutions. Since the objective is to improve the level of ergonomics and to reduce the cost, we can make local perturbation to all the solutions in the pool provided by Cplex to improve the values of objective functions.

Figure 1 depicts the pseudo-code of the ILS algorithm. We start by generating a pool of feasible solutions S, with different ergonomics level and different cost values that constitute our initial search space. Afterward, for each solution in S, we apply sequential local search procedures. Local search explores the search space, moving from a solution to neighborhood solutions that improves the objective functions.

Algorithm: Multi-objective Iterative Local Search

1: S=GeneratePool()
2: **for each** s_i in S **do**
3:     **do**
4:         $s^{break}=s_i$
5:         LocalSearchTask(s_i)
6:         LocalSearchEquipment(s_i)
7:     **while** ($s^{break} \neq s_i$)
8: **end for**
9: S=Filter(S)
10: **return** {S}

Fig. 1. Pseudo-code of the ILS algorithm

We start first with a neighborhood with operations, we apply sequentially the classical swap and shift neighborhood, as defined in [4]. The neighborhood applied in "LocalSearchTask" consists of all transformed solutions, which are obtained by a single feasible swap or shift move of operations, without changing the equipment already assigned in each workstation. A swap or shift select the operation to move from the critical workstation (i.e., the most charged workstation with the lowest ergonomics level) since it is likely what could maximize our ergonomics objective function. To improve the ergonomics level, we choose the steepest descent or best-fit procedure that chooses a move leading to the maximum improvement of the current ergonomics level.

Afterward, we apply a local search to optimize the cost "LocalSearchEquipment", without changing the assignment of operations and without decreasing the value of the ergonomics level. For all workstations, we swap the already existing equipment with another one, which is less expensive. The solution is kept when feasible, and when it improves the value of the OF2.

We apply the same two local search procedures as long as the solution stored at the beginning denoted s^{break} is different (i.e., different objective functions) from the solution at the end of the two local search procedures, to ensure that no better solution is still possible.

A filtering stage is applied to keep in the set S only potentially non-dominated points. We use the Pareto Dominance rules to decide if a solution is better than another with respect to both objectives (i.e., a set containing points not dominated by any other points generated by the algorithm constraint so far and using the Pareto dominance rules).

5 Illustrative Case Study

We illustrate the approach proposed in this paper with a case study. We use the Buxey ALBP instance from the benchmark of Scholl [4], precedence graph, operation's processing time data are available in https://assembly-line-balancing.de/.

The Buxey's instance has 29 operations; the takt time is equal to 1500 s with 14 workstations to assemble the product. Since there are no equipment and physical workload in the literature, we generate the missing data to apply our approach. We generate 10 equipment, with different corresponding costs. The most expensive equipment is better than the others in terms of productivity (lower processing times of operations $t_{i,j}$) and better ergonomics influence (lower physical load of operations $Fload_{i,j}$).

We apply the algorithm ILS to generate the potentially non-dominated points for this instance. We use Cplex V12.8.0 as a solver with default parameters. The application of the algorithm to the case has required computational time of 40 s and has led to the solutions represented in Fig. 2. First, the algorithm generated with the use of Cplex a pool of 30 feasible solutions, Fig. 2 represents the set of initial solutions with bleu diamonds. This initial pool constitutes the input of the ILS algorithm.

With ILS, we obtain 4 potentially non-dominated points, represented with the orange square in the figure. The potentially non-dominated points are obtained with ILS by improving the initial pool of solutions.

By comparing the difference in each criterion between the average solution in the initial pool and the solutions obtained by ILS, we found that, on average, the ergonomics level obtained with ILS is 4.56% better than the average solution of the pool. Also, the average cost is 2.07% lower with ILS than the average solution of the pool.

The approach we proposed is promising to optimize the values of the ergonomics and the total investment cost of assembly lines. Besides, the results are obtained quickly, especially for medium and long term assembly line design problem.

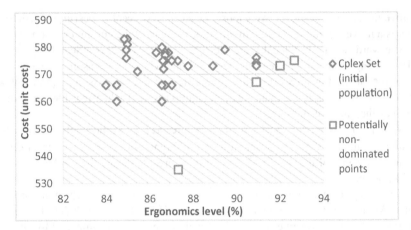

Fig. 2. Representation of solutions in the objective space; the x-axis represents the ergonomics level represented in percentage (%) that we seek to maximize, and the y-axis represents the total investment cost, represented in cost unit – Blue diamonds represent the pool obtained in the generation of initial solutions set with Cplex; Orange square represents the potentially non-dominated points, obtained with the ILS algorithm. (Color figure online)

6 Conclusion and Perspectives

The integration of ergonomics in manufacturing systems design has gained a growing interest in the last years, particularly for assembly lines. The present work has proposed a new approach with a CALDP model and solving approach, to design semi-automatic assembly systems by taking into account the ergonomics during the execution of operations, with the use of fatigue and recovery of workers as ergonomics criteria (i.e., ergonomics level). The objective functions aim at minimizing both the equipment total cost and the ergonomics level. The consideration of ergonomics in the design stage will also allow reducing the cost of future intervention on already existing systems, and enhance the Human-Machine collaboration. The application of the model to an illustrative case study from the literature shows its competitive computational time as well as its practical usefulness to define a set of potentially non-dominated points. The aim is to provide decision-makers with a model and fast multi-objective algorithm to identify the interesting trade-off between the conflicting objectives.

The Human-Machine collaboration in semi-automated assembly lines is motivated by the increased need for flexibility in manufacturing systems. An essential precondition for effective interaction between humans and machines is the ergonomics of the worker, not only physical but also cognitive. As perspectives, to enable safe sharing of the same physical space by humans and advanced robots and machines, cognitive ergonomics could be considered with the acceptability of new technologies by workers, to improve their acceptance and adoption of sophisticated technologies.

References

1. Krüger, J., Lien, T.K., Verl, A.: Cooperation of human and machines in assembly lines. CIRP Ann. **58**(2), 628–646 (2009)
2. Ruppert, T., Jaskó, S., Holczinger, T., Abonyi, J.: Enabling technologies for operator 4.0: a Survey. Appl. Sci. **8**(9), 16–50 (2018)
3. Battaïa, O., Dolgui, A.: A taxonomy of line balancing problems and their solution approaches. Int. J. Prod. Econ. **142**(2), 259–277 (2013)
4. Scholl, A.: Balancing and Sequencing of Assembly Lines. Physica-Verlag, Heidelberg (1999)
5. Baybars, İ.: A survey of exact algorithms for the simple assembly line balancing problem. Manage. Sci. **32**(8), 909–932 (1986)
6. Bukchin, J., Tzur, M.: Design of flexible assembly line to minimize equipment cost. IIE Trans. **32**(7), 585–598 (2000)
7. Bukchin, J., Rubinovitz, J.: A weighted approach for assembly line design with station paralleling and equipment selection. IIE Trans. **35**(1), 73–85 (2003)
8. Rubinovitz, J., Bukchin, J., Lenz, E.: RALB – a heuristic algorithm for design and balancing of robotic assembly lines. CIRP Ann. **42**(1), 497–500 (1993)
9. Borba, L., Ritt, M., Miralles, C.: Exact and heuristic methods for solving the Robotic Assembly Line Balancing Problem. Eur. J. Oper. Res. **270**(1), 146–156 (2018)
10. Delorme, X., Dolgui, A., Kovalyov, M.Y.: Combinatorial design of a minimum cost transfer line. Omega **40**(1), 31–41 (2012)
11. Battaïa, O., Dolgui, A., Guschinsky, N., Levin, G.: Integrated configurable equipment selection and line balancing for mass production with serial-parallel machining systems. Eng. Optim. **46**(10), 1369–1388 (2014)
12. Oesterle, J., Amodeo, L., Yalaoui, F.: A comparative study of multi-objective algorithms for the assembly line balancing and equipment selection problem under consideration of product design alternatives. J. Intell. Manuf. **30**(3), 1021–1046 (2017). https://doi.org/10.1007/s10845-017-1298-2
13. Delorme, X., Battaïa, O., Dolgui, A.: Multi-objective approaches for design of assembly lines. In: Benyoucef, L., Hennet, J.C., Tiwari, M. (eds.) Applications of Multi-Criteria and Game Theory Approaches. Springer Series in Advanced Manufacturing, pp. 31–56. Springer, London (2014). https://doi.org/10.1007/978-1-4471-5295-8_2
14. Finco, S., Abdous, M.-A., Calzavara, M., Battini, D., Delorme, X.: A bi-objective model to include workers' vibration exposure in assembly line design. Int. J. Prod. Res. (2020). 16 pages. https://doi.org/10.1080/00207543.2020.1756512
15. Pekin, N., Azizoglu, M.: Bi criteria flexible assembly line design problem with equipment decisions. Int. J. Prod. Res. **46**(22), 6323–6343 (2008)
16. Hazır, Ö., Delorme, X., Dolgui, A.: A review of cost and profit-oriented line design and balancing problems and solution approaches. Annu. Rev. Control **40**, 14–24 (2015)
17. Bevan, S.: Economic impact of musculoskeletal disorders (MSDs) on work in Europe. Best Pract. Res. Clin. Rheumatol. **29**(3), 356–373 (2015)
18. Otto, A., Scholl, A.: Incorporating ergonomic risks into assembly line balancing. Eur. J. Oper. Res. **212**(2), 277–286 (2011)
19. Choi, G.: A goal programming mixed-model line balancing for processing time and physical workload. Comput. Ind. Eng. **57**(1), 395–400 (2009)
20. Abdous, M.-A., Delorme, X., Battini, D., Sgarbossa, F., Berger-Douce, S.: Assembly line balancing problem with consideration of workers fatigue and recovery. In: International Working Seminar on Production Economics (2018). 12 pages

21. Battini, D., Delorme, X., Dolgui, A., Persona, A., Sgarbossa, F.: Ergonomics in assembly line balancing based on energy expenditure: a multi-objective model. Int. J. Prod. Res. **54**(3), 824–845 (2016)
22. Finco, S., Battini, D., Delorme, X., Persona, A., Sgarbossa, F.: Workers' rest allowance and smoothing of the workload in assembly lines. Int. J. Prod. Res. **58**(4), 1255–1270 (2020)
23. Finco, S., Abdous, M.-A., Battini, D., Calzavara, M., Delorme, X.: Assembly line design with tools vibration. IFAC-PapersOnLine **52**(13), 247–252 (2019)
24. Otto, A., Battaïa, O.: Reducing physical ergonomic risks at assembly lines by line balancing and job rotation: a survey. Comput. Ind. Eng. **111**, 467–480 (2017)
25. Ma, L., Chablat, D., Bennis, F., Zhang, W., Guillaume, F.: A new muscle fatigue and recovery model and its ergonomics application in human simulation. Virtual Phys. Prototyp. **5**(3), 123–137 (2010)
26. Abdous, M.-A., Delorme, X., Battini, D., Sgarbossa, F., Berger-Douce, S.: Multi-objective optimization of assembly lines with workers fatigue consideration. IFAC-PapersOnLine **51** (11), 698–703 (2018)
27. Lourenço, H.R., Martin, Olivier C., Stützle, T.: Iterated local search: framework and applications. In: Gendreau, M., Potvin, J.-Y. (eds.) Handbook of Metaheuristics. ISORMS, vol. 272, pp. 129–168. Springer, Cham (2019). https://doi.org/10.1007/978-3-319-91086-4_5
28. Danna, E., Fenelon, M., Gu, Z., Wunderling, R.: Generating multiple solutions for mixed integer programming problems. In: Fischetti, M., Williamson, David P. (eds.) IPCO 2007. LNCS, vol. 4513, pp. 280–294. Springer, Heidelberg (2007). https://doi.org/10.1007/978-3-540-72792-7_22

Analysis of Manufacturing Platforms in the Context of Zero-Defect Process Establishment

Artem A. Nazarenko[1]([⊠]), Joao Sarraipa[1], Luis M. Camarinha-Matos[1], Marc Dorchain[2], and Ricardo Jardim-Goncalves[1]

[1] Faculty of Sciences and Technology & UNINOVA-CTS, Nova University of Lisbon, 2829-516, Monte Caparica, Lisbon, Portugal
a.nazarenko@campus.fct.unl.pt,
{jfss,cam,rg}@uninova.pt
[2] Software AG, Darmstadt, Germany
Marc.Dorchain@softwareag.com

Abstract. The fourth Industrial Revolution sets higher standards for the manufacturing itself and all associated processes. A promising direction in this context is the concept of Zero-Defect Manufacturing (ZDM) aiming at further automatization and optimisation of the production processes to reduce resources and avoid useless elements in the production chains. Moreover, the modern industrial systems are highly complex and require collaboration with other systems for the products' manufacturing and maintenance. This fact leads to the necessity for the better approaches for design, development, evaluation and assessment of manufacturing systems. The goal of this article is to assess some key European research projects on industrial manufacturing to re-use their achievements for design of the ZDM systems. Another goal is to identify the basis for an umbrella platform able to integrate the functionalities of other manufacturing platforms. Thus, interoperability and collaboration issues are also in the scope of this work.

Keywords: Zero Defect Manufacturing · RAMI 4.0 · Industry 4.0 · Systems interoperability · Collaborative Cyber-Physical systems · Business ecosystem

1 Introduction

Technological advancements in recent decades led to a new era of manufacturing or 4th industrial revolution, introducing flexible production processes aligned with the customer's demands [1]. Transition to the new generation of manufacturing systems sets new challenges both at technological and organisational levels [2]. Some of the core challenges are: collaboration, safety and security, standardization, staff training, improved resources use, industrial infrastructure, complexity/cost reduction, real-time coordination and optimisation, interoperability [2–4]. Another important challenge is the digitalisation of manufacturing processes, whereas combining physical and cyber dimensions of industrial systems. Thus, complex industrial systems designed in line with the Industry 4.0 concept are, in fact, complex Cyber Physical Production Systems

Published by Springer Nature Switzerland AG 2020
L. M. Camarinha-Matos et al. (Eds.): PRO-VE 2020, IFIP AICT 598, pp. 583–596, 2020.
https://doi.org/10.1007/978-3-030-62412-5_48

(CPPS) containing collaborative components [2, 5]. CPPS cover the whole conventional automation stack [6]: (i) physics and mechanics of production, (ii) sensing and actuation, (iii) field level control over production process, (iv) execution system, and (v) enterprise resource planning with one additional dimension, namely the intersystems collaboration [2, 7]. However, the manufacturing processes are not limited to the production itself, but also include the whole product life cycle from design to postsale maintenance and even recycling.

Industry 4.0 implies production costs reduction, as well as resources use optimisation. This led to emergence of the Zero-Defect Manufacturing (ZDM) strategy. ZDM is directed towards achieving various benefits: lower energy consumption, lower costs, less scrap output, less material waste, production system resilience, improved production status overview, improved planning ability, etc. [8]. Among recent efforts made in line with ZDM strategy we can mention: the "ForZDM" and "ZAero" European projects. ForZDM implements the ZDM strategy through *"combining sensor readouts, visual inspections, or manual measurements at every production stage in a centralized database"* [9]. The proposed platform follows the "state of the art" architecture including the shop-floor layer, cyber layer, and the middleware layer. ZAero on the other hand targets the inline quality control for aerospace parts production merged with decision support systems and simulation [10].

This work is done in the context of providing the basis for the technological and standardization approach for the EU project Zero Defect Manufacturing Platform (ZDMP). ZDMP focuses on both Process and Product quality for pre-, during, supervisory, and postproduction quality issues. ZDMP targets an open Industry 4.0 environment where a new generation of developed zero-defect service applications will be available in a marketplace, contributing to create a collaborative business ecosystem [11] where ZDMP stakeholders would be able to interact with each other.

The remaining of this paper is structured as follows: Sect. 2 gives a brief overview of reference models for manufacturing systems; Sect. 3 discusses the strategy for manufacturing platforms assessment; Sect. 4 proceeds with the analysis of selected projects based on identified topics and discusses standardisation efforts towards ZDM strategy; and finally, Sect. 5 presents some conclusions and directions for further work.

2   Reference Architecture Models for Intelligent Manufacturing

It is very important that designed systems follow some standard or widely recognised architectural approach. In fact, the reference architectures can be used not only for designing new industrial manufacturing systems, but also to assess already developed systems. The use of reference models improves understanding if and how some of the elements of already developed systems can be reused in the newly designed systems considering collaborative and interoperability issues. Several efforts are undertaken towards establishment of common architectural approaches to industrial manufacturing platforms in regard to their functionality, technologies, and organizational structure. Some architectural approaches are of particular interest [12–15], such as: Industrial Internet Reference Architecture (IIRA), International Data Spaces Reference

Architecture (IDS RAM), Intelligent Manufacturing System Architecture (IMSA), Reference Architecture Model for Industry 4.0 (RAMI 4.0), and a Reference model for Collaborative Networks (ARCON) [16]. Some research activities target how the mentioned models can be aligned in terms of layers' concordance. Remarkable works are the joint report of Sino-German Industry 4.0 working group [17] addressing the alignment of IMSA and RAMI 4.0 architectural approaches, or the functional mapping of IIRA and RAMI 4.0 [18].

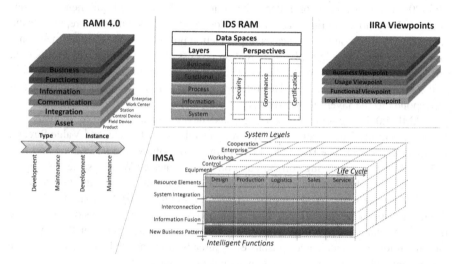

Fig. 1. RAMI 4.0, IIRA, IDS RAM and IMSA architecture approaches.

Figure 1 represents 4 reference models RAMI 4.0, IMSA, IDS RAM, and IIRA, which focus mostly on a single enterprise. For better understanding of layers' alignment and interoperability of different models, same colours are used to mark either completely interoperable system layers (horizontal layers) or layers with same functionality. Thus, Business layer, Business Viewpoint, or New Business Pattern are marked with the same colour; the same logic is applied to other layers.

IIRA is an open architecture for Industrial Information Systems (IIS) based on ISO/IEC/IEEE 42010:2011 standard [19]. The core four viewpoints of IIRA are: (i) Business, (ii) Usage, (iii) Functional, and (iv) Implementation. Business viewpoint serves the goal to assess the system from the business context, i.e. stakeholders' identification, visions, objectives, and high-level representation of how functionalities of the system are meeting the stated objectives. On the Usage layer a set of activities required for providing the system's functionality is presented. The system's structure along with core components, internal relations, and relation patterns with outer elements and systems are in the scope of the Functional layer. The Implementation layer copes with technologies for embodiment of functional blocks, communication schemes, and lifecycles of the designed systems.

The IDS RAM is an architecture aimed at *"generalisation of concepts, functionality, and overall processes involved in the creation of a secure "network of trusted data*" [12]. In spite of the fact that IDS RAM is mostly focused on processes around data, including generation, exchange, formats, and licensing, the model can be considered as relevant from the cyber perspective of CPPS. This model also partially follows the ISO 42010 standard and is similar to IIRA offering a common basis for compatibility. This architecture includes five layers: (i) Business, (ii) Functional, (iii) Process, (iv) Information, and (v) System, and three perspectives valid across all layers, that are: (i) Security, (ii) Certification, and (iii) Governance.

IMSA is a three-dimensional model, in some works referred as "Chinese Industry 4.0" [20]. The first dimension reflects the system levels [17]: (i) Equipment, (ii) Control, (iii) Workshop, (iv) Enterprise, and (v) Cooperation. This dimension represents the hierarchy of entities on various scales of production processes. The second dimension – Lifecycle, covers the stages of value creation process [15]: (i) Design, (ii) Production, (iii) Logistics, (iv) Sales, and (v) Services, i.e. form the products design and assembly to the after-sales maintenance. The Intelligent Functions is the third dimension and corresponds to the layers in RAMI 4.0.

RAMI 4.0 is focused on the design and development process of Industry 4.0 systems regarding 3 dimensions: (i) Hierarchy Levels, (ii) Lifecycle, and Value Stream, and (iii) Layers [13]. The Hierarchy Levels dimension follows the IEC 62264 and IEC 61512 standards considering collaboration on the "Connected World" scale and degree of product's involvement on every manufacturing or maintenance stage in "Product" [21]. Other levels are: (i) Enterprise, (ii) Work Centres, (iii) Station, (iv) Control Device, and Field Device (v). The Life Cycle and Value Stream dimension follows the IEC 62890 standard, whereas introducing the differentiation between the "type" – virtual prototype, model, and "instance" – already implemented object or software component, subdivided onto development/and maintenance stages.

The Layers dimension of RAMI 4.0 introduces the building blocks from which the system comprises. There are 6 sub-layers within the "Layers" dimension: (i) Business, (ii) Functional, (iii) Information, (iv) Communication, (v) Integration, and (vi) Asset, covering the whole CPPS stack from machines to high-level business processes.

Although the mentioned models briefly refer to the "collaboration perspective", a core enabler of Industry 4.0 [2], they are mostly focused on the "internals" of a single enterprise. On a completely different direction, ARCON [16, 22] is focused on collaborative networks, thus better addressing the value chain perspective and distributed manufacturing systems. ARCON considers 3 main dimensions (Fig. 2): (i) Life-cycle, (ii), Environment characteristics, and (iii) Modelling intent. The environment characteristics include the Endogenous Elements of the CN (E1- Structural, E2- Componential, E3- Functional, E4- Behavioural) and the Exogenous Interactions of the CN (I1-Market, I2- Support, I3- Societal, I4-Constituency).

3   Strategy for Manufacturing Platforms Assessment

The analysis of current manufacturing initiatives and projects can give a good indication for the establishment of the manufacturing platforms assessment strategy, allowing getting the best practices, as well as avoiding unnecessary efforts to develop components from the scratch. Moreover, the marketplace being developed within the

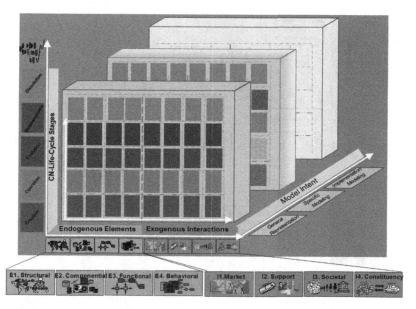

Fig. 2. ARCON reference model framework for collaborative networks (based on [16]).

ZDMP project can benefit from collaboration with other manufacturing platforms and services. This may enrich the marketplace and create a kind of "umbrella" platform, integrating the European efforts towards intelligent manufacturing systems. As ZDMP follows the RAMI 4.0 architectural approach, the studied manufacturing platforms were analysed using the same reference model in order to have a common basis, which is crucial for compatibility and interoperability of the ZDMP platform with other manufacturing platforms. To summarise the efforts undertaken to fulfil the stated goals, the high-level vision of the steps required is introduced:

The methodology to analyse deliverables of manufacturing research projects in order to establish the manufacturing platforms assessment strategy has three stages: Alignment, Analysis, and Estimation (Fig. 3). At the first stage the requirements and goals are identified and set, followed by the focus points such as security, privacy, application/user metadata, underlying technologies, and licensing. The second stage presumes the application of RAMI 4.0 architectural framework to the analysed projects in order to identify which components of the manufacturing platforms are covering the previously mentioned focus points and how they are addressed, in other words, what technologies and approaches are used. During the last stage the important goal is to understand how the identified technologies suit the focus points and how they are compatible (Layers in RAMI 4.0) with the ZDMP platform being developed. A final task is to develop a strategy or a common approach for integration/adoption of manufacturing applications into the common ecosystem. It is important to mention that this particular work is mostly focused on second stage that is Analysis.

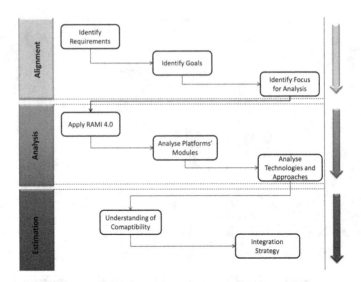

Fig. 3. High-level vision of platforms assessment strategy

4 Manufacturing Platforms Assessment Results and Discussion

The architectural approaches described in the second section serve the purpose of common understanding of standards, technologies, protocols and use-cases. System design by following one of the mentioned architectural approaches should simplify further collaboration, enable the modular system composition and contribute to inter-operability. This means that required functionality can be delivered on demand without requiring enormous efforts to align blocks developed in different platforms but following the same approach.

For this work the RAMI 4.0 was chosen, based on various reasons: (i) RAMI 4.0 is compatible with other reference models, (ii) some analysed projects already follow this methodology, as for instance BEinCPPS [23], (iii) ZDMP project is making use of the RAMI 4.0 [13], (iv) RAMI 4.0 is compatible with OSI and Internet Protocol Stack Model (Fig. 4), (v) RAMI 4.0 improves the collective understanding of standards and use-cases in the context of Industry 4.0. It helps to map manufacturing requirements with standards to facilitate development of Industry 4.0 related products. Moreover, RAMI 4.0 specifies the Asset Administration Shell (AAS) [29] that is a digital shell of the physical asset containing all data for linking the assets together and with digital platform. In its turn, the AAS is used to describe the digital dimension of the physical Asset in a standardized way.

Since the work is focused mostly on inside the manufacturing company, and not on networked enterprises, this option is reasonable instead of a more collaboration-oriented model such as ARCON. In terms of compatibility with RAMI 4.0, the Endogenous and to some extent Exogenous elements of ARCON are close to the Layers and Hierarchy Levels of RAMI 4.0. The Life Cycles in both models represent

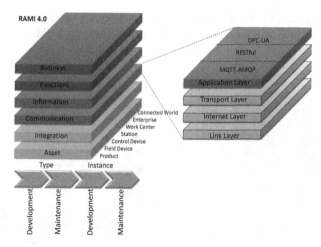

Fig. 4. RAMI 4.0, internet protocol stack and RAMI 4.0 communication layer.

the stages of a product or a system life time. The RAMI 4.0 also presumes some space for collaboration within the Hierarchy Levels, on the last level "Connected World", although less elaborated than in ARCON. In this particular work, platforms are analysed individually to establish a technological foundation for platforms integration. This is also justified by the fact that the ZDMP project is a member of 4DMP cluster interlinking several ongoing projects in the area of digital manufacturing: ZDMP, QUALITY, EFPF, Kyklos 4.0, digiPRIME and SHOP4CF. Thus, the main goal is to analyse innovative manufacturing platforms to establish the interoperability within 4DMP cluster. The core focus layers of the RAMI 4.0 considered in this work are Information and Communication layers for their particular importance for the AAS. The following aspects are in focus: security, privacy, user and application metadata and underlying technologies, as well as licensing issues.

The inter-platform linking and interoperability with external platforms is essential in the context of reusing deliverables of projects from the area of Internet of Things and CPPS. The following research projects are considered in this study: vf-OS, Disrupt, MANTIS, CREMA, BEinCPPS, I-BiDaaS, DIGICOR, RestAssured, GO0DMAN. One of the main goals of the 4DMP cluster is to establish a fundament for integration of some functionality/services developed within various European research projects; in a later phase also interlinking to commercial platforms is targeted. Thus, understanding of underlying communication basis is important for the establishment of interfaces for integration of different modules. To give the common basis for interoperability assessment, the RAMI 4.0 model is applied to the platforms' architectures.

In Fig. 5 the architectures of vf-OS, BiDaaS and RestAssured are analysed and the functional blocks responsible for "Information" and "Communication" layers are identified. The black arrows point on the blocks that correspond to "Information" layer and the red arrows to blocks belonging to the "Communication" layers. Thus, system integrators having a look on these blocks can develop a high-level strategy on interoperability opportunities and difficulties. After this step, every block can be zoomed in and analysed in detail with all corresponding technologies, approaches, and protocols that are used, which will result in a set of concrete steps for building the integration middleware.

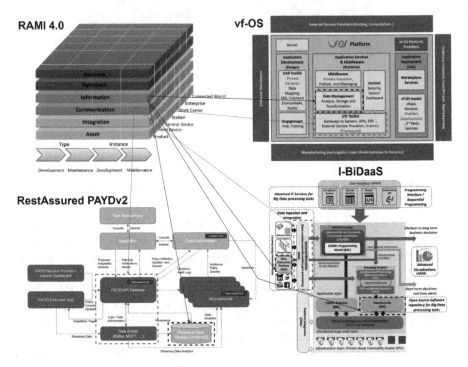

Fig. 5. RAMI 4.0 applied to I-BiDaaS, Restassured and vf-OS architectures

Table 1 presents an analysis of the above motioned projects based on 5 core aspects: security, privacy, licensing, and App/User data with underlying technologies. On its turn, each aspect contains several analysis points that are important for establishing the vision of how various platforms can be combined within one marketplace either directly, by inclusion of functional blocks or through linking the corresponding platform. The inputs for the table are based on the public available deliverables form those projects. Thus, some information might be not available for the public; if no data is available the table's cell contains the "no details" label.

Most of the reviewed projects use two communication paradigms: the Restful and the Publish/Subscribe. The restful approach follows the classical client-server architecture utilising basic HTTP methods: GET, PUT, POST and DELETE. At the same time, using the publish/subscribe approach allows implementation of the asynchronous messaging which is useful in communication with edge devices [24]. The main messaging protocols are AMQP and MQTT requiring a broker to ensure the asynchronous communication when publisher and subscriber do not need to be available at the same time, but the broker guarantees the message delivery.

Table 1. Analysis of manufacturing projects against identified aspects

Technical Level zApps (high-level)	App/User data (underlying technologies)							Security				Privacy			
	Data Format (Messages)	Protocols (Messaging)	Message Broker	Architecture	Communication Paradigm, API	Docker services	Storage	Encryption	Data Integrity	Identity Management	Authentication	Data Confidentiality	Access control	Licensing	Marketplace
vf-OS [26,36]	JSON	AMQP	RabbitMQ	SOA	Pub/Sub, Restful	yes	MongoDB, ZooKeeper	yes (KeyRock)	Yes (TLS/SSL)	yes (security token)	Fiware KeyRock	Fiware KeyRock	RBAC (Role based AC)	Apache License	yes
Disrupt [39,40]	JSON	MQTT, JMS	available	SOA	Pub/Sub, Restful	no details	Cassandra	no details	no details	yes	yes	yes	RBAC	Apache License v2	yes
MANTIS [34,35]	JSON	AMQP	RabbitMQ	SOA	Pub/Sub, Restful	yes	Cassandra, Apache Hadoop	Yes (EEBus)	yes	Yes (PAP, Oauth 2.0)	yes (RFC 4949)		RBAC/ABAC (attribute based)	no details	no
CREMA [32,33]	JSON	AMQP	Apache ActiveMQ	SOA	Pub/Sub, Restful	yes	MongoDB, Sesame	yes (SSL)	yes (security token)	yes (login, password)	no details		RBAC	Apache L v2, AGPL, LGPL	yes
BEinCPPS [23,31]	JSON	MQTT, OPC-UA, AMQP	RabbitMQ	SOA	Pub/Sub, Restful	no details	no details	yes	Optional (SSL)	Yes (OAuth protocol)	yes	no details	RBAC	Apache License v2/ Proprietary	no
I-BiDaaS [43,44]	JSON	MQTT	available	SOA	Publish/Subscribe, Restful	no details	Cassandra/ Hecuba	Preserving Encryption (FPE), Order	yes (SSL)	yes	yes	yes	RBAC	GNU Public Licence/ Proprietary	no
DIGICOR [41,42]	JSON	MQTT, OPC-UA, AMQP	AmazonMQ	SOA	Pub/Sub, Restful	yes	no details	Yes (OPC UA Server)	SSL/TLS	yes	yes	yes	RBAC/ ABAC	no details	yes
RestAssured [37,38]	JSON	no details	no details	SOA	Pub/Sub, Restful	yes	MySQL/Maria DB	yes (IBM)	yes	Keycloack	Keycloack (Kebreros)	JWT token introspection	CBAC (context based AC)	Apache License 2.0/ Proprietary	no
GOODMAN [45,46]	JSON	MQTT, OPC-UA	available	SOA	Pub/Sub, Restful	no details	no details	no details	no details	no details	no details	no details	no details	Freeware/ Proprietary	no

The commonly used format for the payload in MQTT is JSON, especially in the edge layer, including fetching sensor data. The combination of these paradigms allows to use the Restful approach to communicate with end applications and messaging middleware [25] to act as a bridge between the edge devices and end applications, as well as for inter-component communication within the platform. However, the de-facto standard communication approach for the marketplace considering the analysed projects is the RESTful one, mostly using JSON documents for transmitting the user and application metadata or even security related data.

For storage both SQL and NoSQL approaches are widely used. Examples are MongoDB – a document-oriented NoSQL DB enabling storage of JSON documents, Apache Zookeper – a NoSQL database for storing the key-value pairs, Sesame for storing the RDF triples, but also conventional SQL databases, such as MySQL. It is hard to identify a common approach regarding storage tools selection, as it largely depends on the particular type, context, and form of the stored data. For instance, vf-OS is based on the polyglot persistence paradigm [24] combining various DB types in order to utilize different DBs to the best of their potential. An example is the user or application related data which are sent as JSON documents and stored in MongoDB without a need for excessive Extract Transform Load (ETL) operations.

Docker containers are wildly used to enable encapsulation of components as services to be further exposed as software packages [26]. This fact is related to the growing trend to "*move from the monolithic software architecture where many components of a software system run in a single process*" [27]. Docker is a platform used to run applications as a set of containers at the same time on the same host. This means that the functional blocks of the system are composed of many small services delivered as containers [28].

The analysis made shows that various projects are using their own developed security and privacy tools. Just a few utilize third-party solutions such as KeyRock Fiware Generic Enabler or the Keycloak. KeyRock, used in vf-OS, is based on OAuth 2.0 protocol supporting basic authorisation, encryption, authentication and data confidentiality. This protocol supports the Identity Management using "security tokens" that are issued to the client to access protected resources. Security tokens contain all the necessary data about the client, issuing entity and the lifetime of the token. Keycloak on its turn supports both the OAuth 2.0 protocol and the Security Assertion Markup Language (SAML 2.0). Integrity and Encryption are usually assured using the Transport Layer Security (TLS) or Secure Sockets Layer (SSL), used by the majority of the analysed projects. As for the access control, the mostly used approach is the Role Based Access Control (RBAC), in some cases in conjunction with Attribute Based (ABAC) and in one case with Context Based (CBAC). The RBAC approach is based on roles and privileges mechanism, where every user acquires a role to access resources, whereas CBAC is used for traffic filtering and in ABAC access rights are provided through policies combining Boolean attributes.

Most of the technologies and third-party services used in the projects are open source or community editions of commercial software. However, some manufacturing partners might insist on making some parts of the platform available against a fee and thus distributed under proprietary licenses. Sometimes the project goals require utilization of proprietary software, so the resulting platform includes the fee of this component. However, most solutions follow the Apache 2.0 licence, e.g. Keycloak, Cassandra, Hadoop or GNU Public Licence as MySQL or MariaDB. However, a marketplace encapsulating several platforms should be able to cope with multiply licenses.

Whereas implementing the assessment, several limitations were identified, as for instance, integration of platforms and solutions provided by third-parties due to different interfaces, data formats and licensing schemas used. An illustrative example here is the fact that there are more than 25 available vendor-specific industrial Ethernet protocols [30]. These difficulties appear during the Estimation stage of the assessment. An additional difficulty can be the fact that the same functional block in the platform architecture can be aligned with several Layers of the RAMI 4.0 fulfilling the tasks from several layers. An additional challenge can be further alignment of the functional block with the Hierarchy Levels and Life Cycle dimensions of the RAMi 4.0, whereas the current work's focus was on only one dimension – Layers.

5 Conclusions and Further Work

The fourth industrial revolution sets new challenges for design and development of manufacturing systems and platforms. One of those challenges is the strategy of Zero-Defect Manufacturing focusing on improving and optimising the production processes. This can be accomplished in various ways such as defects prediction, production optimisation using intelligent algorithms, strict measures to control the production flow, etc. The European ZDMP initiative aims at implementing this strategy through development of novel manufacturing applications, but also to establish a marketplace for encapsulation of manufacturing applications developed within other European manufacturing research projects and thus enrich the production ecosystem.

In this work we introduced the approach for analysis of European projects based on predefined focus points such as security, privacy, data and communication solutions, and licensing, whereas using RAMI 4.0 architectural approach as the basis. Moreover, issues of compatibility of RAMI 4.0 with other up to date reference models were also in the scope of the work. The strategy for assessment of the digital manufacturing platforms developed within several European projects such as vf-OS, Disrupt, MANTIS, CREMA, BEinCPPS, I-BiDaaS, DIGICOR, RestAssured, GO0DMAN, was proposed. It consists of three phases Alignment, Analysis, and Estimation, whereas the current work was mostly focused on the Analysis stage. During the assessment process, several limitations and challenges were identified: proprietary solutions even based on well standardised protocols and approaches, some platform functional blocks can be aligned with several RAMI 4.0 Layers, some assessment points, for instance, "Data Format" are not enough for deeper analysis, as they only state the syntax used (JSON), without giving an insight on the corresponding semantics and structure. Furthermore, the results of the assessment and analysis base on identified criteria were presented.

Further work will require efforts towards the Estimation phase of the methodology to finalise the analysis of the manufacturing platforms and choose the proper strategy for establishing the interoperability among the marketplaces of the manufacturing platforms and integrate manufacturing applications into the ZDMP marketplace.

Moreover, alignment of the assessed platforms with other 2 dimensions of the RAMI 4.0 – Hierarchy Levels and Life Cycle, can be considered as a part of future work.

Acknowledgments. This work was supported in part by the European Union H2020 Program under grant agreement No. 825631 "Zero Defect Manufacturing Platform (ZDMP)", and by the Portuguese FCT foundation through the program UIDB/00066/2020.

References

1. Dombrowski, U., Wagner, T.: Mental strain as field of action in the 4th industrial revolution. Procedia CIRP **17**, 100–105 (2014). https://doi.org/10.1016/j.procir.2014.01.077
2. Camarinha-Matos, L.M., Fornasiero, R., Ramezani, J., Ferrada, F.: Collaborative networks: a pillar of digital transformation. Appl. Sci. **9**(24), 5431 (2019). https://doi.org/10.3390/app9245431
3. Zhou, K., Liu, T. Zhou, L.: Industry 4.0: towards future industrial opportunities and challenges. In: 2015 12th International Conference on Fuzzy Systems and Knowledge Discovery (FSKD) (2015). https://doi.org/10.1109/fskd.2015.7382284
4. Bigliardi, B., Bottani, E., Casella, G.: Enabling technologies, application areas and impact of industry 4.0: a bibliographic analysis Procedia Manuf. **42**, 322–326 (2020)
5. Nazarenko, A.A., Camarinha-Matos, L.M.: Basis for an approach to design collaborative cyber-physical systems. In: Camarinha-Matos, L.M., Almeida, R., Oliveira, J. (eds.) DoCEIS 2019. IAICT, vol. 553, pp. 193–205. Springer, Cham (2019). https://doi.org/10.1007/978-3-030-17771-3_16
6. Ribeiro, L., Bjorkman, M.: Transitioning from standard automation solutions to cyber-physical production systems: an assessment of critical conceptual and technical challenges. IEEE Syst. J., 1–13 (2017). https://doi.org/10.1109/jsyst.2017.2771139
7. Nazarenko, A., Camarinha-Matos, L.M.: Towards collaborative cyber-physical systems. In: 2017 International Young Engineers Forum on Electrical and Computer Engineering (YEF-ECE), Costa da Caparica, Portugal, pp. 12–17. IEEE Xplore (2017). https://doi.org/10.1109/yef-ece.2017.7935633
8. Lindström, J., et al.: Towards intelligent and sustainable production systems with a zero-defect manufacturing approach in an Industry 4.0 context. Procedia CIRP **81**, 880–885 (2019)
9. Eger, F., Tempel, P., Magnanini, M.C., Reiff, C., Colledani, M., Verl, A.: Part variation modeling in multi-stage production systems for zero-defect manufacturing. In: 2019 IEEE International Conference on Industrial Technology (ICIT) (2019). https://doi.org/10.1109/icit.2019.8754964
10. Steringer, R., Zörrer, H., Zambal, S., Eitzinger, C.: Using discrete event simulation in multiple system life cycles to support zero-defect composite manufacturing in aerospace industry. IFAC-PapersOnLine **52**(13), 1467–1472 (2019)
11. Graça, P., Camarinha-Matos, L.M.: Performance indicators for collaborative business ecosystems – literature review and trends. Technol. Forecast. Soc. Change **116**, 237–255 (2017). https://doi.org/10.1016/j.techfore.2016.10.012
12. International Data Spaces Association. Reference Architecture Model https://www.fraunhofer.de/content/dam/zv/en/fields-of-research/industrial-data-space/IDS-Reference-Architecture-Model.pdf. Accessed 18 Apr 2020
13. Fraile, F., Sanchis, R., Poler, R., Ortiz, A.: Reference models for digital manufacturing platforms. Appl. Sci. **9**, 4433 (2019)

14. Bader, S.R., Maleshkova, M., Lohmann, S.: Structuring reference architectures for the industrial internet of things. Fut. Internet **11**, 151 (2019)

15. Wei, S., Hu, J., Cheng, Y., Ma, Y., Yu, Y.: The essential elements of intelligent Manufacturing System Architecture. In: 2017 13th IEEE Conference on Automation Science and Engineering (CASE), Xi'an, pp. 1006–1011 (2017)

16. Camarinha-Matos, L.M., Afsarmanesh, H., Ermilova, E., Ferrada, F., Klen, A., Jarimo, T.: Arcon reference models for collaborative networks. In: Camarinha-Matos, L.M., Afsarmanesh, H. (eds.) Collaborative Networks: Reference Modeling, pp. 83–112. Springer, Boston (2008). https://doi.org/10.1007/978-0-387-79426-6_8

17. Sino-German Industrie 4.0/Intelligent Manufacturing Standardisation Sub-Working Group. Alignment Report for Reference Architectural Model for Industrie 4.0/Intelligent Manufacturing System Architecture (2018). https://sci40.com/files/assets_sci40.com/img/sci40/Alignment%20Report%20RAMI.pdf. Accessed 17 Apr 2020

18. Industrial Internet Consortium and Plattform Industrie 4.0. Architecture Alignment and Interoperability. Joint Whitepaper (2017). https://www.iiconsortium.org/pdf/JTG2_Whitepaper_final_20171205.pdf. Accessed 10 Apr 2020

19. Industrial Internet Consortium. Industrial Internet Reference Architecture (2014). https://www.iiconsortium.org/IIC_PUB_G1_V1.80_2017-01-31.pdf. Accessed 10 Apr 2020

20. Li, Q., et al.: Smart manufacturing standardization: architectures, reference models and standards framework. Comput. Ind. **101**, 91–106 (2018). https://doi.org/10.1016/j.compind.2018.06.005

21. DIN/DKE. GERMAN STANDARDIZATION ROADMAP. Industry 4.0 Version 2 (2016) https://sci40.com/files/assets_sci40.com/pdf/german-standardization-roadmap-industry-4-0-version-2-data.pdf. Accessed 09 Apr 2020

22. Camarinha-Matos, L.M., Afsarmanesh, H., Galeano, N., Molina, A.: Collaborative networked organizations - concepts and practice in manufacturing enterprises. J. Comput. Ind. Eng. **57**(2009), 46–60 (2009). https://doi.org/10.1016/j.cie.2008.11.024

23. D2.2 – BEinCPPS Architecture & Business Processes. https://6d5a66e7-aea5-4aab-9548-6ced0d99e05c.filesusr.com/ugd/03d390_b6a39ea817ca4c2d97b3ba9171868041.pdf. Accessed 12 Apr 2020

24. Nazarenko, A.A., Giao, J., Sarraipa, J., Saiz, O.J., Perales, O.G., Jardim-Gonçalves, R.: Data Management component for virtual factories systems. In: Zelm, M., Jaekel, F.-W., Doumeingts, G., Wollschlaeger, M. (eds.) Enterprise Interoperability: Smart Services and Business Impact of Enterprise Interoperability, pp. 99–106. ISTE Ltd., London, UK (2018)

25. Giao, J., Sarraipa, J., Jardim-Gonçalves, R.: Open modular components in the industry using vf-OS components. In: Camarinha-Matos, Luis M., Almeida, R., Oliveira, J. (eds.) DoCEIS 2019. IAICT, vol. 553, pp. 238–246. Springer, Cham (2019). https://doi.org/10.1007/978-3-030-17771-3_20

26. vf-OS D2.1: Global Architecture Definition – Vs: 1.2.2 (2017). https://ef136c81-3047-408f-b1ec-2955e8231f38.filesusr.com/ugd/0cf731_286b3f51e13141fa8aca27228b06aa87.pdf. Accessed 11 Apr 2020

27. Stubbs, J., Moreira, W., Dooley, R.: Distributed systems of microservices using Docker and Serfnode. In: 2015 7th International Workshop on Science Gateways (2015). https://doi.org/10.1109/iwsg.2015.16

28. Corista, P., Giao, J., Sarraipa, J., Garcia Perales, O., Almeida, R., Moalla, N.: Enablers Framework: Developing Applications Using FIWARE. Enterp. Interoperab. 83–89 (2018). https://doi.org/10.1002/9781119564034.ch10

29. ZDMP D2.4: Manufacturing Reference Model Analysis Document (2019). https://c53c19bc-6460-4dea-a74f-97b851e7af75.filesusr.com/ugd/851c99_57042ac5fb6a4adea44bf9ff81010f5e.pdf. Accessed 02 Aug 2020

30. Givehchi, O., Landsdorf, K., Simoens, P., Colombo, A.W.: Interoperability for industrial cyber-physical systems: an approach for legacy systems. IEEE Trans. Ind. Inf. **13**(6), 3370–3378 (2017). https://doi.org/10.1109/tii.2017.2740434

31. BEinCPPS D2.4 – IoT Platform Federation (2017). https://6d5a66e7-aea5-4aab-9548-6ced0d99e05c.filesusr.com/ugd/03d390_6264ca6f678642edb48b62cf697fa903.pdf. Accessed 15 Apr 2020

32. CREMA D3.3 Technical Specification. (2015). https://www.crema-project.eu/media/1082/t33-d33-technical-specification-v100.pdf. Accessed 15 Apr 2020

33. CREMA D3.2: Functional Specification (2015). https://www.crema-project.eu/media/1086/t32-d32-functional-specification-v100.pdf. Accessed 15 Apr 2020

34. MANTIS D2.9 Reference architecture and design specification (2018). http://www.mantis-project.eu/wp-content/uploads/2018/07/D2.9_Reference_Architecture_and_Design_Specification_Final_.pdf. Accessed 14 Apr 2020

35. MANTIS D2.10 Interface, Protocol and Functional Interoperability Guidance and Specification (2018). http://www.mantis-project.eu/wp-content/uploads/2015/10/D2.10_Interface_protocol_and_functional_interoperability_guidance_and_specification_v1.1.pdf. Accessed 14 Apr 2020

36. vf-OS D1.2: User Scenarios Characterisation – Vs:1.11 (2018). https://ef136c81-3047-408f-b1ec-2955e8231f38.filesusr.com/ugd/0cf731_f0083b20243747619993661dfe6c7d22.pdf. Accessed 15 Apr 2020

37. RestAssured Deliverable D9.6 Final RestAssured Handbook. Release 1.0 (2019). https://restassuredh2020.eu/wp-content/uploads/2019/12/D9.6.pdf. Accessed 14 Apr 2020

38. RestAssured Deliverable D3.3 Final High-Level Architecture & Methodology. Release 1.0 (2019). https://restassuredh2020.eu/wp-content/uploads/2019/12/D3.3.pdf. Accessed 14 Apr 2020

39. DISRUPT Deliverable D2.3 The DISRUPT Platform Integration Plan (2019). http://www.disrupt-project.eu/Files/Deliverables/D2.3-The%20DISRUPT%20Platform%20Integration%20Plan.pdf. Accessed 12 Apr 2020

40. DISRUPT Deliverable 4.2. Data Analytics Toolkit (2019). http://www.disrupt-project.eu/Files/Deliverables/D4.2-Data_Analytics_Toolkit.pdf. Accessed 12 Apr 2020

41. DIGICOR D6.2: Knowledge Protection Specification (2018). https://6c97d07e-2d66-4f14-9c19-8c5872c4c3ba.filesusr.com/ugd/2512a7_6256f94aca924310a507df5b8ed7bd8d.pdf. Accessed 15 Apr 2020

42. DIGICOR D 5.8: Data access API & Reference data store (2019). https://6c97d07e-2d66-4f14-9c19-8c5872c4c3ba.filesusr.com/ugd/2512a7_a332d527b55e46a3935463fdd722453f.pdf. Accessed 15 Apr 2020

43. I-BiDaaS D6.2: Experiments implementation – initial version (2019). http://www.ibidaas.eu/sites/default/files/docs/ibidaas-d6.2.pdf. Accessed 12 Apr 2020

44. I-BiDaaS Deliverable D1.3: Positioning of I-BiDaaS (2018) http://www.ibidaas.eu/sites/default/files/docs/Ibidaas-d1.3.pdf. Accessed 12 Apr 2020

45. GO0DMAN Deliverable 2.1. Multi-Agent Architecture Specification (2017). http://go0dman-project.eu/wp-content/uploads/2016/10/GO0D-MAN-Deliverable-2.1.pdf. Accessed 16 Apr 2020

46. GO0DMAN Deliverable 1.2 ZDM Management Methodology (2017). http://go0dman-project.eu/wp-content/uploads/2016/10/GO0D-MAN-Deliverable-1.2.pdf. Accessed 16 Apr 2020

Towards a Reference Model for Configuring Services Portfolio of Digital Innovation Hubs: The ETBSD Model

Claudio Sassanelli[1]([⊠]), Hervé Panetto[2], Wided Guedria[3],
Sergio Terzi[1], and Guy Doumeingts[4]

[1] Department of Management, Economics and Industrial Engineering,
Politecnico di Milano, Piazza Leonardo da Vinci, 32, 20133 Milan, Italy
{claudio.sassanelli,sergio.terzi}@polimi.it
[2] Université de Lorraine, CNRS, CRAN, 54000 Nancy, France
Herve.Panetto@univ-lorraine.fr
[3] Luxembourg Institute of Science and Technology (LIST), 5, Avenue des
Hauts-Fourneaux, 4362 Esch-sur-Alzette, Luxembourg
wided.guedria@list.lu
[4] University of Bordeaux, INTEROP-Vlab, Bordeaux, France
guy.doumeingts@interop-vlab.eu

Abstract. In today's manufacturing domain, companies need to be able to join the Industry 4.0 paradigm and, more in particular, the Cyber-Physical Systems (CPS) revolution. However, along this transition, often for companies it could be not enough to deploy new digital technologies in their plant, demonstrating a digital technology readiness. They need to be able to adequately employ this kind of technologies and exploit their potentialities for reaching a suitable digital maturity. In this context, technical expertise, experimental capabilities, and specialist knowledge often represent for companies, and more particularly for SMEs, relevant gaps in the CPS application domains. To lower barriers, especially for SMEs, and to realise the potential of growing autonomy in CPSs, competence centres and, with a broader perspective, (regional/pan-EU) Digital Innovation Hubs (DIH) are arising. This paper introduces the conceptual Ecosystem-Technology-Business-Skills-Data (ETBSD) reference model that DIHs can use to configure their services portfolios unveiling new technological and business opportunities.

Keywords: Digital Innovation Hub (DIH) · Service portfolio configuration · Reference model

1 Introduction

Digital technology's role is rapidly moving from being a driver for marginally enhancing efficiency to becoming an enabler of fundamental innovation and disruption [1]. However, along this transition, often for companies, it could be not enough to deploy new digital technologies in their manufacturing plant, to demonstrate a suitable digital technology readiness. They need to be able to adequately employ these kind of

© IFIP International Federation for Information Processing 2020
Published by Springer Nature Switzerland AG 2020
L. M. Camarinha-Matos et al. (Eds.): PRO-VE 2020, IFIP AICT 598, pp. 597–607, 2020.
https://doi.org/10.1007/978-3-030-62412-5_49

technologies in value-added processes for exploiting their full potentialities, and thus reaching a suitable digital maturity [2]. Rüßmann et al. [3] grounded the Industry 4.0 (I4.0) paradigm on nine building blocks: big data and analytics, autonomous robots and vehicles, additive manufacturing, simulation, augmented and virtual reality, horizontal/ vertical system integration, Internet of Things (IoT), cloud fog and edge technologies, and blockchain and cyber-security [3]. In this context, connected systems can interact between each other using standard Internet-based protocols and can analyse data to predict failure, configure themselves, and self-adapt to changes [3], in other words, being sustainable and resilient.

However, mostly focusing on the CPS application domains, technical expertise, experimental capabilities, and specialist knowledge often represent, for companies, and more particularly for SMEs, relevant gaps. Moreover, several boundary challenges and hurdles (e.g. always changing customer expectations, cultural transformation, updated regulations and skills, etc.) contribute to hamper the digital transition. In this context, industry and government leaders need to manage these challenges to reveal and make exploitable the set of benefits digital technologies offer to both society and industry [1]. Indeed, to properly support the products upgrade, processes improvement and business models adaptation to the digital age, several initiatives have been launched both at European and international level [1, 4, 5] leading to the creation of Digital Innovation Hubs (DIHs). They are defined as support facilities that assist companies (in particular SMEs, start-ups and mid-caps) to improve their competitiveness, through innovations, fostering the implementation of up-to-date digital technologies [4, 6]. These organi-sations, involve different stakeholders belonging to a heterogeneous ecosystem in a people-public-private partnership (PPPP). They provide a set of supportive services that helps companies to become more competitive by improving their business/ production processes by means of digital technology. This paper aims at introducing the conceptual Ecosystem-Technology-Business-Skills-Data (ETBSD) reference model, a tool designed to configure the services portfolio of DIHs and unveiling new business and technological opportunities. The paper is structured as follows. Section 2 provides a brief overview about DIHs. Section 3 presents the proposed conceptual ETBSD reference model. Finally, Sect. 4 discusses the role of the model in the extant DIHs networks and concludes the paper, also providing limitations of the study and proposing further researches.

2 Research Context: Digital Innovation Hubs

Digital Innovation Hubs (DIHs) are, together with Partnerships & Platforms, Skills & Jobs and Regulatory Framework, one of the four key elements of the Digitizing European Industry (DEI) strategy, launched by the European Platform of national ini-tiatives on digitizing industry [5]. Its paramount scope is to enable European industries (of whatever type, sector, and dimension) to fully take advantage from digital innova-tions for empowering their solutions portfolios, also enhancing their processes and fitting their business models to the new digital era. In this context, the DIHs act as a one-stop-shop, providing their stakeholders with several assets, i.e. test before invest, sup-port to find investments, innovation ecosystem and networking skills and training [4].

In the EU roadmap, the plan is to have in each region of the European territory, a DIH that could support companies at a working distance. Several investments (i.e. regional, national and European) have been done both locally and globally in Europe to establish the DIHs infrastructure. Moreover, the European Commission (EC) is also fostering the collaboration and networking among the network of DIHs, financing the foundation of extended pan-European DIHs. These directives started in 2013 with the ICT Innovation for Manufacturing SMEs (I4MS) and continued in 2015 with the Smart Anything Everywhere initiative (SAE). Their common paramount goal is to allow SMEs, start-ups, and mid-caps to empower their products and services through the adoption of innovative digital technologies.

In particular, the I4MS is a European program thanks to which SMEs can partic-ipate to open calls asking for technological and financial support to carry out small experiments and test digital innovations in their business. The I4MS initiative is now in its third phase. Each phase has complementary objectives and mutually focuses on four technology areas (additive manufacturing, CPS and IoT, robotics, HPC), all strategic for the manufacturing companies' digital shift [7].

The SAE program [4] belongs to the EC Digitising European Industry (DEI) Strategy [5]. DIHs have the role of supporting the connection of technology providers and suppliers not only among them but also with the other users dealing with non-core activities (business support services, collaborators, capital providers, aca-demics, HR). The SAE initiative is divided in two phases, both aimed at the creation of consolidated ecosystems around regional DIHs in four technology areas: (i) Cyber-Physical and Embedded Systems; (ii) Customized low energy computing powering CPS and the IoT; (iii) Advanced micro-electronics components and Smart System Integration; (iv) Organic and large area electronics.

In particular, this research is aimed at supporting the first technology area whose goal is to aid companies from any sector in raising the quality and performance of their solutions (products, services and system of them) with advanced embedded ICT components and systems and to sustain eco-system building for promising platforms.

3   The Proposed Conceptual Reference Model

With the main scope of configuring DIHs services portfolios in a systematic way, the Ecosystem-Technology-Business-Skill-Data (ETBSD) reference model (Fig. 1) is proposed. It is grounded on the threefold Ecosystem-Technology-Business (ETB) I4MS [4] service model, the only existing reference model for DIHs. In par-ticular, it has been developed in the context of the Access to I4MS (XS2I4MS) pro-posal (a support action to advance the I4MS ecosystem) and it is actually used in all the DIHNET.eu [8] projects. The three categories composing the ETB model have been elaborated based on the experience of DIHs stakeholders and also from the experi-mented researches in the frame of several projects from the EC I4MS calls. The ETBSD model extends it to the particular domain of Embedded and Cyber-Physical Systems (ECPS) [7]. The ETBSD reference model is grounded on five main macro-classes (Fig. 1), representing the main context in which the DIH can operate, delivering services to its stakeholders. Data and Skills *macro-classes* of services have been introduced since the ETB classes belonging to the previous configuration were not able to cover them fully and exhaustively. Indeed, these two new classes represent core components of the new digitized domain where can intervene paradigms such as the I4.0, comprising up-to-date technologies such as CPS and Artificial Intelligence (AI). Indeed, a major role DIHs must play is to raise the awareness of European manufacturing companies' decision makers (especially of SMEs, start-ups and mid-caps) about the opportunities that the digitization can bring to their company. DIHs should not only transfer and drive technology in their ecosystems in an accessible way but also provide to their stakeholders the consistent staff with adequate skills to utilise and exploit digital technologies. This follows the objective of dedicating at least 10–20% of the efforts employed in application experiments devoted to skills development [4]: these services would not only empower people working in European companies but also enhance the daily working processes and contribute to the digitization of portfolios and business models. For this reason, a special heed has been dedicated in the ETBSD reference model to the Skills and Data *macro-classes*, introducing services able to provide companies with new skills to manage new technologies and to exploit the data connected to them.

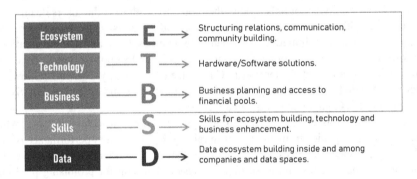

Fig. 1. Extension of the ETB model to the ETBSD reference model

Each one of the five *classes* considered in the proposed ETBSD reference model can be declined in several *types* of services, as shown in the Fig. 2 below. The *types* of services represent the main categories of services provided by the DIH to its stakeholders in each of the five specific macro-*classes*.

Furthermore, each *type* of service can be further detailed in different *classes* of services to be provided by the DIH.

The first *macro-class*, Ecosystem, is aimed at creating, nurturing, expanding and connecting the local SME constituency, involving in the SME digital transformation process different stakeholders as technology providers, technology users, competence centers, education and training hubs, market development experts, regional development associations. Its three main *types* of services are declined in several *classes* of services:

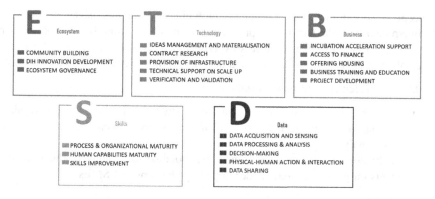

Fig. 2. Types of services in the ETBSD reference model

1. Community building:

- SME and people engagement & brokerage: creating a community around the DIH that connects the members of the innovation ecosystem;
- Innovation incitation, awards, challenges:
  a. Stimulating/rewarding collaborative innovation & problem solving;
  b. Offering innovation spaces to encourage ecosystem members to interact and share ideas as well as spaces for experimentation and pilot manufacturing (including data ecosystem and spaces);
  - Technology scouting: for companies seeking innovative technologies to incorporate into their portfolio (define customer + needs + ecosystem);
  - Communication:
  a. Sharing best practices experiences,
  b. Inviting business/experts to give talks and interact with (potential) customers and partners (study visits and roadshows);

2. DIH Innovation Development:

- Communication and trend watching: providing information on the trends in the market, assessment of market potential (business model), use of trend intelligence platforms and development of trend reports;
- Visioning and strategy development: supporting start-ups and SMEs in shaping their vision and strategies as well as large corporates requiring fresh thinking to remain relevant and competitive in the marketplace;

3. Ecosystem Governance:

- Services impact assessment: assessment of performed services (KPIs);
- Ecosystem management: engagement rules, statute, governance structure. Facilitation of relationships both within the DIHs ecosystems and between DIHs of the network.

As well, the Technology macro-*class* is aimed at following the whole lifecycle of digital technologies from conception and idea generation, through design and proof of concept, up to minimum viable product prototyping and commercialisation. They can be interpreted from the technology providers viewpoint and from the technology users viewpoint, through the steps of access-experiment-experience spiral model. Five main *types* of services have been detected and declined in more detailed *classes* of services:

1. Ideas management and materialization:

   • Ideas generation, assessment. feasibility study: collecting innovation ideas, refining and targeting them in a collaboration environment; preliminary feasibility analysis;
   • Technology readiness assessment: DIHs conduct technology readiness assessments on products/solutions developed by start-ups and SMEs

2. Contract research:

   • Strategic and Specific R&D: strategic perspective: collaborative R&D projects to support the translation of innovative ideas into demonstrable concepts. Applying technological innovation to develop new products/services or improving existing ones;
   • Technology concept development/Proof of Concept (PoC): planning and defining new business services solutions and demonstrating the feasibility of an idea or project through its temporary realisation;

3. Provision of infrastructure:

   • Access to infrastructure and technological platforms: provision of a large range of services (e.g. renting equipment, providing platform technology infrastructure, lab facilities, support to low rate production);

4. Technical support on scale up:

   • Concept validation: developing minimum viable products that can be validated with real customers and/or in an industrially relevant setting;
   • Prototyping: designing prototypes to explore ideas and emerging technologies before going into production by also considering potential opportunities offered by small series production;

5. Verification and validation:

   • Product qualification and certification: support in certifying that the product has passed functional, performance and quality assurance tests;
   • Product demonstration: promotion showrooms and demo-cases in which a product is demonstrated in front of clients.

The third *macro-class*, Business, intervenes in more advanced scenarios (with higher TRL solutions), identifying, modelling and sustaining viable business models, including also fund raising services (e.g. private matchmaking or access to public funding opportunities). It can be declined in five *types* of services detailed in several *classes* of services:

1. Incubation acceleration support:

- Basic facilities: providing access to physical infrastructure (offices, café, meeting rooms, laboratories, co-working areas, libraries, etc.);
- Specialized facilities: providing access to telecommunication infrastructure, HPCs, video conferencing, labs and data ecosystem;
- Business development: coaches and mentors, entrepreneurs in residence, dedicated programs to assist entrepreneurs in the process of business development (funnel, SMEs use case communication and assessment);
- Guidance: offering technical/fiscal/legal advice, regulatory assistance.

2. Access to finance:

- Financial engineering: providing support in addressing financial issues and/or advise on innovative financial products;
- Connection to funding sources: facilitating access to different funding sources (EU, national, regional, and private) aiming at achieving an effective mix of funds (conversation, lobbying, projects);

3. Business training and education:

- Methods and tools, business operations modelling: providing training and development in business skills and entrepreneurship (e.g. formal courses, workshops, seminars) and influence academia;
- Secondment: facilitating the exchange of personnel (e.g. researchers) and core competences among organizations, including IPR;

4. Project development:

- Identification of opportunities: support in the identification of new business opportunities through strategic analysis and trend watching;
- Creating consortia: encouraging cooperation and collaboration among organizations for exploiting common opportunities (e.g. business, research, funding, match-making, open innovation);
- Development of proposals: providing technical assistance in the proposal development process to comply with specific proposal requirements (e.g. for project funding).

In the following, the two additional *macro-classes*, Skills and Data, are fully detailed. Concerning the Skill *macro-class*, it has a twofold aim. The first is to assess the status quo of the companies that want to approach digitization, in terms of both process/organization and skills maturity, and to set an adequate roadmap to empower it. The second is to support the skill empowerment through not only educational programs, up-skilling and re-skilling training but also sharing channels, structure contacts and collaborations for scouting and brokerage aimed at knowledge-transfer. Three main *types* have been declined in the following *classes* of services:

1. Process & organizational maturity:

- Maturity assessment: assessment of company readiness for I4.0 (tech, organizational, and ecosystem readiness);
- Maturity strategy development: definition of a roadmap starting from the characteristics of the single enterprise or part of it;

2. Human capabilities maturity:

- Human skills maturity: support in capabilities screening through on-site visits, interviews, etc. Definition of actual level of I4.0 skills maturity;
- Skills strategy development: gap analysis between the AS-IS and the desired level of skills, action plan definition/support to implementation;

3. Skills improvement:

- Human up-skilling, re-skilling training: life-long training on technical and soft skills at corporate, operational and technology specific level;
- Educational programs: attracting and skilling next generation talents, forming I4.0 employees and workers;
- Scouting and brokerage: support in identifying channels, structure contacts and collaborations intended to knowledge-transfer, etc.

The last *macro-class*, Data, is pivotal for adequately exploiting digital technologies potentialities through services dealing with different phases of the data lifecycle: from data acquisition and sensing, through data processing & analysis, up to decision-making and data sharing, not neglecting aspects as physical-human action & interaction. It includes five *types* of services, detailed in the following service *classes*:

1. Data acquisition and sensing:

- Data acquisition: data in motion models and services for Industrial IoT;
- Data protection: data anonymization, confidentiality, encryption and privacy preservation services;

2. Data processing & analysis:

- Data storage: data spaces, data lake, linked data, distributed storage, knowledge representation services;
- Data analytics: semantic analysis, data discovery, advanced data analytics (edge analytics, cloud analytics) services;

3. Decision-making:

- Cognitive big data architectures: configuration and deployment architectures for big data;
- Decision support and development: cognition, prediction, prescription, simulation, machine learning, reinforcement, DNNs, formal logics;

4. Physical-human action & interaction:

- Collaborative intelligence: human-machine interface, human-robot interaction, human-data interaction, multi-lingual AI;
- User experience: navigation, user experience, exploration;
- Feedbacks loop: control/actuation, cognitive mechatronics;

5. Data sharing:

- GDPR and data sovereignty compliance: consultancy services for personal and non-personal data sharing and exchange business processes modelling, rules of governance and contracts;
- Data spaces: data models/ontologies for trusted secure data exchange;
- Data platform: HW/SW architectures/components, connectors services.

4   Discussions, Conclusions, and Future Work

This paper has the aim of introducing the conceptual ETBSD reference model. It has the paramount aim of supporting the configuration of the services portfolio that a DIH should provide to support companies in adopting digital technologies, grouped under the umbrella of I4.0, with a special focus on CPSs. The ETBSD reference model could be a good reference model for modelling collaborative networks 4.0 in which DIHs will be one of the pillars because of their "by-design" innovation skills. It could also be considered a strategic tool designed for several scopes:

- to classify their extant services (as-is), identifying overlaps and gaps;
- to identify new services (to-be) to be provided in the future (maybe imitating and replicating initiatives of other DIHs in a pan-European ecosystem);
- to identify opportunities for collaboration among DIHs and their stakeholders to-be-joint in a pan-European DIH of three types:
  - Joint provision (more stakeholders put together existing services);
  - Joint development (new services jointly created, putting together skills);
  - Joint matchmaking (for stakeholders looking for partnerships and specific assets in the DIH network).

In particular, the ETBSD reference model will be tested in the DIH4CPS project [9]. DIH4CPS is a EU project aiming at consolidating a pan-European DIH, coordinating the different smart specializations of its poles. DIH4CPS poles are regional/national DIHs with their members (competence centres, technology providers, technology users). Specific services of each pole can be concretely provided by one of its users. However, it is the pole itself that disseminates and communicates the event and creates the audience, trying to sell it wherever, or to create a new service together with the user (based on a cross-fertilization process). This is done under the DIH4CPS network's supervision, which discovers overlaps, competitions and gaps to be filled thanks to the use of ETBSD reference model.

Among the potentialities of this reference model, it has to be highlighted the opportunity of generalization provided by it. Indeed, the reference model is made of classes while an instance of the reference model is "the model" of a specific DIH providing specific services belonging to the reference classes. While the ETBSD reference model has been presented at "class" level, the expected actual services to be provided by DIHs should be declined at the "instance" level (e.g. for Ecosystem macro-class – Community building type - SME and People Engagement Service Class, the Service instances could be DIH Annual Community Event, Industrial events, Academic conferences and workshop). Indeed, a further declination of the service classes is needed. Each service class should need to be characterized with:

- specific service instances,
- the service provider (pan-European DIH, DIH pole, technology provider, academic partner),
- the service customers (technology user, DIH pole, technology/solution provider, academic partner),
- the service output (e.g. events, scouting, funding, training, assessment, consultancy, sharing of assets and ideas, etc.),
- classification of service (networking, skills and training, test before investing, access to funding).

Concerning the service provider, the ETBSD reference model deals with services offered by DIHs to its local/regional ecosystem (perhaps actually provided by some members). Often, the DIH services are sold by them but provided by other users. In this sense, the business model inside the DIH is very important.

Among the limitations, we would underline that the ETBSD reference model could lack of a mechanism to allow its evolution in a sustainable way. Regarding this, it has been planned to validate the presented conceptual version of the reference model and to further improve it through a survey to be run with a twofold approach. The first, top-down, will be submitted to the regional DIHs belonging to the DIH4CPS pan-European network for defining the related as-is services portfolios. The second, bottom-up, will be submitted to the SMEs belonging to the same network for grasping and realising which are the services needing more heed in the ECPS domain.

A limitation of this paper is the application of the reference model to only one of the areas of SAE, Embedded and Cyber-Physical Systems: this concurrently gives evidence to the possibility to extend the adoption of the reference model to all the four areas. Concerning this point, a strong compatibility of the ETBSD reference model has been found with the white paper discussing services that DIHs can provide in the IoT domain, redacted by an EC initiated DIH network in IoT (AIOTIDIHN) [10]. The AIOTIDIHN services portfolio can help to further refine, differentiate, extend or validate the ETBSD reference model: a comparison with it is planned after the run of the survey. Finally, a combination of the ETBSD with the ECOGRAI model [11] can be relevant to measure the sustainability of the DIH ecosystem with adequate KPIs.

Acknowledgments. This work has received funding from the European Union's Horizon 2020 research and innovation programme under grant agreement No 872548.

References

1. World Economic Forum: Digital Transformation of Industries. Demystifying Digital and Securing $100 trillion for Society and Industry by 2025 (2016). https://reports.weforum.org/digital-transformation/wp-content/blogs.dir/94/mp/files/pages/files/wef1601-digitaltransformation-1401.pdf. Accessed 16 Jan 2020
2. Sassanelli, C., Rossi, M., Terzi, S.: Evaluating the smart maturity of manufacturing companies along the product development process to set a PLM project roadmap. Int. J. Prod. Lifecycle Manag. **12**(3), 185–209 (2020)
3. Lasi, H., et al.: Industry 4.0. Bus. Inf. Syst. Eng. **6**(4), 239–242 (2014). https://doi.org/10.1007/s12599-014-0334-4
4. European Commission: Smart Anything Everywhere - Digital Innovation Hubs - Accelerators for the broad digital transformation of the European industry (2018). https://ec.europa.eu/digital-single-market/en/news/communication-digitising-european-industry-reaping-full-benefits-digital-single-market. Accessed 04 Feb 2020
5. European Commission: Digitising European Industry. Reaping the full benefits of a Digital Single Market (2016). https://ec.europa.eu/digital-single-market/en/news/communication-digitising-european-industry-reaping-full-benefits-digital-single-market. Accessed 04 Feb 2020
6. European Commission: Digital Innovation Hubs in Smart Specialisation Strategies. Early lessons from European regions (2018). https://doi.org/10.2760/475335
7. I4MS. https://i4ms.eu/about. Accessed 06 May 2020
8. DIHNET.eu. https://dihnet.eu/. Accessed 30 July 2020
9. DIH4CPS – Digital Innovation Hub for Cyber-Physical Systems. http://dih4cps.eu/. Accessed 09 May 2020
10. IoT Digital Innovation Hub (AIOTIDIHN): Mission and Activities of IoT Digital Innovation Hubs Network (2019). https://aioti.eu/wp-content/uploads/2019/10/AIOTI-WG2-White-Paper-DIH-Network-Activities-Published.pdf. Accessed 30 July 2020
11. Vallespir, B., Ducq, Y., Doumeingts, G.: Enterprise modelling and performance - part 1: implementation of performance indicators. Int. J. Bus. Perform. Manag. **1**(2), 134–153 (1999). https://doi.org/10.1504/IJBPM.1999.004434

Developing Digital Capabilities for SMEs: SMART4ALL's Cross-Border Experiments for Emerging Technology Development and Adoption

Anna K. Lopez-Hernandez[✉] and J. Francisco Blanes Noguera[✉]

Institute for Automation and Industrial Computing (Instituto ai2), Universitat Politècnica de València, Camí de Vera, 46022 València, Spain
anloher3@upv.edu.es, pblanes@ai2.upv.es

Abstract. This paper outline a proposal to study the build-up process of digital capabilities in SMEs and technology-based startups that are produced through the exchange of complementary knowledge between external stakeholders. The SMART4ALL consortium aims to accelerate the launch and adoption of emerging technologies that potentially ensure the improvement of digital infrastructure of the SMEs located in South- Eastern and Central Europe. The introduction of Pathfinder Application Experiments are cross-border experiments that pursue the use of cross-domain of CLEC, CPS and the IoT technologies based co-opetition, co-evolution and co-specialization processes which will be combined in parallel with expertise in R&D, networking and business strategies. Most of these innovation activities are geared towards the development of digital capabilities apply in agriculture, transport, environment and the interconnection of anything, which are considered to be low-embedded digitalization. The research proposal aims to answer what elements influence the fast track build-up of digital capabilities in SMEs and start-ups participants and what organizational elements are influenced by digital capabilities support the launch and adoption of emerging technology?

Keywords: Digital capabilities · New capabilities building · Cross-border experiments · Pathfinder Application Experiments · Emerging technology development

1 Introduction

According to the European Commission the small-medium size enterprises' (SMEs) activities are the core of the European economy. They are responsible of the 67% of the employment meanwhile large companies cover the 33%, the SMEs´ activities represent the 76% of the EU economy and they have important effects in five areas, such as, manufacturing, construction, business services (professional, scientific & technical activities), accommodation and food, wholesale and retail trade, which represent the 71% of the economy net contribution [1]. Added to that, the status of the digital economy and society reports, during 2019, reveal and highlight the relevancy to

© IFIP International Federation for Information Processing 2020
Published by Springer Nature Switzerland AG 2020
L. M. Camarinha-Matos et al. (Eds.): PRO-VE 2020, IFIP AICT 598, pp. 608–620, 2020.
https://doi.org/10.1007/978-3-030-62412-5_50

support the SMEs' sustainability where the urgency to boots new digital capabilities, and the use of new technologies [2] in agriculture, transport, environment and the interconnection of anything sectors that report a high deficiency [3]. The development of digital capabilities are critical in activities regarding operations in e-commerce, teleworking, online training, and cybersecurity services [2].

Since 2014, the EU Commission has started the quest to build a unique digital market to standardized the digital operability of the economic activities to allow State Members' governments, companies, universities and citizens having access to digital equal conditions [4]. Under this context, with the COVID-19 pandemic contingency, the social distancing provoked a new paradigm with the halt of the global economic activities conditions that affected all industrial activities, and also many small businesses broke down. The social distancing shows the real need of digitizing and automation of some activities such as food provision, transport in delivery and business operability [5, 6]. Since then there is an urgency to upgrade the digital operability infrastructure between the State Members in these economic areas, specially to prioritize those country members with low access to the digital groundwork [7, 8].

The current strategic vision of the European Commission towards the creation of a European digital single market encourages collaboration and know-how sharing between member States and associates, through public procurement [9] primarily to support SMEs and to stimulate the economy [10]. Nevertheless, the conditions of a unified digital market in the EU will inevitably bring about aggressive international competition to most SMEs. They themselves undoubtedly have to carry out this digital transformation, which is accompanied by an internal organisational shifting process to build new digital capabilities linked to the uncertainty of adopting the appropriate technology [11]. And on the other hand, regarding emerging technology proposals, considered as potential startups, it is necessary to support digital capabilities building to bridge the gap to the market [12].

This article draws the research proposal to study the digital capabilities building process in the SMART4ALL's Pathfinder Application Experiments (PAEs), which consist on cross-border experiments between SMEs and potential innovations. The following research questions are supported by theoretical approach regarding: What elements influence the fast track build-up of digital capabilities in SMEs and technology-based startups participants and what organizational elements are influenced by digital capabilities to support the launch and adoption of emerging technology. Therefore, this document is structured as follows: the section two is a brief explanation of the theoretical background of Dynamic Capabilities as an approach to explain the concept of fast track of capabilities building, digital capabilities and the emerging technology co-creation through technological complementarity both grounded on innovation and strategic management literature. The third section introduces SMART4ALL consortium as the case study. The fourth section provides details of SMART4ALL's cross-border experiments programme characteristics. The fifth introduces the methodology of data collection and future analysis regarding digital capabilities' indicators to identify the expected impacts and possible implications to the theory. The final section exposes the expected outcomes.

2 Dynamic Capabilities: New Capabilities Building

Given the current turbulent conditions of the economic activities that put pressure to the operability of many SMEs, the digitization process gains an important role toward their sustainability. The theoretical element that gives an explanation of how firms address changes to overcome rapid contextual change are Dynamic Capabilities [13]. The dynamic capabilities most common and primary definition is: *"the firm's ability to integrate, build, and reconfigure internal and external competences to address and shape rapidly changing environments"* [13, 14]. It refers to a systemic approach, where the firm develops in short time extraordinary organizational capabilities [15, 16] that allows it to sensing, seizing and reconfiguring capacities under difficult environmental conditions. These capabilities let firms create and scale up their value, but also allow them to escape from zero profit to survive to the turbulent conditions [17, 18]. Becoming these new abilities or capabilities, as excel and unique internal conditions which in the long run will become a sustainable advantage, and an intangible asset difficult to replicate [19, 20].

The study of the origin of fast-track and specialized new capabilities building under turbulent conditions, in firms and technology-based startups has been undertaken under the umbrella of the dynamic capabilities. It has been identified four common approaches of analysis to study the origin of new capabilities in innovation environments, the first is from the resource-based view that refers to the combination of tangible and intangible assets used to overcome turbulent conditions [21, 22], the second relates to the intangible sources or knowledge-based view of the firm, where the value is created by the knowledge and expertise of the firms' human resources and its valuable intangibles assets that the firm owns such as, the logo, its mission and values, licenses, intellectual property, market strategies, business models [23]; the third is from microfoundations of dynamic capabilities approach [24–26] that pursues the study of dynamic capabilities as the introduction of new routines and capabilities as organizational and managerial structures, systems, processes and procedures [27], in addition of new skills available that readapt the organization [28]. Finally through the team interaction approach as the origin of new capabilities from specific information exchange and interdependencies, based on team collaboration capabilities leveraging the operational capabilities [29, 30], supported by orchestrating and reconfiguring the firms' resources from internal and external know-how. Hence the harnessing of the team interaction is essential where the 'cross-functional cooperation' [31], that refers to constant interactions and exchange of information between the team's members to configure and adapt the firms' operations according to the market conditions [32].

2.1 Digital Capabilities

The European digital market integration is grounded on collaboration between EU State members. The SMEs digitization processes will catapult a new technology era to business, people, communications, production, economic and trade activities including traditional practices [33, 34]. The digitalization of SMEs and the fast-track the launch of emerging technologies involves multidisciplinary interactions and a systemic reconfiguration at strategic, organization, information technology, supply chains and marketing levels [35]. Here we introduce our first research question apply to the SMART4ALL's Pathfinder Application Experiments (PAEs):

What elements influence the fast track build-up of digital capabilities in SMEs and technology-based startups participants?

To answer this question, it was necessary to conceptualize theoretically the organizational knowledge creation process, and design hypotheses to be tested empirically. First of all, the digital capabilities involve adoption of new business concepts, new technology, specialized knowledge, skills, communications and activities human-machine interaction [36]. The conceptual basis of new capabilities building, dynamic capabilities, depend on the previous settlement of organizational and operative structures inside the SMEs, and in technology-based startups the definition of team organization with specific responsibilities [37]. According to Winter in established firms [38, p. 984]: *'to create a significant new capability, an organization must typically make a set of specific and highly complementary investments in tangible assets, in process development, and in the establishment of relationships that cross the boundaries of the organizational unit in which the process is deemed to reside'*. The interaction and collaboration, in innovative contexts and networking [38], produce in SMEs and startups the abilities to harness and enhance their operational capabilities through a set adaptive capabilities to survive under uncertain conditions [19, 32]. Moreover, this means that the SMEs and scientific teams working on developing emerging technology–as potential startups require, external knowledge accompanied by collaborative behaviour [39] as teamwork integration to acquire and assimilate external knowledge.

Hypothesis 1. Organizational teamwork influences the rapid creation of new digital skills [32].

Hypothesis 2. The type of investment in resources - for example, man-hours (in training), operating costs and acquisition of new technologies - influences the rapid creation of new digital capabilities.

Hypothesis 3a. The involvement of new stakeholders in their environment - with new technical knowledge - influences the rapid accumulation of new digital skills.

Hypothesis 3b. The intervention of new stakeholders in their environment - with complementary specialized knowledge - influences the rapid accumulation of new digital capabilities.

2.2   Complementarities in Technological Environment

To understand the innovation dynamics it is necessary to insight that technologic environment around the SMEs' and startups' activities, then their environment is constantly shaping their innovation, and it is also where technological opportunities are appearing and disappearing [39, 40]. Technological complementarities occur when two or more factors increase the return compared with each isolated factor's income as reference [40]. Teece defines that *"complementary relationships [occur between] heterogeneous factors [outside and] inside the firm (and that these can impact firm performance), the contexts in which such interfaces [happen] is yet to be adequately specified"* [40, p. 720]. Complementary technologies demand high levels of absorptive capabilities it means fast learning and applying of multidisciplinary know-how in different areas of the organization [41]. Then our second question is:

What organizational elements are influenced by digital capabilities support the launch and adoption of emerging technology?

The technological complementarity goals, pursue cospecialization goals where all the stakeholders acquire knowledge from their interaction [15, 16] It is based on the collective collaboration and knowledge exchange activities between established innovation ecosystems and respective networks [42], where the partners combine their expertise [43]. The technology cospecialization involves external know-how exchange –from the partners' network [44], applied through internal learning and adaptation of organizational processes. These will be reflected on the firm growth as indicators [45], that will be revealed on their innovation performance as outcome e.g. sales, number of clients, market share [46].

Hypothesis 4. Digital capabilities are linked to the type of complementary knowledge that is applied on strategic actions regarding new business models design, identification of new markets, application of materials.

Hypothesis 5. Digital capabilities are linked to technical areas regarding new product development/new market development/or in addition to external knowledge from the stakeholders' network.

Hypothesis 6. Digital capabilities are linked to management and internal operation regarding logistic, transport, providers.

3   Case Study: SMART4ALL Consortium

The Europe digitization target to spread the benefits and opportunities to all economic activities through a consortium [30]. The role of a consortium is to integrate the multi-actor activities where their members work and contribute in different activities to develop opportunities aiming at a common goal, but at the same time sharing the risks and benefits [47]. The European Commission has an umbrella of different funding programs, in this case Horizon Europe offers support to initiatives that backing SMEs and mid-caps through research and innovation in their quest to digitization [48].

The SMART4ALL consortium is a supranational collaborative network and a Horizon Europe funded action, that combines multicultural ecosystems, with interdisciplinary skills and know-how to establish a Pan European network of Digital Innovation Hubs. It pursues an extended impact across South, Eastern and Central Europe envisioning the production of digital innovation through ICT technologies [49]. The SMART4ALL's mission is to strengthen the inter-European innovation network supporting SMEs, who represent the 90% of businesses in the EU [50].

The SMART4ALL is composed by 25 partners from 15 countries, its goal is to support collaborative cross-border network activities and knowledge transfer through experiments that join academia and industry [49]. It is shaped by a diversity of regional stakeholders, such as universities, research institutes, Investors, networking organizations, SMEs, Digital Innovation Hubs, and NGOs.

Some of the characteristics that stand out this consortium are the integration of cultural diversity, geographical location, but also contribution of specialized capabilities to provide the support required to scientific activities and proposals that are

considered "hidden treasures of innovation", with great deficit on technology application, investment and business vision [51]. The underestimated areas selected are
digitized transport, digitized environment, digitized agriculture and digitized anything,
becoming these the innovation impacts that SMART4ALL seeks to achieve.

The consortium introduce a unique concept named Marketplace-as-a-Service
(MaaS), as strategic service to catapult and back up an idea to prototype/test through
simulation and providing to the participants with tailored services to offer (1) practical
technical tools/services to accelerate design, development, prototyping and manufacturing phases and (2) brokerage, coaching and guidance to access funds and pave the
path towards market growth and investment. The consortium partners are involved in
the performance stages with different technologies domains through their extended
network [47]. All these to reduce the time to market gap of a new technology. Because
of the high level of research components behind the SMART4ALL's innovation, its
activities are pursuing to frame and promote good practices in innovation and ethical
behaviour in research [52, 53], particularly focus on those who involve cross-boards
experimentation activities [54].

4 Pathfinder Application Experiments (PAEs)

The strategic tasks are distributed between the partners according to their expertise
areas applied on four domains targeted: Digitized transport, Digitized Agriculture
Digitized environment, and Digitized Anything (See Fig. 1). The digitized transport
tasks identify concepts regarding digital transport, mobility of goods and people, all
digitally connected with low carbon impacts [32]. Digitized Agriculture tasks, highlights the introduction of intelligent farms systems, following the Industry 4.0 systemic
approach, customizing products, efficiency and mass-production [33]. Digitized
Environment is linking to Digitized Anything tasks, respectively both refers to the
interest to show IoT solutions as open challenges [34] where there are needs of connectivity of intelligent products, devices, services, technical solutions and developing
new ways of interaction with the environment without negative impacts.

These activities pursue to create more value through collaborative activities and
scientific support from competence centres who will provide access to tests and prototype in parallel with the business networks [56]. to find investment, partnership,
identify potential clients and development of business models activities [57].

4.1 The Cross-Border Experiments: Pathfinder Application Experiments

The SMART4ALL consortium introduces three relevant pathway methods through
which it could be possible to implement specialized knowledge based on scientific and
technological sources. The Pathfinder Application Experiments (PAEs) [49, 55] are
technology transfer experiments that will be developed and promoted by the
technology-based partners. It pursues that all PAEs content an intensive collaboration
of scientific and technological activities, including the dissemination activities. Its
objective is bridging technological solutions to the traditional industry activities. These
activities involve the application of digital technologies such as Customized Low

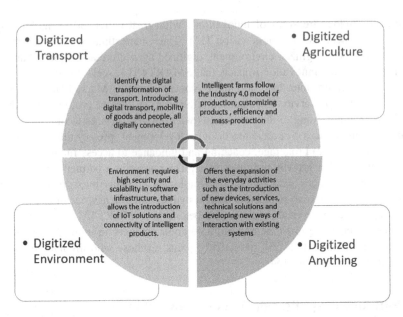

Fig. 1. SMAR4ALL four thematic digitized areas: *Transport, Agriculture, Environment and Anything* [55]

Energy Computing (CLEC), Cyber Physical System (CPS) and Internet of Things (IoT) in South Eastern Europe (SEE). All will apply in agriculture, transport, environment and the interconnection of anything [55].

The PAEs' knowledge transfers content co-opetition, co-evolution and co-specialization as ingredients that aim to robust the novelty with high value added integrated by smart technologies, business and digital skills in a package. The co-opetition is embedded by collaboration and competition that create value, with the opportunity to improve the innovation under a practical and constructive approach [58]. The co-evolution as an approach in technology environments involves creativity, nature and effects of innovation processes such as exploration, development and exploitation [59–61]. Finally, cospecialization as an element that involves the diverse synergies added from the partners to accelerate the R&D processes such as design, development, prototyping and manufacturing phases. The knowledge transference services are possible throughout the training, coaching and expertise guidance providing new skills development to SMEs [17, 62].

The consortium complements cross-board knowledge transfer. The PAEs' calls' are divided in three types: (1) KTE: Knowledge Transfer Experiments, (2) FTTE: Focused Technology Transfer Experiments and (3) CTTE: Cross-domain Technology Transfer Experiments winners will be accompanied during their prototyping processes to be launched into the market and being available to the SMEs [55]. The PAE's program foresees the solution -product-service- development in three stages: 1) the concept/solution description: responsible person/team, objective, processes and activities; 2) second stage, focus on the development and definition of the solution; and 3) third stage, the market launch of the solution. The expected participants shall perform cross boarder activities with their respective partners, then they should belong and established in one EU member state o any EU associated country, because of the PAEs' nature they require the participation of at least two different EU countries and/or associated countries. The participants could be Universities or Academic Institutions; SME and Slightly Bigger Companies and System Integrators and/or Technology Providers.

SMART4ALL will carry out 9 open calls throughout 2020–2022 with the aim of selecting 66 most relevant projects. The selection process will be carried out under an impartial and competitive procedure to evaluate and select the best technological proposal, as part of the SMART4ALL programme. Initially participants will be accompanied by SMART4ALL partners, who have two roles, firstly to support them with complementary expertise and their network during the PAEs and their preparation for market launch. During the experiments performance there are special interventions that will address the development of new products and commercial development. They include access to specialized coaching related to the development, attract investment and identify market growth strategies. [47] (Table 1).

Table 1. The PAEs' processes involve [55]

PAEs	Brief description	Scheme	Budget	Duration
KTEs Knowledge Transfer Experiments	Support small projects, or less mature ideas to be presented, tested and thus potentially find the fertile ground to grow and reveal its product potentials. KTEs act as internships/traineeships, apprenticeships and short-term training programs for unemployed people for vacant digital jobs	Internships projects between two different entities from two different EU Countries: one Academic or Industrial partner	up to 8,000€ to cover mobility allowance for implementing the internship	Short-term (3 months)
FTTEs Focused Technology Transfer Experiments	This one party transfers to the receiving partner a specific HW or SW technology in order to enable improved product or processes	Two different entities from two different EU Countries: one Academic and one Industrial or two industrials	up to 80,000€ to cover staff, travel and equipment	Short-term (up to 9 months)
CTTEs Cross-domain Technology Transfer Experiments	Complex multidisciplinary transfers and prototyping the novelty from CLEC CPS and the IoT technologies to wider markets	Three (3) entities from at least two different EU Countries (at least one SME; the experiment should be led by the SME)	up to 80,000 € to cover staff, travel and equipment	Short-term (12 months)

5 Methodology

The SMART4ALL consortium's cross-board experiments will be combined with specific training and couching of diverse capabilities building around new technologies adoption and organizational adaptation. This is aiming the identification of those capabilities that could be directly and indirectly related to digital capabilities. The development of digital innovation in the different identified areas, anticipating the high potential for adoption of emerging e-products and services, but also the creation of more e-businesses and more new jobs as a result.

A survey design integrates different theoretical indicators, values assigned on ordinal scale. We consider the Likert scales from 1–7, where 1 represented the lowest or most negative value, and 7 represented the highest or most positive value. These numeric values will represent their opinions allowing the quantification of their responses will be distributed among PAEs' participants, such as SMEs and technology-based companies, involving the SMART4ALL partners involved in each PAE. The sample will cover a wide range of stakeholders involved with the aim to analyse the data collected in relation to the process of digital capabilities building through the PAEs' experiments' participants, considering the dates of the Open Calls (Table 2).

Table 2. Open calls program

PAE type		Call 1	Call 2	Call 3
Knowledge Transfer Experiments (KTE)	Call Announcement:	Apr 15th, 2020	Mar 2021	Mar 2022
	Submission Deadline:	Sep 15th, 2020	May 2021	May 2022
Focused Technology Transfer Experiments (FTTE)	Call Announcement:	Jul 1st, 2020	Jun 2021	Jun 2022
	Submission Deadline:	Sep 30th, 2020	Aug 2021	Aug 2022
Cross Domain Technology Transfer Experiments (CTTE)	Call Announcement:	Dec 2020	Sep 2021	Sep 2022
	Submission Deadline:	Feb 2021	Nov 2021	Nov 2022

The study will be a complementary part of mixed-method research, in which qualitative data collection will be considered ensure the specificity of the sample purposes and quantitative data will be necessary to undertake the model estimation to assess each hypothesis through constructs. We are considering the data analysis through the Structural Equation Model (SEM), which is a component-based estimation for cause and effect modelling with latent variables through least squares (PLS) system using the Smart PLS 3 software.

6 Expected Benefits

This paper pursues to introduce a new concept about the digital capabilities building, which requires a systemic understanding of the digital market framework. The digital transformation of SMEs and the launch of emerging technologies require important internal organizational efforts from the PAEs participants and collaborative behaviour from SMART4ALL's partners. This research proposal aims to contribute to the innovation and strategic management literature regarding the digital capabilities building as a new paradigm that require a broad and systemic understanding to build the future of the new industry in the EU. The SMART4ALL consortium's cross-border experiments pursue to diminish the risk between innovators and their potential customers by helping them in their journey of adaptation to change. It should be noted that PAEs are an instrument that encourages and supports cross-border interaction between different actors and their respective networks, forming a supranational innovation ecosystem in the EU.

The SMEs' challenges are pointing to fast tracking digital solutions and building up new technological capabilities that can be economical and environmentally sustainable, but also social and cultural inclusive. The multi-actor collaboration requires a collective effort and commitment, particularly in collaborative environments, which essentially pursue building new capabilities and create more value between the partners involved. Also, the role of the SMEs is to assume huge compromise to continue the efforts of collaboration and influence in their ecosystems through their activities supporting similar companies and providers. Considering that it is expecting that they pursue their sustainability in the long term.

Acknowledgements. SMART4ALL has received funding from the European Union's Horizon 2020 research and innovation programme under Grant Agreement No 872614. We thank to the reviewers for their detailed and insightful feedback to improve this document.

References

1. European Commission: Annual report on European SMEs 2018/2019 (2019)
2. European Commission: Digital Economy and Society Index (DESI) 2020: Thematic chapters (2020)
3. European Commission: The European Green Deal (2019)
4. European Commission: Shaping Europe's Digital Future (2020)
5. Randewich, N.: Coronavirus, oil collapse erase $5 trillion from U.S. stocks. Reuters (2020). https://www.reuters.com/article/us-health-coronavirus-stocks-carnage/coronavirus-then-oil-collapse-erase-5-trillion-from-u-s-stocks-idUSKBN20W2TJ. Accessed 29 Apr 2020
6. Cifuentes-Faura, J.: Crisis del coronavirus: impacto y medidas económicas en Europa y en el mundo. Espaço e Econ. Rev. Bras. Geogr. económica **18**, 1–7 (2020)
7. Maciejewski, M., Ratcliff, C.: The ubiquitous digital single market. European Parlament (2019). https://www.europarl.europa.eu/factsheets/en/sheet/43/the-ubiquitous-digital-single-market. Accessed 30 Apr 2020
8. European Parlament: European Parliament resolution of 11 December 2012 on completing the Digital Single Market (2012/2030[INI]). European Commission (2012). https://www.europarl.europa.eu/sides/getDoc.do?pubRef=-//EP//TEXT+TA+P7-TA-2012-0468+0+DOC+XML+V0//EN
9. Guarnieri, P., Gomes, R.C.: Can public procurement be strategic? A future agenda proposition. J. Public Procure. **19**(4), 295–321 (2019)

10. Kiper, M.: Technology transfer and the knowledge economy. In: Yülek, M., Taylor, T. (eds.) Designing Public Procurement Policy in Developing Countries. Springer, New York (2012). https://doi.org/10.1007/978-1-4614-1442-1_5

11. Li, L., Su, F., Zhang, W., Mao, J.Y.: Digital transformation by SME entrepreneurs: a capability perspective. Inf. Syst. J. **28**(6), 1129–1157 (2018)

12. Bhagavatula, L., Garzillo, C., Simpson, R.: Bridging the gap between science and practice: an ICLEI perspective. J. Clean. Prod. **50**, 205–211 (2013)

13. Teece, D.J., Pisano, G., Shuen, A.: Dynamic capabilities and strategic management. Strateg. Manag. J. **18**(7), 509–533 (1999)

14. Teece, D.J., Pisano, G.: The dynamic capabilities of firms: an introduction. Ind. Corp. Chang. **3**(3), 537–556 (1994)

15. Zollo, M., Winter, S.G.: Deliberate learning and the evolution of dynamic capabilities. Organ. Sci. **13**(3), 339–351 (2002)

16. Winter, S.G.: Understanding dynamic capabilities. Strateg. Manag. J. **24**(10), 991–995 (2003)

17. Teece, D.J.: Explicating dynamic capabilities: the nature and microfoundations of (sustainable) enterprise performance. Strateg. Manag. J. **298**(13), 1319–1350 (2007)

18. Inigo, E.A., Albareda, L., Ritala, P.: Business model innovation for sustainability: exploring evolutionary and radical approaches through dynamic capabilities. Ind. Innov. **24**(5), 515–542 (2017)

19. Dixon, S., Meyer, K., Day, M.: Building dynamic capabilities of adaptation and innovation: a study of micro-foundations in a transition economy. Long Range Plann. **47**(4), 186–205 (2014)

20. Helfat, C.E., Peteraf, M.A.: Managerial cognitive capabilities and the microfoundations of dynamic capabilities. Strateg. Manag. J. **36**(6), 831–850 (2015)

21. Wernerfelt, B.: A resource-based view of the firm. Strateg. Manag. J. **5**(2), 171–180 (1984)

22. Helfat, C.E., Peteraf, M.A.: Understanding dynamic capabilities: progress along a developmental path. Strateg. Organ. **7**(1), 91–102 (2009)

23. Nonaka, I., Kodama, M., Hirose, A., Kohlbacher, F.: Dynamic fractal organizations for promoting knowledge-based transformation - a new paradigm for organizational theory. Eur. Manag. J. **32**(1), 137–146 (2014)

24. Felin, T., Foss, N.J.: Strategic organization: a field in search of micro-foundations. Strateg. Organ. **3**(4), 441–455 (2005)

25. Felin, T., Foss, N.J., Heimeriks, K.H., Madsen, T.L.: Microfoundations of routines and capabilities: individuals, processes, and structure. J. Manag. Stud. **49**(8), 1351–1374 (2012)

26. Barney, J., Felin, T.: What are microfoundations? Acad. Manag. Perspect. **27**(2), 138–155 (2013)

27. Schneckenberg, D., Truong, Y., Mazloomi, H.: Microfoundations of innovative capabilities: the leverage of collaborative technologies on organizational learning and knowledge management in a multinational corporation. Technol. Forecast. Soc. Change **100**, 356–368 (2015)

28. Teece, D.J.: Dynamic capabilities: routines versus entrepreneurial action. J. Manag. Stud. **49**(8), 1395–1401 (2012)

29. Clarke, A.H., Nissen, A.H., Evald, M.R.: Knowledge sharing in heterogeneous teams through collaboration and cooperation: exemplified through Public-Private-Innovation partnerships. Ind. Mark. Manag. **43**(3), 473–482 (2014)

30. Lopez Hernandez, A.K., Fernandez-Mesa, A., Edwards-Schachter, M.: Team collaboration capabilities as a factor in startup success. J. Technol. Manag. Innov. **13**(4), 13–23 (2019)

31. Pinto, M.B., Pinto, J.K.: Project team communication and cross-functional cooperation in new program development. J. Prod. Innov. Manag. **7**(SEPTEMBER), 200–212 (1990)

32. Lopez-Hernandez, A.K.: Team collaboration capabilities as drivers for innovation performance: the case of Spanish technology-based startups. Universitat Politecnica de Valencia (2019)

33. OECD: Higher Education Management and Policy, vol. 17, no. 3 Special Issue on Entrepreneurship: Special Issue on Entrepreneurship. OECD Publishing (2005)

34. Petrillo, A., De Felice, F., Cioffi, R., Zomparelli, F.: Fourth industrial revolution: current practices, challenges, and opportunities. Digit. Transform. Smart Manuf. i, 1–20 (2018)

35. Verhoef, P.C., et al.: Digital transformation: a multidisciplinary reflection and research agenda. J. Bus. Res. (2019)

36. Jisc: Jisc digital capabilities framework: the six elements defined, pp. 1–8 (2019)

37. Helfat, C.E., Lieberman, M.B.: The birth of capabilities: market entry and the importance of pre-history. Ind. Corp. Chang. 11(4), 725–760 (2002)

38. O'Connor, G.C.: Major innovation as a dynamic capability: a system approach. J. Prod. Innov. Manag. 25(4), 313–330 (2008)

39. Teece, D.J.: Firm organization, industrial structure, and technological innovation. J. Econ. Behav. Organ. 31(2), 193–224 (1996)

40. Teece, D.J.: Technological innovation and the theory of the firm: the role of enterprise-level knowledge, complementarities, and (dynamic) capabilities. In: Hall, B.H., Rosenberg, N. (eds.) Handbook Economics of Innovation, vol. 01, pp. 679–730. Elsevier, Amsterdam (2010)

41. Zahra, S.S.A., George, G.: Absorptive capacity: a review, reconceptualization, and extension. Acad. Manag. Rev. 27(2), 185 (2002)

42. Cantner, U., Meder, A., Ter Wal, A.: Innovator networks and regional knowledge base. Technovation 30(9–10), 496–507 (2010)

43. Anderson, E.G., Parker, G.G.: Integration and cospecialization of emerging complementary technologies by startups. Prod. Oper. Manag. 22(6), 1356–1373 (2013)

44. Van Rijnsoever, F.J., Van Den Berg, J., Koch, J., Hekkert, M.P.: Smart innovation policy: how network position and project composition affect the diversity of an emerging technology. Res. Policy 44(5), 1094–1107 (2015)

45. Kim, S.M., Anand, G., Larson, E.C., Mahoney, J.: Resource co-specialization in outsourcing of enterprise systems software: impact on exchange success and firm growth. J. Sci. Technol. Policy Manag. 10(5), 1015–1046 (2019)

46. Stieglitz, N., Heine, K.: Innovations and the role of complementarities in a strategic theory of the firm. Strateg. Manag. J. 28(1), 1–15 (2007)

47. Nepelski, D., Piroli, G.: Organizational diversity and innovation potential of EU-funded research projects. J. Technol. Transf. 43(3), 615–639 (2017). https://doi.org/10.1007/s10961-017-9624-6

48. European Commission: Horizon Europe programme (2019)

49. European Commission: SMART4ALL, Self-Sustained Cross-Border Customized Cyber-physical System experiments for capacity building among European stakeholders (2020). https://cordis.europa.eu/project/id/872614

50. European Commission: Digitising European Industry Reaping the full benefits of a Digital Single Market (2016)

51. Kalff, D., Renda, A.: Hidden treasures. Mapping Europe's sources of competitive advantage in doing business, vol. 27, no. 7. Centre for European Policy Studies, Belgium (2019)

52. Stilgoe, J., Owen, R., Macnaghten, P.: Towards a framework of responsible innovation: from concept to practice through an experiment at the UK research councils. Res. Policy 42(9), 1568–1580 (2011)

53. Pearson, J., Gianni, R., Ikonen, V., Haick, H.: From technology assessment to responsible research and innovation (RRI). In: FTC 2016 - Proceedings Future Technologies Conference, April, pp. 1189–1198 (2017)

54. Foray, D., et al.: Guide to Research and Innovation Strategies for Smart Specialization (RIS3), March 2012, p. 114 (2012)

55. SMART4ALL: smart4all EU project. University of Peloponnese (Greece) (2019). https://smart4all-project.eu/

56. Clarysse, B., Wright, M., Bruneel, J., Mahajan, A.: Creating value in ecosystems: crossing the chasm between knowledge and business ecosystems. Res. Policy **43**(7), 1164–1176 (2014)

57. Bruhn, M., McKenzie, D.: Can grants to consortia spur innovation and science-industry Collaboration? Regression-discontinuity evidence from Poland. World Bank Econ. Rev. **33** (3), 690–716 (2019)

58. Soekijad, M., Andriessen, E.: Conditions for knowledge sharing in competitive alliances. Eur. Manag. J. **21**(5), 578–587 (2003)

59. Schumpeter, J.A.: Capitalism and the process of creative destruction. Monop. Power Econ. Perform. 19–38 (1942)

60. Teece, D.: Profiting from technological innovation: Implications for integration, collaboration, licensing and public policy. Res. Policy **15**(February), 285–305 (1996)

61. Duhamel, F., Reboud, S., Santi, M.: Capturing value from innovations: the importance of rent configurations. Manag. Decis. **52**(1), 122–143 (2014)

62. Harris, P.R., Harris, K.G.: Managing effectively through teams. Team Perform. Manag. **2**(3), 23–36 (1996)

Collaborative Networks for Health and Wellness Data Management

A Framework for the Collaborative Evaluation of Service Outsourcing Contracts in Pharmaceutical Logistics

Elena Pessot[1]([✉]) and Gianni De Togni[2]

[1] Institute of Intelligent Industrial Technologies and Systems for Advanced Manufacturing, National Research Council of Italy, Via Alfonso Corti 12, 20133 Milan, Italy
elena.pessot@stiima.cnr.it
[2] Fondazione Scuola Nazionale Servizi, Viale Aldo Moro 16, 40127 Bologna, Italy
g.detogni@scuolanazionaleservizi.it

Abstract. The management of pharmaceutical logistics is mainly outsourced to external service providers as it requires an efficient organization of warehouses and drug flows, and an optimized and long-term process planning in collaboration with several healthcare stakeholders. This work develops a reference tool to evaluate the efficiency of the Pharmaceutical Logistics Service Outsourcing Contract, which includes the technical specifications and the operating procedures of the logistic service. It structures the data to be collected and analysed, from the viewpoint of the several stakeholders of the drug logistics service, for evaluating the elements of: Complexity, Price, Management system, and Quality.

Keywords: Healthcare supply chain management · Drug logistics · Assessment tool · Contractual agreement · Service quality

1 Introduction

The pharmaceutical logistics sector deals with the delivery, storage and distribution of a high variety of products that differ from each other but are strongly integrated: medicines, healthcare goods, medical devices and economic goods. The logistics and supply of these categories constitute a vital element in the functioning of hospitals, clinics, consortia, pharmaceutical companies and in general healthcare facilities [1]. Specifically, the drug logistics process comprises all the operations ranging from medical prescription to the administration of drugs to patients, including the management of purchases, the handling of materials from suppliers to the hospital or healthcare facility, the management of central and peripheral warehouses (e.g.: of single wards), the physical distribution of drugs to patients, as well as the management of related information and financial flows [2]. Therefore, it entails a specific complexity, high personalized characteristic and relevance in terms of performance and impact on costs and schedule [3]. Even if it is considered a non-core service, it requires a critical organization with efficient management of warehouses and drug flows,

© IFIP International Federation for Information Processing 2020
Published by Springer Nature Switzerland AG 2020
L. M. Camarinha-Matos et al. (Eds.): PRO-VE 2020, IFIP AICT 598, pp. 623–633, 2020.
https://doi.org/10.1007/978-3-030-62412-5_51

optimization patterns and long-term process planning, especially in the complex and highly regulated pharmaceutical industry [4]. Hospitals, clinics and in general healthcare facilities need to optimize their management system to reduce expenses while ensuring the accomplishment of patients' needs and the quality of patient care [5]. For this reason, the drug logistics service is often outsourced to an external service provider, with short- or long-term contracts [1]. To cope with the complexity of logistics service and improve performance, especially in terms of cost savings and patient satisfaction, it is important to foster collaborative partnerships in the network of supplying companies [6].

The service outsourcing contract, including the technical specifications and the related operating procedures, establishes the contractual relationship between the supplier (service provider) and the client. Beyond the compliance with the requirements (and reciprocal commitments) in terms of system, process and result, the complexity and the impacts of the service on the overall pharmaceutical supply chain require even more that the service provider is able to establish a collaborative relationship with the other involved stakeholders, from the client (e.g. the hospital) to the public institutions investing in healthcare, to the final users [1, 7]. Moreover, the logistics provider has to manage the several contact points during both the transport, delivery and storage of medicines, healthcare goods and medical devices. This implies a substantial effort to collect and analyse data from different sources to demonstrate the quality of service delivered, also in compliance with the contractual requirements.

This work aims to develop a reference tool that identifies the fundamental elements to be considered in the evaluation of the contract of pharmaceutical logistics service outsourcing. The resulting framework summarizes the data collected from the assessments of the stakeholders involved and the service performance. The output of the framework will feed a simulation model that identifies the critical success factors and the minimum quality standards in the planning, implementation and monitoring of the service to be achieved in contracts of pharmaceutical logistics outsourcing.

2   Theoretical Background

The literature dealing with the management of contracts and their assessment in the healthcare and hospital logistics is limited, even if there is a growing interest considered the complexity and importance of these services for the overall society [2]. This is fostered by a collective recognition of the importance of an industrial approach (i.e. the management of a company operations) and good practices for efficiency in transportation and storage of materials (together with drugs, medical devices and economic goods) [7, 8].

Nowadays, many hospitals and healthcare facilities are adopting innovative systems, driving an industrialization and reengineering of the drug logistics, a rationalization of costs and an organizational innovation, towards an integrated evolution that takes into account the needs and specificities of each organization in the supplying network [6]. In particular, the approach of "lean hospital" applies the themes of lean organization and lean thinking from the management of the production systems to the hospital setting management, and is achieving importance [2]. The most innovative structures are also moving towards the development of new commercial strategies focused on the patient needs; or the integration of the most advanced technologies such as RFID, automated warehouses and the Internet of Things, to support the optimization of material flow management, the complete traceability of drugs and the computerization of the prescription [6, 9]. Another key theme are the strategic decisions on logistics and clinical-care processes, which also include extensive outsourcing of logistics services, in particular warehouse and transportation management [10]. From the one side, contracting to external service providers leads to financial benefits, with a reduction in central warehouse stocks and an increase in the turnover index of stored goods, a rationalization of operating costs and an increase in the overall quality of the service, with a reduction in errors [8]. From the other side, the outsourcing relationship requires a combination of formal and informal governance mechanisms to be effectively managed [11], including the sharing of appropriate assessment systems and benchmarks [12].

Contributions on measurements of the drug logistics service mainly concern the perceived quality and the user satisfaction regarding the performance of the service. Related frameworks are generally based on data collected through questionnaires, and measuring the quality of the service, user satisfaction and the classification of the main attributes to be taken into account in the provision of the service, with methods as the Multi-Attribute Utility Theory [13]. Other tools evaluate the configuration and management of the distribution model, taking into consideration the users' and functional requirements [9].

When services are outsourced, the design must take into account the level of customer service, the services considered as value-added, the launch of new generic drugs, packaging activities, order management processes, IT check and validation [4]. The evaluation of the outsourced warehouses management takes into account management costs, the level of criticality of the drugs and the level of quality of patient care obtained [8, 10]. As regards the management of the outsourcing contract, the factors taken into account in current models include: strategy (e.g.: need to reduce costs) and maturity of the single organization, required service performance (reliability, responsiveness, flexibility, quality), technical and IT skills, factors related to the specificity and complexity of the logistics of the drug, such as infrastructure (warehouses, vehicles and equipment) and risk assessment [3, 13]. Effective collaborations and coordination across the logistics process, also for accomplishing sustainability performance, should be supported also by a sharing of benchmark and proper monitoring of the contract [11, 12].

While there is a clear focus on the operations and customers' perspectives, an integrated framework that considers also the governance issues, e.g. the contractual arrangements, is still missing. There is the need to improve existing logistics outsourcing analytical models and to highlight the synergistic relationships between the components of the service as well as the stakeholders involved [14]. These have to demonstrate problem solving skills, experience in the management of the demand for drugs, improved business incentives, and a governance structure that includes the communication and coordination mechanisms between supplier and client [12, 14].

3   A Framework for Evaluating the Pharmaceutical Logistics Service Outsourcing Contract

3.1   Sources of Data for Framework Development

This work develops an innovative tool for evaluating the management and performance of pharmaceutical logistics contracts. It supports a collaborative assessment of the outsourcing contract, based on 1) the key elements of the service that go beyond the cost performance, and 2) the data collected and issues raised by different stakeholders on both inputs and outputs of the service and related contractual specificities. It addresses the call for new assessment systems and benchmarks in pharmaceutical supply chain [12] and highlights main issues and best practices implemented by service companies from a collaborative effort of all the stakeholders of the service (including national/regional governments, clients and final users).

The process of identification, analysis and test of factors and variables to be included in the assessment of the Pharmaceutical Logistics Service Outsourcing Contract considered multiple sources of data. This allowed to enable completeness, accuracy and validity of the developed tool. Specifically, the main elements and sub-areas included in the framework were obtained from:

1) a desk research on national and international guidelines on drug logistics, specific contractual agreements and bids;
2) a literature review, including scientific and industrial publications, on pharmaceutical logistics service and assessment models;
3) a case study performed in a consortium of clinics in Central Italy;
4) a set of focus groups and interviews with experts representing the stakeholders of the service.

As regards the case study, data were collected from face-to-face interviews with key roles involved in the management of the centralized logistics process from both perspectives of customer (the consortium of clinics) and the service provider of th current contract. Interviews data were further triangulated with internal documentation provided by informants. The case study was relevant to deepen the peculiarities of the service in a contextualized setting, and to test the framework in the final steps of development.

The focus groups and interviews involved experts from local associations; academics with expertise in transportation, warehouse and logistics management, representatives of department responsible for healthcare logistics in the regional government; experts of certification, training and inspection services; other pharmaceutical logistics service suppliers. Specifically, involved experts were asked to provide their point of view on the dynamics characterizing the drug logistics service, its outsourcing, and the usefulness of a tool for the assessment of the logistics contract based on a collaborative effort of all stakeholder involved. Collected data were integrated with the insights from the case study, and the variables identified in the phases of literature review desk research, to inform the elements and areas included in the framework.

3.2   The Elements of the Framework

To identify a standard for the drug logistics service as reference for ongoing and future contracts, the productivity and efficiency of the service were identified as key performance to be assessed. Beyond the evaluation of quality by service stakeholders, it has to be considered that pharmaceutical logistics is a relevant part of the budget of healthcare facilities, and cost savings can be made [5]. The productivity is measured as the ratio between the quality of the service obtained (output of the service provider) and price (input for the service provider). The efficiency of the service is calculated by comparing the quality/price ratio obtained for the healthcare facility (and its warehouses) under analysis with the results obtained for the structure defined as the benchmark (i.e. the healthcare facility with the best quality/price ratio).

The performance index of the drug logistics service are obtained by analysing four fundamental elements of the framework:

1. The *Quality of the service* provided to the client and users;
2. The (unit) *Price of the service* paid by the client for the service received, and based on the phases supplied and managed externally by the service provider;
3. The *Complexity of the service* provided to the client;
4. The *Management system* adopted by the service provider to guarantee the regular (and optimal) functioning of the service in healthcare facilities.

Figure 1 summarizes the framework and its constituent elements.

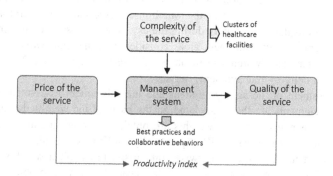

Fig. 1. Framework to evaluate the Pharmaceutical Logistics Service Outsourcing Contract.

The assessment of each area requires the participation and collaborative effort of both service supply and demand side. Specifically, the measurement of complexity is necessary to create groups of homogeneous healthcare structures (and their warehouses), or clusters characterized by a similar level of complexity of providing the service. The comparison between the quality and price levels of the service is made only between healthcare facilities (and their warehouses) defined "similar" in terms of complexity, in order to perform an effective benchmarking.

In addition, the assessment of the management system of the drug logistics service (including training, information systems, control systems, etc.) is fundamental to identify the critical success factors that enabled the service provider (supplier) to reach higher service levels in the most efficient healthcare facilities and warehouses, from the point of view of a correct management of the drug logistics service. Specifically, practices for a collaborative coordination of the process and monitoring of the contract, and elements demonstrating an effort towards collaborative behaviours of both parties (outsourcer and supplier) are highlighted.

3.3   Measurement Areas for Evaluating the Service Outsourcing Contract

The fundamental elements of the service are divided into measurement areas, i.e. the items that define and describe the object of measurement in detail. Each area in turn includes a set of sub-areas, identified and measured through a series of questions and standardized checks that allow a homogeneous comparison between the healthcare structures and their warehouses. The measurement areas can be then aggregated to determine the four fundamental elements of the service defined in Sect. 3.2. A set of questionnaire items corresponds to each sub-area, with answers to be evaluated on a 10-point scale.

During the development of the framework, and specifically the case study performed in a consortium of clinics in Central Italy, it became clear that the many phases characterizing the logistics service required to separate the items considered in the assessment. Moreover, some experts highlighted that in many cases the outsourcing contracts and regional/national tenders are separated for the "warehouse management" service (regarding the operations within the warehouses) and "transport and delivery management" service (from and to the warehouse or the facility). Therefore, the two processes are considered separately during the assessment phase, then integrated in the final assessment. The measurement areas considered in the framework are shown in Table 1, as regard the "warehouse management" service, and Table 2, as regard the "transport and delivery management" service.

The assessment of the aggregate areas and the subsequent assessment of the four fundamental elements are then calculated on the basis of the weighted average of the individual assessments, with the weights are obtained through the application of the Analytical Hierarchy Process (AHP). Specifically, AHP was selected as it is a method based on expert judgement and pairwise comparison to establish weights and scales. Moreover, AHP has been widely used in healthcare for solving problems in several decision areas such as provider selection, diagnosis and treatment, performance evaluation, risk management, and resource planning [15].

3.4   Data Collection and Analysis of Results

The questionnaire items per each sub-area are compiled through a web-based questionnaire with 10-point scale answers, integrated by the official documentation of the service contract. The data collected through the questionnaire are aggregated and assigned to each area, taking into account also the competences and completeness of information of each respondent (i.e. stakeholder). Indeed, the structure of the framework requires a vision of both the inputs and outputs of the logistics service, encompassing technical, organizational and relational aspects. In case of contrasting

Table 1. Elements and measurement areas for "warehouse management" service outsourcing contract.

Element	Area	Sub-area
Complexity of the service	Extent and complexity of contract	• Extent and complexity of warehouse management service
		• Extent of additional services
		• Criticality of expected level of service (e.g. urgent deliveries)
	Typology and distribution of served healthcare facilities	• Infrastructural factors of facilities included in the logistic network
		• Territorial distribution and other logistical criticalities
Cost of the service	Total expenditure	• Price for the service
		• Normalization of specific costs (e.g. investments)
Management system	Organization	• Supplier-client relationship
	Warehouse management	• Warehouse equipment
		• Systems and safety issues
		• Environmental sustainability issues
		• Organization and management
	Information system	• Information system
	Control system	• Control of system requirements
		• Control of result (e.g. stocked products) requirements
		• Control of process (i.e. preparation and delivery) requirements
	Human resources management	• Training of personnel
		• Operational management of personnel
Quality of the service	Quality of compliance	• Compliance of the system
		• Compliance with rules and conditions
		• Compliance with other conditions
	Quality of result	• Ordinary requirements
		• Urgency requirements and emergencies
	Quality of satisfaction	• Level of client satisfaction
		• Level of user satisfaction

Table 2. Elements and measurement areas for "transport and delivery management" service outsourcing contract.

Element	Area	Sub-area
Complexity of the service	Extent and complexity of contract	• Extent and complexity of transport management service
		• Extent of additional services
		• Criticality of expected level of service (e.g. urgent deliveries)
	Typology and distribution of served healthcare facilities	• Infrastructural factors of facilities included in the logistic network
		• Territorial distribution and other logistical criticalities
Cost of the service	Total expenditure	• Price for the service
		• Normalization of specific costs (e.g. investments)
Management system	Organization	• Supplier-client relationship
	Transportation and delivery management	• Means of transportation and service equipment
		• Safety issues
		• Environmental sustainability issues
		• Organization and management
	Information system	• Information system
	Control system	• Control of system requirements
		• Control of result (e.g. loading) requirements
		• Control of process (transportation and delivery) requirements
	Human resources management	• Training of personnel
		• Operational management of personnel
Quality of the service	Quality of compliance	• Compliance of the system
		• Compliance with rules and conditions
		• Compliance with other conditions
	Quality of result	• Ordinary requirements
		• Urgency requirements and emergencies
	Quality of satisfaction	• Level of client satisfaction
		• Level of user satisfaction

assessment, further interviews are conducted with the stakeholders that raise specific issues regarding the different parts. In this sense, involved stakeholders have to demonstrate since the beginning a systematic and collaborative attitude towards reaching a consensus or alternatively areas for improvement.

The integration between the quantitative and qualitative data collected allow to obtain richer insights on the final evaluation, integrate different viewpoints and make mechanisms and collaborative behaviors emerge. The calculation of the performance of productivity of the healthcare facilities taking part to the same contract allows then to feed a simulation model that identifies the benchmark as the most efficient facility (and related warehouse), and to reveal best practices and collaborative behaviours in the management of the pharmaceutical logistics service (e.g. in terms of safety issues, or employees training).

4 Discussion and Conclusions

This work aimed at developing a framework for the collaborative assessment of the outsourcing contract in the pharmaceutical logistics service. It is based on the key elements of complexity of the service, cost of the service, management system and quality of the service, and requires a systemic collection of data from involved stakeholders. The framework for the evaluation of the Pharmaceutical Logistics Service Outsourcing Contract enables to:

- measure the productivity and efficiency of the drug logistics service delivered;
- compare both the clients and the healthcare structures served (hospitals, clinics and other facilities) in a simulation model. This allows to consider the contextual complexity and to identify the critical success factors and best practices in the planning, implementation and monitoring of the service;
- define a standard for the logistics service that has to be reached, taking into account the peculiarities of the contracts, the application areas and the stakeholders to be involved accordingly;
- foster a collaborative attitude of stakeholders of drug logistics process, in adopting assessment tools for both complying with contractual arrangements and enabling continuous improvements;
- identify critical points for improving performance and collaboration between clients, service providers (suppliers of the service) and the other stakeholders involved in each healthcare facility that adopts the tool.

As regards the latter, hidden costs of outsourcing that can occur in the management of the relationship between supplier and outsourcer, and in making changes to the service contract, can emerge and open further discussions for improvements [11].

The structure of the framework allows an analysis along different levels of aggregation and administration, i.e. 1) the "size" of the single client requiring the assessment (i.e. the single hospital, clinic, or an overall consortium of healthcare facilities), 2) the type of respondent according to its specific needs, including the personnel of the service provider, 3) the supply chain process or phase considered, i.e. the warehouse management and/or the transport and delivery management, even if they are managed internally by the facility personnel, as requiring a further coordination with the external service provider.

The developed framework represents also a useful tool to be considered as a sort of "checking list" in the design of contractual arrangements and the bid phase. It can be a reference to simplify the procedures for finalising contracts between outsources (both public and private hospitals and healthcare facilities) and suppliers, to encourage competition between supplying firms through transparent selection practices, and to improve the efficiency and effectiveness of the contract monitoring [11].

Further developments should extend the application of the framework to different outsourcing contracts, encompassing different geographical areas or number of healthcare facilities.

Acknowledgments. This research has been funded by Fondazione Scuola Nazionale Servizi, Italy.

References

1. Gardas, B.B., Raut, R.D., Narkhede, B.E.: Analysing the 3PL service provider's evaluation criteria through a sustainable approach. Int. J. Prod. Perform. Manag. **68**(5), 958–980 (2019)
2. Ho, S., Martin, J., Baccarani, C., Pinna, R., Carrus, P.P., Marras, F.: The drug logistics process: an innovative experience. TQM J. **27**(2), 214–230 (2015)
3. El Mokrini, A., El Mhamedi, A., Berrado, A.: A decision framework for outsourcing logistics in the pharmaceutical supply chain. In: 2015 International Conference on Industrial Engineering and Systems Management (IESM), pp. 748–756. IEEE (2015)
4. Baglio, M., Garagiola, E., Dallari, F.: Outsourcing strategies and distribution models in Italian Pharma Supply Chain. In: 2017 IEEE International Conference on Service Operations and Logistics, and Informatics (SOLI), pp. 175–180. IEEE (2017)
5. Benzekri, S., El Wartiti, M.A., Bennana, A.: Pharmaceutical supply chain: review of the literature. J. Pharm. Clin. **37**(4), 195–203 (2018)
6. Paltriccia, C., Tiacci, L.: Supplying networks in the healthcare sector: a new outsourcing model for materials management. Ind. Manag. Data Syst. **116**(8), 1493–1519 (2016)
7. Law, K.M.: How schedule issues affect drug logistics operations: an empirical study in hospitals in China. Ind. Manag. Data Syst. **116**(3), 369–387 (2016)
8. Kumar, N., Jha, A.: Application of principles of supply chain management to the pharmaceutical good transportation practices. Int. J. Pharm. Healthc. Mark. **13**(3), 306–330 (2019)
9. Aloini, D., Benevento, E., Stefanini, A.: Conceptual design of a tool supporting the "last mile" logistics in hospitals. In 12th IADIS International Conference Information Systems 2019 (IS 2019), pp. 245–249. IADIS Press (2019)
10. Singh, R.-K., Kumar, R., Kumar, P.: Strategic issues in pharmaceutical supply chains: a review. Int. J. Pharm. Healthc. Mark. **10**(3), 234–257 (2016)
11. Skipworth, H., Delbufalo, E., Mena, C.: Logistics and procurement outsourcing in the healthcare sector: a comparative analysis. Europ. Manag. J. **38**(3), 518–532 (2020)
12. Ding, B.: Pharma industry 4.0: literature review and research opportunities in sustainable pharmaceutical supply chains. Proc. Saf. Environ. Protect. **119**, 115–130 (2018)

13. Laghrabli, S., Benabbou, L., Berrado, A.: Multi-criteria decision aid model for transportation supplier selection: case of a pharmaceutical supply chain. In: 3rd International Conference on Logistics Operations Management (GOL), pp. 1–6. IEEE (2016)
14. Beaulieu, M., Roy, J., Landry, S.: Logistics outsourcing in the healthcare sector: lessons from a Canadian experience. Canad. J. Admin. Sci. **35**, 635–648 (2018)
15. El Mokrini, A., Benabbou, L., Berrado, A.: Multi-criteria distribution network redesign-case of the public sector pharmaceutical supply chain in Morocco. Supply Chain Forum Int. J. **19** (1), 42–54 (2018)

Towards a Collaborative Ontology-Based Decision Support System to Foster Healthy and Tailored Diets

Daniele Spoladore[1,2(✉)] and Marco Sacco[1]

[1] Institute of Intelligent Industrial Technologies and Systems for Advanced Manufacturing (STIIMA), National Research Council of Italy (CNR), 23900 Lecco, Italy
{daniele.spoladore,marco.sacco}@stiima.cnr.it
[2] Department of Pure and Applied Sciences, Insubria University, Via Ottorino Rossi 9, 21100 Varese, Italy

Abstract. Nutrition-related diseases can considerably contribute to many different health-related problems and can impact on several segments of the population. Promoting balanced diet plans is therefore pivotal; however, this is not a trivial task as it requires different stakeholders (nutrition experts, agro-industrial businesses and consumers) to cooperate. This work introduces a prototypical ontology-based decision support system to enable such a cooperation, allowing nutrition experts to rely on a support tool when developing diet plans, consumers to received tailored suggestions and to be informed regarding new food products that could have an effect on specific their health condition, and agro-industrial companies to divulge characteristics of novel food products and their expected effects. These stakeholders can also exchange comments, suggestions and observations. The decision support system relies on widely-adopted ontologies and its use is introduced by two scenarios.

Keywords: Decision support system · Ontology engineering · Food ontology · Nutrition ontology

1 Introduction

Unhealthy nutrition can considerably contribute to many different health-related problems. Nutritional diseases – i.e. any nutrient-related condition that causes illness to humans – can range from obesity to eating disorders and include chronic diseases such as cardiovascular disease, cancer, diabetes mellitus, hypertension; another branch of nutritional diseases encompasses metabolic disorders, food allergies and intolerances. Moreover, nutrition can play a pivotal role in influencing and/or preventing other conditions, such as stroke, osteoporosis and mental conditions (depression, anxiety) [1].

According to the World Health Organization (WHO) [2], Europe is facing an increase in overweight and obesity (especially in southern countries), with particular incidence among children and adolescents: the age-standardized prevalence of overweight in EU amount to 58%. Relevant noncommunicable and diet-related diseases –

L. M. Camarinha-Matos et al. (Eds.): PRO-VE 2020, IFIP AICT 598, pp. 634–643, 2020.
https://doi.org/10.1007/978-3-030-62412-5_52

diabetes, cardiovascular diseases, cancer, chronic respiratory diseases, mental disorders – account for more than 77% of deaths in EU [2]. With regard to ageing population, the EU reported that over 20 million elderlies are at risk of undernutrition, a situation that – associated with other health conditions – can impact on social care costs up to 120 EUR billion per year and can potentially aggravate age-related conditions [3].

For these reasons, researches and clinical personnel stressed the importance of following a healthy and balanced diet to maintain or improve a healthy status. This recommendation is particularly relevant for those segments of the population that are more vulnerable to chronic conditions or suffer from allergies and intolerances, like the elderly, people with an impaired immune system, individuals characterized by frailty or neuromuscular conditions, etc. Promoting healthy and balanced diet plans can foster the prevention of the above-mentioned diseases and conditions, but the task of developing and implementing these diet plans is not easy. In the past ten years many mobile phone apps have been developed with the aim of supporting people in engaging themselves in a healthier nutrition, but the majority of them did not reach the goal of fostering the adoption of a balanced nutrition and failed in proving their effectiveness in both medium and long term [4].

Therefore, health professionals remain the most reliable and qualified option in creating healthy diets, while agro-industrial companies strengthen their efforts in developing novel and nutritionally-balanced food products – some of them specifically dedicated to certain segments of the population. In fact, as every person has his/her own health condition, each diet plan needs to be tailored on the individual's specific needs. This complex process could benefit enormously from the cooperation of both clinical and non-clinical professionals, who need to be provided with the means to exchange different data (health-related, food products' and nutrition-related data) in a collaborative effort involving different domains of knowledge. Reaching this goal could therefore enable the development of customized and well-balanced diet plans, specifically studied on the needs of the individuals.

A promising approach for cross-domains knowledge exchange is the ontology, a shared and formal logic-based description of the concepts composing a domain, and of the relationships that hold between them [5]. The ontology, cornerstone of the Semantic Web technologies, can be used to provide information interoperability among different stakeholders. Its adoption is well-established in different health-related domains, and it can be used as backbone for Decision Support Systems (DSSs), as it allows to elicit new pieces of information through semantic reasoning processes.

This work introduces a prototypical ontology-based DSS to enable the cooperation between health professionals, food and nutrition experts and agro-industrial businesses. The DSS is one of the expected results of the Lombardy Region research project sPATIALS[3], started in 2020 and aimed at enhancing agro-industrial productions for a safer, healthier and sustainable nutrition. The ontology behind the DSS allows health professionals, nutrition experts and agro-industrial businesses to exchange knowledge related to both existing and innovative food products' characteristics and their expected effects on health. The knowledge formalized in the DSS serves as a supporting tool for nutrition professionals – as they can have more information related to food products and their effects – and for the consumers, who can benefit from tailored dietary recommendations. Moreover, thanks to the contribution of food companies, the DSS can also encompass the characteristics of novel food products, specifying the segments of the population who could benefit most from them. All the above-mentioned stakeholders can exchange comments, suggestions and observation among them.

The remainder of this paper is organized as follows: Sect. 2 delves into the ontology – backbone of the DSS and named Nutrition and Health Ontology (NutrHe) –, describing its modules in detail (the standards they rely on and the long-standing ontologies it reuses). Section 3 provides two scenarios that help clarifying how the DSS works with health professionals, consumers and agro-industrial businesses. Finally, the Conclusions summarize the main outcomes of this paper and sketch the future directions of this research.

2 Related Work

Domain ontology is widely adopted in DSSs, since it allows to formalize knowledge and enables semantic reasoning. There exist many examples of ontology-based DSS in healthcare, and some of them are focused on nutrition-related problems – both for general and specific target users. Bianchini et al. [6] designed a recommender system to provide users with personalized and healthy menus, taking into account user's preferences and medical prescriptions. An ontology is used to combine people's profile (health and cultural constraints) with recipes. In the context of a semantic-based platform for supporting healthy lifestyles, Dragoni et al. [7] leveraged ontology to provide a description of foods and their macronutrients components (carbohydrate, protein, lipids, etc.). Similarly, NutElCare [8] provides a representation of foods' macronutrients into an ontology with the aim of providing healthy recommendations to elderlies.

Ontology-based technologies cover a relevant role also in many other food-related research fields. Subramaniyaswamy et al. [9] developed a food recommendation system within tourism activities that leverages on ontological representations of users' profile; by comparing different users and adopting filtering mechanisms, the system is able to provide each user with a list of tailored food recommendation. In the field of agriculture, [10] described a DSS aimed at help farmers to plan intercropping, while [11] proposed a DSS to evaluate food quality in agri-food chains.

NutrHe tries to link users' health condition and foods' characterization recurring to widely-adopted ontologies, with the aim of creating a DSS that can be used by different stakeholders. While nutrition professionals can use NutrHe as a support tool in decision making, agro-industrial companies can add their products and consumers can take advantage of tailored suggestions.

3 Development of NutrHe

NutrHe is developed by following the NeOn Methodology for ontology engineering [12]. As many methodologies for ontology development, NeOn fosters the reuse of already existing and long-standing models, which are already adopted in many other projects. NutrHe is divided into four main modules: the first dedicated to the Person, the second dedicated to Food description and the third describing the effects of foods on human health; a fourth module provides a set of rules to trigger some inferences (as further illustrated in Sect. 3.4). The ontology is developed using the editor Protégé [13] and exploits Resource Description Framework (RDF) [14] and Ontology Web Language (OWL) [15] – W3C recommendation languages – with Semantic Web Rule Languages (SWRL) [16].

3.1 Persons and Health Conditions Module

The description of the consumers – persons characterized by a specific health condition – relies on the Friend Of A Friend (FOAF) vocabulary [17] to represent personal data (age, place of birth, contacts, tax identification number, etc.): FOAF is widely adopted due to its simplicity and it allows to formalize the most relevant pieces of information related to a person. NutrHe reuses a limited number of FOAF entities (the `foaf:Person` class and the properties `foaf:age`, `foaf:givenName`, `foaf:familyName`, `foaf:gender`) and adds a few properties to complete a consumer's description (`nutrhe:TINnum`, `nutrhe:address`, `nutrhe:email`, `nutrhe:phone`). Each person is represented with an individual (belonging to `foaf:Person` class) and is linked to an individual representing a health condition via the `nutrhe:healthCondition`.

A person's health condition is described by recurring to two WHO's standard classifications: in fact, to increase health information interoperability and to enhance the cooperation between medical and non-medical professionals, NutrHe adopts the International Classification of Diseases and Related Health Problems (ICD-11) [18] and the International Classification of Functioning, Disability and Health (ICF) [19]. The ICD enables a classification of diseases for diagnostic purposes and can also provide the means to record and analyze the general health situations of populations groups (monitoring the incidence of diseases and other health problems). The ICF focuses instead on the formalization of the functional description of an individual, conceptualizing the interactions between a person's health condition and the environment. The classifications present a similar taxonomical structure: they divide their respective domains of knowledge into Chapters (24 for the stem codes of ICD, and 30 for all the four components constituting the ICF), which are further deepened by subcategories (as exemplified by the excerpts of ICD and ICF reproduced in Fig. 1). The deeper is the subcategory, the more detailed is the information provided by the code.

The ICD stem codes comprised in the 24 chapters (for a total of more than 10.000 codes) can be used alone to represent diseases and conditions, while the 1400 ICF codes can provide a description of the functioning of a person – even within a specific context. Due to their structure, degree of diffusion among health and non-health professionals, and granularity in representing knowledge, both the classifications have been modelled into two ontologies, which are used in the development of ontology-based DSSs involving the management of health-related information [20, 21]. NutrHe prototype reuses parts of these classifications, specifically: for the ICD, the first 15 chapters, for the ICF the whole Body functions component.

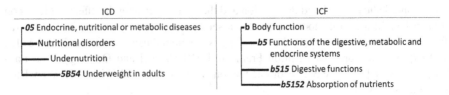

Fig. 1. Two excerpts of the ICD (left) and ICF (right) classifications; both the WHO standards organize the domains of knowledge into a hierarchical taxonomy, starting from the most general category (the "chapters") to the most specific. In this figure, "05 Endocrine, nutritional or metabolic diseases" and "b5 Functions of the digestive, metabolic and endocrine systems" are chapters of – respectively – ICD and ICF; "b Body functions" represents one of the four ICF components.

Each ICD and ICF code is represented in NutrHe with a class and the hierarchical relationships among classes are described using the rdfs:subclassOf property. The bottommost classes – those representing 4- and 5-digits ICF codes and 4-characters codes in ICD – are populated with one individual, named after the class.

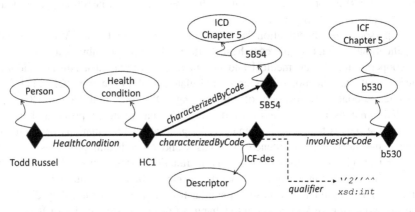

Fig. 2. A graphical representation of a person and his health condition; since in NutrHe it is possible to specify a qualifier for ICF codes, to avoid reification (following an ontology design pattern presented in [22]) a descriptor individual is adopted. Concepts are represented with ellipses, individuals with diamonds, and roles with arrows (dashed arrows indicate datatype properties, full-line arrows indicate object properties); the type of an individual is stated with a curved arrow.

A health condition, represented as an individual of the class nutrhe:HealthCondition, can therefore be specified using the nutrhe:characterizedByCode followed by the individuals representing the ICD or ICF codes – the latter specified by a qualifier ranging from 0 (no impairment) to 4 (complete impairment). Figure 2 provides a graphical representation of a person's health condition in NutrHe.

3.2   Foods and Their Characteristics Module

Formalization of foods reuses the Food Ontology (FoodOn) [23], a large and comprehensive model formalizing more than 9.600 food products in a formal hierarchy. FoodOn is compatible with the Basic Formal Ontology and formalizes classes and properties for the description of food products, their transformation processes and their packaging or containers. NutrHe reuses FoodOn since it allows to describe multiple points of view related to food products: for instance, crisps – potato chips derived from slicing and frying potatoes – can be classified as a `foodon:40370` – `potato crisps from potato slice` (following the Foodex2 classification of the European Food Safety Authority modelled in FoodOn), and also as a fried product (`foodon:food(fried)`) to represent it as a `foodon:food_product_by_process`, or as a `foodon:potato_crips` product (subclass of `foodon:snack_(potato-based)`).

3.3   Food and Health Module

NutrHe's third module links foods from `foodon:food_product_type` to the diseases and conditions represented with ICD and to the impairments of the body described with ICF. NutrHe captures the relationships between food products and health conditions adopting two object property, `nutrhe:canHarm` (and its inverse property `nutrhe:worsenedBy`) and `nutrhe:hasBenefitsOn` (and its inverse property `nutrhe:benefitsFrom`). The first property links those foods that are known to worsen a specific disease, while the second is used to link products whose effects can be good for a specific condition. For instance, a salty food product, like a `foodon:hungarian-type_salami`, or a fat product, like `foodon:butter`, are linked to the ICD code BA00 (Essential hypertension) via the `nutrhe:canHarm` property (and, therefore, the same ICD code is linked to the same food product via `nutrhe:worsenedBy`). On the contrary, `foodon:beet(whole, raw)` and `foodon:tomato(whole, raw)` are linked to the same ICD code via `nutrhe:hasBenefitsOn`. Thanks to FoodOn's structure, it is also possible to account for the same food being prepared differently – and, therefore, having different effects on a certain health condition. For example, a dish (represented as an individual) composed of a piece of `foodon:salmon(frozen)` which is `foodon:output_of` a `foodon:steaming_without_pressure` (a subclass of `foodon:food_cooking_process`) can be linked to ICD BA00 via the `nutrhe:hasBenefitsOn` property. Instead, a dish made of `foodon:salmon(frozen)` undergone a `foodon:deep-frying_process` can be linked to ICD BA00 via the `nutrhe:canHarm` property. In this way, NutrHe can account also for complex foods and their cooking methods, which can deeply modify foods' effects on health.

The aim of this module is to represent a "map" of the relationships between food products and specific health conditions. This task requires expertise from nutrition professionals and food product-related knowledge from agro-industrial companies – especially for complex food products which undergo to several different transformation processes. NutrHe prototype represents the relationships between osteoporosis (ICD code FB83.1), hypertension (ICD code BA00), IBS syndromes (ICD codes DD91.00, DD91.01), gastritis (DA42).

3.4 SWRL Rules

A set of SWRL rules is designed to help clinical personnel to determine food products that can be suggested to persons whose health condition is characterized by specific diseases or conditions. Simple rules like:

```
food_material(?dish),   has_ingredient    (?dish,   ?ing),
foodon_product_type (?ing), hasBenefitsOn (?ing, ?code), not
(canHarm(?ing,   ?code))  ICD_Code   (?code),   Person   (?p),
healthCondition (?p, ?hc), characterizedByCode (?hc, ?code) -
> potentialSuggestionFor (?dish, ?p)
```

can detect those food products containing any ingredient healthy for a person with a healthy effect on the same ICD (or ICF) code. The product is therefore suggested for a specific person, after medical personnel advice. A similar rule identifies food products containing any ingredient that could harm a health condition characterized by a specific ICD (or ICF) code.

A second set of rules checks for specific ICD (or ICF) codes (like, for example, the code describing hypertension) whether or not among food products suggested for a person (having the condition described by the code) the ingredients are processed with an unsuitable method, which may hinder the person's diet and health (as described in Sect. 3.3).

4 Scenarios

This Section introduces two scenarios with the aim of illustrating the use of NutrHe by different stakeholders.

Scenario 1: Medical Personnel and Consumers. A nutritionist adopts an application based on NutrHe to understand whether some (complex) food products can harm or be benefic for one of his patient's health condition. Through automatic reasoning process, each food product modelled in the ontology is suggested (or advised against) for a specific individual, whose health condition is provided as an input and is characterized by ICD and ICF codes. The nutritionist is also informed that new food products specifically designed for helping consumers characterized by the same health condition of his patient are now available. Through the DSS, the nutritionist can therefore evaluate them and insert them into his patients' diet plans. Moreover, the nutritionist can annotate other effects – not explicit in NutrHe – he observed and inform the food company of his findings. Consumers can receive tailored suggestions based on their health status, including the offer of new food products. Suggestions can be received through an application, which also shows consumers only the lists of harmful and benefic foods – thus hiding from them the complexity of the health condition modelling. Also consumers can annotate effects they observed and believe to be connected with a specific food consumption; in this way, the nutritionist could be informed of the alleged effects and evaluate them. NutrHe can facilitate the communication between patients and nutrition professionals, by letting the former aware of which foods can harm them and which can have a positive effect on their health; NutrHe – via application – can inform both consumers and clinical personnel whenever a new product is added to the ontology.

Scenario 2: Agro-industrial Companies and New Products. Companies developing new food products can model them inside NutrHe. For example, if a company develops a new probiotic dietary supplement for consumers suffering from IBS syndrome, it can add the new product in NutrHe (using FoodOn classes) and can indicate the benefits the product is expected to have on the specific health conditions. Following the same pattern, a company producing nutraceutical prepared foods for elderly, can add its products (`foodon:prepare_food_product`) and model the expected benefits in the ontology. The products added in this way can be retrieved by nutrition professionals and consumers, as described in Scenario 1. The same company can also receive comments, suggestions and clinical observation by other stakeholders (consumers and nutrition professionals) regarding the effects linked to the consumption of their products.

5 Conclusions and Further Work

This paper described a prototypical ontology-based DSS designed for helping nutritionists in taking nutrition-related decisions, providing consumers with suggestions tailored on their health condition, and supporting agro-industrial companies in divulging novel food products specifically developed for target users. The main modules composing NutrHe and the decision behind its engineering are exposed, also taking advantage of explanatory scenarios.

Although the main components of the NutrHe ontology are identified, there are some further steps that need to be tackled before the DSS is fully developed. A first important step foresees the further development of the relationships between ICD and ICF codes describing diseases and conditions and food products: several other conditions (such as food allergies or food intolerances, kidney diseases, diabetes, etc.) can be modelled in NutrHe and the effects of foods (benefits and harms) on these conditions can be specified in the ontology as well. This would lead to a larger number of consumers being able to find tailored information and could support nutrition professionals more efficiently.

With regard to adding information to NutrHe, the sPATIALS[3] research project foresees the participation of three agro-industrial companies operating in the Lombardy Region; these companies are expected to develop novel nutraceutical food products (ready meals, food products prepared through new processes) and can test NutrHe's ability to properly represent products' characteristics. In this way, it is possible to test NutrHe in enhancing the cooperation among companies, nutrition professionals and consumers.

Information retrieval from NutrHe also covers a pivotal role and is expected to be conducted using the W3C recommendation language SPARQL [24]; this language can efficiently filter RDF data by combining several triple patterns, thus providing in-depth views of the ontology and the relationships among its entities. Data filtering with SPARQL can also help the retrieval of tailored products for consumers suffering from comorbidities.

Finally, as depicted in Sect. 4, the DSS should be used via applications (dedicated to clinical personnel, consumers and companies), each of which should be tested by the respective targets.

Acknowledgments. sPATIALS3 project is financed by the European Regional Development Fund under the ROP of the Lombardy Region ERDF 2014–2020 - Axis I "Strengthen technological research, development and innovation" - Action 1.b.1.3 "Support for co-operative R&D activities to develop new sustainable technologies, products and services" - Call Hub.

References

1. Rao, T.S., Asha, M., Ramesh, B., Rao, K.J.: Understanding nutrition, depression and mental illnesses. Indian J. Psychiatry. **50**, 77 (2008)
2. World Health Organization: European food and nutrition action plan 2015–2020 (2015)
3. Science and Policy Report by the Joint Research Centre of the European Commission: The Role of Nutrition in Active and Healthy Ageing - For prevention and treatment of age-related diseases: evidence so far (2014)
4. West, J.H., Hall, P.C., Arredondo, V., Berrett, B., Guerra, B., Farrell, J.: Health behavior theories in diet apps. J. Consum. Health Internet **17**, 10–24 (2013)
5. Gruber, T.R., et al.: A translation approach to portable ontology specifications. Knowl. Acquis. **5**, 199–221 (1993)
6. Bianchini, D., De Antonellis, V., De Franceschi, N., Melchiori, M.: PREFer: a prescription-based food recommender system. Comput. Stand. Interfaces. **54**, 64–75 (2017)
7. Dragoni, M., Bailoni, T., Eccher, C., Guerini, M., Maimone, R.: A semantic-enabled platform for supporting healthy lifestyles. In: Proceedings of the Symposium on Applied Computing, pp. 315–322 (2017)
8. Espín, V., Hurtado, M.V., Noguera, M.: Nutrition for elder care: a nutritional semantic recommender system for the elderly. Expert Syst. **33**, 201–210 (2016)
9. Subramaniyaswamy, V., et al.: An ontology-driven personalized food recommendation in IoT-based healthcare system. J. Supercomput. **75**(6), 3184–3216 (2018). https://doi.org/10.1007/s11227-018-2331-8
10. Phoksawat, K., Mahmuddin, M.: Ontology-based knowledge and optimization model for decision support system to intercropping. In: 2016 International Computer Science and Engineering Conference (ICSEC), pp. 1–6. IEEE (2016)
11. Thomopoulos, R., Croitoru, M., Tamani, N.: Decision support for agri-food chains: a reverse engineering argumentation-based approach. Ecol. Inform. **26**, 182–191 (2015)
12. Suárez-Figueroa, M.C., Gómez-Pérez, A., Fernández-López, M.: The NeOn methodology for ontology engineering. In: Suárez-Figueroa, M.C., Gómez-Pérez, A., Motta, E., Gangemi, A. (eds.) Ontology Engineering in a Networked World, pp. 9–34. Springer, Heidelberg (2012). https://doi.org/10.1007/978-3-642-24794-1_2

13. Musen, M.A.: The protégé project: a look back and a look forward. AI Matters **1**, 4–12 (2015)
14. Pan, J.Z.: Resource description framework. In: Staab, S., Studer, R. (eds.) Handbook on Ontologies. IHIS, pp. 71–90. Springer, Heidelberg (2009). https://doi.org/10.1007/978-3-540-92673-3_3
15. Antoniou, G., Van Harmelen, F.: Web ontology language: OWL. In: Staab, S., Studer, R. (eds.) Handbook on Ontologies, pp. 67–92. Springer, Heidelberg (2004). https://doi.org/10.1007/978-3-540-24750-0_4
16. Horrocks, I., et al.: SWRL: a semantic web rule language combining OWL and RuleML. W3C Memb. Submiss. **21**, 1–31 (2004)
17. Graves, M., Constabaris, A., Brickley, D.: FOAF: connecting people on the semantic web. Cat. Classif. Q. **43**, 191–202 (2007)
18. World Health Organization: ICD-11 (International Classification of Diseases for Mortality and Morbidity Statistics, Eleventh Revision) - Reference Guide
19. World Health Organization: How to use the ICF - A Practical Manual for using the International Classification of Functioning, Disability and Health (ICF)
20. Abas, H.I., Yusof, M.M., Noah, S.A.M.: The application of ontology in a clinical decision support system for acute postoperative pain management. In: 2011 International Conference on Semantic Technology and Information Retrieval, pp. 106–112. IEEE (2011)
21. Spoladore, D.: Ontology-based decision support systems for health data management to support collaboration in ambient assisted living and work reintegration. In: Camarinha-Matos, L., Afsarmanesh, H., Fornasiero, R. (eds.) PRO-VE 2017. IAICT, vol. 506, pp. 341–352. Springer, Cham (2017). https://doi.org/10.1007/978-3-319-65151-4_32
22. Spoladore, D., Sacco, M.: Semantic and dweller-based decision support system for the reconfiguration of domestic environments: RecAAL. Electronics **7**, 179 (2018)
23. Dooley, D.M., et al.: FoodOn: a harmonized food ontology to increase global food traceability, quality control and data integration. npj Sci. Food **2**, 1–10 (2018)
24. Pérez, J., Arenas, M., Gutierrez, C.: Semantics and complexity of SPARQL. In: Cruz, I., et al. (eds.) ISWC 2006. LNCS, vol. 4273, pp. 30–43. Springer, Heidelberg (2006). https://doi.org/10.1007/11926078_3

Leveraging on Enterprise Building Information Models in Health Care Services: The Case of St. Olav University Hospital

Sobah Abbas Petersen[2]([✉]), Tor Åsmund Evjen[1],
Seyed Reza Hosseini Raviz[2], and John Krogstie[2]

[1] St. Olavs University Hospital, Trondheim, Norway
tor.asmund.evjen@icloud.com
[2] Department of Computer Science, Norwegian University of Science
and Technology, Trondheim, Norway
{sap,seyed.r.h.raviz,krogstie}@ntnu.no

Abstract. Building Information Models (BIM) play a central role in the construction phase of buildings. At St. Olav University Hospital in Norway, the focus has been on generating value from BIM during the entire lifecycle of the many buildings that comprise the hospital and supporting the core business processes of the hospital during the operations phase. St. Olav University Hospital has been at the forefront of developing Enterprise BIM, where the information from BIM are utilized together with other data and information, such as availability, positioning and movements of equipment and use of the different physical spaces. In this paper, we focus on the use of EBIM and how they could support Collaborative Networks of different stakeholders and their interactions with one another, with the building facilities and the relevant equipment for supporting daily operations.

Keywords: Building lifecycle · Enterprise BIM · Health care services ·
Enterprise processes · Indoor positioning

1 Introduction

Hospitals are complex buildings that serve a variety of stakeholders and support a variety of direct and indirect complex relationships among them [1]. The ability of a hospital or any health care institution to provide the best care with the least resources have been one of the drivers. Similarly, the agility to rapidly reorganise resources and adapt to arising needs is of utmost importance to ensure the wellbeing of patients and health care personnel. Building Information Models (BIM) have received a lot of attention as a technology that could support efficient design and construction of hospitals; e.g. [1, 2]. More recently, BIM have been considered beyond the early life cycles of building, to support hospitals during their operations phases. Some of these areas of application include Facility Management (FM) [3], asset management and refurbishing of older buildings [4].

At St. Olav University Hospital in Trondheim, Norway (St. Olav hereafter), the concept of Enterprise BIM (EBIM) has been explored [5]. EBIM brings together

© IFIP International Federation for Information Processing 2020
Published by Springer Nature Switzerland AG 2020
L. M. Camarinha-Matos et al. (Eds.): PRO-VE 2020, IFIP AICT 598, pp. 644–653, 2020.
https://doi.org/10.1007/978-3-030-62412-5_53

information from BIM models and other enterprise information systems, to provide relevant information and data that could support the daily operations of the hospital and support effective collaboration among stakeholders. In this paper, we describe how St. Olav takes BIM beyond the design and construction phases and FM to support the operations phase of the lifecycle of the hospital buildings. St. Olav has developed an EBIM and utilises information from EBIM along with other relevant data and information to support enterprise processes. Information in BIM models contribute to the development of 3D visualisations of the physical context and layout of buildings. This can be leveraged to create value to a number of stakeholders in hospitals including the management and patients. The aim of this paper is to explore the benefits of EBIM to support a diverse set of stakeholders in hospitals. The main research focus is to investigate possible ways that EBIM could be used to support daily operations in the hospital. By using the Case Study research method [6], we describe some of the approaches taken by St. Olav to utilise information available in their BIM models to create more value for their enterprise processes. To achieve this, St. Olav has developed several prototype applications to explore the possibilities and demonstrate the value of EBIM.

In this paper, we describe briefly three prototype applications that have been developed and tested follows: Sect. 2 provides a brief overview of related work on BIM and EBIM; Sect. 3 describes the case of St. Olav and how EBIM is used to develop three prototype applications and Sect. 4 summarises the paper and outlines future plans.

2 BIM, EBIM and Collaborative Networks

BIM modeling was introduced in the early 2000s in pilot projects to support the building design in the architecture and engineering sectors. As a result, the main research trends focused on enhancing and development of pre-planning and design, visualization, collision detection, quantification, cost and data management [4]. Construction projects involve complex sets of linkages between stakeholders with different professional backgrounds [7]. Therefore it was necessary to change the emphasis from a fragmented approach to a concerted and collaborative effort to support the owner's goals [8]. More recently, the use of BIM has evolved to support the entire lifecycle of buildings or sets of buildings such as a hospital complex, and to support a variety of business and organizational processes such as facility management and asset management. The use of BIM has numerous benefits for a variety of stakeholders in hospitals [9]. Some of the advantages of BIM are the fact that they can represent the different mechanical systems in the buildings such as the ventilation system (HVAC); they enable the building to be considered as a system in itself [9], and they can contain data related to equipment. The possibility to represent the different systems and equipment within a physical and spatial context provides huge advantages in decision making during the entire lifecycle of a building.

BIM have been considered as a significant contribution for Facility Management (FM), where the BIM models were handed over from the entrepreneurs and other relevant actors in the construction phase to the owners and/or operators of the building;

in the case of hospitals, the hospital facility managers. BIM models provide value to FM as they already contain relevant information and thus will reduce the cost and time required to collect and build FM systems [10]. This resulted in the continued use of information in BIM to support cleaning processes [11], proactive maintenance practices and tracking of equipment [12, 13], among others [14]. BIM are also recommended as a tool for supporting the refurbishment of existing buildings and the use of BIM in refurbishment are discussed in detail in [15].

More recently, building owners and operators have focused on leveraging value from the BIM models, or the virtual real estate they represent, by using the information available to support core organizational processes, reduce operating costs and management decision making. In fact, the operational phase of a building has been identified as the main contributor to the building lifecycle cost [10]. The concept EBIM is defined as "a virtual holistic representation of buildings adapted for optimized business management, knowledge sharing and collaboration" [5]. The use of EBIM can facilitate the integration of BIM and other relevant information, through the use of standardised IFC (ISO 16739) models and other information models, in a model server. This opens up for the use of EBIM in making decisions, supported by data and visual components, that are relevant for the operations of the enterprise. The main difference between BIM and EBIM is that EBIM considers the whole enterprise (e.g. the hospital) rather than just the building and puts the core business processes into focus (owner, director, personnel, patient, authorities, manager and builder). For example, such operations could be optimal asset management, efficient collaboration or indeed making critical decisions involving the use of assets and facilities during an unforeseen emergency situation [16].

A lot of the work has focused on BIM-based construction networks to support collaboration and to support collaboration during the design and construction phases; e.g. [17, 18]. Similar to the design and constructive phases, the benefits of information and experience sharing and collaboration among the different stakeholders are significant during the other phases of the lifecycle. In particular, supporting Collaborative Networks [19] outside the context of a project is challenging. Collaborative networks in the health care operations have been addressed by researchers; e.g. Noran analysed the collaborative networks in various tasks performed in hospital operations, where the focus was on the collaboration among different stakeholders [20]. Collaborative Networks in healthcare and interactions across different heath care institutions in processes such as request for investigations and information and physical material (e.g. blood samples) flow were analysed in [21]. Challenges identified include locating physical material that should flow along with their information counterparts, within the IT systems.

Some of the operational activities in an enterprise often comprise of tasks that arise where communication and coordination among individuals or teams from different specialised areas are important; e.g. in a hospital, medical personnel may need to know the availability of specific medical equipment in a specific area of the hospital or about the availability of a medication. Such activities require collaboration among some of the medical staff with FM or people interacting with procurement and logistics. They are strictly teams, but the need for communication (perhaps indirect) is essential. There have been a few attempts at addressing such challenges; e.g. by integrating a workflow engine and a multi-model BIM collaboration platform [22].

3   Example Case – St. Olav University Hospital

St. Olav, located in Trondheim, Norway, is made up of many buildings. Both old and new buildings have been incorporated in this complex, that have to be kept in proper or good condition in the course of the decades of lifetime. The hospital needs to identify a homogenized and standardized open platform with a view to develop and maintain their amenities. Today, all the buildings that constitute St. Olav, approximately 350000m^2 of building area, have been modelled according to the openBIM standards [23]. By considering BIM as a digital interaction paradigm for all types of properties through all lifecycle phases, where everyone can initially share and gain insight through different digital interfaces, the focus has shifted from the project-centric to see BIM in a business perspective. St. Olav and Central Norway's Health Authority set up a collaborative project called Lifecycle BIM in 2012, to build up a lifecycle BIM based on a FM platform. The result was to implement an EBIM philosophy, where information from BIM are considered in hospital operations.

The main research focus is to investigate possible ways that EBIM could be used to support daily operations in St. Olav. The Case Study research method [6] is used to identify and describe different approaches that could be used to create value from EBIM to support enterprise processes. The primary information sources are three ICT prototypes that have been developed by MSc students [24–26], and informal discussions with the staff in St Olav's Property Department. The prototypes were developed based on documentation available from the Property Department and semi-formal interviews with the staff, which helped identify the requirements. The evaluations were focused on the proof of concepts.

3.1   EBIM at St. Olav University Hospital

At St. Olav's, EBIM is defined as a discrete information database aimed to support the many enterprise aspects and enable the integration of the core business and the various processes of the hospital [27]. Traditionally, when the building construction phase is completed, the BIM models are made available to the FM activities. The EBIM concept at St Olav considers the BIM models to be available as a part of the EBIM, which brings together other ICT applications and data that support enterprise operations and strategic decision making, such as facility management, patient related activities, logistics, ERP systems and procurement. This is illustrated in Fig. 1, where EBIM relates the BIM models to the other operational activities.

The main objective of EBIM is to strive for a comprehensive and rational digital management of the building stock that reflects as best as possible the real building structures and functions. In order to meet this objective, a BIM server has been acquired for St. Olav, which is used as the main tool for validating, storing and communicating all building technical information. The system has features that support operation and maintenance, rental agreements, retrieval and tracking of mobile

equipment and people, as well as web-based real estate portal and wireless communications in the field. One of the main technical challenges in adopting BIM-based
models and achieving EBIM is interoperability among different IT systems [28, 29]. At
St. Olav, an application for visualizing and management of EBIM, called Model Server
Manager (MSM) has been developed. The application is object-oriented and based on
open standards such as IFC and EXPRESS data specification language, defined in ISO
10303-11 [30]. All of St. Olav's building models are stored in a database on a BIM
server and the MSM can retrieve and update these models. The application allows a
display of multiple models in the same view.

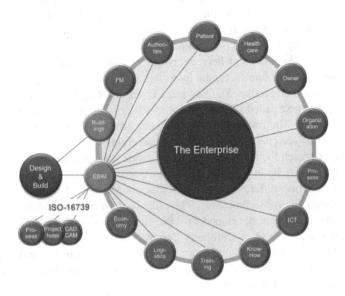

Fig. 1. EBIM and enterprise processes

Information from the EBIM models have been used to develop data driven models
and simulations [1]. Furthermore, several prototype implementations to explore the
value of EBIM for enterprise processes have been developed. They are also aimed at
supporting interaction among the stakeholders and between the building and objects
within it, and users of the hospital facilities and services. In the following subsections,
we describe briefly some of the ways in which St. Olav uses EBIM and other information in the model server to support enterprise operations and decision making. The
technical details for the prototypes are beyond the scope of this paper.

3.2 3D Visualisation of Buildings and Objects

A web-based prototype, using the WebGL API and BIM models has been developed as
the foundation for a 3D scene, to explore the possibilities that 3D WebGL applications
can offer in a virtual hospital context. It includes objects to interact with, which could
likely feature in the virtual hospital arena, and in various enterprise processes such as

logistics, optimization, training or simulations [26]. Information from EBIM models were used to create a 3D visualisation of one of the hospital buildings from 1930. The types of models used were architectural models (ARK) which included elements such as walls, windows, doors, ceiling, roof, beams, benches; and electrical models (RIE), which included lamps, emergency door openers, sockets, card readers, elbow switches, emergency exit signs and more. An additional layer of information was added to include objects placed in the building.

The main aim of the implementation was for users; e.g. facility managers or patients, to walk around in the virtual building and interact with the building and various objects within the building. St. Olav owns a large collection of art. Thus, the prototype chose presentation of the artwork and paintings in the virtual hospital building, where the user could identify their locations and interact with the paintings to learn about them and update information about them as relevant; see Fig. 2. Users could also select a room in the building and access presentations and videos that have been presented in the room. Such a functionality is aimed at enhancing implicit collaboration, communication and knowledge sharing among different stakeholders of the hospital.

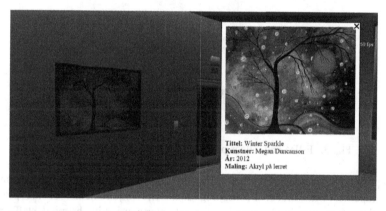

Fig. 2. Interaction with a painting, in a 3D visualisation of a BIM model [26]

The benefits of such a functionality include the possibilities to use information from EBIM for creating a sense of the physical space in a virtual environment. A game to support navigation was created using the 3D visualisation. The main advantage of using BIM information as the basis for modelling the physical environment in the game was the level of detail of the building that was available; a digital twin of the hospital buildings. A usability test was conducted with 17 users from the hospital. A short questionnaire indicated positive responses and over 85% of the respondents saw a value in these types of applications for familiarizing themselves in real buildings, while 69% thought that web-based 3D applications have a potential in educational scenarios. The value of such applications can be for facility managers, health care personnel as well as patients and visitors.

3.3   Asset Management

Asset management involves the balancing of costs, opportunities and risks against the desired performance of assets, to support decision making, planning and execution of activities and tasks of assets as desired by building owners and operators [13]. Hospitals have a need to locate medical equipment as equipment, such as robots and Automated Guided Vehicles (AGV), hospital beds and wheelchairs tend to move relatively frequently. Smaller medical apparatus (e.g. insulin pumps, nebulisers) and other equipment are often borrowed from one section within the hospital to another and in some cases they are never returned. The possibility to efficiently locate such equipment would save time and thus effort and costs to the hospital staff including the health care personnel.

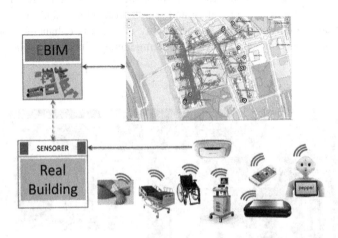

Fig. 3.   EBIM and indoor positioning system for assets management

A prototype has been developed, using the information in the BIM models and the MSM together with Indoor Positioning data. The requirements for the prototype application were identified through informal interviews with hospital staff and by creating scenarios of how various types of personnel would use such a systems; e.g. a maintenance staff, a porter and a project manager for remodelling. Smart asset tags on hospital equipment and wireless technologies were used to trace the movements of equipment and they were located using the CISCO location server. The position and time related data was then saved in an xml file, and visualized in the spatial context with the virtual hospital environment [25]. The movements of an electrical scooter through the hospital buildings within a 3 month period is visualised in Fig. 3.

One very importat aspect of being able to track the location of an equipment and trace their movements is also safety and security; e.g. w.r.t. to the possibility of contamination and the reduction of the risk of infections. The movement and usage of equipment can also be used to manage the "fleet of equipment", e.g. the no. of wheelchairs or AGVs, to an optimal amount, thereby reducing the costs and the effective management and maintenance of the assets.

3.4   Dynamic Cleaning

One of the beneficiaries of BIM are facility managers and examples of benefits include efficient cleaning of equipment and physical spaces. At St. Oav's, EBIM models have been used by the property owners to calculate the area for cleaning so that this information could be used to negotiate the price with the cleaning company [11]. Traditionally, cleaning is a routine process that is conducted at regular intervals, or at hospitals, related to specific activities in specific rooms such as operation theatres. At St. Olav's, an explorative study has been conducted to use information from EBIM and the Model Server to create dynamic cleaning plans based on the use of equipment and spaces. Information such as mobile phone traffic within a specific physical space, (respecting privacy compliance), could be made available on the model server. A prototype, a mobile solution available on an iPad using 3D visualizations, has been developed to explore possibilities for dynamic cleaning routines rather than fixed routines [24].

The requirement for the application were developed by interviewing employees from the cleaning company, who provides the service in several Norwegian hospitals. In addition, staff in the property department were included in the discussions. The prototype was evaluated by employees from the hospital's cleaning department, working with coordination and administrative tasks. The overall response was very positive and they could appreciate the benefits of such an application. Such an application could make cleaning routines more effective while reducing the overall cost of cleaning.

4   Summary and Future Work

In this paper, we have described the concept of EBIM and how St. Olav could create value to its stakeholders through utilising information from EBIM models along with other relevant data and information to support enterprise processes. The main contribution of this work is a demonstration of how BIM data could be operationalised during the operations phase of a hospital. Three prototype applications have been developed to support the operations phase of the lifecycle of the hospital buildings, using information from BIM models. In the first prototype, a 3D virtual hospital arena has been developed, where users could view and interact with objects such as artworks and paintings within the building as well as navigate through a virtual hospital. In the second prototype, indoor positioning data was collected for equipment within the hospital, and their movements were visualised using information in the BIM models. In the third prototype, EBIM information was used with other data to support dynamic cleaning routines, based on the actual use of rooms. The prototypes were based on the use of the IFC standard and a model server to overcome interoperability challenges.

The prototypes demonstrated the benefits for hospital operations in efficient and optimum assets management, updating of information related to equipment and buildings, reduced effort in locating and ensuring the safety of equipment reduction in costs in routine processes such as cleaning. In addition, the possibility to interact with objects in a virtual 3D hospital environment supported efficient update of information in the models as well the value of the models for supporting people to find their way around the buildings efficiently.

The prototype applications that were described in this paper focussed mainly on the technological solutions and little emphasis was given to supporting Collaborative Networks. Our next step will be to consider these within the contexts of workflow and collaborative tasks and how they can benefit collaborative tasks within the healthcare operations. Work also continues in the design and development of new applications that could be built upon the rich data that is available from the EBIM and to explore the value for specific organisational processes and stakeholders.

Acknowledgements. The co-author Raviz has been supported by ERCIM. The authors would like to thank St. Olav University Hospital for letting us use their EBIM applications as a part of the case study and the students that have developed the prototype applications.

References

1. Zwart, J.V.D., Evjen, T.Å.: Data driven simulation model for hospital architecture: modelling and simulating clinical process, architectural layout and patient logistics in a hospital's building information model. In: Viana, D.L., Morais, F., Vaz, J.V. (eds.) Formal Methods in Architecture and Urbanism, pp. 223–236. Cambridge Scholars Publishing, Newcastle upon Tyne (2018)
2. Sanchez, A., Hampson, K., Vaux, S.: Delivering Value with BIM – A Whole-of-life Approach. Routledge, New York (2016)
3. Soliman, A.A., Khodeir, L.M.: Efficient Stakeholders Management: The Impact of Applying the Integrated Building Information Modeling/Facility Management Approach, A Literature Review. Sustainable Mega Projects, Egypt (2016)
4. Volk, R., Stengel, J., Schultmann, F.: Building information modeling (BIM) for existing buildings – literature review and future needs. Autom. Constr. **38**, 109–127 (2014)
5. Evjen, T.Å.: Smart hospital and enterprise BIM. In: 7th International Megaprojects Workshop. University of Quebec, Montreal, Canada (2019)
6. Yin, R.K.: Case Study Research: Design and Methods. SAGE Publications, Thousand Oaks (2014)
7. Latiffi, A.A., Brahim, J., Fathi, M.S.: The development of building information modeling (BIM) definition. Appl. Mech. Mater. **567**, 625–630 (2014)
8. Allen, C., Shakantu, W.: The BIM revolution: a literature review on rethinking the business of construction. In: Galiano-Garrigos, A. (ed.) The Sustainable City XI, WIT Transactions on Ecology and the Environment, pp. 919–930. WIT Press, Southampton (2016)
9. Sanchez, A., Hampson, K., Mohamed, S.: Perth Children's Hospital Case Study Report. Sustainable Built Environment National Research Centre
10. Kelly, G., Serginson, M., Lockley, S., Dawood, N., Kassem, M.: BIM for facility management and a review and a case study investigating the value and challenges. In: 13th Int. Conference on Construction Applications of Virtual Reality, London, UK (2013)
11. Reehaug, B.: BIM – Et Hjelpeverktøy for renholdskontrakter? Høgskolen i Gjøvik (2015)
12. Love, P., Zhou, J., Matthews, J., Sing, C., Carey, B.: A systems information model for managing electrical, control, and instrumentation assets. Built Environ. Project Asset Manage. **5**, 278–289 (2015)

13. Love, P.E.D., Matthews, J., Lockley, S.: BIM for built asset management. Built Environ. Project Asset Manage. **5**, 261–277 (2015)

14. Galliano-Garrigós, A., Andújar-Montoya, M.D.: Building information modelling in operations of maintenance at the University of Alicante. Int. J. Sus. Dev. Plann. **13**, 1–11 (2018)

15. Sheth, A.Z., Price, A.D.F., Glass, J.: BIM and refurbishment of existing healthcare facilities. In: Egbu, C. (ed.) Proceedings of the 26th Annual ARCOM Conference, Leeds, United Kingdom, vol. 2, pp. 1497–1506 (2010)

16. Krugler, P., et al.: Asset management literature review and potential applications of simulation, optimization, and decision analysis techniques for right-of-way and transportation planning and programming. Texas Transportation Institute The Texas A&M University System (2007)

17. Oraee, M., Hosseini, M.R., Edwards, D.J., Li, H., Papadonikolaki, E., Cao, D.: Collaboration barriers in BIM-based construction networks: a conceptual model. Int. J. Project Manage. **37** (6), 839–854 (2019)

18. Merschbrock, C., Munkvold, B.E.: Succeeding with building information modeling: a case study of bim diffusion in a healthcare construction project. In: 47th Hawaii International Conference on System Science, Hawaii (2014)

19. Camarinha-Matos, L., Afsarmanesh, H.: Collaborative networks: a new scientific discipline. J. Intell. Manuf. **16**, 439–452 (2005)

20. Noran, O.: Enhancing collaborative healthcare synergy. In: Camarinha-Matos, L.M., Scherer, R.J. (eds.) PRO-VE 2013. IAICT, vol. 408, pp. 459–467. Springer, Heidelberg (2013). https://doi.org/10.1007/978-3-642-40543-3_49

21. Petersen, S.A., Bach, G., Svarlein, A.B.: Patient care across health care institutions: an enterprise modelling approach. In: van Bommel, P., Hoppenbrouwers, S., Overbeek, S., Proper, E., Barjis, J. (eds.) PoEM 2010. LNBIP, vol. 68, pp. 91–105. Springer, Heidelberg (2010). https://doi.org/10.1007/978-3-642-16782-9_7

22. Gürtler, M., Baumgärtel, K., Scherer, Raimar J.: Towards a workflow-driven multi-model BIM collaboration platform. In: Camarinha-Matos, L., Bénaben, F., Picard, W. (eds.) PRO-VE 2015. IAICT, vol. 463, pp. 235–242. Springer, Cham (2015). https://doi.org/10.1007/978-3-319-24141-8_21

23. http://open.bimreal.com/bim/index.php/

24. Tenstad, A., Halvor, B.M., Thorkildsen, M.K., Eidem, M.R., Ødegaard, O.K., Latif, S.M.: Smart Cleaning. Dept. of Computer Science, MSc. Norwegian University of Science and Technology (2018)

25. Jørstad, F.K.: Smart Hospital: Indoor positioning with BIM. Dept. of Computer Science, Specialisation Project. Norwegian University of Science and Technology, Trondheim, Norway (2016)

26. Hestman, L.M.: The Potential of Utilizing BIM Models With the WebGL Technology for Building Virtual Environments: A Web-Based Prototype Within the Virtual Hospital Field. Dept. of Computer Science. Norwegian University of Science and Technology, Trondheim, Norway (2015)

27. Aksnes, E.Ø.: Indoor Positioning Integrated in EBIM. Norwegian University of Science and Technology, Trondheim, Norway (2016)

28. Azhar, S., Hein, M.F., Blake, S.: Building information modeling (BIM): benefits, risks and challenges. In: ASC Annual Conference (2008)

29. Criminale, A., Langar, S.: Challenges with BIM implementation: a review of literature. In: 53rd ASC Annual International Conference Proceedings (2017)

30. Huse, P.: FDVU/FM med EDMmodelserver. BuildingSMART members' meeting. Jotne EPM Technology AS (2015)

Correction to: Boosting Collaborative Networks 4.0

Luis M. Camarinha-Matos⑩, Hamideh Afsarmanesh⑩,
and Angel Ortiz⑩

Correction to:
L. M. Camarinha-Matos et al. (Eds.):
Boosting Collaborative Networks 4.0, **IFIP AICT 598,**
https://doi.org/10.1007/978-3-030-62412-5

The original version of Chapter 11, "A Semantic Data Model to Represent Building Material Data in AEC Collaborative Workflows," was revised. The last name of Jari Shemeikka was spelled incorrectly as "Shemeika." This was corrected.

The original version of Chapter 14, "Bitcoin Adoption as a New Technology for Payment Mechanism in a Tourism Collaborative Network," was revised. The affiliations of Mehdi Daryaei and Abbas Khamseh were corrected.

The updated version of these chapters can be found at
https://doi.org/10.1007/978-3-030-62412-5_11
https://doi.org/10.1007/978-3-030-62412-5_14

L. M. Camarinha-Matos et al. (Eds.): PRO-VE 2020, IFIP AICT 598, p. C1, 2021.
https://doi.org/10.1007/978-3-030-62412-5_54

Author Index

Printed in the United States
by Baker & Taylor Publisher Services